Theology of Wagner's *Ring* Cycle II

Theology of Wagner's *Ring* Cycle II

Theological and Ethical Issues

Richard H. Bell

CASCADE *Books* • Eugene, Oregon

THEOLOGY OF WAGNER'S *RING* CYCLE II
Theological and Ethical Issues

Copyright © 2020 Richard H. Bell. All rights reserved. Except for brief quotations in critical publications or reviews, no part of this book may be reproduced in any manner without prior written permission from the publisher. Write: Permissions, Wipf and Stock Publishers, 199 W. 8th Ave., Suite 3, Eugene, OR 97401.

Cascade Books
An Imprint of Wipf and Stock Publishers
199 W. 8th Ave., Suite 3
Eugene, OR 97401

www.wipfandstock.com

PAPERBACK ISBN: 978-1-4982-3572-3
HARDCOVER ISBN: 978-1-4982-3574-7
EBOOK ISBN: 978-1-4982-3573-0

Cataloguing-in-Publication data:

Names: Bell, Richard H., 1954–, author.

Title: Theology of Wagner's *Ring* cycle II : theological and ethical issues / Richard H. Bell.

Description: Eugene, OR: Cascade Books, 2020 | Includes bibliographical references and index.

Identifiers: ISBN 978-1-4982-3572-3 (paperback) | ISBN 978-1-4982-3574-7 (hardcover) | ISBN 978-1-4982-3573-0 (ebook)

Subjects: LCSH: Wagner, Richard, 1813–1833 | Wagner, Richard, 1813–1833—Ring des Nibelungen | Wagner, Richard, 1813–1833—Religion | Music—Religious aspects | Theology

Classification: ML410.W15 B45 2020 (print) | ML410.W15 (ebook)

Musical examples are reproduced by kind permission of B. Schott (Examples 4.1, 10.1–4) and Bärenreuther (Example 11.6).

Manufactured in the U.S.A.   08/12/20

For Cameron

Contents

List of Musical Examples | viii
List of Figures | viii
Preface | ix
Acknowledgements | xi
Abbreviations | xiii

1 Introduction to the Theology of the *Ring* | 1
2 *Jesus of Nazareth* Sketches | 3
3 God and the Gods | 19
4 Nature | 52
5 Fall, Power, Desecration of Nature, and Capitalism | 89
6 Love | 113
7 Sexual Ethics and Law | 172
8 Death and Immortality | 189
9 Freedom, Necessity, and Providence | 207
10 Siegfried and Brünnhilde | 219
11 Redemption | 245
12 Aesthetics, Allegory, and Myth | 277

Bibliography | 289
Index of Authors | 307
Index of Biblical Texts | 313
Index of Wagner's Works | 317
Index of Subjects and Names | 321

Musical Examples

Example 4.1: *Rheingold* bars 1–50 | 62

Example 4.2: *Rheingold* bars 49–52 | 68

Example 4.3: *Rheingold* bars 137–51 | 70

Example 4.4: *Walküre* Act I bars 1099–1114 | 81

Example 6.1: *Siegfried* Act III bars 1067–78 | 148

Example 6.2: *Rheingold* bars 2664–68 | 149

Example 6.3: *Siegfried* Act III bars 1668–77 | 154

Example 7.1: *Walküre* Act II bars 253–60 | 176

Example 10.1: *Siegfried* Act III bars 1040–50 | 231

Example 10.2: *Götterdämmerung* Act II bars 1034–40 | 232

Example 10.3: *Götterdämmerung* Act II bars 1143–56 | 234

Example 10.4: *Götterdämmerung* Act II bars 1179–91 | 235

Example 11.1: *Walküre* Act III bars 1647–51 | 255

Example 11.2: *Walküre* Act III bars 980–1036 | 257

Example 11.3: *Rheingold* bars 617–28 | 260

Example 11.4: *Rheingold* bars 1338–43; *Walküre* Act III bars 1608–29 | 262

Example 11.5: *Götterdämmerung* Act III bars 579–85; "Mich dürstet" | 267

Example 11.6: Bach *St John Passion*; "Mich dürstet" | 268

Figures

Figure 4.1: The Harmonic Series | 67

Figure 6.1: Antigone and Artwork of the Future | 130

Figure 11.1: Renunciation, Siegfried, and Woman's Worth | 261

Preface

In the first volume of my study I considered the genesis and development of the *Ring* cycle together with Wagner's appropriation of sources (Germanic, Norse, and Greek), artists, philosophers, and theologians. This second volume now looks at the various theological and ethical themes of the *Ring* such as nature, power and love, law and sexual ethics, death and immortality, freedom and necessity, sin, incarnation, and redemption, together with questions such as authority, gender, and human psychology. All this will be preceded by a chapter on Wagner's sketches *Jesus of Nazareth*, which, I claim, unlocks many theological secrets of the *Ring*, and a chapter on the question of "God" and the "Gods."

This volume is complete in itself but most will be gained by using it in conjunction with volume 1.

Acknowledgements

These volumes were written during my time of a being a holder of a Leverhulme Major Research Fellowship at the University of Nottingham. I am extremely grateful to the Leverhulme Trust not only for freeing me from undergraduate teaching and administration (and financing my excellent replacement Dr Sara Parks) but also for funding me to visit the libraries of Oxford and Cambridge and the archives in Bayreuth. The staff of the University Library, Cambridge, have also been helpful in locating books in their vast collection. The staff of the Bodleian library, Oxford, have with kindness and good humor helped me access some rare books across the disciplines of music, theology, philosophy, and German literature. My annual visits to the Nationalarchiv der Richard Wagner-Stiftung/Richard Wagner Gedenkstätte have been invaluable and I record my special thanks to Frau Kristine Unger for her assistance and chats about some details of the works I have consulted in the archives. The library at the University of Nottingham has kindly allowed me to borrow a large number of books (I understand I have broken a University record) and it has always been a pleasure to chat with the dedicated staff, many of whom have taken an interest in my project.

The ideas for these volumes were partly developed in University teaching at Undergraduate and Masters level when I taught a module "Wagner's *The Valkyrie*" for a small but highly dedicated group of students. I have also given seminars in Nottingham (Department of Theology and Religious Studies), Oxford (Centre for the Reception History of the Bible; Centre for Theology and Modern European Thought), St Andrews (Institute for Theology, Imagination and the Arts), and Glasgow (School of Critical Studies), together with public lectures at Westminster College, Cambridge (Vacation Term in Biblical Studies), Nottingham Lakeside Arts (for the Opera North *Ring* production, 2016), St Mary the Virgin, Nottingham, Rutland Theological Society, Hull Theological Society, and the Nottingham Viking Open Day (2018). Public interest in the project has been enhanced by the work of Michael Timmins (who produced the website Wagner and Theology: www.nottingham.ac.uk/go/wagnertheology) and the encouragement of Keith Elliott, Peter Watts, Anna Walas, Carly Crouch, and Tom O'Loughlin. Launching this project was greatly helped by the encouragement of Chris Rowland, George Pattison, and Barry Millington. In addition to those who have read and discussed my work with me (see below) I have learned much from conversations (via e-mail or face to face) with Roger Allen, Lionel Friend, Barry Millington, Derrick Everett, Mark Berry, Barbara Eichner, Kevin Hilliard, Luke Murphy, Carolyne Larrington, Bennett Zon, Kertin Bußmann, Roland Bauer, Ryan Häcker, Joanne Cormac, Laura Goede, and Alan Sommerstein. Writing these volumes has involved working across various disciplines, some of which have been fairly new to me, and I have been enormously helped by those who have given their time and effort to read through sections or whole chapters and to make corrections and suggestions for improvement (and I mention those who have read material from either volume or in some case both): Stephen Houlgate, Maike Oergel, Philip Goodchild, John Deathridge, Laura Tunbridge, Judith Jesch, Christina Lee, Dennis Vanden Auweele, Charlotte Alderwick, Jem Bloomfield, Stephen McClatchie, Oliver Thomas, Stephen Hodkinson, and Bob Morgan.

The staff of Wipf & Stock have been wonderfully efficient in bringing this work to publication, always answering my questions promptly and I thank especially Robin Parry, Calvin Jaffarian, and Savanah Landerholm. I should highlight that Robin, as well as working through the text at the copy-editing stage, was always on hand to offer advice, and Calvin has done magnificent work at the type-setting stage on a manuscript that was not always entirely straightforward. I am grateful to Matt Davies and Joe Bell for introducing me to the means of producing musical examples and diagrams and to Jeremie Cauchois for help with computer problems. I thank my Oxford friends who offered practical help when I was using the Bodleian library: Bob and Pru Morgan gave me hospitality and much intellectual stimulation; Bruce Kinsey gave me splendid facilities to use at Balliol College; David and Anita Wright gave me wonderful hospitality on a number of occasions; and Wycliffe Hall kindly offered parking facilities. Finally, I thank those who have cared for me in my annual visits to Bayreuth: Joachim Korb (sadly no longer with us), Eva Graf, Reinhard and Ulrike Feldmeier, Eva Deyerling, and Marie-Luise and Jörg Rasch, and my favorite Mädel von Fürth, Diemut Meiners.

Abbreviations

Abbreviations follow the SBL Handbook of Style. References to Wagner's stage works are made by the German title (abbreviated if necessary), Act and bar (e.g. Act I bars 1–7 is expressed as I.1–7) or to the page number in *Sämtliche Werke* (*SW*) or the libretto given in the translation of Stuart Spencer (*WagRS*). Unless otherwise indicated, all bible quotations in English are taken from the New Revised Standard Version (*NRSV*). Quotations of the German of Wagner's prose works are usually taken from *Gesammelte Schriften und Dichtungen* (*GSD*) and for the English I have generally used *Richard Wagner's Prose Works* (*PW*), translated by William Ashton Ellis.

Unless otherwise stated, and all emphasis is that given in the source.

ASSW	*Arthur Schopenhauer Sämtliche Werke, textkritisch bearbeitet von Wolfgang Frhr. von Löhneysen.* 5 vols. 1968. Reprint. Darmstadt: Wissenschaftliche Buchgesellschaft, 2004.
BBH-K	*Bremer Biblische Hand-Konkordanz.* Stuttgart: Anker/Christlichen Verlagshaus, 1979.
Braunes Buch	Joachim Bergfeld, ed., *Richard Wagner, Das Braune Buch: Tagebuchaufzeichnungen 1865–1882.* Zurich/Freiburg in Breisgau: Atlantis, 1975.
Brown Book	Joachim Bergfeld, *The Diary of Richard Wagner 1865–1882: The Brown Book.* Translated by George Bird. London: Victor Gollanz, 1980.
BSELK	*Bekenntnisschriften der evangelisch-lutherischen Kirche.* 10th ed. Göttingen: Vandenhoeck & Ruprecht, 1986.
BWL	*Briefwechsel zwischen Wagner und Liszt.* 2 vols. Leipzig: Breitkopf und Härtel, 1887.
CCSL	*Corpus Christianorum: Series Latina.* 222 vols. Turnhout: Brepols, 1953–2019.
CD	Martin Gregor-Dellin and Dietrich Mack, eds., *Cosima Wagner's Diaries.* 2 vols. Translated by Geoffrey Skelton. New York: Harcourt Brace, 1978–80.

CT	Martin Gregor-Dellin and Dietrich Mack, eds., *Cosima Wagner: Die Tagebücher*. 2 vols. Munich/Zurich: R. Piper, 1976.
CWE	Nicholas Vazsonyi, ed., *The Cambridge Wagner Encyclopedia*. Cambridge: Cambridge University Press, 2013.
CWL	*Correspondence of Wagner and Liszt*. Translated by Francis Hueffer. 2 vols. New York: Haskell, 1969.
DBE²	*Deutsche Biographische Enzyklopädie*. 2nd ed. München: K. G. Saur, 2005–8.
DCT	Alan Richardson, ed., *A Dictionary of Christian Theology*. London: SCM, 1969.
DEBRN	Werner Breig and Hartmut Fladt, eds., *Dokumente zur Entstehungsgeschichte des Bühnenfestspiels Der Ring des Nibelungen*. SW 29,I. Mainz: B. Schott, 1976.
DL-L³	*Deutsches Literatur-Lexikon*. 3rd ed. Vols. 1–28: Zurich/Munich: K. G. Saur; vols. 29–38: Berlin: Walter de Gruyter, 1968–2019.
DL-LE³	*Deutsches Literatur-Lexikon, Ergängungsbände*. 6 vols. Zurich/Munich: K. G. Saur, 1994–99.
DTB	Isolde Vetter and Egon Voss, eds., *Dokumente und Texte zu unvollendeten Bühnenwerken*. SW 31. Mainz: B. Schott, 2005.
FBSW	Franz Hoffmann and Julius Humberger, eds., *Franz Xaver von Baader: Sämtliche Werke*. 16 vols. 1851–60. Reprint. Aalen: Scientia, 1987.
FHSWB	Michael Knaupp, ed., *Friedrich Hölderlin: Sämtliche Werke und Briefe*. 3 vols. Darmstadt: Wissenschaftliche Buchgesellschaft, 1998.
FNKSA	Giorgi Colli and Mazzino Montinari, eds. *Friedrich Nietzsche, Sämtliche Werke: Kritische Studienausgabe*. 15 vols. Berlin: Walter de Gruyter, 1999.
FSSW	Gerhard Fricke and Herbert G. Göpfert, eds., *Friedrich Schiller: Sämtliche Werke*. 5 vols. Darmstadt: Wissenschaftliche Buchgesellschaft, 1980.
FW	Immanuel Hermann Fichte, ed., *Fichtes Werke*. 8 vols. 1845–46. Reprint. Berlin: Walter de Gruyter, 1971.
GELW	Herbert G. Göpfert, *Gotthold Ephraim Lessing: Werke*. 8 vols. Darmstadt; Wissenschaftliche Buchgesellschaft, 1996.
GSD	*Gesammelte Schriften und Dichtungen von Richard Wagner*. 10 vols. 3rd ed. Leipzig: E. W. Fritzsch, 1897.
GWBDK	*Goethe Werke*. Bibliothek deutscher Klassiker. Introduction by Walter Dietze. Commentated by Jochen Golz. 12 vols. Berlin: Aufbau-Verlag, 1981.

ABBREVIATIONS

GWJA   Friedmar Apel et al., eds., *Goethe Werke: Jubiläumsasugabe*. 6 vols. Darmstadt: Wissenschaftliche Buchgesellschaft, 1998.

HHW   G.W.F. Hegel: *Hauptwerke in sechs Bänden*. Hamburg: Felix Meiner, 1999.

JA   Dieter Borchmeyer, ed., *Richard Wagner. Dichtungen und Schriften: Jubiläumsasugabe*. 10 vols. Frankfurt am Main: Insel, 1983.

JGFAW   Fritz Medicus, ed., *Johann Gottlieb Fichte; Ausgewählte Werke in sechs Bänden*. 6 vols. Darmstadt: Lambert Schneider, 2013.

KB   Otto Strobel, ed., *König Ludwig II. und Richard Wagner: Briefwechsel*. 5 vols. Karlsruhe: G. Braun, 1936.

KFSA   Ernst Behler, ed., *Kritische Friedrich-Schlegel-Ausgabe*. 35 vols. Munich: Ferdinand Schöningh/Zurich: Thomas-Verlag, 1963–95.

KGB   Giorgio Colli and Mazzino Montinari, eds., *Friedrich Nietzsche Briefwechsel: Kritische Gesamtausgabe*. 25 vols. Berlin: Walter de Gruyter, 1975–2004.

KGW   Giorgio Colli and Mazzino Montinari, eds., *Friedrich Nietzsche Werke: Kritische Gesamtausgabe*. 24 vols. Berlin: Walter de Gruyter, 1967–2006.

KSA   Giorgio Colli and Mazzino Montinari, eds., *Friedrich Nietzsche, Sämtliche Werke: Kritische Studienausgabe*. 15 vols. Berlin: Walter de Gruyter, 1999.

LchI   Engelbert Kirschbaum, ed., *Lexikon der christlichen Ikonographie*. 5 vols. Rome: Herder, 1968.

LFW   Erich Thies, ed., *Ludwig Feuerbach: Werke in sechs Bänden*. 6 vols. Frankfurt am M.: Suhrkamp, 1975.

LW   J. Pelikan and H. T. Lehmann, eds., *Luther Works*. 55 vols. Philadelphia: Fortress, 1943–86.

Mein Leben   Richard Wagner, *Mein Leben*. 2 vols. 1963. Reprint. Edited by Martin Gregor-Dellin. Munich: Paul List, 1969.

MEW   *Karl Marx/Friedrich Engels: Werke*. Institut für Marxismus-Leninismus. 41 vols. Berlin: Dietz, 1966–70.

MGG²   Ludwig Finscher, ed., *Musik in Geschichte und Gegenwart*. 29 vols. 2nd ed. Stuttgart: J. B. Metler/Basel: Bärenreiter, 1994–2008.

MPG   Jaques Paul Migne, ed., *Patrologia Graeca*. 161 vols. Paris, 1857–66.

My Life   Richard Wagner, *My Life*. Translated by Andrew Gray. Edited by Mary Whittall. Cambridge: Cambridge University Press, 1983.

NDCT   Alan Richardson and John Bowden, eds. *A New Dictionary of Christian Theology*. London: SCM, 1983.

NGDO   Stanley Sadie, ed., *The New Grove Dictionary of Opera*. 4 vols. London: Macmillan, 1992.

ABBREVIATIONS

NibE	*The Nibelungenlied: The Lay of the Nibelungs*. Translated with an Introduction and Notes by Cyril Edwards. Oxford: Oxford University Press, 2010.
NibR	*Das Nibelungenlied: Song of the Nibelungs*. Translated from the Middle High German by Burton Raffel. Foreword by Michael Dirda. Introduction by Edward R. Haymes. New Haven: Yale University Press, 2006.
NibS	*Das Nibelungenlied, Mittelhochdeutsch und Neuhochdeutsch. Auf Grund der Übersetzung von Karl Simrock bearbeitet von Prof. Dr. Andreas Heusler*. Die Tempel-Klassiker. Wiesbaden: Emil Vollmer, n.d.
NPNF1	Philip Schaff, ed., *Nicene and Post-Nicene Fathers: First Series*. 14 vols. 1890–1900. Reprint. Peabody, MA: Hendrickson 1994.
NRSV	*The Holy Bible containing the Old and New Testaments with the Apocryphal/Deuterocanonical Books: New Revised Standard Version*. Edited by Martin H. Manser, John Barton, and Bruce M. Metzger. Oxford: Oxford University Press, 2003.
NWSEB	Dieter Borchmeyer and Jörg Salaquarda, eds., *Nietzsche und Wagner: Stationen einer epochalen Begegnung*. 2 vols. Frankfurt am M.: Insel, 1994.
OCD³	Simon Hornblower and Antony Spawforth, eds., *The Oxford Classical Dictionary*. 3rd ed. Oxford: Oxford University Press, 1996.
OCP	Ted Honderich, ed., *The Oxford Companion to Philosophy*. Oxford: Oxford University Press, 1995.
OD	Klaus Kropfinger, ed., *Richard Wagner: Oper und Drama*. 1984. Reprint. Stuttgart: Philipp Reclam, 2000.
PP	Arthur Schopenhauer, *Parerga and Paralipomena*. 2 vols. 1974. Reprint. Translated by E. F. J. Payne. Oxford: Clarendon, 2000.
PW	*Richard Wagner's Prose Works*. Translated by William Ashton Ellis. 8 vols. New York: Broude Brothers, 1892–99.
RWWSB	*Richard Wagner: Werke, Schriften und Briefe*. Edited by Sven Friedrich. Berlin, 2004 (CD-ROM).
SB	*Richard Wagner: Sämtliche Briefe*. Edited by Gertrud Strobel and Werner Wolf (vols. 1–5), Hans-Joachim Bauer and Johannes Forner (vols. 6–8), Klaus Burmeister and Johannes Forner (vol. 9), Andreas Mielke and Isabel Kraft (vols. 10, 14–15, 18), Martin Dürrer and Isabel Kraft (vols. 11–13, 16–17), Margret Jestremski (vol. 19), Andreas Mielke (vols. 21, 23), Martin Dürrer (vol. 22), Martin Dürrer and Hans Gebhardt (vol. 24), Angela Steinsiek (vol. 25). Leipzig: Deutscher Verlag für Musik, 1967–2000 (vols. 1–9); Wiesbaden: Breitkopf & Härtel, 2000–2017 (vols. 10–25).

ABBREVIATIONS

SL   *Selected Letters of Richard Wagner.* Translated and edited by Stewart Spencer and Barry Millington. New York: W. W. Norton, 1987.

SSD   *Richard Wagner: Sämtliche Schriften und Dichtungen,* Volks-Ausgabe. 16 vols. Leipzig: Breitkopf & Härtel and C.F.W. Siegel (R. Linnemann), 1911 (vols. 1–12) 1914 (vols. 13–16).

SW   *Richard Wagner: Sämtliche Werke* 31 vols. (projected). Mainz: B. Schott, 1970–.

SWMJ   Manfred Schröter, ed., *Schellings Werke, Münchner Jubiläumsdruck.* 12 vols. Munich: C. H. Beck, 1965.

TBRN1   Gabriele E. Meyer, ed., *Texte zum Bühnenfestspiel "Der Ring des Nibelungen" 1 (1848–1853).* SW 29,IIA. Mainz: B. Schott, 2012.

TBRN2   Gabriele E. Meyer, ed., *Texte zum Bühnenfestspiel "Der Ring des Nibelungen" 2 (1853–1876).* SW 29,IIB. Mainz: B. Schott, 2018.

WA   *D. Martin Luthers Werke, kritische Gesamtausgabe.* Weimar: Hermann Böhlaus, 1883–

WBV   Werner Breig, Martin Dürrer, and Andreas Mielke, eds., *Wagner Briefe Verzeichnis: Chronologisches Verzeichnis der Briefe von Richard Wagner.* Wiesbaden: Breitkopf & Härtel, 1998.

WagPS   Lionel Salter, "Libretto." In *Parsifal: Overture Opera Guides,* 105–237. London: Oneworld Classics, 2011.

WagRS   Stewart Spencer, "The Ring of the Nibelung." In *Wagner's Ring of the Nibelung: A Companion,* edited by Stewart Spencer and Barry Millington, 53–372. 1993. Reprint. London: Thames & Hudson, 2010.

WagTS   *Libretto for Richard Wagner's Tristan and Isolde.* Translated by Lionel Salter. Booklet accompanying the Compact Disk recording, conducted by Leonard Bernstein, Philips, 1993.

WBAW   *Walter Benjamin: Ausgewählte Werke.* 5 vols. Darmstadt: Wissenschaftliche Buchgesellschaft, 2015.

WDS   *Wagner: A Documentary Study.* Compiled and edited by Herbart Barth, Dietrich Mack, and Egon Voss. Preface by Pierre Boulez. London: Thames and Hudson, 1975.

WWR   Arthur Schopenhauer, *World as Will and Representation.* 2 vols. 1958. Reprint. Translated by E. F. J. Payne. New York: Dover, 1966.

WWV   John Deathridge, Martin Geck, and Egon Voss, eds., *Wagner-Werk-Verzeichnis: Verzeichnis der musikalischen Werke Richard Wagners und ihrer Quellen.* Mainz: B. Schott, 1986–87.

— 1 —

Introduction to the Theology of the *Ring*

Wagner had an exalted view of art and despised the commercialisation of opera; but he did not hold to the view of "art for art's sake." Rather, he believed his art had the function of transforming not only the human person but also society, and this is especially true of his *Ring* cycle of four operas: *Das Rheingold* (*The Rhinegold*), *Die Walküre* (*The Valkyrie*), *Siegfried*, and *Götterdämmerung* (*Twilight of the Gods*). Regarding the individual person, his *Ring* addresses a whole gamut of existential issues, such as abandonment, loneliness, and anxiety. On a corporate level he addresses, among other things, the dangers of power and "capital," the sickness of society, and the desecration of nature. Hence, his *Ring* addresses a vast spectrum of ethical issues all of which cry out for a theological analysis. The challenge that the *Ring* presents is not only to *understand* the artwork itself but how it may be used to make the world a better place. One could almost apply Marx's dictum from his Thesis XI on Feuerbach: "The philosophers have *interpreted* the world in various ways; the point however is to *change* it."[1] I therefore make the bold suggestion that through an artwork such as the *Ring* lives can be changed for the better and, in particular, such a work can endow them with genuine significance. All this requires a theological analysis, which this volume will seek to provide.

At the end of volume 1 I raised very briefly the significance of Wagner's proposed opera *Jesus of Nazareth* for the *Ring*. Virtually every single issue of the *Ring* addressed in this volume is also addressed by the *Jesus of Nazareth* sketches.[2] These two works came to have these common concerns in the following way. In the Autumn of 1848 Wagner composed his outline of the whole *Ring* drama in the form of his *Der Nibelungen-Mythus: Als Entwurf zu einem Drama* (*The Nibelungs Myth as a Sketch for a Drama*) and then wrote the libretto for *Siegfried's Tod* (*Siegfried's Death*), which was modified over the next years and renamed *Götterdämmerung* in 1856. Elements of these initial

---

1. Engels, *Feuerbach*, 84; *MEW* 3:7. The theses were written by Marx in Brussels in the spring of 1845 in an old notebook and found after Marx's death by Engels, forty years later, who prepared them for publication.

2. Note, however, that the theme of nature, so prominent in the *Ring* (see chapter 4 below) is only discussed briefly in the *Jesus of Nazareth* sketches.

works fed into the *Jesus of Nazareth* sketches, which he composed shortly afterwards. But these sketches included so many other insights that then in turn fed into the *Ring* as it further evolved. Hence, *Jesus of Nazareth* and the *Ring* came mutually to inform one another and interpret one another on the issues of "god," fall, power and "capitalism," love, sexual ethics and law, death and immortality, freedom and necessity, and finally redemption. In this volume I will examine these themes together with Wagner's central concern with nature and I will close by considering some essential issues of interpretation of the *Ring* in relation to myth and allegory. But first I turn to consider more closely the *Jesus of Nazareth* sketches, which provide a linchpin for a theological interpretation of the *Ring*.

— 2 —

Jesus of Nazareth Sketches

Introduction

We only have "sketches" for this proposed five-act drama *Jesus of Nazareth* but they are quite detailed. They consists of two parts: first an outline of the drama (I); secondly a theological commentary (II.1), which is then followed by systematically (in canonical order)[1] quoting the relevant verses from the New Testament (II.2).[2] The drama was composed soon after completing the libretto for *Siegfried's Tod* (*Siegfried's Death*, November 1848).[3] In his autobiography Wagner says the Jesus drama was "sketched out at year-end"[4] but the first entry for the *Annals* of 1849 give "New Testament: sketch of 'Jesus of Nazareth' in 5 Acts."[5] Although the *Annals* were first written as late as February 1868 the date of early 1849 is highly likely. First, from December 1848 Wagner's writing changed to using the lower case for nouns (with the exception of proper nouns or after full stops) and had moved from the German script to the Latin script; here he was following the example of Jacob Grimm.[6] This is precisely the writing style for the *Jesus* sketches.[7] The use of the lower case is found in letters into 1852. There is, however, a lack of consistency in that with writing his *Opera and Drama* in the Winter of 1850–51 and presenting to the publisher a manuscript with the normal upper case we see corresponding changes in his letters.[8] He continued

---

1. This canonical order is stressed by Zegowitz, *Opern*, 191–92.

2. For the three sections, see *PW* 8:285–97, 297–323, 323–40; *DTB* 241–46, 248–59, 259–67. Bell, "Prose Sketches," 263–64, argues that he wrote these sections in the order II.2; I; II.1.

3. See *A Communication to my Friends* (*PW* 1:378; *GSD* 4:331).

4. *My Life* 389; *Mein Leben* 1:403.

5. *Brown Book* 96; *Braunes Buch* 114.

6. See, e.g., Grimm, *Mythologie*, passim. Sometimes Grimm's sentences can even begin without capital letters. See *Mythologie*, 1:XXXVII-VIII. My references to the German will be to the second edition of 1844, which Wagner had in his Dresden library; but his first reading in 1843 would be of the first edition.

7. Capitals are generally reserved for names, places, titles (e.g., "Messias") and the first letter of sentences. *WWV* 339 and *DTB* 241 point out that Eduard Devrient's writing for *Geschichte der deutschen Schauspielkunst*, composed early 1849, is very similar (facsimile in Engel, *Bilde*, 175).

8. Once the manuscript was submitted (20 January 1851), he did go back to using lower case letters

using the lower case into 1852 but reverted to the normal upper case letters in the last months of 1852.[9] The second factor for dating is that he discussed his sketches with Bakunin, whom we know was lodging with Rockel[10] from early 1849.[11] Wagner explains that Bakunin had no interest in the "Nibelung project" but then adds:

> Inspired by a recent reading of the gospels, I had at that time just produced a sketch for a tragedy to be performed in the ideal theatre of the future and to be entitled *Jesus von Nazareth*. Bakunin asked me to spare him any details about it; yet as I seemingly won him over by saying a few words about my general plan, he wished me luck but requested me with great vehemence to make certain Jesus would be represented as a weak character. As to the music, he advised me to compose only one passage but in all possible variations: the tenor was to sing: "Off with his head!," the soprano "To the gallows," and the basso continuo "Fire, fire!"[12]

The third factor to consider for dating is Eduard Devrient's diary entry for 16 April 1849 recording that Wagner on his visit had explained that he had been working on a "tragedy" called "Christus" but had given up on it (and suggests he had given up on all composition).[13] Such a "Christus" must correspond to his *Jesus of Nazareth*. It is striking that in the "Entwurf" itself and in the commentary the title "Christus" is not

---

(from 20 February 1851; *SB* 4:5).

9. It is perhaps significant that among the last to receive letters with lower case letters for nouns were those he considered "revolutionary": see the letter to Liszt of 9 November 1852 (*SB* 5:93–97) and those to Uhlig of 27 November and 6 December 1852 (*SB* 5:120–24). Whether his near consistent use of the old German script for his wife Minna was because she was regarded as "belonging to the 'old' order" (Deathridge, *Good and Evil*, 257 n. 36) or whether he used it simply because she had difficulty reading the Latin script is a subject for debate. The one exceptional use of the Latin script for Minna of which we know is the letter with a postmark of 17 September 1851. Half way through the letter Wagner realized he has used the Latin script and then switched to the German script. *SB* 4:115 n. 277 gives the explanation that Minna had difficulty reading the Latin script.

10. *My Life* 384; *Mein Leben* 1:398.

11. Carr, *Bakunin*, 186, tells us that Bakunin on his journey to Prague passed through Dresden and got to know Röckel, editor of the radical weekly Volksblatt. Then in Röckel's house Bakunin met Wagner and the *Annals* for 1849 tell us that the composer had "[e]xtensive association with him in secret" and at the beginning of the new year had "walks with Bakunin" (*Brown Book* 96; *Braunes Buch* 114). Wagner tells in *My Life* 384 (*Mein Leben* 1:397–98) that the general rehearsal for Beethoven's Ninth (to be performed on Palm Sunday 1849) "had been attended, in secret and without knowledge of the police, by Michael Bakunin." "[A]fter it was over he came up to me unabashedly in the orchestra in order to call out to me that, if all music were to be lost in the coming world conflagration, we should risk our own lives to preserve this symphony." Wagner explains in his report on *Beethoven's Choral Symphony at Dresden* how it came to be performed on Palm Sunday (*PW* 7:241; *GSD* 2:50). There were performances in 1846, 1847, 1849 (the Eighth Symphony was played in 1848).

12. *My Life* 387; *Mein Leben* 1:401. Bakunin is changing the crowd calling for Jesus' crucifixion to other methods of execution (beheading, hanging, burning).

13. Devrient, *Tagebücher*, 1:475: "Besuch von Kapellmeister Wagner. Er sagte, er habe die Zeit her an einer Tragödie 'Christus' gearbeitet, das Unternehmen aber aufgegeben. Nun will er nichts tun als gesund werden, und dazu läuft er spazieren. Auch recht! Ein toller, gescheiter Kerl." Note that Wagner also refers to the work as a "tragedy" in *My Life* 387; *Mein Leben* 1:400.

employed and only occurs in the extensive series of quoted verses from the New Testament (there are four such texts). But we do have a musical sketch entitled "Christus im Schiffe" ("Christ in the ship").[14] This appears on the reverse side of a sheet from the score of *Lohengrin* and would seem to be a musical setting of the scene in Act II where we read of Jesus' teaching the people from the boat.[15] This does raise the intriguing possibility that had he further developed the sketches he may have introduced the title "Christus" into the proposed opera.

All this evidence points to the time of composition as the early months of 1849. But perhaps one can be more precise.[16] Devrient also records an earlier meeting with Wagner on 31 March 1849 where they discuss Wagner's ideas of making the world a better place ("seine weltverbessernden Theorien").[17] If Devrient's diary entry of 16 April 1849 gives a *terminus ad quem* for the sketches, the entry for the previous visit of 31 March may possibly offer a *terminus a quo*. This is because on 31 March every single idea they discuss appears in the *Jesus* sketches, yet nothing is said of the sketches themselves. In their discussion, Wagner proposes the abolition of property in order to achieve moral improvement ("durch Vernichtung des Besitzes alle Versittlichung zu erreichen"), Devrient "a new religious rebirth of Europe" ("eine neue religiöse Wiedergeburt Europas") in order to attenuate egoism ("Selbstsucht"), the mother of all social ills. Wagner considers the destruction of all deficiency ("[e]r denkt an Aufhebung aller Mangelhaftigkeit") and believes in the absolute original perfection of the human race, which has been lost because of the state ("[er] glaubt an die absoluten ursprüngliche Vollkommenheit des menschlichen Geschlechtes, die nur durch den Staat verlorengegangen sei"). Wagner comments on the foolishness of the human development over six thousand years[18] for which the state-mechanism ("Staatsmechanismus") is to blame. The only hope is a moral improvement of our misery ("eine sittliche Verbesserung unserer Misere") which can be achieved by the state structures being guided by the "law of love" ("Gesetz der Liebe"). Devrient thinks the lamentable bankruptcy of the current political situation can only be solved by a great religious inspiration, by God's total intervention.[19] I suspect that Wagner had already given much thought to the sketches but that after the discussion of 31 March 1849 he was propelled to get them committed to paper.

---

14. The music is given in *WWV* 339. It is not immediately clear so to why he avoids using "Christus" in the drama outline and commentary. He is happy to use the title elsewhere including five times in *Die Wibelungen*, which was composed around the same time. Did he have a momentary aversion to Jewish messianic expectation?

15. *PW* 8:289: "Jesus, standing on board, preaches to the Folk" (*DTB*: "Jesus, im Schiffe stehend, lehret das Volk").

16. Cf. *WWV* 339.

17. Devrient, *Tagebücher*, 1:473.

18. I do not think this necessarily points to Wagner's belief in a creation in 4004 BC.

19. Devrient, *Tagebücher*, 1:473–74.

The work was certainly intended as an opera[20] and we do have that one musical sketch, but of just eleven bars. It is significant that this is on the reverse of a page from the score of *Lohengrin*. Had he composed the music, the opera would probably be "choral" rather like *Lohengrin*. (Note that the next opera he turned to, *Siegfried's Tod*, was also "choral" in nature). *Jesus von Nazareth* occupied Wagner's thinking for much of 1849 and we find a series of discussions about the work. On fleeing Dresden and arriving in Weimar he discussed it with Liszt and Carolyne von Sayn-Wittgenstein; that he was able to discuss it, despite the turmoil in his life, is significant. Further, he discussed the work in a series of letters. On 9 August 1849 he writes to Uhlig that Liszt was "damnably keen" for him to write an opera for Paris (he was feeling some pressure from Liszt since he had financed Wagner's journey out of Germany, given him some money, and said he should "seek his salvation in Paris and offer the Grand Opéra a new work").[21] Wagner explains that "a well-known poet" (Gustave Vaëz) was prepared to translate a full libretto into French and Wagner would receive a commission to compose the music.[22] He explains that apart from *Siegfried's Tod* he has two tragic subjects and two comic ones. The tragic ones may be identified with *Achilleus* and *Alexander the Great* and the two comic ones may be *Meistersinger* and *Der junge Siegfried*.[23] None of these though he felt were suitable for a production in French. But he adds: "I now have a 5th one, of which it is a matter of indifference to me in what language it first sees the light of day: 'Jesus of Nazareth'. I intend offering this subject to my French associate and in this way hope to be rid of the whole affair, since I can well imagine the look of horror on his face when he sees the poem."[24] The reference to the "poem" may possibly suggest that he had written the libretto; however, a number of factors cast doubt on this. First, there is no other reference to his writing the poem and when he refers to the work it is always to the sketches.[25] Secondly, although this letter refers to a "poem" other texts point to the difficulty in producing a libretto for Paris. So he explains to Liszt in a letter of 5 June 1849: "A libretto of Scribe or Dumas I cannot set to music" ("Ein Scribesches oder Dumassches libretto kann ich nicht komponiren").[26] In the last months of 1849 he was still toying with the idea of writing the opera for Paris, but one can see clear signs of indecision. So on 14 October

---

20. Ellis, writing in 1899, believes the work was not intended as a *musical* drama (*PW* 8:xv–xvi). Further, Nolte, *Fragmenten*, 62–63, writing in 1917, also thinks it was a spoken drama. Perhaps he deduced this from *Mein Leben*, which refers to the work as a "tragedy" and "drama." But Wagner envisaged including the work in volume 4 of collected works: "Entwurf zu einem grossen musikalischen Drama 'Jesus von Nazareth.'—(Im Besitz der Fürstin Caroline von Wittgenstein—in Bonn.)" (*KB* 1:48, 6 January 1865).

21. Gregor-Dellin, *Life*, 184.

22. *SL* 174; *SB* 3:109.

23. *SL* 175 n. 2.

24. *SL* 175; *SB* 3:110.

25. See below on the problems he faced in trying to get the sketches from Princess Carolyne.

26. *SB* 3:74.

he writes to Liszt; "Subjects which I should have been prepared to execute for Paris (such as *Jesus of Nazareth*) turn out to be impossible for manifold reasons when I come to consider the practical bearings of the thing, and I must therefore have time and leisure to wait for inspiration, which I can expect only from some remote region of my nature."[27] But on 19 November he writes to Ferdinand Heine, words that may imply further work on the opera: "I shall spend the next few days elaborating my sketch for there [i.e., Paris]; it is: *Jesus of Nazareth*."[28] But a letter of 4 December to Heine suggests no further work had been undertaken since, he writes, *Jesus von Nazareth* appears as a full chimera.[29] His giving up on Paris is further underlined in a letter the following day to Liszt: "What operatic subjects I had in my head would not have done for Paris, and this was the cause of my hesitation in the whole affair which you had initiated so well."[30]

Wagner took a fresh interest in the work again after being rescued by Ludwig, but Wagner had lent the sketches to Carolyne von Wittgenstein, who prevented the publication of the work and refused to return it. We do not know when or how she came in possession of it, but it must have been before King Ludwig asked the composer for the sketches twice in 1865.[31] Ludwig then turned to Cosima, asking in a letter of 26 January 1866 if there was no manuscript of *Jesus von Nazareth*, explaining that his longing for this (and other pure dramatic works) was like a hart longing for the spring or a prisoner longing for freedom.[32] Cosima explained that the text "is locked up on the Altenburg in Weimar" ("ist eingesperrt auf der Altenburg in Weimar"), belongs to Carolyne von Wittgenstein, and she has said she will return from Rome to Germany, sort out her papers, and will pass on the manuscript for Ludwig. But she has not yet done this![33] Ludwig's enthusiasm for the work is reflected in Wagner's letter to Praeger, the authenticity of which is unclear. Here Wagner says Ludwig wished to put on "Christus" and that Wagner himself still found the idea of "Christus" stimulating, and considered that he might still bring the work to fruition.[34] The sketches were published by Siegfried Wagner in 1887, four years after his

27. *CWL* 1:49; *SB* 3:136.

28. *SL* 179; *SB* 3:150. But note there is no extant evidence though of further work on the opera.

29. *SB* 3:178.

30. *CWL* 1:56; *SB* 3:187. Included among the "operatic subjects" was *Jesus of Nazareth*.

31. Letters of 17 June (*KB* 1:108) and 7 November 1865 (*KB* 1:206).

32. *DTB* 56 (Schad, *Cosima Wagner und Ludwig II*, 133). Ludwig's words "ich sehne mich, wie der Hirsch nach Wasserquelle darnach" probably allude to Psalm 42:1 (Luther's translation Psalm 42:2: "Wie der Hirsch schreitet nach frischem Wasser / So schreitet meine seele Gott zu dir"). Ludwig's comments about "Seinen andern, rein dramatischen Werken" ("His other purely dramatic works") does not mean that the work was not intended as an opera; it is simply that the work was only at present in prose form.

33. *DTB* 56 (Schad, *Cosima Wagner und Ludwig II*, 259).

34. Letter of 8 April 1865 (Praeger, *Wagner*, 340; *WBV* 4151; *DTB* 56): "Er ist ein so schöner Jüngling, dass er den Christus vorstellen könnte, (ein Thema, welches mich immer wieder reizt—vielleicht bringt es mich noch dazu)."

father's death.[35] How Siegfried managed to recover the manuscript is unknown but it is significant that 1887 was the year of Carolyne's death.

But even if Wagner had recovered the sketches, we know from *A Communication to my Friends*, that he had reservations about composing such an opera. In the last year of his life he expressed concerns at least about setting the work to music. Cosima records this conversation: "R. begins, 'One cannot paint Christ, but one can portray him in music.'—I say that I see it as evidence of his great and so significant artistic sagacity that he abandoned the figure of Christ and created Parsifal instead: 'To have Chr. sung by a tenor—what a disgusting idea! (von einem Tenoristen Chr.[istus] gegeben, pfui T.[eufel])' he says."[36] This could of course be referring to the fact that Jesus would have to be a Heldentenor (as it is the case for his other heroes) whereas in the Bach passions he is a bass (and who sings only recitative).[37] Further, Wagner may also have in mind the fact that Christ is a tenor in Beethoven's oratorio *Christus am Ölberg*, a work about which he appears to have had doubts.[38] But the issue is perhaps not so much whether he would be a tenor, bass, or even baritone, but the fact that no human singer could do justice to the Son of God. Hence Wagner's wisdom, as Cosima indicates, that he created *Parsifal* instead.

In Wagner's original plan for his collected works (1865) *Jesus von Nazareth* was to be in volume 4.[39] Wagner made a second plan for the publication on 26 April 1868, this time including *Jesus von Nazareth* in volume 1 under a section headed "Entwürfe" ("sketches").[40] But the Princess was still refusing to return the manuscript, as shown by Wagner's letter to Jessie Laussot of 24 January 1869[41] and by Cosima's entry for that day: "R. is replying to Mme Laussot and demanding through her the manuscript of *Jesus von Nazareth* from Princess Wittgenstein, who, although she was only lent it,

---

35. The work was dedicated to memory of Heinrich von Stein (1857–87). He was a disciple of the antisemite Eugen Dühring. Von Stein was sent to Nietzsche the year after Wagner's death in an effort "to coax him back into the Wagner circle" (Santaniello, "Nietzsche and the Jews," 28). See *Ecce Homo*, "Why I am so Wise," 4 (Nietzsche, *Anti-Christ*, 79; *FNKSA* 6:269–70).

36. *CD* 22 October 1882.

37. The other possibility is that he could he baritone like the Holländer. However, such baritones probably have too many dark associations for the Son of God.

38. In addition to the SATB chorus the angel is a soprano and Peter is a bass. The work was badly received and Beethoven himself was critical of it. The work was conducted by Reissiger on the Palm Sunday performance of Beethoven's Ninth in 1849. Wagner's only reference to the work is as "Christus am Elbberge" (Glasenapp, *Leben*, 2:161 n 3), a reference to Reissiger living "Am Elbberge." Although Wagner had the greatest admiration for Beethoven, he seems to share the general view that it is not one of his greater works and Beethoven himself admitted it was composed in haste (Matthews, *Beethoven*, 196). Further, Wagner had reservations about the medium of the oratorio generally.

39. See n. 20 above.

40. *Brown Book* 131; *Braunes Buch* 156. The other sketches were to be "Die Sarazenin," "Die Bergwerke zu Falun," and "Wiland der Schmied."

41. *SB* 21:47; *DTB* 56.

does not want to give it back. Greed of possession or religious caution? Whichever it is, her cynical effrontery is the same."[42]

I now turn to consider under five headings fundamental theological issues that the sketches and the final *Ring* share: the question of "God"; the problem of power; capital and property; law and freedom, and love; redemption. One of the questions to consider will be whether ideas from the *Mythus* and *Siegfried's Tod* fed into the *Jesus* sketches and whether the ideas from the *Jesus* sketches fed into the further development of the *Ring* as Wagner went on to compose *Der junge Siegfried*, and then *Rheingold* and *Walküre*, and then also making some significant changes to *Siegfried's Tod*.

God

In the dramatic outline itself the word "God" never appears apart from the term "Son of God."[43] This negative result is in itself significant and points to a tendency found throughout most of Wagner's artistic career that divinity is to be focussed in the person of Jesus. Wagner stresses the humanity of God and this is realized in the *Ring* in that the key divine figure is Brünnhilde; it is also significant that even the chief God Wotan is human and in fact turns out to be the most psychologically complex character of all.

In the 1848 *Ring* the gods are aloof and do not suffer. This was all to change as he developed the drama in 1851–52 and one wonders whether the suffering Jesus in some way influenced his portrayal of the suffering Wotan. I will return to this in chapter 3 below.

Power

It has been too easily overlooked that the *Jesus* sketches write of powers from which one needs to be redeemed, the central ones being sin, law, and death,[44] something to which I return when I consider redemption itself. But the power that I need to address here is that which parallels power in the *Ring*, the power exercised by those who would deny love and wish to take over the world.

Throughout the drama Barabbas[45] acts as an antipode to Jesus and Judas is given a much stronger political role than in the Gospels. In the very first scene Barabbas plots with Judas against the Roman yoke (this, with the appropriate symbolism, takes

---

42. *CD* 24 January 1869.

43. Note, however, Jesus speaks of "the Kingdom of Heaven in Man" (*PW* 8:289; *DTB* 243) at the end of Act II. Cf. Luke 17:21 "For, in fact, the kingdom of God is among you." Wagner in using the term "heaven" is adopting a circumlocution for "God," found frequently in Matthew.

44. Compare how the Swedish theologian Nygren, *Romans*, 187–349, analyzed what he considered "Part Two" of the letter, Rom 5–8: free from wrath (5), sin (6), law (7), and death (8). The one element missing in Wagner's sketches is "wrath"!

45. Note that Wagner follows Luther's spelling "Barrabas"; Ellis in his translation replaces this with the correct spelling "Barabbas."

place at night). Another night scene in the *Ring* offers an intriguing parallels: *Götterdämmerung* Act II Scene 1, where Hagen and Alberich are discussing their plans to "inherit the world."[46] When Wagner wrote his *Jesus* sketches, the libretto for what was then called *Siegfried's Tod* was somewhat more extensive[47] in that Alberich has to explain previous events to Hagen, which was not necessary in the final libretto since the previous operas have done that already. But in these different versions we have two dark figures who, quite possibly, are portrayed as "Jewish," just as in the case of Judas and Barabbas, who are trying to achieve this world dominion![48]

Power in Jewish hands is shown to have devastating consequences as Wagner's *Jesus* drama progresses and everything comes to a head in the final act with an uproar caused by Barabbas and then by Jesus (but as polar opposites, it being stressed that Jesus is not a political messiah).[49] The person who tries to exercise power in a good sense is the non-Jew, Pilate. He does not have enough troops to control the situation and is desperately awaiting reinforcements to arrive in Jerusalem. In the trial scene Pilate attempts to delay proceedings hoping that the Syrian reinforcements will arrive.[50] A marginal note at the end of the drama offers the possibility that just after Jesus' death Pilate receives news that his awaited legions are approaching; he despairs at their coming too late, thereby portraying Pilate even more positively than in the Gospels.[51]

It is not only in the trial scene that the Jews are portrayed in a negative light. Throughout the drama the villains are the Jewish leaders, a Pharisee from Tiberias being singled out for censure. He appears first in Act I where he criticizes Jesus for "his familiar intercourse with publicans and sinners."[52] He is also the one who approaches Judas in the plan to betray Jesus.[53] Further "the Pharisees ply the Folk, direct its sympathies to Barabbas [. . .] not Jesus"[54] and, with Caiaphas, they object when Pilate wishes to acquit Jesus.[55] Further, it is the Pharisees who object to Pilate's inscription saying Jesus is of "King of the Jews."[56] In the canonical Gospels the Pharisees are not involved directly in Jesus death[57] but Wagner enhances their

---

46. *WagRS* 310.

47. Haymes, *Ring*, 108–13.

48. Note that whereas in *WagRS* 311 Hagen sings "The ring I shall have" ("Den Ring soll ich haben") in the original *Siegfried's Tod* he tells Alberich "You shall have the ring" ("Den Ring sollst du haben") (Haymes, *Ring*, 112–13).

49. *PW* 8:294; *DTB* 246.

50. *PW* 8:294–95; *DTB* 246.

51. *PW* 8:297; *DTB* 246.

52. *PW* 8:286; *DTB* 242.

53. *PW* 8:291; *DTB* 244 (Act III).

54. *PW* 8:294; *DTB* 245. Contrast Matt 26:20 where it is the "chief priests and the elders."

55. *PW* 8:295; *DTB* 245.

56. *PW* 8:296; *DTB* 246. In John 19:21 it is "the chief priests of the Jews" who object.

57. But see their attempts to destroy him in Mark 3:6; Matt 21:45–46; see especially John 11:57; nevertheless, the Pharisees do tend to move into the background as we approach the passion of Jesus.

involvement.⁵⁸ We have therefore a binary opposition between the positive reading of Pilate and a negative one of the Pharisees.

Pilate's exercise of power in a good sense parallels Wotan's attempt to try to place order on the world. In the *Jesus* sketches, as in the Gospels, the Jewish exercise of power is largely through their Jewish law. Wagner's antisemitism is clearly at work here and it is underlined by the fact that Jesus' Jewishness is relativized. At the beginning of the commentary Wagner explains: "Jesus descended from the house of David, out of which the Redeemer of the Jewish nation was awaited: David's own lineage, however, went back to Adam, the immediate offspring of God, from whom spring all men."⁵⁹ Although Jesus was seen as "the heir of David" at his baptism, Jesus came to a different conclusion in the desert where "he counselled with himself."⁶⁰ "He went still deeper to the founder of his race, to Adam the child of God: might he not gain a superhuman strength, if he felt conscious of that origin from God who stood exalted over Nature? [. . .] So Jesus brushed aside the House of David: through Adam had he sprung from God, and therefore all men were his brothers."⁶¹

It is significant that it was after writing the *Jesus* sketches that Wagner intensified the theme of the dangers of power in the *Ring* and it is probable that it was precisely the work on the *Jesus* sketches that provoked this development in the *Ring*.

Capital and Property

Just as we have Alberich as the (possibly Jewish) capitalist, so in the Jesus sketches there are warnings about capital and property (which could be said to be related to corrupt power). It is often stated that Wagner conceives of Jesus preaching a purely worldly religion of "commonality and communism," advocating "freedom from law and thus liberation from the shackles of the state."⁶² Whilst this does not come over in the drama itself, in the commentary Wagner shows clear sympathy for the views of Proudhon (i.e., property should be fairly distributed). One can say (and many do) that Wagner presented Jesus as a "social revolutionary,"⁶³ although it has to be said that this is just one aspect of Jesus' ministry and in the drama is a minor aspect (it is more important in the commentary). Further, it is a fundamental mistake to associate the Jesus of his drama with Wagner's activities on the barricades of Dresden.⁶⁴

58. Note that Sadducees are not mentioned by name but the "Jewish tribal aristocracy" (*PW* 8:298) can be identified as Sadducees.

59. *PW* 8:297; *DTB* 248.

60. *PW* 8:297; *DTB* 248.

61. *PW* 8:298; *DTB* 248.

62. Kienzle, "A Christian Music Drama?" 84.

63. *WDS* 75.

64. Note that the sketches specifically reject the view that Jesus was a political revolutionary. But Millington, *Wagner*, 36, almost suggests he was, believing that Wagner's portrayal of Jesus is supported by "[m]odern scholarship." He refers to Brandon, *Trial*, whose reconstruction of the trial of

Just as Wagner speaks against property, so he speaks against "possession" in the realm of marriage. Such a "Verfestigung," a central idea in this passage on possession and marriage,[65] enters when law comes into play: "[I]f Man made a law to shackle love, to reach a goal that lies outside of human nature (—namely, power, dominion— above all: the *protection of* property:) he sinned against the law of his own existence, and therewith slew himself."[66] The allusion here is to Proudhon.[67] No works of Proudhon are in his Dresden library (or later in the Wahnfried library) and he most likely knew of him from August Röckel.[68] These words in the *Jesus* sketches are redolent of Sieglinde's words: "Dieß Haus und dieß Weib / sind Hunding's Eigen" ("This house and this wife / are Hunding's own").[69] Further, these words from the commentary to the *Jesus* drama are relevant for Sieglinde: "If a woman was wed by a man for whom she had not love, and he fulfilled the letter of the marriage-law to her, through that law she became his property: the woman's struggle for freedom through love thereby became a sin, actual contentment of her love she could only attain by adultery."[70] Wagner goes on to put words into the mouth of Jesus. First for Act IV: "Through my death there perisheth the Law, inasmuch as I shew you that Love is greater than the Law."[71] Then for Act I: "The commandment saith: Thou shalt not commit adultery! But I say unto you: Ye shall not marry (freien) without love. A marriage without love is broken as soon as entered into, and whoso hath wooed without love, already hath broken the wedding."[72] This is a clear example where ideas of the Jesus sketches have entered the *Ring* as it was developed after 1849.

Utterances on capital and property in the *Jesus* sketches, and how they are extended to marriage, then bring us to the next theme: law, freedom, and love.

Law, Freedom, and Love

As in the drama, there is much negative comment in the commentary on the Jewish law. In preparing for *Jesus of Nazareth* he had read systematically through the whole New Testament and in the commentary it is clear that he had been struck by some

---

Jesus (whereby Jesus was condemned by the Romans as a "zealot" revolutionary) is in direct contradiction to Wagner's drama (see below). It is also worth adding that Brandon's whole Zealot hypothesis has been seriously questioned by those who know rather more about the issues (see Hengel's review of Brandon's *Jesus and the Zealots*).

65. Zegowitz, *Opern*, 188.
66. *PW* 8:301; *DTB* 249.
67. Cf. Proudhon, *Staatsökonomie*, 1:341–46. Wagner's debt to Proudhon is further discussed below (chapter 5).
68. Zegowitz, *Opern*, 188 n. 31.
69. *WagRS* 123.
70. *PW* 8:302; *DTB* 250.
71. *PW* 8:303; *DTB* 250.
72. *PW* 8:303; *DTB* 250. This final sentence is a marginal addition.

radical texts concerning the law. First he reflects a view of law that may be related to Paul although it is often a development of Paul. So Wagner (in the commentary) puts these Pauline words into Jesus' mouth where law and spirit are set against each other:

> I redeem you from Sin by proclaiming to you the everlasting law of the Spirit, which [i.e., the law] is its being, but not its limitation (beschränkung). The Law, as given you heretofore, was the limitation (beschränkung) of your being in the flesh: without that law ye had no sin, but hearkened to the law of Nature: but the Letter (buchstabe) was set up over your flesh [Rom 7:6; 2 Cor 3:6], and the Law, which taught you to regard the nature of the flesh as sinful, brought you to death [Rom 7:9–10]; for now ye sinned in doing what, according to the law, ye should not. But I release you from the Law which slew you [Rom 7:6a], inasmuch as I bring unto you the law of the Spirit [Rom 8:3–4], which giveth life [. . .] now I slay this law, and thereby root up sin: from sin I thus redeem you, inasmuch as I give you Love.[73]

As I have indicated, there are numerous allusions to Paul's letters,[74] the very last phrase indicating how central love was for Wagner.

But as well as presenting Pauline ideas sometimes, as I have suggested, he goes beyond Paul and the question is whether this is a legitimate development. Consider these words (in these cases not put into the mouth of Jesus). First he writes of the "fall": "God was one with the world from the beginning: the earliest races (Adam and Eve) lived and moved in this oneness, innocent, unknowing it: the first step in knowledge was the distinguishing between the helpful and the harmful [Gen. 2:17]; in the human heart the notion of the Harmful developed into that of the Wicked."[75] Then he goes on to speak of the entrance of the law, by which he must mean the Mosaic law. I offer this extended quotation as an example of his interweaving of aspects of biblical thought with that of figures such as Hegel and Feuerbach:

> Human society next sought deliverance through the *Law*: it fastened the notion of Good to the Law, as to something intelligible and perceptible by us all: but what was bound fast to the Law was only a moment [aspect/impulse] of the Good, and since God is eternally generative, fluent and mobile, the Law thus turned against God's self; for, as man can live and move by none save the ur-law of Motion itself (nach dem urgesetze der bewegung selbst) [Acts 17:28],[76] in pursuance of his nature he needs must clash against the Law, i.e., the binding, standing,—thus grow sinful. This is man's suffering, the suffering of God himself, who has not come as yet to consciousness in men (Dies ist das menschliche leiden, das leiden gottes selbst, der sich in den

---

73. *PW* 8:300; *DTB* 249.

74. In addition to those given see also 2 Cor 3:6. Note that in Luther's translation the Greek *gramma* is rendered "Buchstabe."

75. *PW* 8:310; *DTB* 254.

76. Acts 17:23b-29 is quoted in section II.2 (*PW* 8:335–36; *DTB* 264–65).

menschen noch nicht zum bewusstsein gekommen ist). That consciousness we finally attain through taking the essence of Man himself for immediate Godhood, through recognising the eternal law whereby the whole creation moves as the positive and ineluctable, and abolishing the distinction between the helpful and the harmful (den unterschied des nützlichen und schädlichen dadurch aufheben) through our recognition that sub specie aeterni (im Betracht des Ewigen) the two are the selfsame utterance of creative force: the original oneness of God and the World thus is gained anew to our consciousness, and Sin, therefore Suffering, abolished by our abolition (aufgehoben [. . .] aufheben) of the clumsy human law—which opposed itself as State to Nature—through recognition that the *only* God indwells in us and in our unity with Nature—the which, again, we recognise itself as undivided. Jesus removed this conflict (hat diesen zwiespalt aufgehoben), and established the oneness of God, by his proclamation of *Love*.[77]

The idea I extract from this, and which coheres with views expressed at several points throughout the sketches, is that the principle of love and spirit must be followed and not that of law. Love, which for Wagner often takes the role of Hegel's spirit, is flexible and responsive but law is static and inflexible. But at the same time Wagner can speak positively about law as the law of love:[78] "but God is the law of Love, and when once we know it and walk thereby, as every creature walketh without knowing it, we are God himself: for God is the knowledge of self."[79] The divinization of human beings may well have been inspired by John 10:31–33 and 10:34–38,[80] both of which were marked in his New Testament.[81] This idea also occurs a little earlier in the commentary: "Jesus knows and practises God's-love through his teaching of it: in the consciousness of Cause and Effect he accordingly is God and Son of God; but every man is capable of like knowledge and like practice,—and if he attain thereto, he is like unto God and Jesus."[82]

The law of love of which Wagner speaks is not a law that *commands* love. Towards the end of the commentary (II.1) he writes: "The Law is lovelessness; and even should it command me to love, in keeping it I should not practice love, for Love deals only after itself, not after a commandment."[83] It is rather ironic that

---

77. *PW* 8:311; *DTB* 254.

78. As he can concerning the "law of the Spirit" (see above).

79. *PW* 8:312; *DTB* 254.

80. Jesus, answering the accusation of "the Jews" that he blasphemes since as a human being he is making himself God, quotes Psalm 82:6: "Is it not written in your law, 'I said you are gods'?"

81. John 10:31–33 is further marked with the Roman numeral III (i.e., he considered it relevant for Act III of his drama); also the preceding verse, John 10:30 ("The Father and I are one"), is underlined and in the margin he writes what looks like three adjoining crosses in a line.

82. *PW* 8:301; *DTB* 249.

83. *PW* 8:322; *DTB* 259.

although Wagner's views on the Jewish law appear negative, reflecting those of German idealism,[84] his views can bear a certain similarity to those of ancient Judaism whereby "the law would be most appropriately fulfilled if one were to do what corresponds to it *before* the law itself were given."[85] See *Numbers Rabbah* 14:2: "Joseph, you observed the Sabbath before the Torah was given. By your life! I shall repay your grandson by allowing him to present his offering on the Sabbath, an offering which an individual is otherwise not permitted to bring, and I undertake to accept his offering with favour."[86] A little earlier, Job 41:3 is applied to Joseph: "'Whoso hath anticipated Me, I will repay him' speaks of Joseph who early observed the Sabbath before it was given [. . .]."[87] Hence Jüngel argues that "[t]he law [. . .] is the representative of that obviousness of force (Selbstverständlichkeit des Zwanges) to which human exertion and human achievement correspond."[88] To love God and one's neighbor "is the very epitome of the law's demands" (Mark 12:29–34), "[b]ut this demand is fulfilled by one's *exertions*."[89] Hence, Paul has the negative view of "works of law" and seeking to establish one's own righteousness (Rom 10:3). The human being under the law is "chained to himself."[90] Jesus by contrast "anticipated the law out of the obviousness of love (Selbstverständlichkeit der Liebe), and thus more than satisfied the law with a great although new obviousness. And he thereby made plain that one could fulfil the law only by *preceding* it, anticipating it in its fulfilment. That is the only way in which man can show himself to be absolutely *free*."[91] These ideas of anticipating what the law requires found in ancient Jewish texts and developed by Jüngel do elucidate Wagner's view of law and love but we are faced with a historical problem in that Jesus was brought up by his family in the knowledge of the law.

---

84. See, e.g., Hegel, *On Christianity*, 68–69 ("The Positivity of the Christian Religion" Part I), who writes that at the time of Jesus "[t]he Jews were a people [. . .] overwhelmed by a burden of statutory commands which pedantically prescribed a rule for every casual action of daily life and gave the whole people the look of a monastic order. As a result of this system, the holiest of things, namely, the service of God and virtue, the holiest of things, namely, the service of God and virtue, was ordered and compressed in dead formulas, and nothing save pride in this slavish obedience to law not laid down by themselves was left to the Jewish spirit, which already was deeply mortified and embittered by the subjection of the state to a foreign power." Such views are seriously one-sided when compared with those put forward in the ancient Jewish sources. The secondary literature on law in ancient Judaism is vast and I simply refer to Avemarie, *Tora und Leben*, as a model of nuanced analysis of the complex and sometimes contradictory ancient Jewish views on the law.

85. Jüngel, *Mystery*, 358 n. 35 (*Geheimnis*, 491 n. 35), who appeals to a private conversation with his Tübingen colleague H. P. Rüger.

86. Slotki, *Midrash Rabbah: Numbers*, 2:570. This grandson is taken to be "Elishama, son of Ammihud, the leader of the Ephraimites" (Num 7:48).

87. Slotki, *Midrash Rabbah: Numbers*, 2:570.

88. Jüngel, *Mystery*, 358 (*Geheimnis*, 491).

89. Jüngel, *Mystery*, 358 (*Geheimnis*, 491), Jüngel's emphasis.

90. Jüngel, *Mystery*, 359 (*Geheimnis*, 492).

91. Jüngel, *Mystery*, 359 (*Geheimnis*, 492–93).

A correlate of Wagner's view of the law is his view of freedom. One of the striking aspects of Jesus' teaching in the sketches is precisely his idea of freedom, not so much freedom from the law of the state but rather freedom from the law of the Jews. But his view of freedom is sophisticated and in many respects resembles Hegel's view. For Hegel, "[t]rue freedom [. . .] lies not merely in doing or choosing what one wishes, but in being a 'free will which wills the free will.'"[92] The free will therefore derives obligations from itself; it is "a self-legislating and self-determining will."[93] Obligations therefore do not come from some alien authority.

Hegel seems to find that this view coheres with the teaching of Jesus. "This spirit of Jesus, a spirit raised above morality [Kant's view of reason dominating inclination], is visible, directly attacking laws, in the Sermon on the Mount, which is an attempt, elaborated in numerous examples, to strip the laws of legality, of their legal form."[94] Against Kant, Hegel argued that "in love all thought of duties vanishes."[95] "The opposition of duty to inclination has found its unification in the modifications of love, i.e., in the virtues. Since law was opposed to love, not in its content but in its form, it could be taken up into love, though in this process it lost its shape."[96] This is precisely Wagner's understanding of freedom in his sketches and we have again the pattern of ideas from the *Jesus* sketches feeding into the *Ring's* development after 1849.

Redemption and Jesus' Death

Although Wagner described his drama as a "tragedy," this does not necessarily mean that the work ends with the "downfall" of Jesus.[97] The Syrian reinforcements arrive too late for Pilate to save him, but his death is seen as redemptive and is a necessary prerequisite for the bestowing of the Holy Spirit.

The theme of redemption occupied Wagner throughout his creative life and appears in one form or another in every single opera. In the dramatic outline (I) of the sketches Jesus speaks of his "impending sacrificial death"[98] and his "redeeming death" ("erlösungstod," Act II),[99] and his "sacrificial death" ("opfertod," Act IV),[100] stressing that this redemption is for "all people of the earth [. . .] not of the Jew alone";[101] and, as

---

92. Houlgate, *Introduction to Hegel*, 184, quoting *Philosophy of Right* §27 (Knox/Houlgate, *Philosophy of Right*, 46).

93. Houlgate, *Introduction to Hegel*, 185.

94. Hegel, *On Christianity*, 212.

95. Hegel, *On Christianity*, 213.

96. Hegel, *On Christianity*, 225.

97. Cf. Hegel, *Aesthetics*, 2:1218: "the tragic denouement need not every time require the downfall of the participating individuals."

98. *PW* 8:288; *DTB* 243.

99. *PW* 8:289; *DTB* 243.

100. *PW* 8:292; *DTB* 244.

101. *PW* 8:291; *DTB* 244.

we have seen, Peter speaks of "the sacrificial death of Jesus" as he is being crucified.[102] Wagner's understanding of redemption in the sketches comes primarily from reading Luther's New Testament translation and he clearly has a "cultic" understanding of redemption. For example, although the root "erlösen" (to redeem) does not occur in Heb 9:13–14, the placing of words, which unmistakably allude to these verses, in Jesus' mouth in the commentary (II.1) makes the cultic nature of redemption clear: "With an offering of the blood of bulls and rams the High Priest entered once each year into the sanctuary of the Temple, that yet was made by hand of man: with the offering of my own blood once and forever I go into the holiest sanctuary of the temple that was made by hand of God: but the temple of God is mankind."[103] However, although Wagner speaks of Jesus' death as a sacrifice and quotes Hebrews 9:13–14, he does not have a "theory of the atonement." If he did, the closest he comes to one is probably that found in Luther's *Shorter Catechism,* which Wagner probably committed to memory for his confirmation. In the discussion of the creed, the "second article" on the "Son" is actually entitled "Of Redemption" ("Von der Erlösung"). After the article is quoted we have the question "What does this mean?" to which the answer is:

> I believe that Jesus Christ, true God, begotten of the Father from eternity, and also true man, born of the Virgin Mary, is my Lord; who has redeemed me (der mich [. . .] erlöset hat), a lost and condemned human being, secured and delivered me [even] from all sins, from death, and from the power of the devil, not with gold or silver, but with the holy, precious blood, and with his innocent sufferings and death; in order that I might be his own, live under him in his kingdom, and serve him in everlasting righteousness, innocence, and blessedness, even as he is risen from the dead, and lives and reigns forever. This is most certainly true.[104]

Redemption here is understood as release from three powers: those of sin, death, and the devil.

Of these three powers sin and death are the most important in the *Jesus* sketches. Given that there are over six hundred references to the term "devil" ("Teufel") and its derivatives in Wagner's writings[105] it is noticeable that the term only occurs twice in the sketches and in both cases in the scriptural citations in section II.2.[106] As far as redemption *from sin* is concerned, this is not explicitly stated in the dramatic outline but it is a key theme in the commentary (e.g., "I redeem you from Sin").[107]

---

102. *PW* 8:297; *DTB* 246.

103. *PW* 8:309; *DTB* 253. Note that Wagner makes some significant changes to the text of Hebrews.

104. Schaff, *Creeds of Christendom*, 3:79 (*BSELK* 511). This text is further discussed in chapter 11 below.

105. The term "Satan" and derivatives occurs just fifteen times, six of which are in *Der fliegende Holländer*.

106. *PW* 8:323; *DTB* 260 (Matt 11:18) and *PW* 8:339; *DTB* 266 (1 Tim 4:1).

107. *PW* 8:300; *DTB* 249.

Perhaps the most creative aspect of Wagner's theology as found in the sketches is his view of death. He does not speak so much of a redemption *from death* but of a reconciliation *with death*. It is significant that he speaks neither of a resurrection of Jesus nor of a "general resurrection" and it is telling that those verses he marked in 1 Corinthians refer not explicitly to the resurrection from the dead but rather the overcoming of death.[108] Further, in the commentary he implies that ideas of immortality are egotistic, this possibly reflecting Feuerbach's thought: "The last ascension of the individual life into the life of the whole is Death, which is the last and most definite upheaval of egoism."[109]

Conclusions

Wagner's Jesus of Nazareth sketches provide a rich quarry in which to dig for his theological ideas, many of which I believe inform and provide a key for the *Ring* cycle. In subsequent chapters, these themes will be explored, the first of which is the question of God and the gods.

---

108. 1 Cor 15:24–26, 31–32b, 36, 46, 55–56

109. *PW* 8:313; *DTB* 255. "Egoismus" actually occurs thirty-eight times in the sketches and represents a concentration of the term across all of Wagner's writings.

— 3 —

God and the Gods

The Question of God

In the previous chapter I established the possible pivotal role of the *Jesus of Nazareth* sketches for the interpretation of the *Ring*. If I was on the right tracks it suggests that the key divine figure in the *Ring* cycle is not Wotan but his beloved daughter, Brünnhilde, who offers her life as a sacrifice for sin. This coheres with much of Wagner's thought on the question of "god," in particular that divinity must seek its manifestation in the human being. Wagner would fully endorse these words from the Lutheran *Formula of Concord*, which are quoted by Feuerbach, and argue that a saviour God without humanity is unable to redeem the human being: "Here is God, who is not a God for me [. . .]. That would be a miserable Christ to me, who . . . should be nothing but a purely separate God and divine person [. . .] without humanity. No, my friend; where thou givest me God, thou must give me humanity too."[1] My justification for understanding the *Ring* in this way is dependent on my understanding it as an allegory, in particular seeing Brünnhilde as a Christ figure, something further explored in chapters 10 and 11 of the present volume.

Although this idea of the "humanity of God" is the core of Wagner's doctrine of God, there are other voices that emerge from this artwork. To some extent this multiplicity of voices emerges from the instability of allegory to which I turn in the final chapter. So, as I will argue, the death of Siegmund, a death being allowed and even orchestrated by his father, points to God the Father giving up his own Son to death (Rom 8:32);[2] further, Wotan being a "god the father" figure is suggested at the end of

---

1. As quoted in Feuerbach, *Essence*, 39. BSELK 1044.43–1045.13: "hie ist Gott, der nicht Mensch ist und noch nie Mensch worden. Mir aber des Gottes nicht. Dann [. . .] es sollt mir ein schlechter Christus bleiben, der [. . .] allein ein bloßer abgesonderter Gott und göttliche Person sein, ohn Menschheit. Nein, Gesell, wo du mir Gott hinsetzest, da mußt du mir die Menschheit mit hinsetzen."

2. Note that whereas Wotan has many daughters (nine Valkyries and Sieglinde) he has only one son. Cf. John 1:18 where, whichever of the three readings one adopts ("God, the only Son"; "the Son, the only one"; "the only Son"), it is clear that there is only one Son. On these textual variations, see Brown, *John*, 1:17, 36. Contrast *Saga of Ynglings* 4 that Odin "had many sons" (Finlay/Faulkes, *Heimskringla*, 8; Hollander, *Heimskringla*, 9). Wagner's changing to one son is significant. Note also that Donner is not Wotan's son (contrast Thor being Odin's son, *Gylfaginning*, 9 (Faulkes, *Edda*, 13)).

Walküre in the sense that he is sending his daughter into another reality and allowing her to become fully human in her "incarnation." However, much more is actually at work in this scene as we will discover.

God and "Paganism"

Wagner's appropriation of the polytheism of Norse and Germanic mythology in the *Ring* has been well researched; but the emphasis tends to be on what one could call an "antiquarian" interest.[3] My concerns here are primarily theological, asking how a study of Wagner's pantheon can contribute to a Christian theology. This immediately raises two questions. First, is it at all obvious to anyone experiencing the *Ring* that Wagner is preaching Christian theology? I have to say that the vast majority of Wagner enthusiasts see no Christian theology whatsoever in this art-work and a significant number would even say it negates the Christian faith.[4] The second question is this: is there any evidence that Wagner was consciously setting out to do Christian theology in the *Ring*? I have found no such utterance of Wagner specifically for the *Ring* (although one will find many for his final stage-work *Parsifal*). But according to the testimony of the French poet Count Philippe-Auguste Villiers de l'Isle-Adam, Wagner said this when the poet visited him in 1868: "let me inform you that, before all, I am a Christian, and that all the accents of my work which impress you are only inspired and created primarily by that alone."[5] But perhaps more important than this, and this answers both the questions I have put, is what he wrote to August Röckel in a letter of 23 August 1856:

> My dearest friend, your letter, far from making me feel argumentative, has rather served to confirm me in my belief that in this world nothing is ever gained by disputation. That which is most unique to us as individuals we owe not to our conceptualizations (Begriffe) but to our intuitions (Anschauungen): but these latter are so much our own that we can never fully express them nor adequately communicate them, for even the most complete attempt to do so—in what the artist does, namely his work of art—is ultimately apprehended by others, in turn, purely in accordance with their own particular way of apprehending things. But how can an artist hope to find his own intuition

---

3. For one of the early attempts see Golther, *Grundlagen* (1902). The fine study of Magee, *Nibelungs* (1990), remains a benchmark in the study of Wagner and his Norse and Germanic sources, carefully tracing how Wagner used the literature available to him (including what he borrowed). Björnsson, *Volsungs*, 130–274, offers a helpful and clear resource in going systematically through the *Ring* and pointing to the parallels in the primary sources. I have also made my own contribution to this study in volume 1, chapter 3.

4. Hence, there are "atheist" productions of the *Ring* (e.g., that of Keith Warner, Covent Garden, 2012 and 2018) based on the idea that the whole cycle ends with the *twilight* of the gods.

5. Villiers, "Souvenir," 141. In Bell, *Parsifal*, 227–28, I suggest there is no reason to doubt the testimony of Villiers.

(seine eigene Anschauung) perfectly reproduced in those of another person, since he stands before his own work of art—if it really *is* a work of art—as though before some puzzle, which is just as capable of misleading *him* as it can mislead another person.[6]

He goes on to explain that he had through his Nibelung poem set out, relying on his "conceptions" ("Begriffe"), to construct "a Hellenistically optimistic world."[7] But what *transpired* was a work in line with the philosophy of Schopenhauer.[8] This I maintain implies that he saw the *Ring* in many respects as a Christian work. This is because Schopenhauer's "pessimism" in appropriating Paul, Augustine, Luther, etc., for his idea of "original sin" can to some extent be found in the *Ring*.[9] But I should add that Schopenhauer's views of redemption were radically changed by Wagner in the *Ring* (and in *Tristan* and *Parsifal*). Wagner's correction of Schopenhauer was that redemption was not *from* erotic love but *through* erotic love, and such erotic love does not necessarily mean having sex! So although Wagner does not say here that the *Ring* is really a Christian work, ideas of "original sin" are clearly implied and there are utterances elsewhere to suggest that his view of redemption in the *Ring* is a Christian one.[10] Therefore, whether it was Wagner's intention or not to preach Christian theology in the *Ring*, it may nevertheless do so as the artwork takes on a life of its own.[11]

So what are we to say about Wagner's use of the Germanic and Norse gods? For Wagner such "pagan gods" are not simply to be divorced from Christian theology and this can be justified in three respects. First, one can make the general point that Wagner was the father of the structuralist interpretation of myth. So he discusses various equivalences in myths when he looks back at *Holländer* (comparing Odysseus and Wandering Jew) and *Lohengrin* (comparing Zeus/Semele) in *Communication to My Friends*.[12] Although no Norse myths are mentioned here his general view was that myths have a universal character grounded in what he called the "purely-human."[13] Secondly, the Norse myths were not only transmitted in writing by Christians but, in the traditions that have come down to us, Christian theology is often an integral part

---

6. *SL* 356–57 (translation modified); *SB* 8:152.

7. *SL* 357; *SB* 8:153.

8. Wagner writes that the very way he understands the distinction between intuition (Anschauung) and concept (Begriff) comes from "Schopenhauer's profound and happy solution" (*SL* 358; *SB* 8:154).

9. See chapter 5 below, where I point to differences between Wagner's idea of original sin and that of Augustine and Luther.

10. See chapter 11 below.

11. Note that although one can read his comments to Röckel as disguising the fact he knew a fair bit of Schopenhauer's philosophy already in 1852 (see volume 1, chapter 6), they do nevertheless highlight the fact that a work of art can transcend the thoughts and intentions of the artist.

12. *PW* 1:333–35; *GSD* 4:289–90.

13. *PW* 2:182; *GSD* 4:57.

of the mythology.[14] Thirdly, the "pagan myths" of the Germans were always seen in the context of Christianity by Jacob Grimm, who was crucial for Wagner's appreciation of German mythology (and Wagner himself would see the equivalence of pagan and Christian myths) and he was standing in a long tradition of Christian Edda reception.[15] Just three pages into the "Vorrede" ("Preface") of the *Deutsche Mythologie* Grimm makes it clear that in the Germanic mythology we have a revelation of the God of the Christian tradition. "I am met by the arrogant notion, that the life of whole centuries was pervaded by a soulless cheerless barbarism; this would at once contradict the loving kindness of God, who has made His sun give light to all time, and while endowing men with gifts of body and soul, has instilled into them the consciousness of a higher guidance."[16] Then the very opening of the "Einleitung" ("Introduction") to volume 1 starts straightaway with a discussion of the spread of Christianity from Asia to Europe: "From the westernmost shore of Asia, Christianity had turned at once to the opposite one of Europe."[17] Grimm then continues to discuss the evangelization of Europe, the conversion of pagans, but then also the fact that some believed in both the old gods and the God of the Christian faith.[18] Then constantly throughout his discussion he relates this "pagan" mythology to biblical themes.[19] Grimm also relates Tacitus' description of the German mythology to the fact that the Reformation began in Germany! Tacitus writes of the Germans: "Apart from this they deem it incompatible with the majesty of the heavenly host to confine the gods within walls, or to mould them into any likeness of the human face: they consecrate groves and copices, and they give the divine names to that mysterious something which is visible only to the eyes of faith (quod sola reverentia vident)."[20] Grimm then relates this *alleged* lack of images[21] to the fact that the Reformation started in Germany and that other "Germanic" countries such as England and those of Scandinavia (and to some extent France, where "German blood" persisted) were receptive to the Reformation:

---

14. See, e.g., Dronke, *Edda II*, 93–98, discussing the Christian theology in the *Völuspá* (which of all the mythological poems has the highest concentration of such theology).

15. See volume 1, chapter 3.

16. Grimm, *Mythology*, 3:vii; *Mythologie*, 1:VII.

17. Grimm, *Mythology*, 1:1; *Mythologie*, 1:1: "Von Asiens westlicher Küste hatte sich das christenthum gleich herüber nach Europa gewandt."

18. Grimm, *Mythologie*, 1:6–7; *Mythology*, 1:7–8.

19. E.g., "Donar" is related to Elijah's ability to control thunder and rain and Grimm refers to texts such as 1 Kgs 17:1; 18:41, 45; Luke 4:25; Jas 5:17, to which one should add 5:18 (Grimm, *Mythologie*, 1:158; *Mythology* 1:174).

20. Tacitus, *Germania* 9 (Hutton, *Tacitus I*, 144–45), quoted in Grimm, *Mythologie*, 1:XLIII; *Mythology*, 3:xlix.

21. Whether "images" in Norse religion functioned as "idols" is disputed. On images of Thor see Ellis Davidson, *Gods*, 77–80. For a recent discussion of images see Wellendorf, "Idols," 89–110. Grimm clearly assumed from his written sources that there were no "idols."

That notable piece of insight shows us the whole germ of Protestantism. It was no accident, but a necessity, that the Reformation arose first in our country, and we should long ago have given it our undivided allegiance, had not a stir been made against it from abroad. It is remarkable how the same soil of Old-German faith in Scandinavia and Britain proved receptive of Protestant opinion; and how favourable to it a great part of France was, when German blood still held its ground. As in language and myth, so in the religious leanings of a people there is something indestructable.[22]

He then further argues that for German mythology the multiplication of the one highest ungraspable and incomprehensible God into many gods can only occur through their human manifestation with their heavenly and earthly dwellings: "Gods, i.e., a multiplication of the one supreme incomprehensible Deity, could only be conceived of [. . .] under a human form [. . .], and celestial abodes like earthly houses are ascribed to them."[23] Portraying these gods in the form of images is impossible, to which Grimm compares the Old Testament decalogue. Further, Grimm believes that the vaults of medieval churches can be traced back to the transcendence of the Germanic gods represented in the World Ash Tree Yggdrasil, a transcendence that the Greek vaults were unable to match. He also argues that in the ancient German forest-cult there were only a few priests.[24] We know that Wagner highly valued Grimm's *Mythologie* and the comments on the relation between Germanic mythology and the Reformation would no doubt appeal to Wagner as a convinced Protestant and an opponent of Catholicism.

The way Wagner appropriates Grimm, and the Norse mythology that forms the backbone of Grimm's work, reveals some significant things about the evolution of Wagner's *Ring* and its theology. For example, Grimm's portrayal of Wuotan rightly gives a balance of his having a heavenly dwelling and looking down on earth,[25] yet when he appears on earth he is very human; e.g., he "is one-eyed, he wears a broad hat and with a wide mantle."[26] In the "Ring of 1848" (i.e., *Mythus* and *Siegfried's Tod*),

---

22. Grimm, *Mythology*, 3:l; *Mythologie*, 1:XLIII–IV: "Jene merkwürdige beobachtung zeigt uns den vollen keim des protestantismus. es war nicht zufall, sondern nothwendig, dass die reformation gerade in Deutschland aufgieng, das ihr längst ungespalten gehört hätte, würde nicht auswärts dawider angeschürt. nicht zu übersehen ist, wie empfänglich derselbe boden germanischen glaubens in Scandinavien und England für die protestantische ansicht bleibt. wie günstig ihr ein grosser theil Frankreichs war, in dem deutsches blut haftete. gleich sprache und mythus ist auch in der glaubensneigung unter den völkern etwas unvertilgbares."

23. Grimm, *Mythology*, 3:l; *Mythologie*, 1:XLIV: "Götter, d.i. vervielfachung der einen, höchsten unerfasslichen gottheit sind nur als menschlich gestaltet zu fassen [. . .] und himlische wohnungen gleich irdischen häusern werden ihnen beigelegt."

24. Grimm, *Mythology*, 3:li; *Mythologie*, 1:XLIV. Although he concedes that the number of priests did increase in the later temple cult, generally speaking Grimm seems to go out of his way to minimize the presence of priests.

25. Grimm, *Mythology*, 1:135; *Mythologie*, 1:124.

26. Grimm, *Mythology*, 1:146; *Mythologie*, 1:133.

Wagner downplays these human elements. Although Wotan in the *Mythus* has human form (e.g., "Wotan gives the hoard to the giants"),[27] he does not have the psychological complexity we find in the first three operas of the final *Ring*. More striking is that in *Siegfried's Tod* of 1848 (and in subsequent versions and in *Götterdämmerung*) the gods are essentially absent from events on earth. They are prayed to and oaths are made in their name but they do not appear as characters on the stage as in the final *Ring* where *Siegfried's Tod* is prefaced by three "incarnational" operas. There is then a second incarnational shift, and this concerns the children of Wotan. The children of gods in the *Mythus* are spoken of only vaguely: "Mighty human races, bred from divine seed, are already arising."[28] So Wotan is not the direct father of the Volsung twins; rather "a childless marriage of this dynasty was brought to fruition by Wotan through the means of one of Holda's apples, which he caused the pair to eat."[29] The Gibichungs is "[a] second heroic dynasty [. . .] descended from the gods."[30] But there is no indication of the parentage of the Valkyries (including Brünnhilde); and Erda, Brünnhilde's mother in the final *Ring*, is missing entirely from both the *Mythus* and *Siegfried's Tod* of 1848.[31] In *Siegfried's Tod* (1848) Hagen explains that "Volsung was Wotan's son" and from Volsung was born Siegmund and Siegelind, making Siegfried the god's great-grandson. Then in the entire libretto of *Siegfried's Tod* there is only one reference to Brünnhilde being a "child of Wotan," and it is by no means clear how these words on the lips of the dying Siegfried are to be taken: "Brünnhild! Brünnhild! / You radiant child of Wotan!"[32] Whenever Brünnhilde addresses Wotan it is always as a god.[33] One of the odd things about *Siegfried's Tod* (1853) and *Götterdämmerung* is that *taking the libretto alone* it is even less "incarnational" than *Siegfried's Tod* of 1848 in the sense that there is no indication whatsoever that Brünnhilde or Siegfried are related to Wotan in any way![34] But the music of *Götterdämmerung* and knowledge of the previous three operas of the cycle allow one to read incarnation into this final opera.

---

27. Haymes, *Ring*, 44–45.
28. Haymes, *Ring*, 46–47.
29. Haymes, *Ring*, 46–47.
30. Haymes, *Ring*, 48–49.

31. Erda is implicit in the revision of 1852 (*TBRN1* 119) and the *Viertschrift* (*TBRN1* 142; cf. *WagRS* 284 "Zur Mutter!"). Contrast the *Erstschrift* (*TBRN1* 53).

32. Haymes, *Ring*, 78–79, 170–71. When he came to the final revisions at the end of 1852 "Du strahlendes Wodanskind!" ("You radiant child of Wodan!") was removed (together with the lines that follow) and replaced by lines we now know from the final version "Brünnhild! — / heilige braut —" etc (*TBRN1* 200–201).

33. See, e.g., Haymes, *Ring*, 100–101, where she refers to "The ruling god!"

34. Not only is "You radiant child of Wotan!" removed but also Hagen's reference to Siegmund and Sieglinde being descended from Wotan via Volsung (*WagRS* 289). See the *Viertschrift of Siegfried's Tod* where "Von Wodan stammte Wälse" is crossed out (*TBRN1* 148; cf. Haymes, *Ring*, 78–79).

Gods and Nature

Grimm's *Mythologie* covers the whole range of mythological issues from "God" (chapter 2) to subjects such as "heroes" (chapter 15), "wise women" (chapter 16), "giants" (chapter 18), "elements" (chapter 20), "trees and animals" (chapter 21), and "devil" (chapter 33). In his mythological scheme (as in all myth) there is no clear distinction between gods and the world. As Bultmann pointed out: "Mythology is the use of imagery to express the other worldly in terms of this world and the divine in terms of human life, the other side in terms of this side."[35] It is only in demythologized myth that we are able to draw the distinction between god and nature. Hence, although I am discussing "gods" in this chapter and "nature" in the next, they are inseparable in the mythical world of Wagner's *Ring*.

Another reason why gods and nature are inseparable in the *Ring* is because of the Hegelian influence. Hegel had been accused (and in some quarters still is) of pantheism, but he responded by arguing first that pantheism itself is misunderstood and secondly that he is not a pantheist anyway.[36] His key point is that the infinite cannot be kept aloof from the finite: "Without the world God is not God."[37] But for Hegel God cannot be reduced to the world even though he does not transcend it. It may be that Wagner did not grasp this point but he does hold to the view that both history and nature are divinized, and this view may well have been influenced by Hegel's view of God. "In virtue of God's inseparability from the world, Hegel naturalizes and historicizes the divine; but in virtue of his non-reducibility to the world, he divinizes history and nature."[38]

If Wagner is a true disciple of Hegel he then holds to an immanent but not a pantheistic view of God. But one way in which Wagner departs from Hegel is that Wagner's god is the god of mythological texts.[39] Here we have not only Norse myths (colored by the Greeks) but also biblical texts that are essentially mythological in nature (although some may entail their own demythologizing, as in John 1).[40] Although Hegel takes seriously the 'picture thinking' of the mythological view of God, his *philosophical* view of God is the 'Absolute', the source of all truth and the truth of all things.

---

35. Bultmann, "Mythology," 10 n. 2.

36. Hegel, *Philosophy of Religion*, 1:375–76: "It has never occurred to anyone to say that everything, all individual things collectively, in their individuality and contingency, are God [...] Spinozism itself as such, and Oriental pantheism, too, comprise the view that the divine in all things is only the universal aspect of their content, the *essence* of things, but in such a way that it is also represented as the *determinate* essence of things." (*Philosophie der Religion*, 1:273).

37. Hegel, *Philosophy of Religion*, 1:308 n. 97; *Philosophie der Religion*, 1:213 n. This is in Hotho's transcript of the 1824 lectures.

38. Beiser, *Hegel*, 143.

39. On Hegel's view of myth as a lower form of intuition, see Hübner, *Mythos*, 61.

40. See, e.g., Weder, "Mythos."

Another key influence on Wagner's understanding of God and nature was Goethe, whose view of God in many ways coheres with that of Hegel. In "God and World" Goethe writes: "What sort of God would it be who merely gave the universe a push from outside and rotated it with his finger! It befits Him to impart motion to the world from within, to cherish Nature in Himself and Himself in Nature, so that all that lives and moves and has its being in Him is never without His power and His spirit."[41] The penultimate line clearly alludes to Acts 17:28, a verse that was important for Wagner.[42] Further, Goethe has a view of the "World Soul," writing a poem "Weltseele" in "Aus: Gott und Welt"[43] and "Eins und Alles" which also speaks of the "Weltgeist."[44] Such ideas cohere with Schelling and to some extent with Wagner.

However, we must proceed with caution since at least in his later years Wagner was to criticize Goethe's understanding of God: "Take Goethe, who held Christ for problematical, but the good God for wholly proven, albeit retaining the liberty to discover the latter in Nature after his own fashion; which led to all manner of physical assays and experiments, whose continued pursuit was bound, in turn, to lead the present reigning human intellect to the result that there's no God whatever, but only 'Force and Matter.'"[45]

The Gods

It has already been noted above that the Norse and Germanic myths were propagated by Christians and that in the sources one cannot make a clean separation between Christianity and paganism.[46] I now consider the gods of Wagner's pantheon: first, there are the obvious figures of Wotan, Fricka, Freia, Froh, Donner, and Erda; secondly, there is the "half-god" Loge; thirdly, there is Brünnhilde, a daughter of two gods, Wotan and Erda;[47] fourthly, there is the figure of Siegfried who, although classified as a hero, has some god-like characteristics.

---

41. Luke, *Goethe: Selected Verse*, 271. "Was wär' ein Gott, der nur von außen stieße, / Im Kreis das All am Finger laufen ließe! / Ihm ziemt's, die Welt im Innern zu bewegen, / Natur in Sich, Sich in Natur zu hegen, / So daß was in Ihm lebt und webt und ist, / Nie Seine Kraft, nie Seinen Geist vermißt" ("Gott und Welt," *GWJA* 1:221).

42. It was noted in volume 1, chapter 7 that Wagner marked Acts 17:26–29 in his New Testament, adding "!!" See also his quotation of Acts 17:23b–29 in the *Jesus of Nazareth* sketches (*PW* 8:335–36; *DTB* 264–65).

43. *GWJA* 1:223–24.

44. *GWJA* 1:226.

45. *PW* 6:256; *GSD* 10:256. This is from his *What Use Is This Knowledge?* published in *BBl* December 1880.

46. See also the discussion of Wagner's appropriation of Norse and Germanic sources in volume 1, chapter 3.

47. We do not know whether Erda was also the mother of the other eight Valkyries and therefore whether they are to be considered fully divine (in the sense of having both parents as gods).

God and the Gods

Odin and Wotan

Wagner's Wotan has one wife Fricka, corresponding to the Norse Frigg, and several "lovers": the women Fricka alludes to in *Rheingold* Scene 2;[48] the goddess Erda; the mortal mother of Siegmund and Sieglinde; possibly others such as the unknown mother of the eight Valkyries who, as noted, was not necessarily Erda. Odin of the *Elder Edda* also has one wife, Frigg, and one lover, the giantess Iord;[49] Odin of the *Prose Edda*, on the other hand, has several wives: Frigg, Earth, Rind, and Grid,[50] and commits incest in that Earth is also his daughter.[51] In this respect Wagner's Wotan therefore is more similar to the Odin of the *Elder Edda*.

Odin is given an extraordinary number of names. According to *Gylfaginning* 3, Odin has twelve names.[52] The name Snorri first mentions and is emphasized is "All-Father," and we later learn that he is given this name since "he is father of all the gods and of men and of everything that has been brought into being by him and his power."[53] This title is used by Wagner, but only in the very early stages of evolution of the *Ring*, once in the 1848 *Mythus*,[54] three times in *Siegfried's Tod* (1848),[55] and once in the *Erstschrift* for *Der junge Siegfried*.[56] But stage by stage he removed the name "All-Father" such that it does not occur in the final *Ring* libretto. One reason for doing so is probably because he wished to demote Wotan ("All-Father" was showing his pre-eminence among the gods). But another reason is that he wished Wotan to have just one son (i.e., Siegmund) rather than many and this will prove to be highly significant.[57] The sixth name Snorri mentions, "Oski" ("Fulfiller of Desires"), is found in *Grímnismál* 49[58] and is alluded to in *Walküre*.[59] However, this list of twelve names in *Gylfaginning* 3 is by no means exhaustive since additional names are found in the *Elder Edda*, sometimes given as long lists.[60] Two important names which Wagner has

---

48. WagRS 71: "Um des Gatten Treue besorgt / muß traurig ich wohl sinnen, / wie an mich er zu fesseln, / zieht's in die Ferne ihn fort" ("Heedful of my husband's fidelity, / I'm bound in my sadness to brood / on ways of binding him fast / whenever he feels drawn away").

49. Larrington, *Poetic Edda*, xxxiv, gives a family tree.

50. See the family tree in Byock, *Prose Edda*, 131.

51. Faulkes, *Edda*, 13.

52. Faulkes, *Edda*, 8–9.

53. Faulkes, *Edda*, 13 (*Gylfaginning* 9).

54. GSD 2:166; Haymes, *Ring*, 58–59.

55. GSD 2:209, 227–28; Haymes, *Ring*, 144–45 (cf. the *Viertschrift* of *Siegfried's Tod* where "All-vater" is still retained (*TBRN1* 188)), 182–85 (cf. the *Viertschrift* of *Siegfried's Tod* where "Allvater" drops out (*TBRN1* 205–9)).

56. *TBRN1* 322. This sketch is dated 3-24 June 1851.

57. For the many see Faulkes, *Edda*, 13, 21.

58. Orchard, *Elder Edda*, 58.

59. Brünnhilde in Act II Scene 4 tells Siegmund of "Wish-maidens" (Wunschmädchen) in Valhalla (*WagRS* 160). In Act III Scene 2 Wotan tells Brünnhilde: "Wish-Maid (Wunsch-Maid) / you were to me: / but against me you have wished" (*WagRS* 181).

60. E.g., *Grímnismál*, 46–50 (Orchard, *Elder Edda*, 57–58).

appropriated occur in the first poem of the *Elder Edda*, *Völuspá*: "Herjafödr"[61] ("Father of Battles"), which Wagner renders as "Heervater,"[62] and "Sigföðr" ("Father of Victories"),[63] which Wagner renders as "Siegvater."[64]

Gylfaginning 20 explains another name, "Val-father" ("father of the slain"), employed "since all who fall in battle are his adopted sons."[65] Wagner uses "Walvater" at significant points in the drama (all in relation to Valhalla): in *Walküre* Act II Scene 4 where Brünnhilde calls Siegmund to Valhalla;[66] in Act III Scene 1[67] and Scene 3 (Brünnhilde being expelled from Valhalla);[68] in *Götterdämmerung* Act I Scene 3 (Brünnhilde and Waltraute on the state of Valhalla).[69] It could be that although Wotan had just one son (Siegmund), the heroes who fall in battle are his *adopted* sons.

As Brünnhilde is expelled from Valhalla, Wotan essentially loses his power, and in the next opera, *Siegfried*, Wotan is called "Wanderer." This name occurs only once in the *Elder Edda*[70] but there are three poems where Odin journeys on earth under an assumed name: Grímnir,[71] Gagnráðr,[72] and Vegtamr (Way-tamer).[73] Simrock in his notes on *Vafthrúdnismál* writes that these names all refer to Odin as "Wanderer."[74] Wagner's portrayal of the "Wanderer" was also inspired by the *Völsunga Saga*, where Odin appears as an old "venerable" man.[75] In the sketches for *Der junge Siegfried* Wagner describes the "Wanderer" thus: "He is of lofty appearance and one-eyed; brown, curly beard; long, dark-blue cloak; he carries a spear for a staff. On his head he has a large hat with a broad, round brim which hangs down low over the missing eye."[76] It is also likely that Wagner's "Wanderer" was a development of his own Flying Dutchman,[77] as well as

---

61. *Völuspá* 42 (Dronke, *Edda II*, 18). Ettmüller, *Vaulu-spá*, 16, 31, renders the Icelandic and German as "HeriafauÞr" and "Heriafadir."

62. Note the terrible irony in Fricka's referring to her husband as "Heervater" (*WagRS* 147) after she has frustrated his plans to save Siegmund (*Walküre* Act II Scene 1). Four other occurrences are in Act II Scene 1 when Brünnhilde fears facing her father's wrath (*WagRS* 172–74).

63. *Völuspá* 52 (Dronke, *Edda II*, 21). See also *Grímnismál* 48 (Orchard, *Elder Edda*, 58).

64. This occurs just once when Brünnhilde, "shocked and stunned," tells us (*WagRS* 155): "So—sah ich / Siegvater nie" ("Thus have I never seen / Father of Victories").

65. Faulkes, *Edda*, 21. Again this is not one of the twelve names given in *Gylfaginning* 3.

66. *WagRS* 160

67. *WagRS* 170, 173, 175.

68. *WagRS* 188.

69. *WagRS* 301–2.

70. See *Grímnismál*, 46 (Orchard, *Elder Edda*, 57).

71. See *Grímnismál* pr, 47 (Orchard, *Elder Edda*, 49–59).

72. See *Vafthrúdnismál* 8, 9, 11, 13, 15, 17 (Orchard, *Elder Edda*, 40–42).

73. *Baldrs Draumar* 6, 13 (Orchard, *Elder Edda*, 248–49).

74. See Simrock, *Edda*, 346; Magee, *Nibelungs*, 124–25.

75. Finch, *Volsung Saga*, 4.

76. Strobel, *Skizzen*, 118; Magee, *Nibelungs*, 124, whose translation I have used, notes that this is abbreviated in the final *Siegfried* (see *GSD* 6:100).

77. Williams, *Hero*, 89, points out that "[t]he figure in the early music-drama [the Wanderer] most

being influenced by figures such as Byron,[78] and the poems and musical settings of the "Wanderer" in the Romantic period.[79]

A final name to consider, not used by Wagner but to which he may allude, is "Ygg," which means "death," "dread," "terrible one."[80] This name is actually highly ambiguous. On the one hand, it does point to Odin's frightening nature and the suffering he can impose; but at the same time it points to the suffering he himself endures. One could see this double nature as a parallel to the portrayal of Christ in the book of Revelation, who appears as a frightening figure in Rev 1:12–16 but at the same time is the lamb who suffers (Rev 5:12). The World Ash Tree is named "Yggdrasil" and "drasil" can mean either "gallows" or "horse." Hence, "Yggdrasil" could be understood as "deadly gallows" or "Odin's horse." This then offers the intriguing interpretation that when related to *Hávamál* 138–41, Odin rides the tree in that he hangs from it.[81] The tree in *Hávamál* is not named but it is most likely Yggdrasil:[82]

> 138 Óðinn I know that I was hanging
> on a windswept tree (vindga meiði á)
> nine whole nights,
> gashed with a spear
> and given to Óðinn
> —myself to myself—
> on that tree
> of which no one knows
> from roots of what it originates.
> 139 Óðinn They did not hearten me with a loaf
> or a horn of ale.

---

readily recalls is the Flying Dutchman. Initially the Wanderer seems less engaged than the Dutchman, because while the Dutchman longs for a human community he has never experienced, the Wanderer has willingly abandoned one to wander through the world with no desire to be a participant in it."

78. Childe Harold could be considered the most celebrated of Romantic wanderers, "an infinitely self-conscious figure, burdened by guilt from a past he cannot reveal and nostalgic of a transcendent love which cannot be fulfilled" (Williams, *Hero*, 10). Wagner's Wanderer is not searching for love but in other respects this description fits rather well. Further, "[t]he brooding Byronic hero, be he Childe Harold [. . .] or the guilt wracked Manfred, reminds us how close the romantic hero comes to villainy" (Williams, *Hero*, 11). Wagner possessed a twelve-volume edition of Byron's works edited by Adolf Böttger in his Dresden library. The translation "Ritter Harolds Pilgerfahrt" is in volume 1, dedicated to Theodor Apel (Wagner's friend whom he first got to know at the Leipzig Nikolaischule) and Friedrich Günther. "Manfred" is included in volume 7.

79. I noted in volume 1, chapter 5 how Wagner had marked many of Uhland's poems, including "Wanderlieder" (Uhland, *Gedichte*, 79). Turchin, "Wanderlieder," notes how central such poems were for the "Wanderlieder" cycles.

80. See *Vafthrúdnismál* 5; *Grímnismál* 53–54; *Hymiskvida* 2; *Fáfnismál* 43 (Orchard, *Elder Edda*, 40, 58–59, 77, 168).

81. Orchard, *Elder Edda*, 269.

82. Dronke, *Edda III*, 30–31.

> I peered down—prying
> I caught up runes–
> crying out in triumph I caught them.
> Back I fell from beyond.
> 140 Óðinn Nine powerful lays
> I learned from the famous son
> Of Bolþorn, Bestla's father,
> and a drink I procured
> of the priceless mead
> —I, irrigated with Óðrerir!
> 141 Óðinn Then I began to be fertile
> and fruitfully wise
> and to grow and feel good.
> Word for word
> sought a word for me,
> deed from deed
> sought a deed for me.

Turville-Petre is surely right that "[t]he similarities between the scene described here and that of Calvary are undeniable"[83] and is no doubt correct to come to the conclusion of Christian influence.[84] The parallels of this "crucifixion scene" are numerous: Odin is "gashed with a spear" (*Hávamál* 138), which reflects John 19:34; Odin's complaint "They did not hearten me with a loaf / or a horn of ale" (*Hávamál* 139) can be said to reflect "the pathos of the abandoned Christ";[85] Odin's "crying out" as he grasped the runes is reminiscent of Christ's cry of dereliction (Mark 15:34). I think the most arresting issue this text from *Hávamál* raises, and its relationship to Christ's death, is that of "atonement." Odin hangs on a tree, the word "meiðr" being used in v. 138.[86] The New Testament sometimes speaks not of Jesus being hung on a cross but on a tree (*xulon*), as in Acts 5:30, 10:39, 13:29, this being so expressed in order to allude to Deut 21:23, which states that "anyone hung on a tree (*xulon*) is under God's curse." In Gal 3:13 Paul explicitly makes this connection: "Christ redeemed us from the curse of the

---

83. Turville-Petre, *Myth*, 42.

84. It is noted that "nearly every element in the Norse myth can be explained as a part of pagan tradition, and even of the cult of Óðinn" (Turville-Petre, *Myth*, 43). Nevertheless, the myth of Óðinn may have been influenced by Christ's crucifixion. "We could believe that a Viking in the British Isles had seen an image of the dying Christ, whom he identified with the dying Óðinn" (50).

85. Dronke, *Edda III*, 61. Dronke, *Edda III*, 62, also suggests that there is a play on the pre-Christian sense of baptism in "I, irrigated with Óðrerir!" (*Hávamál* 140).

86. From the "Wörterbuch" in his copy of Ettmuller, *Vaulu-spá*, 109–68, Wagner would know of the various Norse words for tree: baðmr, (e.g., *Völuspá* 19), meiðr (Ettmüller, *Vaulu-spá*, 14, 142, gives meiþr), tré (e.g., *Hávamál* 136), þollr (e.g., *Völuspá* 20). See the commentary in Dronke, *Edda III*, 61–63.

law by becoming a curse for us—for it is written, 'Cursed is everyone who hangs on a tree (*xulon*).'" Christ becomes cursed because he identified with the human condition. The question is whether Odin in any sense also identifies with the human condition and atones for sin. The first point to note is that the Norse equivalent to *xulon* is not "meiðr," as in *Hávamál* 138, but rather þollr,[87] used for example in *Völuspá* 20: "From there come maidens / deep in knowledge, / three, from the lake / that lies under the tree (er und þolli stendr)."[88] Secondly, although Christ's sacrifice is *to some extent* "to deal with sin," this does not appear to be the purpose of Odin's sacrifice: his suffering is not related to atoning for sin but rather gaining knowledge.[89] Nevertheless, such knowledge does lead to a form of salvation since Odin "begins [. . .] to grow and feel good" (141).[90] Bearing in mind that Christ's sacrifice is not simply to "deal with sin" but also entails the renewal of the human being,[91] one can say that there are parallels between the sacrifices of Christ and Odin. Further, the sacrifice of Odin is "myself to myself," i.e., "god to god, of such a kind as is related in Scripture of the sacrifice of Christ."[92] Some of the traditional views of the atonement fall down because they stress what Christ as a *human being* achieves (e.g., offering "satisfaction" to God) and fail to take seriously that Christ as *God* suffers and dies. Wagner may well be taking account of this problem in his own way by often bracketing out "God the Father"; hence Christ's sacrifice was, just like Odin's, "God to God."

In addition to Odin's "crucifixion" in *Hávamál* 138–41 we see a pattern in several texts where he appears willingly to accept suffering. In the prose introduction to *Grímnismál* we read how Odin dressed in a blue cloak and calling himself Grímnir came to king Geirröd, revealing nothing about his true identity.

> The king had him tortured to make him speak, and set him between two fires; he sat there for eight nights. King Geirröd had a son, ten years old, called Agnar after his brother. Agnar went to Grímnir and gave him a full horn to drink; he said that the king was behaving wickedly in having an innocent man tortured. Grímnir drank it up; then the fire had come so close that the cloak was burning off Grímnir.[93]

This suffering of Odin has clearly contributed to Wagner's portrayal of Wotan. One of the most arresting aspects of Wagner's chief god is his complexity: we find a figure who

---

87. Wagner could know this from Ettmuller, *Vaulu-spá*, 167.

88. Dronke, *Edda II*, 12.

89. Dronke, *Edda III*, 47: "Óðinn's self-sacrifice on the tree is expressly for an intellectual purpose, not a moral one—no human sins are on his shoulders for expiation."

90. Dronke, *Edda III*, 47.

91. Bell, "Sacrifice and Christology."

92. Turville-Petre, *Myth*, 48.

93. Orchard, *Elder Edda*, 50. The lay ends though by Geirröd accidentally falling on his sword when he realizes that the one he is burning is none other than Odin (59).

wants to rule and have authority over others ("Den Ring muss ich haben!")[94] yet at the same time a figure who endures excruciating mental torment (which is ultimately of his own making): the death of his son, Siegmund, and the loss of his favorite daughter, Brünnhilde. He ends up as a pathetic figure, eloquently portrayed in Waltraute's narration in *Götterdämmerung* Act I Scene 3. His whole world, which he has planned and built up, is slowly falling apart. He is a complex and psychologically convincing figure, having something of Euripides' Agamemnon[95] or Shakespeare's King Lear.

Wotan, like Odin, finally meets his end. According to the *Prose Edda*, Odin is swallowed by the wolf Fenrir at Ragnarök.[96] He is shown no mercy. By contrast, in Wagner's *Götterdämmerung* Wotan at least is offered a sort of sedative before he meets his end in the final conflagration in that Brünnhilde consoles him: "Ruhe! Ruhe, du Gott!" ("Rest now, rest now, you god!").[97]

With this portrayal of Wotan (developed from 1849 onwards, his 1848 *Ring* having rather aloof gods) we may therefore find parallels with Christ, and Wagner actually points to such an identification in *Die Wibelungen*.[98] But is there any way Wotan is related to "Yahweh of the Old Testament"? There are in fact two interesting points of contact. First, Odin was the storm and war god in Norse mythology and to some extent Wagner has retained this in his Wotan, who, as we saw, is "Father of Battles" and "Father of Victories." His entrance in *Walküre* Act III Scene 2, described by the eight Valkyries, when he confronts his disobedient daughter, Brünnhilde, is terrifying:[99]

Weh'!	Alas!
Wüthend schwingt sich	In his fury Wotan dismounts
Wotan vom Roß—	from his horse—
hierher ras't	hither he storms
sein rächender Schritt!	with vengeful step!

Likewise, Yahweh may originally have been a storm and war god: Gerstenberger writes: "Yahweh was not always God in Israel and at every social level. Rather, initially he belongs only to the type of storm and war gods like Baal, Anath, Hadad, Resheph, and Chemosh, who were worshipped in regional alliances or states in closely defined, special situations."[100] Such a view of Yahweh was to be later complemented by many

---

94. *WagRS* 82.
95. See volume 1 chapter 4.
96. Faulkes, *Edda*, 73: "The wolf will swallow Odin. That will be the cause of his death." *Völuspá* 51 tells of Odin going to fight the "wolf" but with the result: "Then shall Frigg's / sweet friend fall" (Dronke, *Edda II*, 21).
97. *WagRS* 349.
98. *PW* 7:287; *GSD* 2:144, discussed in volume 1, chapter 2.
99. *WagRS* 179.
100. Gerstenberger, *Theologies in the Old Testament*, 151. Note the plural *Theologies* in the title. Usually such works employ the singular *Theology* (Gerhard von Rad, Walter Eichrodt, Horst Dietrich

other images (e.g., loving father, mother) but which often do not always sit easily beside each other. Perhaps the most convincing way they do cohere is in the prophetic tradition or in a text such as the song of Moses in Deut 32. Wagner may have been influenced by such texts in his portrayal of the *god* Wotan.

The second point relating Wotan to Yahweh is that although Odin/Wodan/Wotan was originally the god of storm, he became the supreme god, being given the attributes of the heavens. Hébert, one of the first to write about Wagner and theology, puts it like this: "the blue mantle with the stars of gold represent[s] the sky; the hat that covers his face, the cloud that hides the sun; the one eye, the sun."[101] This role of Wotan as a sky god can be easily missed but is suggested by Wagner's sketch noted above and by Doepler's costume designs where both Wotan and the Wanderer have a blue cloak.[102] Wotan as sky god is also indicated at a number of points in the libretto that not only relate to Yahweh being transcendent and in the sky, but also to Yahweh being all seeing since Wotan as sky god is inextricably intertwined with his watching events unfold on earth through his eye, represented by the sun. These relations will then bring together the constellation of Wotan/Apollo/Siegfried, to which I now turn.

Wotan/Siegfried/Apollo the Sun-god

In *Siegfried* Act II Scene 3, after killing the dragon (and Mime), the hero unknown to himself alludes to Wotan keeping an eye on events on earth:[103]

Hoch steht schon die Sonne:	The sun's already high in the heavens:
aus lichtem Blau	its eye stares down
blickt ihr Aug'	on the crown of my head
auf den Scheitel steil mir herab.—	from the brilliant blue above.—

Grimm notes that "[t]he very oldest and most universal image connected with the sun and other luminaries seems [. . .] to be that of the eye"[104] and this is related to the ancient views of vision, emission theories or extramission theories, where that light emitted from the eyes facilitated vision.[105] So here in *Siegfried* Act II Wotan's eye shines from the sky and observes. But is this the eye in his head or the missing eye? Grimm

---

Preuss, Walter Brueggemann).

101. Hébert, *Religious Experience*, 49 n. 46. He assumes the remaining eye is the sun, something I will question below.

102. Doepler, *Figurinen*, 19, 67.

103. *WagRS* 251–52.

104. Grimm, *Mythology*, 2:702; *Mythologie*, 2:664.

105. According to Empedocles, Aphrodite made the eyes out of the four elements, and she lit the fire in the eye which shone out. Emission theories were held by Plato, questioned by Euclid (300 BC), reestablished by Galen, and then finally refuted by Alhazen (c. 965–c. 1040), who established an intramission theory.

argues in *Deutsche Mythologie* that with the remaining eye "the divinity surveys the world, and nothing can escape its peering all-piercing glance."[106] The final *Ring* libretto is unclear, but in the sketch for *Der junge Siegfried* of 3–24 June 1851 the Wanderer makes it clear to Mime in Act I that it was the missing eye that was the sun:[107]

nur ein auge	only one eye
leuchtet an seinem haupt	shines on his head
weil am himmel das andre	because in the heavens the other
als sonne den helden schon glänzt	shines as the sun on the heroes

Magee points out that Wagner's only support for this was Studach, whose translation of the *Edda* Wagner had borrowed from the Dresden Royal Library. Commenting on Odin's lodging his eye "in the famed / fountain of Mímir!"[108] he identified this lost eye with the sun.[109] Therefore, the eye in the spring is identical with the eye in the sky and the two could be identified by seeing the sun's eye as reflected in that of the spring.[110]

If the sun is identified with Wotan's missing eye, we have an explanation as to what is going on in *Siegfried* Act III Scene 2. The Wanderer in replying to Siegfried's taunt seems to be saying that his missing eye is passed on to Siegfried as sun-god:[111]

Mit dem Auge,	With the eye which,
das als and'res mir fehlt,	as my second self, is missing,
erblick'st du selber das eine,	you yourself can glimpse the one
das mir zum Sehen verblieb.	that's left for me to see with.

Siegfried's becoming a "sun-god" may be anticipated when the dragon Fafner addresses him as "You bright-eyed boy, unknown to yourself" ("Du helläugiger Knabe, / unkund deiner selbst").[112] It is significant that Siegfried is so addressed after he has delivered the fatal blow and the dragon is about to die. Wagner relates Siegfried as sun-god to his killing the dragon in *Die Wibelungen*. There he asserts that the "oldest meaning" of the Nibelungen myth is that Siegfried is "God of Light or Sun-god."[113] This is the original meaning of Siegfried's fight with the dragon, which is likened to

---

106. Grimm, *Mythology*, 2:703; *Mythologie*, 2:665. See also Simrock, *Edda*, 336, who, commenting on his *Völuspá* 22 (*Edda*, 6), considers the sun as Odin's eye in his head (Magee, *Nibelungs*, 141).

107. Strobel, *Skizzen*, 123 (quoted by Magee, *Nibelungs*, 141).

108. *Völuspá* 28 (see Dronke, *Edda II*, 14).

109. Studach, *Edda*, 16 n. (which Magee, *Nibelungs*, 141, appears to misquote).

110. Simrock, *Edda*, 336, by speaking of the reflection *distinguishes* the eyes whereas I am identifying them.

111. *WagRS* 262.

112. *WagRS* 242.

113. *PW* 7:263; *GSD* 2:119.

Apollo fighting the dragon Python.[114] Siegfried "conquers and lays low the monster of ur-Chaotic night" and hence light vanquishes darkness. He gains the Nibelungen-hoard but the dragon's heir (the powers of darkness) "drags him down into the gloomy realm of Death."[115] But what is not clear is whether Siegfried is in any sense polluted by slaying the dragon. Foster refers to Müller: "Although the destruction of the Python is characterized as a triumph of the higher and divine power of the deity; yet the victorious god was considered as polluted by the blood of the monster, and obliged to undergo a series of afflictions and woes."[116] It could be suggested that Siegfried is so polluted by what I have just quoted from *Die Wibelungen* but in my judgement this is far from clear.[117]

The Rhinemaidens may possibly allude to Wotan or Siegfried as sun-god in *Götterdämmerung* Act III Scene 1 when they call on "Frau Sonne" to send a hero who will give them back their gold,[118] although there is the obvious problem that they call on a goddess. There may also be an allusion to Wotan as sun-god in *Rheingold* (or again to a sun-goddess) when the sun illumines the gold in Scene 1. Finally, Wotan may be alluding to his missing eye after the rainbow bridge has been formed and before he enters Valhalla with his fellow gods (*Rheingold* Scene 4):[119]

Abendlich strahlt	In evening light
der Sonne Auge;	the sun's eye gleams;
in prächtiger Gluth	in its glittering glow
prangt glänzend die Burg:	the stronghold shines resplendent:

It may be significant that Hegel in his *Phemonenology* devotes a section on "God as Light" in his discussion of "Natural Religion."[120] Further, in Goethe's *Faust I* (which Wagner grew up with and possibly knew by heart) "The Prologue in Heaven" begins with these words of Raphael: "The sun proclaims its old devotion (Die Sonne tönt nach alter Weise) / In rival song (Wettgesang) with brother spheres, / And still completes in thunderous motion / The circuits of its destined years."[121]

---

114. *PW* 7:275; *GSD* 2:131.

115. *PW* 7:276; *GSD* 2:133. This passage is quoted by Golther, *Grundlagen*, 94–95.

116. Foster, *Greeks*, 40. See Müller, *Doric Race*, 1:338.

117. See also *PW* 7:275; *GSD* 2:131–32, where again he likens Siegfried's fight with the dragon to Apollo's fighting the Python: "as Day succumbs to Night, again, as Summer in the end must yield to Winter, Siegfried too is slain at last."

118. *WagRS* 331. *WagRS* 371, n. 172, points to Grimm's discussion of "Frau Sonne" as a goddess in medieval literature (*Mythology* 2:704–5; *Mythologie*, 2:666–68).

119. *WagRS* 116.

120. Miller, *Phenomenology*, 418–20 (§§ 685–88).

121. Luke, *Faust I*, 9; *GWJA* 3:17 (ll. 243–46).

Siegfried and Brünnhilde

Siegfried may not be considered a "god" since he is a "hero"; and although his grandfather was a god, his grandmother was a mortal as were his parents, Siegmund and Sieglinde. He and Brünnhilde will be considered in more detail in chapter 10 below, but in view of the above discussion about Siegfried as "sun-god" it is necessary to tie up some loose ends now.

As we have seen above, Wagner relates Siegfried as sun-god who kills the dragon to Apollo who kills the python. Many hidden things are actually at work here and uncovering them will lead to a fresh appreciation of the theological significance of the hero Siegfried. As was noted in volume 1, Wagner took a special interest in the "Dorian invasion."[122] K. O. Müller, whose work Wagner possessed, traced the invasion by considering the Apollo cult.[123] This god, he thought, was the "totem of the tribe," as Poseidon was for the Ionians.[124] The "Ur-hellene" according to Müller, a view Wagner adopted, were the Pelasgians.[125] Since Müller considered the Doric dialect to have a "northern character"[126] and his portrayal of the Dorians as somewhat "Protestant"[127] it is easy to see how a connection could be made with "Germany."[128] Hence, in Wagner's mind this possible connection would strengthen the Siegfried-Apollo link: not only is he, like Apollo, a "sun-god" but he is related to Apollo via the Dorians. So towards the beginning of *Art and Revolution* Wagner wrote that after the "Greek spirit" had overcome "the raw religion of its Asiatic birth-place" (i.e., the nature worshipping Pelasgians) and "had set the *fair, strong and free humanity* upon the pinnacle of its religious consciousness," it "found its fullest expression in the god Apollo." He explains, as he did in *Die Wibelungen*, that it was this god who slew the Python, the dragon of Chaos ("den chaotischen Drachen"), and that this "fulfiller of the will of Zeus upon the Grecian earth" was known by both Aeschylus and the Spartan youths "[n]ot as the soft companion of the Muses" but rather "with all the traits of energetic earnestness, beautiful but strong."[129] Then there is yet another Spartan link in that the warlike ancestor of the Dorians was Heracles, and this is highly significant in that Siegfried is to some extent modelled on him.

---

122. One of the sources for this was Thucydides, *Peloponnesian War*, 1.12 (Smith, *Thycydides I*, 22–25).

123. Müller, *Doric Race*, 1:227–384 (*Geschichte*, 2:200–370), and others traced the Dorian invasion by considering the cult of Apollo. It is somewhat ironic that Delos, the birth place of Apollo, was colonized by the Ionians (Catling, "Delos," 442).

124. Hall, *Ethnic identity*, 6.

125. Müller, *Doric Race*, 1:6–7.

126. Müller, *Doric Race*, 1:18.

127. See the discussion in volume 1, chapter 4.

128. Müller, *Doric Race*, 1:6–7.

129. *PW* 1:32; *GSD* 3:9–10.

Siegfried as a Volsung, a race despised by Fricka, also chimes in with Apollo's ancestry. He was the son of Zeus and Leto and Hera, jealous wife of Zeus, forbade all lands to receive Leto so she would be unable to give birth to Apollo and his sister Artemis. This problem was then solved in that Zeus caused the island Delos to rise from the sea. Wagner would know of this from the *Homeric Hymn to Apollo* and from Goethe's *Faust* Part II: "Who raised Delos from the sea, / Leto's Isle, that she might bear / Phoebus and his sister there."[130]

Siegfried may also have an association with Apollo in that the god was associated with the Delphic oracle and nearby Mount Parnassus, home of muses. The whole opera *Siegfried* is very much associated with song and lyricism and prophecy, precisely those things for which Apollo was renowned.[131] Although in *Art and Revolution* Wagner may appear to renounce Apollo "as soft companion of the Muses,"[132] the question whether Siegfried displays any "femininity" needs to be discussed when I turn to *Siegfried* Act III Scene 3 in chapter 6 below.

At the end of *Art and Revolution* Wagner links the two figures of Jesus and Apollo as "the two sublimest teachers of mankind."[133] It is therefore no surprise that Wagner saw a fundamental link between Siegfried and Christ. They, together with Apollo, were associated with the "light" and all three conquered the forces of darkness by slaying the "dragon."

Another possible suggestion of Siegfried being a "god" is that his death has certain parallels with the Norse myth of the death of Baldr, which will be discussed later.[134] But, as will be argued later, caution is required here and any divinity of Siegfried is far from explicit.

Although Siegfried's divinity is not explicit in Wagner's *Ring*, Brünnhilde is clearly divine. The key point to bear in mind though is that this is something Wagner himself has introduced, since in the Norse sources Brynhild is a human figure, the daughter not of a god but of Budli. He does, however, agree with his sources that when she is awoken by Siegfried she is not a goddess,[135] since at the end of *Walküre* she loses her divinity.

---

130 Luke, *Faust II*, 94 (a somewhat free translation of ll. 7533–35). It was under the epithet Phoebus ("radiant") that Apollo became identified with sun-god.

131. Müller, *Doric Race*, 2:385–88, argues for the Dorians as originators of lyric. See also Nelis, "Lyric Poetry," 900: "Choral lyric is especially associated with 'Dorian' states (Alcman, Stesichorus, Arion, Ibycus, Pindar), though not exclusively." Note that Orpheus was son of Apollo and a muse.

132. *PW* 1:32; *GSD* 3:10.

133. *PW* 1:65; *GSD* 3:41.

134. See chapter 10 below and the discussion in volume 1, chapter 3.

135. Note that the sleeping one (here Sigrdrífa) is referred to as a "flax goddess" in the words of the nuthatches to Sigurd *Fáfnismál* 43–44 (which very much has influenced *Siegfried* Act III), but this is simply a term for "woman." "I know that a valkyrie sleeps on the fell, / and there plays over her the peril of wood [i.e., fire]; / Dread stabbed her with a thorn: that flax goddess [i.e., woman] / slew another man than he had wished. 44 You can see, lad, that helmeted maid, / who rode from battle on Vingskornir [her horse]; / you cannot rouse Sigrdrífa from sleep, / child of princes, in the face of the norns' decree" (Orchard, *Elder Edda*, 168).

I will discuss Brunnhilde's divinity in more detail in chapter 10 below, but one interesting thing about her is that in *Götterdämmerung* and only here does she "pray" to the gods:[136]

O heilige Götter,	O holy gods,
hehre Geschlechter!	hallowed kinsmen!
Weidet eu'r Aug'	Feast your eyes
an dem weihvollen Paar!	on this blessed pair!

This praying to the gods may be accounted for by the fact that she is in a state whereby she has lost her divinity.[137]

Fricka

In normal circumstances one would expect that among the "Götter" to whom Brünnhilde's prays in the Prologue to *Götterdämmerung* is Fricka: she is after all the goddess of marriage and Brünnhilde's prayer seems to be one of protection for the "blessed pair" ("wehvolle[s] Paar"), a prayer which was clearly not answered. But there is a curious aspect to this. In the *Mythus* Fricka has no part in Siegmund's death and we simply read: "Brünnhild, the Valkyrie, protects Siegmund against Wotan's order, who had condemned him to die to atone for his crime."[138] But in *Siegfried's Tod* of 1848, where the same prayer as in the later *Siegfried's Tod/Götterdämmerung* is found,[139] we learn from Brünnhilde that it was Frikka who commanded Siegmund's death: "For [Siegmund] was outlawed by Frikka's command, / For committing adultery, in order to conceive / The purest son with his own sister."[140] Although this is removed in *Götterdämmerung*, we know from *Walküre* that Fricka demanded Siegmund's death against Wotan's wishes and that there is animosity between Fricka and her step-daughter. Would Brünnhilde wish to pray to such a goddess of marriage?

Fricka's character will be explored in more detail in chapter 7 on sexual ethics and law. We have already noted that she is based on the Norse Frigg, but the obvious difference is that whereas Frigg can be sexually promiscuous, Fricka is quite the opposite. In productions she is often portrayed entirely negatively as the upholder of outdated morals. However, as we shall see in chapter 7, she is actually more complex than this and in *Walküre* Act II wins the argument in her altercation with Wotan.

---

136. *WagRS* 287.

137. In ancient Greek literature the only instance I have found where a god/goddess prays to another god is in the *Odyssey* Book 3, where, on Telemachus' request, Athene prays to Poseidon (Murray/Dimock, *Odyssey I*, 84–85).

138. Haymes, *Ring*, 48–49.

139. Haymes, *Ring*, 74–75; cf. *WagRS* 286. There are minor changes to the spelling and the lines of *Siegfried's Tod* of 1848 are halved.

140. Haymes, *Ring*, 96–97.

Erda

"Earth," although counted among the goddesses in *Gylfaginning* 36, does not have a prominent role in Norse mythology, which is rather surprising since "nature" was so central to this mythology. According to *Gylfaginning* 9, she is the daughter and wife of Odin and as the giantess Jörd/Hlödyn she is the mother of Thor.[141]

Wagner's portrayal of Erda, his Earth goddess, in *Siegfried* Act III Scene 1 (who predated Wagner's Erda of *Rheingold*) is the Vala of the *Völuspá*, who was not an Earth goddess but simply a seeress. Since the Earth goddess of Norse mythology is obscure, Wagner had to turn to the Greek equivalents to develop his Erda. He may well have been struck by the beginning of the *Eumenides*, where Pythia honours Mother Earth as "the first of the gods to prophesy" (l. 2), this gift being eventually passed to Apollo (Phoebus).[142] In the *Ring* Erda makes her first explicit appearance in *Rheingold* Scene 4, although it could be said she is implicitly the very first god of the cycle as we hear the evolution of "nature" in the Prelude.

Another inspiration for Wagner's Erda could be well be Goethe's *Faust*.[143] After opening Nostradamus he reflects on "endless Nature" and her "breasts that flow / With life's whole life,"[144] sees the "Sign of the Earth Spirit" and then experiences her epiphany.[145] Seung may well be correct in suggesting that "the Earth Spirit [is] the real power behind the throne of the Lord in Heaven. [. . .] Thus the monotheism of the Prologue in Heaven is absorbed into Faust's pantheistic naturalism. This is what is meant by the naturalization of Christianity."[146] The Earth Spirit's description of her activities is reminiscent of Wagner's nature in *Rheingold*:[147]

---

141. *Thrymskvida* 1 and *Lokasenna* 58, refer to Thor as "Son of Earth" and *Völuspá* 53 as "the glorious child of Hlödyn."

142. Fagles, *Oresteia*, 231. For this pattern of earth being the first god see Frazer, *Apollodorus I*, 2–3 (I.1), which links her with sky: "Sky (Ouranos) was the first who rule over the whole world. And having wedded Earth, he begat first the Hundred-handed, as they were named."

143. Goethe and Herder formed many compound words with Erde, and initially it was Herder who influenced Goethe in this respect. Among Herder's earth compounds, many of which he himself coined, are "Erdenatur" ("earth-nature"), "Erdegebilde" ("earth-forms"), "Erdegesetze" ("earth-laws"), "Erdeschranken" ("earth-limitations"), "Erdenursprung" ("earth-origin"), "Erdebürger" ("earth-citizens"), and "Erd-Gott" ("earth-god," meaning "humankind"). See Goethe's own favorite was "Erdensohn" ("earth-son") (Luke, *Faust I*, 104; *GWJA* 3:118.). See Mason, *Goethe*, 154; Seung, *Goethe*, 11.

144. Luke, *Faust I*, 17.

145. Luke, *Faust I*, 18.

146. Seung, *Goethe*, 14.

147. Luke, *Faust I*, 19; *GWJA* 3:27 (ll. 501–9).

In Lebensfluten, im Tatensturm	In life like a flood, in deeds like a storm
Wall' ich auf und ab,	I surge to and fro
Wehe hin und her!	Up and down I flow!
Geburt und Grab,	Birth and the grave
Ein ewiges Meer,	An eternal wave,
Ein wechselnd Weben,	Turning, returning,
Ein glühend Leben,	A life ever burning:
So schaff' ich am sausenden Webstuhl der Zeit,	At Time's whirring loom I work and play
Und wirke der Gottheit lebendiges Kleid.	God's living garment I weave and display.

The idea of Earth as a "Mother," something Wagner indicated in the Prologue to *Götterdämmerung* as the Norns descend "Zur Mutter" ("To mother"), is developed in *Faust* Part II. Mephistopheles divulges to Faust the existence of goddesses who have no space or time around them and are called "the Mothers," to which the startled Faust exclaims "Mothers!" Mephistopheles responds: "You dread the name?"[148] Faust (shuddering) a little later explains: "The Mothers! Every time it strikes such fear / Into my heart, this word I dare not hear."[149] But when he decides to rescue Helen he calls on the Mothers for help: "Mothers, Mothers, grant this boon!"[150] The words of the Wanderer in *Siegfried* Act III Scene 1 may allude to these mothers: "The wisdom of primeval mothers / draws towards its end."[151]

But the most important role Erda plays in the *Ring* is as a prophetess, and this is her prominent role in both her appearances. In her first appearance, in *Rheingold* Scene 4, she warns Wotan to shun the ring. The final libretto may suggest that Wotan's downfall will be avoided if he gives up the ring:[152]

Alles was ist, endet.	All things that are—end.
Ein düst'rer Tag	A day of darkness
dämmert den Göttern:	dawns for the gods:
dir rath' ich, meide den Ring!	I counsel you: shun the ring!

This issue bothered Röckel and Wagner addressed it in his letter of 25/26 January 1854, where he points to a change he made in the libretto. He quotes from his *Erstschrift des Textbuches*:[153]

---

148. Luke, *Faust II*, 51; *GWJA* 3:215 (ll. 6213–15). Luke, *Faust II*, xxvi, notes that this opens the central Faust-Helen sequence of the finished Part II.

149. Luke, *Faust II*, 52; *GWJA* 3:217 (ll. 6265–66).

150. Luke, *Faust II*, 62; *GWJA* 3:228 (ll. 6558).

151. *WagRS* 257, 369 n. 122.

152. *WagRS* 112.

153. *TBRN1* 416. In quoting this in his letter (*SB* 6:67) he employs the normal German scheme of capitalization (which he had earlier renounced).

Ein düstrer tag	A day of darkness
dämmert den göttern:	dawns for the gods:
in schmach doch endet	yet in shame will end
dein edles geschlecht,	your noble race,
lässt du den reif nicht los!	should you not let the ring go!

Hence, the issue here is not *whether* the gods will perish but exactly *how* they perish. He offers this rationalization: "We must learn to die, and to die in the fullest sense of the word; fear of the end is the source of all lovelessness, and this fear is generated only when love itself is already beginning to wane."[154] Wagner does not actually explain why he changed the libretto, omitting this clarification, but he clearly still felt that the gods will come to an end anyway but it will be in a shameful way should Wotan not shun the ring. Berry comments that "[t]he ring, through Erda's warning, thus acquires associations of a lust for immortality."[155] Wotan, even after this warning, still wants to gain the ring through "project Siegmund"[156] but he comes to a point of giving up in *Walküre* Act II and especially in *Siegfried* Act III Scenes 1 and 2.[157] The issue then is whether Wotan will meet a shameful or noble end. I suggest that the answer to this is by no means clear partly because Wotan waits too long before deciding to shun the ring.

Freia and the Golden Apples

Although Freia as a goddess of love is absent from the 1848 *Mythus* she does get two mentions in *Siegfried's Tod* Act II Scene 2:[158]

Gudrune:	Gudrune:
Freija grüße dich	May Freija greet you
zu aller Jungfrau'n Ehre!	In honour of all maidens!
Siegfried:	Siegfried:
Freija, die Holde, heiß' ich dich:	I call you Freija, the dear one:
Frikka laß uns nun rufen,	Let us now call Frikka,
Wotan's heilige Gattin,	Wotan's holy spouse,
sie gönne uns gute Ehe!	Let her grant us good marriage.

This was then later reduced to one with the second mention changing to a word-play on her name: "Frei und hold / sei nun mir frohem" ("Be open-handed and well-disposed /

---

154. *SL* 306–7; *SB* 6:67.
155. Berry, *Bonds*, 165.
156. Kitcher and Schacht, *Ending*, 112–20.
157. This may suggest that before Autumn 1854 he already had a reasonable knowledge of Schopenhauer's philosophy. See volume 1, chapter 6.
158. Haymes, *Ring*, 114–17.

to me in my happy state").¹⁵⁹ In the original and later versions of *Siegfried's Tod* Freia is noticeably absent from the gods to whom sacrifices are to be made, Hagen commanding offerings to Froh, Donner, and Frikka.¹⁶⁰ Freia makes no appearance in *Der junge Siegfried* or in *Walküre*, but she has a pivotal role in *Rheingold*.

Grimm defines her as a "love-goddess" whom "lovers do well to call upon her,"¹⁶¹ distinguishing her from Fricka, who "presides over *marriages*."¹⁶² Magee points out that this is a "hard-won distinction" since the "demarcation-lines between the two goddesses were very fluid in the sources."¹⁶³ Further, Grimm discovered that Germanic religion produced a number of similar domestic goddesses, one of which was Frau Holda. Hence, we have the word-play of Fasolt in *Rheingold* Scene 2:¹⁶⁴

Freia, die holde,	Freia the fair,
Holda, die freie	Holda the free

The sources do not link the apples with Freia but rather with Idunn, wife of Bragi: "She keeps in her casket apples which the gods have to feed on when they age, and then they all become young, and so it will go on right up to Ragnarok."¹⁶⁵ Wagner's scene of the gods growing old after Freia has been taken away could be based on *Skaldskaparmal* 1, where, on the theft of Idunn and her apples, the Æsir "soon became grey and old."¹⁶⁶ Wagner's stage direction is: "A pale mist, growing gradually denser, fills the stage, so that the gods acquire an increasingly wan and aged appearance; they all stand gazing anxiously and expectantly at Wotan, who is lost in thought, his eyes fixed firmly on the ground."¹⁶⁷ Included in Loge's commentary that follows is "From your hand, Donner, / your hammer is sinking."¹⁶⁸ A closer parallel to that from *Skaldskaparmal* 1 is

---

159. *WagRS* 313.

160. Haymes, *Ring*, 122–23; *WagRS* 317 (see below). Note that in *Lohengrin* Ortrud calls on her but for the purpose of vengeance (*GSD* 2:87).

161. Grimm, *Mythology*, 1:305; *Mythologie*, 1:282.

162. Grimm, *Mythology*, 1:303–4; *Mythologie*, 1:280. It is somewhat ironic that Grimm adds that "her aid is implored by the childless" (Grimm, *Mythology*, 1:304; *Mythologie*, 1:280) given that Wagner's Fricka is childless.

163. Magee, *Nibelungs*, 190.

164. *WagRS* 74. Magee, *Nibelungs*, 191, compares Grimm, *Mythologie*, 2:842–43: "*Holda* die holde [. . .] *Freyja* die schöne oder frohe"; *Mythology*, 2:889: "*Holda* the gracious [. . .] *Freyja* the fair or happy."

165. Gylfaginning 26; Faulkes, *Edda*, 25. But note that Idunn's apples are not specified as "golden" (Bjornsson, *Volsungs*, 138). Magee, *Nibelungs*, 191, suggests that it was Grimm's reference to Freia as a fertility goddess that prompted Wagner to identify her with Idunn.

166. Faulkes, *Edda*, 60.

167. *WagRS* 85.

168. *WagRS* 85. See also Donner's own words: "My hand is sinking" ("Mir sinkt die Hand"); *WagRS* 86.

Hrafnagaldr Odhins, which was included in Simrock's 1851 *Edda*.[169] This tells of how Idunn sinks down under the earth and the gods lose their power: "Die Kräfte ermatten, / Ermüden die Arme, / Schwindelnd wankt / Der weiße Schwertgott" ("Powers fade, / Arms fail, / The white sword-god / Wavers, irresolute").[170] The spell is broken only when Odin rouses himself in *Vegtamskvida* (Baldr's dreams)[171] as Odin goes to the underworld. In the *Edda* he goes to seek the Wala; in *Rheingold* Wotan goes to seek Alberich.

Loki and Loge

Wagner's Loge was primarily based on the Norse Loki, who plays a prominent role in both Eddas, and the rather obscure figure of Logi, a fire god.[172] Just as Loki's poem *Lokasenna* (*Loki's home-truths*) is perhaps the most entertaining of all the poems of the *Elder Edda*,[173] so Wagner's Loge has some of the best lines in the *Ring*.

As noted in volume 1, chapter 2, Loge does not feature in the 1848 *Ring*, either in the *Mythus* or in *Siegfried's Tod*. Wagner may have first read about him in Grimm's *Mythologie* in 1843. We do have a reference to his reading this section but only as late as 1873.[174] Wagner may have been prompted to include Loge after work on his 1848 *Ring* by reading Weinhold's work on Loki.[175] As Magee notes, Weinhold "was concerned to restore the god to what he regarded as his original stature and dignity."[176] The view in the Eddas of "the court jester of Asgard, who entertains the king, Lord Odin, by gossip and foolery and who sets evil on foot wherever he can" is, for Weinhold, "a late, debased representation of the god."[177] We see this "late" representation in Grimm, who describes him as "a sly, seducing villain."[178] In contrast, for Weinhold "the harm Loge

---

169. Magee, *Nibelungs*, 192–93.

170. Simrock, *Edda*, 36; Magee, *Nibelungs*, 193. This v. 23 in Simrock's edition occurs earlier in Lassen, *Hrafnagaldur Óðins*, 88 (v. 14).

171. This follows in Simrock's edition. Indeed, the work was composed as an introduction to Baldr's dreams.

172. The two feature together in the *Prose Edda* where Loki loses to Logi in an eating contest (Faulkes, *Edda*, 45).

173. Orchard, *Elder Edda*, 82–96.

174. CD 1 October 1873. In his Wahnfried library he had the third edition (1854). The section on Loki/Logi is *Mythologie* 1:220–25; *Mythology*, 1:241–46.

175. Weinhold, "Die Sagen von Loki." This was in the 1849 volume of the *Zeitschrift für deutsches Alterthum* to which Wagner subscribed. However, his 6 volume collection in his Dresden library only extended from 1841–48 (DB 168).

176. Magee, *Nibelungs*, 197.

177. Magee, *Nibelungs*, 197, points to the views of other scholars Wagner was reading all of whom portray Loki negatively.

178. Grimm, *Mythology*, 1:241. He writes of both Logi and Loki: "*Logi* die naturkraft des feuers, das im laut fortgeschobne *Loki* zugleich eine verschiebung des begrifs: aus dem plumpen riesen ist ein schlauer, verführerische bösewicht geworden" (*Mythologie*, 1:221). Cf. Magee, *Nibelungs*, 197.

causes is well-directed, systematic, and purposeful."[179] A somewhat less positive view of Loki is found in Mohr who compares Loki to Goethe's Mephistopheles. Just as Mephistopheles is "Part of that Power which would / Do evil constantly, and constantly does good" ("Ein Teil von jener Kraft, / Die stets das Böse will und stets das Gute schafft")[180] so it is for Loki.[181] The view of Loki in some of the Norse sources can be extremely negative. As noted in volume 1, chapter 3 Loki has something of the biblical devil in him in that he engineers the death of Baldr.

Wagner's view of Loge would appear to be closer to Weinhold than say Grimm. And rather than acting like Mephisto, intending evil but ending up making things better, he appears to wish the good but can end up making everything much worse. In *Rheingold* he genuinely wishes to resolve problems, such as freeing Freia. And it looks as though he has sympathy for Fasolt as the giants quarrel over the hoard and tells him to "look to the ring alone!"[182] But evil consequences follow as Fafner kills Fasolt. Wotan is horrified and shaken: "Fearful now / I find the curse's power!" ("Furchtbar nun / erfind' ich des Fluches Kraft!")[183] Loge's response in consoling Wotan seems to lack empathy and may suggest sociopathetic tendencies: "Wotan, what can compare / with your luck? / Winning the ring / gained you much; / that it's been taken away from you / serves you even more: / behold, your enemies / fell one another / for the sake of the gold that you gave away."[184] At the end of *Rheingold* we see a cluster of aspects that sum up Loge's character (although whether we have an integrated personhood is another question). First, he has insight into what will indeed come to pass ("They're hurrying on towards their end, / though they think they will last for ever").[185] In fact, apart from Erda, Loge is the only one who understands this. Secondly, he and only he has a feeling of shame ("I'm almost ashamed / to share in their dealings").[186] Thirdly, he has a genuine concern for the Rhinemaidens who mourn the loss of the gold; but at the same time he can engage in bitter irony:[187]

---

179. Magee, *Nibelungs*, 197.
180. Luke, *Faust I*, 42; *GWJA* 3:51 (ll. 1336–37).
181. Mohr, "Mephistopheles und Loki," 199.
182. *WagRS* 114.
183. *WagRS* 114.
184. *WagRS* 114.
185. *WagRS* 117.
186. *WagRS* 117.
187. *WagRS* 118.

Ihr da im Wasser!	You there in the water!
was weint ihr herauf?	Why weep at us up here?
Hört, was Wotan euch wünscht.	Hear what Wotan wishes of you:
Glänzt nicht mehr	if the gold no longer
euch Mädchen das Gold,	gleams on you maidens,
in der Götter neuem Glanze	blissfully bask henceforth
sonnt euch selig fortan!	in the gods' new-found splendour!

Such irony may stem from the fact that for Wagner Loge is a half-god: towards the end of Scene 2 of *Rheingold* Loge, perhaps with a dose of Schadenfreude as he observes the gods becoming "old and grey, grizzled and grim," explains that Freia begrudged him the "luscious fruit" since he was merely a half-god.[188]

Loge demonstrates a certain instability[189] and we see at the end of *Rheingold* his desire to turn himself "into guttering flame" ("zur leckende Lohe").[190] He does indeed do this and in *Walküre* Act II Wotan in his monologue explains that "cunningly Loge lured me on / but vanished while roaming the world" (listig verlockte mich Loge, / der schweifend nun verschwand").[191] But he calls upon him at the end of Act III to "enfold the fell with fire"[192] and the ending of *Walküre* suggests that Loge has a protective role, shielding Brünnhilde from any "coward" who may draw near. Further, he only acts with his fire when called upon, as can be seen in this closing scene of *Walküre* and in his role at the end of *Götterdämmerung* when Brünnhilde tells Wotan's ravens:[193]

Fliegt heim, ihr Raben!	Fly home, you ravens!
Raunt es eurem Herren,	Whisper to your lord
was hier am Rhein ihr hörtet!	What you heard here by the Rhine!
An Brünnhilde's Felsen	Make your way
fahrt vorbei:	past Brünnhilde's rock:
der dort noch lodert,	tell Loge, who burns there,
weiset Loge nach Walhall!	to haste to Valhalla!

In *Völuspá* Loki/Loge plays a crucial role in Ragnarök. Not only has he managed to beget the Wolf Fenrir, Hel, and the Midgard Serpent (the mother is the giantess

---

188. *WagRS* 86.

189. This is also represented musically. Rappl, "Weltschöpfung," 19: "when Loge mocks the sedentary character of his fellow-gods Donner and Froh, which he contrasts with his own restless nature ('In Tiefen und Höhen treibt mich mein Hang'), the Valhalla theme is caricatured and belittled, entering three times, on each occasion in a different key, C sharp major, A major and F major. The idea behind this is that Loge is not settled in any key: he is everywhere and nowhere at home."

190. *WagRS* 117.

191. *WagRS* 149.

192. *WagRS* 191.

193. *WagRS* 350.

Angrboda), but he breaks free from his bonds (35) and leads Muspell's troops[194] from the East over the waters (51) but is then killed by Víðar, Odin's son (54).[195] In *Götterdämmerung* Loge appears more as a tool of Wotan rather than being an independent entity as in *Völuspá*. The third Norn prophesies:[196]

Des zerschlag'nen Speeres	The shattered spear's
stechende Splitter	sharp-pointed splinters
taucht einst Wotan	Wotan will one day bury
dem Brünstigen tief in die Brust:	deep in the fire-god's breast:
zehrender Brand	a ravening fire
zündet da auf;	will then flame forth,
den wirft der Gott	which the god will hurl
in der Welt-Esche	on the world-ash's
zu Hauf' geschichtete Scheite.	heaped-up logs.

Wagner does allude to Loki's leading troops with the first entry of the Third Norn: "Loge's Heer / lodert feurig um den Fels" ("Loge's host / burns brightly round the fell").[197] But the reference here is to the flames around Brünnhilde's rock.

Down the centuries many have been traumatized or died from fire from the brutal burning of Njal[198] down to the appalling Grenfell Tower tragedy. The fire unleased at the end of *Götterdämmerung* has the same destructive effect, but, as noted above, at least the god is given a sedative before he is consumed by the flames of Loge.

A significant change Wagner could be said to make is that whereas in the Norse tradition Loki is instrumental in killing Baldr by putting a mistletoe dart in the hand of Höð, Loge plays no part in Siegfried's death. However, not too much should be read into this since the death of Siegfried is largely influenced by the *Nibelungenlied*, where he is killed by Hagen (with the collusion of Prünhilt and Gunther). Nevertheless, it can be said that Wagner portrays Loge sympathetically when one compares him to his Norse counterparts.[199] As far as Greek counterparts are concerned, Loge corresponds to the fire-god Hephaestus. But he also has similarities to Hermes, the subordinate deity who is a messenger god, an expert in technology, and can be mischievous.[200]

---

194. Muspell for the poet is a fire giant.

195. Orchard, *Elder Edda*, 12–13.

196. *WagRS* 283.

197. *WagRS* 280.

198. On the burning of Njal see Magnusson and Pálsson, *Njal's Saga*, 265–73 (chapters 130–31).

199. I find Donington, *Ring*, 81–87, unnecessarily negative towards Loge. Just as I have argued above that he is more humane than Mephistopheles, he has also little in common with Lucifer (contrast Donington, *Ring*, 82).

200. Cf. Donington, *Ring*, 82, who argues Loge is closer to Hermes than Hephaestus. However, I find Donington unnecessarily negative towards Loge (see above).

Donner and Froh

Given that Thor was such a prominent god in the Norse sources, being the central figure in a number of the poems, it is striking that Wagner's Donner has only a minor role in Wagner's *Ring*. Likewise, Froh has a minor part and tracing both these minor gods through the evolution of the *Ring* one can say they progress only to a limited extent from 1848 to 1852 and "remain psychologically undeveloped."[201] In the presentation of these gods in the 1848 *Ring* we are very much in the realm of Grimm's *Mythologie*, as we can see in Hagen's address to the vassels in *Siegfried's Tod* Act II:[202]

Einen Eber fällen sollt ihr für Froh,	You should kill a boar for Froh,
einen stämmigen Bock stechen für Donner;	Stab a brawny ram for Donner;
Schafe aber schlachtet für Frikka,	Sacrifice sheep for Frikka,
daß gute Ehe sie gebe!	So she will bestow a good marriage.

Donner and Froh do become more significant in the final *Ring* in that they do take human form in *Rheingold*. Further, Donner forms a bridge in more senses than one in that he not only brings into existence the rainbow bridge at the end of *Rheingold* (with Froh at his side)[203] but also his leitmotif forms a musical bridge in linking the end of *Rheingold* to the beginning of *Walküre*.[204]

It is worth adding that Wagner has made Donner and Froh brothers of Fricka (and also made Freia her sister). Thus he has eliminated the key distinction in the Norse sources between the Æsir (Odin, Frigg, Thor) and the Vanir (Freyr and Freyja, children of the sea god Njord).[205]

Final Reflections on the Question of God and the Gods

The question remains about the ontological status of the gods in Wagner's *Ring*. Do the gods "Wotan," "Fricka," "Donner," "Froh," "Freia," and "Erda" exist in any sense? The Christian author of the *Prose Edda* certainly did not think so. The very title of the first major section of the Prose Edda "The Deluding of Gylfi" (*Gylfaginning*) makes clear that the three figures Gylfi encounters have deceived him not only in producing a visual illusion of Valhalla but also in spinning the elaborate mythology that Gylfi believes and passes on to others. *Gylfaginning* does not specify who these figures "High"

---

201. Magee, *Nibelungs*, 190.
202. Haymes, *Ring in 1848*, 122–23. Apart from dividing most of the lines, this is unchanged in *Götterdämmerung*.
203. *WagRS* 116.
204. Compare *Rheingold* 3675–701 to *Walküre* I.62–95.
205. Cooke, *End*, 152–53. So Freia refers to Fricka as her sister (*WagRS* 72) and Donner and Froh as her brothers (*WagRS* 73).

("Hár"), "Just-as-High" ("Jafnhár"), and "Third" ("Þriði")[206] are, but Arnkiel identified them with Thor, Odin, and Freyja.[207] It would certainly make sense to see "Just-as-high" as Odin in view of the identification in *Grímnismál* 49.[208]

This euhemerist view of the gods (i.e., believing they were originally historical figures) can be found in the *Prologue* of the *Prose Edda*, which provides a Christian introduction to the body of "pagan mythology." This prologue was actually missing in the editions Wagner possessed and consulted[209] but it was in the edition of Resenius and of Rasmus Rask, Grimm referencing the latter in his *Deutsche Mythologie*. I outline the contents of this Prologue since it highlights what rationalization of the gods entails and how different Wagner's approach is.

At the very beginning of the Prologue theological elements are taken from the Old Testament: "Almighty God created heaven and earth and all things in them, and lastly two humans from whom generations are descended, Adam and Eve, and their stock multiplied and spread over all the world."[210] It goes on to speak of the fall (but relating it to Gen 6 rather than Gen 3), Noah's flood, and the repopulation of the earth by the eight survivors. But humankind "neglected obedience to God" and "forgot the name of God." Nevertheless, God gave them wisdom "so that they could understand all earthly things."[211] There then follows a discussion of the natural order and concludes that humankind failed to "know where his kingdom was" and "understood everything with earthly understanding, for they were not granted spiritual wisdom. Thus they reasoned that everything was created out of some material."[212]

Section two of the Prologue tells of the three parts of the world: Africa, Europe, and Asia. Asia is portrayed as a paradise and contains "the middle of the world" close to which is Troy.[213] One of the kings was Munon or Mennon, married to Troan, daughter of King Priam. They had a son "Tror, the one we call Thor."[214] He was brought up to be a strong man in Thracia and "[w]e call that place Thrudheim."[215] He explored all parts of the world and "defeated unaided all berserks and giants and one of the greatest dragons and many wild animals." In the north he met the prophetess Sibyl (Sif) and married her. A long genealogy is given, which runs through to Fridleif whose son was Woden "that we call Odin." "He was an outstanding person for wisdom" and his wife

---

206. Faulkes, *Edda*, 8.

207. See the image in Arnkiel's *Cimbrische Heyden-Religion* (1702) after p. 58 (this is part I of *Außführliche Eröffnung*). Cf. Krömmelbein, "Schimmelmann," 126.

208. Orchard, *Elder Edda*, 58.

209. See volume 1, chapter 3.

210. Faulkes, *Edda*, 1.

211. Faulkes, *Edda*, 1.

212. Faulkes, *Edda*, 2.

213. Faulkes, *Edda*, 2–3.

214. Faulkes, *Edda*, 3.

215. Faulkes, *Edda*, 3.

GOD AND THE GODS

was "Frigida, whom we call Frigg."[216] Odin and a large following then travelled north and settled for a long time in "Saxony."[217] His three sons then ruled over Europe: Veggdegg in East Saxony, Beldegg (Baldr) in Westphalia, and Siggi in what is now called France.[218] Odin then travelled to Reidgotaland (Jutland) and from his son Skiold are descended the Skioldungs who were to rule Denmark.[219] Odin then travelled to Sweden where king Gylfi went out to meet "the men of Asian (who were called Æsir)."[220] The three, who are suddenly introduced without explanation, may be related to the three on the thrones in *Gylfaginning* 2. Peace and prosperity accompanied their journey and Odin chose a place for a town, which is now called Sigtunir. He then travelled to Norway and placed his son Sæming in power there and his other son Yngvi became king of Sweden (from whom the Ynglings are descended). The Æsir and some of their sons married women from these northern lands and spread throughout "Saxony" and the language of Asia became the "mother tongue" of these lands.[221]

Although this Prologue was missing in the editions Wagner possessed and consulted, he would nevertheless know of such euhemerism from *Heimskringla*, which he did read. But Wagner does not engage in such rationalization and I have found no statement where he said that his gods of the *Ring* cycle do not exist! And one wonders whether despite his anti-Judaism and antisemitism he nevertheless followed many of the earlier texts from the Old Testament that assume that the gods of the nations do exist.[222] The gods of Wagner's *Ring* have an ontological status and it *could* be argued that this comes about because of the language of myth, which does not *depict* reality (this is what metaphors and models do) but rather *forms* its own reality.[223] The concept of "God" is therefore integrally related to the concept of "faith," a view expressed in Luther's *Greater Catechism* in his exposition of the first commandment:

> What is it to have a god? What is God? Answer: A god is that to which we look for all the good and in which we find refuge in every time of need. To have a god is nothing else than to trust and believe in him with our whole heart. As I have often said, the trust and faith of the heart alone make both God and an idol. If your faith and trust is right, then your God is right as well, and again, where the belief is false and wrong, then the right God is absent too. For

---

216. Faulkes, *Edda*, 3. The origin of Odin here contradicts that given in *Gylfaginning* 6 that he was born of Bor and Bestla who had giant connections (Faulkes, *Edda*, 11).

217. Faulkes, *Edda*, 4.

218. Faulkes, *Edda*, 4.

219. Faulkes, *Edda*, 4.

220. Faulkes, *Edda*, 5. Asia here refers to Asia Minor, i.e., Troy.

221. Faulkes, *Edda*, 5.

222. See, e.g., Deut 32:8–9.

223. One can compare Luther's understanding of the creative power of the "word of God" (Ebeling, "Luthers Wirklichkeitsverständnis," 418–20).

these two belong together, faith and God. That to which your heart clings and entrusts is, I say, really your God.[224]

Feuerbach—whose influence on Wagner was discussed in volume 1, chapter 6—was struck by Luther's linking of God and faith and Ebeling writes that in Luther's exposition of the first commandment "[o]ne could almost imagine that one was listening to Ludwig Feuerbach." [225] It should therefore come as no great surprise that Feuerbach considered himself to be a follower of Luther and called himself Luther II.[226]

Although one *could* employ such an argument for the *Ring*, suggesting that its myth is *creating* its own reality, something more complex is going on. Wagner does write of "myth" but he also writes of "mythic allegories." I will discuss allegory in detail in the final chapter, but it is necessary to address this now, in particular the idea of a Christian allegory.

As noted earlier, there had been a tradition of Christian interpretation of the Norse material before Jacob Grimm. Schimmelmann, for example, understood Odin as Adam,[227] Loki as sin, and the Midgard serpent as the devil.[228] The *Völuspá*, he claimed, can be seen as an "Old Testament"[229] and so he came to the view that the *Edda* was nothing other than concerned with matters of the church.[230] This is obviously something that could only be developed by adopting an allegorical interpretation of the Edda. Can Wagner be seen to be doing something similar in the *Ring*?

Christian allegory could be seen at work in a number of key passages. There are the Christian ideas of the father giving up his son (Wotan/Siegmund), incarnation (Brünnhilde becoming fully human), and redemption (Brünnhilde's sacrificial death). The way they are presented in the artwork comes as a surprise and, I claim, speaks anew with a certain freshness that is not possible by simply repeating Christian doctrines and retelling the narratives of the Bible. But perhaps more is at work for the theologian. If Wotan is seen as a "God the Father" figure then we have something essentially absent from the New Testament witnesses: God the Father expressing his thoughts and emotions! In the Old Testament we do have this in that God speaks to his people either directly (e.g., Exod 20:2—31:17) or through his prophets. But when we come to the New Testament God has become so transcendent that we only occasionally hear his voice, as at Jesus' baptism (Mark 1:11) and transfiguration (Mark 9:7 par.). The most vivid voice of God comes in the book of Revelation, but we hear him speak on just two occasions (Rev 1:8; 21:5–8). Otherwise, we have pronouncements

---

224. BSELK 560. The translation (here modified) is taken from Tappert, *Book of Concord*, 365.
225. Ebeling, *Luther*, 250.
226. See Rawidowicz, *Feuerbach*, 161–62, whose source is Feuerbach's student Wilhelm Bolin.
227. Cf. my discussion on Wotan as Adam in chapter 12 below.
228. Krömmelbein, "Schimmelmann," 112.
229. Schimmelmann, *Edda*, 24 (Krömmelbein, "Schimmelmann," 119).
230. Schimmelmann, *Edda*, 8, claimed "der ganze Inhalt der Edda [sei] nichts anderes als Kirchlich." (Krömmelbein, "Schimmelmann," 119).

of his love (John 3:16) or wrath (Rom 1:18). Further, such love and wrath are often discontinuous with human ideas of love and wrath. In Paul's letters God's love can be irresistible (whereas human love risks the possibility of rejection), seen for example in the doctrine of predestination, and God's "wrath" in Paul is not an emotion of God but is rather related to his role as just judge.[231] Hence, God the Father in the New Testament can be somewhat abstract and the exception is Revelation, where the emotions of God the Father can be perceived even though, as pointed out, he only speaks twice. Generally speaking, all the humanity of God seems to be concentrated in the Son: he appears as a human being in the Gospels and as glorified Son of God it is he who usually speaks in the book of Revelation.

It is perhaps no accident, although also surprising, that of all the books of the New Testament, it is Revelation that has the closest resemblance to the *Ring* in relation to expressing the emotions of "God the Father." This is so because both works are concerned with myth and allegory. One approach to Revelation is to argue that in its "apocalyptic eschatology" we find "myth" moving over into allegory, Rev 11:19—12:17 being a possible exception.[232]

If the *Ring* is seen as an allegory, and like all the best allegories it is an inconsistent one,[233] then Wagner shows how God agonizes over the death of his Son, or even how he agonizes over sending his Son into the world. This loss of a child is so graphically shown in *Walküre*. Wotan has to participate in killing his own son Siegmund in Act II and at the end of Act III he has to say a final farewell to his favorite daughter, Brünnhilde. At this point he does not understand what tragedies await her. He simply thinks she will be woken by Siegfried the hero and married to him. It is only in the final act of the next opera, *Siegfried*, that Wotan realizes that she "will work the deed that redeems the world."[234] And it is worth emphasizing that this redemptive death is not an expression of Wotan's love but of Brünnhilde's.

One could take a further controversial step and suggest that Wagner has, through his figure of Wotan, shown that God's suffering is of his own making, and that he has made a world that is fundamentally out of joint.[235] But perhaps it is neither necessary (nor politic) to spell out such heresies since those experiencing the artwork have the freedom to come to their own conclusions and reflect upon them.

---

231. Bell, *No one seeks for God*, 27–33.

232. Bell, *Evil*, 58–59. Koch, *Drachenkampf*, 70, argues that Rev 11:19—12:17 is mythical, not allegorical.

233. See chapter 12 below.

234. *WagRS* 258.

235. Contrast the view of the goodness of creation in the "General Thanksgiving" of the *Book of Common Prayer*.

— 4 —

Nature

Introduction

Wagner believed that his *Ring* concerned "the world's beginning and its end (Untergang)"[1] and also that in it he had glimpsed not "a single phase in the world's evolution (Weltentwicklung)" but rather "the essence (Wesen) of the world itself in all its conceivable phases."[2] In view of this breadth and depth of interest in the world it is hardly surprising that among Wagnerians there have numbered many eminent scientists, mathematicians, and medical practitioners. A good example is the physicist Hermann Helmholtz, in whose work Wagner also took an interest.[3] He was present at Wagner's reading of *Götterdämmerung* on 17 January 1873.[4] On attending the rehearsals in Berlin of *Ring* extracts on 23 April 1875 Cosima notes: "Prof. Helmholtz constantly in tears as he listened to these divine things."[5] He attended the first *Ring* cycle and Cosima records the Grand Duke of Weimar asking Helmholtz "whether he is conducting here!"[6] The tradition of scientists being well represented among Wagnerians became increasingly clear after the composer's death. His son Siegfried noted how well the medical profession was represented in the audience at Bayreuth.[7] William Ashton Ellis, who did so much to promote Wagner in Britain, was

---

1. Letter to Franz Liszt, 11 February 1853 (*SL* 281; *SB* 5:189).

2. Letter to August Röckel, 23 August 1856 (*SL* 358; *SB* 8:153).

3. Wagner possessed the fourth edition (1877) of his work *On the Sensations of Tone* (*Die Lehre von den Tonempfindungen*).

4. See Cosima's letter to Nietzsche of 12 February 1873, where she speaks of her joy in getting to know him (*NWSEB* 1:216). On the chronology see Gregor-Dellin, *Chronik*, 140–41.

5. *CD* 23 April 1875. Two concerts took place on the following two days and after the second one the Wagners went to the Helmholtzes where they were introduced to Theodor Mommsen (*CD* 24–25 April 1875).

6. *CT* 17 August 1876: "Er fragt u.a. Pr. Helmholtz, ob dieser hier dirigiere!" This could be translated (as in *CD*): "Among other things, he asks Prof. Helmholtz whether he is conducting here!" or perhaps "He asks Prof. Helmholtz, among other people, whether he is conducting here!" Whichever translation is adopted, this is an instance where a pun is apparent in the translation but not in the original!

7. Cormack, "Faithful," 42.

a medical practitioner[8] and one of the main twentieth-century Wagner researchers, Curt von Westernhagen, studied medicine (in Berlin) and opened a dentist's practice after the First World War.[9] This interest in Wagner among scientists has continued to this day.[10]

This fascination of scientists for Wagner may have something to do with his endeavor to understand "the essence of the world itself" through his artwork. Of all operas, I judge those of Wagner to show the profoundest insight into "nature" through the intricate interweaving of music, text, and "dance." But although Wagner did take some interest in scientific developments, in his *Ring* he was in the business of "re-mystifying" nature. In doing this he was actually opposing the science of his day, which he felt had turned nature into "prose"; and in view of the "new atheism" prevalent in the UK and USA today, which sees Christianity an inimical to science, it is somewhat ironic that Wagner held Christianity to be largely responsible for fostering the scientific worldview.[11] But the *Ring* looks rather different today with the advent of Quantum theory where "the universe begins to look more like a great thought than like a great machine."[12] This raises a key hermeneutical issue: how to interpret this artwork and its relation to natural science in an age of Quantum Physics.

In this chapter I will consider anew the composer's relationship to science, particularly how it affects his theological outlook.[13] A key to this enquiry is a re-assessment of his appropriation of the philosophers Schelling, Hegel, and Schopenhauer. To some extent this can be perceived not only from his theoretical writings but also from the music itself, as we shall see in considering the opening of *Rheingold*. His appropriation of these philosophers is subtle and provides a good link to a discussion of his relation to science and nature. But first, I turn to consider two of the key aspects of nature in the *Ring*, both of which have a mythological character: the mystery of nature and the "elements" of nature.

Mystery of Nature

Carlyle's very first lecture *On Heroes, Hero-Worship, and the Heroic in History*, largely concerns "Scandinavian Mythology" and his comments on nature are arresting: "The

8. Cormack, "Ellis."

9. Dörte von Westernhagen, "Und was haben Sie vor 1945 gemacht?" 85–86.

10. From Britain alone see, e.g., Martin Rees, Stephen Hawking, Richard Dawkins, Marcus du Sautoy, and Semir Zeki.

11. Note also that his argument in *Public and Popularity* criticizes the "trivial confession of Atheism" (*PW* 6:80; *GSD* 10:88) which could result from Darwin's theories (*PW* 6:75–76; *GSD* 10:84–85).

12. Jeans, *Universe*, 148.

13. Recent examples of Wagner's relationship to science include Melderis, *Raum*, and Chadwick, "Science." Chadwick writes that in the *Ring* there is a "rejection of the gods" (25) and he finds a convergence between the "secularism" in his art and that found in "modern multiverse cosmology" (36). My chapters 2 and 3 above clearly have a different perspective.

essence of the Scandinavian, as indeed of all Pagan Mythologies, we found to be recognition of the divineness of Nature; sincere communion of man with the mysterious invisible Powers visibly seen at work in the world round him. This, I should say, is more sincerely done in the Scandinavian than in any Mythology I know."[14] Carlyle has captured something essential about the Norse mythology and although Wagner may not have read this work of Carlyle by the time he completed the poem for the *Ring* he would no doubt agree with the sentiment here expressed.[15] In appropriating Norse mythology he found gods who were related to the elements of nature: Erda is the obvious example, but there is also Donner who makes thunder, and Wotan as a storm god. The Rhinemaidens, as I will later argue, embody the waves of the river. Fasolt and Fafner may not at first appear to have any nature link but the very first *Rheingold* sketch (November 1851) names the giants as Windfahrer and Reiffrost.[16] A "Fafner" had earlier been introduced in the sketch for *Der junge Siegfried* in May 1851 but this was simply the name given to the dragon;[17] Wagner at that time had not conceived of any metamorphosis of a giant into a dragon. Fasolt first appears in the "Ergänzende Taschenbuchaufzeichnung zu Rheingold" (early 1852)[18] by which time the giant Fafner, who kills Fasolt, is identified with the dragon. Wagner's changing the names does not necessarily mean he gave up on the giants being weather giants. Reiffrost had to be changed to Fafner to enable the identification with the dragon and Fasolt was chosen partly to alliterate with Fafner but also because there was a storm giant named Fasolt in the sources he used. Fasold appears as Eck's brother in *Ecken Ausfahrt* (in the *Heldenbuch* of von der Hagen)[19] and Jacob Grimm understands Fasolt as a storm giant,[20] making the point that in Middle High German names of giants often end in –olt, such as Witolt, Fasolt, and Memerolt.[21]

But it was not just his gods, Rhinemaidens, and giants who were related to nature, even embodying nature. Nature embodied the divine and this was one way in

---

14. Carlyle, *Heroes*, 266–67.

15. The first connection of Wagner to Carlyle I have found is in May 1852 (Wille, *Erinnerungen*, 32). His Wahnfried library contains German translations of Carlyle's key works, including *Heroes*. Much of this he read, often in the evening, as is clear from the numerous references in Cosima's diaries (I found twenty-nine occurrences of "Abends Carlyle"), starting 24 November 1870 and continuing to just a few weeks before his death (the last reference is *CD* 4 January 1883). Although the couple had reservations about his style (*CD* 21 February 1871) Wagner clearly admired him and referred to him in his letters and essays (e.g., the introduction to his *Gesammelte Schriften und Dichtungen*, volumes 3–4 (1872); *PW* 1:23–24; *GSD* 3:1–2). Carlyle also took an interest in Wagner and according to Cosima (letter to Daniela, 3 April 1881), Wagner's *Religion and Kunst* was the last thing Carlyle read before his death on 5 February 1881 (Westernhagen, *Biography*, 1:319).

16. Strobel, *Skizzen*, 203; *TBRN1* 347.

17. Strobel, *Skizzen*, 66; *TBRN1* 211.

18. Strobel, *Skizzen*, 209; *TBRN1* 348.

19. See also W. Grimm, *Heldensage*, 214 where the spelling is "Fasolt." See volume 1, chapter 3.

20. Grimm, *Mythologie*, 1:524, 602; *Mythology*, 2:557, 636.

21. Grimm, *Mythologie*, 1:494; *Mythology*, 2:527.

which Wagner thought about human communion with nature, presented at its most vivid in *Siegfried* Act II Scene 2.[22] This divinizing of nature was found not only in Greek, Norse, and Germanic mythology[23] but was also in the writings of figures such as Goethe and Schiller. Wagner's divinizing of nature went hand in hand with his highly ambivalent view towards natural science,[24] which, as already noted, he associated with Christianity: "Science, which dissected Nature into fragments, without ever finding the real bond between those fragments, could only fortify the Christian view of Nature."[25] Here Wagner was sharing the view expressed by Mephistopheles in *Faust I* as he warns the student of the dangers of studying science:[26]

Wer will was lebendig's erkennen und beschreiben,	When scholars study a thing, they strive
Sucht erst den Geist heraus zu treiben,	To kill it first, if it's alive;
Dann hat er die Teile in seiner Hand,	Then they have the parts and they've lost the whole,
Fehlt leider! nur das geistige Band.	For the link that's missing was the living soul.

Something similar is found in Schiller's poem, *Die Götter Griechenlands* (1788): nature had become empty as a result of Christian demystification (l. 160).[27] Christians had made nature into prose[28] and in the *Ring*, especially in *Rheingold* and *Siegfried*, Wagner was trying to re-mystify nature, achieving this, as we shall see, through his unique welding together of music, poetry, and dance.

Elements of Nature

Anyone who has visited Iceland cannot avoid its overwhelming grandeur of nature with the rugged landscape, waterfalls, and geothermal features. It may be that such aspects informed the Norse mythology,[29] but it is worth emphasizing that the view

22. *WagRS* 238–39.

23. In fact, *Siegfried* Act II Scene 2 itself was probably influenced here by Simrock's *Amelungenlied*, 1:99. See volume 1, chapter 4.

24. This is something he shared with Hegel. See, e.g., Hegel's views on "evolution"; the theory he would know is that of Lamarck whereby lower organisms were generated spontaneously and higher organism then gradually developed from them through, e.g., transmission of acquired characteristics.

25. *PW* 2:158; *GSD* 4:36 (*Opera and Drama*).

26. *GWJA*, 3:69 (ll. 1936–39); Luke, *Faust I*, 58.

27. *FSSW* 1:168 (ll. 155–60). Taylor, *Hegel*, 42, writes that although Schiller shared the Romantic "hunger for unity" he is not generally classed as a Romantic in that "he would not take the ontological step, either as philosopher or writer, to a divinized nature, or an absolute subjectivity."

28. Borchmeyer, *Theatre*, 141: "The prosaic outlook of life which typifies the modern period, and the banishing of the gods from the phenomenal world (in other words, the displacement of imagination and feeling by intellect, science, politics, and history), were developments that, in Wagner's view, must be laid at the door of Christianity."

29. An example is discussed by Nordvig, "Creation."

of nature Wagner appropriated from Iceland (and Scandinavia) was of a mythological rather than a natural landscape. Grimm opens his chapter on the "Elements" by writing of "the simple phenomena of nature, which at all times in their silent greatness wield an immediate power over the human mind. These all-penetrating, all-absorbing primitive substances, which precede the creation of all other things and meet us again everywhere, must be sacred in themselves, even without being brought into closer relation to divine beings."[30]

An instructive example to consider regarding natural versus mythological landscape and Grimm's scheme of "Elements" is the descent into Nibelheim between Scenes 2 and 3 of *Rheingold*. We read in the stage direction: "[Wotan] climbs down into the crevice after Loge: the sulphurous vapours (Schwefeldampf) rising from it spread out over the whole stage, quickly filling it with dense clouds."[31] Wagner never visited Iceland but if he read the "Einleitung" of Rühs' *Edda* he would know that it was "durchaus vulkanisch" ("volcanic throughout")[32] and his general knowledge would suggest that the gases emitted were sulphurous.[33] But another source for his "sulphurous vapours" could be the *Elder Edda*. In the *Völuspá* we read:[34]

Hapt sá hón liggia	A captive she saw lying
undir Hveralundi,	under Cauldrons' Grove,
lægiarn[s] líki	in the shape of malignant
Loka áþekkian.	Loki, unmistakable.

Hot springs are found also in *Grímnismál*.[35] Yet another source for Wagner's "sulphurous vapours" would be the biblical tradition with references to "brimstone" in both Old and New Testaments,[36] taken up in works such as Dante's *Inferno*.[37]

This journey of Wotan and Loge through the sulphurous vapors is the first of four significant journeys in the *Ring*, each taking place in successive operas of the cycle: first, here in *Rheingold* there is the journey through the earth (Wotan and Loge

---

30. Grimm, *Mythology*, 2:582; *Mythologie*, 1:548. Cf. Deathridge, *Ring*, xxix.

31. *WagRS* 87.

32. Rühs, *Edda*, 1. This work was in his Dresden library (DB 119).

33. The main gas is water vapor and the sulphurous gases are Sulphur Dioxide (SO_2), a colorless gas that is pungent and irritating to the skin, eyes, nose, and throat, and Hydrogen Sulphide (H_2S), again a colorless gas but having the characteristic smell of rotten eggs.

34. Dronke, *Edda II*, 16.

35. *Grímnismál* 26 speaks of Hvergelmir and 29 of the two hot springs Kerlaugar (Dronke, *Edda III*, 118–19).

36. "Sulphurous vapor" only occurs in Rev 9:17–18, where it issues from the mouths of horses. Note that Ettmüller, *Vaulu-spá*, 91 (in Wagner's Dresden library), draws attention to this text, comparing Sutr's consuming trees with fire.

37. Cantos 14–17 deal with Level 7 Ring 3. Canto 14:79–81 tells of a stream Bulicame that runs red with sulphur (Kirkpatrick, *Inferno*, 123, 370) and Canto 15:2 of the "vapors" which rise up from the brook (Kirkpatrick, *Inferno*, 129). On Wagner's admiration for Dante, see volume 1, chapter 5.

at the end of Scene 2); second, in *Walküre* there is the journey through air (Valkyries in Act III Scene 1); third, in *Siegfried* there is the journey through fire (Siegfried at the end of Act III Scene 2); fourth, in *Götterdämmerung* there is the journey through water, or rather on water (Siegfried's Rhine Journey at the end of the Prologue).[38] Another way of viewing the elements is to take them in the reverse order, in fact in the order in which Jacob Grimm takes them: water, fire, air, and earth:

> Water, the limpid, flowing, welling up or running dry; Fire the illuminating, kindled or quenched; Air unseen by the eye, but sensible to ear and touch; Earth the nourishing, out of which everything grows, and into which all that has grown dissolved;—these, to mankind from the earliest time, have appeared sacred and venerable; ceremonies, transactions and events in life first receive their solemn consecration from them.[39]

In the *Ring* each element is represented by some mythical figure: "father Rhine" (water), Loge (fire), Wotan (air), and Erda (earth), and each forms a striking image for each opera of the tetralogy: "the underwater beginning of *Rhinegold*, the unforgettable magic fire at the end of *The Valkyrie*, the open air spaces of *Siegfried*, and the earthly feudal community and its rituals in *Twilight of the Gods*."[40]

Wagner's view of nature was not only influenced by Norse mythology; Goethe also played a part. Wagner shared his organic view of nature and although this was a common view at the time, Wagner and Goethe share an interest in the four elements. Wagner's debt to Goethe was discussed in volume 1, chapter 5 but now I focus on how Goethe's *Faust* may possibly have influenced Wagner's *Ring* in relation to nature and the four elements.

The four elements first appear in the study scene "Studierzimmer I" of *Faust I*. This scene was especially important for Wagner, quoting from it in his commentary on Beethoven's Ninth[41] and, more importantly perhaps, his love of Faust's translation of John 1:1, which alludes to Luther translating the New Testament in the Wartburg and being attacked by the devil.[42] So shortly after this translation scene, Faust in an effort to overcome the howling dog "[w]ith fearsome jaws and fiery eyes" ("Mit feurigen Augen, schrecklichem Gebiß"),[43] who will shortly metamorphize into Mephistopheles, exclaims:[44]

---

38. I owe this again to John Deathridge, "Leitmotifs in Wagner's Ring Cycle" (Radio 3 Broadcast, 4 July 2016) who has subsequently written of this in *Ring*, xxix. Note that apart from the journey through air, each journey is represented by an orchestral transition within the Act.

39. Grimm, *Mythology*, 2:583; *Mythologie*, 1:548–49.

40. Deathridge, *Ring*, xxix.

41. *PW* 7:250; *GSD* 2:60. There is a slight change to *GWJA* 3:48 (ll. 1210–11); Luke, *Faust I*, 38.

42. *GWJA* 3:48 (ll. 1224–37); Luke, *Faust I*, 39; see also *Faust I*, 154 n. 27.

43. *GWJA* 3:49 (l. 1255); Luke, *Faust I*, 39.

44. *GWJA* 3:49–50 (ll. 1272–75); Luke, *Faust I*, 40. Luke, *Faust I*, 154 n. 29 explains that "Faust's use of these commands will cause the dog, if it is an elemental, to reveal itself in its true shape; if it is a

Erst zu begegnen dem Tiere,	First, to defeat this beast,
Brauch' ich den Spruch der Viere:	I need the Spell of the Four, at least.
Salamander soll glühen,	Salamander, burn!
Undene sich winden,	Water-nymph, twist and turn!
Silphe verschwinden,	Sylph of the air, dissolve!
Kobold sich mühen.	Goblin, dig and delve!

Then a little later, after Mephistopheles appears, we discover that he, like Loge, has a distinct preference for the element fire:[45]

So geht es fort, man möchte rasend werden!	So it goes on; it drives me mad. The earth,
Der Luft, dem Wasser, wie der Erden	The air, the water, all give birth:
Entwinden tausend Keime sich,	It germinates a thousandfold,
Im Trocknen, Feuchten, Warmen, Kalten!	In dry or wet, in hot or cold!
Hätt' ich mir nicht die Flamme vorbehalten:	Fire is still mine, that elements alone—
Ich hätte nichts Apart's für mich.	Without it, I could call no place my own.

Another favorite scene of Wagner's was the "Classical Walpurgis Night" of *Faust II*,[46] a scene that constitutes the major part of Act II and where the four elements feature strongly. Act II closes by bringing together the power of eros and the four elements:[47]

---

devil it can be conjured with the crucifix (1298–1309) or a symbol of the Trinity (1319)."

45. *GWJA* 3:53 (ll. 1373–78); Luke, *Faust I*, 43.

46. There are numerous references in Cosima's diaries. See, e.g., the following entries: *CD* 5 December 1878: "Speaking last night about the 'Classical Walpurgis Night' he said that it always seems to him to grow shorter, he had imagined Nereus and the Nereids to be much longer; the humor in it becomes ever more apparent"; *CD* 8 April 1882: "he much admires Erichtho's speech, but almost above all else the scene of Mephisto with the griffins and sphinxes, the Chiron—everything, in fact, in this most wonderful of conceptions."

47. *GWJA* 3:288 (ll 8480–87); Luke, *Faust II*, 123. As Seung, *Goethe*, 79, observes, "the Classical Walpurgis Nights ends with the celebration of Eros and her reproductive power."

Sirens:	Sirens:
So herrsche denn Eros der alles begonnen!	Now let Eros, first cause of all, reign and be crowned!
Heil dem Meere! Heil den Wogen!	Hail to the sea, the shifting tide,
Von dem heiligen Feuer umzogen;	By sacred fire beautified!
Heil dem Wasser! Heil dem Feuer!	Hail to the waves, hail to the flame,
Heil dem seltnen Abenteuer!	Hail, this event without name!
All Alle:	Tutissimi:
Heil den mildgewogenen Lüften!	Hail to the mild and gentle breeze!
Heil geheimnisreichen Grüften!	Hail, caverns rich with mysteries!
Hochgefeiert seid allhier	Fire, water, air, and earth as well:
Element' ihr alle vier!	You elements all four, all hail!

To my knowledge we have no extant text where Wagner discusses this particular text at the end of Act II. But it is redolent of the end of the *Ring* in that here the Homunculus, moved by "Eros, first cause of all," experiences what one could call a self-immolation.[48]

The two oppositional elements in the *Ring* are fire and water. As *Rheingold* opens "[t]he top of the stage is filled with billowing waters that flow unceasingly from left to right"[49] and ends when "the whole stage seems to be engulfed in flames," "the Rhine overflows its banks in a mighty flood, surging over the conflagration" and "bright flames seem to fare up in the hall of the gods."[50] The two oppositional forces at work here are "father Rhine" and Loge, showing how his reading of Goethe had been enriched by his subsequent reading of Norse mythology. This opposition of water and fire is also found in *Faust II* where Neptune and Vulcan are both needed for nature's balance.[51] It is also seen in the debate between Thales and Anaxagoras:[52]

---

48. Cf. Luke, *Faust II*, xxxii.

49. *WagRS* 57.

50. *WagRS* 351.

51. It is worth emphasizing that Wagner's reading of *Faust II* would appear to predate his reading of Norse mythology as found in the Eddas (where a water/fire opposition is also found, e.g., in *Völuspá* 54). Wagner quotes from *Faust II* in his 1846 programme notes (albeit just two lines); the only work concerning Norse mythology that we know he read before that was Grimm's *Deutsche Mythologie* (*My Life* 259–60; *Mein Leben* 1:273). This was clearly an important work for him. He also read literature on the *Nibelungenlied* in 1844–45 (see volume 1, chapter 3) but it was only in 1847–48 that he read the Eddas (*My Life* 343; *Mein Leben* 1:356–57).

52. *GWJA* 3:269 (ll. 7861–68); Luke, *Faust II*, 104.

Thales:	Thales:
Nie war Natur und ihr lebendiges Fließen	The peaceful flow of Nature's living powers
Auf Tag und Nacht und Stunden angewiesen;	Needs no constraint of nights or days or hours.
Sie bildet regelnd jegliche Gestalt,	She moulds and rules all forms, and even on
Und selbst im Großen ist es nicht Gewalt.	The greatest scale no violence is done.
Anaxagoras:	Anaxagoras:
Hier aber war's! Plutonisch grimmig Feuer,	It was done here! Monstrous Plutonian heat,
Äolischer Dünste Knallkraft ungeheuer,	Aeolian explosive gas, replete
Durchbrach des flachen Bodens alte Kruste	With rage, burst through the earth's old flat crust, and so
Daß neu ein Berg sogleich entstehen mußte.	At once compelled this great new hill to grow.

As in the *Ring* the element of water is seen as life giving. So although Anaxagoras can claim "I say this rock by fire was created" ("Durch Feuerdunst ist dieser Fels zu Handen"), Thales can reply "In moisture all that lives originated" ("Im Feuchten ist Lebendiges erstanden").[53] Indeed, the Sirens can go as far to say that "Without water there is no salvation" ("Ohne Wasser ist kein Heil!").[54] The element of water in the *Ring* is not only life giving but also has a protective role: in *Rheingold* Scene 1 it is rather as the waters of the womb, protecting the sleeping gold, or it has the association of waves through the various forms of the "wave" leitmotif.[55] Its only negative role is in the drowning of Hagen, which is actually seen as an ultimate blessing in destroying evil!

I maintain then that it is probable that Wagner was inspired in his portrayal of nature not only by Norse mythology but also Goethe, and perhaps the most striking portrayal of nature in any musical work is the very opening of *Rheingold*, to which I now turn.

In the Beginning

In the Norse creation myth we find two contrasting regions: Muspell (an abbreviation of Muspellheim), with its fire in the south and a land of snow and ice in the north. When these two extremes mix there appeared the great giant Ymir and from his body the world was formed.[56] At the beginning of *Rheingold*, as Wagner presents his own creation myth, he has apparently ignored those of his sources. Indeed, there is nothing in the final version of the *Ring* that appeals to Norse creation myths.[57] Instead Wagner

---

53. *GWJA* 3:268 (ll. 7855–56); Luke, *Faust II*, 104.

54. *GWJA* 3:258 (l. 7499); cf. Luke, *Faust II*, 93.

55. See "Reconciliation with Nature" below and the discussion in chapter 6.

56. Faulkes, *Edda*, 9–13. *Grímnismál*, quoted in Snorri's Edda, explains: "From Ymir's flesh was earth created, and from the blood, sea; rocks of bones, trees of hair, and from his skull, the sky. And from his eyelashes the joyous gods made Midgard for men's sons, and from his brains were those cruel clouds all created" (Faulkes, *Edda*, 13).

57. The only instance I have found where there is a reference to the Norse creation myth is in the

gives us a purely musical creation myth (see Example 4.1). Two groups of double basses play almost imperceptibly the note of E♭ in octaves (E♭´ and E♭)[58] and there is no sense of rhythm.[59] In the theatre in Bayreuth, where the first official performance took place, one could not even get a sense of the timing since the conductor (and orchestra) were hidden from view. The double basses are then joined in bars 4–16 by bassoons playing in octaves the note of B♭ (B♭´ and B♭),[60] hence rendering the interval of the fifth, which gives an "empty" sound.[61] The key could be either E♭ major or minor, but as the eighth horn enters (first in bar 17) the note of G (g´) is introduced in bar 18, completing the triad, indicating the key of E♭ major, and also finally giving some sense of rhythm. This G is then sustained in bars 20, 24, 28, 30, etc.[62] The eighth horn introduces in bars 17–20 what has come to be known as the "nature" motif.[63] Then from bar 49 other instruments join in and fill in other notes of the E♭ major scale, adding a stronger sense of rhythm (particularly marked in bars 81ff), the whole presentation of nature lasting for 136 bars.[64] Wagner's choice of E♭ major was not a practical one to choose since the second group of four double basses had to tune down their lowest string E´ by a semi-tone to E♭´.[65] One can speculate about the significance of the key. Perhaps the key had a special character, Deryck Cooke considering it to be "something atavistically secure and affirming"; or perhaps a case can be made that the key has an "epic" quality, being the key of Beethoven's Eroica symphony and Emperor concerto.[66] Another possible reason for choosing E♭ Major is that Haydn's *Creation* opened in the relative key of C minor.[67]

sketches for *Der junge Siegfried*. Bjornsson, *Volsungs*, 191–92, points to the sketches of the Wanderer's reply to Mime on the giants. See Strobel, *Skizzen*, 74 ("frost und hitze hat sie gezeugt") and 121 ("frost gezeugt sie / hitze gebar sie"). But this section of text was changed for the 1853 edition, introducing the figure of Fasolt (*WagRS* 210) to this opera (he was first introduced in the "Ergänzende Taschenbuchaufzeichnung zu Rheingold" (Strobel, *Skizzen*, 209)).

58. The system for specifying the octave is taken from Helmholtz, *Tone*, 22.

59. Notes made for the first Bayreuth performance add that the basses are supported by an "organ pedal tone" ("Orgelpedalton") (*SW* 10.I:1; see Example 4.1 below).

60. Darcy, "Genesis," 93, points out that since the four second bassists playing E♭´ on an open string (tuned down a semi-tone) "the third harmonic is audibly present during the first four measures," hence "when the bassoons enter with B♭, they merely reinforce a pitch that was already sounding." On this phenomenon see Helmholtz, *Tone*, 253–54.

61. Cf. Perschmann, *Tragödie*, 4.

62. Wagner notes that this G should be played piano and with great tenderness (see Example 4.1).

63. Cooke, "Introduction," describes it as the "original nature motif" (Example 4.1), which then transforms into "nature motif (definitive)" (Example 4.2).

64. There are in fact no notes other than the diatonic scale of E♭ major in the Prelude. The first deviation from this is in bar 162 with the introduction of A natural (by Woglinde).

65. He asks for horns in E♭ but he could have chosen another key for them; if natural horns were used attachments (crooks) could be used to give other keys and in fact later they do change to C, F, and even E, the last suiting the double basses since E is the lowest string.

66. Cf. Dawson-Bowling, *Wagner Experience*, 2:219.

67. Wagner admired Haydn and possessed the vocal score for the *Creation* in his Wahnfried library.

Example 4.1: *Rheingold* bars 1–50

On Haydn's "chaos" see his somewhat caustic comments about Rossini (*PW* 4:271 n.; *GSD* 8:223 n).

NATURE

2

It is difficult to pin down the mood of the opening of *Rheingold*. As in Haydn's masterpiece it could suggest a sense of "chaos."[68] In *Pilgrimage to Beethoven* he has the composer utter these words, which are relevant to the openings of both the *Ninth Symphony* and *Rheingold*: "The instruments represent the rudimentary organs of Creation and Nature (die Urorgane der Schöpfung und der Natur); what they express can never be clearly defined or put into words, for they reproduce the primitive feelings (Urgefühle) themselves, those feelings which issued from the chaos of the first Creation, when maybe there was not as yet one human being to take them up into

---

68. Haydn's *Creation* opens with "Die Vorstellung des Chaos" ("The Representation of Chaos").

63

his heart."[69] Such gentle chaos is also suggested by the stage direction (rarely followed today) that the theatre is in total darkness and only at bar 126 does the curtain open to reveal the scene: "On the bed of the Rhine. Greenish twilight, lighter above, darker below."[70] But the sense of darkness and prior knowledge that we are in the Rhine, together with the quiet sustained notes on the basses and bassoons, could also convey a strange sense of security of being in the mother's womb.[71]

One theological question the opening of *Rheingold* raises is whether we can speak of "creation" (implying a "creator" and possibly including *creatio ex nihilo*) or simply of "nature." The quotation above from *Pilgrimage* includes both "creation" and "nature" and in the Prelude to *Rheingold* I think Wagner is being ambiguous and deliberately so. In support of "nature" (rather than "creation") Wagner himself writes of "the plastic nature-motives" of *Rheingold*, which were to evolve and "shape themselves into exponents of the various forms of Passion in the many-membered Action and its characters."[72] In support of "creation" is the probability that the formlessness and chaos as *Rheingold* opens, together with the darkness and the key element of water, alludes to the first creation story of Genesis: "the earth was a formless void and darkness covered the face of the deep, while a wind from God swept over the face of the waters" (Gen 1:2). The very first verse of Genesis has been variously translated, but Wagner would have known it from Luther's translation: "Am Anfang schuf Gott Himmel und Erde" (cf. the King James Version "In the beginning God created heaven and earth").[73] Hence, we have a creation with a definite starting point. However, there are other creation texts that do not speak of such a clearly defined beginning and have a more "mythical" nature.[74] Although Wagner's Prelude has a beginning, its opening with the *piano* of the double basses is quite different to Haydn's opening *forte* on a sustained semibreve.[75] It could even be said that "[i]n an ideal performance [of *Rheingold*], the audience is unable to discern exactly when the initial contrabass tones begin; the listener only gradually becomes aware of a sound that, in effect, has always been there."[76]

---

69. *PW* 7:41–42; *GSD* 1:110.

70. *WagRS* 57; *SW* 10.I:1.

71. The one thing a mother's womb has that is missing in the opening bars of the Prelude is a sense of rhythm. Such a sense only slowly establishes itself as the Prelude progresses.

72. *PW* 3:266; *GSD* 6:266 (Epilogue to the "Nibelung's Ring").

73. Cf. NRSV: "In the beginning when God created the heavens and the earth." On the issue as to whether we have a principal or subordinate clause see Westermann, *Genesis* 1–11, 93–97, who argues for the former.

74. See Isa 51:9: "Was it not you who cut Rahab in pieces, who pierced the dragon?" If this refers to some sort of "creation" of the world (Whybray, *Isaiah* 40–66, 159) there are pre-existing mythological creatures. Brueggemann, *Theology*, 147, points out that such imagery of "struggle in combat, as it relates to creation, is subdued and marginal in the Old Testament."

75. For this first note Haydn employs virtually the full force of his orchestra.

76. Darcy, "Genesis," 92.

Now if Wagner does envisage a "creation" does he also envisage a "creator god"?[77] Again I think he is ambiguous. But it is clear that the chief god Wotan is not a creator god.[78] In the first sketch of *Rheingold* Wotan is present in Scene 1 and bathes with the Rhinemaidens;[79] but even here he is not a creator god. He is removed from Scene 1 in the second sketch (and subsequent versions). In the second sketch (*Prosaentwurf*) "the maidens" do speak of "der vater"[80] and in the *Erstschrift des Textbuches* and then in the final version it is specifically Flosshilde who speaks of a "Father" ("Father warned against such a foe"; "Father told us and bound us over to guard the bright hoard wisely");[81] this father could possibly be a creator (it is not Wotan) but Flosshilde is most likely referring to "father Rhine," the personified river.

If Wagner has no clear idea of a "creator god" how then is creation to be conceived? The opening of the Prelude suggests a "beginning" to nature. Dahlhaus writes that the "nature motif," "a musical image of the elemental, of the *primeval origins of the physical world*, consists of simple sound waves derived from the broken chord of E♭ major."[82] Thomas Mann likewise writes of "beginnings" in the Prelude: "It was too much to ask that they should give the name of 'music' to the E flat major triad that shapes the *Rheingold* Prelude. Nor indeed *was* it music. It was an acoustic idea: the idea of the beginning of all things."[83] Vazsonyi then adds a possible allusion to "creation" in that this "grandest aquatic example [. . .] almost biblically suggests: 'In the beginning was the Sound.'"[84]

Any piece of music inevitably has a beginning and an end but it may be that music can point beyond itself to express different types of beginnings and endings. *Rheingold* has a distinctive type of beginning, as already noted; indeed, it is probably

---

77. Wagner's often uses the word "Schöpfung" for the creation of an artwork. E.g. he uses "Schöpfung" for Mozart's *Don Giovanni* and *Magic Flute* (PW 6:90, 91; GSD 10:97,98) and "Schöpfungsakt" for Liszt's *Dante Symphony* (PW 6:92; GSD 10:100). No doubt Wagner considered this opening of *Rheingold* as a "creation," possibly even as a *creatio ex nihilo*!

78. This is also the case in Norse mythology where Odin appears relatively late in the creation process. In *Völuspá* the seeress tells Corpse-father (Odin) of the creation. After narrating this creation process (1–5), the gods name "night and her offspring" (v. 6), the Æsir are mentioned (v. 7), and Odin is only named in v. 18. Odin may not be the creator but Wagner names him as sustainer of nature in *Die Wibelungen*: "The quintessence of this constant motion, thus of Life, at last in 'Wuotan' (Zeus) found expression as the chiefest God, the Father and Pervader of the All (Vater und Durchdringer des All's). Though his nature marked him as the highest god, and as such he needs must take the place of father to the other deities, yet was he nowise an historically older god, but sprang into existence from man's later, higher consciousness of self" (PW 7:275; GSD 2:132).

79. TBRN1 347.

80. TBRN1 351.

81. WagRS 59, 67 (cf. TBRN1 366, 374).

82. Dahlhaus, *Music Dramas*, 117 (my emphasis).

83. Mann, "Sorrows and Grandeur," 108. Mann, "Leiden und Größe," 29: "Es war zuviel verlangt, den Es-Dur-Dreiklang, der das Rheingoldvorspiel ausmacht, bereits Musik nennen zu sollen. Es war auch keine. Es was ein akustischer Gedanke: der Gedanke des Anfanges aller Dinge."

84. Vazsonyi, *Self-Promotion*, 138, referring to Gen 1:2.

to be considered Wagner's most revolutionary beginnings of all his works if not the most revolutionary up until his time.[85] If one wished to analyze the form of the Prelude one could turn to Lorenz, who divided it into an Introduction (16 bars), Theme (32 bars), Variation I (32 bars), then Variations II, III, IV (each of 16 bars), and finally a Coda (of 8 bars).[86] As noted above, it opens with no sense of rhythm but as the Prelude develops the rhythm becomes progressively more pronounced. Such gradual animation is subtly found in the Introduction even before the entry of the eighth horn with bow changes of the basses (Eb) and tonguing of bassoons (Bb):[87]

1	2	3	4	5	6	7	8	9	10	11	12	13	14	15	16
E♭				B♭				E♭		B♭		E♭		B♭	

However, to focus solely on the temporality of the music (to which I will return) I think misses the point of what the Prelude presents to us. Wagner's intention was that one experiences this in a darkened auditorium and I suggest that this gives a strange sensation of the interpenetration of space and time. In the process of the composition of the Prelude Wagner was already well aware of aspects of Hegel's philosophy and was coming to know something also of Schopenhauer.[88] If one wished to elucidate the opening of *Rheingold* I suggest that one of the most fruitful ways to do so is by considering Hegel's understanding of time and space, which while not *anticipating* Einstein's theories of Special and General Relativity at least can in certain respects *cohere* with them.[89] The essential point I want to draw out from Hegel is that "[t]ime [. . .] is not something independent of space, but simply what space itself logically proves to be."[90]

Wagner therefore presents his *own creation myth* through his music in the Prelude, and it is extremely sophisticated as far as "creation myths" go.[91] He presents an "evolution" in sound, introducing the notes of the harmonic series (the octave, the fifth, the third, etc.; see Figure 4.1) all of which can be said to have a foundation in mathematics and in nature (embodied mathematics).

---

85. An earlier revolutionary beginning which was foremost in Wagner's mind was that of Beethoven's Ninth.

86. Lorenz, *Ring*, 126, which Darcy, "Genesis," 92, considers "difficult to criticize." Concerning Darcy's appropriation of Lorenz, see McClatchie, *Analyzing Wagner's Operas*, 191–92.

87. Lorenz, *Ring*, 126. Darcy, "Genesis," 93, adds that "[t]he overlapping pulsations in mm. 9–16 persist for the remainder of the Prelude."

88. The Prelude was conceived sometime in the period September 1853 to March 1854 (Darcy, "Genesis," 79–81) and "he did not conceive it in its final form until well after the rest of *Das Rheingold* had been composed" (Deathridge, "Cataloguing Wagner," 196). In volume 1, chapter 6 I have argued that Wagner already had a reasonable knowledge of Schopenhauer in 1852.

89. Houlgate, *Introduction to Hegel*, 156–60.

90. Houlgate, *Introduction to Hegel*, 128.

91. See above for the Norse creation myth.

NATURE

Figure 4.1: The Harmonic Series

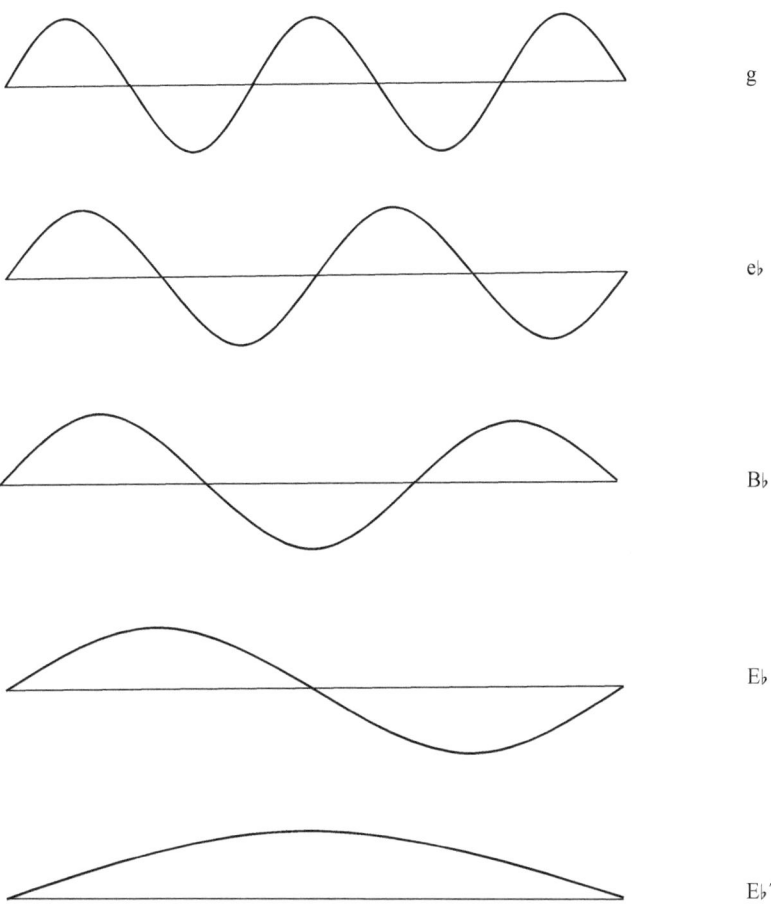

As the music evolves through bars 1–48 these intervals are introduced but from bar 49 (when Lorenz' "Variation I" is introduced) we hear for the first time the interval of the second, the first bassoon tracing out the five notes from E♭ to G, but then jumping to the E♭ and G above. This is the very first example given by Wolzogen in his guide (see Example 4.2), which he calls "the motif of the original element in its simplest form" ("das Motiv des Urelementes in seiner einfachsten Form"):[92]

---

92. Although Wolzogen could be said to have "downgraded Wagner's complex vision to a dictionary of themes and images" he nevertheless "became a model for all subsequent leitmotivic opera analysis to the present day" (Abbate, "Analysis," 117). Note that Wagner "tolerated Wolzogen's efforts but never really welcomed them" (Thorau, "Guides," 136).

Example 4.2: *Rheingold* bars 49–52

From this theme, containing steps and jumps, the essence of the music for the whole cycle can be said to evolve.[93] The "evolution" within the Prelude is represented not only by the introduction of notes of the E♭ major scale together with the introduction of more pronounced, but also by the rhythm and the nature of the crescendo: "Regarding the orchestral prelude as a whole [. . .] Wagner insisted that its huge crescendo should throughout create the impression of a phenomenon of nature developing *quite of its own accord*."[94] Such an "evolution" could be understood either in Hegelian or Schopenhauerian terms and Wagner probably had both in mind at some point. His ambiguity concerning "creation" and "nature" could be elucidated by considering how Hegel relates "God" and the "world" and I will return to questions of Hegel and evolution of nature and culture.[95] Hegel's Berlin opponent, Schopenhauer, could also be said to shine light on the Prelude to *Rheingold* with his evolution of the world will.[96] Wagner was later to write of his *Ring* in this Schopenhauerian vein: "instead of a single phase in the world's evolution, what I had glimpsed was the essence of the world itself in all its conceivable phases, and that I had thereby recognized its nothingness, with the result, of course—since I remained faithful to my intuitions rather than to my conceptions—, what emerged was something totally different from what I had originally intended."[97] Schopenhauer considered music to

---

93. As a rough approximation it can be said that whereas the motifs that run step-wise are concerned with "culture" and "civilization" (e.g., the downward-scale motif of the "spear") those that run on "jumps" are related to "nature" (e.g., "storm") or to the "heroic" (e.g., "sword"). See again Deathridge, "Leitmotifs in Wagner's Ring Cycle."

94. Porges, *Rehearsing the Ring*, 7 (my emphasis).

95. See below on "Wagner's Evolving Universe."

96. Darwin's *Origin* was not published until 1859, but Schopenhauer's thought to some extent coheres with Darwin (Young, *Schopenhauer*, 85–87) even though the philosopher considered Darwin's *Origin* "shallow empiricism" (Hübscher, *Schopenhauers Briefe*, 472). Young, *Schopenhauer*, 85–86, points to the importance of teleology in Schopenhauer's *Will*, book 2.

97. Letter to Röckel, 23 August 1856 (*SL* 358; *SB* 8:153). Peil, *Krise*, 299–300, sees the *Ring* as a revolutionary work with a dose of Schopenhauer, and in the context of discussing this letter to Röckel denies that the *Ring* is a "Kosmogonie" dealing with creation, development, and end of the world. Such a view is difficult to sustain from this passage and also from Wagner's own view that his *Ring* concerned "the world's beginning and its end" (*SL* 281; *SB* 5:189).

be an "Abbild," an "exact copy," of the world will, so the world of phenomena can be understood as embodied music as well as embodied will.⁹⁸

Birth of Consciousness: From Nature to Culture

Not only is Wagner's creation myth of the Prelude his own creation, but the whole first scene is without parallel. Deryck Cooke writes: "We face the extraordinary fact that this opening scene of the tetralogy, despite its profoundly mythic character, is Wagner's own invention."⁹⁹ With the entry of Woglinde in bar 137 "[t]he unexpected conversion of a powerful crescendo into a piano created the effect of a transformation of the waves of water into a single human figure, 'slender and light as though created out of nothing', moving freely and gracefully before us."¹⁰⁰ With nature having given birth to a human being we are then presented with the evolution of "culture" (just as previously there had been an evolution of nature). Such an evolution of "culture" can be discerned in two respects, one musical and another more linguistic. So first, with the entry of the first singer, Woglinde, we hear a pentatonic melody which continues (with Wellgunde's entries) for thirteen bars (see Example 4.3), only to be broken by Woglinde's "Safe from your reach" ("Sicher von dir").¹⁰¹

---

98. *WWR* 1:257; *ASSW* 1:359.

99. Cooke, *End*, 134. So the originality applies not just to the "creation" but also to the story of Alberich being repulsed by the Rhinemaidens, his stealing of the gold, and renunciation of love to form the ring (Cooke, *End*, 134–42).

100. Porges, *Rehearsing the Ring*, 8; the inner quotation is from Schiller.

101. Woglinde's g′′ on "dir" breaks the pentatonic pattern. On the pentatonic scale see Helmholtz, *Tone*, 257–61.

Example 4.3: *Rheingold* bars 137–51

We therefore move from a harmonic structure to a melodic one, in particular a melodic structure associated with a "primordial form of music."[102] As Nattiez argues, this transition reflects Wagner's comments in *Opera and Drama*: "But *that* Melody to whose birth we now are listening, forms a complete antithesis (ein vollkommener Gegensatz) to the primal Mother-melody."[103] Further, Wagner writes of the musician mounting "from the depths, to the surface of the sea of Harmony; and on that surface will be celebrated the glorious marriage of Poetry's begetting Thought with Music's endless power of Birth."[104] A further possible link to the world of *Rheingold* could be perceived again in the words that follow: "That wave-borne (wogende) mirror-image is *Melody*."[105]

The second way we see the evolution of culture is in the idea of mutual linguistic and musical origins. Grey comments that "[a]s Woglinde's 'natural' melody (based on the triad and added sixth) emerges from the crest of the prelude's vast tonic surge, the words move tentatively from playful nonsense syllables to articulate speech and back ('Weia! Waga! / Woge, du Welle, / walle zur Wiege! / Wagalaweia! / Wallala weiala weia!'), experimentally conjoining the various 'musical' vowel sounds with—aptly enough—the 'liquid' consonants 'L' and the vowel-like 'W.'"[106] Wagner is expressing his own theory of the common origin of melody and speech that he had put forward in *Opera and Drama*. He probably gained this view from Rousseau, who argued that "need dictated the first gestures, while the passions stimulated the first words."[107] Therefore,

> [i]t is neither hunger nor thirst but love, hatred, pity, anger, which drew from them the first words. [...] One can take nourishment without speaking. One

---

102. Nattiez, *Androgyne*, 57.
103. Nattiez, *Androgyne*, 57–58; *PW* 2:284 (modified); *GSD* 4:145.
104. *PW* 2:280; *GSD* 4:142.
105. *PW* 2:280; *GSD* 4:142.
106. Grey, *Musical Prose*, 266.
107. Rousseau, "*Origin*," 11.

stalks in silence the prey on which one would feast. But for moving a young heart, or repelling an unjust aggressor, nature dictates accents, cries, lamentations. There we have the invention of the most ancient words; and that is why the first languages were singable and passionate before they became simple and methodical.[108]

Wagner appears to be following Rousseau here when he argues that "[t]he primal organ of utterance of the inner man [. . .] is *Tone-speech* (*Tonsprache*), as the most spontaneous expression (als unwillkürlichster Ausdruck) of the inner Feeling stimulated from without."[109] Further, he appears also to be following Rousseau[110] and Herder[111] that vowel sounds were the remnants of such an instinctive musical speech, when he continues: "A mode of Expression similar to that still proper to the beast was [. . .] alike the first employed by Man." This can be reproduced "by removing from our Word-speech its dumb articulations, and leaving nothing but the open sounds."[112] Woglinde, in her first entry in *Rheingold*, would appear to be harking back to the origins of human song and speech. Darwin, writing after Wagner composed *Rheingold*, also suggested that song came before speech,[113] something that intuitively seems correct. If originally music and language belonged together but have become divorced from each other, Wagner's project was to bring speech and music back together.

As well as this evolution of "nature" and "culture" we find that the two are interconnected in a way that is not found in "scientific" discourse. An extreme way this interpenetration of nature and culture is found is in the gold of the Rhine itself.[114] Wellgunde and Woglinde tell Alberich that from this gold there is the possibility of fashioning a ring so as to gain "limitless power," but only for the one who foreswears love. Such a logic is, of course, the logic of myth, not of natural science. Another striking fact is that not only is the distinction between nature and culture eroded but so is the distinction between the organic and inorganic world; inorganic nature also seems to have a "life." Again, concerning the gold, Flosshilde speaks of "the sleeping gold." Later when the sun shines into the water, we see again this interpenetration of the organic and inorganic. Woglinde: "The waking sun (Die Weckerin) smiles into the deep." Wellgunde: "she greets the glad sleeper." Flosshilde: "she kisses [the gold's] eyelid that it may open." Wellgunde: "See how he smiles in the gleaming light."[115]

Earlier I mentioned that Wagner may have had the first creation story in view with the water and the darkness (Gen 1:2). He may also have had the second creation

---

108. Rousseau, "*Origin*," 12. Cf. Grey, *Musical* Prose, 259–60.
109. *PW* 2:224; *GSD* 4:91.
110. Rousseau, "*Origin*," 14.
111. Herder, "*Origin*," 87–91.
112. *PW* 2:224–25; *GSD* 4:91–92.
113. See Darwin, *Descent of Man*, in *Evolutionary Writings*, 237–42.
114. Bell, *Evil*, 44.
115. *WagRS* 65.

story in mind, especially with the appearance of the Rhinegold later in the scene. Genesis 2:11–12 tells of the river Pishon that "flows around the whole land of Havilah, where there is gold, and the gold of that land is good."[116] For Wagner it is not just the gold that is good but, as in Genesis 1–2, the whole creation has a certain goodness and innocence. One can speculate whether this is expressed by the key of E♭ major; but what is clear is that this innocence is expressed by the music and words of Woglinde's entry in bar 137: "Weia! Waga! Woge, du Welle (Heave, you wave)! Walle zur Wiege (wave around the cradle)! Wagalaweia! Wallala weiala weia!" Wagner explained in an open letter to Nietzsche (12 June 1872) that he had moulded Jacob Grimm's "Heilawâc" into "Weiawaga" and likens this to the familiar word "Weihwasser" ("consecrated water"). What is particularly interesting, and Wagner does not mention this in his letter, is that Grimm in his chapter on "Elements" writes of such water being created at a holy time, namely at midnight before the rising of the sun: "Water drawn at a holy season, at midnight, before sunrise, and in solemn silence, bore till a recent time the name *heilawâc, heilwâc, heilwœge*."[117] Likewise, *Rheingold* begins before the rising of the sun and it is only at bar 509 that the stage direction tells that "an increasingly bright glow penetrates the floodwaters from above"[118] and at bars 518–19 that Woglinde announces "The wakening sun smiles into the deep" ("Die weckerin lacht in den Grund").[119] In his letter Wagner then explains that from "Weiawaga" he passed on to "its next of kin," "wogen" (to heave) and "wiegen" (to rock), "wellen" (to billow) and "wallen" (to seethe) "and thus built up a root-syllabic melody for my watermaidens, after the analogy of the 'Eia popeia' ['hushabye'] of our nursery-songs."[120] Wagner commented to his wife Cosima that "the movement of the waves in *Das Rheingold* [. . .] is, so to speak, the world's lullaby."[121] Supporting the idea of the "world's lullaby" is the fact that Woglinde's words are "soft." The vowels, which predominate, have a natural softness, but the same goes for the consonants, all of which bar one (z) Wagner considered to be soft: so we have here W, G, D, L,[122] as opposed to what Wagner considered "energetic consonants" such as K, R, P, T or strengthened ones such as Schr,

---

116. Hübner, "Christentum," 276, points to this parallel. He also notes the rough correspondence between the world ash tree and tree of life (Gen 2:9).

117. Grimm, *Mythology*, 2:585. *Mythologie*, 1:551: "Wasser, zu heiliger zeit, mitternachts vor sonnenaufgang, in feierlicher stille, geschöpft, führt noch späterhin den namen *heilawâc, heilwâc, heilwœge*."

118. *WagRS* 65. *SW* 10.I:55: "Durch die Flut ist von oben her ein immer lichterer Schein gedrungen."

119. *WagRS* 65; *SW* 10.I:56.

120. *PW* 5:297; *GSD* 9:300. "eia pop eia" in Greek means "now then, ha, now then." The German song begins: "Eia, popeia, was raschelt im Stroh?"

121. *CD* 17 July 1869.

122. The letter "l," which predominates, is considered by linguists as a liquid consonant—perhaps appropriate since we find ourselves on the bed of the river Rhine. Note the l is always used here between two vowels, hence giving a clear l rather than a dark l, as in "Gold."

Sp, St, Pr.[123] There is therefore this clear expression of innocence both in nature and in the Rhinemaidens (including their song), the sort of picture of "paradise" one finds in Irenaeus' interpretation of Genesis 2.[124] Note that the first minor chord and first accidental comes with Flosshilde at bar 162: "besser bewacht / des Schlummernden Bett, / sonst büß't ihr beide das Spiel!" ("pay better heed / to the slumberer's bed / or you'll both atone for your sport.")[125]

But in addition there is also another possible aspect of nature: the verb "wogen" ("to heave") can be used not only of the heaving of the surface of water but also for the movement of a woman's breast.[126] To a child the mother's breast is a source of comfort and nourishment. But for an adult male the effect can be rather different, as seen later in the scene where Alberich tells Wellgunde how he would like to nestle up to her "heaving breast" ("schwellende Brust"). Nature is manifest in the waves of the Rhine and the waves in turn are manifest in the Rhinemaidens; the names Woglinde and Wellgunde are derived from the waves of the Rhine,[127] and in the heaving of their breasts.[128] These maidens therefore display an innocence but also a sexual character.[129]

The words and melody of the Rhinemaidens certainly suggest a rocking movement. But implicit in all this is a certain seductiveness, which is manifest when they meet Alberich. But what Hegel calls "Entzweiung" ("bifurcation," "diremtion") and consequent "fall" comes about not simply because of a "third party" (Alberich/serpent of Genesis 3) but, as Hegel emphasized, because of something rooted in the individual.[130] So the "fall" Wagner presents corresponds to Hegel's view that the "Entzweiung"

---

123. *PW* 2:271; *GSD* 4:134. For an example of these strengthened consonants see Alberich's third entry: "Stör' ich eu'r Spiel, / wenn staunend ich still hier steh'?" ("Would it spoil your sport / if I stood here in silent amazement"; *WagRS* 59).

124. See Irenaeus, *Proof of the Apostolic Preaching* 12, in Smith, *Proof*, 55: "the man was a little one, and his discretion still undeveloped, wherefore also he was easily misled by the deceiver." Smith, *Proof*, 150 n. 70, also points to Clement of Alexandria, *Protrepticus* who calls Adam a "child of God" ("paidion tou theou") but when he was seduced by pleasure and lusts he "grew old in disobedience" ("andrizomenos apeitheia") (Clement, "Exhortation," 100 (chapter 11); *MPG* 8:228). Note that Corse, *Consciousness*, 74, denies this innocence of nature. "Wagner did not [...] postulate this natural world of the prelude as an idealized nature that is unequivocally good." On this, see my discussion below.

125. *WagRS* 58.

126. It is significant that in Wagner's essay *Opera and Drama* "the sea as emotion and music are to be associated with that of music as a woman" (Dyson, "Sea," 20).

127. "Woglinde" is derived from "wogen" ("to heave" or "to billow") and Middle High German "linde" ("gentle"). "Wellgunde" is derived from "Welle" ("wave") and possibly from ON gunnr ("battle").

128. Note that the third Rhinemaiden, Flosshilde, has a name not derived from the waves but from the "fin" (Flosse") and "hilt" ("battle"). Note that she is the one who has the sense of responsibility in warning her sisters to guard the gold.

129. Fricka in Rheingold considers the "watery brood" as dangerously seductive (*WagRS* 83).

130. As we have seen in Wellgunde's "heaving breast," the "negative" of being "sexually seductive" emerges out of the "positive" of "comforting" and the "nourishing."

is immanent in the human being and not imposed from outside.[131] After this "diremtion" there is the "sublation" ("Aufhebung") whereby a position of greater maturity is reached and culminates at the end of the *Ring* cycle when they gives Brünnhilde "sincere counsel." This is how Wagner in *Artwork of the Future* presents the spontaneous emergence of human life from nature, the birth of consciousness, and the fall into error, all of which occur in *Rheingold* Scene 1.

> From the moment (Von dem Augenblicke) we humans became aware of our difference from nature, the very moment we began to develop as human beings and to break away from our unconscious, animal existence as children of nature to wake to conscious life—when we set ourselves apart from nature and, from that first sensation of dependence on nature, thought began to develop within us—this was the moment we went astray, error as the first expression of consciousness. Yet out of error knowledge is born and the history of the birth of knowledge out of error is the history of the human species from primitive myth to the present day.[132]

In the following chapter I will look more closely at the "fall" presented here in *Rheingold* and elsewhere in the *Ring*. Hegel's idea of "bifurcation" ("Entzweiung") will be seen to be a key to understanding what is happening in the fall in *Rheingold* and the alienation from nature. But now I focus on how Hegel and others can illumine the process of "evolution" that we have seen not only in the realm of nature[133] but also of culture.

Wagner's Evolving Universe

Wagner's own creation myth, in contrast to those in his Norse sources, is "teleological," but is *internally*, not externally so. The sense of purpose is immanent, no external intervention or manipulation being involved.[134] Wagner thus presents an organic view of the world, and so stands not only with Hegel but also with Herder,[135] Schelling,[136] Goethe,[137] and others who reacted against the mechanistic views of the world found in

---

131. Inwood, *Hegel*, 95.

132. Warner, "Artwork," 13; *GSD* 3:43. Cf *PW* 1:70.

133. Note, however, that Hegel himself rejected an idea of evolution in the natural world and this was rooted in that fact that he was interested in "the *logical* and not the *temporal* relations between phenomena in nature" (Houlgate, *Introduction to Hegel*, 173). However, one could argue that in principle his philosophy of nature does not necessarily entail a rejection of evolution including Darwin (174).

134. Cf. Inwood, *Hegel*, 246–47.

135. See *Ideen zur Philosophie der Geschichte der Menschheit* (1784–91), a work included in Wagner's one-volume edition of Herder's selected works.

136. See *Ideas for a Philosophy of Nature* (1797) and *On the World Soul* (1799).

137. To take just one example from Faust I (Night): "How it all lives and moves and weaves / Into a whole! Each part gives and receives" (Luke, *Faust I*, 17); *GWJA* 3:25 (ll. 447–48): "Wie alles sich zum

seventeenth-century science. Such mechanistic views, originating with Descartes, saw the world in terms of matter, inertness, impact, efficient causality, and atomism. But at the close of the eighteenth century there was a move to more organic views, and this was partly propelled by a rather different scientific worldview associated with attraction, magnetism and electricity, chemistry, epigenesis (i.e., organisms grow and develop by their own power and are not preformed), and human sciences.[138] The father of this alternative was Leibniz (who revived Aristotelian ideas of an organic universe).

One of the remarkable things about the flowering of thought and culture in the age of German idealism is the interaction between "philosophers" and "poets."[139] For example, Goethe, who, we have seen, was central for Wagner's view of nature, was indebted to Schelling's *Naturphilosophie*,[140] writing a poem "World-soul" ("Weltseele").[141] Goethe shared Schelling's view that we can only know nature when we commune with it, and not by dominating or subjecting it to the categories of analytic understanding.[142]

The one to develop the most sophisticated organic view of the world was Hegel. Although his views were interwoven with the developments of "Naturphilosophie," he was originally inspired by classical and platonic ideas. In the Tübinger Stift, Hegel, together with Schelling and Hölderlin, were enthusiastic about Plato, especially the *Timaeus*.[143] But even more important for his teleology[144] was theology, as can be seen in his use of John 1:1–4 in the *Spirit of Christianity*.[145] Therefore, the relation of the Father to the Son "is not a conceptual unity" but rather "a living relation of living beings."[146] What may be contradictory in the realm of the dead is not in the realm of life. "A tree which has three branches makes up with them one tree; but every 'son' of the tree, every branch . . . is itself a tree."[147] Such an organic view not only helps

---

Ganzen webt, / Eins in dem andern wikt und lebt!"

138. Beiser, *Hegel*, 84–85.

139. I have pointed this out already in volume 1, chapters 5 and 6.

140. Nisbet, "Religion and Philosophy," 228.

141. *GWJA* 1:223–24.

142. See "Aus: Zahme Xenien" (*GWJA* 1:250): "Wär' nicht das Auge sonnenhaft, / Die Sonne könnt' es nie erblicken; / Läg' nicht in uns des Gottes eigne Kraft, / Wie könnt' uns Göttliches entzücken?"

143. Beiser, *Hegel*, 87, points to *Timaeus* 30D: "God constructed it as a Living Creature, one and visible" (Bury, *Plato IX*, 54–55) and 33B (Plato speaks of "that Living Creature which is designed to embrace within itself all living creatures" (Bury, *Plato IX*, 60–61). Note that Wagner had the works of Plato in his Dresden library in Schleiermacher's translation, but *Timaeus* (together with *Critias* and *Laws*) were not included in this edition.

144. "Teleology" is derived from two Greek words, telos (goal) and logos (word); hence teleology concerns the goal to which nature is heading and the process of design.

145. Hegel, *On Christianity*, 256, argues that "the predicates [of the logos] are not concepts, not universals" but rather "something being and living." Further, "in him [the Logos] was life" (John 1:4).

146. Hegel, *On Christianity*, 260.

147. Hegel, *On Christianity*, 261.

explain the Trinity but also, if applied to nature, overcomes the alienation between the individual and nature.[148]

What then was Wagner's own distinctive contribution to teleology in his appropriation of Hegel? His genius does not lie in his cumbersome prose, even though I think he does have some remarkable insights. Rather his genius lies in his music and his drama. Nietzsche expresses it so in the fourth of his *Untimely Meditations*, *Richard Wagner in Bayreuth*:

> The *poetic element* in Wagner is disclosed by the fact that he thinks in visible and palpable events, not in concepts; that is to say, he thinks mythically, as the folk has always thought. The myth is not founded on a thought, as the children of an artificial culture believe, it is itself a mode of thinking; it communicates an idea of the world, but as a succession of events, actions and sufferings. *Der Ring des Nibelungen* is a tremendous system of thought without the conceptual form of thought. Perhaps a philosopher could set beside it something exactly corresponding to it but lacking all image or action and speaking to us merely in concepts: one would then have presented the same thing in two disparate spheres, once for the folk and once for the antithesis of the folk, the theoretical man. Thus Wagner does not address himself to the latter; for the theoretical man understands of the poetical, of the myth, precisely as much as a deaf man does of music, that is to say both behold a movement which seems to them meaningless.[149]

Therefore in respect to Hegel, Wagner expresses the Hegelian dialectic by means of the musical and dramatic temporal sequence. Wagner himself expressed this at the end of Part II chapter 6 of *Opera and Drama*: "The genuine Drama, then, is influenced no longer by aught that lies outside it; but it is an *organic Be-ing and Becom-ing* (*ein organisch Seiendes und Werdendes*), evolving and shaping itself by those inner conditions [. . .]."[150]

Reconciliation with Nature

Wagner's view of nature was largely feminine. This was partly because of the mythological traditions he appropriated with their earth goddesses. Wagner intensifies this feminine aspect of nature through the Rhinemaidens, who are the figures most closely associated with nature. But there were masculine elements too in that we have "father" Rhine and gods of nature (Donner and Wotan) and, as we have seen, the giants have an association also.

---

148. Beiser, *Hegel*, 88.
149. Nietzsche, *Untimely Meditations*, 236–37.
150. *PW* 2:350; *GSD* 4:204.

As we shall see in the next chapter, humankind comes to be alienated from nature through various means and Wagner has a number of ways of being reconciled to nature. One is through the process of love itself and the other is through the "eternal feminine." The "eternal feminine" was central for Wagner, the expression being found at the end of *Faust II*. It refers to Gretchen, who although passing into the background in part II is central to part I. Seung argues that Faust "is approaching Gretchen not simply as a girl, but as the vital medium for reuniting himself with Mother Nature. This is the most important point for understanding his relationship with Gretchen and the ensuing tragedy."[151] One clue to this is "Abend" when Faust, after drawing aside a curtain from the bed of Gretchen, exclaims: "What fierce joy seizes me! I could / Stand gazing here for ever. Nature, you / Worked this sweet wonder, here the inborn angel grew / Through gentle dreams to womanhood. / Here the child lay, her tender heart / Full of warm life, here the pure love / Of God's creative forces wove / His likeness by their sacred art!"[152] Then once their love has in some sense been sealed we have in the scene "Forest and Cavern" ("Wald und Höhle")[153] Faust's "magnificent blank-verse prayer of thanks to the sublime spirit that gave him full access to nature." His description of nature "connects passion and calm, perception and memory, in which the silver forms of the past (who exist independently of Faust) 'calm the severe pleasure' of his contemplation (3239)."[154] The "Sublime Spirit" ("Erhabener Geist") is the earth spirit of "Night" who has given Faust Gretchen, giving him access to "Nature's splendor."[155] Then in "Martha's Garden" when Gretchen raises the issue of "religion" he expresses his longing for consummation: "Oh, tell me whether / We can have some peaceful hour together, / Lie breast to breast and mingle soul with soul!"[156]

Earlier in "Night" Faust was in wonder about the "powers of Nature all about," "[h]ow it all lives and moves and weaves / Into a whole" and then these words, which in a modified form were included in Wagner's 1846 commentary on Beethoven's Ninth:[157] "How great a spectacle! But that, I fear, / Is all it is. Oh, endless Nature, where / Shall I embrace you? Where, you breasts that flow / With life's whole life? All earth and heaven hangs / On you, who slake the thirsty pangs / Of every heart—and must I languish vainly so?"[158] Therefore, what he spoke of in his (gothic) study of Nature's "Nurtur-

---

151. Sueng, *Goethe*, 30–31.

152. Luke, *Faust I*, 85; *GWJA* 3:97 (ll. 2709–16). Cf. Sueng, *Goethe*, 30.

153. Luke, *Faust I*, 102–3; *GWJA* 3:116–17. Luke, *Faust I*, 162–63 notes that in the Fragment the scene follows scenes 19 and 20, and hence was originally meant to follow the seduction of Gretchen. Hence some lines (eg 3249–50; 3307–10; 3336–37; 3345–65) read rather oddly.

154. Brown, "Faust," 93 (see *GWJA* 3:117 (l. 3239): "Und lindern der Betrachtung strenge Lust").

155. Luke, *Faust I*, 102; *GWJA* 3:116 (l. 3220).

156. Luke, *Faust I*, 111; *GWJA* 3:125 (ll. 3503–5): "Ach kann ich nie / Ein Stündchen ruhig dir am Busen hängen, / Und Brust an Brust und Seel' in Seele drängen?"

157. *PW* 7: 251; *GSD* 2:60 (on the fourth movement). "Welch Schauspiel! aber ach! ein Schauspiel nur!" is changed to "Welch' holder Wahn,—doch ach, ein Wähnen nur!"

158. Luke, *Faust I*, 17; *GWJA* 3:25 (ll 454–59): "Welch Schauspiel! aber ach! ein Schauspiel nur! /

ing breasts" he now identifies with his beloved Gretchen. This movement from the scholar's study to embodied nature is something Wagner reflected on when speaking of the Homunculus of *Faust II*: "The Homunculus, demanding birth, R. sees as the German spirit, which must turn from the scholar's study to Nature."[159]

So how does Wagner in the *Ring* express this reconciliation with nature through love? The first example of true passionate love in the *Ring* is that between Siegmund and Sieglinde and their love, although flouting law, is in harmony with nature. Towards the end of Act I the darkness of Hunding's hut is overcome by the full moon which shines in and, as Siegmund exclaims, "Spring shines into the hall!" This could be seen as an "Easter" moment (since we have both spring and full moon),[160] but it is also a call back to nature. The use of the moon imagery in *Faust* may also elucidate this "Easter" moment. In the Classical Walpurgis Night Anaxagoras calls on Moon:[161] "Goddess, unageing on thy heavenly throne, / Thou of three names, three shapes in one: / Now in my people's woe I call on thee, / Diana, Luna, Hecate!" Later in the same scene the Telchines call to the moon, relating her as Artemis (Diana) to her brother Apollo, the sun-god (both born of Zeus and goddess Leto): "Sweet goddess high up in the zenith, rejoice / For your brother the sun is extolled with one voice!"[162] This symbol of Artemis/moon appears in *Faust I* in two scenes that relate to Faust's love for Gretchen. First in "Abend," when he enters Gretchen's room with Mephisto after Gretchen has left, we hear him inspired by her love: "Welcome, sweet twilight, shining dim all through / This sanctuary! Now let love's sweet pain / That lives on hope's refreshing dew / Seize and consume my heart again!"[163] Then in that great monologue encountered above (Wald und Höhle: "Erhabener Geist" "Oh sublime Spirit!") after Faust has fallen in love with Gretchen, Faust speaks of the "pure moon" that "lifts its soothing light."[164] Therefore, instead of the "sad full moon"[165] in the "high-vaulted, narrow Gothic room" of the "Night" scene, we have the soothing light.[166]

Wo fass' ich dich, unendliche Natur? / Euch Brüste, wo? Ihr Quellen alles Lebens, / An denen Himmel und Erde hängt, / Dahin die welke Brust sich drängt—/ Ihr quellt, ihr tränkt, und schmacht' ich so vergebens?"

159. *CD* 6 December 1873.

160. Easter is calculated as the first Sunday after the paschal full moon that occurs on or after the vernal equinox.

161. *GWJA* 3:270 (ll. 7902–5); Luke, *Faust II*, 105 (see also the note 277). Anaxagoras was associated with the fall of a large meteorite at Aegospotami in Thrace c. 467 BC (Smith, "Anaxagoras," 85).

162. Luke, *Faust II*, 117. *GWJA* 3:282 (ll. 8289–90): "Allieblichste Göttin am Bogen da droben / Du horst mit Entzücken den Bruder beloben."

163. Luke, *Faust I*, 84. *GWJA* 3:96 (ll. 2687–90): "Willkommen süßer Dämmerschein! / Der du dies Heiligtum durchwebst. / Ergreif mein Herz, du süße Liebespein! / Die du vom Tau der Hoffnung schmachtend lebst."

164. *GWJA* 3:117 (ll. 3235–36): Luke, *Faust I*, 103.

165. *GWJA* 3:24 (l. 386); Luke, *Faust I*, 16.

166. Cf. Seung, *Goethe*, 34.

Gretchen is the means by which Faust is reconciled with nature. When the Volsung twins fall in love in *Walküre* Act I, we see also a call back to nature. For Wagner their incest was by no means unnatural and he justified incest in the realm of myth in his essay *Opera and Drama*. Wagner expresses this call back to nature in both the words and music. When the moon shines onto the scene and Siegmund speaks of the "gentle light" of the moon, reminiscent of the Faust scenes just mentioned, the consonants W and L, which, as we saw, predominate in Woglinde first entry, occur again:[167]

Winterstürme wichen	Winter's storms have waned
dem Wonnemond,	at May's awakening;
in mildem Lichte	in gentle light
leuchtet der Lenz;	Spring is aglow;
auf linden Lüften	on balmy breezes,
leicht und lieblich,	light and lovely,
Wunder webend	working wonders
er sich wiegt.	he wafts this way.

These words not only share the "w" and "l" of Woglinde's first entry, but we also have "lind" (meaning gentle) and the verb "wiegen" (to rock). (Compare Woglinde's use of "Wiege" and note that the name "Woglinde" comes from "wogen" to billow and "lind" gentle.)

---

167. *WagRS* 134–35 (modified).

Example 4.4: *Walküre* Act I bars 1099–1114

Musically the call back to nature is suggested by the cello line of 8 bars before Siegmund's entry (Example 4.4), which gives roughly the first two thirds of the theme on violins when the Rhinemaidens greet "Rheingold."[168] This theme recurs through-

---

168. See the first and second violin lines which happen to appear on the front cover of volume I of the present work.

out *Rheingold* Scene 1, either as a good nature theme (bars 540–68) but also indicating the waves with the terrible theft of the gold (bars 709–746). Cooke calls this a wave motif, one of the nature motifs in the *Ring*. It is also found when Loge introduces "Weibes Wonne und Werth" (bars 1340–72) in *Rheingold* Scene 2 and when Siegfried reflects on nature in Act II of *Siegfried* (bars 819–30). The world of nature to which the love of the Volsung twins point is the world of nature that their son Siegfried inhabits, a world of forest murmurs, of the woodbird who prophecies that he will awake the maiden sleeping on the rock. And it would appear that it was in the drafting of *Der junge Siegfried* that Wagner's *Ring* took on this intense interest in nature.

Nature and Knowledge

Grimm notes that the intelligence of the giants is innate rather than learned: "They stand as specimens of a fallen or falling race, which with the strength combines also the innocence and wisdom of the old world, an intelligence more objective and imparted at creation than self-acquired."[169] Magee comments that this is reflected in Wagner's Fasolt in *Rheingold* Scene 2, who despite his naïvity "is nevertheless upright and trustworthy and better able to speak for moral integrity than anyone else there present."[170]

Wagner can present wisdom as innate to the non-human world. The First Norn relates that in the shade of the World Ash Tree "there plashed a spring, / whispering wisdom, / its ripples ran" ("rauscht' ein Quell, / Weisheit raunend / rann sein Gewell'").[171] By drinking at the spring Wotan gave up an eye to gain wisdom. Wagner reflected on this physical loss of an eye to enable greater intellectual power:[172]

> Regarding the strangeness of Melusina's children R. says, "The urge to individualize figures caused people to depict gods and creatures of divine origin (Götter und Wesen göttlicher Abkunft) with physical defects, Wotan with one eye, etc." [. . .] "That also expresses the belief that spiritual power (geistige Gewalt) precludes regular physical beauty; just as we know no genius of regular beauty, the women took Hephaestion to be the King, for he seemed more beautiful to them than Alexander. Wherever this thoroughbred (racenhafte), regular beauty appears, the brain is reduced in potency—Nature had intended something different."[173]

One can also add that Wotan's gaining "knowledge" is related to the "fall," an issue I take up in chapters 5 and 9 below.

169. Grimm, *Mythology*, 2:529; *Mythologie*, 1:495–96.

170. Magee, *Nibelungs*, 195–96.

171. *WagRS* 281. Hence Wagner's mythical world is the very opposite of Kant's dualism of reason and nature.

172. Cf. Borchmeyer, *Ahasvers*, 296: "Der Verlust des Auges, also die Depotenzierung seiner Physis bedeutet für Wotan umgekehrt die höchste Steigerung seiner geistigen Kraft."

173. *CD* 23 June 1872; that morning Cosima had been reading to "Lusch" (Daniela) the story of Melusina.

The other significant gaining of knowledge in the *Ring* is at the end of the cycle when Brünnhilde explains that to atone for the gods' guilt Siegfried had to betray her "that a woman might grow wise."[174] She did not gain knowledge as Wotan did through a physical imperfection; rather she gained it by the most agonizing experience of betrayal.

Rheingold, Philosophy, and Cosmology

At around the time Wagner was writing the libretto for the *Ring* (i.e., 1848–53) it was known for some time that the age of the earth was much older than was suggested by the biblical account.[175] A view developed that as far as inorganic matter was concerned there was a move from chaos to order, which Weinert describes as "a very early anticipation of the Big Bang theory."[176] Such a view is found in Kant, who argued in *Theory of the Heavens* (1755) that the whole cosmos was "a vast network of systems and subsystems, all locked into Newtonian regularities."[177] For such inorganic nature there was no "teleology" as such. The situation with organic matter though was quite different; here design was at work, a view Kant put forward both in his 1755 work[178] and in his third critique of 1790, the *Critique of the Power of Judgment*.[179] Observable mechanisms "must be interpreted *as if* they were operating according to a hidden blueprint (Bauplan)."[180] Teleology, finding its origins in Aristotle's final causes, had been applied to the physical world and human action until the time of Galileo, and had been abandoned by Descartes. Kant, however, introduced a limited role for teleology. Teleological judgements may supplement determinant judgement as a regulative principle; but final causes do not interfere with physical causality.[181]

---

174. *WagRS* 349.

175. The Scottish geologist James Hutton (1726–97) was beginning to doubt the traditional view on the age of the earth as had Immanuel Kant. In his *Theory of the Heavens* (1755) Kant speculated that "a number of millions of years has passed before the sphere of formed nature in which we find ourselves has grown to the perfection that now attends it" (Kant, *Natural Science*, 266; Weischedel, *Kant*, 1:334). Note that although Wagner speaks of a six-thousand-year human development ("Menschheitsentwicklung") in conversation with Eduard Devrient in April 1849 (Devrient, *Tagebücher*, 1:473–74), this does not necessarily mean he believed in a "young earth."

176. Weinert, *Darwin*, 95.

177. Weinert, *Darwin*, 95.

178. Kant nevertheless does not exclude a mechanical explanation for organic matter. He just says a mechanical explanation will first be found for inorganic matter. See Kant, *Natural Science*, 201; Weischedel, *Kant*, 1:237.

179. This principle is emphasized in §§ 61, 80–84 (Kant, *Judgment*, 233–34, 286–303; Weischedel, *Kant*, 8:469–70, 537–51).

180. Weinert, *Darwin*, 95.

181. Kant, *Judgment*, 250–51; Weischedel, *Kant*, 8:492 §67: "It is self-evident that this is not a principle for the determining but only for the reflecting power of judgment (die reflektierende Urteilskraft), that it is regulative and not constitutive, and that by its means we acquire only a guideline for considering things in nature, in relation to a determining ground that is already given, in accordance with a new, lawful order, and for extending natural science in accordance with another principle,

Following Kant we find an acute interest in teleology in Schelling and Hegel. Schelling particularly admired Kant's third critique and anticipated Hegel's spirit (Geist) and Schopenhauer's "will." He wrote: "In the final and highest judgment there is no other Being than will. Will is primal being to which alone all predicates of Being apply."[182] But the person to develop teleology to the full was Hegel.[183] As we have seen Wagner knew of the philosophy of Schelling and Hegel through uncle and through Weisse and by the time he composed the *Ring* had actually read some of their work.[184] The signs of Hegel in Wagner's theoretical writings are unmistakeable and when one reads *Artwork of the Future* (1849) some sections seem to offer a suitable commentary on creation and fall in *Rheingold* (although in some sections he denies Hegel's fundamental role of spirit (Geist)).[185] So at the beginning of the essay he writes of the development from nature to humans to art not in terms of an external teleology, but an internal one as in Hegel:[186] "Once nature had developed the right conditions for humans to exist then humans came spontaneously into being: as soon as human life develops the conditions for art to emerge, so art springs spontaneously to life."[187] At the point when humans became aware of their difference to nature, error came into being as "the first expression of consciousness." Yet this had a positive role since "out of error knowledge is born and the history of the birth of knowledge out of error is the history of the human species from primitive myth to the present day."[188]

Wagner and Science

One of the things Wagner was doing in the *Ring* was to re-mythicize nature, and hence to bring back its mystery. Wagner had negative views on experimental science, especially when the subjects were animals. In his "Against Vivisection" (1879) he calls for "unconditional abolishing" of vivisection[189] and twice he appeals to Mephistopheles. First, he refers to his words from the "Prologue in Heaven" that reason (Vernunft) has only increased humankind's power "to be beastlier than a beast."[190] Secondly, he

---

namely that of final causes, yet without harm to the mechanism of nature." Note, however, that he entitles §80 "On the necessary subordination of the principle of mechanism to the teleological principle in the explanation of a thing as a natural end" (Kant, *Judgment*, 286; Weischedel, *Kant*, 8:537).

182. Schelling, *Human Freedom*, 21; *SWMJ* 4:242" "Es gibt in der letzten und höchsten Instanz gar kein anderes Seyn als Wollen. Wollen ist Urseyn, und auf dieses allein passen alle Prädicate desselben." Knatz, *Geschichte*, 287, n. 129, notes, however, that Schelling's "Wollen" is not a metaphysical substance as in Schopenhauer's "Wille."

183. See Onnasch, "Teleologie," 439–41.

184. See volume 1, chapter 6.

185. See Warner, "Artwork," 20; *GSD* 3:56; cf. *PW* 1:83. See chapter 9 below.

186. Inwood, *Hegel*, 246–47.

187. Warner, "Artwork," 13; *GSD* 3:42; cf. *PW* 1:69.

188. Warner, "Artwork," 13; *GSD* 3:43; cf. *PW* 1:70.

189. *PW* 6:210; *GSD* 10:209.

190. *PW* 6:206; *GSD* 10:206: "nur thierischer als jedes Thier zu sein." Luke, *Faust I*, 10; *GWJA* 3:18

refers to the "Studierzimmer II" scene: "When Mephistopheles warns us of the 'hidden bane' of Theology, we may take that warning for just as sinister as his suspicious praise of Medicine, whose practical results, for the comfort of doctors, he commits to the 'pleasure of God.'"[191] Mephistopheles explains to the student who is keen on studying medicine: "The art of Medicine's easily defined. / You study the whole world, both great and small, / Only to find / That God's creation can't be changed at all."[192]

Goethe's own views of science were not as negative as those of Mephistopheles, but he opposed the orthodoxy of Newton and others, publishing works that set out his alternative views on a wide range of scientific issues (plants, colors, etc). For Goethe nature was unified and continuous, a view that can be traced to Leibniz (1646–1716), where nature is a single "great chain of being" and to the principle that "nature makes no leaps" (Carl Linnaeus, 1707–78). But nature is not just an object of scientific study but also something to be experienced "in the most direct, immediate way."[193] It is a "sensuous maternal presence."[194] Goethe opposed the mechanical view of nature that had developed with the scientific revolution, arguing that "there were no raw facts, independent of the viewer's preconceptions."[195] As he writes in *Betrachtungen im Sinne der Wanderer* nr 136: "The supreme goal would be to grasp that everything is already theory. The blue of the sky reveals to us the basic law of chromatics. Do not look for anything behind the phenomena: they themselves are the doctrine." ("Das Höchste wäre, zu begreifen, daß alles Faktische schon Theorie ist. Die Bläue des Himmels offenbart uns das Grundgesetz der Chromatik. Man suche nur nichts hinter den Phänomenen; sie selbst sind die Lehre.")[196] So there is nothing behind the phenomena and nothing to be explained.[197]

Wagner may well have shared this idea of Goethe. Much earlier Goethe seems to use the word "Theorie" in a different sense: "My friend, all theory is grey, and green / The golden tree of life" ("Grau, teurer Freund, ist alle Theorie, / Und grün des Lebens goldner Baum").[198] Mephistopheles' words of advice to the student in "Studierzimmer (II)" belong already in the Ur-Faust so are fairly early (1772–75) and are alluded to in Wagner's poem "An Helmholtz": "Grau wäre alle Theorie? / Dagegen sag' ich, Freund, mit Stolz: / uns wird zum Klang die Harmonie, / fügt sich zum Helm ein edles Holz."[199]

(ll. 285–86).

191. *PW* 6:200; *GSD* 10:199. Cf. Luke, *Faust I*, 60; *GWJA* 3:70–71.

192. Luke, *Faust I*, 60; *GWJA* 3:71 (ll. 2011–14): "Der Geist der Medizin ist leicht zu fassen; / Ihr durchstudiert die groß' und kleine Welt, / Um es am Ende gehn zu lassen, / Wie's Gott gefällt."

193. Robertson, *Goethe*, 24.

194. Robertson, *Goethe*, 26.

195. Robertson, *Goethe*, 30.

196. *GWJA* 6:501.

197. Robertson, *Goethe*, 30. It may interest theologians that this was appealed to by Lohmeyer, *Grundlagen*, 2–3, and Jüngel, *Paulus und Jesus*, 4,

198. Luke, *Faust I*, 61; *GWJA* 3:72 (ll. 2038–39).

199. *SSD* 12:387.

Wagner's interests in Goethe's understanding of nature raises the question whether he appropriated the idea of the "Urphänomen."[200] Wagner had a love of compounds formed with the prefix "Ur-"[201] but "Urphänomen" appears not to be one of them, at least in the extant writings.

Animals and Humans

In the *Ring* Wagner presents a range of living beings that have their place in the cosmos. After Fafner refuses to give up the ring to Alberich in *Siegfried* Act II Scene 1 the Wanderer tells him:[202]

Nun, Alberich, das schlug fehl!	Well, Alberich, that miscarried!
Doch schilt mich nicht mehr Schelm!	But call me a knave no longer!
Dieß Eine, rath' ich,	This one thing—I advise you—
achte noch wohl:	heed it well:
Alles ist nach seiner Art;	all things go their different ways;
an ihr wirst du nichts ändern.—	you can alter nothing.—

That matters of creation and their order are in mind are suggested by two things. First with the words "Alles ist nach seiner Art" we hear, most clearly in the orchestra, the Erda motif. Secondly, there is most likely an allusion to Genesis 1 where "ein jeder/jedes nach seiner Art" "each according to its kind" (RSV) is repeated three times (vv. 12 (day 3 for vegetation), 21 (day 5 for sea creatures and birds), 25 (day 6 for creatures on earth). This interest in the "kinds" found in the "Priestly writing"[203] is found in the *Ring* with its giants, dwarves, and human beings.[204] Hence, because everything is according to its own kind Alberich can alter nothing. The irony here though is that one kind (giant) can be metamorphosed into another (serpent)!

The Wanderer's words "Alles ist nach seiner Art" also probably allude to "Night: The street outside Gretchen's door" in *Faust I*, where Valentin exclaims in the context of how his friends boast of their girlfriends "Alles nach seiner Art!" ("Each to his taste!"),[205] adding that no one can match his Gretchen. The sense of the allusion is

---

200. Robertson, *Goethe*, 31.

201. *Die Wibelungen* is full of such compounds (see volume 1, chapter 2). On "Urgesetz" see chapter 7 below.

202. *WagRS* 233.

203. See also Gen 6:20; 7:14; Lev 11:14–29 (Wenham, *Genesis 1–15*, 21).

204. See the Wanderer's reply to Mime's questions "what is the race" ("welches Geschlecht?") in *Siegfried* Act I Scene 2 (*WagRS* 210). Fricka mocks Wotan in fathering a couple of "common mortals" ("gemeiner Menschen / ein Paar zu erzeugen") in *Walküre* Act II Scene 1 (*WagRS* 143). Huber, *Ring*, 236, comments: "Die Wirklichkeit besteht aus unzähligen, je für sich eigentümlich gearteten Einzelwesen mit ganz verschiedenen Anlagen, Fähigkeiten, Antriebsrichtungen und Zielsetzungen."

205. *GWJA* 3:130 (l. 3630); Swanwick, *Faust*, 129 (cf. Fairley, *Faust*, 63: "Every man to his taste"). Luke, *Faust I*, 115, has "All honour where honour's due!"

not entirely clear but it is significant that these are words uttered by Valentine shortly before he is killed by Faust.[206] Like Fafner he speaks of what has befallen him and what is to come, and as he dies he expresses the sort of determinism the Wanderer expresses ("you can alter nothing") as he tells Gretchen "What's done is done, I'm sorry to say, / And things must go their usual way."[207]

Wagner was well known for his love of animals, keeping dogs and parrots as pets. One of the striking aspects of the *Ring*, indeed of most of Wagner's operas, is the prominence of animals, and with one exception (to which I shortly turn) they are portrayed as good and innocent. In this connection it is interesting that of the two passages marked in Wagner's copy of Hegel's *Philosophy of History*, one of them concerns the status of animals (it is section III, chapter 2 "Christianity"):

> For the state of innocence, the paradisaical condition, is that of the brute (der tierische). Paradise is a park, where only brutes (Tiere), not men, can remain. For the brute is one with God, only implicitly [not consciously]. Only the human being is Spirit (that is) has a self-cognizant existence. This existence for self, this consciousness, is at the same time separation from the Universal and Divine Spirit. If I hold to my abstract Freedom, in contraposition to the Good, I adopt the stand-point of Evil.[208]

Hegel then continues to speak of the fall as "the eternal Mythus of Man—in fact the very transition by which he becomes man."[209] He then refers to a verse from Psalm 51, a psalm that was central to theological discussion of "original sin": "Lord, create for me a pure heart, a new *steadfast Spirit*" (Psalm 51:10).[210]

The presence of animals is especially strong in *Siegfried*. The bear of Act I seems to be largely harmless, Siegfried using it to taunt Mime ("Gobble him up, gobble him up").[211] Siegfried sings of the care animals have for their young such that it was here that he learned "the meaning of love."[212] In Acts II and III Wagner presents the woodbird and Grane respectively, who are both good and innocent. The one truly fearful creature is the "Wurm." But it is significant that the *one* negative image of an animal we have in the *Ring* is a transformed human figure, albeit a giant. The background to

206. Luke, *Faust I*, 119; *GWJA* 3:135.

207. Luke, *Faust I*, 118; *GWJA* 3:134 (ll. 3734–35): "Geschehen ist leider nun geschehen, / Und wie es gehn kann, so wird's gehn."

208. Sibree, *History*, 321 (modified; the brackets are Sibree's). *Geschichte*, 389: "Denn der Zustand der Unschuld, dieser paradiesische Zustand, ist der tierische. Das Paradies ist ein Park, wo nur die Tiere und nicht die Menschen bleiben können. Denn das Tier ist mit Gott eins, aber nur an sich. Nur der Mensch ist Geist, d.h. für sich selbst. Dieses Fürsichsein, dieses Bewußtsein ist aber zugleich die Trennung von dem allgemeinen göttlichen Geist. Halte ich mich in meiner abstrakten Freiheit gegen das Gute, so ist dies eben der Standpunkt des Bösen."

209. Sibree, *History*, 321–22; *Geschichte*, 389.

210. Psalm 51:12 in Luther's translation.

211. *WagRS* 196.

212. *WagRS* 201–2.

the "Wurm" is particularly rich. Wagner stressed that the "Wurm" should be a serpent and not a dragon,[213] the term being used right from the origin of the *Ring* in the *Mythus* of 1848.[214] Wagner's term "Wurm" is the OHG equivalent to "ormr" meaning snake, serpent,[215] the word being used in *Völuspá* 47, 53,[216] *Hávamál* 86,[217] *Grímnismál* 34,[218] *Skírnismál* 27,[219] and "gleaming serpent" in *Fáfnismál* 19;[220] further, the term is used for the "midgard serpent" ("Midgardsormr").[221] Also Fouqué wrote of Siegfried as the serpent killer ("Schlangentödtner"). However, the *Nibelungenlied* tells us that Sivrit killed a lintrachen (Lindrachen).[222] Further, *Die Wibelungen* always has "dragon" rather than serpent: so we have Siegfried's "fight with the Dragon" ("Drachenkampf"), which is likened to Apollo who "fought against the dragon Python" ("gegen den Drachen Python stritt").[223] Likewise it speaks of the "dragon's heir" ("der Erbe des Drachen")[224] and of night "*that held its ghostly, gloomy, dragon's-wings spread fearsomely above the world's rich stores*" ("*ihre düsteren Drachenflügel über die reichen Schätze der Welt gespenstisch grauenhaft ausgebreitet hielt*").[225] Finally Rothbart sits in the Kyffhäuser "all round him the treasures of the Nibelungen, by his side the sharp sword that one-time slew the dread Dragon (Drachen)."[226]

Hence, the "Wurm," the transformed giant, is the only fearful animal of *Siegfried*, indeed of the whole *Ring*. Conversely, of the human figures in the *Ring* it is those who most closely resemble animals that are the most innocent, namely the Rhinemaidens. This brings us to the subject of the next chapter, the "fall," which affects humans (and gods!) and the associated themes of power, the desecration of nature, and capitalism.

213. See *CD* 3 April 1878.
214. Haymes, *Ring*, 48 ("Wurm," "Riesenwurm").
215. Cleasby, *Icelandic-English Dictionary*.
216. Dronke, *Edda II*, 20, 22.
217. Dronke, *Edda III*, 19.
218. This refers to the serpents that lie under Yggdrasil. Whereas Orchard, *Elder Edda*, 56, translates "More serpents lie under the ash Yggdrasil," Dronke *Edda III*, 120, renders as "More worms are a-bed /beneath Yggdrasil's Ash."
219. Dronke, *Edda II*, 382.
220. Orchard, *Elder Edda*, 164. Here the word is translated "Wurm" by both Ettmüller, *Lieder*, 16 ("Schillernder Wurm"), and Simrock, *Edda*, 163 ("Du funkelnder Wurm"), works which Wagner employed.
221. *Gylfaginning* 51 (Faulkes, *Edda*, 53–54).
222. Av 3 (100); *NibE* 14; *NibS* 34–35.
223. *PW* 7:275; *GSD* 2:131. Cf. *Art and Revolution* where again Apollo "had slain the Python, the dragon of Chaos (den chaotischen Drachen Python)" (*PW* 1:32; *GSD* 3:10).
224. *PW* 7:276; *GSD* 2:133.
225. *PW* 7:276; *GSD* 2:133.
226. *PW* 7:298; *GSD* 2:155.

— 5 —

Fall, Power, Desecration of Nature, and Capitalism

Introduction

In the previous chapter we saw how there was a goodness and innocence in nature as presented in the opening of *Rheingold*, but that there was always that possibility, perhaps inevitability, that such a state of innocence could not last. In this chapter I examine the "fall" as presented by Wagner. This is linked to issues of power in that in both instances of the "first sin" the lust for power is involved, such power being incompatible with love: Alberich curses love in order to fashion the ring and Wotan tears the branch from the World Ash Tree in order to exercise his power, which also means he has ultimately to deny love. This denial of love is worked out in the utter lovelessness we find in *Rheingold*; it is also found in the subsequent operas of the *Ring* (e.g., the marriage of Wotan and Fricka, the fraternal relationship of Mime and Alberich, the filial relationship of Alberich and Hagen). The issue of the fall is also related to the rise of capitalism (Alberich's sin gives rise to his accumulation of wealth for the sake of wealth) and the desecration of nature (Wotan's sin gives rise to the destruction of the World Ash Tree). Wotan's imposition of law is not only linked to the desecration of nature (i.e., he had to tear the branch to form his spear on which his laws were inscribed) but again works to destroy love, not only in the sense that it leads to his own denial of love but also that such "law" is incompatible with love.[1]

The "Fall"

The language of "fall" I am using is theological and deliberately so. The key biblical texts are Genesis 3, as understood in the Christian tradition,[2] and Romans 5 and 7. Although one can finds traces of such tradition in the *Ring* it is also sometimes more subtle. So, as we have seen in the previous chapter and as we shall further discuss, sin can come into being not because of a "serpent" or personified "sin" ("hamartia" in Rom 7:8) but rather

---

1. See chapter 7 below.

2. The Jewish tradition does not have the same understanding of the "fall" as the Christian tradition and does not share the view of "original sin." See Bell, *No one seeks for God*, 118–25.

can come into being because of the inherent nature of human beings (and gods): they are thinking and conscious beings, and as such there is a process which Hegel termed "bifurcation" ("Entzweiung"). But I start with the two most obvious explanations of sin's origin, ones that have more of a biblical flavor.

The first is Scene 1 of *Rheingold* where Alberich's amorous advances are rejected by each of the Rhinemaidens in turn and he decides that fulfilment lies in the renunciation of "love" and "rape" of the Rhinegold. But what is the nature of such "love"? Both Flosshilde and Wellgunde say he is "in love" ("verliebt").[3] All three ask: "Why, faint-hearted dwarf, / did you fail to bind fast / the maiden that you love (das du minnst)?"[4] As the sunlight shines into the deep, the gold of the river Rhine is revealed in its glory. Woglinde introduces the possible renunciation of "love": "Only the man who forswears / love's sway (der Minne Macht), / only he who disdains / love's delights (der Liebe Lust) / can master the magic spell / that rounds a ring from the gold."[5] But Wellgunde explains that they are safe "since all that lives must love (denn was nur lebt will lieben); / no one wants to abjure its delights."[6] Wellgunde adds "Least of all he, / the lecherous elf: / he's almost dying / of lustful desire (Liebesgier)!" Flosshilde speaks of "the flames of his lust (Minne Brunst)."[7] Wellgunde adds "with the frenzy of love (vor Zorn der Liebe) / he sizzles aloud."[8] Finally, after he decides to take the gold, all three sing that "love (Minne) has driven him mad!"[9] The Rhinemaidens therefore seem to jumble "love" and "lechery" but they could be ironic, giving his lust the exalted name of love ("Liebe," "Minne").[10] Alberich also confuses lust and "Minne": "In every limb / a blazing fire / burns and glows! / Rage and desire (Minne), / wild and all-powerful, / throw my thoughts into turmoil!"[11] However, he also seems to think more clearly as he contemplates stealing the gold, making a distinction between love itself ("Liebe") and the "delights" ("Lust") it can confer: "Though love can't be gained by force, / through cunning might I enforce its delights?"[12]

The key moment of the "fall" occurs when Alberich steals the gold and curses love:[13]

---

3. *WagRS* 59, 61.
4. *WagRS* 64.
5. *WagRS* 68.
6. *WagRS* 68.
7. *WagRS* 68.
8. *WagRS* 68.
9. *WagRS* 69.
10. *WagRS* 364 n. 7 suggests that the term "Minne" in the *Ring* has a more sexual connotation than "Liebe."
11. *WagRS* 65.
12. *WagRS* 68. Note though that the German "Lust" does not have the negative associations of the English "lust."
13. *WagRS* 69.

Bangt euch noch nicht?	Still not afraid?
So buhlt nun im Finstern,	Then whore in the dark,
feuchtes Gezücht!	you watery brood!
Das Licht lösch' ich euch aus,	Your light I'll put out,
entreiße dem Riff das Gold,	wrench the gold from the rock
schmiede den rächenden Ring:	and forge the avenging ring:
denn hör' es die Fluth—	so hear me, you waters:—
so verfluch' ich die Liebe!	thus I lay a curse on love!

I earlier wrote of the "rape" of the Rhinegold because the language in the stage direction for his subsequent stealing of the gold sounds like the rape of a woman: "he tears the gold from the rock with terrible force" and then adds: "Impenetrable darkness suddenly descends on all sides."[14] This darkness contrasts starkly with the brightness of the Rhinegold. The language in the 1848 *Mythus* stresses the purity and nobility of the Rhinegold: "Alberich seized the clear and noble Rhine-gold, abducting it from the depths of the water" ("Des klaren edlen Rheingoldes bemächtigte sich Alberich, entführte es den Tiefen der Wässer").[15]

The "love" Alberich renounces is not simply sexual activity[16] but it does seem to involve this. The "love" he renounces is what one could call true erotic love, the deep fulfilling relationship between human beings that involves sexual relations. Such love Alberich renounces, but he still wants sex of a debased nature. This becomes clear in his dialogue with Wotan in Scene 3: "Beware! / Beware!— / For when your menfolk / yield to my power, / your pretty women, / who spurned my wooing, / shall forcibly sate the lust (Lust) of the dwarf, / though love (Liebe) may no longer smile upon him."[17] The "fall" therefore involves divorcing sex from love and as in Genesis 3 the "fall" in *Rheingold* has a sexual element.[18]

One could argue that Alberich already had a propensity to "sin" since, as Wotan tells Brünnhilde, he was "born of the night."[19] Whether he has any diminished responsibility for his part in the "fall" could be debated but one can certainly say the fall is exacerbated by the gods' susceptibility to evil. Wagner, in his key letter to Röckel of 25/26 January 1854, suggests that it was the loveless marriage of Wotan to Fricka that caused the evil: "it is not the fact that Alberich was repulsed by the Rhine-daughters which is the definitive source of all evil—for it was entirely natural for them to repulse

---

14. *WagRS* 69.

15. Haymes, *Ring*, 45 (my literal translation).

16. It would be too easy to equate the two. Magee, *Wagner and Philosophy*, 120–21, tends to equate them on the basis of *Rheingold* Scene 1.

17. *WagRS* 96–97.

18. Note that the view of "fall" in the Christian tradition clearly intensifies anything found in the Jewish tradition and its interpretation of Genesis 3. Cf. Barr, *Eden*, 63–65, 69–70.

19. *WagRS* 149: "den Nacht gebar, / der bange Nibelung, / Alberich brach ihren Bund."

him." Further, "Alberich and his ring could not have harmed the gods unless the latter had already been susceptible to evil." The "germ of this evil" ("Keim dieses Unheils") is in the "mutual torment of a loveless union."[20]

The second sin to consider is that of the chief god Wotan. In the sketches of 1848 and in *Siegfried's Death*, there is no story of Wotan forming his spear out of the branch of the World Ash Tree. His sin and that of the gods appears to some extent to be a *response* to this first sin of Alberich in their attempts to impose order on the world,[21] but doing this "through violence and cunning."[22] But in the later *Siegfried's Tod/Götterdämmerung* Wotan's sin could even be seen to pre-date that of Alberich. In the Prologue the first Norn explains that once the World Ash Tree stood tall and strong, and in its shade was a spring from which wisdom came. But a "dauntless god," i.e., Wotan, was so desperate to drink from this spring so he could attain wisdom that he gave up one of his eyes. Then he broke off a branch from the sacred World Ash Tree to form his spear, which came to represent his power and authority and his laws. The tree had been "tall and strong," having "a forest of sacred branches," but the wound made by Wotan "consumed the wood" and leaves fell. The tree grew rotten and the well-spring, previously protected by the shade of the tree, ran dry.[23] Wagner hence presents the association of law and knowledge with the desecration of nature.

Another way this fall affects the future development of human affairs is by introducing a poisonous callousness. *Rheingold* is saturated with lovelessness. Wotan does not love his wife and has no genuine concern for the abducted Freia. Wotan's concern to free Freia only comes to a head when he starts to lose his immortality as the golden apples dry out and wither.[24] Earlier he was willing, it seems, to forsake her, i.e., forsake love! The only ones who appear to have any humanity are the Rhinemaidens and occasionally the half-god Loge, who sympathizes with their loss:[25]

Traulich und treu	Trusty and true
ist's nur in der Tiefe:	it is here in the depths alone:
falsch und feig	false and fated
ist was dort oben sich freut!	is all that rejoices above!

---

20. *SL* 307; *SB* 6:67.
21. See volume 1, chapter 2.
22. Haymes, *Ring*, 46–47.
23. *WagRS* 280–81.
24. *WagRS* 86.
25. *WagRS* 118. Wagner may be alluding to these words in his "morning confession" ("Morgenbeichte") to Mathilde Wesendonck (7 April 1858, *SL* 383; *SB* 9:231): "Only inside, within us, only deep down does salvation dwell!"

Influences on Wagner's View of the Fall

There are four possible sources that influenced Wagner's view of the fall in the *Ring*: the Bible, German philosophy, the Greeks, and Romanticism.

The biblical account of a "good creation" (Gen 1:31a) that is ruined by "sin" (Gen 3), an idea developed by St Paul,[26] is clearly reflected in *Rheingold* Scene 1. As noted in the previous chapter, creation does indeed seem to be "very good" with the life-giving river Rhine and the "light-bringing joy" of the Rhinegold (cf. Gen 2:11–12). The command of "father" not to divulge the secrets of the power of the ring[27] parallels Gen 2:16–17 where God warns Adam not to eat the fruit of the tree of the knowledge of good and evil. Hence, in both *Rheingold* and Genesis the "fall" concerns the danger of "knowledge," a crucial Wagnerian theme. Once the demonic figure of Alberich enters, the potential for catastrophe is there. He "lusts" after the Rhinemaidens,[28] who in turn tease him. On being rejected he then "lusts" after the Rhinegold. His "fall" certainly has a sexual element and, as we have seen, even his stealing of the Rhinegold uses vocabulary and phrases usually used for the rape of a woman.[29] The only explanation given for Alberich's dark character is that he was "born of the night,"[30] therefore having a propensity to bring "sin" into the world as did the serpent in Genesis 3. His "fall" then leads to disastrous consequences for everyone.

Just as Alberich's sin has links to Genesis 1–3, so it is with Wotan's sin. We have the issue of "knowledge" again (Gen 2:16–17), here in Wotan's search for wisdom,[31] and this link between "error" and "knowledge" is central for the beginning of the *Artwork of the Future*.[32]

As far as philosophy is concerned, Schopenhauer, whose "pessimism" was inspired by St Paul, Luther, and Augustine,[33] could no doubt influence him, especially if, as I argued in volume 1, Wagner came to a reasonably good knowledge of Schopenhauer already in 1852 while he was still working on the libretto. The sage of Frankfurt may well have been at the back of his mind when he wrote this to Liszt (7 October 1854) shortly after he completed *Das Rheingold*: "let us treat the world only

---

26. Rom 5:12: "Therefore, just as sin came into the world through one man, and death came through sin, and so death spread to all because all have sinned." Note also Rom 5:18 which was doubly marked in Wagner's New Testament and quoted in the *Jesus of Nazareth* sketches (*PW* 8:338; *DTB* 266).

27. Flosshilde warns: "Father told us / and bound us over / to guard the bright hoard widely / that no false thief should filch it from the flood: / be silent, then, you babbling brood!" (*WagRS* 67).

28. Wellgunde exclaims "The lecherous rogue!" ("Der lüsterne Kauz!") (*WagRS* 59).

29. *WagRS* 69: "He tears the gold from the rock with terrible force" ("Er reisst mit furchtbarer Gewalt das Gold aus dem Riffe").

30. *WagRS* 149.

31. This is missing in the original *Nibelungen-Mythus* and *Siegfried's Tod* of 1848.

32. *PW* 1:69–70; *GSD* 3:43.

33. Wagner, as we have seen, greatly admired Paul and Luther, although there is little reference to Augustine in Wagner's writings and recorded utterances. See Bell, *Parsifal*, 136 n. 3.

with contempt; for it deserves no better [. . .]. It is evil, *evil, fundamentally evil* [. . .]. It belongs to Alberich: no one else!! Away with it!"[34] Another philosophical influence was Hegel but this is actually much more subtle and is related to "Entzweiung" (diremption), which was discussed in the previous chapter.

Another element contributing to his idea of fall could be early Greek thought.[35] Nestor in the *Iliad* speaks of heroes of former times: "Ere now have I consorted with warriors that were better men than ye, and never did they set me at naught. Such warriors have I never since seen, nor shall see, as Peirithous was and Dryas, shepherd of the host, and Caeneus and Exadius and godlike Polyphemus, and Theseus, son of Aegeus, peer of the immortals."[36] No one now, he avers, can match such heroes; "with them could no man fight of all mortals that now are upon the earth."[37] Wagner, we know, was an admirer of Homer, one of his indispensables,[38] and he possessed his works in both the Dresden and Wahnfried libraries.[39] However, we do not have a parallel with the sort of "fall" we find in *Rheingold*. We may be on slightly firmer ground with Hesiod, although I have found no explicit references to him in Wagner's works.[40] Foster considers Hesiod *Works and Days* 11–26, which compares two "strifes," a good one "inspiring healthy competition" and an evil one causing "strife, war, and feud."[41] Foster sees this evil strife which caused Perses (supposed brother of Hesiod) to take more than his fair share of the family inheritance to be reflected in the antagonism between Alberich and Mime.[42] There may be some parallels in that Mime is the wronged brother[43] but the parallels are not particularly strong. One could also consider Hesiod *Works and Days* 42–105; 106–26, in particular 90–95, which tells the story of Pandora: "For previously the tribes of men used to live upon the earth entirely apart from evils, and without grievous toil and distressful diseases, which give death to men. [For in misery mortals grow old at

---

34. *SL* 319; *SB* 6:249.
35. See Ruffell, *Prometheus Bound*, 58–61, on this "lapsarian" ideology of the Greeks.
36. *Iliad* 1.260–65 (Murray, *Homer I*, 23).
37. *Iliad* 1.271–72 (Murray, *Homer I*, 23).
38. *CD* 4 June 1871.

39. For the editions of Homer in the Dresden library, see Westernhagen, *Bibliothek*, 94. His admiration for Homer is reflected in the multiple editions he had of his works in the Wahnfried library (Greek editions of Wilhelm Dindorf and Wilhelm Baeumlein; German translations of Johann Heinrich Voss).

40. Note that there are no works of Hesiod in his Dresden library. But included in his Wahnfried library was a German edition of Hesiod's works edited by Eyth (second edition of 1865), and Lehrs' edition of *Carmina* (1862) (Lehrs had been a key influence on Wagner in his Paris years). There is a possible allusion to Hesiod (as Foster, *Greeks*, 89–90, seems to suggest) in the late essay *Religion and Art* (1880) where he writes some lines on "Greek Theogony" (*PW* 6:216). Note also *CD* 1 February 1873 which notes that Nietzsche sent a copy of his "Der Florentinische Tractat über Homer und Hesiod."

41. Foster, *Greeks*, 86.
42. Foster, *Greeks*, 86–87.
43. Foster, *Greeks*, 88, also considers the strife between Fafner and Fasolt.

once.] But the woman removed the great lid from the storage jar with her hands and scattered all its contents abroad—she wrought baneful evils for human beings."[44] However, in *Rheingold* the "fall," as I suggested in the previous chapter, is something much more subtle, reflecting Hegel's idea of "Entzweiung."

A final influence to consider is that of Romantic writers, who themselves were influenced by the Bible, idealism, and the Greeks. One such figure is Freidrich Schlegel who set forward views of human development, employing biblical categories such as paradise, fall, and redemption.[45]

Industrialization, the Desecration of Nature, and Capitalism

The transition from Scene 2 to Scene 3 of *Rheingold* can be shocking, and familiarity with it can dampen the shock. It is perhaps ironic that the horror of the industrial landscape of Nibelheim, which is first represented by the "incessant dotted rhythm" on the anvils, may reflect Beethoven's joyful Seventh Symphony ("the apotheosis of the dance"),[46] which Wagner had conducted shortly before composing the music.[47] Over twenty years later, as Wagner left London on 25 May 1877, he noted: "This is Alberich's dream come true—Nibelheim, world dominion, activity, work, everywhere the oppressive feeling of steam and fog."[48]

George Bernard Shaw in his allegorical interpretation famously drew attention to how Nibelheim represents the worst aspects of factories and capitalism. Commenting on Scene 3, he wrote: "This gloomy place need not be a mine: it might just as well be a match factory, with yellow phosphorous, phossy jaw, a large dividend, and plenty of clergymen shareholders. Or it might be a whitelead factory, or a chemical works, or a pottery, or a railway shunting yard [. . .] or any other of the places where human life and welfare are daily sacrificed in order that some greedy foolish creature may be able to hymn exultantly to his Plutonic idol."[49] The most telling passage on the folly of accumulating capital is in Scene 3 of *Rheingold* where Wotan asks Alberich: "What good is the hoard / since Nibelheim's joyless / and naught can be bought here with wealth?"[50] Alberich responds: "To create yet more wealth / and to hide away wealth."[51] Wagner always associated capitalism with the Jew who "rules, and will rule, so long as Money

---

44. Most, *Hesiod I*, 95 (n. 6 explains that the sentence in brackets is only found in the margin or text of very few manuscripts and is generally rejected as a gloss).

45. See volume 1, chapter 5.

46. *PW* 1:124; *GSD* 3:94 (*Artwork of the Future*).

47. Matthews, *Beethoven*, 184.

48. *CD* 25 May 1877. No doubt Wagner was attracted to Balzac for his portrayal of human misery in society. Writing forty years ago, Gregor-Dellin, *Leben*, 854, noted that a sociological and psychological study on Wagner and Balzac had not yet appeared. To my knowledge we are still waiting.

49. Laurence, *Shaw's Music III*, 434.

50. *WagRS* 96. "Nibelheim" means "land of mists" ("Nebelheim") (Haymes, *Ring*, 44–45).

51. *WagRS* 96.

remains the power before which all our doings and our dealing lose their force."[52] No doubt he saw Alberich in these terms. Likewise, he had a negative view of the Roman equivalent of Hermes, Mercury, "the god of merchants."[53]

With the rise of Alberich's "capitalism" work becomes alienating. Mime tells Wotan and Loge that before the "fall":[54]

Sorglose Schmiede,	Carefree smiths,
schufen wir sonst wohl	we used to fashion
Schmuck uns'ren Weibern,	trinkets for our womenfolk,
wonnig Geschmied,	delightful gems and
niedlichen Nibelungentand:	delicate Nibelung toys:
wir lachten lustig der Müh'.	we cheerfully laughed at our pains.

Alberich becomes the arch-capitalist; Wotan is not interested in capital as such but he longs for power, including that which the ring can confer: "I must have the ring!" ("Den Ring muß ich haben!")[55] It is with Wotan's plan to obtain the ring that, according to Borchmeyer, we have the circulation of radical evil ("Kreislauf des radikal Bösen"),[56] such a view of radical evil being prominent in Kant.[57] This brings us to the question of power and how it can have a positive and negative connotation.

Power: Positive and Negative

The commonplace understanding of the *Ring* is that it concerns the conflict between love and power; more precisely it concerns the conflict between love of power versus power of love. So power in itself is neutral (rather as money is)[58] but the poison enters when power is made one's God.[59] In the *Ring* power in its most ominous sense is achieved by renouncing love. This is highlighted when one considers a case where power is apparently sought without the explicit renunciation of love, as seen in the figure of Mime. His desire for the ring is not so much motivated by a desire for power

---

52. *PW* 3:81; *GSD* 5:68.
53. *PW* 1:41–42; *GSD* 3:18–19.
54. *WagRS* 91.
55. *WagRS* 82.

56. Borchmeyer, "Anfang," 19. Zegowitz, *Opern*, 197, suggests that as Wotan hears of the ring in *Rheingold* Scene 2 that he is prepared to give up Freia. However, at this stage Wotan does not know of the demand of the giants for "the Nibelung's bright red gold" (*WagRS* 83) as a substitute for Freia.

57. Kant, *Religion*, 45–73.

58. Hence, the significant wording in 1 Tim 6:10: "For the *love* of money is the root of all kinds of evil."

59. Cf. Luther's *Greater Catechism*, *BSELK* 560 (quoted in chapter 3 above).

itself, but rather in hate for and rivalry with his brother Alberich: had he ever gained the ring he would not really know what to do with it in exercising power.[60]

Hence, the menacing exercise of power is seen in those instances where it is gained by renouncing love, expressed musically by the so-called "Entsagungsmotiv" ("renunciation motif"), which first appears in *Rheingold* Scene 1.[61] But it is not just Alberich who renounces love, for Wotan is his "unwitting mirror" as he "renounces love in his own way, seeking in its stead power over the world."[62] This mirroring is expressed by the fact that they are both "Alberich": "Licht-Alberich" and "Schwarz-Alberich"[63] But one can also say "Whereas Alberich renounces love in favour of the pursuit of power, Wotan finds his power diminished just because he cannot imagine a life without love. As the drama unfolds, they each lose both power and love."[64] Alberich's and Wotan's renunciation of love for the sake of power could be reflected in the use of the "Entsagungsmotiv" as Siegmund pulls Nothung out of the ash tree. Cooke shows the clear parallels between the music and the words in the first occurrence of the motif in *Rheingold* Scene 1 and in *Walküre* Act I Scene 3: "Minne" and "Liebe" in both instances are sung on E♭ and then D.[65] Cooke argues that "Siegmund is drawing the sword from the tree, not only to win Sieglinde for his bride, as it seems to him, but also, unwittingly, to regain for Wotan the ring of absolute power which was originally made by Alberich at the cost of renouncing love."[66]

Before proceeding with the question of positive and negative power in the *Ring* I consider two possible influences on Wagner in this respect, Norse Mythology and Hegel, which may or may not illumine Wagner's understanding of power.

Norse Mythology and Power

In Norse Mythology the gods, despite their many failings, do at least attempt to create order in the cosmos at it emerges from the world of giants, wood-ogresses, etc. We read of their giving names to parts of the day (*Völuspá* 6), engaging in building projects (*Völuspá* 7), and trying to prevent what they see as the disaster of Ragnarök. This idea of their imposition of order in the *Edda* may well come from Genesis, where we see an ordering of the cosmos in terms of "separation" (Gen 1:1–19, days 1–4) and naming of animals (Gen 2:20), etc. The idea of imposing order is found in the *Ring*, especially in reference to Wotan's spear. But although Wagner could learn of Odin as lawgiver from

---

60. For this insight I am grateful to Richard Roberts who sang Mime in the 2016 Opera North production of the *Ring*.
61. See Example 11.3 below.
62. Schofield, *Redeemer Reborn*, 40.
63. *WagRS* 210–11.
64. Winterbourne, "Freedom," 349.
65. Cooke, *End*, 3.
66. Cooke, *End*, 4.

his Norse sources, there is nothing there to relate this to his spear.[67] Magee thinks that the source for this connection can only be Wilhelm Müller, who writes: "We may also quite rightly surmise that under the protection of the god [Odin] were particularly such legal matters in which symbols were formerly used which we also find associated with him. Thus the spear Gungnir was Odin's chief weapon."[68] Hence in *Rheingold* Wotan is represented as the chief of the gods, "ruler of the world with a basically civilizing mission, symbolized by his spear."[69] Although Wotan may have had a good motive in imposing such order, such exercise of power also has a corrupting influence.

Wotan's spear does not just represent his ordering of the world but also acts as a weapon. Sometimes it is a weapon in preventing strife, as when he intervenes in *Rheingold* Scene 2 to prevent Donner first from attacking the giants[70] or Loge.[71] At other times his spear actively determines the outcome of battle, and we see the devastating consequences of this in *Walküre* Act II.

Hegel and the Master/Slave

It is not clear how much of Hegel's philosophy of power Wagner fully understood, but there are possible instances in the *Ring* that witness to his ideas of domination and the counter-intuitive idea that it is in fact the slave who has the greatest freedom. Hegel's view of the master/slave is set forth in the section on self-consciousness in the *Phänomenologie*, a text with which Wagner was to some extent familiar, even if he did not understand every word of this demanding work. The master/slave relation Hegel examines "is not embedded in the world" in the sense that he is not speaking of slavery in ancient Greece or Rome but simply considers the relation of a master, who dominates his slave and consumes things around him, and the one subject to him.[72] "The lord is the consciousness that exists *for itself*, but no longer merely the Notion of such a consciousness. Rather, it is a consciousness existing *for itself* which is mediated with itself through another consciousness, i.e. through a consciousness whose nature it is to be bound up with an existence that is independent, or thinghood in general."[73] The master as master may feel autonomous but according to Hegel's understanding his consciousness is recognized by the consciousness of the other, the slave. He thinks that his selfhood resides in "the sheer negation of the thing, or the

---

67. Magee, *Nibelungs*, 185, refers to *Ynlinga saga* Chapter 8 (in *Heimskringla*). See also Björnsson, *Volsungs*, 139: "Odin established in his land [Sweden] the same laws which had formerly been current among the Æsir."

68. Magee, *Nibelungs*, 186, translating Müller, *Geschichte und System*, 193.

69. Cooke, *End*, 316.

70. *WagRS* 77: "Stop, you firebrand! / Nothing by force! / My spearshaft / safeguards contracts: / spare your hammer's haft."

71. *WagRS* 79.

72. Houlgate, *Phenomenology*, 95.

73. Miller, *Phenomenology*, 115 (§190); *HHW* 2:112–13.

enjoyment (Genuß) of it."[74] Whereas "desire" ("Begierde") comes face to face with the independence of the other, in the case of "enjoyment" the master is simply a consumer[75] and does not grow since he sees the slave as a thing and not as an autonomous agent.[76] The slave on the other hand recognizes the independence of the master and as opposed to being a consumer he is a worker. Whereas Marx applied Hegel master-slave relationship to the necessity of the transformation of society, Hegel was interested "solely in tracing the changes in *self-understanding* that the master and the slave undergo."[77] The counter-intuitive outcome is that "just as lordship showed that its essential nature is the reverse of what it wants to be, so too servitude in its consummation will really turn into the opposite of what it immediately is; as a consciousness forced back into itself, it will withdraw into itself and be transformed into a truly independent consciousness."[78] For Hegel "through the combination of labour and the fear of death, the slave comes to realize that, within his servitude, he is essentially *free*."[79] The sense of freedom therefore arises not through labour alone but also through the indispensable condition of fear of death.[80]

Towards the end of the section on master-slave Hegel focuses on fear: "In the lord, the being-for-self is an 'other' for the bondsman, or is only *for* him [i.e., is not his own] (Im Herrn ist ihm das Fürsichsein *ein anderes* oder nur *für es*; in der Furcht ist das Fürsichsein *an ihm selbst*); in fear, the being-for-self is present in the bondsman himself; in fashioning the thing, he becomes aware that being-for-self belongs to *him*, that he himself exists essentially and actually in his own right."[81]

Turning to the *Ring*, one often sees a pattern of master/slave relationship but it does not always follow Hegel's scheme. In the Alberich/Mime relationship in *Rheingold* Scene 3 Alberich views his "slave" as a thing and not as an autonomous agent, but beyond this I am unsure what Hegel's analysis can offer. A rather better example of the slave who is the real instrument of a new consciousness is "woman in her traditional roles as wife and lover."[82] As Millington elaborates: "Erda is subjugated by Wotan, Sieglinde by Hunding, the young unnamed woman in Siegmund's narration by her kinsmen, Grimhilde by Alberich, Brünnhilde first by Siegfried disguised as Gunther, and then by Gunther himself."[83] This subjugation is something of which women also break out; however, it is not quite in the way Hegel envisages. So the description of

---

74. Miller, *Phenomenology*, 116 (§190); *HHW* 2:113. Cf. Houlgate, *Phenomenology*, 95.
75. Houlgate, *Phenomenology*, 96.
76. Corse, *Consciousness*, 29.
77. Houlgate, *Phenomenology*, 97.
78. Miller, *Phenomenology*, 117 (§193); *HHW* 2:114. Cf. Houlgate, *Phenomenology*, 98.
79. Houlgate, *Phenomenology*, 100.
80. Houlgate, *Phenomenology*, 100.
81. Miller, *Phenomenology*, 118 (§196); *HHW* 2:115.
82. Corse, *Consciousness*, 30.
83. Millington, "The Ring and Its Times," 24.

the slave's consciousness that Corse quotes from the *Phenomenology* hardly applies to Brünnhilde's immolation as she suggests.[84] Likewise, although I can agree that "[w]omen in the *Ring* are the natural subjects of domination and fear" I am unsure the following words using Hegel's analysis really illumine the drama: "Brünnhilde fears Wotan's wrath, but she conquers this negativity of being (symbolised by her long sleep) rising to a new self-consciousness that her own fear has taught her."[85] I am also unsure of Corse's argument that for the hero Siegfried, the necessary component of fear for the slave's psychology has been removed such that "Brunnhilde learns fear for Siegfried and passes her 'wisdom,' the knowledge she has gained through fear, to him."[86] One problem with this is that it overlooks the fact that he already learns fear directly on finding Brünnhilde asleep on the rock. Siegfried in learning such fear is truly transformed.

Hence, I think there are limitations as to how Hegel's master/slave analysis opens up an understanding of the power structures in the *Ring*, important though the philosopher was to Wagner in other respects.

Walküre Act II Scene 1

Perhaps the most interesting and subtle "master/slave" relationship in the *Ring* is that of Wotan and Brünnhilde, but it springs a number of surprises. Nike Wagner describes Brünnhilde's entrance thus: "From behind a clump of rocks, a young girl in armour bursts upon the stage, jubilant, fierce, childlike—Brünnhilde. Her overbrimming *joie de vivre* is evident from her exuberant cries, leaping from high to low and back again—'Heiaha! Hojotoho!' Headstrong, angular and jagged, her song is like the mountains all around: it echoes the world of nature that surrounds the Valkyries, the nature that is Brünnhilde's home." The Valkyrie "leads an untroubled existence" in that she "is at one with herself because she is at ease with her appointed role, and the task that so fulfils her has been assigned to her by Wotan, her father."[87] Her warrior character reflects that of her father who, as we saw in chapter 2 above, adopts three of Odin's titles from the *Edda*: Valfadir, Herfadir, and Sigföðr. As we saw Valfadir = father of the slain (Walvater for Wagner) (Wal = slain, Vater = father), Herfadir = father of hosts (Heervater), and Sigföðr = father of victory (Siegvater). Then Valkyrja = chooser of the slain (Walküre) and Valholl = hall of the slain (Walhall/Walhalla).

At the beginning of *Walküre* Act II Wotan tells Brünnhilde to harness her horse for there is to be a "furious fight" ("brünstiger Streit").[88] She is to give victory to Sieg-

---

84. Corse, *Consciousness*, 30, quotes Hegel's *Phenomenology* (cf. Baillie, *Phenomenology*, 237; Miller, *Phenomenology*, 117 (§194)).
85. Corse, *Consciousness*, 30.
86. Corse, *Consciousness*, 30.
87. N. Wagner, *Wagners*, 72.
88. *WagRS* 140.

FALL, POWER, DESECRATION OF NATURE, AND CAPITALISM

mund—Hunding should die and Wotan adds that he does not want him in Valhalla. Nike Wagner comments: "It does not occur to her that her mission—luring heroes to their death so that they can reside in Valhalla—is a bloody and ugly one. For her, the justness of her assignments is guaranteed by the fact that her father, whom she loves, commands them."[89] This is a remarkable relationship. She "rides with Wotan through storms and foul weather, hands him his beer at table and lets herself be kissed by him at all times. Her childlike femininity enchants without offending, her boyish masculinity conceals no Oedipal threats."[90] As Wish-Maid she fulfils her father's fantasies. Magee points out that one of Wotan's names in Old Norse is "Oski" and in Middle High German "Wunsch"; therefore the Valkyries are "Wunschmädchen" or "daughters of Wunsch/Wotan."[91] So the wish maids who will serve Siegmund in Valhalla are daughters of Wotan.[92] However, there is another aspect to this in that Brünnhilde is the "creative womb of his wishes."[93] She appears to exercise no power herself and in this sense she could be considered Wotan's "slave" as he explains in *Walküre* Act III:[94]

Keine wie sie	No one, as she did,
kannte mein innerstes Sinnen;	knew my innermost thinking;
keine wie sie	no one, as she did
wußte den Quell meines Willens;	watched at the well-spring of my will;
sie selbst war	she herself was
meines Wunsches schaffender Schooß:—	my wish's life-giving womb:—

However, although she should have been Wotan's "slave" she defied him, even though later she argues that she had been true to his deepest wishes since Fricka had made him an enemy of himself.[95] Wotan speaks of his "slave's rebellion" thus:[96]

Wunsch-Maid	Wish-Maid
war'st du mir:	you were to me:
gegen mich doch hast du gewünscht	but against me you have wished

However, as I will argue in subsequent chapters, the irony of Wotan as "master" is that through punishing Brünnhilde he comes to lose power (and thereby comes to grow personally) and his "slave" will later come to take over the world with her

---

89. N. Wagner, *Wagners*, 72.

90. N. Wagner, *Wagners*, 72. This is summed up in Wotan's words to his daughter in *Walküre* Act III (*WagRS* 181, 190–91) his kisses being *non-sexual*.

91. Magee, *Nibelungs*, 175–78.

92. *WagRS* 160.

93. Magee, *Nibelungs*, 176.

94. *WagRS* 180.

95. *WagRS* 184.

96. *WagRS* 181.

husband Siegfried. However, this all happens in ways that do not really correspond to Hegel's analysis in the *Phenomenology*.

Siegfried, the Positive View of Power, Revolution, Anarchy, and Property

We have seen the menace of Alberich's and Wotan's lust for power and money. The opposite pole is Siegfried. He is precisely the one who can exercise power in a positive sense and correspondingly he is the one who has no interest in "money." As he emerges from Fafner's cave he has little interest in the treasure he has gained from killing the dragon:[97]

Was ihr mir nützt,	What use you are
weiß ich nicht:	I do not know:
doch nahm ich euch	but I took you
aus des Hort's gehäuftem Gold,	from the heaped-up gold of the hoard
weil guter Rath mir es rieth.	since goodly counsel counselled me to do so.

Likewise, when Hagen in *Götterdämmerung* Act I Scene 2 hails Siegfried as the "lord of the Nibelung hoard" he responds: "I'd almost forgotten the treasure, / so little I treasure its barren worth."[98]

Wagner's portrayal of Siegfried has been justly likened to revolutionaries such as Bakunin. Shaw write that Siegfried is "a totally unmoral person, a born anarchist, the ideal Bakoonin, an anticipation of the 'overman' of Nietzsche."[99] He is not only rude and cruel to his step-father Mime, but his attitude to his grandfather can be painful to experience: "But under it [the huge hat] one of your eyes is missing [. . .]. Be off with you now! / Or else you could easily / lose the other one, too."[100] Perhaps less obviously a "Siegfried" was Wagner's friend and colleague in Dresden August Röckel who, Wagner noted, had undergone "the strange transformation":[101] "On the basis of the socialist theories of Proudhon and others pertaining to the annihilation of the power of capital by direct productive labor, he constructed a whole new moral order of things to which [. . .] he little by little converted me, to the point where I began to rebuild upon it my hopes for the realization of my artistic ideals."[102] As Wagner started composing the *Ring* he was indeed influenced by French socialists such as Proudhon.[103] In *Artwork*

---

97. *WagRS* 246 (*Siegfried* Act II Scene 3).
98. *WagRS* 294.
99. Laurence, *Shaw's Music III*, 457–58; he goes on to call him "Siegfried Bakoonin" (458–68).
100. *WagRS* 261.
101. *My Life* 372; *Mein Leben* 1:386.
102. *My Life* 373; *Mein Leben* 1:387.
103. Although Proudhon is not mentioned by name in *Die Wibelungen* there are certainly echoes

of the Future he writes: "Nothing has been more destructive of human happiness, than this frenzied haste to regulate the Life of the Future by given present laws. This loathly care about the Future, which indeed is the sole heritage of moody, absolute Egoism, at bottom seeks but to *preserve,* to *ensure* what we possess to-day, for all our lifetime. It holds fast to Property—the to-all-eternity to be clinched and riveted, *property*—as the only worthy object of busy human forethought."[104] There is a clear allusion to Proudhon in this final sentence (cf. his comments quoted above on his influence on Rockel). His *Qu'est-ce que la propriéte* was published in 1840 when Wagner was actually living there and his slogan "property is theft" "is encapsulated in the symbol of the ring" and "as a source of wealth, it puts temptation in everybody's way and invites theft."[105]

But despite such negative views on "property" in the *Ring* it is worth saying that in the *Jesus* sketches a more realistic view of property is put forward and actually represents Proudhon's views fairly accurately.[106] He clarified his slogan "property is theft" by saying it was polemically formulated and that property could even be the basis for the freedom of the individual over against the state.[107] Property is only problematic when it turns into power over human beings and this of course is the fundamental problem with Alberich's and Wotan's longing for the ring. Wagner's Jesus does not demand the total abolition of property but simply a just distribution of it, a view that was also not unlike that of Marx and Engels.[108]

Nationalism

Whereas twentieth- and twenty-first-century nationalism is generally associated with right-wing politics, in much of the nineteenth it was associated with socialism, hence Wagner's involvement in the 1849 Dresden revolution. Wagner's nationalism has associations with figures such as Herder and Fichte,[109] but categorizing his nationalism, like his antisemitism, is not always straightforward. He held to a cultural nationalism rather like Herder,[110] but it is striking that although the *Nibelungenlied* was associated with such German nationalism, Wagner does not appear to appeal to this epic to support his nationalist sentiments. As far as Fichte is concerned, Wagner certainly shared

of his thought (*PW* 7:295–96; *GSD* 2:153; see volume 1, chapter 2).

104. *PW* 1:206; *GSD* 3:171.

105. Millington, "The Ring and Its Times," 19.

106. See Proudhon, *Staatsökonomie*, 1:341–46.

107. Kreckel, *Frühsozialisten*, 104–6.

108. Marx and Engels, *Communist Manifesto*, 235: "The distinguishing feature of Communism is not the abolition of property generally, but the abolition of bourgeois property. But modern bourgeois private property is the final and most complete expression of the system of producing and appropriating products, that is based on class antagonisms, on the exploitation of the many by the few."

109. Wagner's relationship with these two figures was discussed in volume 1, chapters 5 and 6 respectively.

110. This is seen clearly in Hans Sachs' final words in *Meistersinger* (Berger, *Beyond Reason*, 28).

his view that the nation was more fundamental than the state. In his *Orations to the German Nation*,[111] Fichte writes "the state, as the mere regiment of human life proceeding along its usual peaceful course, is not something primary, existing for itself, but is merely the means to a higher end, that of the ever-uniform and continuing development of the purely human (Ausbildung des rein Menschlichen) in this nation."[112] His likening of Germany to Greece in this respect would be music to Wagner's ears: "As was the case only among the ancient Greeks before them, among the Germans the state and the nation were actually separate from each other."[113]

Although Wagner explained how his art could lead to a new order (and hence a genuine German nationalism) in his Zurich essays, a key to this being the appropriation of Greek tragedy, he nevertheless argued that Germany could only be revitalized through the Greeks after a revolution.[114] Therefore Wagner "incites his audience to overthrow the present state in order to rebuild the nation along more natural lines. Only after this revolution might Germany be able to sponsor a drama such as Athens sponsored for its citizens."[115]

Wagner's nationalism had not only a "Greek" element but also a strong "Christian" component as we shall shortly see when I consider Friedrich Barbarossa. But this Christian component was essentially Protestant, and Wagner often relates the Reformation to his German nationalism, and he considered "Rome" an alien element. Cosima relates her husband's only extant allusion to Arminius: "'So far,' R. says, 'we have been great in *defence*, dispelling alien elements which we could not assimilate; the Teutoburger Wald was a rejection of the Roman influence, the Reformation also a rejection, our great literature a rejection of the influence of the French; the only positive thing so far has been our music—Beethoven.'"[116]

Wagner certainly believed that in composing the *Ring* he was creating Germany, and the inscription on the titles page of the first printed score of *Das Rheingold* (dated 20 March 1873) certainly witnesses to a nationalism:[117]

---

111. The 1859 edition complied by Fichte's son, Immanuel Hermann Fichte, was in Wagner's Wahnfried library.

112. Fichte, *Address*, 111 (eighth address; *JGFAW* 5:502–3); note Fichte's use of the "purely human," a key idea for Wagner.

113. Fichte, *Address*, 111 (*JGFAW* 5:503); cf. Berger, *Beyond Reason*, 29–30. On the *Orations* and whether they are hostile to human liberty see Wood, "Philosophy of Right," 185, and Aichelle, "Ending Individuality," 248–72.

114. Foster, *Greeks*, 209, writes that for Wagner Germany would need to "return to the more universal world of nature in order to 'replant' the nation in a richer and purer cultural soil and thus, in a sense, do for itself what Wagner did for Siegfried, namely, provide a natural education." He refers to *Artwork of the Future* (PW 1:203; GSD 3:168): "Our modern *States* are thus far the most unnatural unions of fellow men."

115. Foster, *Greeks*, 209, referring to *Art and Revolution* (PW 1:54–55; GSD 3:30–31).

116. *CD* 19 February 1872.

117. *DEBRN* 5, 172.

Der Ring des Nibelungen	The Ring of the Nibelung
Ein Bühnenfestspiel	A Festival Stage Play
für drei Tage und einen Vorabend	for Three Days and a Preliminary Evening
Im Vertrauen auf den deutschen Geist entworfen	Conceived in faith in the German spirit
und zum Ruhme seines erhabenen Wohltäters	and completed for the greater glory of its noble benefactor
des Königs	King
Ludwig II	Ludwig II
von Bayern	of Bavaria,
vollendet von	by
Richard Wagner	Richard Wagner

Wagner believed after his rescue from financial disaster by King Ludwig II in 1864 that Bavaria would provide the context for his art renewing the nation. However, his hopes were frustrated by the Bavarian politicians and press. He then pinned his hopes on Prussia and Bismarck in the process of which he was to celebrate the new establishment of the German Reich in 1871 after the Franco-Prussian war. But Bismarck also was to prove to be a bitter disappointment and Wagner's hopes for change in society were rooted again in his art and not in politics.[118] But despite being so disillusioned with current political leaders, he could at least take some comfort from the great leaders of the past. After 1871 he took a special interest in Friedrich der Grosse, considering him one of the "very rare geniuses"[119] and entertained writing a stage work about him.[120] He read Carlyle's biography,[121] and two writers who influenced Wagner, Ranke and Droysen, both took a special interest in Friedrich der Grosse, extolling his achievements. However, the dominating political (and to some extent "spiritual") figure for Wagner for much of his creative life was to be Friedrich Barbarossa.

---

118. Bermbach, *Wahn*, 343–44.

119. *CD* 26 January 1871.

120. *CD* 30 January 1871: "'If I were a young fellow,' R. said, 'how I should like now to complete my Barbarossa, my Bernhard von Weimar! Frederick the Great still occupies my thoughts, his state of mind is in fact a true picture of our own up till now; the imagination French, but the essential being thoroughly German; this division ought to give the work an extremely interesting profile." Just over a week later he received Mathilde Wesendonck's *Friedrich der Grosse: dramatische Bilder nach Franz Kugler* (published 1871 and based on Kugler's *Geschichte Friedrichs des Großen*, Leipzig 1840). But according to Cosima, "R. is utterly opposed to women's venturing into the market in this way, he sees it as a sign of lack of taste." I am unsure whether this is an accurate representation of the composer's views.

121. *CD* 4 June 1871.

Hohenstaufens

Wagner read Raumer's history of the Hohenstaufens at the end of 1841[122] in his Paris years[123] when he was sketching his proposed five-act opera *Die Sarazenin*,[124] a work that concerns Manfred, the son of Friedrich II. This was not the first time he dealt with the Staufer theme since already in 1832 he had composed an Overture "König Enzio" (WWV 24; *WWV* 88–91).[125] But the figure who was to fascinate Wagner was Friedrich Barbarossa, as can be seen in the sketches for his opera *Friedrich I*[126] and in *Die Wibelungen*.[127] Raumer's work in six volumes first appeared in 1823–35 and Wagner possessed volumes 1, 2, and 4 of the second edition of 1840–41 (volume 2 being concerned with Friedrich I).[128] Whereas A. W. Schlegel and Ranke viewed the Hohenstaufens in terms of a Roman/German medieval world, Raumer portrayed a Romantic "Christian-German" history whereby the emperors were not seen in terms of real power but rather as an ethical idea.[129] Munz argued that over the century the sometimes sober assessments of Barbarossa's career was to be transformed[130] such that by the time we come to Prutz's three-volume work *Kaiser Friedrich I* (1871–74) we find Barbarossa portrayed as a heroic figure and his reign a golden age[131] such that it was understandable that the Kyffhäuser legend (see below) could have developed.[132]

The *Friedrich I* sketches are brief but *Die Wibelungen* is an extensive work and holds many clues for the *Ring*.[133] Wagner writes of conflict between the "Welfen" and the "Wibelungen," the significant point being that whereas the Welfen were submissive to the papacy, the Wibelungen wished to dominate. The Hohenstaufens were preceded by the Salian emperors who ruled 1024–1125, the last being Henry V (reigned 1106–25) who died childless, appointing his nephew Friedrich of Swabia of the house

---

122. Gregor-Dellin, *Chronik*, 31.

123. *My Life* 210; *Mein Leben* 1:221.

124. *My Life* 210–12; *Mein Leben* 1:221–23. On *Die Sarazenin* (WWV 66; *DTB* 205–21) see *PW* 1:313–14; *GSD* 3:270–71 (*Communication to my Friends*).

125. Zegowitz, *Opern*, 110.

126. The sketches were composed over the period 1846–49 (see volume 1, chapter 2 on the issue of dating).

127. Wagner worked on this in late 1848 and in early 1849.

128. Note also that Ranke, *Reformation*, 1:36–37, deals briefly with Friedrich Barbarossa's relationship to the papacy (Wagner possessed Ranke's five-volume history of Germany at the time of the Reformation in his Dresden library).

129. Kaul, *Barbarossa*, 1:79.

130. Munz, *Barbarossa*, 4, claims that in Raumer's work "nothing spectacular is attributed to Frederick, and his reign does not appear to have been particularly golden." Note, however, that Raumer writes of the Roncaglia diet in glowing terms (*Hohenstaufen*, 2:101).

131. Prutz, *Kaiser Friedrich I*, 3:353–56, offers a concluding "doxology." This work was in Wagner's Wahnfried library.

132. Prutz, *Kaiser Friedrich I*, 1:4.

133. See volume 1, chapter 2.

of Hohenstaufen as his successor. But the ecclesiastical and lay princes elected Lothar (a Welf). Wagner contrasts Henry V and Lothar thus: "Heinrich V., previously supported by the Church against his hapless father, had scarcely reached the rank of Kaiser than he felt the fateful craving to renew his father's wrestle with the Church" realizing that his "world-dominion" should include "dominion of the Church herself."[134] On the other hand, the Welf Lothar III (reigned 1125–37) "adopted an attitude of peaceful submission to the Church: he did not fathom what the Kaiser-rank implied; *his* claims did not extend to world-dominion,—those were the heirloom of the Wibelungen, the old-legitimist contenders for the Hoard. But clearly and plainly as none before, great *Friedrich I.* took up the heir-idea in its sublimest sense."[135] Hence Friedrich I came to have such an important place in Wagner's thinking. In his autobiography he comments in the context of his *Friedrich I* drama: "The idea of a ruler was to be grasped here in its most powerful and momentous significance; his dignified resignation at the impossibility of realizing his highest ideals was to lead, while arousing sympathy for the hero as well, to a true insight into the manifold complexity of all action in this world."[136] Part of Wagner's admiration for Friedrich was clearly that he opposed the power of the pope; he added "Holy" to the "Holy Roman Empire" (in 1157), the epithet "reflecting his aim to dominate Italy and the papacy, as well as the areas north of the Alps."[137] In *Die Wibelungen* Wagner related Barbarossa to both Siegfried and Christ, all three being in their different ways "saviour" figures.[138] The close link Wagner made between Barbarossa and Siegfried is also seen in the fact that in the *Annals* for 1848 he writes: "Old German studies. Sketched out in my head Barbarossa in five acts. Passed on to Siegfried by way of a prose work on his historical significance: *Die Wibelungen*."[139]

While Friedrich was viewed by Wagner as a parallel to Siegfried (and to Christ) in positive terms, he was also viewed as a parallel to Wotan, but in ways that are not always positive. There is the parallel to Wotan in that Friedrich, according to the legend, sleeps in the Kyffhäuser mountain with his ravens circling above.[140] But there is also the entirely negative association in that Wotan was prepared to sacrifice his son, Siegmund. Cosima records: "Talked about Barbarossa and Arnold of Brescia, the great sin of the former in delivering him up, an act avenged on his whole

134. *PW* 7:288; *GSD* 2:145.

135. *PW* 7:288; *GSD* 2:146.

136. *My Life* 376; *Mein Leben* 1:390.

137. Whaley, *Germany I*, 17.

138. See volume 1, chapter 2. As well as Wagner's linking Barbarossa and Christ see the connection made in the painting (1837) and copperplate engraving (1858; E. Bendemann and E. A. Goldfriedrich) "Christus streitet für uns" (Kaul, *Barbarossa*, 2:3–4).

139. *Brown Book* 95; *Braunes Buch* 113. Note, however, that these *Annals* were rewritten in 1868 and certain details were falsified. See volume 1, chapter 2.

140. In certain respects (but only certain respects) this resembles Waltraute's description of Wotan in *Götterdämmerung* Act I Scene 3: "So he sits, / says not a word, / silent and grave / on his hallowed seat" (*WagRS* 303). But note Friedrich will return to *save* Germany; Wotan is simply awaiting his end.

family like—*Der Ring des Nibelungen*, Wotan's sin."[141] Arnold of Brescia was a radical preacher who attacked the wealth of the clergy, advocated their complete poverty, and led a rebellion against the pope.[142] Pope Hadrian demanded that Friedrich capture and hand over Arnold, which he did;[143] Hadrian in turn handed him over to the prefect of Rome, who had him executed,[144] something Friedrich later bitterly regretted (since Arnold may have been useful to his cause).[145]

Friedrich I as an opponent of the pope also became important for Luther, and this connection was not lost on Wagner as a keen Protestant. Cosima records her husband's words in 1869, the year he earnestly started working again on the *Ring* after his so-called twelve-year break: "When I have finished the *Nibelungen* [. . .] I shall write some plays for the theater: Luther's marriage with C[atherine] v[von] Bora, Bernard von Weimar [. . .] and also Barbarossa."[146] Wagner's associating Barbarossa with Luther was not accidental.

There are two key sources for Wagner concerning the legendary and mythological stories of Friedrich: Jacob Grimm's *Deutsche Mythologie*, which he read in 1843, and then the *Volksbuch* of 1519, which was republished in 1845. Grimm tells of the legend that Friedrich I had not in fact died but that he had been taken to the Kyffhäuser in Thüringen where he sleeps, sitting on a round stone table, his beard growing over the table.[147] Friedrich asks a shepherd if the ravens were still encircling the mountain, and as the shepherd said yes, Friedrich said that he must then sleep for another hundred years.[148] Grimm then goes on to speak of the tradition of the final battle: "When the beard has for the third time reached the last corner of the table, the *end of the world* begins, a *bloody battle* is fought for the Walserfeld, *Antichrist* appears,

---

141. CD 27 October 1876.

142. Munz, *Barbarossa*, 29, 59, 61.

143. Munz, *Barbarossa*, 80.

144. Munz, *Barbarossa*, 87.

145. Munz, *Barbarossa*, 87, 247.

146. CD 27 June 1869.

147. Grimm's *Mythologie*, 2:906; *Mythology*, 3:955. The legend originally was attached to Friedrich I's grandson, Friedrich II. The idea that it was Frederick I was first made popular by Rückert's poem *Barbarossa*, composed in 1816 and published in 1817 (Kaul, *Barbarossa*, 1:102). It tells of his never dying (strophe 2) and his returning the glory to Germany (strophe 3: "Er hat hinabgenommen / Des Reiches Herrlichkeit, / Und wird einst wiederkommen, / Mit ihr, zu seiner Zeit"). It ends thus: "Er spricht im Schlaf zum Knaben: / Geh' hin vor's Schloß, o Zwerg, / Und sieh, ob noch die Raben / Herfliegen um den Berg! / Und wenn die alten Raben / Noch fliegen immerdar, / So muß ich auch noch schlafen, / Verzaubert hundert Jahr" (Rückert, *Gedichte*, 172–73). Further, linking the legend with Friedrich I was "given the seal of scholarly approval by the publication of Grimm's *Deutsche Mythologie*" (Munz, *Barbarossa*, 15), which was first published in 1835. Grimm did in fact link the legend to Barbarossa back in 1816 when his *Deutsche Sagen* (written with his brother Wilhelm) was published. But whereas his main source Johannes Praetorius had doubts about the identity of the emperor, Grimm, it appears, had none (Munz, *Barbarossa*, 15, n. 4).

148. Grimm, *Mythologie*, 2:906–7: *Mythology*, 3:955–56.

the angel-trumpets peal, and the *Last of Days* has dawned."[149] He then gives the older tradition, including that of the religious poem of the sixteenth century (Gräter's Odina) that tells of "Herzog Friedrich," "who is to win back the H[oly] Sepulchre, and hang his shield on a leafless tree; and Antichrist is brought in too."[150] This, we will see, is related to the tradition found in the 1519 *Volksbuch*.

Hence, Grimm explains: "That the *common people* disbelieved the death of Emp. Frederick, and expected him to come back, is plain from the passages which expressly refer to 'old peasants'"[151] and adds that "it had most likely been the same in the preceding (thirteenth) cent., and was long after."[152] Such a "coming back," his "wiederkehr," exactly the term Wagner's Jesus of the *Jesus of Nazareth* sketches employs for the "second coming," will occur once the ravens ceased to encircle the mountain.[153] These ravens are clearly Wotan's birds but the precise nature of his association with the mountain is unclear.[154] This discussion of Friedrich appears in Grimm's *Mythologie* chapter 32 headed "Entrückung" ("rapture")[155] and in a section specifically on "Bergentrückte Helden," ("heroes taken up into mountains") and immediately before the discussion of Friedrich I there is brief mention of Siegfried who, it is believed, lives with other heroes in the old Geroldseck Castle and will appear when the German people are facing greatest need.[156] Wagner developed these legends in *Die Wibelungen* which, as was seen in volume 1, is a strange but important work for understanding the *Ring*, in particular the

---

149. Grimm, *Mythology*, 3:956; *Mythologie*, 2:908: "hat der bart zum drittenmale die letzte tischecke erreicht, so tritt das *weltende* ein, auf dem Walserfeld erfolgt eine *blutige schlachte*, der *antichrist* erscheint, die engelposaunen tönen und der *jüngste tag* ist angebrochen."

150. Grimm, *Mythology*, 3:956; *Mythologie*, 2:908.

151. Grimm, *Mythology*, 3:958; *Mythologie*, 2:910: "Dass kaiser Friedrichs tod *unter dem volk* bezweifelt und seine wiederkehr geglaubt wurde, lehren die angeführten stellen, die sich ausdrücklich auf alte bauern beziehen." See also the *Jesus of Nazareth* sketches, which speak of Jesus' "wiederkehr." Berry, *Bonds*, 41, refers to Heine who speaks of Barbarossa as "holding in his hand the divine sceptre of liberty, and carrying upon his head the imperial crown without a Cross" ("tenant dans sa main le sceptre divinatoire de la liberté, et portant sur sa tête la couronne impériale sans croix" (*Werke*, 9:191)).

152. Grimm, *Mythology*, 3:958; *Mythologie*, 2:910.

153. When Wagner included *Die Wibelungen* in his collected writings in 1871 he omitted the "supernatural conversation with Barbarossa in the underworld" (Köhler, *Titans*, 255). "'When will you return, Frederick, O glorious Siegfried! and slay the evil gnawing worm of humanity?' 'Two ravens are flying round my mountain,—they are glutted on the spoils of the empire. From the South-east pecks the one, from North-east the other:—drive away the ravens and the hoard is yours. But leave me in peace in my mountain of the gods!'" See *SSD* 12:229 (entitled "Die Wibelungen (1848) (Schlußworte)"): "'Wann kommst du wieder, Friedrich, du herrlicher Siegfried! und schlägst den bösen nagenden Wurm der Menschheit?'—'Zwei Raben fliegen um meinen Berg,—sie mästeten sich fett vom Raube des Reiches!—Von Südost hackt der eine, von Nordost hackt der andere:—verjagt die Raben und der Hort ist euer! Mich aber laßt ruhig in meinem Götterberge!'"

154. Munz, *Barbarossa*, 12.

155. Grimm, *Mythologie*, 2:903. *Mythology*, 3:951 render "Entrückung": as "Translation."

156. Grimm, *Mythologie*, 2:906; *Mythology*, 3:955. Castle Geroldseck is in Alsace and overlooks Haegen.

issue of its German character, questions about race, and the links between Siegfried (who is like Apollo killing Python),[157] Friedrich Barbarossa, and Christ, and then again links from Friedrich and Christ to Wotan.[158]

The second work to consider is the *Volksbuch* of 1519, which was important regarding Friedrich's confrontation with the papacy.[159] It was originally published in Augsburg, had a wide circulation, and went through many editions.[160] Then in the nineteenth century it was republished in the *Zeitschrift für deutsches Alterthum* in volume 5 of 1845 (together with other Friedrich I material), which was in Wagner's Dresden library.[161] I think it is very likely Wagner read the section of Friedrich since it was in 1846 that he produced his first sketch for his opera *Friedrich I* and chose to write this on Reformation Day (31 October). The *Volksbuch* recounts four stories concerning Friedrich, all of which are essentially legendary. The first includes Friedrich's capture of Jerusalem.[162] The second concerns a story that Pope Alexander III envied Friedrich, ordered a portrait be produced which was sent to the Sultan of Babylon, who was asked to find Friedrich in Armenia on his crusade. Friedrich and his chaplain were captured, imprisoned, but were eventually released by the Sultan. Friedrich returned to his empire and planned vengeance on the pope.[163] The third story concerns his capture of Venice (to where the pope had fled), his making St Mark's basilica a stall for his horses, and ploughing up St Mark's square to sow corn.[164] This story ends by Friedrich humbling himself before the pope on the advice of the Bishop Hartman of Brixen but confessing that he is obedient to St Peter, not to the pope (even though he is his successor).[165] All ends peacefully between Friedrich and Alexander.[166] The fourth story tells of the deaths of the two figures. The pope's final act is to call a counsel and he dies in the twenty-first year of his papacy. But no one knows where Friedrich is buried. The *Volksbuch* ends by telling of the tradition of Barbarossa living still in a mountain, having been being taken up. He is expected to return when he will punish the clergy, and hang his shield on the

---

157. Spencer, "Romantic operas," 298 n. 37, suggests that Wagner drew the Siegfried/Fafner and Apollo/Python parallelism from Grimm, *Mythologie*, 1:345; *Mythology*, 1:371–72.

158. The most detailed discussion I have found is that of Wilberg, *Mythische Welt*, 77–184. This work is especially helpful in relating Wagner to the fundamentally important work of Hübner, *Mythos*. Among other things she gives a helpful summary of earlier work on *Die Wibelungen* (89–95).

159. Stadtwald, *Roman Popes*, 52–57.

160. Munz, *Barbarossa*, 14.

161. Wagner possessed volumes 1–6 (1841–48) (Westernhagen, *Bibliothek*, 110). In addition to the "Volksbüchlein" itself (253–67) there was an introduction by Pfeiffer (250–52), a text from 1572 ("Eusebii chronica aller christ. kirchen"), which includes an outline of the pope's various attempt to kill Friedrich (267–68), and a poem "Kaiser Friedrich aus Enenkels Weltchronik" (268–93).

162. Pfeiffer, "Volksbüchlein," 253–59.

163. Pfeiffer, "Volksbüchlein," 259–65.

164. Pfeiffer, "Volksbüchlein," 265–66.

165. Pfeiffer, "Volksbüchlein," 266: "ich bin nit dir, sonder Petro, des nachkomen du bist, gehorsam."

166. Pfeiffer, "Volksbüchlein," 265–67.

barren tree that is guarded by the Sultan.[167] This is the first extant reference to the figure in the Kyffhäuser being Friedrich I.[168]

Although such stories have little basis in history, and Wagner was clearly aware of this, one has to take seriously his utterance that Cosima reports: "what human beings have themselves thought out and imagined is more important than what really happened."[169] Such stories concerning Friedrich were part of the German collective consciousness of the nineteenth century and fashioned the way they thought of the nation and its relationship to the papacy. In addition to the stories related in the *Volksbuch* of 1519, but possibly growing out of it, is that Friedrich on his return will avenge the blood of the peasants in the battle of Frankenhausen (1525). According to the *Volksbuch*, Friedrich in taking Jerusalem was helped by the son of a Bavarian miller who was carrying the flag of the "pundtschuoch" ("Bundschuh"),[170] the "peasants' boot," which was to be the symbol of the peasants' revolt of 1525.[171] It may be purely a coincidence but the final battle of the revolt took place in Bad Frankenhausen, situated at the southern slope of the Kyffhäuser range. A tradition developed in that region that on Good Friday peasants would assemble on the Kyffhäuser, Friedrich would be resurrected, and he would avenge the innocent blood spilt at Frankenhausen.[172] We do not know if Wagner knew of this tradition, but if he did it would clearly appeal to his political sympathies.

Wagner's fascination with Barbarossa was to continue and in 1871 he said that if he were young again he would like to complete the play.[173] In November, whilst making corrections on *Die Wibelungen* (for publication of *Collected Writings*) Cosima records: "he says he is in fact still thinking of doing something on Friedrich Barbarossa, in order to bring out this one single feature—his magnificent, barbaric, noble, and indeed divine inexperience."[174] This description of Friedrich is clearly fitting for Siegfried.[175] He then speaks as though the "Holy Roman Empire" still exists

---

167. Pfeiffer, 267: "Die pawrn und schwartzen künstner sagen, er sey noch lebendig in ainem holen perg, soll noch herwider komen und die gaistlichen straffen und sein schilt noch an den dürren paum hengken, welchs paums all Soldan noch fleissig hüeten lassen. Das ist war das des paums gehüet wirt, und sein hüeter darzu gestifft: wölcher kaiser aber seinen schilt sol daran hengken, das waiss got." This barren tree is presumably the one Jesus cursed in Mark 11:12–14, 20–21; Matt 21:18–20.

168. There was also a tradition that it was in fact Barbarossa's grandson, Friedrich II, who was the figure of the Kyffhäuser legend (Munz, *Barbarossa*, 6–15). See above on Wagner's interests in Friedrich II.

169. *CD* 17 November 1879.

170. Pfeiffer, "Volksbüchlein," 256–57.

171. On Wagner's interest in the peasant's war see the letters of 10 April 1845 (to Ferdinand Hiller, *SB* 2:425) and 24 October 1846 (to Johann Kittl, *SB* 2:529).

172. Munz, *Barbarossa*, 10, who refers to Eberhardt, "Kyffhäuserburgen," 97.

173. *CD* 30 January 1871.

174. *CD* 12 November 1871.

175. See chapter 10 below on Siegfried's character.

(perhaps because of Wilhelm I of Prussia being proclaimed emperor on 18 January 1871 in the Hall of Mirrors, Versailles).

> "And how inconceivable it is," R. adds, "that this German Empire, the most inconceivable thing of all, is probably something which will outlast all monarchies."—"I am glad," he says, "that I have an eye for this connection between legend and history. In the popular view Caesar was connected with Ilium, and Saint Gregory of Tours speaks of a Frankish Pharamund who was a descendant of Priam. The compilation of the Nibelung Saga, which was hardly understood anymore, began with Friedrich I."[176]

Then a year later Cosima records: "we talked yesterday about this wonderful race (diese herrliche Race) of Hohenstaufens, who appear before us like all the magnificent figures of the ancient world."[177]

Wagner's interest in Friedrich was no doubt fed by Hegel's emphasizing the greatness of Friedrich Barbarossa. The first sketch for *Friedrich I* was made in 1846, he read Hegel's *Philosophy of History* in 1847 and then made further sketches in 1848–49 and composed *Die Wibelungen* at around the same time. Hegel writes:

> In the brilliant period of the *Hohenstaufen* dynasty, individuals of commanding character sustained the dignity of the throne; sovereigns like Frederick Barbarossa, in whom the imperial power manifested itself in its greatest majesty, and who by his personal qualities succeeded in attaching the subject princes to his interests. Yet brilliant as the history of the Hohenstaufen dynasty may appear, and stirring as might have been the contest with the Church, the former [Hohenstaufen dynasty] presents on the whole nothing more than the tragedy of this house itself [and of Germany], and the latter [the Church] had no important result in the sphere of Spirit.[178]

---

176. *CD* 12 November 1871. Note he had a copy of Lobell, *Gregor von Tours*, in both his Dresden and Wahnfried libraries.

177. *CD* 8 November 1872. This was in relation to reading on 7 November a poem by Heinrich VI, son of Barbarossa.

178. Hegel, *History*, 388. *Geschichte*, 466: "In der glänzenden Periode der Hohenstaufen behaupteten Individuen von großem Charakter den Thron, wie Friedrich Barbarossa, in welchem sich die kaiserliche Macht in ihrer größten Herrlichkeit darstellte und welcher durch seine Persönlichkeit auch die ihm untergebenen Fürsten an sich zu halten wußte. So glänzend die Geschichte der Hohenstaufen erscheint, so lärmend der Kampf mit der Kirche war, so stellt jene doch im ganzen nur die Tragödie der Familie dieses Hauses und Deutschlands dar, und dieser hat geistig kein großes Resultat gehabt."

— 6 —

Love

Introduction

If love is the greatest power for good then its absence is the source of evil; hence Wagner came to the idea of renunciation of love.[1] There is no hint of the denial of love in either the *Mythus* of 1848 or *Siegfried's Death* (1848). It first enters in the earliest sketch for *Rheingold*, which was drafted in early November 1851, and to which he refers in letters to Uhlig (3 and 12 November 1851)[2] and Liszt (20 November 1851).[3] Then as the *Ring* further evolved, love came to be one of the very central themes of the cycle with the heart-wrenching tale of Siegmund and Sieglinde and Brünnhilde's transformation as she witnesses their love and her own expression of self-sacrificial love, which brings about the redemption of the world. However, Wagner does not just compose a drama *about* love; love, he wrote, is built into the very structure of his mode of composition: "I cannot conceive the spirit of Music as aught but *Love*."[4]

As we proceed through this chapter I will be asking questions about the nature of this love, how and why it came to have such a key role in the *Ring*, and the possible influences upon on the composer regarding love. But first in order to gain our bearings I consider matters synchronically (rather than diachronically) in asking some basic questions about the types of love in the *Ring*.

1. Windell, "Hegel," 35.

2. *SL* 233; *SB* 4:175 (12 November 1851): "it begins with Alberich, fired by erotic desire (liebesgelüste), pursuing the three watermaidens of the Rhine and being spurned by each of them [. . .] so that he finally steals (stiehlt) the Rheingold in his fury:—in itself this gold is only a glittering trinket [. . .] but another power resides within it which can be coaxed from it only by *the man who* renounces *love*." Winterbourne, "Freedom," 352 n. 4, claims "Alberich does not *steal* the gold" since "by forswearing love, Alberich is literally entitled to take it." But he *does* steal it and forswearing love entitles him to forge the ring (*WagRS* 68).

3. *SL* 238–39; *SB* 4:188.

4. *PW* 1:306; *GSD* 4:264 (*Communication to my Friends*). He goes to speak of "the Need-of-Love downtrodden by that loveless formalism (das Bedürfniß der Liebe unter dem Drucke eben jenes lieblosen Formalismus)." On the problem of writing *about* love, see Bultmann, "What Does It Mean to Speak of God?" 53: "one cannot speak *about* love at all unless the speaking about it is itself an act of love. Any other talk about love does not speak about *love*, for it stands outside love." If Bultmann is correct, this chapter, one of the most difficult to compose, has its limitations.

Types of Love

The theme of love occurs in virtually all opera and Wagner is no exception. But Wagner stands out in that rarely does one find the depth and sophistication of Wagner's treatment of love. One key aspect is that when, e.g., Siegmund and Sieglinde fall in love it is not simply a tragic story of doomed love. It is, as we have seen, part of a larger canvas. Although other composers have also placed their love stories within a larger narrative in many cases it simply serves as a useful backdrop to the romance (e.g., the political circumstances in Puccini's *Tosca*), although Berlioz, *Les Troyens* and Prokofiev, *War and Peace*, partly owing to the genius of their sources, do bring out the drama of both the love story and the wider narrative. One of Wagner's masterstrokes in the *Ring* is the way his love stories are so fully integrated into the wider narrative and the way this wider narrative propels the love story and vice versa. So who else would be able to make a love scene herald the downfall of the gods as we find in *Siegfried* Act III Scene 3?

Wagner wrote much about love in his letters and essays but before delving into these and examining his principles of love I outline the three basic types of love we find in the *Ring* cycle, that between man and woman (I call this "sexual love" for convenience), that between parent and child, and love for our "neighbor."

Sexual Love

There are a wide variety of "sexual" loves in Wagner's *Ring*. One of the striking aspects, and this has perhaps been overlooked in the frequent emphasis of Wagner being an iconoclast, is that all the noble cases of sexual love fall into the category of what one could call "marriage" and most of the exploitative cases of intercourse occur outside "marriage." But there are also loveless marriages, the prime example being that between Sieglinde and Hunding.

As far as erotic love in marriage is concerned one can say that generally speaking the more conventional the relationship the less passionate it is and conversely the less conventional the more passionate it is. So the most erotic music we find in the *Ring* is found in the passionate love between Siegmund and Sieglinde, clearly the most unconventional of all the *Ring* relationships. Although they are not married they clearly see themselves as about to get married in that Siegmund calls Sieglinde his "bride."[5] And, incidentally, this relationship is only seen as "sinful" from the perspective of Fricka. No one else condemns it and, as we shall see, Wotan specifically praises it.[6] At the opposite extreme is the marriage of Sieglinde and Hunding, and Wagner's work as a consummate dramatist places the two extremes of "marriage" side by side in *Walküre* Acts I and II. Sieglinde as Hunding's possession is made

---

5. *WagRS* 139, 157.
6. See chapter 7 below.

clear in some of her earliest words to Siegmund: "This house and this wife / are Hunding's own (Hunding's Eigen)."[7]

A less abusive marriage, but one nevertheless that has gone sour, is that between Wotan and Fricka. It is portrayed as a loveless marriage and Wagner may have intended to portray their marriage even more negatively by making it childless,[8] in this respect paralleling the marriage of Sieglinde and Hunding and contrasting that of Sieglinde and Siegmund. On Wotan and Fricka, Wagner writes: "The firm bond which binds them both, sprung from the involuntary error of a love that seeks to prolong itself beyond the stage of necessary change and to obtain mutual guarantees in contravention of what is eternally new and subject to change in the phenomenal world—this bond constrains them both to the mutual torment of a loveless union."[9] He even goes to the point of saying that it was this, not Alberich and the ring, which was "the germ" of the evil portrayed in his drama.[10] However, it could be that there was once love between them since Wotan was at least prepared to *offer* an eye to gain Fricka. I maintain he did not *actually* sacrifice an eye for Fricka.[11] As Millington points out "When Wotan staked a pledge for Fricka it was not *one of his eyes* but *his one eye* ('mein eines Auge setzt' ich werbend daran'); in other words, having already sacrificed one eye at the Well of Wisdom, he pledged the remaining one for Fricka but was not, in the event, called upon to forfeit it."[12] An alternative interpretation (which although interesting is ultimately unsatisfactory) is that Wotan *did* lose an eye for Fricka since she is the protector of the treatises, which are the outcome of the wisdom she embodies.[13] However, although Fricka came to be the protector of marriage and by extension "law," she is not a figure of Wisdom, a role that of course falls to Erda. However, Erda is not involved in this first search for wisdom at the Well of Wisdom but she is the key for his second search (in events between *Rheingold* and *Walküre*) as we shall soon see.

7. *WagRS* 123. Berry, *Bonds*, 188–89, compares this to Marx's analysis of bourgeois marriage in the communist manifesto.

8. Note that their counterparts in Norse mythology, Odin and Frigg, do have children (Baldr, Höd, and Vidar). The same be said for their Greek counterparts Zeus and Hera. See Hesiod, *Theogony*, 921–22 (Most, *Hesiod I*, 76–77): "[Zeus] made Hera his vigorous wife; and she, mingling in love with the king of gods and men, gave birth to Hebe and Ares and Eileithyia." Even if Wagner had not read Hesiod when composing the *Ring* libretto (Hesiod was in his Wahnfried but not in the Dresden library) he had been a close friend of the Hesiod scholar Samuel Lehrs in his Paris years (1839–42). In any case, he would know of Zeus and Hera having as children Hebe (Homer, *Odyssey*, 11.603), Hephaestus (Homer, *Iliad*, 1.578; 14.338 (but in Hesiod, *Theogony*, 927, Hera conceives him without a male partner)) and possibly Eris (Homer, *Iliad*, 4.440, named as "sister of Ares").

9. Letter to Röckel, 25/26 January 1854 (*SL* 307; *SB* 6:67–68).

10. *SL* 307; *SB* 6:67–68. See chapter 5 above.

11. Skelton, "Conflict," 8.

12. Millington, "Myths and Legends," 136. See *WagRS* 72 and *TBRN1* 352 (*Prosaentwurf* 23 March 1852): "*Wodan* erinnert sie daran, dass er, um Fricka einst zu gewinnen, er willig ja sein eigenes eines auge ihren trotzigen sippen verpfändet."

13. Borchmeyer, "Mythos vom Anfang und Ende der Welt," 17: "Sie verkörpert die Intelligenz, die Wotan durch den Verlust des Auges gewonnen hat."

Other marriages in the *Ring* that are also disastrous (but in a different sense) are those between Gunther and Brünnhilde and between Siegfried and Gutrune in *Götterdämmerung*. The use of opera comique in Act II for the pairing of Siegfried and Gutrune was noted by Wagner himself.[14] The reference in particular is to Auber's *La Muette de Portici*, which Wagner discusses in *Opera and Drama*[15] and considers this "Stumme" as "the dumb-struck Muse of Drama."[16] Indeed, the melody employed in Act II as Gutrune rejoins Siegfried ("Freia grüsse dich") is virtually identical to that of the bridal chorus in Act I of Auber's *La Muette de Portici* (composed in 1828).[17] Whereas Gutrune sings "Freia grüße dich / zu aller Frauen Ehre" the chorus in *La Muette de Portici* sing something similar: "Daigne exaucer notre prière et bénis, bénis ces heureux époux" (Deign to hear our prayer and bless, bless this happy couple").[18] Nattiez rightly draws attention to the fact that when Wagner was composing the music of *Götterdämmerung* one morning he sang to Cosima "a pretty theme by Auber"[19] and on another occasion played excerpts from Auber on the piano.[20] Wagner clearly knew the score of *La Muette de Portici* having rehearsed the work when he was chorus master in Würzburg;[21] also Auber attended one of Wagner's concerts in Paris in 1860 and the two became acquainted with each other.[22] Wagner admired *La Muette de Portici*, considering it Eugène Scribe's best libretto,[23] and what greater compliment could be offered by noting that the work provoked riots, "was recognised as the obvious theatrical precursor of the July revolution," and that "seldom has an artistic product stood in closer connection with a world-event."[24] Although the work was a five-act

---

14. Porges, *Rehearsing the Ring*, 129 (see below). See also Boulez, "A partir du present," 34.

15. *GSD* 3:265; *PW* 2:56–57. Later he describes French Opera as "Kokette" ("coquette") (*GSD* 3:318; *OD* 120; *PW* 2:112–13). Note that for the opera's first Leipzig performance on 28 September 1829, his sister Roslie played the dumb girl (Newman, *Life*, 1:80; Gregor-Dellin, *Life*, 41).

16. *GSD* 3:265; *PW* 2:57.

17. *Götterdämmerung* Act II (bars 274–75); Auber, *Muette*, 1:173–81 (the melody reappears in Act II (1:330)). The pitches of the notes are identical: g' e" d" c" b' a' g' (although the rhythm is somewhat different). Whereas Auber places the melody in C major Wagner moves from C to G Major. Nattiez, *Androgyne*, 86 comments that the orchestra in *Götterdämmerung* Act II doubles the vocal line (but note the "doubling" is complex and imprecise) and compares Flosshilde's flirtation with Alberich in *Rheingold* Scene 1 (bars 368–82; Nattiez, *Androgyne*, 65). Further one can add that the violins and flute double as the bridal chorus melody is first introduced (Auber, *Muette*, 1:173–74).

18. Auber, *Muette*, 176–81.

19. *CD* 19 March 1873.

20. *CD* 8 August 1874.

21. Millington, *Wagner*, 11.

22. Gregor-Dellin, *Life*, 458, 465. There is only one extant letter from Wagner to Auber (8 February 1861; *SB* 13:40).

23. *PW* 5:39; *GSD* 9:45 (the libretto was actually by both Eugène Scribe and Germain Delavigne).

24. *PW* 5:53; *GSD* 9:58 (*Reminiscences of Auber*, which appeared in November 1871). There are numerous references to Auber in Wagner's writings and in his very first published essay (*On German Opera*, 1834) he notes that it was the French "from Grétry to Auber," not the German or Italians, who had appropriated Gluck's "Dramatic Music" (*PW* 8:56; *SSD* 12:2).

tragedy, the reference to the "comic opera" in the notes made by Porges for the "conversation [. . .] between Gutrune, Hagen and the returned Siegfried" must refer to Auber's work: "'A very detailed dialogue'—'a kind of lively conversation on the stage to be kept wholly in the style of comic opera': these are the clues Wagner gave and only if they are strictly followed can the right effect be created."[25]

The relationship between Siegfried and Brünnhilde is considered a "marriage" in that Brünnhilde declares that she is "wed" to Siegfried ("dem Manne dort / bin ich vermählt").[26] There is certainly *some* passion between the two in *Siegfried* Act III, but it certainly lacks that between the Volsung twins. There is also what may appear a curious toning down of the passion between Siegfried and Brünnhilde as he worked on the libretto. So in the sketch completed on 1 June 1851, the final stage direction reads "Brunnhilde sturzt sich in Siegfrieds arme: sie weilen verschlungen, mund an mund" ("Brunnhilde falls into Siegfried's arms: They remain intertwined with one another, mouth to mouth").[27] However, in just under a month as he wrote his *Dichtung* he had second thoughts, and Brünnhilde simply "falls into his arms."[28] In the Prologue to *Götterdämmerung* we also find that their relationship lacks the intensity of the Volsung twins: Siegfried appears to get bored and decides, with Brunnhilde's blessing, to go on his new adventures. Her very first words are:[29]

Zu neuen Thaten,	To new adventures,
theurer Helde,	beloved hero,
wie liebt' ich dich—	what would my love be worth
ließ' ich dich nicht?	if I did not let you go forth?

Going on such adventures was, as we know, to prove disastrous: Act I ends in tragedy when, under the power of the drink of forgetfulness, "S. overpowers Br. and she subconsciously recognises him."[30] I will discuss this scene in more detail in chapter 10, where the issue of whether Siegfried had intercourse with Brunnhilde after overpowering her will be considered.

This then brings us to those cases of attempted seduction and of sexual assault. Wotan tells Brünnhilde that he "mastered the vala / with love's magic spell / and broke

---

25. Porges, *Rehearsing the Ring*, 129. The tragic ending of Auber's opera, with Fenella throwing herself into the lava flowing from Vesuvius, clearly influenced the close of *Götterdämmerung*. The nobility of Fenella contrasts sharply with Gutrune's superficiality who really is the woman of "opera comique."

26. WagRS 322. This is also stressed in her Schlussgesang ("Die Gattin trügend"; "False to his wife" (WagRS 348); "Selig grüßt dich dein Weib!"; "In bliss your wife bids you welcome!" (WagRS 351)).

27. Strobel, *Skizzen*, 96; TBRN1 235.

28. Strobel, *Skizzen*, 196; TBRN1 330 (cf. GSD 6:176). Likewise, Siegfried's words "saug' ich deinen athem dir vom munde" in *Der große Prosaentwurf* are changed to "aug' in auge, mund an mund" in the *Dichtung* and final poem (Strobel, *Skizzen*, 95, 193; GSD 6:174). Cf. Dreyfus, *Erotic Impulse*, 94–95.

29. WagRS 284.

30. CD 4 June 1870.

her wisdoms pride [. . .]. Knowledge I gained from her; / from me though she gained a pledge: / the world's wisest woman / bore to me, Brünnhilde, you."[31] This would appear to be a violation of Erda, and we get the same impression in *Siegfried* Act III Scene 1 where Erda tells Wotan as Wanderer: "wise though I am / a ruler once tamed me."[32] The comments of the composer recorded by Cosima may cause some alarm: "What a strange night that must have been when Wotan subjugated Erda! That is my own invention entirely—I know nothing about Zeus and Gaea [. . .]. The night when Brünnhilde was begotten—it can only be seen as something divine; the urge to subjugate this prophetic woman, to learn all from her! Such outbreaks of natural force I have witnessed in the animal world—our only analogue for the divine is in the animal world."[33] At worst these remarks could be taken to suggest that when we act like animals then rights and responsibilities are irrelevant (and the same applies for the gods!) At best though they could be taken to mean that it is possible for sex to involve no shame when we act like animals, a point to which I will return.

Wagner clearly portrays negatively the seduction of Grimhilde by Alberich where he gave her gold (stolen from the Rhinemaidens) for sex, suggesting at worse a form of prostitution ("the dwarf had had his way with a woman, / whose favours gold had gained him")[34] and the Vala's prophecy tells of when Alberich "begets a son in his fury" ("zürnend zeugt einen Sohn").[35] On the other hand, his attempted seduction of the Rhinemaidens seems to be viewed at least by the composer as fairly harmless and he even had some sympathy for him![36]

Love between Parents and Children

Just as we encounter no passionate sexual love in the early stages of the *Ring*, there are also no tender parent–child relationships. But in *Der junge Siegfried* we find Siegfried having tender thoughts about his parents he never knew[37] and when Wagner turned to work on *Walküre* his portrayal of relationships with children is remarkable.

In *Walküre* we encounter those crucial parent–child relationships, the most complex being those of Wotan to Siegmund and especially to Brünnhilde (both children growing up without a mother). In one sense, it could he said be *uses* his children in that between *Rheingold* and *Walküre* he begets them simply to further his own plans;

---

31. WagRS 150.
32. Wag RS 256.
33. CD 8 May 1874.
34. WagRS 154.
35. WagRS 153.
36. CD 2 March 1878: "R. tells me that he once felt every sympathy for Alberich, who represents the ugly person's longing for beauty."
37. See the sketch completed 24 June 1851 (Strobel, *Skizzen*, 150–51; TBRN1 287–88) and WagRS 238–39.

but he does grow to love them (or at least some of them). Although he begat Siegmund in order to recover the ring, he clearly came to love him and hence his excruciating mental anguish in Act II Scene 2: "what I love I must relinquish, / murder him whom I cherish."[38] This love is reciprocated by Siegmund, whose trust in his father is so cruelly crushed as witnessed in Wotan's next two lines: "and foully betray / him who trusts me!"[39] Siegmund had enjoyed adventures with his father but had been separated from him and in Act II Scene 4 Siegmund, when faced with Brünnhilde's calling him to Valhalla, wonders if he will see his father there. Then when we turn to the Valkyries, Wotan begat them to recover fallen heroes from the battle field to fight at what the Norse Mythology called Ragnarök. But he grew to love Brünnhilde and she became his favorite daughter with whom he enjoyed an "untroubled form of affectionate companionship."[40] Brünnhilde's love for her father is intimate and touching and is shown, e.g., when the stage direction in Act II Scene 2 (just after she pleads with her father to confide in her) tells us: "Lovingly and anxiously she rests her head and hands on his knees and lap."[41] Then in Act III Scene 3, in somewhat different circumstances, she pleads again: "O tell me, father! Look in my eyes and silence your anger."[42]

Brünnhilde grows up without her mother, perhaps not even knowing who she is, and appears to show little interest in her.[43] Siegfried grows up without both parents, even without any knowledge of them, and it is only when he threatens his step-father that he learns about their fate.[44] Siegfried's relationship to his parents only exists on the level of his thinking about them as in the touching scene in *Siegfried* Act II when, as we have seen, he wonders what his father and especially his mother looked like.[45] The most moving association with his parents comes in Siegfried's funeral march where we hear in turn the motifs of the Volsungs, Sieglinde, and the sword (associated with his father).[46]

The most dysfunctional parent-child relationship is that between Mime and Siegfried, his adoptive son. The relationship is built upon deceit in that Mime claims he is "father and mother in one."[47] It is notable that in the *Jesus of Nazareth* sketches

38. *WagRS* 153.

39. *WagRS* 153.

40. Skelton, "Conflict," 7. Skelton (8) believes Wotan once had such feeling for Fricka.

41. *WagRS* 148.

42. *WagRS* 184. Her words sung in part to the descending scale characteristic of much of this scene is accompanied by a tender form of "Wotan's frustration" on the English horn and oboe (bars 1030–36). See Example 11.2 (chapter 11) below.

43. It is unclear whether Wotan's words in his *Walküre* Act II monologue is the first she knows of her mother (*WagRS* 150).

44. *WagRS* 203–6.

45. *WagRS* 238–39.

46. Here we find "the most powerful function of the leitmotif" as an "evocation of things *past*" (Grey, "Leitmotif," 109) as opposed to its use for "prophecy" or "action" (98–109).

47. *WagRS* 202.

Wagner stresses the lovelessness of "gratitude" ("Dankbarkeit"). Gratitude is the love of a child "to its begetters, nourishers and bringers up."[48] But he goes on to say gratitude is no love and is associated with duty and a wish to compensate.[49] This is a theme in Act I of *Siegfried* where Mime tells Siegfried he should show some gratitude for his having brought him up.[50] Mime explains that he found his mother, Sieglinde, in the forest in labour pains. He helped her into a cave where she gave birth to Siegfried and as she died she handed Siegfried over to Mime's care who brought him up. Then the gratitude theme changes towards the end of Act I and into Act II to the sinister plot that Mime will kill Siegfried once Siegfried has killed Fafner.

Another dysfunctional father–son relationship is that between Alberich and Hagen. Like Wotan, Alberich begat a son for his own purposes, but the very conception was hateful and colors Hagen's whole being. Wotan explains to Brünnhilde:[51]

Des Hasses Frucht	A woman harbours
hegt eine Frau;	the seed of hate;
des Neides Kraft	the force of envy
kreiß't ihr im Schooß:	stirs in her womb:
das Wunder gelang	this wonder befell
dem Liebelosen.	the loveless dwarf.

There is little love between father and son even though Alberich closes their dialogue in *Götterdämmerung* Act II Scene 1 by calling Hagen "[t]rauter Held" ("beloved hero");[52] Hagen though does not mince his words, addressing his father as "schlimmer Albe" ("evil elf")![53]

Love for Our "Neighbor"

The third type of love I consider is that love of which the New Testament most often speaks, a love not for those in one's family, but a universal love of the "neighbor." As we found in chapter 2 above, this is the love that features so prominently in the *Jesus of Nazareth* sketches. The *Ring* is full of lovelessness and the only person who one can say truly practises such love is Brünnhilde, and although the word is rarely used, there can be no doubt that the sacrifice she makes in attempting to save Siegmund and her final self-sacrifice at the end of the cycle are acts of love. Concerning love for Siegmund,

---

48. *PW* 8:314; *DTB* 257.
49. *PW* 8:314–15; *DTB* 257.
50. E.g., *WagRS* 198–99.
51. *WagRS* 154.
52. *WagRS* 312.
53. *WagRS* 309.

Sieglinde says "For him whom *we* loved"[54] and later Brunnhilde tells her father of the love in her heart for Siegmund:[55]

Der diese Liebe	Inwardly true
mir in's Herz gehaucht,	to the will
dem Willen, der	which inspired
dem Wälsung mich gesellt,	this love in my heart
ihm innig vertraut—	and which bound me to the Wälsung—
trotzt' ich deinem Gebot.	I flouted your command.

But Wotan replies that "out of my love for the world, / I was forced to staunch the well-spring of love."[56] Such "love for the world" could *perhaps* be compared to the love of God who was prepared to send his Son into the world, the love of John 3:16 ("For God so loved the world that he gave his only Son").

But the focus of the loving character in the *Ring* is without doubt Brünnhilde. As Wagner puts it, "she had renounced her divinity for the sake of love."[57] These words from Feuerbach's *Essence* are pertinent: "Love determined God to the renunciation of his divinity. Not because of his Godhead as such, according to which he is the *subject* in the proposition, God is love, but because of his love, of the *predicate*, is it that he renounced his Godhead; thus love is a higher power and truth than deity. Love conquers God. It was love to which God sacrificed his divine majesty."[58] Hence for Feuerbach love is more important than God.[59] Then to the question "Who then is our Saviour and Redeemer: God or Love?" he answers: "Love; for God as God has not saved us, but Love, which transcends the difference between the divine and human personality. As God has renounced himself out of love, so we, out of love, should renounce God; for if we do not sacrifice God to love, we sacrifice love to God, and, in spite of the predicate of love, we have the God—the evil being—of religious fanaticism."[60]

As far as her self-immolation is concerned, although the word "love" does not appear in her "Schlussgesang" and although her thoughts are also focused on her husband Siegfried, her act is nevertheless a loving act which redeems the world ("erlösende Weltenthat").[61]

---

54. *WagRS* 178 (my emphasis).
55. *WagRS* 186.
56. *WagRS* 186.
57. *SL* 309; *SB* 6:71.
58. Feuerbach, *Essence,* 53; *LFW* 5:60.
59. Harvey, *Feuerbach,* 47.
60. Feuerbach, *Essence,* 53; *LFW* 5:61.
61. *WagRS* 258.

Development of Wagner's Principles of Love

The above discussion of Wagner's understanding of love in terms of sexual love, love between parents and children, and love of neighbor has been conducted *syn*chronically (at a *point* of time), considering the final form of the *Ring*. I turn now to looking at Wagner's understanding of love more in terms of its development, that is *dia*chronically (*through* time), which will, I claim, reveal patterns that a synchronic approach can systematically ignore.[62]

His operas of the 1840s, *Der fliegende Holländer*, *Tannhäuser*, and *Lohengrin* all concern the redemption through love;[63] although this is also found in the *Ring*, the idea of love has become also much more complex as a result of his further studies and development as an artist. The principal influences concerning love—which seemed to change his views from around 1845 (when he started work on *Lohengrin*)[64] through to the end of 1852 (when he completed the *Ring* libretto)—was his intensive work on the Greeks (especially Sophocles, *Antigone, Oedipus Tyrannus, Oedipus at Colonus*), his reading of Hegel and Feuerbach, and his study of the New Testament. There were other influences, such as Plato and Romanticism, that no doubt also played a role in his understanding of love, but the time at which they influenced Wagner is harder to date. Again we are dealing with a creative appropriation and I consider first the Bible and Romanticism, and then in more detail Hegel, Feuerbach, and the Greeks.

Bible

As noted in chapter 2 above, Wagner's study of the New Testament had a key role in the development of his *Ring* and this included the understanding of love. Love was seen as a key element in the message of Jesus, such love being essentially opposed to law. This will prove to be a key element in *Walküre* Acts I and II.[65] But the biblical message of love was also seen through the lens of Hegel and Feuerbach. Hegel's idea on the centrality of love, found throughout his writings, was to inform Wagner's interpretation of the Bible. Jesus' teaching that it is through giving of oneself to others that one discovers oneself forms a central part of Hegel's philosophy and was clearly central also for Wagner.[66] The idea of God as love in the First letter of John was important for

---

62. It is perhaps worth saying here that this is why a study of the *history* of philosophy is so important, revealing truth which may otherwise be missed.

63. There are also other types of love in these operas. E.g., in *Tannhäuser* there is the so-called "sacred" and "profane" love, the relationship of which is often misunderstood (as explained in Bell, *Parsifal*, 162). Note also that Wagner later came to reinterpret love in these works as in *Communication to my Friends* (see below).

64. The poem was composed July/August to November 1845 (*WWV* 305) and read before a group of friends and colleagues on 17 November (Gregor-Dellin, *Chronik*, 39).

65. See below and the following chapter on law and sexual ethics.

66. See, e.g., *Philosophy of Religion*, 3:286; *Philosophie der Religion* 3:211 (quoted in Houlgate,

Wagner[67] and most likely became even more important with his reading of Feuerbach, for whom 1 John 4:8 ("God is love") became so central: "God is love. The human loves, but God is love."[68] Wagner was also most likely aware of the rich varieties of love in the Bible from the love of God in Christ in Rom 5:6–8[69] right through to the erotic love in the Old Testament book of *Song of Songs*.[70]

Romanticism

Romantic writers such as Friedrich Schlegel influenced Wagner, and in volume 1, chapter 5 I considered the possible influence of his novel *Lucinde*. Eichner writes of Schlegel's understanding of the motif of Liebestod (love's death): "The ultimate reason for the death wish is the conviction that everything finite, and hence even the lovers' bliss in each other's arms, is imperfect. Anyone who has the 'feeling for the universe' which is the essence of religion will always be tormented by this thirst for the infinite—a thirst that can only be quenched through reunion with God or the Absolute in death."[71] This religious dimension of passionate love with its association with death is famously found in *Tristan* but it is prefigured in the *Ring*.[72] Wagner writes of this love/death link in his letter to Röckel of January 25/26 1854: "We must learn *to die*, and *to die*, in the fullest sense of the word; fear of the end is the source of all lovelessness, and this fear is generated only when love itself is already beginning to wane. [. . .] Wodan rises to the tragic heights of *willing* his own destruction. This is all that we need to learn from the history of mankind: *to will what is necessary* and to bring it about ourselves. The final creative product of this supreme, self-destructive will is a *fearless* human being, one who never ceases to *love: Siegfried*."[73]

Introduction to Hegel, 262): "In friendship and love I give up my abstract personality and thereby win it back as concrete. The truth of personality is found precisely in winning it back through this immersion, this being immersed in the other (durch das Versenken, Versenktsein in das Andere)."

67. In Wagner's New Testament, the first letter of John has a number of marginal markings (/ indicates a stroke; the Roman numeral indicates the Act of *Jesus of Nazareth* for which the verse is relevant): 1 John 2:7 // I IV; 3:3–8; 3:9 //; 3:10// I IV; 3:15–24; 4:9–12; 5:3–4 // IV. Note, however, that 1 John 4:8 itself "God is love" is not marked. But as in Wagner's not marking Schiller's "Ode to Joy" (see volume 1, chapter 5) this could mean that he was already well acquainted with the verse and hence had no need to mark it.

68. Feuerbach, *Thoughts*, 19; *LFW* 1:98. See also volume 1, chapter 6.

69. See chapter 2 above.

70. Wagner had Friedrich, *Das sogenannte hohe Lied Salomonis*, in his Wahnfried library. But it is not clear when he purchased (or read) it.

71. Eichner, *Schlegel*, 155 n. 6.

72. This is found in *Siegfried* Act III Scene 3 with the associations of love and death. See below.

73. *SL* 306–7; *SB* 6:67–68. Not only is there the influence of Romanticism but the phrase "*to will what is necessary* and to bring it about ourselves" is reminiscent of Hegel, *History*, 441 (*Werke* 12:523): "Luther [. . .] triumphantly established the position that man's eternal destiny [. . .] must be wrought out *in himself*" (i.e., as Sibree elucidates, it "cannot be an *opus operatum*, a work performed *for him*").

Together with Schlegel one should also consider his friend Schleiermacher,[74] who wrote a positive review of *Lucinde* emphasizing that the work shows not only the poetic but also the religious and moral aspects of love.[75] I have found no reference to Schleiermacher in Wagner's writings and it may be that the only way he knew of him was through his translations of and introductions to Plato's dialogues. But nevertheless Wagner and Schleiermacher appear to share much on the issue of love. In the context of discussing the love between Siegmund and Sieglinde in *Walküre* Act I Berry points to the Romanticism of Schleiermacher,[76] in particular his criticism of Kant and Fichte, whose ethics of duty cannot explain the importance of love:

> Yes, love, you power of attraction of the spiritual world! No individual or development is possible without you. Without you everything must degenerate into a crude, homogenous mass! Those who do not desire to be anything in their own right do not need you; for them laws and duties, uniform action and justice are sufficient. The holy feeling of love would be a useless ornament to them. [. . .] But for us, you are the alpha and omega.[77]

Hegel

Wagner's appropriation of Hegel and the Greeks (to which I later turn) on the issue of love is extremely rich such that he relates love to questions that one would not usually associate with it: these range from ultimate questions of consciousness right through to questions of the state and revolution. To some extent I think this accounts for the virtually unique way Wagner can present a "love story" as having such philosophical, political, and religious implications as we find in the *Ring*.[78]

As noted in volume 1, chapter 6, Wagner read Hegel's *Phenomenology of Spirit* around 1846–47. As is well known, it is not an easy work and I reserve a more detailed analysis of the work to another occasion.[79] Coming to grips with the first sections of this remarkable work may help one to *articulate* ideas of love as found in the *Ring*, but one can still understand the essence of Wagner's understanding of love by simply enjoying the drama, and part of his genius is presenting difficult philosophical ideas in the form of an artwork, just as for Hegel religion is able to articulate them in a ready digestible form, communicating "rational truths" in a "non-rational, non-conceptual

---

74. Schlegel moved into Schleiermacher's Berlin apartment and enjoyed a great friendship (Behler, *Schlegel*, 57–58). Also as noted in volume 1, chapters 4 and 5, they planned to work together on translating Plato.

75. Dischner, *Lucinde*, 135.

76. Berry, *Bonds*, 188.

77. Beiser, *German Romantics*, 179 (*Monologues II*). Note also Schleiermacher's view of androgyny discussed below.

78. See my comments above as I introduce "Types of Love."

79. I plan a study on theological anthropology that will involve engaging in Hegel's *Phenomenology*.

way."[80] But I will nevertheless outline how Wagner may have understood love as derived from the subject–object relationship explored by Hegel.

Love for Wagner was not simply physical, emotional, and irrational. He saw it as the fundamental human relationship and stressed its rational aspect in mutual recognition (as did Hegel). The cognitive nature of love, and the probable Hegelian influence, can be discerned in *Opera and Drama*. The cognitive element here relates to that of the artist, in particular the poet: "Art, by the very meaning of the term, is nothing but the fulfilment of a longing (die Erfüllung des Verlangens) to know oneself (sich selbst zu erkennen) in the likeness of an object of one's love or adoration, to find oneself again in the things of the outer world, thus conquered by their representment (Darstellung)."[81]

Hegel tried to overcome the subject–object gap by "a dialectical understanding of history."[82] According to Feenberg, "Hegel's great advance over Kant and Fichte" was "his concept of being as continuous becoming."[83] Wagner adopted this in the *Ring* in that he "emphasized the continuous becoming of the individual and society."[84] Corse argues that "the heroic individual who reflects self-consciousness achieved through a combination of sensuality and rationality in love (Wagner's concept, which combines elements of Hegelian and Feuerbachian thought) is Wotan (early and late), Siegmund, Sieglinde, Siegfried, and Brünnhilde—not any of them singly but all of them collectively. Brünnhilde, however, reaches a level of self-awareness the others do not, but it is a level impossible without their contributions. [. . .] This concept of the self as *becoming*, as object of history as well as subject, is what makes the *Ring* cycle so compelling."[85]

Hegel's idea of finding oneself in another is clearly expressed in his addition on love in *Philosophy of Right*. The first part certainly coheres with what Wagner presents in the *Ring*: "Love means in general terms the consciousness of my unity with another, so that I am not in isolation of myself but win my self-consciousness only through the renunciation of my independence (Fürsichsein) and through knowing myself as the unity of myself with another and of the other with me."[86] Hegel then writes something that Wagner denies in the *Ring* but that he no doubt would affirm in real life (see his real need to be legally married to Cosima!), namely that although love is a "feeling,"

---

80. Houlgate, *Introduction to Hegel*, 245.

81. *PW* 2:155; *GSD* 4:32–33. As Ellis notes, Wagner here derives "Kunst" from "kennen" (to know) whereas in *Artwork* he derives it from können (*PW* 1:100; *GSD* 3:72). The cognitive aspect of love at the close of Section II of *Opera and Drama* (*PW* 2:236; *GSD* 4:102–3) will be discussed below under "Incest."

82. Corse, *Consciousness*, 13.

83. Feenberg, *Sources of Critical Theory*, 11 (cf. Corse, *Consciousness*, 13).

84. Corse, *Consciousness*, 13.

85. Corse, *Consciousness*, 13.

86. Knox/Houlgate, *Philosophy of Right*, 162 (§158).

such feeling disappears "[i]n the state" where "we are conscious of unity as law."[87] Hegel then continues:

> The first moment in love is that I do not wish to be a self-subsistent and independent person and that, if I were, then I would feel defective and incomplete. The second moment is that I find myself in another person, that I count for something in the other, while the other in turn comes to count for something in me. Love, therefore, is the most tremendous contradiction; the understanding cannot resolve it since there is nothing more stubborn than this point (Punktualität) of self-consciousness which is negated and which nevertheless I ought to possess as affirmative. Love is at once the producing and the resolving of this contradiction.[88]

Such love of which Hegel speaks would appear to be that between "partners"; i.e., it is not fully applicable to say parent/child.

Wagner on Oedipus, State, Power, Love, Incest, and Antigone

Wagner discusses human personhood (which has clear implications for love) in Hegelian terms in Part II chapter 4 of *Opera and Drama*. He wrote this in 1850–51[89] and many of the ideas he expresses there are found in *Siegfried* (he first sketched *Der junge Siegfried* 3–10 May 1851) and *Walküre* (first sketched c. 11–20 November 1851). But to understand how Wagner brings together the constellation of incest, state, love, gods, one must follow through his argument from chapter 3 to the end of chapter 6 of Part II.

Wagner's discussion early on in chapter 3 of the Oedipus myth examines not only the question of incest but also the opposing roles of state and love. Oedipus' exposure by his father Laius demonstrates how the state became "the representative of *im*morality and hypocrisy."[90] So he argues: "*Quiet* and *Order* (*Ruhe* und *Ordnung*), even at the cost of the most despicable outrage on human nature and the wonted morality (die gewohnte Sittlichkeit) itself,—at the cost of a conscious, deliberate murder of a child by its own father, prompted by the most unfatherly self-regard,—this Quiet and Order were at any rate more worth considering that the most natural of human sentiments, which bids a father sacrifice himself to his children, not them to *him*."[91] Then in Creon the people recognized "the legitimate successor to Laïus and Eteocles"[92] and his polar oppo-

---

87. Knox/Houlgate, *Philosophy of Right*, 162 (§158).
88. Knox/Houlgate, *Philosophy of Right*, 162 (§158).
89. Gregor-Dellin, *Chronik*, 61, gives the completion date for the whole work as 10 January 1851. He sent part II to Uhlig at the beginning of Feb 1851 and tells Uhlig that part III will follow in fourteen days (*SB* 3:501; cf, *SB* 3:427).
90. *PW* 2:188; *GSD* 4:61. Cf. Borchmeyer, *Theatre*, 294.
91. *PW* 2:187–88; *GSD* 4:61.
92. *PW* 2:188; *GSD* 4:62.

site was Antigone: "In this State there was but one sorrowing heart, in which the feeling of Humanity had sought a shelter:—it was the heart of a sweet maiden (Jungfrau), from whose soul there sprang into all-puissant beauty the flower *of Love*. Antigone knew nothing of politics;—*she loved*."[93] Whereas Creon was the "State personified,"[94] in Antigone we see "the fullest flower of *pure Human-love*" ("die reichste Blume *reiner Menschenliebe*").[95] In her challenging the citizens of Thebes to condemn her for dealing "from pure human-love alone" we find that "*the love-curse of Antigone annulled the State! (der Liebesfluch Antigone's vernichtete den Staat!)*."[96] Three things should be noted. First, whereas Alberich's "love-curse" ("Liebesfluch") is to be understood as an objective genitive ("a curse on love"), as in Froh's words regarding the ring ("It's easily won now, / without cursing love (ohne Liebesfluch),"[97] Antigone's "Liebesfluch" is a subjective genitive, the curse *of* love, love's *own* curse. Love is a curse *in relation to the state*. Secondly, Wagner, in opposition to Hegel (who thought that both Creon and Antigone had a valid view point),[98] emphasizes that one side is in the right and the other in the wrong! Thirdly, Wagner goes on to declare Antigone as a redeemer figure: "*O holy Antigone! on thee I cry! Let wave thy banner, that beneath it we destroy and yet redeem!*"[99] She was motived by the love we find in the redeemer figures of Brünnhilde and Christ; however, in the cases of Christ and Brünnhilde we find an added dimension: their death as a redeeming sacrifice.

After discussing the Oedipus myth Wagner reflects more generally on the subject of myth: "[t]he incomparable thing about the Mythos is, that it is true for all time, and its content [. . .] is inexhaustible throughout the ages." He adds: "The only task of the Poet, was to expound it (ihn zu deuten)."[100] He believes that at the present time "we only need to faithfully expound the *myth of Oedipus* in its inmost essence" and that thereby one can see the whole history of mankind "from the beginnings of Society to the inevitable downfall of the State (bis zum nothwendigen Untergange des Staates)."[101] After discussing issues of "fate"[102] he concludes again on the theme of annulling the state: "to bring *the unconscious part* of human nature to consciousness within society [. . .] is as good as to say, *annul the State*."[103]

---

93. *PW* 2:188–89; *GSD* 4:62.
94. *PW* 2:190; *GSD* 4:63.
95. *PW* 2:189; *GSD* 4:63.
96. *PW* 2:189; *GSD* 4:63.
97. *WagRS* 82.
98. Houlgate, "Tragedy," 155–56. See my discussion in volume 1, chapter 4.
99. *PW* 2:190; *GSD* 4:63–64.
100. *PW* 2:191; *GSD* 4:64.
101. *PW* 2:191; *GSD* 4:65.
102. *PW* 2:193; *GSD* 4:66.
103. *PW* 2:193–94; *GSD* 4:66–67.

He begins chapter 4 by relating art to the *"annulling of the State"* (*"Vernichtung des Staates"*)[104] and how the poet's task is "to display the battle ([d]ie Darstellung des Kampfes) in which the Individual sought to free himself from the political State or religious dogma."[105] Wagner then speaks of the individual within society in Hegelian terms: "The Individual without Society is completely unthinkable by us, *as an individuality*; for first in intercourse with other individuals, is shewn the thing wherein we differ from them, wherein we are peculiar to ourselves."[106] If the surrounding ("Umgebung") is natural, "giving ample breathing-space to the development of the individuality" then all well and good, but society has grown into a political state, which is not a flexible surrounding "but a stiff, dogmatic, fettering and domineering might; which lays down for the individual in advance, 'So shalt thou think and deal!'"[107] Wagner does not say this here, but Corse believes it must be implied, that the hero must come from outside society.[108] This "very un-Hegelian notion" would therefore explain why Wagner's heroes are all in some sense "outsiders," seen in the *Ring* at its clearest with Siegmund and Siegfried.[109]

He begins the next paragraph by writing: "The dangerous corner of the human brain (Den gefährlichen Winkel des menschlichen Hirnes) into which the entire individuality had fled for refuge,—the State endeavoured to sweep it out as well, by the aid of religious Dogma," but it is *"from thinking* ([a]us dem Denken) that there first arose the force to withstand the State" and this involved "warding off the bondage of religious dogma."[110] But the poet "who had to portray the battle of the Individuality against the State could *portray* (*darstellen*) the State alone; but the free Individuality he could merely *suggest to the thought* (*dem Gedanken andeuten*)."[111] Hence, the Drama has been *"an appeal to the Understanding* (*Verstand*),*—not to the Feeling* (*Gefühl*)"[112] thereby taking the place of the "Didactic-poem."[113] On the other hand, "the poet who turns towards the Feeling (Gefühl) must be already so at one with himself (so einig mit sich sein), that he can dispense with any aid from the mechanism of Logic and address himself with full consciousness to the infallible receptive powers of the unconscious (an das untrügliche Empfängiß des unbewußten), [of the] purely human

---

104. *PW* 2:195; *GSD* 4:67.

105. *PW* 2:195; *GSD* 4:67.

106. *PW* 2:195–96 (emphasis added by Ellis); *GSD* 4:67.

107. *PW* 2:196; *GSD* 4:68.

108. Corse, *Consciousness*, 36.

109. In a different way there are also the outsider figures of the Dutchman, Tannhäuser, Lohengrin, Walther, and Parsifal.

110. *PW* 2:196–97; *GSD* 4:68. Note that "Hirn" is not a Hegelian term.

111. *PW* 2:197; *GSD* 4:69.

112. *PW* 2:197; *GSD* 4:69.

113. *PW* 2:197–98; *GSD* 4:69). Wagner's argument here parallels the one later in Part III (*PW* 2:282–83; *GSD* 4:143) discussed in volume 1, chapter 4.

Feeling (rein menschlichen Gefühles)."[114] Hence the modern poet wishes to address the understanding (Verstand). But "[t]he return from Understanding to Feeling will be the march of the Drama of the Future, in so far as we shall advance from the *thought-out* individuality to the genuine one."[115]

Wagner's view that art can only be renewed with a revolution is reflected in his comments that the drama (of the future) will be shaped by the "Going-under (Untergang) of the State" and "by the rise of an organically healthy Society."[116] And the "Going-under of the State can mean nothing else but *the self-realisement of Society's religious conviction (das sich verwirklichende religiöse Bewußtsein der Gesellschaft) of its purely-human essence*."[117] Such a conviction cannot be a "Dogma stamped upon us from without" such as historical traditions. So it is not a matter of "outward duty" but of "Religious Conscience" when "we *so* act as we cannot act otherwise."[118] But he thinks that a Religious Conscience must be a Universal one and it can only be so if "it knows the Unconscious, the Instinctive, the Purely-human, as the only true and necessary thing."[119] This implies that love and not law is the fundamental ethical principle.[120]

I will return to *Opera and Drama* Part II, discussing chapter 4 (concerning "fate"), in chapter 9. But now I conclude this section by stressing that the issue of incest in the Oedipus myth is central not only to particular plots and scenes in Wagner's stage works but also goes the heart of how he understood art, state, law, society, and, of course, love. It is very much related to the idea of the "purely-human," which occurs throughout *Opera and Drama*. The purely-human contrasts with the historical or culturally variable[121] and consists of "natural instincts" ("natürliche Willkür") as Wagner perceived in the actions of Oedipus and Jocasta.[122] Further, as Wagner was later to explicate in *Communication to my Friends*, the "purely-human" points to the universality of myths.[123]

The centrality of the Oedipus myth for Wagner's art is well expressed by Borchmeyer: "Antigone is very much cast as the patron saint of musical drama."[124] This is because at the end of Part II of *Opera and Drama* when discussing the sexual union of music (as feminine) and poetry (as masculine), he points to how feeling ("das

---

114. *PW* 2:198; *GSD* 4:69–70.

115. *PW* 2:200; *GSD* 4:72.

116. *PW* 2:201; *GSD* 4:72.

117. *PW* 2:201; *GSD* 4:72.

118. *PW* 2:201; *GSD* 4:72.

119. *PW* 2:201; *GSD* 4:72.

120. See the discussion in the following chapter.

121. *PW* 2:170–71; *GSD* 4:46–47. Cf. Young, *Philosophies*, 58.

122. *PW* 2:182; *GSD* 4:57.

123. *PW* 1:333–35; *GSD* 4:289–90. So the Flying Dutchman is the wandering Jew and Odysseus; Lohengrin and Elsa are Zeus and Semele.

124. Borchmeyer, *Theatre*, 296.

Gefühl" but understood as feminine) precedes and gives rise to understanding ("der Verstand" as masculine), feeling and understanding standing in a mother–son relationship. He writes of the "mother element, the womanly, from whose womb—the *ur*-melodic expressional-faculty,—there issued Word and Word-speech (das Wort und die Wortsprache)."[125] But then the "understanding" needs to fecundate the "feeling"[126] and through such fecundation finds itself "justified" ("gerechtfertigt").[127] He then adds in a footnote the parallel in the Oedipus myth: "Would it be thought trivial of me, if I were to remind the reader—with reference to my exposition of that myth—of Oedipus, who was born of Jocasta, and who begot with Jocasta the redemptrix, Antigone?"[128] We therefore have these relationships which Nattiez sets out in a helpful diagram (see Figure 6.1).[129]

Figure 6.1: Antigone and Artwork of the Future

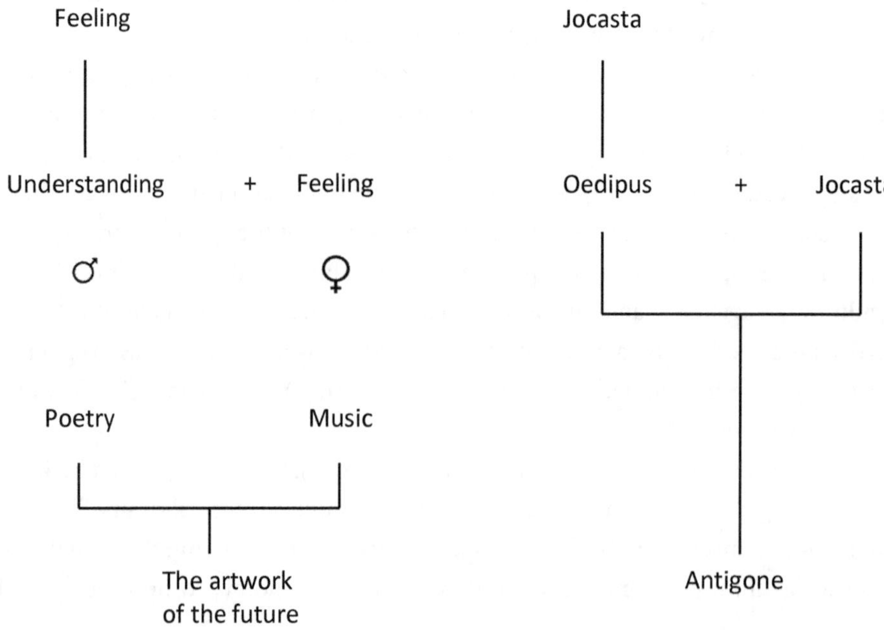

```
    Feeling                              Jocasta
       |                                    |
       |                                    |
Understanding  +  Feeling          Oedipus  +  Jocasta
       ♂           ♀                   |_____|
                                            |
   Poetry        Music                      |
      |_____|                         |
            |                               |
      The artwork                       Antigone
      of the future
```

In order for this fecundation to occur the (male) understanding needs a "stimulus" ("Reiz") and he must pour himself into that object's full reality.[130] This "stimulus" is the

125. *PW* 2:235 (emphasis added by Ellis); *GSD* 4:102.

126. *PW* 2:235; *GSD* 4:102.

127. *PW* 2:235-36; *GSD* 4:102. Note the theological verb "to justify." Wagner also in his complex metaphor speaks of the understanding being "mirrored back" (*PW* 2:236; *GSD* 4:102), recalling his metaphor of the sea of music (*PW* 2:285; *GSD* 4:146, discussed below).

128. *PW* 2:236 n; *GSD* 4:102 n.

129. Nattiez, *Androgyne*, 92.

130. *PW* 2:236; *GSD* 4:102. He uses the verb "ergiessen." Compare Fichte's use of "Entäusserung"

"mediatrix" ("Vermittlerin") between the feeling and understanding and is "Phantasy" and is identified with the "eternal womanly," alluding to the end of *Faust II*.[131]

> This charm (Reiz) is the influence of the "eternal womanly," which draws the man-ly Understanding out of its egoism,—and this again is only possible through the Womanly attracting that thing in it which is kindred to itself: but That in which the Understanding is akin to the Feeing is *the purely-human*, that which makes-out the essence of the human *species* as such. In this Purely-human are nurtured both the Manly and the Womanly, which only *by their union through Love become first the Human Being*. The impetus necessary to the poetic intellect, in this its poesis, is therefore *Love*,—and that the love *of man to woman*. (Der nothwendige Drang des dichtenden Verstandes in diesem Dichten ist daher *die Liebe*,—und zwar die Liebe *des Mannes zum Weibe*.) Yet not that frivolous, carnal love, in which man only seeks to satisfy an appetite, but the deep yearning to know himself redeemed from his egoism through his sharing in the rapture of the loving woman; and *this yearning* is *the creative moment* (*das dichtende Moment*) of the Understanding. The necessary bestowal, the seed that only in the most ardent transports of Love can condense itself from his noblest forces—*this procreative seed is the poetic Aim, which brings to the glorious loving woman, Music, the Stuff for bearing*.[132]

He follows with these words, hence concluding Part II of *Opera and Drama* (The Play and the Nature of Dramatic Poetry) and looking forward to Part III (The Arts of Poetry and Tone in the Drama of the Future): "Let us now lend ear to this act of Birth."[133]

Love, Passion, and "Sensuality"?

The operas composed before the *Ring* certainly present "sensuality" (Tannhäuser and Venus) and a certain degree of "passion" (Lohengrin and Elsa), but in composing the *Ring* passion and sensuality are brought to a completely different level. This change is often attributed to Feuerbach's influence on Wagner's understanding of love. It is claimed that Feuerbach's "equivalence of reality and sensuality" would have "extraordinary appeal to one with the strong sexuality of Wagner."[134] However, one needs to ask what Feuerbach means by "sinnlich": the emphasis it not best rendered by the English "sensual" (which could have a sexual connotation) but simply by "sensuous," pertaining to the senses. Hence, "Sinnlichkeit" means "sensuousness" and is "the link between the

---

(Heath and Lachs, *Wissenschaftslehre*, 154; *FW* 1:165) where the subject empties itself out into the object.

131. *PW* 2:236; *GSD* 4:102.
132. *PW* 2:236; *GSD* 4:102–3.
133. *PW* 2:236; *GSD* 4:103.
134. Windell, "Hegel," 35.

body and the psyche."[135] Hence, the opening of section 32 of *Principles* is best translated thus: "The real *in its reality* or taken *as real* is the real *as an object of the senses* (*als Objekt des Sinnes*); it is the *sensuous* (das *Sinnliche*). *Truth, reality,* and *sensation* (*Sinnlichkeit*) are identical. Only a sensuous being is a *true* and a *real* being."[136] However, Feuerbach did come to influence Wagner's understanding of love, but he appropriated the philosopher in his characteristically creative way as we shall see.

The first indication of Wagner's new understanding of "passionate love" is in *Artwork of the Future*.[137] Here we find not simply the romantic concept of love but love as a simple human need.

> But the Life-need (Lebensbedürfniß) of man's life-needs is the *need of Love* (*Liebesbedürfniß*). As the conditions of natural human life are contained in the love-bond of subordinated nature-forces, which craved for their agreement, their redemption, their adoption into the higher principle, Man; so does man find his agreement, his redemption, his appeasement (Befriedigung), likewise in something higher; and this higher thing is the *human race* (*menschliche Gattung*), *the fellowship of man,* for there is but one thing higher than *man's* self, and that is—*Men* (*die* Menschen).[138]

Hence "the *highest* human need is *Love*" ("das *höchste* menschliche Bedürfniß [...] ist die Liebe").[139]

A telling passage in *Opera and Drama* clearly links Feuerbach with passionate love. In Part II he writes that the sense of "Necessity" was once placed "*above*" but "one at last had grown convinced of both the artistic and the scientific barrenness of this view."[140] He then hints at Feuerbach (suggested by the word "species"),[141] although he does not mention him and indeed speaks just of "thinkers and poets":

> so thinkers and poets now sought for this explanatory Necessity *below*, among the foundations of all history. The soil of history is *man's social nature*: from the individual's need to unite himself with the essence of his species (Gattung) [...]. The historic phenomena are the outward manifestments of an inner movement, whose core is the Social Nature of man. But the prime motor of

---

135. Harvey, *Feuerbach*, 143.

136. Feuerbach, *Principles*, 51 (§32); *LFW* 3:298. I have added emphasis to Vogel's translation to reflect that in the original. Note that Windell, "Hegel," 35, translates using "sensuality" and "sensual."

137. The slightly earlier Zurich essay, *Art and Revolution*, does speak of love but in the Greek tragic sense of "Love-offering of [...] Death" (*PW* 1:58; GSD 3:35).

138. *PW* 1:96; *GSD* 3:68.

139. *PW* 1:97 (modified); *GSD* 3:69.

140. *PW* 2:174; *GSD* 4:50.

141. We find this key word at the very beginning of Feuerbach, *Essence*, 1 (*LFW* 5:17): "Consciousness in the strictest sense is present only in a being to whom his species, his essential nature, is an object of thought." It occurs also in earlier works (*Thoughts*, 108 (1830)).

this nature is the *Individual*, who only in the satisfaction of his instinctive longing for Love (*Liebesverlangen*) can appease his bent-to-happiness.[142]

This term "Liebesverlangen" occurs again later in *Opera and Drama*[143] and twice in *Communication to my Friends*.[144] We can compare these occurrences with the first sketch (c. 11–20 November 1851) for *Walküre*, which for the end of Act I speaks of "immer brennenderes liebesverlangen" ("constant burning longing for love").[145]

But when then did Wagner make his key change to the idea of "passionate love" we find in *Walküre*? It is true that the passionate *music* can be accounted for by his love of Mathilde Wesendonck. But the libretto itself expresses the passion between the Volsung twins even in the very first sketch.[146] This, as already noted, was written c. 11–20 November 1851,[147] and he did not meet Mathilde until February 1852 and the first sign of being in love with her is in a letter to Liszt of 30 May 1853.[148] I think a key to understanding love in *Walküre* Act I is his *Communication to My Friends*, which was completed just three months (August 1851)[149] before the first *Walküre* sketch. Here he puts forward two opposing views of "love." First he writes of "the fantastic debauchery of German student-life" and confesses that this "over-indulgence" had become abhorrent to him.[150] Dreyfus comments: "To counteract this descent into illicit sensuality, Wagner—now strongly under the thumb of Ludwig Feuerbach—searches for a true form of love to cure the ills of the modern world."[151] So later in *Communication* Wagner writes: "In contrast to the directly experienced hedonism (Genußsinnlichkeit) which surrounded modern life and art, [my desire was for] a pure, chaste, virginal, unapproachable and intangible form of love."[152] Wagner's view of love as here expressed is, as Dreyfus puts it, "utterly amorphous."[153] He thinks this reflects Feuerbach's view (to which I will return). Such a view may be found in *Artwork of the Future*: "He now can only will the universal, true, and unconditional; he yields himself, not to a love for this or that particular object, but to wide *Love* itself. Thus does the egoist become

---

142. *PW* 2:174–75; *GSD* 4:50.

143. *PW* 2:285; *GSD* 146.

144. He uses the term when he looks back on his composing *Tannhäuser* (*PW* 1:323; *GSD* 4:279) and Lohengrin (*PW* 1:335; *GSD* 4:290).

145. *TBRN1* 424; Strobel, *Skizzen*, 204.

146. The *Prosaskizzen* tells of Siegmund's wild passion for Sieglinde and includes "Siegmund: 'Weib und schwester, so [. . .] glühe denn Welsungenblut!'—Er umfasst sie mit wüthendem feuer" (*TBRN1* 424; Strobel, *Skizzen*, 204).

147. *TBRN1* 423.

148. *SB* 5:304.

149. See Wagner's letter to Uhlig written some time after 24 August 1851 (*SB* 4:96).

150. The translation of Dreyfus, *Erotic Impulse*, 50 (cf. *PW* 1:294). *GSD* 4:253. See also the section of *Communication* that Wagner later deleted but is given in Ellis' appendix (*PW* 1:396).

151. Dreyfus, *Erotic Impulse*, 50.

152. Dreyfus' translation, *Erotic Impulse* 50. Cf. *PW* 1:322–23; *GSD* 4:279.

153. Dreyfus, *Erotic Impulse* 51.

a communist, the unit of all, the man God, the art-variety Art."[154] Earlier, in a letter to Karl Ritter of 21 November 1849, Wagner praised Feuerbach (he had enclosed a copy of *Artwork of the Future*[155] completed on 4 November 1849 and published 1850). This letter shows how he appreciated Feuerbach's "natural healthy process."

> I expect that by now you will have grown more familiar with Feuerbach. You should probably have begun with his essay on death and immortality. [. . .] In order to express the most basic truth, the writer must write God knows how much, and what's worse, he becomes in the process not a human being but merely a writer once more. But Feuerbach ends up by becoming a human being, and on this point he is so weighty an authority, particularly in relation to absolute philosophy in which the human being is completely subsumed by the philosopher. Nowhere have I found the natural healthy process so clearly and so consciously expressed as by Feuerbach, and I confess that I am greatly indebted to him: the same thing will presumable happen to you, too.[156]

At the time of writing *Communication* Wagner was grappling with a new Romantic view of love, which, as Dreyfus puts it, was "a confused relation between love, sexual urges, and eroticism," a love "that wants to rise above bases desires and that at the same time cannot exclude a sexual element."[157] Dreyfus outlines the opposing poles in Wagner's understanding of love around 1851–54. He quotes a passage from a letter to Liszt where he points to the "two conflicting elements of desire within me, one of which I sought to appease by means of my art, while periodically giving vent to the other my means of passionate, fantastical [and sensual] extravagances."[158] But then he goes on to claim to have brought these two together in *Lohengrin* where he claims there is "a single unity in true *love*."[159]

I suggest that it is not so much in *Lohengrin* itself that such love is portrayed but rather in his later reflections on the opera in *Communication*,[160] which, as I noted above, was completed just three months (August 1851) before the first *Walküre* sketch (November 1851). In this passage he reflects on the parallel to Lohengrin and Elsa, namely Zeus and Semele, and we see here a view of love that goes both beyond the conventional romantic view and beyond Hegel and Feuerbach:[161] "'Twas no *God*, that

---

154. *PW* 1:94; *GSD* 3:67. Note the Feuerbachian interest in egoism. Also in the previous sentence Wagner writes of the human being as "species" ("Gattung").

155. *SB* 3:160 n. 4

156. *SL* 180–81; *SB* 3:161.

157. Dreyfus, *Erotic Impulse*, 51.

158. *SL* 297; *SB* 5:495.

159. *SL* 297; *SB* 5:495 (this is not quoted by Dreyfus).

160. *PW* 1:335 (quoted above).

161. I do not think there is here "a baffling incoherence about [Wagner's] concept of Love" (Dreyfus, *Erotic Impulse*, 53).

sang the meeting of Zeus and Semele; but *Man*, in his humanest of yearnings (der *Mensch* in seiner allermenschlichen Sehnsucht)."¹⁶² A little later he then asks:

> What then is the inmost essence of this Human Nature, whereto the desire which reaches forth to farthest distance turns back at last, for its only possible appeasement? It is the *Necessity of Love* (die *Nothwendigkeit der Liebe*); and the essence of this love, in its truest utterance, is the *longing for utmost physical reality* (*Verlangen nach voller sinnlicher Wirklichkeit*), for fruition in an object that can be grasped by all the senses, held fast with all the force of actual being.¹⁶³

Wagner as I read him is taking Feuerbach's "amorphous" view of love¹⁶⁴ and giving it form! And this is precisely what he does in *Walküre* Act I to which I now turn.

Walküre Act I

Walküre Act I contains "the only intentionally erotic scene in the entire *Ring* [...] when the twins Siegmund and Sieglinde fall in love and find themselves incapable of resisting their impulses."¹⁶⁵ One of the most remarkable aspects is the sense of constraint in the first scene and the way the attraction between the Volsung twins is resisted until that final scene. In considering this Act (and part of Act II) I consider the eroticism, questions of embodiment, and the way three key witnesses respond (Wotan, Fricka, and Brünnhilde), who also represent the way different audiences have responded. I will then move on to a systematic discussion of incest and the Oedipus myth.

Eroticism

The eroticism of Act I is highlighted by the fact that *Rheingold* is almost entirely without love; the nearest one comes to any sense of affection are in the lines of Fasolt (Scene 2) of having a woman in the home (and he seems to be oblivious to the fact that the woman he has in mind, Freia, has not given consent):¹⁶⁶

---

162. *PW* 1:335; *GSD* 4:290.
163. *PW* 1:335; *GSD* 4:290.
164. This is how Dreyfus, *Erotic Impulse* 50, describes Feuerbach's and Wagner's view of love. Although it is seen in some of Wagner's words (*PW* 1:322–23; *GSD* 4:279 (*Communication to my Friends*) and *PW* 1:94; *GSD* 3:67 (*Artwork*), quoted above), at this point in *Communication* I would not consider it amorphous.
165. Dreyfus, *Erotic Impulse*, 95.
166. *WagRS* 75.

Wir Plumpen plagen uns	We blunderheads toil away,
schwitzend mit schwieliger Hand,	sweating with blistered hand,
ein Weib zu gewinnen,	to win a wife
das wonnig and mild	who, fair and meek,
bei uns armen wohne:—	would dwell with us poor creatures:—

The last three lines are accompanied by the extended love motif played on the oboe. The next best thing to this tender expression of love in *Rheingold* is found in the same scene where Loge praises of love;[167] however, it is a somewhat clinical analysis of love and suggests that Loge has no first-hand knowledge of it! Then Fricka's desire for her husband is more to keep him in check: "Heedful of my husband's fidelity, / I'm bound in my sadness to brood / on ways of binding him fast / whenever he feels drawn away."[168] But she complains that "domestic bliss" ("wonniger Hausrath") fails to satisfy him, to which Wotan responds that if he is held "fast in his fortress" then his wife should grant that he "might win [. . .] the world outside."[169] Such sentiments resemble more a suburban abode of comfort as a base for gaining power than any passion for his wife. No doubt many couples will recognize this pattern of settling into domestic comfort and the focus of attention moving from love for one another to "conquering the world."

It is in *Walküre* Act I that for the first time we find in the *Ring* a true and authentic love. In fact, in the love between the Volsung twins we find for the first time in any of his works a truly charged erotic love in the best sense of the word. The earlier operas do deal with redemption through love but the love between Senta and the Dutchman, Tannhäuser and Elisabeth, and Elsa and Lohengrin,[170] although deep and profound, lacks that passion we find between Siegmund and Sieglinde. And it is worth adding that the relationship between Tannhäuser and Venus is simply "pornographic" and leads to Tannhäuser being bored, feeling oppressed amid the "rosy perfumes" of the Venusberg, and longing "for the woodland breezes, / for the clear blue of our skies, / for the fresh green of our meadows, / for the sweet song of our little birds, / for the dear sound of our bells."[171]

The remarkable thing about Siegmund and Sieglinde is that they recognize something of themselves in the other and one could say this corresponds to Hegel's idea of mutual recognition. So this was not possible for Tannhäuser when he was with Venus. Perhaps it was not even so for the Dutchman and Senta, or Lohengrin and Elsa. In fact, in the last case it is the *contrast* between the two that brought them together. On

167. *WagRS* 79–80.
168. *WagRS* 71.
169. *WagRS* 71–72.
170. Note, though, Wagner's comments quoted above on Elsa, comment though made in 1851, three years after completing *Lohengrin*.
171. *GSD* 2:7.

a superficial level this appears as Elsa, the accused, is rescued by Lohengrin, a "knight in shining armour"; but on a more profound level, Elsa is meant to redeem Lohengrin, who, one could argue, wishes to "use" Elsa so that he may become fully human. In a sense Siegmund and Sieglinde also rescue each other, but also they *find something of themselves in the other*. And *one way* Wagner represents this is to cast them as twins, the likeness being commented upon by Hunding.[172] But at the same time there are differences in that they find in each other what they each lack. It could be argued that this is what happens between Lohengrin and Elsa, but the relationship between Siegmund and Sieglinde is qualitatively different. In Scene 3 Siegmund sings (note the Stabreim and chiasmus pattern of abba):[173]

Was je ich ersehnt	Whatever I longed for
ersah' ich in dir;	I saw in you;
in dir fand ich	in you I found
was je mir gefehlt!	whatever I lacked!

Likewise Sieglinde sings:[174]

Du bist der Lenz,	You are the Spring
nach dem ich verlangte	for which I longed
in frostigen Winters Frist;	in frostly wintertime;

But at the same time she finds in Siegmund something of herself, an idea we found in Hegel's reflections on "love":[175]

Doch dich kannt' ich	But you I recognized
deutlich und klar:	plainly and clearly:
als mein Auge dich sah,	when my eye beheld you,
war'st du mein Eigen:	you were my own:
was im Busen ich barg,	*what I hid in my breast*
was ich bin,	and what I am,
hell wie der Tag	it came to me
taucht' es mir auf,	as bright as day;
wie tönender Schall	like an echoing sound
schlug's an mein Ohr,	it struck my ear,
als in frostig öder Fremde	when in frostily foreign wasteland
zuerst ich den Freund ersah.	I first beheld my friend.

172. *WagRS* 126.
173. *WagRS* 134.
174. *WagRS* 135.
175. *WagRS* 136 (my emphasis).

And again, a little later:[176]

Im Bach erblickt' ich	My own likeness
mein eigen Bild—	I glimpsed in the brook—
und jetzt gewahr' ich es wieder:	and now I see it again:
wie einst dem Teich es enttaucht,	as once it rose from the pool,
bietest mein Bild mir nun du!	to me now you show that likeness!

Siegmund responds:[177]

Du bist das Bild,	You are the likeness
das ich in mir barg.	I hid within me.

In the "rejected version" of *Walküre* Act II Scene 1 (*Erstschrift des Textbuches*) Wotan even goes to the point of implying that as a result Siegmund and Sieglinde growing together in their mother's womb, "unwittingly" ("unbewußt") lying there together, they have now come "unwittingly" ("unbewußt") to love each other.[178]

Embodiment (Eyes and the "Blick")

As we have seen, Wagner in his portrayal of love in the *Ring* is influenced by both Hegel and Feuerbach. Both take embodiment seriously,[179] as does Wagner, who is often emphasizing the physical (sinnlich). It is therefore worth asking questions about embodiment in relation to the Volsung twins.

One reason Wagner chose to have the lovers as twins goes back to the Norse sources, although some significant changes have been made.[180] But there are some interesting physical, psychological, and physiological matters to consider. Wagner focusses very much on the eyes and the glance ("Blick"), which also play such a crucial role in *Tristan* and *Parsifal*.[181] Shortly after his entrance Hunding comments that Siegmund looks like Sieglinde, especially regarding their eyes:[182]

---

176. *WagRS* 137.
177. *WagRS* 137 (my emphasis).
178. *WagRS* 355; *TBRN1* 470. See chapter 7 below for further discussion of this "rejected version."
179. Hegel is misunderstood if it is thought he does not take the physical world or science seriously. See Houlgate, *Introduction to Hegel*, 15, 122–60.
180. See volume 1, chapter 3.
181. See Bell, *Parsifal*, 97.
182. *WagRS* 126. "The sign of the serpent or dragon indicates Wälsung blood" (*WagRS* 365 n. 39, referring to Magee, *Niblungs*, 156).

Wie gleicht er dem Weibe!	How like the woman he looks!
Der gleißende Wurm	The selfsame glittering serpent
glänzt auch ihm aus dem Auge.	is glinting in his eye, too.

Siegmund alludes to Sieglinde's eyes in Scene 3 when he sees the "glimmering light" of the sword in the tree but doesn't recognize it as such:[183]

Was gleißt dort hell	What glints there so bright
im Glimmerschein?	In the glimmering light?

Siegmund wonders whether it is the glinting look of Sieglinde:[184]

Ist es der Blick	Is it the glorious
der blühenden Frau,	woman's glance,
den dort haftend	which she left behind her,
sie hinter sich ließ,	clinging there,
als aus dem Saal sie schied?	when she passed out of the hall?

Then the stage direction indicates "From this point on, the fire in the hearth gradually dies out" and he continues:[185]

Nächtiges Dunkel	Nighttime's shadows
deckte mein Aug';	shielded my eyes;
ihres Blickes Strahl	the flash of her gaze
streifte mich da:	then glanced upon me,
Wärme gewann ich und Tag.	bringing me warmth and light.

The shining of the eyes and the "Blick" was last heard in Scene 4 of *Rheingold* in a somewhat different relationship, when Fasolt speaks of Freia's "Blick":[186]

Weh! noch blitzt	Alas! Her glance
ihr Blick zu mir her;	still gleams on me here;
des Auges Stern	her starry eye
strahlt mich noch an:	still shines upon me:
durch eine Spalte	I cannot but see it
muß ich's erspäh'n! —	through the crack! —
Seh' ich dieß wonnige Auge,	While I still see this lovely eye,
von dem Weibe lass' ich nicht ab.	I'll not give up the woman.

  183. *WagRS* 131.
  184. *WagRS* 131.
  185. *WagRS* 131–32.
  186. *WagRS* 110.

There are striking cases in both literature and real life of siblings or even twins falling in love with each other.[187] "Genetic Sexual Attraction" is a recognized phenomenon and can occur when family members have been separated at an early age and later reunited.[188] Although we are inhabiting a mythical world in *Walküre* Act I, considering such questions is perhaps not so inappropriate given that the composer is constantly asking questions about embodied life, as was Feuerbach.[189]

Wotan as Witness

As the drama of *Walküre* Act I unfolds, Wotan is watching. According to my argument in chapter 3 he would be watching with his missing eye. Further, although he does not appear on the stage, his presence is felt. In fact, in the 1852 prose sketch Wotan (Wodan) enters the stage after Hunding's outburst, which begins "I know an unruly race" ("Ein wildes geschlecht ward mir bekannt").[190] Wodan thrusts his sword into the ash tree, Hunding unsuccessfully tries to take it out, but Siegmund manages to do so. Then Wodan unnoticed disappears ("Wodan ist unbemerkt verschwunden").[191] Removing Wotan from the stage in the final version does not mean he is not present; it simply means he is present in a different sort of way. He not only observes through his missing eye but according to Fricka he guided him to where he may find the sword that Wotan fashioned for him.[192]

The first possible reference to Wotan in *Walküre* Act I is when Siegmund tells Sieglinde:[193]

Einen Unseligen labtest du:—	You've tended an ill-fated man:—
Unheil wende	May Wotan avert
der Wunsch von dir!	ill-fortune from you!

---

187. E.g., Daniel Defoe, *Moll Flanders*, where Moll unwittingly marries her half-brother.

188. One theory is that by being separated the so-called "Westermarck Effect" has not been experienced. Named after the Finnish anthropologist Edvard Westermarck (1862–1939), this hypothesis was put forward in his 1891 *The History of Marriage* and concerns how those living in close proximity within a "family" (however that may be interpreted) become desensitized to any later sexual attraction. Although the view is considered antiquated in some quarters, scientific papers are still appearing on the subject.

189. See Feuerbach, *Essence*, 268–69; *LFW* 5:316: "The species is not an abstraction; it exists in feeling, in the moral sentiment, in the energy of love. It is the species which infuses love into me. A loving heart is the heart of the species throbbing in the individual. Thus Christ, as the consciousness of love, is the consciousness of the species. We are all one in Christ. Christ is the consciousness of our identity. He therefore who loves man for the sake of man, who rises to the love of the species, to universal love, adequate to the nature of the species, he is a Christian, is Christ himself."

190. *TBRN1* 430; Strobel, *Skizzen*, 234. Cf. "Ich weiß ein wildes Geschlecht" (*WagRS* 130).

191. *TBRN1* 431; Strobel, *Skizzen*, 235.

192. *WagRS* 145.

193. *WagRS* 124.

"Wunsch" is here translated as "Wotan" on the basis of his names in Old Norse ("Oski") and Middle High German ("Wunsch").[194] Wotan is, of course, referred to in what follows: Siegmund tells of his adventures with "Wolfe," his father;[195] Siegmund sings of the sword his father promised him, which he would find in greatest need;[196] Sieglinde sings of the "stranger" ("Fremder") who entered at the wedding feast and lodged the sword in the ash tree;[197] and she reveals that they must both be Volsungs, children of "Wälse."[198] The key to Siegmund being a son of "Wälse" is in his "smouldering glance":[199]

Deines Auges Gluth	Your eye's smouldering glance
erglänzte mir schon:—	glinted upon me ere now:—
so blickte der Greis	so the greybeard looked
grüßend auf mich,	as he greeted me once
als der Traurigen Trost er gab.	and brought comfort to me on my sadness.
An dem Blick	By his glance
erkannt' ihn sein Kind—	His child knew who he was—

Many will share Wotan's reaction to the love between the Volsung twins and, as we shall see in the next chapter, he effectively becomes Wagner's mouthpiece. Also one could say that just as Wagner was the one to bring the twins together in love, so Wotan was doing the same.

An inspiration for this Act was Mathilde Wesendonck. She was Sieglinde to Wagner's Siegmund. There are in fact seventeen coded messages to her in the composition sketch of Act I. For example, when Siegmund and Sieglinde "gaze raptly into each other's eyes with the utmost emotion" he adds "L.d.m.M??": "Liebst du mich, Mathilde??" ("Do you love me, Mathilde??") And when Siegmund sings to Sieglinde "Die Sonne lacht mir nun neu" ("But sunlight laughs on me now") he notes "I.l.d.gr.": "Ich liebe dich grenzenlos" ("I love you beyond measure").[200] In addition to what has been described as this "affair" (although I suspect it was never "consummated") there were also the "Hegelian Left" influences upon Wagner, which attacked bourgeoise middle-class values,[201] and this was precisely what Wotan as Wagner's mouthpiece was doing.

---

194. *WagRS* 365 n. 38; Huber, *Ring*, 177. Hence "Wunschmädchen" are daughters of Wotan.
195. *WagRS* 127–28.
196. *WagRS* 131.
197. *WagRS* 133.
198. *WagRS* 138.
199. *WagRS* 137.
200. Newman, *Life*, 2:485.
201. Deathridge, *Good and Evil*, 57–58.

Fricka as Witness

Fricka learns, through Hunding's prayer to her for vengeance, of the doings in his household.[202] Not only has adultery been committed but also incest:[203]

Mir schaudert das Herz,	My heart is quaking,
es schwindelt mein Hirn:	my brain is reeling:
bräutlich umfing	as bride a sister
die Schwester den Bruder!	embraced her brother!

Fricka's moral outrage may even be intensified by the fact that it was not just a man from outside breaking up a marriage but also that the wife was being positively unfaithful. It can certainly be said that "Siegmund's passion reaches its white heat in response to hers; she leads the way, opening the doors to it, and then releasing the floodgates for it."[204] Further, the reading given above explicitly says Sieglinde takes the initiative. The reading "den Bruder," making Siegmund the object, is found in the scores of Schott[205] and Peters. However, the *Collected Writings and Poems*[206] and the Breitkopf & Härtel scores read "der Bruder," thus making Siegmund the subject. Unfortunately the fair copy is not available,[207] although we have the *Partiturerschrift*.[208] The "rejected" version of the scene also has Siegmund as the subject. On balance, I prefer the reading that makes Sieglinde the subject.[209] Note Siegmund unconsciously relates "love" ("die Liebe") to Sieglinde, who lures him as "Spring" ("der Lenz") when he declares tenderly "Love has lured Spring here" ("die Liebe locket den Lenz") and Sieglinde explicitly identifies Siegmund as the "Spring" when she responds "You are the Spring / for which I longed" ("Du bist der Lenz, / nach dem ich verlangte").[210] Further, one could say such an interpretation of the woman being the steering force coheres with Wagner's view of women in the early 1850s.[211]

---

202. *WagRS* 141.
203. *WagRS* 142.
204. Kitcher and Schacht, *Ending*, 142.
205. *SW* 11.2:39 (bars 227–28).
206. *GSD* 6:27 (see also *JA* 3:98).
207. The assumption is that it was destroyed in the conflagration in Hitler's bunker (together with the fair copy of *Das Rheingold* and the autograph scores of *Die Feen*, *Das Liebesverbot* and *Rienzi*). As Darcy, "Autograph Manuscripts," 221, points out: "Although rumours of their survival continue to circulate, the whole incident must be judged as Hitler's final contribution to the cause of Wagner scholarship."
208. *WWV* 367.
209. Weight has to be given to *SW* 11.2:39.
210. *WagRS* 135.
211. See *WagRS* 366 n. 52, who point to Wagner's letter to Röckel of 24 August 1851: "we shall not become what we can and must be until such time as—*womankind* has been *wakened*" (*SL* 228; *SB* 4:95). The meaning of these words, however, are by no means clear (see below).

LOVE

Fricka's moral outrage was shared by the agnostic Schopenhauer, to whom Wagner sent a copy of his *Ring* libretto. It is perhaps significant though that he was so outraged on the basis of the libretto alone. Had he experienced the work in the theatre (or even heard some of the music) he may have felt otherwise. But not so Max Kalbeck, who was outraged despite having seen it performed in Bayreuth in 1876.[212] He argues that Act I may be beautiful and moving but "its ethical anarchy is outrageous and provocative, a slap in the face for all religious feeling."[213] Kalbeck writes that although incest occurs elsewhere in literature it does so in an entirely different way. Oedipus sleeps with his mother but is entirely unaware of this. In contrast "Wotan's children pursue their culpable passion knowingly and go to their destruction with 'seeing eyes.'"[214] So as Siegmund declares in the final moments of Act I: "Bride and sister / you are to your brother—/ so let the blood of the Wälsungs blossom!"[215] And in addition to entering this relationship with open eyes one can add that Wagner manages to get the listener on the side of the Volsung twins, this demonstrating what a skilled (and some would say manipulative) dramatist he was.

Brünnhilde as Witness

Of the three witnesses I am discussing, Brünnhilde is the crucial one. In fact, the second opera of the *Ring* is called "The Valkyrie" simply because Brünnhilde is the focus, and the great turning point in the opera is when she witnesses the love of Siegmund for Sieglinde, which engenders the fundamental change in her. Never before has she witnessed such love between two human beings. So it is not Siegmund as hero who impresses her, but rather Siegmund as lover, who is prepared to sacrifice everything, even immortality, for his beloved.[216] At first she cannot believe the intensity of his love for Sieglinde, which even entails rejecting the everlasting bliss ("ewige Wonne") of Valhalla:[217]

---

212. Kalbeck became Brahms' official biographer and it is worth mentioning that he "provided his readers with a number of fantasies masquerading as facts" (Walker, *Hans von Bülow*, 308 n. 35). Walker points to Kalbeck's description of von Bülow's extreme reaction as he received news of Wagner's death and stories about Brahms playing the piano in saloons and brothels to make ends meet (on which point see Hofmann, "Hamburg musician," 13–14).

213. Deathridge, *Good and Evil*, 57, quoting Großmann-Vendrey, *Bayreuth in der deutschen Presse I*, 193 (who in turn quotes Kalbeck, "Erste Aufführung").

214. Deathridge, *Good and Evil*, 57, quoting Großmann-Vendrey, *Bayreuth in der deutschen Presse I*, 194.

215. *WagRS* 139.

216. Kitcher and Schacht, *Ending*, 144.

217. *WagRS* 162.

Alles wär' dir	Is she all to you,
das arme Weib,	this pitiful woman
das müd' und harmvoll	who, tired and sorrowful,
matt auf dem Schooße dir hängt?	lies there, faint, in your lap?
Nichts sonst hieltest du hehr?	Is there nothing else you hold dear?

Siegmund "gazing up at her, bitterly," responds: "Young and fair / though you shimmer before me: / cold and hard / my heart now knows you to be!"[218] Kitcher and Schacht remark that Brünnhilde is "pierced by his charge that she (whose emotions have resonated in anguish to her father's pain) is cold and hard."[219] "The truth and ultimacy of their love [. . .] is precisely what becomes so profoundly authoritative in Brünnhilde's eyes,"[220] and she sees an authority that transcends that of her father.

I imagine that all who experience *Walküre* have at some point experienced or witnessed the passionate love between two human beings that can lead them to extraordinary sacrificial acts. Nevertheless, *Walküre* presents in its extreme way what erotic sacrificial love can entail; and it can be the most inspiring form of love to witness. In the love of Siegmund for Sieglinde we may appear to be distanced from the sexual restraint enjoined by the New Testament. However, the letter to the Ephesians does tell of the witness that husband and wife can play, the husband pointing to Christ's willingness to give himself up for his church: "Husbands, love your wives, just as Christ loved the church and gave himself up for her" (Eph 5:25).

Incest and Sexual Morality

We have already seen how the Oedipus myth, discussed in *Opera and Drama* Part II, has wide ranging implications for questions of state, love, ethics, art, and mythology itself. Apart from ethics, many experiencing the *Ring* will be oblivious to these issues and understandably so: they are interested in the drama and not reading Wagner's theories in a long essay that is not always easy to read. I will discuss law and sexual ethics in the next chapter but it may be worth making some essential points here about the ethics.

As far as incest in the *Ring* is concerned, "we are not dealing here with real family relationships, but with fantasised, fantastical one."[221] Incest is an important theme in mythology: we have the sibling marriages of Zeus and Hera (son and daughter of Chronus and Rhea; they were not twins) and of Isis and Osiris (who were twins). Njord had sex with his sister,[222] giving birth to the twins Freyr and Freyja, whom

---

218. *WagRS* 163.
219. Kitcher and Schacht, *Ending*, 146.
220. Kitcher and Schacht, *Ending*, 146.
221. N. Wagner, *Wagners*, 58.
222. *Lokasenna* 36 (Orchard, *Elder Edda*, 90). See also *Ynglinga Saga* 4: "While Njorth lived with the

Loki accused of incest.[223] Further, incest is be found in Wagner's main sources. The *Völsunga Saga* tells of the twins Sigmund and Signy[224] who slept with each other. But the significant difference is that here Sigmund was not aware he was sleeping with his sister since she had changed shape with the sorceress.[225] Further, Signy's motive for sleeping with him is that she wanted to have a strong son to avenge the killing of her father; and through this liason she did in fact have a son, Sinfjotli, who was "tall, strong and handsome."[226] This motif of incest is missing in both the *Elder Edda* and the *Prose Edda*.

Cooke offers an excellent comparison of the *Völsunga Saga* and *Walküre* Act I and is probably correct to argue that of all the acts of the tetralogy adapting "this discursive and bloodthirsty narrative" proved to be the most difficult.[227] Among other things he makes the point that the Saga has four generations between Odin and Sigmund[228] which Wagner reduces to one, Siggeir[229] is replaced by Hunding,[230] and Sieglinde, Signy's equivalent, has no murdered father for which she needs to avenge.

Wagner never described Oedipus' relationship with his mother as "unnatural" or as a "violation of human nature."[231] Although this relationship "fills us with horror and loathing" (since it offends our "*customary* (*gewohnten*) relations with our mother")[232] Oedipus did not "offend against this Human Nature" since "from their union had sprung an enrichment of human Society, in the persons of two lusty sons and two noble daughters."[233] So Wagner's view is that incest is not a problem for "nature"; it is only a problem for "culture" or "civilization."[234]

Vanir he had his sister as wife, because that was the custom among them. [. . .] But among the Æsir it was forbidden to marry so near a kin" (Hollander, *Heimskringla*, 8; cf. Finlay/Faulkes, *Heimskringla I*, 8).

223. *Lokasenna* 32 (Orchard, *Elder Edda*, 89).

224. *Völsunga Saga* 2 (Finch, *Volsungs*, 3–4).

225. *Völsunga Saga* 7 (Finch, *Volsungs*, 9): "[Signy] joined [Sigmund] in the shelter and they sat down to a meal. He often glanced at her and she appeared to be a good-looking and attractive woman. And when they were satisfied, he told her that he wanted them to sleep together that night. She made no objection and for three nights in succession he laid her next to him." Note that Sigmund here takes the initiative (cf. Sieglinde in *Walküre*).

226. *Völsunga Saga* 7 (Finch, *Volsungs*, 10). Cf. Wagner's observation that Jocasta and Oedipus produced "two lusty sons and two noble daughters" (*PW* 2:182; *GSD* 4:56). See the discussion below.

227. Cooke, *End*, 290, points out that "his three successive prose-sketches for [Act I] were from the start misconceived in one respect, and the finished text was (luckily) different from all of them." For the sketches see *TBRN1* 423–43, and volume 1, chapter 2.

228. Cooke, *End*, 282. So we have Odin—Sigi—Rerir—Volsung—Sigmund (Finch, *Volsungs*, 1–3).

229. Cooke, *End*, 285, argues that Siggeir "was impossible for Wagner, since it was old Norse," and even if Germanized, would have been totally inappropriate since the opening syllable "Sieg" would be too near to "Siegmund" and "Siegfried."

230. We know of him from the *Elder Edda* (the two songs of Helgi, the slayer of Hunding).

231. Borchmeyer, *Theatre*, 291.

232. *PW* 2:182 (modified); *GSD* 4:56 (Wagner's emphasis).

233. *PW* 2:182; *GSD* 4:56.

234. Cf. *CD* 14 March 1873, discussed below.

I now move to discussing a scene that appears to lack the eroticism of *Walküre* Act I: Siegfried's awakening of Brunnhilde and their falling in love. I have to confess that when I first listened to this scene in my student days I was somewhat dumbfounded to know what to make of it. But it contains many clues as to how Wagner understood love and its relationship to the state (for which he prepared in Part II of *Opera and Drama*) and his views on gender (for which he prepared in Part III of *Opera and Drama*). After discussing aspects of this scene I will then move to a more systematic discussion of gender, androgyny, and sexuality.

Siegfried Act III Scene Three

Although the Woodbird has told Siegfried he will find a woman on the rock, Siegfried sees what he assumes is a man. The stage direction tells us that Brünnhilde "lies asleep in full shining armour, her helmet on her head, her long shield covering her."[235] Siegfried emphasizes the "glittering steel" that "bedazzles" his gaze, his light as sungod being reflected in her armor. But there is a hint already that the one beneath the shining armor is a woman with the reference to the "celestial lake":[236]

Schimmernde Wolken	Shimmering clouds
säumen in Wellen	have fringed a shining
den hellen Himmelssee:	celestial lake with their waves:
leuchtender Sonne	the radiant sunlight's
lachendes Bild	smiling likeness
strahlt durch das Wogengewölk!	shines through a billowing bank of clouds!

The sun from Siegfried shines on and through the waves of Brünnhilde's hair described as a "bright celestial lake," the sea referring to the woman.[237] We therefore are presented with Brünnhilde's ambiguous gender, although Siegfried himself assumes it is a man. It is then only on removing the breast plate that Siegfried realizes it is a not a man. It is now that Siegfried learns fear, the stage direction telling us that "[h]e stares at the sleeping woman in a state of utter turmoil." He sings: "Burning enchantment / charms my heart; / fiery terror / transfixes my eyes: / my senses stagger and swoon!" He then calls on his mother: "To save me, whom shall I / call on to help me?— / Mother! Mother! / Remember me!"[238] He then wonders how he could bear the light of her eyes if he were to awaken her. This looks back to Wotan's farewell in *Walküre* Act III where he speaks of "That radiant pair of eyes" and "this glittering

---

235. *WagRS* 265.
236. *WagRS* 265–66.
237. Cf. Nattiez, *Androgyne*, 76–77. Nattiez, despite his extensive discussion of the link between the female and the sea, does not actually comment on the "Himmelssee."
238. *WagRS* 266.

pair of eyes / which often glistened on me in the storm" and that a day will come when "On a happier man / their stars shall shine."[239]

Siegfried asks whether he could bear the light of her eyes. "Around me everything floats / and sways and swims; / searing desire / consumes my senses: / on my quaking heart / my hand is trembling!—/ What is this, coward, that I feel?—/ Is this what it is to fear?—/ O mother! Mother! / Your mettlesome child!" Then "very tenderly" he adds "A woman lies asleep:—/ she has taught him the meaning of fear!"[240] The idea of the light of her eyes (and the earlier shining armor) points to her being a "Siegfried"; indeed it looks as though she too has become almost a sun-goddess (although if she is an "Artemis," Apollo's twin sister, she is a lunar goddess).[241] Nattiez suggests that "this fear is not only the result of his discovery of sexuality and the otherness of the female sex, it is also caused by his confrontation with the irremediable breakdown of the original unity, the realization, in short, that *half of himself* exists outside himself."[242] Siegfried then asks "How can I overcome my fear? / How can I summon up courage?—/ That I myself may awaken, / I must waken the maid!"[243]

The key idea behind his fear of the woman is that she will be portrayed as a "Wurm." Before he wakes her there are two possible anticipations of her "Wurm" character: he speaks of "her burgeoning mouth" and "fragrance of that breath,"[244] an anti-type to characteristics of the Wurm, killed in Act II. So Mime warns Siegfried of the "awesome jaws" ("schrecklicher Rachen") of the Wurm. Further:[245]

Giftig gießt sich	Poisonous spittle
ein Geifer ihm aus:	spews from his lips:
wen mit des Speichels	whoever gets spattered
Schweiß er bespei't,	by gobbets of spit,
dem schwinden wohl Fleisch und Gebein.	your flesh and bones will waste away.

When Siegfried decides to kiss Brünnhilde he realizes that this may well bring about his own death: "So I suck life / from the sweetest of lips—/ though I should perish and die!" The stage direction then adds "He sinks, as though dying, on the sleeping woman."[246] After playing *Siegfried* Act III to Cosima on the piano, Wagner com-

---

239. *WagRS* 190–91.
240. *WagRS* 266.
241. See the discussion in chapter 4 above.
242. Nattiez, *Androgyne*, 77.
243. *WagRS* 266–67.
244. *WagRS* 267.
245. *WagRS* 235 (modified; cf. Deathridge, *Ring*, 435).
246. *WagRS* 267.

mented: "The kiss of love is the first intimation of death, the cessation of individuality, that is why a person is so terrified by it."[247]

This association of sex and death will prove to be central for our study of sexuality in the *Ring*.[248] The upper notes of the first four key chords that accompany the awakening of Brünnhilde (see Example 6.1) are precisely those of the "serpent," ("Wurm"; Example 6.2) and this will become significant later in the scene.[249]

Example 6.1: *Siegfried* Act III bars 1067–78

---

247. *CD* 15 August 1869. One wonders whether these comments are related in any way to the fact that this was the Feast of the Assumption and earlier that day Cosima showed the children Titian's Assumpta?

248. See chapter 7 below.

249. Note also that this Wurm theme is often used for the *waking* of the Wurm.

Example 6.2: *Rheingold* bars 2664–68

Her words on awakening "Hail to you, sun! / Hail to you, light!"[250] refer not simply to her seeing the sun and light for the first time in many years,[251] the stage direction indicating that she "welcomes her return to an awareness of earth and sky"; they also refer to the fact that Siegfried here appears as the "God of Light or Sun-god,"[252] i.e., Apollo.

Siegfried gives thanks for the mother who gave him birth and alludes to Wotan in that he says "I saw the eye / that smiles on me now in my bliss!"[253] Brünnhilde again points to Siegfried as sun-god: "You waker of life, / all conquering light!" and tells how she always loved him: "I nurtured you, you tender child, / before you were begotten; / even before you were born, / my shield already sheltered you: / so long have I loved you, Siegfried!"[254]

Siegfried then misunderstands her, reflecting "softly and shyly": "So my mother did not die? / Was the lovely woman merely asleep?" Brünnhilde explains that his mother will not come back; rather "Your own self am I, / if you but love me in my bliss." She then utters something that parallels what Wagner called "emotionalising of the intellect" ("Gefühlswerdung des Verstandes.")[255] She refers to Wotan's "thought" ("Gedanke") about the whole sequence of events leading up to her awakening by Siegfried, a "thought" she did not conceive but rather "felt".[256]

---

250. Note *Sigrdrífumál* 3: "Hail, Day, hail, Day's sons" (Orchard, *Elder Edda*, 169).

251. If Siegfried is here eighteen then she has been sleeping for around eighteen years and nine months.

252. *PW* 7:263; *GSD* 2:119 (*Die Wibelungen*).

253. *WagRS* 268.

254. *WagRS* 268.

255. *GSD* 4:78. *PW* 2:208. Note also his use of "Gefühlsverständniß" (*GSD* 4:82; *PW* 2:213; *GSD* 4:137; *PW* 2:274; *GSD* 4:210; *PW* 2:357). For discussion of this see volume 1, chapter 6.

256. *WagRS* 269.

Der Gedanke, den ich	The thought which I
nie nennen durfte;	could never name;
den ich nicht dachte,	the thought I did not think
sondern nur fühlte;	but only felt;
für den ich focht,	the thought for which I fought,
kämpfte und stritt;	did battle and have striven;
für den ich trotzte	for which I flouted
dem, der ihn dachte;	him who thought it;
für den ich büßte,	for which I atoned,
Strafe mich band,	incurring chastisement,
weil ich nicht ihn dachte	because, not thinking,
und nur empfand!	I only felt it!
Denn der Gedanke—	Because that thought—
dürftest du's lösen!—	could you only guess it!—
mir war es nur Liebe zu dir.	was but my love for you.

Brünnhilde appears to be referring back to *Walküre* Act II Scene 2, where Wotan *speaks* to her. She asks him; "Tell me (Sage), what ails you?"[257] "To Wotan's will you speak (spricht du) / when you tell me (sag'st du) what you will." He then tells her: "What in words (in Worten) I reveal to no one, / let it stay / unspoken (unausgesprochen) for ever: / with myself I commune / when I speak (red' ich) with you)."[258] But whereas Wotan *speaks* to her, Brünnhilde has just *sung* to Siegfried, as he explains:[259]

Wie Wunder tönt	Wondrous it sounds
was wonnig du sing'st;	what you blissfully sing;
doch dunkel dünkt mich der Sinn.	but its meaning seems obscure to me.
[. . .]	[. . .]
deiner Stimme Singen	the sound of your singing
hör' ich süß:	is sweet to hear:
doch was du singend mir sag'st,	but what you say to me singing,
staunend versteh' ich's nicht.	stunned, I cannot understand.

And a little later she *sings* again, as Siegfried observes:[260]

---

257. *WagRS* 148.
258. *WagRS* 149.
259. *WagRS* 269.
260. *WagRS* 271. Note also the earlier "Dichtung" of 3–24 June 1851 (Strobel, *Skizzen*, 185; *TBRN1* 321): "O rede, singe! / töne in worten! / Nie vernahm mein ohr / solch edlen schall. / töne mir wunder, / singe mir wonnen, / sag' mir, du hehre, / was ich noch nie gehört!"

Sang'st du mir nicht,	Did you not sing
dein Wissen sei	that your knowledge stemmed
das Leuchten der Liebe zu mir?	from the shining light of your love for me?

To refer to someone singing in the *Ring* is rare, although it is frequent in *Meistersinger*. The other key character to "sing" is the Woodbird. It may be significant that when Siegfried first hears the bird singing, he refers to "it" ("das Vöglein")[261] speaking ("He must be telling me something"; "Gewiß sagt' es mir 'was"). Then to confuse matters, Siegfried *sings*: "I'll sing his language in that way / and no doubt grasp what he's saying" ("sing' ich so seine Sprache, / versteh' ich wohl auch was er spricht"). But then Siegfried moves over to chattering ("I'll chatter away then!"; "so schwatz' ich denn los!").[262] Once he has tasted the dragon's blood he refers to the communication of the Woodbird mostly as singing: "what is it singing to me?" ("was singt es mir?");[263] "I'd be glad to hear your song"; "now sing, I'll list your song";[264] "O welcome song!"; "you lovely songster."[265] This switch over to the Woodbird *singing* rather than *speaking* correlates with the further emergence of her feminine characteristics, i.e., a soprano!

There is therefore a parallel between the feminine Woodbird singing and the feminine Brünnhilde singing as a means of communicating key insights to Siegfried. And although this may confuse the parallelism, we also find that Siegfried comes to understanding after he takes Fafner's blood into his mouth and when he takes Brünnhilde's "juices" into his mouth. Brünnhilde therefore is both a Woodbird and a Fafner!

Regarding the former (Woodbird), we can say that Brünnhilde embodies music. As Nattiez argues, "[e]verything about Brünnhilde as a character corresponds with the features that Wagner ascribes to music, which [. . .] is described as feeling impregnated by understanding."[266] There are numerous instances where Wagner draws this comparison between woman and music. In his letter to Liszt of 25 November 1850 he writes: "My essay on the nature of opera, the final fruits of my deliberations, has assumed greater dimensions than I had first supposed: but if I wish to demonstrate that music (as a woman) must necessarily be impregnated by a poet (as a man), then I must ensure that this glorious woman is not abandoned to the first passing libertine, but that she is made pregnant only by the man who yearns for womankind with true, irresistible love."[267] Compare *Opera and Drama* 1.3: "unshamed the bloom lays bare its dainty stamens, and offers them, with horrible indifference, to the prying nose

---

261. *WagRS* 238: "Du holdes Vög'lein!"
262. *WagRS* 239. He moves over to the masculine, presumably because it is "*der* Waldvogel."
263. *WagRS* 243.
264. *WagRS* 252.
265. *WagRS* 253.
266. Nattiez, *Androgyne*, 80.
267. *SL* 220–21; *SB* 3:467.

of every ribald rake."²⁶⁸ The stress in these two texts is on the *male* poet ("der Dichter") and the *female* music ("die Musik"). The same sort of polarity is found also in *Opera and Drama* 3.3, but matters are slightly more complex for we have also the "musician" ("der Musiker," who is masculine) and the "word-verse" ("Wortvers," also masculine).²⁶⁹ He writes about a melody that

> rose from the immeasurable depths of *Beethoven's* music, in the "Ninth Symphony" to greet the shining light of day. The appearance of this melody on the surface of the Harmonic sea was made possible [. . .] solely by the urgence of the Musician to look upon the Poet eye to eye [. . .]. This melody was the love-greeting of the woman to the man, and the open-armed "Eternal Womanly" (ewig Weibliche) here shewed itself more loveable than the egoistic Man-ly (egoistische Männliche). [. . .] Only the poet whose Aim we have here expounded, will feel driven so irresistibly to a heart-alliance with the "eternal womanly" (mit dem "ewig Weiblichen") of Tone-art, that in these nuptials he shall celebrate alike his own redemption.²⁷⁰

The key things to draw out are that the melody comes about through the *musician* ("der Musiker") looking upon the *poet* ("der Dichter") eye to eye (i.e., man to man). Secondly, he writes about a contrast between music or melody as the "Eternal Womanly" (ewig Weibliche) and the poet as the "egoistic Man-ly" (egoistische Männliche).

That the egoistically Manly is the poet rather than the "Word-verse" is suggested by the next paragraph:

> Through the redeeming love-kiss of that Melody the poet is now inducted into the deep, unending mysteries of Woman's nature: he sees with other eyes, and feels with other senses. To him the bottomless sea of Harmony, from which that beatific vision rose to meet him, is no longer an object of dread, of fear, of terror, such as earlier it seemed in his imaginings of the strange and unknown element; now, not only can he float upon the surface of this ocean, but—gifted with new senses—he dives into its lowest depth. From out the lonely, fearsome reaches of her mother-home the woman had been self-driven (Aus seinem einsamen, furchtbar weiten Mutterhaufe hatte es das Weib hinausgetrieben), to wait the nearing of the beloved; now, with his bride, he sinks him down, and learns the hidden wonders of the deep.²⁷¹

---

268. *PW* 2:52; *GSD* 3:261; "schamlos enthüllt sie ihre edlen Zeugungsglieder und bietet sie mit grauenvoller Gleichgültigkeit der riechenden Nase jedes gaunerischen Wollüstlings dar." Compare Brunnhilde's complaint to Wotan: "If fettering sleep / is to bind me fast, / as easy prey / to the basest of cowards, / this one thing alone you must grant me / that holy fear entreats of you" (*WagRS* 189).

269. *PW* 2:285; *GSD* 4:146. He also writes of "Word-speech" ("Wortsprache"), grammatically feminine, but he relates this to "Melodie."

270. *PW* 2:285; *GSD* 4:146.

271. *PW* 2:285–86; *GSD* 4:146–47.

Ellis points to the clear parallels to *Siegfried* Act III where the hero overcomes his fear.[272] The text also highlights the role of the "mother-home"[273] and the way the woman drags down the male under the surface of the waters. Wagner continues that the poet's "insight pierces, clear and tranquil, sheer to the ocean's primal fount; whence he sends the wave-shafts mounting to the surface, to run in ripples at the sun-rays, to softly plash beneath the soughing west-wind, or manlike rear their crests against the north-wind's storm."[274]

But at the same time Brünnhilde, although portrayed as the feminine music and appears vulnerable on awaking, also demonstrates a certain strength. Nattiez[275] appeals to *Artwork of the Future*: "And exactly in degree as woman, in perfected womanhood, through love to man and sinking of herself within his being, has developed the manly element of that womanhood and brought it to a thorough balance with the purely womanly, and thus in measure as she is no longer merely man's *beloved* but his *friend*—can man find fullest satisfaction in the love of woman."[276] The highly significant thing about this text is that it is preceded and followed by a discussion of Spartan love between men, to which I turn below.

Nattiez notes that "Brünnhilde has inherited Wotan's masculinity on several counts."[277] In *Walküre* Act II she tells her father that she is his will and he responds by saying that he communes with himself when he speaks with her.[278] Her "male" element is also revealed in her passion for Siegfried a little later in the scene:[279]

---

272. PW 2:286 n.

273. This could be a possible reference to Erda.

274. PW 2:286; GSD 4:147: "Sein verständiger Sinn durchdringt Alles klar und besonnen bis auf den Urquell, von dem aus er die Wogensäulen ordnet, die zum Sonnenlichte emporsteigen sollen, um an seinem Scheine in wonnigen Wellen dahinzuwallen, nach dem Säuseln des Westes sanft zu plätschern, oder nach den Stürmen des Nordes sich männlich zu bäumen." Ellis (PW 2:286 n.) points to the intentional Stabreim in the German.

275. Nattiez, *Androgyne*, 81.

276. PW 1:167; GSD 3:135.

277. Nattiez, *Androgyne*, 81.

278. One could also add that her "riding" theme represents "[t]he Valkyries as the masculine element in women" (Donington, *Symbols*, 293).

279. WagRS 274.

Wie mein Blick dich verzehrt,	As my gaze consumes you,
erblindest du nicht?	are you not blinded:
Wie mein Arm dich preßt,	As my arm holds you tight,
entbrenn'st du mir nicht?	don't you burn for me?
Wie in Strömen mein Blut	As my blood streams
entgegen dir stürmt,	in torrents towards you,
das wilde Feuer,	do you not feel
fühlst du es nicht?	its furious fire?
Fürchtest du, Siegfried,	Do you not fear, Siegfried,
fürchest du nicht	do you not fear
das wild wüthende Weib?	the wildly raging woman?

At precisely those points I have emphasized the "Wurm" motif is played on 'cellos and basses (see Example 6.3).

Example 6.3: *Siegfried* Act III bars 1668–77

In fact, in this section we have all the bodily correspondences between the Wurm and Brünnhilde enunciated (the eyes, the limbs, the blood, and the fire) summed up in the fear of "the wildly raging woman." The reference to the fire of her blood is highly significant since when Siegfried's hand comes into contact with the serpent's blood "Its blood is burning like fire."[280] Note Fafner's breast is the source of blood and

---

280. *WagRS* 242.

corresponds to Brünnhilde fiery blood from her breast. Then when she asks whether he fears she sings her Valkyrie cry and Siegfried "in joyful terror" sings of the blood in their veins that ignites and "our flashing glances" that "consume one another."[281] Note that in Act II Mime emphasizes the terror not only of the sight of the Wurm but also of the sound and it is both the sight and sound of Brünnhilde that has terrorized Siegfried. Mime warns Siegfried:[282]

Wart' es nur ab!	Just wait awhile!
Was ich dir sage,	For all that I say
dünke dich tauber Schall:	may seem to you empty sound:
ihn selber mußt du	you have to see
hören und seh'n,	and hear him himself,
die Sinne vergeh'n dir dann schon!	then your senses will surely fail you!

In the final duet Brünnhilde issues her fourfold "laughing," linking it to love, blindness, perishing, and doom:[283]

Lachend muß ich dich lieben;	Laughing I must love you;
lachend will ich erblinden;	laughing I must grow blind;
lachend lass' uns verderben—	laughing let us perish—
lachend zu Grunde geh'n!	laughing go to our doom!

Then apart from the names and use of pronouns and a slightly different line, both Brünnhilde and Siegfried end with the same words:[284]

Mir strahlt zur Stunde/Prangend strahlt	Siegfried's/Brünnhilde's star
Siegfried's Stern;/mir Brünnhilde's Stern!	now shines upon me;
er/Sie ist mir ewig,	He's/she's mine forever,
ist mir immer,	always mine,
Erb' und Eigen,	my heritage and own,
ein' und all':	my one and all:
leuchtende Liebe,	light-bringing love
lachender Tod!	and laughing death!

This love duet ending Act III is virtually unparalleled in Opera. The only competitor in my view is the love duet of *Tristan* Act II. Both relate love to death but in a quite

---

281. *WagRS* 275.
282. *WagRS* 236. See the discussion below on the "wondrous sounds."
283. *WagRS* 275. Ellis in *PW* 1:133 n comments on the Stabreim.
284. *WagRS* 276.

different way.²⁸⁵ Nattiez sums up the end of *Siegfried* is a suitably arresting manner: "the kiss that presages death enables the couple to break down the egoism of the I in favor of that supreme unity through which one can taste immortality, a prelude to a return to the state of nature, the downfall of the gods, and the advent of a free society prepared for by Siegfried, that modern incarnation of Christ."²⁸⁶ I return to the question of "immortality" of Brunnhilde in chapter 8 below.

Androgyny and Overcoming Individuation

I have argued that it is Brünnhilde who is the androgynous character in *Siegfried* Act III Scene 3; in fact, this is seen in her first appearance in *Walküre* Act II Scene 1. I will further develop this idea in the discussion of redemption in chapter 11 below: the tragedy of *Götterdämmerung* is that Siegfried and Brünnhilde become separated as a result of the "potion in the chest,"²⁸⁷ but they do come together at the end in that in the final scene when Brünnhilde recovers her divinity, she can be understood to incorporate Siegfried in an androgynous unity.²⁸⁸ Her sacrifice is then the complete sacrifice of the complete human being, both male and female: she takes on again her Valkyrie (male) status and her death parallels that of the death of the androgynous Christ. Hence, it is the female who is androgynous, as in *Wieland der Schmied*, a work Wagner was sketching in 1849–50.²⁸⁹ In Act II Scene 3 Neiding tells his daughter Bathilde: "some mighty King I'd wish to mate with thee as bridegroom!" She responds: "Let me become that mighty man: I need alone a woman for a mate (ich brauche nur ein Weib zum Manne)." Neiding is shocked: "Thou braggart, dauntless child! Wilt thou re-bear thyself as Man?"²⁹⁰

I cannot find anything in the libretto to suggest that Siegfried is androgynous; in fact, it is difficult to find any ideas that the male can be so in any of Wagner's writings. In a letter to Röckel (24 August 1851) Wagner tells Röckel that he has written the poem of *Der junge Siegfried* and, explaining Act III Scene 3, writes: "Siegfried passes through the fire and awakens Brünnhilde—womankind (das *Weib*)—in the most blissful of love's embraces." He then later adds: "we shall not become what we can and must

---

285. Cf. Nattiez, *Androgyne*, 126: "It would be wrong [. . .] to confuse the Liebestod announced and hoped for at the end of *Siegfried* with the Schopenhauerian *Liebestod* that forms the climax of *Tristan und Isolde*." Whilst agreeing with the differences I add that the ending of *Tristan* is Schopenhauerian only to a limited degree.

286. Nattiez, *Androgyne*, 126.

287. *WagRS* 291.

288. Cf. his comments in *Artwork of the Future* where he speaks of "a woman who loves a man from the fullness of her femininity and by losing herself in him develops the masculine element within this femininity" (Warner, *Artwork*, 64).

289. See volume 1, chapter 2. Wieland is discussed by Natttiez, *Androgyne*, 43–52.

290. *PW* 1:234; *GSD* 3:193–94.

be until such time as—womankind (das *Weib*) has been wakened."[291] This had been a topic of their "animated conversations."[292] However, it is by no means clear that Wagner is saying womankind is awakened *within* man. He may be referring to ideas, as in Goethe's "das ewig Weibliche," that woman is the redeeming figure.

I find that although I am in many respects in sympathy and even agreement with Nattiez' approach to the *Ring* and androgyny, I fail to see how this applies to Siegfried, even though I find many aspects of his interpretation of Siegfried convincing. I outline briefly how I understand his union with Brünnhilde, in many respects following Nattiez, but departing from him regarding his crucial point on Siegfried's androgyny. So Brünnhilde is the "female incarnation of Wotan's deepest desires"[293] and as Siegfried's symbolic mother she saves Sieglinde so he can be born. Siegfried is the sun, "the antithesis of chaos, the night, and ignorance."[294] The fear he sought in vain is fear of his other half, "a fear that he must feel in order to rediscover the joyful sensation of quintessential unity and to escape the drama of individuation."[295] In one and the same person he discovers woman who invented him and who embodies the other half of humanity. So far I can follow Nattiez argument; but I find the following unwarranted: "Siegfried seeks to rediscover the original sense of androgynous unity with her, inasmuch as she is the image of the woman who gave him birth."[296] But it *is* the case that Siegfried discovers on kissing her that unity is only attainable through death. So he must renounce egotistic individuality (Feuerbach) in favor of the other[297] and hence the couple end by rejoicing in laughing death.[298]

I think some confusion has arisen regarding androgyny, because the idea of the union of lovers and their being interchangeable has been interpreted by Nattiez as pointing to androgyny. But this does not have to be the case. When the lovers next appear in *Götterdämmerung*, after they have consummated their love, we find this interpenetration. Siegfried tells Brünnhilde: "Through your virtue alone / shall I undertake adventures? [. . .] Upon your stallion's back, / within the shelter of your shield, / no more do I think of myself as Siegfried, / I am Brünnhilde's arm alone!"[299] Brünnhilde even suggests "So you yourself would be Siegfried and Brünnhild'?" to

---

291. *SL* 228; *SB* 4:95.

292. *SL* 228; *SB* 4:95.

293. Nattiez, *Androgyne*, 280.

294. Nattiez, *Androgyne*, 280.

295. Nattiez, *Androgyne*, 280.

296. Nattiez, *Androgyne*, 280.

297. Nattiez, *Androgyne*, 280–81.

298. I have some sympathy with the view of Nattiez, *Androgyne*, 280, that we do not need psychoanalysis to analyze this scene; we have this tautegorical approach. But nevertheless Wagner does, I believe, anticipate some of the insights of psychoanalysis.

299. *WagRS* 286–87.

which Siegfried answers "Wherever I am, both will be safe," to which she replies, "So my mountain hall is deserted?" He replies: "United, it holds us both."[300]

The idea of the union of lovers is also found in *Tristan und Isolde*. But the question again is whether this is a matter of "androgyny." Is it not simply that there is an interpenetration of their persons and their gender is unaltered? One can compare the Christological debate on the union of the human and divine natures where the two natures although *fused* are not *confused*.[301] But unlike the Christological debate there is no "communication of attributes" or, as one could put it, "communication of genders." So in sexual union one loses individuality, which *could* be understood as the man losing his maleness and woman her femaleness. But in Wagner's understanding it appears that gender is retained. In sexual union a death also takes place, the man giving up his egoism and the woman offering her eternal womanly characteristics.

Perhaps a more convincing argument for the "communication of genders" is to consider again the poet and music. Wagner sees music "as a direct, instinctive expression of the self."[302] Further, he sees music as female and poet as male. "*Music is a woman*. The nature of Woman is *love*: but this love is a *receiving*, and in receival an unreservedly *surrendering*, love" ("*Die Musik ist ein Weib. Die Natur des Weibes ist die Liebe: aber diese Liebe ist die empfangende und in der Empfängniß rückhaltlos sich hingebende.*")[303] Whereas woman is the "bearing woman" ("die Gebärerin") the poet is the "begetter" ("der Erzeuger").[304] Drama comes about through this marriage. But through this marriage there is not just the "offspring," the drama; for through this sexual union there comes about a "communication of attributes" as in Christology, reflected in that Wagner "affirms the musicality of language (especially in his theories of the origin of language) and the linguistic nature of music (in the leitmotif)."[305] Hence, in love there is a mutual interpenetration of subjects, a "perichoresis."

What were the sources for such thinking on androgyny that could have influenced Wagner? The first obvious work to consider is Plato's *Symposion*, which Wagner first read in 1847[306] and was to become "indispensable."[307] Plato's works in six volumes, translated by Schleiermacher, were clearly among his prize possessions in his Dresden library.[308] I suggest two ways in which Plato's *Symposion* could have influenced Wagner

---

300. *WagRS* 287.

301. See the "Symbol of Chalcedon" (451) in Schaff, *Creeds of Christendom*, 2:62: Christ is "to be acknowledged in two natures inconfusedly, unchangeably, indivisibly, inseparably," and "the distinction of natures being by no means taken away by the union."

302. Corse, *Consciousness*, 14.

303. *PW* 2:111; *GSD* 3:316.

304. *PW* 2:111; *GSD* 3:316.

305. Corse, *Consciousness*, 14; cf. Mann, "Sorrows, 108.

306. *My Life* 343; *Mein Leben* 1:356. Nattiez, *Androgyne*, 119, dates this reading between 18 June and 2 August.

307. *CD* 4 June 1871.

308. *Symposion* was in volume 2.2, 384–468, preceded by Schleiermacher's introduction, 369–83.

on androgyny. The first relates to the language and music. Part of Wagner's agenda was to bring together two things that had in the past been together but had been separated. Here we have two feminine nouns, "Sprache" and "Musik." Correspondingly, we have two male figures bringing these into being, the "poet" ("der Dichter") and the "musician" ("der Musiker"). Again Wagner was concerned to bring them back together in one person. It is perhaps significant that Wagner's first reading of Plato's *Symposion* was in 1847, and the first we know of Wagner's sexualization of musical ideas is his "Toast," given after a concert to mark the tercentenary of the "Royal Kapelle at Dresden" on 22 September 1848.[309] Then thirteen days later he completed the *Nibelungen-Mythus* (4 October) and then followed *Siegfried's Tod*. Androgyny is not clear in this *Ring* of 1848 but it was to become clear as he worked on *Der junge Siegfried* in 1851.

In addition to Plato, there was also a tradition of androgynous thinking in the late eighteenth century and early nineteenth centuries among scientists and Romantic thinkers. We have here tradition that combined science (especially electricity and magnetism) with religious thinking whereby opposites could be reconciled. We know that Wagner took an interest in such theories, for example that of animal magnetism, proposed by Anton Mesmer (1734–1815).[310] Johann Wilhelm Ritter (1776–1810) was a chemist, physicist, and philosopher who belonged to the Romantic movement (he was strongly influenced by Schelling). He saw Eve as a female Christ and prophesied that "One day a Christ will come who will be androgynous." He pointed to the symmetry between Eve and Christ: "Eve was born of man without the help of a woman, Christ of a woman without the help of a man; the androgyne will be born of both at once. Both will dissolve completely into a blaze of glory."[311] So "[t]he androgyne that is born of Eve and Christ will be a sexless androgyne but as immortal as the gold of the alchemists."[312] This sort of idea was continued by Franz von Baader (1765–1841),

---

I noted in volume 1 that Schleiermacher's translation of and introductions to Plato's works was significant not just for the study of Plato but also for the wider philosophical, philological, and literary context.

309. See *PW* 7:317 (*GSD* 2:232): "If ['man'] is to live up to the level of his destiny, he must be hale and blithe: [. . .]. But if he is to feel quite whole and well, the man requires a *wife*, i.e., the Instrumental Orchestra requires an equally healthy Vocal Institute entrusted to its keeping: this I call a woman, since we all know that the existing Orchestra has issued from the womb of a Choir."

310. I have found no reference to Mesmer in Wagner's writings but the stage direction in *Holländer* Act II Scene 2 is an unmistakable allusion to mesmerism: "bei dem Beginn von Erik's Erzählung versinkt sie [Senta] wie in magnetischen Schlaf [. . .]" (*GSD* 1:276).

311. Ritter, *Fragmente aus dem Nachlaß eines jungen Physikers*, 2:188–89 (Fragment 602): "Eva war ein weiblicher Christus; sie erlößte die Thiere, und sündigte als Mensch. — Alle Geburt Sünde, aller Tod Erlösung. Es ist hier aber von höheren Individuen, deren Gliedmaßen bloß sichtbar sind, die Rede. Es ist aber ein Christus zukünftig, welcher Androgyn seyn wird. Eva war ohne Weib vom Manne geboren, Christus ohne Mann vom Weibe, der Androgyn aber wird von beyden geboren werden. Aber sie werden im Glanz zerfließen ganz und gar, das wird das Wunder seyn, und der Glanz in einen Leib sich bilden, in einen Leib ohne Geschlecht, und also unsterblich." Nattiez, *Androgyne*, 113, quotes part of this remarkable passage.

312. Nattiez, *Androgyne*, 113.

whose work bears a resemblance to that of Böhme's *Mysterium Magnum*,[313] which was in Wagner's Wahnfried library. Baader, whom Nattiez considers "without doubt the most important and influential exponent of the theory of androgyny during the whole of the Romantic period,"[314] believed that "without the concept of androgyny, the central concept of religion, namely the image of God, remains unintelligible" ("ohne den Begriff der Androgyne der Centralbegiff der Religion, nemlich jener des Bildes Gottes unverstanden bleibt").[315] The image of God first occurs in Gen 1:27, where, according to Baader, an androgynous Adam was created in the image of an androgynous God.[316] The first chapter of Genesis 1 tells us "that God created the human being as male and female, and that everything was good, whereas in the second chapter the separation of the human being into man and woman is narrated, because it is no longer good, that the human being succeeds without this separation."[317] Man was tempted by the woman and lost his androgyneity. "If woman was created from man, it is simply because at the time of his first temptation or in the very first moment of that temptation, he felt the same kind of desire for *external* assistance in self-multiplication as is felt by animals, so that he lost the desire for inner assistance."[318] Christ will restore our "natural humanity" and love will strive to recreate the original androgyny. "The higher significance of sexual love (in the sense of not being simply the desire to propagate) is [. . .] none other than to help the man and women to complement one another inwardly (in mind and spirit) and form the complete human being, in other words, the original image of God."[319]

---

313. Baader gave eighteen lectures on this work (*FBSW* 13:159–236) together with lectures focussing on "Von der Gnadenwahl" (*FBSW* 13:57–158, 237–330).

314. Nattiez, *Androgyne*, 113.

315. *FBSW* 3:303–4; Cf. Nattiez, *Androgyne*, 113.

316. This idea of an androgynous Adam was later put forward by Schwally in 1906 on a linguistic basis. He noted that with Luther's translation of Gen 1:27 exegetes have in mind Adam and Eve: "und er schuf sie, ein Männlein und Fräulein." Schwally proposes reading "ihn" ("him," "otham") rather than "sie" ("them," otham) since Gen 1:27 a, b refers to creating Adam. Hence he translates: "Und Elohim schuf den Menschen nach seinem Bilde . . . . männlich und weiblich schuf er ihn." He adds "Wir erfahren aus diesem Texte die überraschende Tatsache, daß Adam ein doppelgeschlechtiges Wesen war" ("Schöpfungsberichte," 172–73). There was in fact a Jewish view of man being born with two faces as a hermaphrodite (b. ber. 61a; b. 'erub 18a; Bereshith Rabba 8.1) and this in included among the traditions Schwally goes on to mention. His work is discussed and rejected by König, *Genesis*, 160, Procksch, *Genesis*, 450, and Cassuto, *Genesis*, 1:58.

317. *FBSW* 9:210. So contrast Gen 1:31 where "God saw everything that he had made, and indeed, it was very good" with Gen 2:18 that "it is not good that man should be alone."

318. *FBSW* 7:229: "Nur also weil der Mensch in der ersten Versuchung oder im ersten Momente derselben nicht bestand und in ihm die Lust nach einem äusseren Gehilfen zur Selbstmultipliation, wie solchen die Thiere haben, aufging, hiemit aber die Lust an dem inneren Gehilfen [. . .] in ihm unterging, wurde das Weib aus ihm geschaffen." Cf. Nattiez, *Androgyne*, 113.

319. *FBSW* 3:309: "Die höhere Bedeutung der Geschlechtsliebe als nicht, mit dem Fortpflanzungs-Triebe identisch ist folglich, [. . .] keine geringe, als dass sie dem Manne, wie dem Weibe behilflich sein soll, sich innerlich (in Gemüth und Geist) zum ganzen Menschenbild zu ergänzen, die zum ursprünglichen Gottesbild." Cf. Nattiez, *Androgyne*, 114.

From the Romantic period Friedrich Schlegel (among others) could have influenced Wagner on androgyny, especially *Lucinde*.[320] The idea is also found in Schleiermacher's "Idea for a Rational Catechism for Noblewomen" in the *Athenaeum Fragments* (number 364); we do not know if Wagner knew this, but if he did I imagine he would approve.[321] Feuerbach is a more likely source. Reflecting on Gen 2:21–23 in *Thoughts on Death and Immortality* and introducing ideas from Aristophanes' speech in Plato's *Symposion*, he writes: "In sleep the woman emerged from the man; / In sleep his body was split in two."[322] Then later in *Essence of Christianity* he writes: "God the Father is *I*, God the Son *Thou*. The *I* is understanding, the *Thou* love. But love with understanding and understanding with love is mind, and mind is the totality of man as such—the total man."[323] Then a little later in the same chapter ("The Mystery of the Trinity") he writes:

> The Son is the mild, gentle, forgiving, conciliating being—the womanly sentiment of God (das weibliche Gemüt Gottes) [. . .]. The Son is thus the feminine feeling of dependence in the Godhead (das weibliche Abhängigkeitsgefühl in Gott); the Son implicitly urges upon us the need of a real feminine being. The son—I mean the natural, human son—considered as such, is an intermediate being between the masculine nature of the father and the feminine nature of the mother; he is, as it were, still half a man, half a woman, inasmuch as he has not the full, rigorous consciousness of independence which characterises the man, and feels himself drawn rather to the mother than to the father. The love of the son to the mother is the *first* love of the masculine being for the feminine.[324]

---

320. Nattiez, *Androgyne*, 115. See also *On Diotima* (1795) where, in the context of discussing the Greeks' understanding of the masculine and feminine, writes: "If we separate the essential from the accidental, then this fundamental principle is irrefutable: the feminine, like the masculine, is to be cleansed so as to yield a higher humanity." *FSKA* 1.1:92: "Trennen wir aber das Wesentliche vom Zufälligen, so ist der Grundsatz unwiderleglich: die Weiblichkeit soll wie die Männlichkeit zur höheren Menschlichkeit gereinigt werden." Cf. Nattiez, *Androgyne*, 114.

321. The first part of this "Catechism" is a re-writing of the ten commandments and then there is a three-part confession of faith (as in Luther's *Shorter Catechism*), the first two being: "(1) I believe in infinite humanity, which was before it assumed the garment of masculinity and femininity (ehe sie die Hülle der Männlichkeit und der Weiblichkeit annahm). (2) I believe that I do not live to obey commands or to seek diversions, but rather to be and to become; and I believe in the power of the will and of education to make me draw near once more to the infinite, to deliver me from the chains of miseducation, and to make me independent of the restraints of sex (den Schranken des Geschlechts)" (Schlegel, *Fragments*, 220–21; Schleiermacher, *Schriften aus der Berliner Zeit*, 154; cf. Nattiez, *Androgyne*, 114). Of the 451 aphorisms, twenty-nine were by Schleiermacher, 320 by Friedrich Schlegel, eighty-five by A. W. Schlegel, 134 by Novalis, and four were jointly written (Beiser, *German Romantics*, 115 n).

322. Feuerbach, *Thoughts*, 150; *LFW* 1:244: "Im Schlaf entstieg dem Mann sein Weib, / Im Schlaf entzweite sich sein Leib." Cf *Symposium* 189C-193E (Lamb, *Plato III*, 132–47).

323. Feuerbach, *Essence*, 67. Note the wording in *LFW* 5:78n: "Gott ohne Sohn ist *Ich*, Gott mit Sohn ist *Du*. *Ich* ist *Verstand*, *Du* ist *Liebe*. *Liebe* aber *mit Verstand* und *Verstand mit Liebe* ist *Geist*; *Geist* aber die *Totalität* des Menchen als solchen, der *totale Mensch*."

324. Feuerbach, *Essence*, 71 (emphasis added to match *LFW* 5:83–84).

Much later, after work on the *Ring* had been completed, Wagner read Gfrörer's ideas on the Trinity, which could suggest an androgynous Christ,[325] and told Cosima that in *Parsifal* "he gave the words to a chorus so that the effect would be neither masculine nor feminine, Christ must be entirely sexless, neither man nor woman; Leonardo, too, in the *Cena*, attempted that, depicting an almost feminine face, adorned with a beard."[326]

So to clarify finally on the issue of androgyny regarding Brünnhilde and Siegfried, it is not to be based on any idea of "perichoresis" (i.e., interpenetration) which no doubt is at work but on the basis of Brünnhilde incorporating Siegfried into her personhood. She, like Christ, is a "corporate personality."

Loge and Sexuality

Concerning issues of sexuality, Loge is perhaps the most complex figure in the *Ring* cycle. In Norse mythology Loki has a fluid gender and sexuality. He changes sex when he becomes a mare giving birth to Odin's horse Sleipnir.[327] In *Lokasenna* 23 Odin tells him: "eight winters / you were under the earth / a milker-of-cows and a matron, / and there you've borne babies—/ and that I thought an unmanly nature."[328] Larrington comments: "His gender is [...] subject to slippage: he's the mother of the eight-legged horse, Sleipnir [...]; he becomes pregnant from eating a half-cooked female heart; and, as Óðinn claims, he seems to have spent eight winters underground as a woman."[329] Again we see his unmanly nature in the closing verses of *Lokasenna* (57, 59, 61, 63) where Thor repeats four times: "Hold your tongue, you unmanly imp (rög vættr)!"[330] and threatens him with his hammer. This confrontation between Loki and Thor is reflected in Scene 2 of *Rheingold* whereby Donner threatens Loge, but with no reference to his being unmanly: "Accursèd flame, / I'll snuff you out!" ("Verfluchte Lohe, / dich lösch' ich aus!")[331] Fuchs writes that whereas the gods are "honourable, open, sincere, upright: in short, they are men" ("ehrlich, offen, gerade: kurz, sie sind Männer") Loki reminds one of a woman in that he is "the one who is deceitful, quick-witted, false, cunning" ("der Listige, Behende, Falsche, Verschlagene").[332] Fuchs' view of Loge in *Rheingold* is that the half-god finds it difficult truly to understand why a man would be so passionate about a woman:[333] in the words of Elizabeth Förster-Nietzsche, describing

---

325. CD 6 Jan 1875. See also Bell, *Parsifal*, 251.
326. CD 27 June 1880.
327. Byock, *Prose Edda*, xxi.
328. Dronke, *Edda II*, 338.
329. Larrington, *Norse Myths*, 41.
330. Dronke, *Edda II*, 345–47.
331. WagRS 79.
332. Fuchs, *Homosexualität*, 140.
333. Fuchs, *Homosexualität*, 146.

her brother's dismay at human passion: "And all that just about a little woman" ("Und das alles um ein kleines Mädchen"),[334] a sentiment he finds expressed in Loge's praise of "womans' delights and worth" ("Weibes Wonne und Wert"),[335] which despite his words fails somewhat to portray what erotic love for a woman is like.

An added argument for Loge's homosexuality is that Loki has a number of similarities to Mephistopheles.[336] On the issue of homosexuality, the key scene is towards the end of *Faust II* where Mephistopheles is somewhat distracted by the beautiful angels: "You're pretty! I must give you all a kiss" ("Ihr seid so hübsch, fürwahr ich möcht euch küssen").[337] Note, however, that Mephistopheles is attracted to *boys*, whom he addresses as "nice boys" ("die allerliebsten Jungen").[338] We also have an element of humor thrown in, that "when angels descend from heaven, the sight of their pretty bottoms distracts the paedophilic Mephisto and gives him an inkling that there may really be such a thing as love after all. When Mephisto is not looking, Faust's immortal part is carried up to heaven, leaving Mephisto with the useless mortal part and the bitter realization that he has utterly failed."[339]

Heterosexuality and Homosexuality

A view has been put forward that "[s]exual love in the *Ring* is emphatically a relation between man and woman [. . . ,] the 'otherness' of the other sex being a crucial factor in how their love is conceived."[340] This view is defended by appealing to Wagner's extended letter to Röckel (25–26 January 1854). Wagner argues that "to be consumed by truth is to abandon oneself as a sentient human being to total reality"[341] but for such a consummation "we must abandon completely our search for the 'whole.'"

> [T]he whole reveals itself to us only in the individual manifestation, for this alone is capable of being *apprehended* in the true sense of the word; we can *really "grasp"* a phenomenon only if we can allow ourselves to be fully absorbed by it, just as we must in turn be able to assimilate it fully within us. How is this marvellous process most fully achieved? ask nature! Only through *love!*—everything that I cannot love remains outside me, and I remain outside it: the philosopher may no doubt imagine that he can grasp what is going on here, but not the true human being. But the full reality of love is possible only

---

334. Fuchs, *Homosexualität*, 144.
335. WagRS 79.
336. Fuchs, *Homosexualität*, 33–35.
337. Luke, *Faust II*, 229; GWJA 3:394, l. 11771.
338. Luke, *Faust II*, 229; GWJA 3:393, l. 11763.
339. Robertson, *Goethe*, 99.
340. Scruton, *Ring*, 252. Note that one of the most insightful books on Wagner and sexuality, Nattiez, *Androgyne*, is simply dismissed by Scruton.
341. SL 303; SB 6:62.

between the sexes: only as *man* and *woman* can we *human beings* really love, whereas all other forms of love are mere derivatives of it, originating in it, related to it or an unnatural imitation of it. It is wrong to regard this love as only *one* manifestation of love in general, and to assume that other and higher forms must therefore exist *alongside* it.[342]

In order to evaluate whether these words have anything to say on the issue of love between those of the same sex it is necessary to bear two things in mind. First, Wagner's view regarding androgyny, as we have seen, is that one is only a whole human being with both the masculine and feminine components, something Wagner highlighted in that same letter of 25/26 January 1854 a little later: "but the true human being is both man and woman, and only in the union of man and woman does the true human being exist, and only through love, therefore, do man and woman become human."[343] This partly explains how the bringing together of Siegmund and Sieglinde and Brünnhilde and Siegfried is seen as "salvation" ("Heil").[344] Note, however, that there is a certain asymmetry in that the emphasis is on how the woman brings salvation to the man, and in the case of Brünnhilde she effectively "saves" Siegfried by incorporating him into her being.[345]

A second reason Wagner supports this view of heterosexuality is because he views the *poet* as male and the *music* (*not* the composer) as female. Hence, he speaks of the sexual union of poet and music in *Opera and Drama*. But note that he also speaks of the musician looking upon the poet eye-to-eye.[346] And when we come to the end of *Opera and Drama* (3.7) Wagner considers the poet and musician as "an ideal symbiosis of two men differing in age."[347] The younger stands closer "to Life's instinctive utterance" and in their working together "there would bloom that fairest, noblest Love (die schöne edelste Liebe), which we have learnt to recognize as the enabling force of Art-work."[348] Wagner refers back to this in a letter to Ludwig of September 1865: "I suspected this highest possibility of [our] Love: near the end of *Opera and Drama*, I longingly pictured this relationship: the love which binds the older to the younger man."[349]

So when the poet and *musician* rather than the poet and *music* are considered, a different picture emerges, but however much they are bound in love or however "homoerotic"[350] the relationship is one of "eye-to-eye"! Dreyfus points to the "scorch-

---

342. SL 303; SB 6:62.
343. SL 303; SB 6:63.
344. WagRS 132, 272. These passages are discussed in chapter 8 below.
345. See the discussion above on "Androgyny."
346. PW 2:285; GSD 4:146. See above.
347. Dreyfus, *Erotic Impulse*, 196.
348. PW 2:355; GSD 4:208–9.
349. KB 1:170–71, translated in Dreyfus, *Erotic Impulse*, 202.
350. Dreyfus, *Erotic Impulse*, 195.

ing heat of homophile passion"[351] in the letters of Ludwig to the composer and gives as an example that of 2 November 1865 where, for example, he writes: "How I love you, I love you my only one, my most cherished possession."[352] Wagner's letters can be almost as passionate, although the stress is on "eye-to-eye," as can be seen in the close of the letter of 20 April 1865, written just a few months before the premiere of *Tristan*, where he writes of "a last glance up to your eyes":

> Dear, Dear heavenly Friend! How you brighten my poor harassed existence. I feel so deeply, deeply satisfied and elevated through your love, through my—through our love! No words can express what this wonderful relationship between us means. Might I die—on the evening of my *Tristan*, with a last glance up to your eyes, with a last grasp of your hand!
>
> Affectionate, blessed, divine Friend!
>
> How deep, how deep is the bottom of our Love!
>
> Suffering, but blissful—
>
> Eternally yours
>
> Richard Wagner.[353]

Fuchs and Dreyfus note how Wagner's writings may well have introduced Ludwig for the first time to the question of love between men.[354] Ludwig read *Artwork of the Future* in 1857 (when he was twelve)[355] and Dreyfus notes that "Wagner—surprisingly—grounds the idea for a woman's selfless love in unselfish devotion shown by male lovers in ancient Sparta."[356] He writes in *Artwork of the Future*:

> This beautiful naked human is at the very core of the Spartan identity: true joy in the beauty of the most perfect human, the *male* body, gave rise to *love between men* [*Männerliebe*] that permeated and shaped the Spartans' entire

---

351. Dreyfus, *Erotic Impulse*, 198.

352. *KB* 1:204. Note that in this letter Ludwig appeals to words of Tristan from Act II ("da erdämmerte mild / erhab'ner Macht / im Busen mir die Nacht; / mein Tag war da vollbracht" ("then gently dawns from within my breast the night of sublime power, my day came to an end"; *GSD* 7:42) when he writes: "Uns dämmert mild erhabener Macht die Nacht, Unser Tag, er wird 'vollbracht'!" ("For us dawns gently the night of sublime power, our day, it comes to an end"). This part is not quoted by Dreyfus.

353. *KB* 1:86; translation given in Dreyfus, *Erotic Impulse*, 199, who rightly argues that these words cannot simply be dismissed as opportunistic since he confessed of these feelings towards the king to his closest friends. So he writes in May 1864 to Eliza Wille: "At last a love relationship (ein Liebesverhältnis) which does not lead to suffering and torments! That is how it is when I see this magnificent youth so before me [. . .]. He stays mostly in a little castle in my proximity; in 10 minutes the carriage takes me to him. Our conversations are ravishing. I always fly to him as to a lover" (Wille, *Erinnerungen*, 79; translation given in Dreyfus, *Erotic Impulse*, 199).

354. Fuchs, *Homosexualität*, 196; Dreyfus, *Erotic Impulse*, 196–97.

355. Ludwig's dates are 25 August 1845–13 June 1886.

356. Dreyfus, *Erotic Impulse*, 194.

state. We perceive this love in its original purity and most selfless expression of human beauty. Whereas man's love for woman, in its most natural form, is fundamentally selfish, hedonistic love in which, while finding satisfaction in a certain physical pleasure, he is incapable of resolving himself in his whole being—man's love for his fellow man represents a far higher affection, precisely because it causes him *not* to long for particularly physical satisfaction but rather to sink *his entire being* into the being of the other, to lose himself in the object of his love; and only as long as a woman who loves a man from the fullness of her femininity and by losing herself in him develops the masculine element within this femininity; thus complementing the purely feminine, is the man, to the extent that she is not only his *lover* but also his *friend*, able to find full satisfaction in a woman's love.[357]

As Dreyfus comments, "[t]his affection is none other than that of Romantic friendship."[358] Wagner then continues:

> The higher element of that love of man for man (Männerliebe) lay precisely in the fact that it excluded the motive of physical (sinnlich), selfish pleasure. Yet the bond of friendship was *not* a purely spiritual one but rather the spiritual friendship was merely the flowering, the total enjoyment of sensual friendship (der vollendete Genuß der sinnlichen Freundschaft): this came directly from joy in beauty, indeed in the physical, sensual beauty of the beloved man. Yet that joy was no selfish longing but rather a stepping out of the self into perfect empathy with the joy of the beloved in himself, involuntarily expressed in his joyful bearing born of beauty. This love, which was grounded in the noblest physical and spiritual pleasure—not the epistolary, cerebral, businesslike, sober transactions we call friendship—was the sole tutor of the young Spartan, the forever youthful teacher of boy and man, the marshal of communal festivities and daring exploits, the inspiration on the battlefield.[359]

So he praises such "love of man for man (Männerliebe)," which excluded "the motive of physical, selfish pleasure," but he was clearly unhappy about "pederasty." In notes on *What is German?* he writes: "We must understand a thing in *our* language if we want to understand it properly. (barbaros—un-German. Luther.) That is the sense of a *German* culture. What we cannot ever or in any language understand about the Greek way, is what wholly separates us from it, e.g., their love—in—pederasty."[360] Wagner's reference to "barbarous" and its translation by Luther as "un-German" ("undeutsch") can be made comprehensible by referring to 1 Cor 14:11, discussed in *Shall We Hope?*[361]

---

357. Warner, "Artwork," 63–64. I have added emphasis to correspond to *GSD* 3:134–35.
358. Dreyfus, *Erotic Impulse*, 195.
359. Warner, "Artwork," 64. I have added emphasis to correspond to *GSD* 3:135.
360. *Brown Book* 194; *Braunes Buch* 232.
361. *PW* 6:123; *GSD* 10:128–29.

Wagner made some striking notes that are relevant for the question of homosexuality.³⁶² They are quoted by Fuchs and I give the translation made by Dreyfus (and complete it using Ellis):

> No individual can be happy before we all are, because no individual can be free before we all are.
>
> *Strength*–drive–will–enjoyment
>
> *Love*–drive: sexual love Family love (the idea)
>
> *Love between men* [Männerliebe] (society)
>
> *Reason*–reduction of all ideas to nature (truth)
>
> Reason: measure of life
>
> *Freedom* (i.e., Reality)
>
> The more independent and free, the stronger the love: / compare the maternal love of a lioness with that of a cow, and the conjugal love of wolves with that of sheep.³⁶³

The striking word here is "Männerliebe," which Dreyfus rightly translates "love between men" and which Ellis manages to obfuscate with his translation "love towards men."³⁶⁴ These notes on happiness, freedom, and love are placed in a significant context. They are preceded first by sketches for "Achilles," whose relationship with Patroclus is one of the most celebrated gay relationships in Greek literature.³⁶⁵ Then immediately before the lines quoted above ("No individual can be happy" etc.) are some line on "Reason" ("Vernunft"). Following the lines "The more independent and free" is a poem "So wär' verloren der völker ehre . . ." and then another part of the "Achilles" sketch.³⁶⁶ I will return to these sketches in chapter 8 below since they concern important insights into Wagner's views on immortality.

Two important influences on Wagner's view of homosexuality were Schiller and Goethe. Schiller's poem "Die Freundschaft" (1782) vv 3–5 was discussed by Fuchs.³⁶⁷ Not only do these verses have a strong sense of spiritual homoeroticism but, as

---

362. *SSD* 12:275-76.

363. Fuchs, *Homosexualität*, 133; Dreyfus, *Erotic Impulse*, 196 (who does not translate the last half sentence); *PW* 8:368.

364. *PW* 8:368.

365. *PW* 8:367-38. Patroclus is not mentioned though in these brief sketches. Note that Homer indicates no sexual relationship, but this was to change in later literature. See Aeschylus fr. 134a (Brown, "Achilles," 7).

366. Neither *SSD* 12:274-76 nor *PW* 8:366-68 represent Wagner's ordering of his thoughts. The correct ordering is given in *DTB* 268.

367. Fuchs, *Homosexualität*, 68-69. See Dreyfus, *Erotic Impulse*, 193-94, who offers a translation of these three verses. Fuchs, *Homosexualität*, 69-71, also quotes from what he considers homoerotic lines from *Don Carlos*.

Dreyfus has pointed out, "the italics of the original almost betoken a strong sensation of touching."[368] The striking thing about this poem and the Wagner connection is that the very end of "Die Freundschaft" is quoted (freely) at the very end of Hegel's *Phenomenology*![369] Further, the ending of Wagner's *A Happy Evening*[370] could have been inspired by *Die Freundschaft*: "Raphael, an *deinem* Arm—o Wonne!" (verse 3); "Arm in Arme, höher stets höher" (verse 9).[371] *Happy Evening* ends on a note that reflects the mood of Schiller's poem: "'So here's to Happiness, to Joy! Here's to Courage, that enheartens us in fight with our fate! [. . .] To Love, which crowns our courage; to friendship, that keeps firm our Faith! To Hope, which weds itself to our foreboding! [. . .]. And three cheers for Music and her high priests! Forever be God adored and worshipped, the god of Joy and Happiness,—the god who created Music! Amen.'—Arm-in-arm we took our journey home; we pressed each other's hand, and not a word more did we say."[372]

We have seen already Goethe's influence on Wagner, and it is significant that Goethe also had an interest in homosexual love, but specifically as put alongside heterosexual sexual love. Dreyfus quotes Fuchs: "it is highly significant that both of the greatest German minds, Goethe and Wagner, juxtaposed same-sexual feelings of love (die gleichgeschlechtlichen Liebesempfindungen) next to heterosexual feelings of love; they concern themselves not with the purely homosexual but rather with the bisexual man who is able sensually to love both man and woman."[373] Dreyfus points to the "erotic intensity" in *Wilhelm Meisters Wanderjahre*[374] also found scattered in other works, "some with more or less oblique references."[375] Goethe's "Winckelmann und sein Jahrhundert" specifically addresses his homosexuality,[376] arguing that Winkelmann felt he was born for such friendship.[377] Fuchs offers an extended quotation,[378] fo-

---

368. Dreyfus, *Erotic Impulse*, 194.

369. Miller, *Phenomenology*, 493; *HHW* 2:433–34; cf. *FSSW* 1:93. See volume 1, chapter 6.

370. See *PW* 7:70–81 (*GSD* 2:136–49, *Ein glückliche Abend*) written 12 May 1841 in Meudon. The original title was Über Instrumentalmusik (Kühnel, "Prose Writings," 639). The work was originally published as "Une soirée heureuse: Fantaisie sur la musique pittoresque," *Revue et Gazette Musicale* 24 October and 7 November 1841.

371. Schiller, *FSSW* 1:91, 92.

372. *PW* 7:81; *GSD* 1:149.

373. Fuchs, *Homosexualität*, 137 (quoted in Dreyfus, *Impulse*, 195).

374. See Book 2, chapter 11 (*GWBDK* 7:278–83). Both Fuchs, *Homosexualität*, 36–38 and Dreyfus, *Impulse*, 192, mistakenly refer to Book 2, chapter 12.

375. Dreyfus, *Erotic Impulse*, 192–93, names *Faust, Roman Elegies, Venetian Epigrams, Letters from Switzerland*, and *West-Easterly Divan*. This last work (in volume 4 of Wagner's forty-volume edition in his Dresden library) was frequently marked.

376. Kuzniar, "Introduction," *Outing Goethe*, 9–16.

377. *GWJA* 6:254: "Zu einer Freundschaft dieser Art fühlte W. sich geboren [. . .]"

378. Fuchs, *Homosexualität*, 41–45; Cf *GWJA* 6:253–56.

cussing on Goethe's phrase "man fühlt sich beschämt" ("one feels oneself ashamed")[379] and in this connection quotes from Nietzsche, *Der Fall Wagner* 3:[380]

> You know what happened to Goethe in moralistic, old-maidish Germany. The Germans were always scandalized by him [. . .]. What did they blame Goethe for? The "mount of Venus" and the fact that he wrote the *Venetian Epigrams*. Even Klopstock preached ethics at him; there was a time when Herder liked using the word "Priapus" when talking about Goethe [. . .]. But above all, the superior brand of old maid (die höhere Jungfrau) was infuriated: all the petty courts, all types of "Wartburgs" in Germany crossed themselves against Goethe, against the "unclean spirit" in Goethe.[381]

Goethe's phrase "man fühlt sich beschämt" ("one feels almost ashamed of oneself") is somewhat ambiguous and Fuchs questions whether it points to "a gentle admission to a unobjectionable sexuality" ("ein leises Eingeständnis einer nicht einwandfreien Sexualität").[382] But he in fact comes to the conclusion that for Goethe it is a confession "in the matter of love—be it in love of the man for a woman or in the love of a man for a man—as something noble and good, as an apparent ideal, as an ideal however to whose height he could never himself soar" ("in der Liebe—sei es in der Liebe des Mannes zum Weibe oder in der Liebe des Mannes zum Manne—als edel und gut, als Ideal erschien, als ein Ideal allerdings, zu dessen Höhen er sich niemals aufschwingen konnte").[383]

Erotic Love and Shame

I close this chapter by considering the issue of erotic love and shame, which is relevant for every kind of sexuality, and which will be followed through in the next chapter on sexual ethics and law.

The Jewish tradition relates nakedness to a sense of being embarrassed (Genesis 2–3)[384] and the Christian tradition went further in relating sex to shame, the seeds of this being found in St Paul.[385] Feuerbach reacted against this tradition, as did Wagner. In the *Ring* sex becomes shameful when it is related to civilization; but in its original context of nature there is no shame. Wagner's wife, Cosima, records in her diary words

---

379. Cf *GWJA* 6:254.

380. Fuchs, *Homosexualität*, 45.

381. Nietzsche, *Anti-Christ*, 238–39 (*FNKSA* 6:18–19; §3). The references to the "mount of Venus" and "Wartburg" are, of course, primarily to *Tannhäuser* (cf. *Anti-Christ*, 238 n. 12).

382. Fuchs, *Homosexualität*, 45.

383. Fuchs, *Homosexualität*, 45–46.

384. Barr, *Eden*, 63–65, 69–70.

385. Paul has an ontological view of sin, i.e., it is primarily to do with who we are ("sinners") than what we do (Bell, *No one seeks for God*, 213). His view of sexual sin in particular (e.g., Rom 1:24–32) colored the thinking of theologians such as St Augustine.

of her husband that suggest that in some sexual acts, when humans behave like animals, then there is no sin. They discuss the controversy over the ending of Act I of *Walküre* when incest appears to be "proclaimed." Wagner says "this union of Siegm[und] and Siegl[inde] looks like an act of Nature (eine Naturnotwendigkeit) [. . .] so nothing immoral has been suggested (nichts Unmoralisches dargestellt ist)."[386] The German "eine Naturnotwendigkeit" is literally "a necessity of nature." Then eight years later he made similar remarks about Siegfried and Brünnhilde. Cosima records that her husband "plays Siegfried's awakening of Brünnhilde, is pleased with the character of this work, its trueness to Nature: 'Like two animals,' he says of Br. and Sieg. 'Here there is no doubt, no sin,' he continues, and in his Wotan he recognizes the true god of the Aryans."[387] If we take both these comments and relate them to Wagner's utterance about Wotan and Erda conceiving Brünnhilde, where "[s]uch outbreaks of natural force I have witnessed in the animal world—our only analogue for the divine is in the animal world,"[388] then one could argue that with the love-making of Siegmund and Sieglinde and of Siegfried and Brünnhilde, we see humans acting like gods.

To some extent Wagner's ideas on sex resemble those of Feuerbach. We have no evidence that Wagner read the *Lectures on the Essence of Religion* and indeed when his friend, the poet Georg Herwegh, opened its pages in front of him he writes: "I closed the book with a bang before his very eyes."[389] But ideas in these *Lectures* correspond to some extent to what Wagner said about sex and animals and it may well be that he received these ideas via the "oral tradition":

> The Christian sets aside his sensuous nature; he wants to hear nothing of the common, "bestial" urge to eat and drink, the common, "bestial" instincts of sexuality and love of young; he regards the body as a congenital taint on his nobility, a blemish on his spiritual pride, a temporarily necessary degradation and denial of his true essence, a soiled traveling garment, a vulgar incognito concealing his heavenly status.[390]

But Wagner goes beyond Feuerbach in two respects, namely that the animal activity of sex among humans involves no sin and that we see here the divine activity. To understand the background to his thinking it is important to highlight the way in which he appropriated the philosopher Schopenhauer and how he modified him. Wagner came to know first-hand Schopenhauer's philosophy around 1852–54. Schopenhauer's view of sex and sin was influenced by figures such as Paul, Augustine, and Luther. His view was entirely negative and he saw redemption as being

---

386. *CD* 14 March 1873. This discussion was precipitated by Wagner reporting that Prof. Fries had asked him whether the end of *Walküre* Act I would shock the "general public."

387. *CD* 5 September 1882.

388. *CD* 8 May 1874. See the fuller quote above.

389. *My Life* 431; *Mein Leben* 1:443.

390. Feuerbach, *Religion*, 260.

released from the curse of sexual arousal. But as Wagner was composing *Tristan und Isolde* he came to see that this was mistaken, and he wrote of this in a letter to Mathilde Wesendonck, a woman with whom he was deeply in love (and the erotic nature of the music he composed for *Walküre* Act I was inspired by her).[391] In this letter we have an answer to the Christian obsession with guilt, shame, and sin concerning sex and Wagner's correction of Schopenhauer was that redemption was not *from* erotic love but *through* erotic love.

> [I]t involves a more detailed explanation of the state in which we become capable of recognizing ideas, and of genius in general, which I no longer conceive of as a state in which the intellect is divorced from the will (Losgerissenheit des Intellectes vom Willen), but rather as an intensification of the individual intellect to the point where it becomes the organ of perception of the genus or species (eine Steigerung des Intellectes des Individuums zum Erkenntnissorgan der Gattung), and thus of the will itself, which is the thing in itself; herein lies the only possible explanation for that marvellous and enthusiastic joy and ecstasy felt by any genius at the highest moments of perception, moments which Sch. seems scarcely to recognize, since he is able to find them only in a state of calm and in the silencing of the individual affects of the will (in der Ruhe und im Schweigen der individuellen Willens-Affecte). Entirely analogous to this view, however, I have succeeded in demonstrating beyond doubt that in love there lies the possibility of raising oneself above the individual impulse of the will to a point where total mastery over the latter is achieved, and the generic will (Gattungs-Wille) becomes fully conscious of itself, a consciousness which, at this level, is necessarily synonymous with total pacification (vollkommener Beruhigung).[392]

Writing of the "generic will (Gattungs-Wille) is reminiscent of Feuerbach for whom the Gattung (species) was central for his understanding of the human being.

The questions of erotic love and shame naturally lead to the theme of the next chapter: sexual ethics and law.

---

391. See the various marginal comments discussed above.
392. *SL* 432 (Golther, *Mathilde Wesendonk*, 79–80); letter of 1 December 1858.

— 7 —

Sexual Ethics and Law

Introduction

In the previous chapter we have seen how love is the fundamental criterion in regard to ethics for Wagner and this was related to his understanding of the "purely human." In this chapter I turn to another principle of ethics, namely law, and how this relates to sexual ethics. The two key issues that arise in the *Ring*, particularly in *Walküre*, are those of incest and adultery. In the previous chapter these were seen in context of love in Act I. But once we enter the very different world of Act II, where law comes into consideration, everything changes.

The Debate over Adultery and Incest in *Walküre* Act II Scene 1

As we move from Act I to Act II of *Walküre* Wagner keeps our sympathies with the Volsung twins and, in order to focus on this, he does not bring in Fricka straightaway but shows us "Wotan sporting briefly with his daughter Brünnhilde." So we see him "happily enjoying love in the way he tends to see it: as a simple, untroubled form of affectionate companionship."[1]

Brünnhilde sees Fricka approaching on her chariot drawn by "a team of rams." The portrayal of Fricka for the animal loving composer could hardly be less flattering and we appear to have a blatant manifestation of wicked power, which, as we shall see, in encapsulated in "law":[2]

Hei! Wie die gold'ne	Ha! How she whirls
Geißel sie schwingt;	the golden whip;
die armen Thiere	the pitiful beasts
ächzen vor Angst	are bleating with fear

---

1. Skelton, "Conflict," 7.
2. *WagRS* 140.

Brünnhilde adds that although she is fond of "brave men's battles" she cares not to fight "[i]n strife of this kind."[3] She "disappears behind the high rock" and as Fricka enters the atmosphere changes.[4] We hear a motif that is reminiscent of the Erda motif, which functions to point to Siegmund's impending doom.[5]

The altercation between Wotan and Fricka concerning Siegmund's fate has no parallel in Norse mythology, although there are some arguments between Odin and Frigg that, in comparison to *Walküre* Act II, concern minor matters.[6] One should also note that Frigg, in complete contrast to Fricka, is sexually promiscuous.[7] In the ensuing argument one can say that Fricka fairly wins (this is perhaps more clearly seen in the "rejected" version) and Wotan is forced to give in to her wishes. As Cooke comments: "Perhaps it is because she is *so* right that she receives such little sympathy."[8]

In tracing the drama and the altercation I begin with Fricka relating that Hunding had called on her for vengeance and that she as "Wedlock's guardian" answered his prayer and "promised to punish / severely the deed / of that brazenly impious pair."[9] Wotan asks what was so wrong in what they did. Was it not "Love's enchantment" ("Der Minne Zauber") that had cast its magic spell upon them?[10] And so Wotan (as Wagner's mouth-piece) puts forward his "new morality." Wotan sees nothing wrong in the relationship between Siegmund and Sieglinde:[11]

Was so schlimmes	What was so wrong
schuf das Paar,	that was done by the couple
das liebend einte der Lenz?	that Spring united in love?
Der Minne Zauber	Love's enchantment
entzückte sie:	had cast upon them its magic spell:
wer büßt mir der Minne Macht?	who'll make me amends for the power of love?

Fricka is shocked by Wotan's attitude: has not "wedlock's a holy vow" been broken? Wotan avers that a vow that binds unloving hearts is "unholy." In the final version it may appear that Wotan makes this valid point, which Fricka appears then to evade

---

3. *WagRS* 140.

4. *WagRS* 141.

5. See Sabor, *Walküre*, 73; although he says it is the Erda motif, it is rather a variation of it (bars 163–66).

6. See the prose introduction of *Grímnismál* (Orchard, *Elder Edda*, 50). Cooke, *End*, 127–28, also points to Paulus Diaconus, *History of the Lombards* (c. 787), where Wodan is tricked by his wife "Freia" into granting victory to the Winniles rather than the tribe he favoured, the Vandals.

7. Saxo Grammaticus, *Gesta Danorum*, 1:53, discussed in volume 1, chapter 3.

8. Cooke, *End*, 325.

9. *WagRS* 141.

10. *WagRS* 141. Cf. *Tristan* Act II Scene 1: "Know you not the goddess of love / and the power of her magic" ("Frau Minne kenntest du nicht? / Nicht ihres Zaubers Macht?" (*WagTS* 106; *SW* 8.II bars 375–82). *GSD* 7:34 has "Miracle's power" ("Wunders macht").

11. *WagRS* 141.

by changing the subject to that of incest. So in the final version Wotan expresses his view thus:[12]

Unheilig	Unholy
acht' ich den Eid,	I deem the vow
der Unliebende eint;	that binds unloving hearts;
und mir wahrlich	and, in truth, you cannot
muthe nicht zu,	expect me now
daß mit Zwang ich halte	to bind by force
was dir nicht haftet:	what won't be bound by you:
denn wo kühn Kräfte sich regen,	wherever forces are boldly stirring,
da rath' ich offen zum Krieg.	I openly counsel war.

However, in the "rejected" (longer) version, a different picture emerges[13] and this "Erstschrift des Textbuches" shows how Wagner struggled to fashion this part of the dialogue.[14] So before moving to the subject of incest Fricka gives an answer to Wotan's point that even she cannot sanction a marriage entered involuntarily. She argues that it is *Wotan* who is to blame for Sieglinde's unhappy marriage. She challenges him: "You never shield the weak / but only help the strong. [. . .] When Hunding once used force /—which weak as I am, I couldn't prevent—/ you brazenly let him have his way."[15] This crucial point is omitted in the final version (although she does make the point in relation to Siegmund that Wotan has ultimate control of events).[16] She then adds another crucial point that Hunding atoned for his guilt (this is missing in the final version):[17]

sühnte er dann	when he then atoned
des Frevels Schuld,	for the guilt of his outrage,
Freundin ward ihm da Fricka	Fricka became his friend
durch heiliger Ehe Eid:	through holy wedlock's vow:
so vergess' ich	thus I forget
was je er beging,	whatever his fault
mit meinem Schutze	and raise my shield
schirm' ich sein Recht.	to shelter his rights.
Der nicht seinem Frevel gesteuert,	Let him who failed to hinder his outrage
meinen Frieden stör' er nun nicht!	refrain from disturbing my peace of mind!

12. *WagRS* 142.
13. Cf. Oberkogler, *Ring*, 130–31.
14. See the markings in *TBRN1* 467–70.
15. *WagRS* 353; *TBRN1* 468.
16. *WagRS* 144–45.
17. *WagRS* 353–54; *TBRN1* 469.

This obviously raises the question whether atoning for forcing someone into marriage can then legitimise that marriage. In this rejected version Wotan then responds, claiming that he has not interfered with Fricka's realm:[18]

Stört' ich dich je	Have I ever disturbed you
in deinem Walten?	in your dominion?
Gewähren ließ ich dich stets.	I always let you have your way.
Knüpfe du bindender	Tie the bonds
Knoten Band,	of binding ties,
fess'le was nicht sich fügt.	fetter what doesn't fit.

So according to Wotan, she actually has the power to prevent an unloving marriage (and she does not seem to dispute this point), although he then adds rather acerbically that she can play the hypocrite ("heuch'le") when vows are made of "pretended love."[19]

In both the rejected and final versions Fricka's one weakness in her argument is that she changes the subject! She asserts that if he deems the "breach of wedlock" to be worthy of praise then why not say their incest is also holy:[20]

Mir schaudert das Herz,	My heart is quaking,
es schwindelt mein Hirn:	my brain is reeling:
bräutlich umfing	as bride a sister
die Schwester den Bruder!	embraced her brother!

Wotan tells her that something new may be happening that she should bless:[21]

Heut'—hast du's erlebt:	Today you have witnessed it happen:
erfahre so,	learn thus that a thing
was von selbst sich fügt,	might befall of itself
sei zuvor auch noch nie es gescheh'n.	though it never happened before.

He then asks Fricka to bless their bond.[22] The stage direction indicates that Fricka "break[s] out in the most violent indignation."[23] The "Z motif" employed here (see Example 7.1) represents the obstacle between an intention and its fulfilment,[24] and

18. *WagRS* 354; *TBRN1* 469.

19. *WagRS* 354; *TBRN1* 469.

20. *WagRS* 142. Cf. *WagRS* 354; *TBRN1* 469. On the reading "den Bruder" (rather than "der Bruder") see chapter 6 above.

21. *WagRS* 142.

22. *WagRS* 142.

23. *WagRS* 142.

24. Cooke, "Musical Language," 254–68, discusses what he calls the Z motif. See "Musical Language," 261 Ex. 33.

here it is Fricka who "firmly stands between Wotan and the fulfilment of his plan, and also between the lovers (Siegmund and Sieglinde) and the fulfilment of their love, since that is part of Wotan's plan."[25]

Example 7.1: *Walküre* Act II bars 253–60

In her lengthy tirade (in which the Volsung twins are variously referred to as "dissolute Wälsungs," "impious twin-born pair," "she-wolf's litter")[26] Fricka moves the subject to the end of the gods.[27] This will come about because Wotan has defied his own laws, something made clearer in the rejected version.[28] She adds that he was the first to infringe them, and castigates him for his adultery.

Wotan responds, arguing that all Fricka can grasp is "Age-old custom" ("Stets Gewohntes"),[29] whereas his thoughts "seek to encompass / what's never yet come to pass."[30] He then puts forward his argument that he needs a hero to accomplish his purposes, a hero who lacks godly protection, someone who "breaks loose from the

---

25. Cooke, "Musical Language," 260–61.

26. *WagRS* 142–43.

27. *WagRS* 142: "So is this the end / of the blessed immortals[?]" ("So ist es denn aus / mit den ewigen Göttern[?]").

28. See the discussion of "Law" below.

29. *WagRS* 144.

30. *WagRS* 144.

law of the gods (Göttergesetz)."³¹ However, Fricka manages to show that his argument simply does not work since Siegmund is nevertheless under his control.³² Wotan comes to realize that his argument is baseless and is eventually forced to agree to his wife's demand. In theory he could have defied his wife and allowed Siegmund to live but he is constrained by his own laws, to which I will return. It is also worth adding that despite Erda's warning in *Rheingold* Scene 4 that the gods will come to an end, at this point Wotan probably still thinks he can avert the end of the gods.

Before she leaves she emphasizes twice the issue of her "honour" ("Ehre") by means of an inclusion:³³

Deiner ew'gen Gattin	Your eternal spouse's
heilige Ehre	sacred honour
beschirme heut' ihr Schild!	her shield must defend today.
[...]	[...]
Der Wälsung fällt meiner Ehre:—	The Wälsung falls for my honour's sake:—
empfah' ich von Wotan den Eid?	will Wotan give me his oath?

As Brünnhilde returns on the scene Fricka addresses her with words of terrible irony (he is hardly "Lord of Battles" and neither has he "chosen" this course of action):³⁴

Heervater	The Lord of Battles
harret dein:	awaits you:
lass' ihn dir künden	let him explain
wie das Loos er gekies't!	the fate he has chosen!

I will return to the confrontation between Wotan and Fricka in chapter 9 below where the issue of the freedom of the gods will be considered.

Law

This scene, like a number of others in the *Ring* cycle, raises the issue of Wagner's understanding of "law." This is then in turn related to a number of issues such as "society," "the state," ethics, and morality, all of which are addressed in one way or another in the *Ring* and for which there are a number of parallels in *Jesus of Nazareth*, which I examine below.

One of the complex issues in *Walküre* Act II is the relation of "Wotan's law" to what we could call "Fricka's law." Fricka clearly does represent law as George Bernard

---

31. *WagRS* 144.
32. This is a question of divine and human agency which will be discussed in chapter 9.
33. *WagRS* 147.
34. *WagRS* 147.

Shaw recognized.³⁵ But, of course, the person who is meant to uphold the law is Wotan. In the rejected version, which, as we have seen, gives us more detail of what Wagner had been thinking, Fricka asks:³⁶

Wohin renn'st du,	Where are you heading,
rasender Gott,	you headstrong god,
reißest die Schöpfung du ein,	destroying the world you created,
der selbst das Gesetz du gab'st?	a world whose law you made yourself?

Wotan's original "law" corresponded to Fricka's law. But with his "project Siegmund," whereby he is attempting to get back the ring, he is trying to circumvent these laws. Cooke argues that although Wotan does not realize it, this old side is far stronger than the new, progressive side, and this is why he loses the argument with Fricka.

> It is not that Fricka "outwits" Wotan: she defeats him fairly in argument because she appeals to that side of his character which originally led him to make her his wife—the old conservative, power-dominated side responsible for his creation of his authoritarian world with its immutable laws. Although he does not realise it, this side is still far stronger than his new, progressive side, committed to circumventing these law through his children the Volsungs, since this new side has as yet no real appreciation of the value of love.³⁷

So he is tied to his old law and I suspect that it is this sense of obligation to law rather than fear of the end of the gods that drives him finally to give Fricka his oath.³⁸ Hence, I think it can be said that in respect to the old law Wotan is concerned primarily with establishing some sort of order in the world (a sort of state law) and this corresponds to Fricka's upholding some view of sexual ethics, in particular that concerning marriage.

We saw in the previous chapter how Wagner sees an opposition between the state and the principle of love. He sees the original "society" as having the potential for good but everything goes awry with the foundation of the "state." To *some* extent Wagner could agree with Rousseau that the original state of nature was "good."³⁹ But also society had the potential to go astray as we saw in Hegel's "Entzweiung." Further, in view of possible anarchism that could emerge,⁴⁰ Wotan attempted to halt this through his treaties. Reference to these has been seen in *Rheingold* Scene 2, but the significance of such

---

35. He describes her as "the Law" (Laurence, *Shaw's Music III*, 452) and writes of Wotan being "dependent on the laws of Fricka" and hence being "shackled and bound" (440).
36. *WagRS* 355; *TBRN1* 470.
37. Cooke, *End*, 324.
38. *WagRS* 147.
39. See volume 1, chapter 5.
40. Zegowitz, *Opern*, 196, points to the concerns of Fasolt and Fafner as to how Alberich, in possession of the gold, will "think up new ways to harm [them]" (*WagRS* 81).

treaties is not really developed until *Walküre* Act II Scene 2 and further in the Prologue to *Götterdämmerung*;[41] there is also a brief reference in *Siegfried* Act I Scene 2.[42]

Wotan's treatises raise the fundamental question whether political power is in itself evil[43] or whether it is the problem with Wotan's motives. Unscrupulous motives are certainly involved, Zegowitz seeing the problem in Wotan's egoism.[44] Wotan's monologue in *Walküre* Act II points explicitly to his base motives in gaining power and making treaties. In a passage, strong in Stabreim, he tells Brünnhilde how, "when youthful love's delights had faded," he longed for power. Power was meant to fulfil what sexual love had previously fulfilled:[45]

Als junger Liebe	When youthful love's
Lust mir verblich,	delight had faded,
verlangte nach Macht mein Muth:	I longed in my heart for power:
von jäher Wünsche	impelled by the rage
Wüthen gejagt,	of impulsive desires,
gewann ich mir die Welt.	I won for myself the world.

He then goes on to admit that he acted unfairly but says that he did so unknowingly:[46]

Unwissend trugvoll	Unwittingly false
Untreue übt' ich,	I acted unfairly,
band durch Verträge	binding by treaties
was Unheil barg.	what boded ill.

Some of the blame he places on Loge:[47]

| listig verlockte mich Loge, | cunningly Loge lured me on |
| der schweifend nun verschwand. | but vanished while roaming the world. |

However, there is a more fundamental law at work in the *Ring*, the "Urgesetz" ("primeval/primal law"), to which I now turn.

---

41. *WagRS* 281.

42. *WagRS* 211.

43. See the issue in Genesis 1–2 and whether "political power" was there before the fall. Apart from having dominion over fish, birds, and "every living thing" (Gen 1:28) and having the power to name them there are no other hints of political power before the "fall."

44. Zegowitz, *Opern*, 197.

45. *WagRS* 149.

46. *WagRS* 149. Note the distinction made in the Priestly writing between unwitting sins and sins with a high hand. See, e.g., Num 15:27–31.

47. *WagRS* 149. I noted in chapter 3 above that in some respects Loge is a Mephistopheles-like figure.

Urgesetz—Primeval Law

The term "Urgesetz" occurs in the first sketch for the *Ring*, the *Mythus* of 1848. First it is found in the scene (corresponding to *Siegfried's Tod*/*Götterdämmerung* Act III Scene 1) where Siegfried tells the mermaids (Meerfrauen) that "[t]he curse and your threats I don't count for a single hair. Whatever my courage drives me to do, that is my eternal law (Urgesetz)."[48] This then is later taken up in *Götterdämmerung* III Scene 1 where the Rhinemaidens (Rheintöchter) tell Siegfried that the "Night-spinning Norns" have woven the curse of the ring "into the rope of primeval law."[49] Siegfried replies that "primeval law's / eternal rope [. . .] / Nothung [i.e., the sword] will hew from the hands of the Norns!"[50]

The term "Urgesetz" is used towards the end of the *Mythus* where Brünnhilde, taking the ring from her murdered husband, says "I recognize the runes on this ring. I now also recognize the runes of the original law ([d]es Urgesetzes Runen), the ancient lore of the Norns (der Nornen alten Spruch)!"[51] That this is a fundamental law, one to which the gods are subject, is suggested by the next lines: "Hear now, you lordly gods; your injustice has been erased. Thank him, the hero, who took your guilt upon himself."[52] The gods being subject to the "runes of the original law" coheres with Odin's hanging on the tree to gain knowledge of the runes.[53]

However, the rejected version of *Walküre* Act II Scene 1, which I considered earlier, may suggest Wotan could have been in some sense the author of the "Urgesetz" in that he *applied* it to the created order. We have seen how Fricka criticizes him: he destroys the very world he created, a world he himself made.[54] In his reply he explains that he applied one primal law in respect to nature and that power he also applied to the Volsung twins as they lay in their mother's womb, a power that anticipated their later falling in love:[55]

---

48. *GSD* 2:163; Haymes, *Ring*, 54–55.
49. *WagRS* 336. *Siegfried's Tod* was similar (Haymes, *Ring*, 154–55).
50. *WagRS* 336. Cf. Haymes, *Ring*, 156–57.
51. *GSD* 2:166; Haymes, *Ring*, 58–59. In the corresponding part of *Siegfried's Tod* Brünnhilde recognizes the ring's runes but the reference to Urgesetz is dropped (*GSD* 2:226; Haymes, *Ring*, 180–81).
52. *GSD* 2:166; Haymes, *Ring*, 58–59.
53. *Hávamál* 138–41 (Dronke, *Edda III*, 30–31). See chapter 3 above.
54. *WagRS* 355; *TBRN1* 470.
55. *WagRS* 355; *TBRN1* 470.

Des Urgesetzes	One primal law
walt' ich vor Allem:	I obey above all others:
wo Kräfte zeugen und kreisen,	wherever forces stir and strive,
zieh' ich meines Wirkens Kreis;	I circumscribe my sphere of action;
wohin er läuft	I guide the flood
leit' ich den Strom,	wherever it flows
den Quell hüt' ich	and guard the well-spring
aus dem er quillt:	from which it wells:
wo Leibes- und Liebeskraft,	where strength of limb and love is found,
da wahrt' ich mir Lebensmacht.	I've exercised power over life.
Das Zwillingspaar	That power
zwang meine Macht:	the twin-born pair has felt:
Minne nährt' es	love nurtured them
im Mutterschooß;	within their mother's womb;
umbewußt lag es einst dort,	unwittingly, they lay there once,
unbewußt liebt' es sich jetzt.	unwittingly, they love each other now.

These two ideas of "Urgesetz" being related to the created order and to fundamental love is also given in the *Jesus of Nazareth* sketches. I discussed in chapter 2 above the idea Wagner expresses in the commentary to the drama that "man can live and move by none save the ur-law of Motion itself (nach dem urgesetze der bewegung selbst)"[56] which results in the human's clash against the law.[57] Then later he writes of the link between "Urgesetz" and love: "But Love is mightier than the Law, for it is the Ur-law of life" ("Die liebe ist aber mächtiger als das gesetz, denn sie ist das urgesetz des lebens").[58] Then in the theoretical writings the term appears twice. First in *Art and Revolution*: "Apollo [...] through his priestess at Delphi, had proclaimed to questioning man the fundamental laws of the Grecian race and nation (das Urgesetz griechischen Geistes und Wesens)."[59] Secondly, in *Epilogue to the "Nibelung's Ring"* he writes of Tristan and Siegfried who both "woo for another their own eternally-predestined bride (das ihm nach dem Urgesetze bestimmte Weib)."[60]

Hence, although the term "Urgesetz" is not used frequently it is nevertheless significant. Wagner was fond of compound words formed with the prefix "ur," many of which occur in the *Ring*, such as "urweise," "Urwissend," "Urmütter," "Ursorge," and "Urgesetz" itself.[61] Further, such words are particularly frequent in *Die Wibelungen*

---

56. The allusion here is to Acts 17:28.
57. *PW* 8:311; *DTB* 254.
58. *PW* 8:321; *DTB* 259.
59. *PW* 1:32; *GSD* 3:10.
60. *PW* 3:268; *GSD* 6:268.
61. Schuler, *Language*, 94.

where a process of conscious archaizing is at work.[62] The prefix "ur-" is taken to mean "primeval,"[63] although it originally meant "out of," "forth," or "from within," being equivalent to "er-," as in "Erscheinung" ("appearance").[64]

The term "Urgesetz" was used by figures who influenced Wagner either directly or indirectly, and I offer some of the notable instances of its use in chronological order. First, Fichte in his *Wissenschaftslehre* of 1804 writes that eternal life is to know God and he whom he sent (John 17:3) and this means perceiving the "Urgesetz" and its eternal image, and this is not only a perception to life but life itself.[65] In view of Fichte's views of God at this time, "Urgesetz" would presumably mean the moral law. The second instance is from Schelling, who writes of the moral "Urgesetz,"[66] and a third example of its use can be found in Wagner's lecturer in aesthetics, C. H. Weisse.[67] Fourthly, Feuerbach used the term in *Essence*, and it is perhaps significant that this was used in relation to Odin: "To the ancient Germans the highest virtues were those of the warrior; therefore their supreme god was the god of war, Odin,—war, 'the original or oldest law.'"[68] Then after Wagner we find its use, and this cannot be accidental, in Nietzsche's *Richard Wagner in Bayreuth*. He writes of Wagner's art that it "shows in general that true music is a piece of fate and primal law (daß wahre Musik ein Stück Fatum und Urgesetz ist)."[69] Although not mentioning Wagner, what he writes in *Beyond Good and Evil* does seem very much to correspond to Siegfried's "Urgesetz":

> At the risk of annoying innocent ears I will propose this: egoism belongs to the essence of the noble soul. I mean that firm belief that other beings will, by nature, have to be subordinate to a being "like us" and will have to sacrifice themselves. The noble soul accepts this fact of its egoism without any question-mark, and also without feeling any harshness, compulsion, or caprice in it, but rather as something that may well be grounded in the primordial law

---

62. Full details are given in the discussion of the *Die Wibelungen* in volume 1, chapter 2.

63. Goethe was fond of such usage as in "Urpflanze" ("proto-plant, archetypal plant") or "Urphänomen" ("proto-phenomenon"). See Inwood, *Hegel Dictionary*, 8, and chapter 3 above.

64. Inwood, *Hegel Dictionary*, 8, points out that the original sense of "Ursprung" was the "springing forth," especially of water.

65. *JGFAW* 4:369: "Worin besteht denn nun das ewige Leben? Dies ist das ewige Leben, heißt es, daß sie dich, und den du gesandt hast, d.h. bei uns, das Urgesetz und sein ewiges Bild, *erkennen*; bloß *erkennen*; und zwar führt nicht etwa nur dieses Erkennen zum Leben, sondern es *ist* das Leben" (Lecture 25).

66. *Vom Ich als Prinzip der Philosophie oder über das Unbedingte im menschlichen Wissen* (1795), §14 (*SWMJ* 1:123).

67. Weisse, *Grundzüge der Metaphysik*, 457, 465.

68. Feuerbach, *Essence*, 21. Cf. *LFW* 5:38 this section is missing in the 1841 edition and inserted in that of the 1843 edition.

69. Nietzsche, *Meditations*, 221; *FNKSA* 1:464. Note that he goes on to write of "die ur-bestimmte Natur" (*FNKSA* 1:465): "Primordially determined nature (die ur-bestimmte Natur) through which music speaks to the world of appearance is thus the most enigmatic thing under the sun, an abyss in which force and goodness dwell together, a bridge between the self and the non-self" (*Meditations*, 222).

of things (im Urgesetz der Dinge). If the noble soul were to try to name this phenomenon, it would call it "justice itself."[70]

Jesus of Nazareth, Law, and Sexual Ethics

Wagner's commentary on the *Jesus of Nazareth* drama sketch (Part II.1) discusses themes of Jesus' sonship, law, love, property, marriage, death, and "the woman." I have argued elsewhere that this commentary was written after the drama had been sketched.[71] Wagner's theoretical discussion is often followed by utterances of Jesus and others, many of which are non-biblical, but there are cases of quotations from or allusions to the New Testament. Often the sayings are preceded by Roman numerals, which refer to the relevant Act, often two numerals being given, suggesting Wagner was unsure for which Act the utterance was relevant. A good number of the sayings are too cumbersome to be included in a libretto, but this does not exclude the possibility of their being adopted.[72]

The point that is particularly relevant in section II for the present discussion is the contrast between law and Spirit/love. I give a few examples of words Wagner puts into Jesus' mouth: "I redeem you from Sin by proclaiming to you the everlasting law of the Spirit." "I release you from the Law which slew you." "[N]ow I slay this law, and thereby root up sin: from sin I thus redeem you, inasmuch as I give you Love."[73] But when law comes into the realm of marriage, "possession," and love, then we have a "Verfestigung" (a "stiffening"), a key idea in this passage.[74] Wagner does not use the noun but rather the verb "verfestigen" on three occasions, which Ellis translates with different verbs. So first, we have "verfestigen" applied to marriage: "As a first law, *Marriage* was entrenched by transferring the law of Love to it" ("Als ein erstes gesetz verfestigte sich die *ehe*, indem das gesetz der liebe auf sie übergetragen wurde").[75] Secondly, it is applied to the question of "possession" ("besitz"): "To this complete relationship [i.e., family relationships based on love] became attached the concept of Possession: the man belonged to the woman, the woman to the man, the children to the parents, the parents to the children,—love gave duration (dauer) to this state of Belonging (angehören), and continuous Belonging stiffened (verfestigte) to the concept of Possession."[76] Thirdly, "verfestigen" is applied to love itself. Through the "law of Property (gesetz des eigenthumes) [. . .] the love which expresses itself in

---

70. Nietzsche, *Beyond Good and Evil*, 162; *FNKSA* 5:219–20 (§265) "Was ist Vornehm."

71. Bell, "Jesus of Nazareth," 263–64.

72. Hence I disagree with Zegowitz, *Opern*, 188, who assumes that II.1 was written before the drama outline.

73. *PW* 8:300; *DTB* 249.

74. Zegowitz, *Opern*, 188.

75. *PW* 8:301; *DTB* 249.

76. *PW* 8:301; *DTB* 250.

Man as the bent to satisfaction through the enjoyment of Nature and her products, became hardened (verfestigt) into the unit's exclusive right over Nature beyond her capacity for enjoyment."[77]

Hence, for Wagner "law" is opposed to "love," and these fundamental ideas of the *Jesus of Nazareth* sketches fed into the *Walküre* libretto, developed in 1851–52. So in the *Jesus* sketches, law makes marriage into a matter of "property": "[I]f Man made a law to shackle love (ein gesetz zur beschränkung der liebe), to reach a goal that lies outside of human nature (—namely, power, dominion—above all: the *protection of property* (der *schutz* des *besitz*):), he sinned against the law of his own existence, and therewith slew himself."[78] Wagner here hints of a connection between the issue of "property" and "marriage," which then later becomes explicit: "If a woman was wed by a man for whom she had not love, and he fulfilled the letter of the marriage-law to her, through that law she became his property (eigenthum): the woman's struggle for freedom through love thereby became a sin, actual contentment of her love she could only attain by adultery."[79] The parallel to Sieglinde's unhappy marriage to Hunding is obvious. The *Mythus* sketch of 1848 did contain the seeds of this part of the drama: "Siegmund takes a wife; Sieglinde is married to a man (Hunding); but both their marriages remain childless. In order to bring forth a true Volsung, brother and sister come together themselves."[80] But I suggest the writing of the *Jesus* sketches propelled Wagner to make changes and highlight the issue of the incompatibility of love and law and to make marriage (or at least bad marriages) into a matter of "possession." And so Sieglinde explains to Siegmund in Act I: "This house and this wife / are Hunding's own" ("Dieß Haus und dieß Weib / sind Hunding's Eigen").[81]

Further words put into the mouth of Jesus are also relevant for *Walküre* Act I. So for Act IV Jesus says: "Through my death there perisheth the Law, inasmuch as I shew you that Love is greater than the Law."[82] Then for Act I: "The commandment saith: Thou shalt not commit adultery! But I say unto you: Ye shall not marry without love. A marriage without love is broken as soon as entered into, and whoso hath wooed without love, already hath broken the wedding."[83] Such words raise the thorny issue of Jesus' attitude to the Mosaic law in "history" and in the Gospels themselves. Among New Testament scholars there is actually little consensus, some arguing that Jesus was a law-observant Jew[84] and others arguing that he had a radical view of the

---

77. *PW* 8:302; *DTB* 250. This is one of the few occasions where "nature" appears in the sketches. See my comments in chapter 1 above.

78. *PW* 8:301; *DTB* 249. The words corresponding to "to reach a goal" through to "*protection of property*" are a marginal addition in the original manuscript.

79. *PW* 8:302; *DTB* 250.

80. Haymes, *Ring*, 46–49.

81. *WagRS* 123.

82. *PW* 8:303; *DTB* 250.

83. *PW* 8:303; *DTB* 250. This final sentence is a marginal addition.

84. E.g., Crossley, *Date of Mark's Gospel*.

Jewish law and prepared for its "abolition" by St Paul.[85] Whichever view one holds to, it is significant that according to the Gospels Jesus in his teaching on marriage relativizes the law on divorce in Deut 24:1–4 and goes back to the creation story of Genesis 1–2. Wagner doubly marked Matt 19:5–6, placing a "I" by it, indicating its relevance for Act I of the *Jesus* sketches.[86] Further in section II.2 of the *Jesus* sketches he wrote out the section Matt 19:3b–8, which he considered relevant for Act I, which begins with the Pharisees' question "Is it lawful also for a man to put away his wife for any cause?"[87] He continues:

> Jesus: "Have ye not read that he which made them at the beginning, he made them male and female? For this cause shall a man leave his father and mother, and cleave to his wife; and the twain shall be one flesh. What therefore God hath joined together, let not man put asunder."—They say unto him: "Why then did Moses command to give a writing of divorcement, and to put her away." Jesus: "Moses because of the hardness of your hearts suffered you to put away your wives: but from the beginning it was not so."[88]

Wagner then adds: "And following verses.—Verse 16 to end: scene with the rich young man."[89]

Hence, whatever one may fling at Wagner for his unorthodox Christian faith, he was faithful to the Bible ("bibeltreu")[90] in that he related love to creation and "nature." But in putting forward his views on marriage he was also clearly influenced by Proudhon's radical views on property and this was then related to the issue of marriage.[91] No works of Proudhon are in his Dresden library (indeed, there were no political books), but he most likely knew of his work from August Röckel.[92] Indeed, Wagner in his autobiography explains the implication of Proudhon on property as

---

85. E.g., Käsemann, *Jesus means Freedom*, 16–41.

86. Note, however, that the only way this text is relevant for Act I is that Jesus attacks the Pharisees for their hypocrisy and Jesus "expounds his doctrine of Love" (*PW* 8:286–87; *DTB* 242).

87. *PW* 8:325; *DTB* 260.

88. *PW* 8:325; *DTB* 260 (Wagner mistakenly ascribes this passage to Matthew chapter 18). Ellis, *PW* 8:323 n., explains that in his translation he has used the Authorised Version (1611) and Revised Version (1881) and subjected them to revision in the light of Wagner's original.

89. *PW* 8:325; *DTB* 260. This is marked "II" in his copy of the New Testament and was in fact employed for Act II (*PW* 8:288; *DTB* 242–43).

90. I encountered the frequent use of the term "bibeltreu" among the "Neupietisten" of the "Württembergische Landeskirche" whilst studying in Tübingen (1986–90).

91. See Proudhon: "What is property; Property is theft" and the discussion in chapter 5 above. Proudhon seems to have influenced Wagner to the end of his life. On seeing the unoccupied palaces in Venice, he comments: "That is property! The root of all evil (Der Grund alles Verderbens). Proudhon took a far too material view of it, for property brings about marriages for its sake, and in consequence causes the degeneration of the race (Degeneration der Race)" (See *CD* 5 February 1883).

92. See chapter 5 above.

developed by his friend Röckel: "he wanted to do away completely with the institution of marriage as he knew it."[93]

Implications for Current Debates on Sexuality

Although Wagner saw nothing wrong in the incest of the Volsungs or indeed in the myth of Oedipus, he would clearly use a different logic were he addressing a "real" situation (e.g., something happening in his own household). Considering the rightness of such incest in terms of consequences, neither Siegfried nor the children of Oedipus suffered from genetic complications; indeed, as we have seen, the composer emphasizes that Oedipus' children were all healthy. In the real world though things work out somewhat differently.

If his "mythical world" is so removed from the "real world," does Wagner's *Ring* then have anything practical to say about sexual ethics? One thing I think he was trying to achieve in the *Ring* was to establish a form of "situation ethics" whereby the primacy of the principle of love is emphasized: in a given situation one should follow the most loving course of action, and although laws and principles may offer some guidance as to what the most loving action is, in a given circumstance they can be rejected if necessary.[94] By taking the most extreme example, a case not only of adultery but also of incest, Wagner (using the voice of Wotan) was making a vivid point: Sieglinde and Siegmund are in love, the vow of marriage between Sieglinde and Hunding is not only void but "unholy," and therefore the bond between the Volsung twins should be blessed.[95]

Through Wotan's worldview Wagner is presenting a radical form of "situation ethics" to which I return. In terms of German idealism, one can say that he is opposing Kant's categorical imperative. Conversely, *to some extent* he could be seen to align himself with Hegel in the following way. Hegel argued that "[t]rue freedom [. . .] lies not merely in doing or choosing what one wishes, but in being a 'free will which wills the free will.'"[96] The free will therefore derives obligations from itself; it is "a self-legislating and self-determining will."[97] Obligations therefore do not come from some alien authority, a view Wagner would appear to support. If he knew Hegel's *Spirit of Christianity* (1799) he would also find views with which he would readily

---

93. In *My Life* 373; *Mein Leben* 1:387.

94. Fletcher, *Situation Ethics*, 86: "the Christ of the Christian ethic leaves no doubt whatsoever that *the ruling norm of Christian decision is love: nothing else.*" For a summary of the different forms of situation ethics, see Childress, "Situation Ethics," 586–88. Related theories are "Intuitionism" (a version of which is defended by McNaughton, "Intuitionism") and "Particularism" (debated in Hooker/Little, *Moral Particularism*).

95. WagRS 142.

96. Houlgate, *Introduction to Hegel*, 184, quoting *Philosophy of Right* §27 (Knox/Houlgate, *Philosophy of Right*, 46).

97. Houlgate, *Introduction to Hegel*, 185.

agree: "This spirit of Jesus, a spirit raised above morality [Kant's view of reason dominating inclination], is visible, directly attacking laws, in the Sermon on the Mount, which is an attempt, elaborated in numerous examples, to strip the laws of legality, of their legal form."[98] As we saw in chapter 2, Hegel argued against Kant that "in love all thought of duties vanishes."[99] "The opposition of duty to inclination has found its unification in the modifications of love, i.e., in the virtues. Since law was opposed to love, not in its content but in its form, it could be taken up into love, though in this process it lost its shape."[100] Such a view of morality is precisely that put forward by Wagner in both the *Ring* and in his *Jesus of Nazareth* sketches.

There then remains the question whether law is at all useful in ethical discussion. Fricka, we have seen, represents "law," and Wagner no doubt had in mind "Jewish law." Fricka, like the Pharisees in the *Jesus of Nazareth* sketches, embodies three of Wagner's "targets": Jews, Jesuits, and Lawyers.[101] She has few defenders among those writing on Wagner (and I imagine few defenders among Wagner audiences). One of those was Newman who, in an early study of 1899, thinks that Wagner has oversimplified questions of morality. He questions Wagner's setting forward "Fricka, as guardian of the conventional marriage law, and his Brynhild as the upholder of Love against traditional morality." He continues: "Even the most thoroughgoing revolutionary must draw back in amazement at this childlike mode of settling a huge social question. Has 'traditional morality' no justification?"[102] The question is though whether Wagner actually makes matters so simple. Many productions do present a one-sided view of Fricka as a nagging wife obsessed with "law"; but one of the few productions to present a more nuanced and dignified Fricka is that of Chereau.[103]

One can certainly say that Wagner opposes any legalistic religion and he has here in his sights Judaism and Catholicism (or at least the Jesuits). However, he perceived (rightly in my view) that Christianity can provide a framework that avoids such legalism. In preparing his sketches for *Jesus of Nazareth* Wagner had read systematically through the whole New Testament and had clearly considered carefully the Sermon on the Mount and the antitheses: "You have heard that it was said to the men of old

---

98. Hegel, *On Christianity*, 212.

99. Hegel, *On Christianity*, 213.

100. Hegel, *On Christianity*, 225.

101. In *What is German?* Wagner employs a "Stabreim" (*PW* 4:158n) in attacking "Junker" (young Prussian aristocracy), "Juristen" (lawyers), and "Juden" (Jews) (*GSD* 10:43). This was published in the *Bayreuther Blättter* for February 1878. Two months later Cosima actually refers to the "Jurist" as the "4th J" (*CD* 30 April 1878). To the three Js of *What is German?* one can add "Jesuiten" (Jesuits) and "Journalisten" (Journalists) "in which [Wagner] sees summed up all the negative features of his age" (Kühnel, "Prose Writings," 613).

102. Newman, *Study*, 226. Another notable defender of Fricka was Louise Otto in her review of the Leipzig *Ring* of 1878 in *Neue Bahnen* 13 (1878) 87 (McManus "Louise Otto," 182–83).

103. I am grateful to Ro Mody for highlighting this for me. Fricka here is played by Hanna Schwarz.

[. . .] But I say unto you [. . .]."[104] Not only were passages from Matt 5.17–48 marked[105] but some were earmarked for his drama and quoted in section II.2 of the sketches.[106] Had Wagner lived one century later I suspect that one of his favorite New Testament scholars would be Ernst Käsemann. As well as being a warrior for social justice, he underlined the radical nature of Jesus' teaching. He wrote that Jesus' repeated refrain in the Sermon on the Mount "But I say unto you" embodies "a claim to an authority which rivals and challenges that of Moses."[107] Jesus overcame the world of the demonic by the power of the Spirit of God[108] and by such inspiration "the Sabbath commandment and the law of purification are assailed" and "the demand for intelligent love is set up and placed in opposition to the demand of the rabbinate for blind obedience."[109] Likewise, Wagner saw that Jesus was not putting forward a "new law" in the sense of the law of Moses; rather he was setting out the "law of love," an idea he may well have taken from Rom 13:8–10.[110] He was also familiar with other passages of Paul's letters, which set out life in the Spirit and freedom from law.[111]

Wagner visited Britain on three occasions (1839, 1855, 1877) and if he were to visit again, but in the twentieth century, I think he would have little time for the socially awkward John A. T. Robinson. But I think he would certainly have some sympathy with these words of that controversial bishop:

> The moral precepts of Jesus are not intended to be understood legalistically, as prescribing what all Christians must do, whatever the circumstances, and pronouncing certain courses of action universally right and others universally wrong. They are not legislation laying down what love always demands of every one: they are illustrations of what love may at any moment require of anyone. They are, as it were, parables of the Kingdom in his moral claims—flashlight pictures of the uncompromising demand which the Kingdom must make on any who would respond to it.[112]

---

104. See Matt 5:21–48. This formula is found in vv. 21, 27, 31, 33, 38, 43. The first two (concerning anger and adultery) intensify the law of Moses, but the last four (concerning divorce, oaths, retaliation, and lover for enemies) oppose it. Stuhlmacher, *Biblische Theologie I*, 103, argues that in addition to the first two, antithesis 6 also is an intensification; some also argue for the fourth being an intensification.

105. He had marked vv. 17, 33–36, 45, 48.

106. Matt 5:17 for Act III (*PW* 8:333), 5:45, 48 for Act I (*PW* 8:323).

107. Käsemann, "Historical Jesus," 37.

108. Käsemann, "Historical Jesus," 41, referring to Matt 12:28.

109. Käsemann, "Historical Jesus," 42.

110. He marked Rom 13:8–9 and 13:10, considering them for use in Acts I and II respectively, although he did not quote them in section II.2.

111. E.g., he doubly marked Rom 7:7 (quoted for Act II, *PW* 8:332) and triply marked Rom 8:2 (quoted for Act V, *PW* 8:340).

112. Robinson, *Honest to God*, 110–11. He goes on (116–19) to appeal to Fletcher, "Christian Ethics."

— 8 —

Death and Immortality

Introduction

In the discussion of death and immortality in the *Ring* cycle a crucial distinction needs to be borne in mind. First, there is the question of the immortal gods. They are not naturally immortal since they need to eat Freia's golden apples in order to attain this (once the apples are no longer accessible as in *Rheingold* Scene 2 the strength of the gods wanes).[1] Secondly, there is the question whether mortal humans can attain some sort of immortality in the sense of a life beyond death (and related to this is the question of the immortal "soul").

Immortality of the Gods

Questions of the immortality of the gods are raised already with Erda's warning in *Rheingold* of the downfall of the gods:[2]

Alles was ist, endet.	All things that are—end.
Ein düst'rer Tag	A day of darkness
dämmert den Göttern:	dawns for the gods:
dir rath' ich, meide den Ring!	I counsel you [Wotan]: shun the ring!

One may think, as many do, that if Wotan were to give up the ring he can avoid the gods' downfall and end; and as we shall see this in fact is what Wotan does assume. But Erda's warning in *Rheingold* Scene 4 is not that Wotan can avoid the end if he gives up the ring, but that he will gain a different sort of end if he does so. This position is supported by the earlier version and Wagner points to this in his comments to Röckel where he quotes from this earlier version: "a gloomy day dawns on the gods: in shame shall end your noble race, if you do not give up the ring!"[3] However, the

---

1. *WagRS* 85–86.
2. *WagRS* 112.
3. *SL* 306; *SB* 6:67.

issue now is whether Wotan *understood* Erda correctly. In his monologue in *Walküre* Act II Scene 2 he recalls Erda's warning:[4]

Die Alles weiß	She who knows all
was einstens war,	that ever was,
Erda, die weihlich	Erda, the awesomely
weiseste Wala,	all-wise vala,
rieth mir ab von dem Ring,	told me to give up the ring
warnte vor ewigem Ende.	and warned of an end everlasting.
(*etwas heftiger*)	(*somewhat more forcefully*)
Von dem Ende wollt' ich	Of that end I wanted
mehr noch wissen;	to know yet more;
(*zurückhaltend*)	(*guardedly*)
doch schweigend entschwand mir das Weib.	but the woman vanished in silence.

This could suggest that he accepts that there is to be an "end" and perhaps now and again he did think so. But the drama suggests that he actually thought he could avoid the end. This is demonstrated by the idea of the "sword" at the end of *Rheingold* when Wotan declares: "Thus I salute the stronghold, safe from dread and dismay" with the stage direction "very resolutely, as though seized by a grandiose idea"[5] and with the second trumpet playing the sword motif.[6] Further, any acceptance he did have of the end of the gods was short lived; for in his monologue he goes on to tell how he visited Erda "in the womb of the world" and effectively raped her. He had a fascination with the goddess and managed to manipulate her ("I [. . .] mastered the vala (*zwang ich die Wala*) / with love's magic spell")[7] such that he could break her "wisdom's pride":[8]

Da verlor ich den leichten Muth;	Then I lost all lightness of heart;
zu wissen begehrt' es den Gott:	the god desired knowledge:
in den *Schooß* der Welt	into the *womb* of the world
schwang ich mich hinab,	I descended,
mit Liebes-Zauber	mastered the vala
zwang ich die Wala,	with love's magic spell
stört' ihres Wissens Stolz,	and broke her wisdom's pride,
daß sie Rede nun mir stand.	that she gave account of herself.

---

    4. *WagRS* 149–50; *SW* 11.II:94–95.

    5. *WagRS* 116.

    6. *SW* 10.II:392–93.

    7. *WagRS* 150 (my emphasis). Cf *Siegfried* III.1 (*WagRS* 256).

    8. *WagRS* 150 (my emphasis to highlight the textual variants). Note these variants: *SW* 11.II:95 (bar 729) has the spelling "Schoß" rather than "Schooß"; *GSD* 6:38 has "barg" instead of "empfing" (*WagRS* 367 n. 57); *SW* 11.II:96 has "Kind" rather than "Pfand."

Kunde empfing ich von ihr;	Knowledge I gained from her;
von mir doch *empfing* sie ein *Pfand*:	from me though she *gained* a *pledge*;
der Welt weisestes Weib	the world's wisest woman
gebar mir, Brünnhilde, dich.	bore to me, Brünnhilde, you.

The irony is that although claiming to have gained knowledge, Wotan actually became more confused through this sexual encounter. He embarked upon a new project producing children between *Rheingold* and *Walküre*.⁹ So "project Siegmund" was precisely planned to avoid the downfall of the gods. Siegmund was begotten so he could kill the dragon and recover the ring (to be returned to Wotan (not the Rhinemaidens)). The Valkyries were begotten so that Wotan would have an army to defend Valhalla against onslaught from his enemy (der Feind), namely Alberich. Wotan explains:¹⁰

durch euch Walküren	through you valkyries
wollt' ich wenden,	I hoped to avert
was mir die Wala	the fate that the vala
zu fürchten schuf—	had made me fear—
ein schmähliches Ende der Ew'gen.	*a shameful end of the gods everlasting.*
Daß stark zum Streit	That our foe might find us
uns fände der Feind,	stalwart in strife
hieß ich euch Helden mir schaffen:	I bade you bring me heroes:
die herrisch wir sonst	those men whom, high-handed,
in Gesetzen hielten,	we tamed by our laws,
die Männer, denen	those men whose mettle
den Muth wir gewehrt,	we held in check
die durch trüber Verträge	by binding them to us
trügende Bande	in blind allegiance
zu blindem Gehorsam	through troubled treaties'
wir uns gebunden—	treacherous bonds—
die solltet zu Sturm—	you'd to spur them on
(immer belebter, doch mit gemäßigter Stärke)	*(increasingly animated, but with muted force)*
und Streite ihr stacheln,	to onslaught and strife,
ihre Kraft reizen	honing their strength
zu rauhem Krieg,	for hot-blooded battle,
daß kühner Kämpfer Schaaren	so that hosts of valiant warriors
ich samm'le in Walhall's Saal.	I'd gather in Valhalla's hall.

9. Kitcher and Schacht, *End*, passim, seem to think that Wotan understands that the gods' downfall was inevitable right from Erda's warning. But this ignores what they call "project Siegmund" (112), an attempt to avert Wotan's downfall. Further, they admit that in Act II Scene 2 Wotan comes to a new understanding here (*WagRS* 153) but claim he has always been aware that he must come to an end.

10. *WagRS* 150 (my emphasis of the libretto); *SW* 11.II:98–102.

There is a certain ambiguity in "a shameful end of the gods everlasting": in its context it could indicate that he accepts an end, but not a shameful end, or he wants to avoid an end altogether. Wotan then explains that Erda warned him of Alberich's threat:[11]

Durch Alberich's Heer	Through Alberich's host
droht uns das Ende:	our end now threatens:
mit neidischem Grimm	burning with envious rage,
grollt mir der Niblung;	the Nibelung bears me ill-will:
(*belebend*)	(*more animated*)
doch scheu' ich nun nicht	but I'm not now afraid
seine nächtigen Schaaren—	of his forces of night—
meine Helden schüfen mir Sieg.	my heroes would defeat him.
(*gedämpfter*)	(*more muted*)
Nur wenn je den Ring	Only were he
zurück er gewänne—	to win back the ring
(*noch gedämpfter*)	(*even more muted*)
dann wäre Walhall verloren:	would Valhalla then be lost:
der der Liebe fluchte,	he who laid a curse on love,
er allein	he alone
nützte neidisch	in his envy would use
des Ringes Runen	the runes of the ring
zu aller Edlen	to the noble gods'
endloser Schmach;	unending shame;
der Helden Muth	my heroes' hearts
(*belebend*)	(*more animated*)
entwendet' er mir;	he'd turn against me,
die kühnen selber	forcing the brave
zwäng' er zum Kampf;	to battle with me
mit ihrer Kraft	and, with their strength,
bekriegte er mich.	wage war against me.

Wotan then goes on to explain his project Siegmund: he would beget a hero who could act independently of him. But after his argument with Fricka Wotan came to see how he had deceived himself and admits to Brünnhilde: "How slyly I sought / to deceive myself!"[12] That Wotan only comes to understand that his end is inevitable in *Walküre* Act II is further underlined by Erda's mysterious words. After saying he wishes "the end," he explains:[13]

---

11. *WagRS* 151; *SW* 11.II:104–7.
12. *WagRS* 153.
13. *WagRS* 153–54 (my emphasis); *SW* 11.II:129–30.

Und für das Ende	And Alberich will see
sorgt Alberich!—	to that end!—
Jetzt versteh' ich	*Only now* do I fathom
den stummen Sinn	the silent sense
des wilden Wortes der Wala:—	of the vala's mysterious words:—
"Wenn der Liebe finst'rer Feind	"When love's dark foe
zürnend zeugt einen Sohn,	begets a son in his fury,
der Sel'gen Ende	the end of the gods
säumt dann nicht!"	won't long be delayed!"

He explains that the dwarf has had his way with a woman and that she "harbours the seed of hate."[14] Therefore, I conclude that Wotan does seems to think between the end of *Rheingold* through to the confrontation with Fricka in *Walküre* Acts II that he can save his immortal status.

Turning to the other gods, Fricka herself seems naïve about the gods' destiny, assuming that they are immortal. She refers to herself as the "immortal goddess" ("Ew'gen").[15] She does ask whether Wotan's begetting the Volsung twins means "the end" of the "blessed immortals" but only in the sense that their moral authority would be compromised:[16]

So ist es denn aus	So is this the end
mit den ewigen Göttern,	of the blessed immortals,
seit du die wilden	since you begot
Wälsungen zeugtest?	those dissolute Wälsungs?

Further she criticizes her husband for "laughingly loosening / heaven's hold (Himmels Haft)"[17] in trying to support Siegmund.

In *Götterdämmerung* Act I Scene 3 Brünnhilde speaks to Waltraute of the "immortal gods"[18] and "glory of the immortals."[19] This is striking in view of her final words in *Siegfried* Act III: "Dusk of the gods (Götter-Dämm'rung), / let your darkness arise!"[20] Note also that in *Götterdämmerung* Act I Scene 3 Waltraute speaks of the fear of the lesser gods, i.e., their fear of death:[21]

---

14. *WagRS* 154.
15. *WagRS* 144.
16. *WagRS* 142.
17. *WagRS* 143.
18. *WagRS* 302.
19. *WagRS* 305.
20. *WagRS* 275.
21. *WagRS* 303.

Der Götter Rath	He convened
ließ er berufen;	the council of gods;
den Hochsitz nahm	his high seat
heilig er ein:	he solemnly took
ihm zu Seiten	and on either side
hieß er die bangen sich setzen	bade the anxious gods be seated

Wotan seems to have gladly given up on any hope of immortality, and Waltraute tells us he is even refusing Holda's apples:[22]

Holda's Äpfel	Holda's apples
rührt er nicht an:	he does not touch:
Staunen und Bangen	wonder and fear
binden starr die Götter.—	hold the gods in thrall.—

It would therefore appear that it is the lesser gods who are "anxious gods" for whom "wonder and fear" hold them "in thrall";[23] but Wotan himself is not anxious, his change of heart coming about in *Siegfried* Act III Scene 1. And in the following scene he has his one and only encounter with Siegfried, who "is infinitely wise, for he knows the highest truth, that death is better than a life of fear."[24]

So such is the end of the immortality of the gods, essentially caused by Wotan's mishandling a whole series of events from the fashioning of his spear from a branch of the World Ash Tree, through to building Valhalla, and making treacherous treaties. There are, however, two other gods to consider, in fact, goddesses: Erda and her daughter Brünnhilde. Erda has eternal qualities and in contrast to the "end of the gods" ("Götter Ende") of which Wotan speaks in *Siegfried* Act III Scene 1, he leaves her "to ageless sleep!" ("zu ew'gem Schlaf!")[25] Brünnhilde's immortality, however, is more involved to which I now turn.

In *Walküre* Act II Scene 2 Wotan tells Brünnhilde that what in words he reveals to no one "let it stay / unspoken for ever (ewig): / with myself I commune / when I speak with you."[26] Then in Act III Scene 3 Brünnhilde pleads with Wotan not "to dishonour / that part of you which is eternal (Dein ewig Theil)."[27] This suggests that there is a communion between father and daughter that is reflected in their immortality.

---

22. *WagRS* 303.
23. *WagRS* 303.
24. *LS* 309; *SB* 6:70 (letter to Röckel, 25/26 January 1854).
25. *WagRS* 257–58.
26. *WagRS* 149.
27. *WagRS* 187 (modified).

However, she comes to lose that immortality at the end of the Act as he kisses away her divinity ("so küßt er die Gottheit von dir").[28]

The word "eternal" ("ewig") is used a number of times in *Siegfried* Act III Scene 3. In a sense, this is ironic since Brünnhilde has lost her eternity and Siegfried is a mortal. One way of taking this word "ewig" is in a loose sense of "always," interpreting it in the light of Brünnhilde declaration: "O Siegfried! Yours / was I always! (war ich von je!)"[29] This could parallel Siegmund's words to Sieglinde, where there is no idea of "eternity":[30]

Was je ich ersehnt	Whatever I longed for
ersah' ich in dir;	I saw in you;
in dir fand ich	in you I found
was je mir gefehlt!	whatever I lacked!

However, it may be that more is actually going on in *Siegfried* Act III Scene 3; these words, a little earlier, may point to her eternity and what they mean for Siegfried:[31]

Ewig war ich,	Ever was I,
ewig bin ich,	Ever am I,
ewig in süß	ever beset by
sehnender Wonne—	sweet-yearning bliss—
doch ewig zu deinem Heil!	yet ever working for your salvation!

There is a significant "textual variant" that to my knowledge has not been discussed. What I have quoted corresponds to the words in the score.[32] However, the "Collected Writings" have for the second line "ewig wäre ich" ("I would be eternal") and this is also the reading in the *Dichtung* of 3–24 June 1851.[33] The line is missing in the *Prosaentwurf* of 24 May–1 June 1851, which simply runs "Ever was I, ever for your salvation" ("Ewig war ich, ewig zu deinem heil!").[34] If "ewig" has some sense of eternity then the version in the "Collected Writings" would make more sense, since Brünnhilde has lost her divinity. Translating "ewig" as "eternal" in the first line affirms her former immortality; whether it affirms her "pre-existence," as Huber suggests, is perhaps speculating a little too much.[35]

---

28. *WagRS* 191. This will be further explored in chapter 11 below.
29. *WagRS* 273 (modified).
30. *WagRS* 134.
31. *WagRS* 272 (modified).
32. *SW* 12.III:296.
33. *GSD* 6:172; Strobel, *Skizzen*, 192; *TBRN1* 327.
34. Strobel, *Skizzen*, 95; *TBRN1* 234.
35. Huber, *Ring*, 261. But note that he takes the reading "Ewig bin ich" (92).

When it comes to speaking of the eternal love between Brünnhilde and Siegfried (as when in the final moments of Act III when they declare "er/sie ist mir ewig")[36] I suggest the word "ewig" points to a different *quality* of time rather than everlasting *duration*,[37] a point that Nattiez seems to imply.[38] Wagner suggests this in his letter to Röckel, writing that the "unique nature" of love is that "it resembles the ebb and flow of the tide, changing, ending and living anew."[39] This contrasts with a love that is abstract and falsely praised because it has "permanence."[40] "The mere possibility of its indefinite continuance proves how non-essential is this kind of love." Then he describes what true eternity involves: "'Eternal'—in the true sense of the word—is that which negates (aufhebt) finitude (or rather: the concept of finitude): the concept of finitude is unsuited to 'reality' (das 'Wirkliche'), for reality, i.e. something that is constantly changing, new and multifarious—is precisely the negation (Aufhebung) of all that is merely imagined and conceived as finite: the infinitude of metaphysics is eternal unreality."[41] A number of terms and ideas are clearly Hegelian and one can compare what Hegel writes about spirit and this gives some support to the view that Wagner replaces "spirit" with "love."[42] Hegel argues that "Spirit is eternal" but adds that "[e]ternity is not mere duration but *knowing*—the knowing of what is eternal."[43] So "humanity is immortal only through cognitive knowledge, for only in the activity of thinking is its soul pure and free rather than moral and animallike. Cognition and thought are the root of human life, of human immortality as a totality within itself."[44] On the basis of such a text (and there are not many) one could possibly make a case that individual immortality is a consequence of Hegel's system.[45]

---

36. *WagRS* 275–76.

37. For this qualitative rather than quantitative understanding of "eternal" one can compare Wotan's leaving his inheritance to Siegfried, "dem ewig Jungen" (*WagRS* 258).

38. Nattiez, *Androgyne*, 126, writes about Siegfried and Brünnhilde breaking down their egoism and enjoying the "supreme unity through which one can taste immortality" (see the fuller quotation in chapter 6 above).

39. *SL* 303; *SB* 6:63.

40. *SL* 304; *SB* 6:63.

41. *SL* 304; *SB* 6:63–64.

42. Corse, *Consciousness*, 21.

43. Hegel, *Philosophy of Religion*, 3:208–9; *Philosophie der Religion*, 3:140–41.

44. Hegel, *Philosophy of Religion*, 3:304; *Philosophie der Religion*, 3:227–28.

45. Note, however, that those who claim Hegel can support immortality are in a minority. Shortly after Hegel's death two works to argue that Hegel's philosophy can at least support the basis for immortality were those of the "Right Hegelians" Weisse, *Unsterblichkeit* (1834) and Göschel, *Unsterblichkeit* (1835) (Stewart, "Religion," 85). Note that Weisse's work was published just two years after Wagner had heard him lecture on aesthetics at the University of Leipzig. As noted in volume 1, chapter 6 the general thrust of Hegel's view is not in the direction of the traditional view of immortality and Houlgate, *Introduction to Hegel*, 266, puts his finger on the subtlety of Hegel's position: "Eternal life does not begin or continue when we have physically passed away, for Hegel. It comes rather when one has accepted the finality of death in the faith that death is not ultimately a barrier or threat to our lives, but that Christ-like acceptance of death will take away death's sting, set us free from the empty concern

The other issue to address in Brünnhilde's words to Siegfried quoted above is how to understand "Heil" in the phrase "doch ewig zu deinem Heil!" Spencer translates "but ever working for your own weal"[46] and Mann is similar "but always caring for your good."[47] Deathridge though translates "but also for ever to save you"[48] and I have translated "Heil" as "salvation." The use of "Heil" in *Walküre* Act I Scene 3 may shed some light. Sieglinde, having drugged Hunding, tells Siegmund: "Use night's cover to save your life! (Nütze die Nacht dir zum Heil!)" He responds: "Your coming brings me life! (Heil macht mich dein Nah'n!)"[49] Although Spencer translates "Heil" as "life" a salvific meaning of "Heil" may well be here,[50] and he and Millington point to the ambiguous meaning of the word, "its meaning extending from physical safety and well-being to eschatological salvation."[51] Further, for Wagner the word "seems to have been associated additionally with that sense of 'wholeness' which comes through mutual recognition."[52] Hence, both *Walküre* Act I Scene 3 and *Siegfried* Act III Scene 3 could be seen in Hegelian terms of wholeness coming about through mutual recognition. Siegmund and Sieglinde see something of each other in their partner; for Siegfried and Brünnhilde matters may be more complex since, as argued in chapter 6 above, Brünnhilde may be understood as incorporating Siegfried into her being and hence offering him "salvation" ("Heil").

Hence, Brünnhilde *was* eternal, and she loses her immortality because she did the right and loving thing, defending Siegmund, whom she knew her father loved. She lost her immortality because she realized what true erotic love involved as she witnessed Siegmund's love for Sieglinde. The point at which she loses her immortality is as Wotan kisses the godhead from her at the end of *Walküre*. This, I will argue, can be understood as an allegory for Jesus' incarnation. Further, Brünnhilde gladly accepts her "incarnation," although there is also a tragic aspect: separation from her beloved father. She will no longer be able to bring heroes to Valhalla or hand Wotan his drinking horn at the gods' "friendly feast." Nevermore will Wotan "fawn" on her "childlike mouth";[53] she will be cut off from the "kin of immortals."[54]

In view of Brünnhilde's loss of immortality it would be instructive to consider what the sketches *Jesus of Nazareth* say about Jesus' own immortality. The earthly Jesus

---

for ourselves and fill us with Christ's love."

46. *WagRS* 272.
47. Mann, *Siegfried*, 100.
48. Deathridge, *Ring*, 529.
49. *WagRS* 132. Note how the German offers a pleasing mirror image: "Nütze die *Nacht* dir zum Heil! / Heil *macht* mich dein Nah'n!"
50. Berry, *Bonds*, 189. See also Deathridge, *Ring*, 181: "Use the night for your salvation! / Your return is my salvation!"
51. *WagRS* 366 n. 44.
52. *WagRS* 366 n. 44; they point to Corse, *Consciousness*, 116–19.
53. *WagRS* 181.
54. *WagRS* 182.

is obviously subject to aging and death and it is often said that in *Jesus of Nazareth* there is no sense of immortality. There is certainly no resurrection of Jesus (there is a resurrection of Levi's daughter, but she was brought back to life only to die again).[55] However, the sketches do suggest a "second coming" and this surely presupposes some form of "immortal soul" or something similar for Jesus. Wagner in fact uses the terms "wiederkunft" / "wiederkehr" (second coming), which are precisely the terms used in Christian dogmatics. Towards the end of Act II Jesus "foreshadows his redeeming death and second advent (wiederkunft) for the liberation of mankind."[56] Then in the middle of Act IV, after we read that the disciples will come to understand Jesus "through his sacrificial death, after which the Holy Ghost shall be sent to them,"[57] he adds in the margin "Announcement of his future and return (wiederkehr)" together with "That I may be ever with you, I now must depart from you."[58] In part II.1 of the sketches there is a reference to the second coming. These words are put into Jesus' mouth: "I am the Messiah and the son of God: I tell you this that ye may not be led astray and look (wartet) for any other."[59] Wagner adds that for the second coming (wiederkunft) of Jesus one should note 2 Thess 2:8–12.[60]

Immortality of Humans

In the *Ring* human beings are not created immortal and there is nothing about an "immortal soul." But there is the hope of an afterlife in Valhalla for the heroes who die on the battlefield and this brings us to the scene where Brünnhilde calls Siegmund to Valhalla.

The opening of *Walküre* Act II Scene 4 presents Brünnhilde's "announcement of death" ("Todesverkündigung"). As she enters, she is accompanied by solemn hymn-like music played by the Wagner tubas. Siegmund's response to her call "Siegmund!—/ Look on Me! / I am she / whom you'll follow soon" suggests that her appearance may be understood as a "supernatural one":[61]

Wer bist du, sag',	Who are you, say,
die so schön und ernst mir *erscheint*?	who *appears* before me so fair and solemn?

This is confirmed by her reply:[62]

55. *PW* 8:285; *DTB* 241.
56. *PW* 8:289; *DTB* 243.
57. Wagner references the Gospel of John.
58. *PW* 8:292; *DTB* 244.
59. *PW* 8:308; *DTB* 253.
60. *PW* 8:308; *DTB* 253.
61. *WagRS* 159 (my emphasis).
62. *WagRS* 159.

DEATH AND IMMORTALITY

Nur Todgeweihten	The death-doomed alone
taugt mein Anblick:	are destined to look on me:
wer mich erschaut,	he who beholds me
der scheidet vom Lebens-Licht.	goes hence from life's light.
Auf der Walstatt allein	In battle alone
erschein' ich Edlen:	I appear before heroes:
wer mich gewahrt,	him who perceives me
zur Wal kor ich ihn mir.	I've chosen as one of the slain.

Hence, Siegmund has been *chosen* to receive such an "appearance" as one not simply *doomed* to death but, as "Todgeweihten" and the *context* of the scene could also suggest, *consecrated* to death. In the ensuing scene there is no physical contact between the two. Brünnhilde does, however, have physical contact with Sieglinde at the end of the act as the stage direction indicates: "She lifts Sieglinde on to her horse [...] and immediately *disappears* with her."[63] Sieglinde seems to enter a supernatural realm with Brünnhilde!

Returning to Siegmund's encounter with the Valkyrie, she tells him that "The Lord of the Slain (Walvater) / has chosen you."[64] Siegmund then asks a series of questions. Will he find Walvater alone? Might he find his own father, Wälse?[65] Will a woman greet him in Valhalla? To this last question Brünnhilde tells him that "Wotan's daughter" will hand him his drink, whom Siegmund correctly understands will be Brünnhilde herself. Then comes the crucial question:[66]

Hehr bist du,	Awesome are you,
und heilig gewahr' ich	and Wotan's child
das Wotanskind:	I behold with holy wonder:
doch Eines sag' mir, du Ew'ge!	but tell me one thing, immortal!
Begleitet den Bruder	Will the sister-bride
die bräutliche Schwester?	go with her brother?
Umfängt Siegmund	Will Siegmund embrace
Sieglinde dort?	Sieglinde there?

And then comes the devastating reply:[67]

---

63. *WagRS* 166 (my emphasis).
64. *WagRS* 160.
65. *WagRS* 160. Siegmund does not realize that the "Lord of the Slain" and his father "Wälse" are in fact the same.
66. *WagRS* 160.
67. *WagRS* 160.

Erdenluft	Earthly air
muß sie noch athmen:	she must breathe awhile:
Sieglinde	Siegmund
sieht Siegmund dort nicht!	will not see Sieglinde there!

It is a sign of Wagner's genius that Siegmund does not immediately react with any sense of outrage. The stage direction simply indicates: "bending gently over Sieglinde, kissing her softly on the brow and turning calmly to Brünnhilde once more."[68] Then Siegmund sings with a melody of nobility (almost hymn-like):[69]

So grüße mir Walhall,	Then greet for me Valhalla,
grüße mir Wotan,	greet for me Wotan,
grüße mir Wälse	greet for me Wälse
und alle Helden—	and all the heroes—
grüß' auch die holden	greet, too, Wotan's
Wunsches-Mädchen:—	gracious daughters:—

Then he adds "very emphatically" the crucial words: "to them I follow you not." At this point the hymn-like music then suddenly changes as Siegmund rejects Brünnhilde's offer of immortality[70] and is accompanied by a motif (at bar 1619) sometimes called "Siegmund's rebellion."[71] This recurs at a number of points as the Act progresses (e.g., bars 1621–26, 1629–60, 1714, 1719–24, 1726–30), including at the point of Siegmund's death (bars 2001–2, 2003–4) and later in Brünnhilde's dialogue with Wotan in Act III Scene 3 (bars 1019–1025).

Looking back at this part of the scene we see that Siegmund not only rejects the pleasures of Valhalla but also his own father and the god himself; but he does not reject immortality itself but rather the fact that he cannot share this with Sieglinde. The reason he speaks of "Valhalla's cold delights"[72] is not because he rejects Valhalla in principle but because Sieglinde will not be with him.

I now turn to the question as to how Wagner's approach to immortality could be related to the philosophical trends of his time. Although Kant was able to champion immortality as a prerequisite for practical reason, a case can be made that it virtually disappeared in Hegel's thought and this was further developed by Feuerbach. Many

---

68. *WagRS* 161.

69. *WagRS* 161. His response suggests that Siegmund identifies Walvater with Wotan (but not with Wälse).

70. The idea of Siegmund's rejection of immortality is first found in the second prose sketch for *Walküre* dated 17–26 May 1852 (Strobel, *Skizzen*, 243; *TBRN1* 437).

71. Sabor, *Walküre*, 113.

72. *WagRS* 163.

have related Siegmund's rejection of immortality to Feuerbach's 1830 work *Thoughts on Death and Immortality* and Berry points to this passage, to which I add the German:[73]

Der Himmel dann die Erde hier	Once in heaven, this earth
Das schöne Jenseits wär' sie dir.	Would become for you the beautiful hereafter.
Du würdest die Unsterblichkeit	You would gladly give up immortality
Gern geben hin für diese Zeit,	For this time,
Und aus dem leid'gen Engelsstand	And, in the land of death, you
Dich sehnen in des Todes Land,	Would long to leave the tiresome angelic state
Um wieder auf dieser Erden	To become a loving human
Ein lieb'nder Mensch zu werden.	Once again on this earth.
Denn Hier ist ja das schönste Land,	For the most beautiful land, the best condition
Ein Mensch zu sein, der höchste Stand,	For being a human is here;
Nur wo es Kampf und Leiden gibt,	Only where there are conflict and suffering,
Und Schmerz der Seele Hellung trübt,	Where pain clouds the clarity of soul,
Da ist mein wahres Vaterland,	Only there is my true fatherland;
Schmerz ist des Geistes Unterpfand.	Pain is the pledge of Spirit.
Es mögen feige Pfaffen	Let cowardly clerics
Ins Jenseits sich vergaffen!	Fall in love with the hereafter!
Mir bleibe nur mein Schmerz,	Only my pain is left to me,
Mein liebend heißes Herz.	Only my loving, burning heart.
Und wollten Alle himmlisch sein,	And if the whole world wished to be divine,
Und gingen in den Himmel ein	And to go to heaven—
—Was aber ich nicht glauben kann,	Which I cannot believe,
Es gibt noch manchen tapfern Mann—	For three still are some brave men—
Ich bliebe draußen stehen,	I would stay outside,
Ich möcht' nicht hinein gehen.	I would not go in.

Wagner writes on reading Feuerbach's *Thoughts on Death and Immortality*: "I found it elevating and consoling to be assured that the sole authentic immortality adheres only to sublime deeds and inspired works of art."[74] So one may well find echoes of this work of Feuerbach in Wagner's world of thought. Wagner, like Feuerbach, had some contempt for the established church in his early and middle years, and Feuerbach's reference in the passage above to "cowardly clerics" ("feige Pfaffen") may be reflected in the name "Fafner," who, although hardly a coward, could be seen to be a representative of the clerics and the papacy.[75] More significant is that the composer certainly came to stress the centrality of sensuous love in this world.[76] However, as far

---

73. Berry, *Bonds*, 166. Feuerbach, *Thoughts*, 145–46; *LFW* 1:239–40.

74. *My Life* 430; *Mein Leben* 1:442.

75. See the discussion in chapter 10 below.

76. See, for example, *Artisthood of the Future* (*PW* 8:349): "Only the sensuous (sinnlich) is also

as *Walküre* Act II Scene 4 is concerned, it is essential to note that Siegmund does not reject immortality in itself. He is certainly fascinated by this world of Valhalla where he would be able to meet his father again, and one could say there is no indication that Valhalla is "the tiresome angelic state," as in Feuerbach. Indeed, in some respects Wagner has made Valhalla especially attractive and his concept of Valhalla transcends the afterlife of Norse and Germanic mythology. Brünnhilde describes it to Siegmund as "bliss everlasting" ("ewige Wonne").[77] There is none of the rather macabre routine of *Vafthrúdnismál* where the Einherjar (fallen heroes) fight with each other every day only to be brought back to life to feast with Odin and to fight anew the next day.[78] But the main problem is that apart from the Wünschmächen there are no women, thus corresponding to the general view of the Norse sources.[79] Apart from women being barred entry, Brünnhilde presents Valhalla in the most positive terms; and if Sieglinde could come with him there is no doubt he would gladly follow Brünnhilde to Valhalla. One can say that whereas Wotan has a rejection of "will to life," Siegmund stands more firmly in Feuerbach's line and demonstrates true courage.[80]

Some find a parallel to Siegmund's rejection of immortality in Achilles' rejection of immortality in Wagner's sketches for his play, composed when he started work on the *Ring*.[81] Here we read: "Achilles waives the immortality his mother Thetis offers him, an immortality without delight: the delight he is to reap from vengeance allows him to spurn the joys of immortality. (His mother acknowledges that Ach. is greater than the elements (the gods). Man is the completion of god. The eternal gods are the elements for the begetting of man. In man, therefore, creation finds its end. Achilles is higher and more perfect than the elemental Thetis."[82] Gregor-Dellin believes that this idea of

---

sensible (sinnig): the non-sensuous is also nonsensical: the sensible is the perfection of the physical;—the senseless the true purport of the non-physical world."

77. *WagRS* 162.

78. *Vafthrúdnismál* 41 (Orchard, *Elder Edda*, 46); *Gylfaginning* 41 (Faulkes, *Edda*, 34). See Ellis Davidson, *Gods*, 152.

79. Ellis Davidson, *Gods*, 150–52. Huber, *Ring*, 212, points out that the exclusion of women in Valhalla means nothing other than that the whole of the human person does not enter there but only "das Heldenhafte und Kämpferische" and that the individuality of the person is lost. "Daher bleibt die Walhallvorstellung unbefriedigend."

80. Berry, *Bonds*, 167 argues that he is courageous rather than fearless (as Siegfried is).

81. *DTB* 268 dates these sketches to the first half of 1849. Such a dating is suggested not only by his *Annals 1846–1867* (*Brown Book* 96, *Braunes Buch* 114; see also *DTB* 57) but also by the Latin script together with the general use of small letters which he started using in December 1848. The sketch concerns just the third act. Cf. *CD* 1 April 1878: "I also sketched the third act of an Achilles [. . .]."

82. *PW* 8:367–68. *DTB* 268 (*WWV* 81): "Achilleus weisst die unsterblichkeit, die ihm seine mutter Thetis anbietet, von sich, diese unsterblichkeit ohne genuss: der genuss, den ihm die befriedigung seine<r>s rachedurstes gewähren soll, lässt ihn die freu<nd>den der unsterblichkeit verachtungsvoll entsagen. (Seiner mutter erkennt an, dass Ach: grösser sei als die elemente (d. götter.) / Der mensch ist die vervollkommnung gottes. Die ewigen götter sind die elemente die erst den menschen zeugen. In dem menschen findet die schöpfung somit ihren abschluss. Achilleus ist höher und vollendeter als die elementare Thetis." The phrase "vervollkommnung gottes" could also be translated "consummation of god" (cf. Gregor-Dellin, *Life*, 172). Note that the problem in nesting the brackets is found in the

human being as the consummation of god and the accomplishment of creation is "one of the basic ideas of the *Ring*."[83] However, there are differences: Achilles simply rejects it because otherwise he could not exact vengeance for the killing of Patroculus.

Returning to our scene, it is one of the most moving in the whole *Ring* cycle.[84] As Brünnhilde approaches at the beginning of the scene we hear the motif of "fate" or "mutual recognition" (bars 1462–64, 1466–68, 1474–76, 1478–80) and the timpani which tells of death. Also introduced is a four bar theme that is associated with Siegmund's impending death and recurs through this scene with variations. Sabor calls this motif "death" and points out that the first two bars derive from the Wälsung motif and the next two from the fate motif.[85] Brünnhilde's calling of Siegmund to Valhalla alludes to the scene in Marschner's *Hans Heiling* where the Queen of the Earth Spirits tells Anna (a mortal) that she must release Hans Heiling from the "net of her love magic" so he may return to his otherworldly throne.[86] The point to emphasize in *Walküre* Act II is that Siegmund rejects immortality because he puts his love of Sieglinde first. It is in a way an expression of the decision many have taken whether to put love for a human being before religious beliefs.[87] We know that Wagner understood the scene in this sort of way from Cosima's diary: "He tells of Radbod, the Prince of Frisia, who, with one foot already in the font, leaped back when he heard that he would not meet his heathen father in Heaven (Siegmund!)."[88] Siegmund's response to the offer of immortality is in fact more radical, since he says he will choose "Hella" to be with his beloved.

Brünnhilde cannot understand why Siegmund would choose to be with Sieglinde. Siegmund's response is that though Brünnhilde is "young and fair" and shimmers before him, she is also "cold and hard" and "unfeeling."[89] But, as was discussed in chapter 5 above, Brünnhilde in witnessing Siegmund's love for Sieglinde is fundamentally transformed, and provides one of the key turning points for the whole *Ring* cycle.

Immortality of Siegfried and Brünnhilde

One issue of immortality that seems unclear is that of Siegfried and Brünnhilde. *Brynhild's Hel-ride* has a view of immortality in that after her being burned on her funeral

---

original.

83. Gregor-Dellin, *Life*, 172; *Leben*, 267.

84. I noted in volume 1, chapter 2 that it is said that Liszt was moved to tears in the scene with Brünnhilde and Siegmund.

85. Sabor, *Walküre*, 69.

86. Warrack, "Musical Background," 110 (Ex. 13). See Act II no 9 (Marschner, *Heiling*, 102–3). Wagner conducted the opera in January 1844 (Newman, *Life*, 1:361; reviews in Kirchmeyer, *Wagner-Bild II*, nos. 310, 312).

87. Adding an "unscientific" observation, I was particularly struck by this issue when I worked in a Church in London. See volume 1, chapter 1.

88. *CD* 21 July 1871. Ortrud in *Lohengrin* is the daughter of Radbod.

89. *WagRS* 163.

pyre she "drove in her wagon along the road to Hel" and ends her altercation with the giantess (who challenges her right to go to hel) with the words: "we too shall never be torn apart, / Sigurd and I together: sink yourself, giantess-spawn!"[90] Sigurd does not go to Valhalla since he was not killed on the battlefield; rather he, and Brynhild, go to the land of the dead, Hel (this corresponds to the Greek Hades and Hebrew Sheol).

In Wagner's *Siegfried's Tod* of 1848 the hero does enter Valhalla despite not dying on the battlefield. Brünnhilde confidently declares:[91]

Allvater! Herrlicher du!	All-father! Magnificent one!
Freue dich des freiesten Helden!	Rejoice in the freest of heroes!
Siegfried führ' ich dir zu:	Siegfried I bring to you:
biet' ihm minnlichen Gruß,	Give him a loving greeting,
dem Bürgen ewiger Macht!	The protector of eternal power!

In case there should be any doubt about the destiny of Siegfried (and Brünnhilde), it is debated by the women and the vassals and it is finally affirmed that "Valhalla can greet them / United in eternal bliss!"[92]

---

90. Orchard, *Elder Edda*, 193, 195.
91. Haymes, *Ring*, 182–83.
92. Haymes, *Ring*, 182–85.

Die Frauen:	The women:
Fiel er im Streit? Starb er im Haus?	Did he fall in battle? Did he die at home?
Geht er nach Hellja's Hof?	Is he going to Hellja's court?
Die Mannen	The vassals:
Der ihn erschlug, besiegte ihn nicht,	The one who killed him did not conquer him,
nach Walhall wandert der Held.	The hero goes now to Valhalla.
Die Frauen:	The women:
Wer folgt ihm nach, daß nicht auf die Ferse	Who follows him, so that Valhalla's doors
Walhall's Thüre ihm fällt?	Do not strike him on the heels?
Die Mannen	The vassals:
Ihm folgt sein Weib in den Weihebrand,	His wife follows him to the sacrificial fire,
ihm folgt sein rüstiges Roß.	His mighty steed follows him.
Die Mannen und Frauen zusammen:	The vassals and women together:
Wotan! Wotan! Waltender Gott!	Wotan! Wotan! Ruling god!
Wotan, weihe den Brand!	Wotan, bless the pyre!
Brenne Held und Braut,	Burn hero and bride,
brenne das treue Roß:	Burn the faithful steed:
daß wundenheil und rein,	So that free of wounds and pure,
Allvater's freie Genossen,	All-father's free companions,
Walhall froh sie begrüßen	Valhalla can greet them
zu ewiger Wonne vereint!	United in eternal bliss!

The stage direction also clearly implies that they do enter Valhalla since Brünnhilde "as a Valkyrie" "leads Siegfried by the hand through the air."[93]

The picture in *Götterdämmerung* is somewhat different, partly because Wagner changes the whole structure of the ending: the gods no longer rule and there will be no Valhalla for Siegfried and Brünnhilde to enter! The close of *Götterdämmerung* is ambiguous, probably deliberately so. Brünnhilde prepares to greet Siegfried but the stage directions are silent about the couple's destiny since the focus then moves to the ensuing conflagration, the overflow of the Rhine and the twilight of the gods. Addressing Grane, she asks: "Do you know my friend, / where I'm taking you now?" ("Weißt du auch, mein Freund, wohin ich dich führe?"). The answer is not Valhalla but simply to be with Siegfried, her final words being "Siegfried! Siegfried! See! / In bliss your wife bids you welcome (Selig grüßt dich dein Weib!)."[94] They are in some sense reunited, but how exactly is unclear.[95]

---

93. Haymes, *Ring*, 184–85.
94. *WagRS* 350–51.
95. See chapter 10 below on the numinous aspects of the final scene.

Concluding Thoughts

This chapter has raised some fundamental existential issues regarding death and any hope for immortality. Wagner addresses death in the commentary of his *Jesus of Nazareth* sketches: "The most complete divestment of my Me (die vollständigste entäusserung meines Ich's) takes place through death;—for inasmuch as I completely upheave (aufhebe) my Me, thus make it naught, I mount completely to the Universal (gehe ich vollständig in das allgemeine auf), which henceforth is something substantial and stands in the same relation to me through my death as I stood to it through my birth."[96] To some extent what he writes reflects Feuerbach's *Thoughts*: "Death is the total and complete dissolution of your entire being; there exists only one death, which is total."[97] But he does add another dimension in that how the Universal stands to me through my death is how I stand to it through my birth. By so arguing he is pointing to the symmetry between birth and death. Plato's view of the pre-existence of souls,[98] which was held also by early Christian theologians such as Origen,[99] is often thought to be a rather odd idea. But Flew comments that Plato in insisting on both pre-existence and immortality "was adopting a less arbitrary position than that of those who assert immortality only. It was not without reason that in the Ancient World spokesmen for human mortality made much of the comparison between our nothingness before conception and our annihilation in death. [...] As Santayana once remarked: 'The fact of being born is a poor augury of immortality.'"[100]

Although there is little about the hope of any immortal life in the *Ring*, in later life Wagner was clearly drawn to the idea, partly because he increasingly appropriated the philosophy of Kant and Schopenhauer; so although the body in the world of the phenomena may die, the thing-in-itself transcends space and time and may be said to "remain."[101]

---

96. *PW* 8:318; *DTB* 257.
97. Feuerbach, *Thoughts*, 22; *LFW* 1:101.
98. *Phaedo* 75C–77B (Fowler, *Plato I*, 262–69).
99. Trigg, *Origen*, 107, 213.
100. Flew, *Death*, 13–14.
101. Bell, *Parsifal*, 257–58.

— 9 —

Freedom, Necessity, and Providence

Introduction

The theme of freedom and necessity is one that runs throughout the *Ring* cycle and is reflected not only in the drama but is actually part of the discussion between some of the protagonists, as we shall see in *Walküre* Act II. The issue of freedom and necessity also occupied Wagner in his Zurich essays, written as he worked on the *Ring* libretto; in fact, it occupied him for the rest of his life, not only in stage works but again also in essays, especially *Religion and Art*.[1] Alongside the question of freedom and necessity is that of providence, and as one experiences the *Ring* this sense of providence is unmistakable. Wagner's interest in freedom and necessity largely concern human beings, but they are also relevant to God or gods, and it is to this topic that I first turn.

Freedom of the Gods

In some strands of Christian theology the freedom of God is stressed. So Rom 9:7–29, a rather unpalatable text that speaks of God predestining one group to salvation and another to damnation, is at the same time an expression of God's freedom (see especially Rom 9:18, 19–21). However, there is a certain irony in this freedom, for God is himself constrained, and this is something Paul comes to see a little later on, in Romans 11. For since God has made promises to Israel he must be faithful to such promises, otherwise his character would be seriously impugned. Therefore, he has to see that "all Israel" comes through to final salvation (Rom 11:25–27), "for the gifts and calling of God are irrevocable" (Rom 11:28). Hence, he "contradicts" his earlier statement in Rom 9:27 (a quotation from Isa 10:22): "Though the number of the children of Israel were like the sand of the sea, only a remnant of them will be saved."[2] The reason the question of Israel's salvation was so important to Paul was because if God went back on his promises to Israel he could just as well go against any promises made to Christians, thus jeopardizing their salvation. Hence, in Romans

---
1. See Bell, *Parsifal*, 164–80.
2. On the understanding of this "contradiction" see Bell, *Provoked to Jealousy*, 139–40.

9–11 Paul in many ways deals with the question of the "perseverance of the saints," that is assuring Christians of their final salvation.

In the *Ring* the god who finds himself in the terrible conflicts of keeping to his promises is, of course, Wotan and this is an issue that arises particularly in *Walküre* Act II Scene 2, to which I turn.

Walküre Act II Scene 2: Wotan's Promises

Wotan is constrained by promises he made. All the constraints appear to go back to the treaty he made with the giants (i.e., he has to pay them for their work in building Valhalla). Then by stealing the gold from Alberich one thing led to another such that now he says that he has bound himself in his own fetters;[3] his bonds hold him "in thrall" and he is "a slave to those treaties."[4] Being bound to such treatises leads to the great tragedy in *Walküre*. He has to see his own son, whom he dearly loves (or perhaps one should say has grown to love), die:[5]

Der Fluch, den ich floh,	The curse that I fled
nicht flieht er nun mich:—	won't flee from me now:—
was ich liebe, muß ich verlassen,	what I love I must relinquish,
morden, wen je ich minne,	murder him whom I cherish
trügend verrathen	and foully betray
wer mir traut!—	him who trusts me!—

This is an example, I believe, where a Christian allegorical interpretation of *Walküre* is possible. In the Christian theology of sin and redemption there is the central idea that God has issued various laws that human beings are powerless to keep. One can debate whether these are good laws (cf. Rom 7:12) or bad ones (animal sacrifice, brutal punishments such as stoning, etc).[6] Wotan's are a mixture of the two. His intention is to give good laws and create order in the world, but he also speaks of treacherous bonds. In Christian theology the fact that laws have been contravened means that some reparation is necessary and some sort of atonement (at-one-ment) is required. This is achieved through Christ's sacrificial death; whether one deals with penal substitution or with a levitical type of sacrifice, some sort of atonement is necessary.[7] The

---

3. *WagRS* 148.
4. *WagRS* 152.
5. *WagRS* 153.
6. Wagner is critical of Old Testament laws, blaming them for the negative view of animals (*PW* 6:203; *GSD* 10:203). See also Bell, *Parsifal*, 190–91.
7. Penal substitution is the view that God must punish human beings because they have broken his laws and that Jesus Christ is punished as their substitute (hence, there is an "exclusive place-taking"). In contrast, the levitical sin offering, upon which Paul most likely built his theology of the sacrifice of Christ, deals with an "inclusive place-taking" whereby human beings participate in Christ's death (see

parallel between the necessity of Christ's death and that of Siegmund's is clear. And in Act III Wotan tells Brünnhilde that it was out of love for the world that Siegmund had to die.[8] But there are also clear differences between God of Christian theology and Wotan, the key being that the biblical God is presented as "holy" whereas Wotan "falls" and is guilty. But both are presented as struggling with dilemmas. So like Wotan we see Yahweh tearing out his heart as he wonders how to deal with Israel.[9]

The intriguing aspect of Wotan's struggle is that, as Wagner puts it, he "rises to the tragic heights of willing his own destruction." He adds: "This is all that we need to learn from the history of mankind: *to will what is necessary* and to bring it about ourselves."[10]

Walküre Act II Scene 1: Siegmund's Agency

Freedom and necessity is raised in the altercation between Wotan and Fricka in *Walküre* Act II Scene 1. Here we are dealing not so much with how sin may restrict freedom but with the question of human and divine agency. Wotan argues that he needs a hero who can act independently of the gods:[11]

Noth thut ein Held,	A hero is needed
der, ledig göttlichen Schutzes,	who, lacking godly protection,
sich löse vom Göttergesetz:	breaks loose from the law of the gods;
so nur taugt er	thus alone is he fit
zu wirken die That,	to perform that feat
die, wie noth sie den Göttern,	which, needful though it is to the gods,
dem Gott doch zu wirken verwehrt.	the god is forbidden to do.

But Fricka asks:[12]

Was hehres sollten	What lofty feat
Helden je wirken,	could heroes perform
das ihren Göttern wäre verwehrt,	that their gods were prevented from doing,
deren Gunst in ihnen nur wirkt?	whose grace informs their actions alone?

Bell, "Sacrifice and Christology"). I will return to these issues in chapter 11 below.

8. *WagRS* 186.

9. See, e.g., Hos 11:8: "How can I give you up, Ephraim? / How can I hand you over, O Israel? / How can I make you like Admah? / How can I treat you like Zeboiim? / My heart recoils within me; / my compassion grows warm and tender."

10. Letter to Röckel of 24/25 January 1854 (*SL* 307; *SB* 6:68).

11. *WagRS* 144.

12. *WagRS* 144.

Two important points are raised here. First, that according to Fricka the gods themselves are free (and therefore why bother with heroes). But, of course, Wagner suggests they are *not* in fact free. Secondly, the gods' grace (Gunst) works within the heroes anyway. However, Wotan thinks Siegmund can act independently of him and therefore asks:[13]

Ihres eig'nen Muthes	Have you no heed
achtest du nicht?	of their own independence?

She responds:[14]

Wer hauchte Menschen ihn ein?	Who breathed it into human kind?
Wer hellte den Blöden den Blick?	Who lighted the coward's eyes?
In deinem Schutz	Sheltered by you,
scheinen sie stark,	they seem to be strong;
durch deinen Stachel	spurred on by you,
streben sie auf:	they strive for the light:
du—reizest sie einzig,	you alone urge them on
die so mir Ew'gen du rühm'st.	whom you thus praise to me, the immortal goddess.

As Donington comments, "Siegmund is no more than Wotan acting vicariously."[15]

The same issue regarding agency arises later in the scene with respect to Brünnhilde, with Fricka telling Wotan that Brünnhilde is a function of his will (and this is what Brünnhilde herself also later says). So in response to Fricka's demand: "Turn the valkyrie from him, too" (Wotan has already agreed that he himself will not protect him), Wotan says "Let the valkyrie choose for herself" ("Die Walküre walte frei").[16] But Fricka objects:[17]

Nicht doch! Deinen Willen	No, no! For it's *your* will
vollbringt sie allein:	alone she carries out:
verbiete ihr Siegmund's Sieg!	forbid her Siegmund's victory!

What Fricka says corresponds exactly to what Frauer writes of the Valkyries: they are expressions of Odin's will and are subordinate beings.[18] They may appear to be act-

---

13. *WagRS* 144; "Muth" usually understood as "courage," is here understood as "independence of mind" (*WagRS* 366 n. 54, see this in the light of Hegel's master/slave).

14. *WagRS* 144.

15. Donington, *Symbols*, 150.

16. *WagRS* 146.

17. *WagRS* 146.

18. Frauer, *Walkyrien*, 44: "Als Vollstreckerinnen von Ôhdins Willen, als seine Mädchen und Dienerinnen sind die Walkyrien eigentlich nur untergeordnete Wesen." I am grateful to Derrick Everrett for drawing my attention to this and the following two passages. According to Minna, Frauer's book

ing freely but they are simply carrying out his will;[19] indeed, when they appear they are nothing other than Odin himself interacting in the lives of heroes.[20] They could therefore be compared to "the angel of the LORD," as in Exod 3:2, who fully represents God. Here the angel appears to Moses "in a flame of fire out of the bush" but then after Moses "turns aside" (Exod 3:3) Yahweh himself calls to him "out of the bush" (Exod 3:5).

Walküre Act II Scene 2: Brünnhilde's Freedom

The issue of Brünnhilde's agency continues into Scene 2. Brünnhilde tells her father that she is none other than Wotan's will:[21]

Zu Wotan's Willen sprichst du,	To Wotan's will you speak
sag'st du mir was du willst:	when you tell me what you will:
wer—bin ich,	who am I
wär' ich dein Wille nicht?	if not your will?

So whereas Siegmund is "the other" (or should we say Wotan deceives himself into thinking that he is "the other"),[22] Brünnhilde is the very essence of his will. But in fact Brünnhilde proves herself to be free whereas Wotan is constrained. Wotan's lack of freedom is stressed on a number of occasions in his monologue: he has bound himself in his own fetters,[23] his bonds hold him "in thrall," and he is "a slave to those treaties."[24] That Wagner considered these issues to be central is shown in his letter to Liszt of 3 October 1855, where he wrote: "This is the most important scene for the development of the whole of the great four-part drama."[25]

It is in Act II Scene 4 that Brünnhilde makes her fundamental decision, demonstrating her freedom. Further, "she carries out [Wotan's] true wishes only when she contravenes his express instructions and helps Siegmund in his encounter with Hunding after the Volsung has been abandoned by the father of the gods."[26] The irony

---

was in Wagner's Dresden Library (Westernhagen, *Bibliothek*, 112).

19. Frauer, *Walkyrien*, 44: "Die Walkyrien werden bei ihrem Einwirken auf bestimmte Verhältnisse meist so dargestellt, als ob sie frei und selbstständig handelten, wodurch sie von selbst ihren Herrn und Meister Ôhdin zurückdrängen und ganz an seine Stelle treten."

20. Frauer, *Walkyrien*, 43: "Sie sind nichts Anderes, als Ôhdin selbst in seinem Eingreifen in das Leben der Helden."

21. *WagRS* 149.

22. Fricka argues that Wotan has tried to deceive her in suggesting that Siegmund is "the other": "in him [Siegmund] I find only you" (*WagRS* 144). Later Wotan suggests to Brünnhilde that he has also deceived himself: "How slyly I sought / to deceived myself! / How easily Fricka / uncovered the fraud! / To my deepest shame / she saw straight through me" (*WagRS* 153).

23. *WagRS* 148.

24. *WagRS* 152.

25. *SL* 352; *SB* 7:283.

26. Borchmeyer, *Drama*, 231.

at the end of *Walküre* is that the seemingly powerful Wotan is proved to be powerless and when he meets his adversary Alberich in *Siegfried* Act II he confesses: "I came to watch / and not to act."[27]

Brünnhilde's freedom reflects that of Antigone in that although she is free she finds herself under the constraints of love. Wagner writes that Antigone's love was "*fully conscious (vollbewußte)*":

> She knew, what she was doing,—but she also knew that do it she must, that she had no choice but to act according to love's Necessity; she knew that she had to listen to this unconscious, strenuous necessity of *self-annihilation (Selbstvernichtung) in the cause of sympathy*; and in this consciousness of Unconscious she was alike the perfect Human Being (vollendete Mensch), the embodiment of Love in its highest fill and potence.[28]

Wagner described her as "a sweet maiden (Jungfrau)"[29] and the term "Jungfrau" could allude to the Virgin Mary. But her being constrained by love could also reflect how Jesus felt constrained in laying down his life. In section II.1 of the *Jesus* sketches Wagner puts these words into Jesus' mouth for the Temple scene in Act III: "openly before all eyes will I suffer death for that Love through which I redeem the world to life eternal."[30]

So although Siegmund is supposed to be "the other," the surprise of *Walküre* is that it is in fact Brünnhilde who turns out to be "the other" ("das Andere"). She turns out to the one who is truly free. The first major idea Wagner presents in his letter to Röckel is that freedom "counts above all else." Freedom is not "licence" ("Willkür") but "integrity" ("Wahrhaftigkeit"). "He who is true to himself, i.e. who acts in accord with his own being, and in perfect harmony with his own nature, is *free*; strictly speaking, outward constraint is powerless unless it succeeds in destroying the integrity of its victim, inducing him to dissemble and to persuade himself and others that he is a different person from the one he really is."[31] And it is surely Brünnhilde "who acts in accord with her own being" and "in perfect harmony with her own nature." This, Wagner argues, is "true servitude."[32]

Wagner then relates this discussion of freedom as "Wahrhaftigkeit" to the issue of "truth."

> I believe that this "integrity" ("Wahrhaftigkeit") is essentially the same as the "truth" ("Wahrheit") of which we read in books on philosophy and theology. "Truth" is a concept and, by its nature, is simply objectified "integrity"; the

---

27. WagRS 229.
28. PW 2:189; GSD 4:63.
29. PW 2:189; GSD 4:62.
30. PW 8:307; DTB 252. See also Zegowitz, *Opern*, 208.
31. SL 301; SB 6:60.
32. SL 301; SB 6:60.

actual content of this "integrity", however, is "reality" pure and simple, or rather: the "real", "what really is", and only what is "material" is "real", whereas the "immaterial" is certainly also "unreal", in other words merely "thought" or "imagined."[33]

This then leads him to what appears to be a Feuerbachian analysis of feeling: "Our surest grasp of reality is through feeling, and true feeling is perceived exclusively through the senses." But he adds: "what we understand here by 'senses' is not what philosophers and theologians mean when they speak with total contempt of the *animal* senses, but the *human* senses which, as is well known, are capable of measuring the stars and imagining their courses."[34]

The essential point here then is that freedom, as true servitude, is integrity, which in turn is related to truth. This is something that Wagner discusses in *Opera and Drama* in relation to fate, the state, and the liberating function of art.

Fate, State, and Art

Fate is a fundamental issue in Greek tragedy and it was briefly discussed in volume 1, chapter 4. The key point about fate is that it is not deterministic since whatever one does the same outcome transpires. A good example is that of Oedipus, who in fact does everything he can to avert his fate, but finds he cannot do so. It is therefore no accident that Wagner's discussion of fate occurs as he deals with questions of the Oedipus myth in *Opera and Drama* (section 2.3). He prefaces his discussion of the Oedipus myth with comments on "Fatum."[35] He opens by noting that "[t]he Greek *Fate* (*Fatum*) is the *inner Nature-necessity* (*die innere Naturnothwendigkeit*), from which the Greek— *because he did not understand it*—sought refuge in the arbitrary political state (in den willkürlichen politischen Staat)." But our fate, he argues, is the arbitrary political state, an outer necessity, from which refuge is sought in the "Nature-necessity." "Nature-necessity utters itself the strongest and the most invincibly in the physical life-bent (Lebenstrieb) of the *Individual*."[36] After the discussion of the Oedipus myth, Wagner then recapitulates: "In their 'Fate' the Greeks mistook the nature of the Individuality, because it disturbed Society's moral-wont: to battle against this Fate, they armed themselves with the political State. Now, our Fate is the political State, in which the free Individuality perceives its destroying Destiny (Schicksal). But the essence of the political State is *caprice* (*Willkür*), whereas the essence of the free Individuality is *necessity* (*Nothwendigkeit*)."[37] At the end of section 2.3 Wagner concludes that bringing

33. *SL* 301; *SB* 6:60–61.
34. *SL* 302; *SB* 6:61.
35. *PW* 2:179–80; *GSD* 4:53–55.
36. *PW* 2:179; *GSD* 4:53–54.
37. *PW* 2:193; *GSD* 4:66.

the unconscious part of human nature to consciousness within society means knowing "nothing other than *the necessity common to every member of society, namely of the Individual's own free self-determining (Nothwendigkeit der freien Selbstbestimmung des Individuums)*," this entailing the annulment of the state whose essence, as noted above, is "caprice" ("Willkür").[38]

Issues of freedom and the state continue in the next section (2.4), but bringing in the role of art that can annul the state.[39] The "Going-under" ("Untergang") of the state and the rise of an "organically healthy society" means "*the self-realisement of Society's religious conviction of its purely-human essence*"[40] and "*[i]n the free self-determining of the Individuality there therefore lies the basis of the social Religion of the Future.*"[41] Art therefore has this fundamental liberating role and central for this is "the *emotionalising of the intellect (die Gefühlswerdung des Verstandes)*."[42] Hence: "In the Drama, we must become *knowers* through *the Feeling* (Im Drama müssen wir *Wissende* werden durch *das Gefühl*). The Understanding tells us: '*So is it,*'—only when the Feeling has told us: '*So must it be.*'"[43]

Section 2.4 closes with the idea of "Wonder" (Wunder"),[44] a word associated with "miracle," and is taken up in the next section: "The Wonder in the Poet's work is distinguished from the Wonder in religious Dogma by this: that it does not, like the latter, *upheave* the nature of things, but the rather makes it *comprehensible* to the Feeling."[45] In Wonder/miracle of the Judaeo-Christian tradition divine will (Wille) stood over Nature and demanded faith but denied understanding. In contrast, "the poetising intellect has absolutely no concern with *Faith*, but only with an *understanding through the Feeling (Gefühlsverständniß)*."[46] I will return to the issue of the "emotionalising of the intellect" and the "understanding through the feeling" in chapter 12 below.

Wagner, Freedom, and Philosophy

As we have seen in volume 1, chapter 6, German idealism was fundamental for Wagner's thinking including the issue of freedom. Immanuel Kant stressed the freedom of the human person, and one of the central concerns in his philosophy was to find a role for freedom, together with God and immortality, within a Newtonian worldview.

---

38. *PW* 2:193–94; *GSD* 4:66–67.
39. *PW* 2:195; *GSD* 4:67.
40. *PW* 2:201; *GSD* 4:72.
41. *PW* 2:202; *GSD* 4:73.
42. *PW* 2:208; *GSD* 4:78.
43. *PW* 2:209; *GSD* 4:78.
44. *PW* 2:212; *GSD* 4:81.
45. *PW* 2:213; *GSD* 4:82.
46. *PW* 2:213; *GSD* 4:82.

Hegel in a different way argued for an all-embracing view of human freedom, a view that Wagner also expressed in the person of Brünnhilde.[47]

Wagner discusses issues of freedom, necessity, and nature in *Artwork of the Future*, written a year after his first work on the *Ring* (i.e., the *Mythus* and *Siegfried' Tod*). He brings in issues of the fall and knowledge (as in Genesis 2–3), but this does not have the same complexion as we find in his final stage work, *Parsifal*, which has a more pessimistic anthropology.[48] In the opening of *Artwork* he writes of a certain determinism in nature, but his argument is quite subtle and could be said to cohere with modern biology in that nature is a "blind watchmaker" and has "no intentions" (absichtslos) as such: "Nature engenders her myriad forms without intention (absichtslos) and without caprice (unwillkürlich), according to her need (Bedürfniß), and therefore of Necessity (Nothwendigkeit). The same Necessity is the generation and formative force of human life. Only that which is without intention (absichtslos) and without caprice (unwillkürlich) can spring from a real need; but on Need alone is based the very principle of Life."[49] Then he goes on to speak of the fall: "From the moment when Man perceived the difference between himself and Nature, and thus commenced his own development as *man*, by breaking loose from the unconsciousness of natural animal life and passing over into conscious life [...] from that moment did Error begin, as the earliest utterance of consciousness. But Error is the [father] of Knowledge [...]."[50] This is relevant for the fall of Wotan: giving up an eye for wisdom and then tearing the branch from the World Ash Tree to form his spear (cf. the fall of Adam and Eve).

Feuerbach has shaped much of his argument in section 1.5 of *Artwork of the Future*,[51] which has important implications for Wagner's view of human freedom. The chapter opens thus: "The beginning and foundation of all that exists and all that is conceivable, is actual physical being (das wirkliche sinnliche Sein)."[52] He continues: "The beginning and foundation of human thought is the inner recognition of his life-need as the *common* life-need of his *species*, in contradistinction to nature and all her countless living species that lie apart from the human being."[53] When considering the activity of the spirit/mind one must start with the real sensuous (sinnlich) human being and the spirit/mind (Geist) must be seen as the last and most conditioned (als

---

47. See above and the further discussion in chapter 10 below.

48. See Bell, *Parsifal*, 135–54.

49. *PW* 1:69 (modified); *GSD* 3:42. Ellis comments that this paragraph and the following sections of the chapter show that Wagner's philosophy is "self-originated." "Except that Wagner does not employ the term 'Will,' but rather 'Necessity,' the whole scheme is Schopenhauerian from beginning to end, and the gradual evolution of the 'Will's' manifestation, from elementary force to Intellect and Spirit, might have been written by that greatest philosopher of the century" (*PW* 1:69 n.). But the ideas are more likely to be Hegelian (Corse, *Consciousness*, 19).

50. *PW* 1:70; *GSD* 3:43. Ellis renders "Vater der Erkenntniß" as "mother of knowledge."

51. Rawidowicz, *Feuerbachs Philosophie*, 394.

52. *PW* 1:82; *GSD* 3:55. Cf. Warner, "Artwork," 20.

53. My own translation, based on *PW* 1:82; *GSD* 3:55. Cf. Warner, "Artwork," 20.

letzte und bedingteste) and not as the foundation and cause of nature (als Grund und Ursache der Natur)."[54] Then he argues, again in Feuerbachian mode:

> If the spirit (Geist) created nature, if thought (der Gedanke) made reality (das Wirkliche), if the philosopher precedes the human then nature, reality (Wirklichkeit) and human beings are no longer necessary (nothwendig), their existence (ihr Dasein) is superfluous, harmful even; most superfluous of all however is the imperfect (das Unvollkommene), once the perfect has come into being (nach dem Vorhandensein des Vollkommenen) [cf. 1 Cor 13.9]. Then nature, reality and human beings only gain meaning, their existence is only justified when the spirit (Geist)—that unconditional spirit (der unbedingte), which is cause, effect and law unto itself—uses them according to its own absolute, sovereign pleasure. If the spirit *in itself* is necessity (Nothwendigkeit) *then it is* life that is arbitrary (das Willkürliche), a fantastic masquerade, an idle distraction, a frivolous whim, a "car tel est notre plaisir" [for such is our pleasure] of the spirit.[55]

Although there are some views expressed here that negate Hegel,[56] Wagner's views on freedom nevertheless often cohere with Hegel. We have seen this in relation to Brünnhilde's freedom at the end of the *Ring* cycle, where desire and reason coincide: what she wishes to do (sacrifice herself) is the right thing to do. On a larger canvas we also see how Wagner's view of providence seems thoroughly Hegelian. Providence was a central element in Hegel's understanding of history as expressed in the *Lectures*, a work we know Wagner read (discussed in volume 1). Similar ideas are expressed in his *Reason in History*. Although there is no evidence Wagner knew this, it sets out ideas that are also in the *Lectures* and sometimes with greater clarity, so is worth quoting.[57] Hegel argues that philosophy brings with it "the idea that reason governs the world, and that world history is therefore a rational process."[58] Further, "the history of the world is a rational process, the rational and necessary evolution of the world spirit. This spirit [is] the substance of history; its nature is always one and the same; and it discloses this nature in the existence of the world."[59] Then he introduces providence: "the world's events are controlled by providence, indeed by divine providence [. . . ;] divine providence is wisdom, coupled with infinite power, which realises its ends, i.e. the absolute and rational design of the world; and reason is freely self-determining thought,

---

54. *PW* 1:83; *GSD* 3:55–56. Cf. Warner, "Artwork," 20.

55. Warner, "Artwork," 20 (emphasis added to correspond to *GSD* 3:56); cf. *PW* 1:83.

56. Wagner to some extent is negating Hegel, who considered spirit as the "cause of the world" ("die Ursache der Welt") and wrote of the "master workman" ("Werkmeister") as "the One Living Spirit" ("der Eine lebendige Geist") (*Encyclopaedia Logic* (Geraets, Suchting, Harris), 32, 38; *HHW* 6:48 (§8), 55 (§13)).

57. Cf. Küng, *Incarnation*, 320–25.

58. Nisbet, *Reason*, 27.

59. Nisbet, *Reason*, 29.

or what the Greeks called 'nous.'"⁶⁰ It was Anaxagoras who "was the first to declare that the world is governed by a 'nous', i.e. by reason or understanding in general."⁶¹ But how are we to reconcile this "lofty speculative course of the World Spirit" with the "inferior, empirical and irrational stuff of which world history is made?"⁶² Hegel's answer lies in the "cunning of reason": "For it is not the universal Idea which enters into opposition, conflict, and danger; it keeps itself in the background, untouched and unharmed, and sends forth the particular interests of passion to fight and wear themselves out in its stead. It is what we may call the *cunning of reason* (*List der Vernunft*) that it sets the passions to work in its service, so that the agents by which it gives itself existence must pay the penalty and suffer the loss."⁶³

Many consider Hegel's approach to world history as inadequate. Küng writes that "we remain saddled with the critical question of how we can go on regarding world history as the speculative history of the rational World Spirit when this process of the Spirit's self-enhancement toward greater freedom is marked by such an infinite volume of waste and debris in terms of individuals, whole peoples and eras [. . .]."⁶⁴ But I think Hodgson rightly argues that Hegel's words on history, which a few pages earlier he described as a "slaughter bench" ("Schlachtbank"),⁶⁵ are not justified in the sense that good can come out of evil.⁶⁶ He points to Jüngel who makes the key point that Hegel's *cunning of reason* "does not rationalize away 'the total mass of concrete evils' in world history."⁶⁷ Rather he takes such evils so seriously that he calls for a reconciliation through judgement of the world, not for the purpose of retribution ("Vergeltung") but for reconciliation ("Versöhnung"). "God justifies godself not by exercising retribution but instead by reconciling."⁶⁸

Fundamental for his idea of reconciliation is the incarnation, where "the divine Idea is revealed as the unity of divine and human nature."⁶⁹ He criticizes religions such as Judaism and Islam for separating the "absolute" from the "finite," where any talk of the "spirit" for the "absolute" "is no more than an empty name."⁷⁰ It is also worth emphasizing that Hegel here also criticizes pantheism.⁷¹ But in the Christian religion there is posited "the unity of Man with God" and in this "Idea of God"

60. Nisbet, *Reason*, 35.
61. Nisbet, *Reason*, 34.
62. Küng, *Incarnation*, 326, who refers to Iljin, *Gotteslehre*, 330–39.
63. Nisbet, *Reason*, 89. The text is very similar in the Hegel, *History*, 33; *Geschichte*, 49.
64. Küng, *Incarnation*, 326.
65. Hegel, *History*, 21; *Geschichte*, 35. See volume 1, chapter 6 above.
66. Hodgson, *Shapes*, 46.
67. Jüngel, "Weltgeschichte," 25. Cf. Nisbet, *Reason*, 43.
68. Jüngel, "Weltgeschichte," 25.
69. Nisbet, *Reason*, 106.
70. Nisbet, *Reason*, 106.
71. Nisbet, *Reason*, 106: "pantheism has no content, for God, as a subject, disappears, because the subject no longer has any distinct existence."

rightly conceived there is "*Reconciliation* (*Versöhnung*) that heals the pain and inward suffering of the human being. For suffering itself is henceforth recognized as an instrument necessary for producing the unity of man with God."[72] This passage occurs in the *Philosophy of History*, just a few pages after one that Wagner had marked;[73] hence it is highly likely he actually read it.

Hegel I think does manage to make sense of the whole philosophy of the spirit's self-enhancement by speaking of the unity of God and the human being and then later his idea of the "death of God."[74] It is on this basis also that Hegel's understanding of world history applies to Wagner's *Ring*. It is a much more profound sense of providence than that found in say the story of Joseph in Genesis 37–50. Wagner could perhaps see "reason" at work as the story of the *Ring* evolves and agree with Anaxgoras that his world at least was governed by "nous."[75] However, like Hegel and unlike Marx's view of history, it was not deterministic.

In the *Ring* we see the working out of the "Geist," as in Hegel's "Weltgeschichte" where, as we have seen, he appeals to Anaxagoras: "As history tells us, the Greek *Anaxagoras* was the first to declare that the world is governed by a 'nous', i.e. by reason or understanding in general. [. . .] For divine providence is wisdom, coupled with infinite power, which realises its ends, i.e. the absolute and rational design of the world; and reason is freely self-determining thought, or what the Greeks called 'nous.'"[76] But another way of viewing the issue of providence in the *Ring* is considering Schopenhauer's idea of the "will" in which Wagner later became so interested. Such a "will" encompassed not only the human will but also the inorganic world: "the will proclaims itself just as directly in the fall of a stone as in the action of man."[77] Such a "will to life" ("Wille zu Leben") was then to be developed by Nietzsche in his "will to power" ("Wille zur Macht"), who likewise encompassed both organic life and inorganic matter in the one term.[78]

---

72. Sibree, *History*, 324 (modified); *Geschichte*, 392.

73. The marked passage in Wagner's copy is *Geschichte* (RW), 391, which corresponds to *Geschichte*, 389; Sibree, *History*, 321. This is quoted above in chapter 4.

74. On the "death of God" see the following chapter together with volume 1, chapter 6.

75. The only extant mention of Anaxagoras in Wagner is *CD* 20 November 1869, where he is criticized as a "Praktiker"; Plato was the first to recognize the ideality of the world. Note the role of Anaxagoras in Goethe, *Faust II*.

76. Nisbet, *Reason*, 34–35.

77. *WWR* 2:299 (2.23) *ASSW* 2:387.

78. Nietzsche's "will to power" first appears in *Zarathustra*, giving little idea of what the term means. Later writings make it a little clearer what it involves. See, for example, *Beyond Good and Evil*, 36 (*FNKSA* 5:55; §36): "The world seen from inside, the world determined and described with respect to its 'intelligible character'—would be just this 'will to power' and nothing else.—"

— 10 —

Siegfried and Brünnhilde

Introduction

In the next chapter the couple Siegfried and Brünnhilde will become fundamental in the discussion of redemption in the *Ring* cycle and in how they draw the whole drama to a close. But first of all it is necessary to discuss the problems they pose. Many commentators have, for understandable reason, been at a loss to know what to make of the hero Siegfried; to some extent there is also a problem with Brünnhilde, who although being the shining focus of *Walküre* presents certain problems in *Götterdämmerung*.

To appreciate these two characters and how they interact it is necessary to delve a little deeper in the Norse and Germanic sources, for therein, and by considering Wagner's appropriation, some answers may be found.

Siegfried: Hero and Comic

A key issue to bear in mind with *Siegfried* is that it was originally called *Der junge Siegfried*[1] and that for Wagner it was a "heroic comedy" ("heroisches Lustspiel") to complement the tragedy of *Siegfried's Tod*. As he wrote in his autobiography: "I conceived *Der junge Siegfried*, a heroic comedy to serve as preface to the tragedy *Siegfrieds Tod*."[2] In forming his Siegfried he combined two traditions. The first was the tragic hero we find in *Nibelungenlied* and *Volsunga Saga*; second, there is the "comic" Siegfried we find in *Thidrek's Saga*, who, like the hero of *Das Lied vom Hürnen Seyfrid*, could be described as "a true comic-strip hero,"[3] provided one bears in mind that this entails a fair amount of violence.

---

1. It is all too easy to forget Siegfried's youth since the Heldentenor performers necessarily require some vocal maturity.
2. *My Life* 465; *Mein Leben* 2:478.
3. Magee, *Nibelungs*, 107. Note, however, that *Thidrek's Saga* also contains the tragic elements of the Sigurd story, such as his mother dying shortly after his birth and the story of his death. See my discussion in volume 1, chapter 3.

To some extent the problems many have when faced with the figure of Siegfried could be ameliorated by considering the youthful Sigurd of *Thidrek's Saga*. In this source we read that when Sigurd was nine years old he was strong and big and "was so hard to deal with that he oppressed Mimir's apprentices and forced them into submission, so that they could scarcely feel comfortable around him."[4] Such aggression of the hero has been carried over into Wagner's Siegfried. But there is another interesting development which Magee has highlighted, namely that in developing the Sigurd tradition by Fouqué and Simrock the physical qualities of the youth has been transformed inwardly in order to enhance his heroic temperament.[5] This is something Wagner appropriated, as can be seen with Siegfried's angry and insulting outburst against Mime, expressing his dissatisfaction with the sword Mime has forged:[6]

Da hast du die Stücken,	There, take the pieces,
schändlicher Stümper:	you shameful bungler:
hätt' ich am Schädel	if only I'd smashed them
die sie zerschlagen!—	against your skull!—
[...]	[...]
mit einem Griff	I can crush the trash
zergreif' ich den Quark!—	in a single grip!—
Wär' mir nicht schier	Were the knave not
zu schäbig der Wicht,	simply scurvy,
ich zerschmiedet' ihn selbst	I'd smash him to pieces
mit seinem Geschmied',	with all his smith-work,
den alten albernen Alp!	the old and addle-headed elf!
Des Ärgers dann hätt' ich ein End'!	My anger were then at an end!

Some clues to Siegfried's character as represented in these lines may be found in the late essay *Herodom and Christendom* (1881), where Wagner notes the similarities between Siegfried and Heracles. Heracles is persecuted by Hera "and kept in menial subjection,"[7] this alluding to "that school of arduous labors in which the noblest Aryan stems and races throve to grandeur of demigods."[8] Such races, like Heracles and Siegfried, "were conscious of divine descent: a lie to them was inconceivable, and a free man meant a truthful man." The root-qualities of the Aryan race are seen plainly "in the contact of the last pure-bred Germanic branches with the falling Roman world."[9]

---

4. Haymes, *Thidrek*, 106.

5. Magee, *Nibelungs*, 108–11, gives examples from Simrock, *Amelungenlied*, 1:93–94; Fouqué, *Sigurd*, 19.

6. *WagRS* 198.

7. *PW* 6:277; *GSD* 10:277.

8. *PW* 6:278; *GSD* 10:278.

9. *PW* 6:278; *GSD* 10:278.

But as in mythic heroes their rise ultimately leads to their fall. "The accident of their becoming masters of the great Latino-Semite realm (des großen lateinischen Semitenreiches) was fatal to them. Pride is a delicate virtue and brooks no compromise, such as crossing of breed: but the Germanic race without this virtue has—naught to tell us. For this pride is the soul of the truthful, of the free through serving." Hence, the member of the Germanic race "knows no fear (*Furcht*), but respect (*Ehrfurcht*)—a virtue whose very name, in its proper sense, is known to none save those oldest Aryan peoples; whilst honour (*Ehre*) itself is the sum of all personal worth, and therefore can neither be given nor received, as is our practice to-day, but, a witness of divine descent, it keeps the hero unashamed even in his most shameful of sufferings."[10] After recommending Gobineau's work *The Inequality of the Human Races* (for a third time in the essay) he argues: "we now must seek the Hero where he turns against the ruin of his race (gegen die Verderbniß seines Stammes), the downfall of its code of honour, and girds his erring will to horror, finding himself again as divine Hero in the *Saint* (im *Heiligen*)."[11]

One has to be cautious is retrojecting all Wagner writes here into his Siegfried. There is the obvious point that Gobineau, who has colored much of what he here writes, first met Wagner in 1876; Wagner read his *Essai sur l'inégalité des races humaines* in 1879[12] and spent much time with him in May-June 1881.[13] Further, in contrast to what Wagner writes in the essay, the hero of his *Siegfried* was not "conscious of divine descent." But there are ideas in the essay that illumine what is at work in his fashioning of the drama. First, the parallel Wagner draws between "the last pure-bred Germanic branches" and Siegfried could suggest he is a figure who subjects the "semitic" world and possibly also the papacy (so he writes of "the great Latino-Semite realm"). He certainly subjects the "Jewish" Mime and there may be a hint of his conquering the "papacy" as represented by Fafner.[14] Secondly, Siegfried's character is characterized by being truthful (so whatever one may feel about the libretto quoted above, at least one can say he was honest). Thirdly, he is, of course, the hero who knows no fear.

However much one is repelled by his character, Siegfried does undergo a transformation: first by falling in love and learning fear from a woman; and then his transfiguration as he dies as a "worthy" hero. He therefore may well be transformed

---

10. *PW* 6:278; *GSD* 10:278. There is not only a word play on "Ehre"/"Ehrfurcht" but also probably on "arisch"/"Ehre." See volume 1, chapter 5.

11. *PW* 6:279 (modified); *GSD* 10:279.

12. This, together with three other works of Gobineau was in his Wahnfried library.

13. Wagner met with Gobineau at Wahnfried 11–24 May 1881, then they travelled to Berlin for Neumann's *Ring*, returned to Bayreuth on 31 May and then Gobineau stayed until 7 June.

14. Note the contemptuous term "Pfaffe" for priest (see chapter 8 above). See, e.g., the words of Mephistopheles on Gretchen (Luke, *Faust I*, 82; GWJA 3:94 (ll. 2621–22)): "Sie kam vor ihrem Pfaffen, / Der sprach sie aller Sünden frei" ("She's just been to her confession. / Her priest gave her full absolution"). See also Luke, *Faust I*, 88; GWJA 3:101 (ll. 2813–14): "Just think those jewels for Gretchen that I got, / A priest (Pfaff) has been and swiped the lot!"

into a Christ-like figure, and as Wagner writes in that late essay, the divine hero becomes the "Saint."

I now turn to two issues that arise in *Götterdämmerung*: Siegfried as lover and deceiver.

Siegfried as Lover and Deceiver

Siegfried's character seems to be rehabilitated to some extent as he falls in love with Brünnhilde in *Siegfried* Act III. However, he seems to take a nosedive again in *Götterdämmerung* as he is involved in the quadrilateral set of relationships of Acts I and II: Siegfried = Gutrune; Gunther = Brünnhilde. This corresponds to what we have in the *Nibelungenlied* (Sivrit = Kriemhilt; Gunther = Prünhilt) and in Norse sources (Sigurd = Gudrun; Gunnar = Brynhild). I will analyze the difficult scenes of the close of Act I and Act II a little later, but the fundamental question is whether it is Siegfried or Brünnhilde who is lying in the bitter mutual accusations in Act II? Did Siegfried have intercourse with Brünnhilde between Act I and Act II as she claims? And even if he did not, is he not being disingenuous concerning when he gained the ring from Brünnhilde? And why did he forcefully take the ring from Brünnhilde at the end of Act I? In order to tackle these problems I need to point to the key relevant events in the first part of the *Nibelungenlied*, together with any parallels in the *Elder Edda*, *Prose Edda*, and *Völsunga Saga*.[15]

Nibelungenlied and Norse Sources

It is in the fifth adventure of the *Nibelungenlied* that Sivrit meets Kriemhilt and falls madly in love with her and in the next adventure Gunther hears of Prünhilt, Queen of Iceland (she is not a Valkyrie) and is desperate to marry her. She, like Sivrit, is extraordinarily strong in all senses of the word and she parallels Sivrit in many respects. Sivrit already knows of Prünhilt's strength and aggression and there is even a hint that he has previously been with her,[16] this to a very limited extent corresponding to the previous "marriage" of Brünnhilde and Siegfried in *Siegfried* Act III and the Prologue to *Götterdämmerung*. Sivrit accompanies Gunther to Iceland to help him woo this formidable woman. Now this wooing involves a show of his strength (throwing a javelin so heavy that three men could hardly carry it and hurling a stone that twelve men could hardly carry—so it was rather like an extreme version of the Highland Games).[17] Prünhilt says "if [Gunther] proves master in [the games], then I'll be his wife."[18] Because Gunther cannot match her strength, Sivrit acts for Gunther using his

---

15. These were not covered in sufficient detail in volume 1, chapter 3.
16. Av 6 (329–30; *NibE* 34).
17. Av 7 (440–50; *NibE* 44–45).
18. Av 7 (423; *NibE* 42).

cloak of invisibility.[19] Prünhilt is won and they all return to Worms where the double wedding takes place. Sivrit marries Kriemhilt and their marriage is consummated, but Prünhilt denies Gunther intercourse, binds him and hangs him on a peg. Sivrit comes to Gunther's aid using again his cloak of invisibility. He breaks down Prünhilt's resistance and after he has overpowered her physically she "became Gunther's wife. She said: 'Noble king, you must let me live! I will make full amends for all that I have done to you. Never again shall I defy your noble love. I have found out for certain that you can be a lady's master.'"[20] But then Sivrit makes his crucial mistake, which partly corresponds to the final moments of *Götterdämmerung* Act I: "Sivrit stood back as if he wanted to take off his clothes, leaving the maiden lying there. He took a golden ring off her finger, without the noble queen ever noticing. He also took her girdle, a fine braid. I don't know if he did that out of his high spirits. He gave it to his wife; that was to cost him dear in time to come."[21] He then leaves her to Gunther to make love. Although Sivrit was foolish in taking her ring and girdle, the text seems fairly clear that there was no intercourse between Sivrit and Prünhilt,[22] this having implications for *Götterdämmerung*.

After this, Sivrit returns to the Netherlands with Kriemhilt (Av. 11). Ten years later Sivrit and Kriemhilt accept Gunther's invitation to festivities in Worms, including a grand service in the minster. But as the two queens are about to enter, an argument begins as to who should have precedence and enter first (Av. 14).[23] Kriemhilt calls Prünhilt a whore and claims that it was Sivrit, not Gunther, who took her virginity. We then have a series of events that lead to Sivrit's betrayal (Av. 15) and death at the hands of Hagen (Av. 16). Sivrit is presented in all this as a noble figure who is killed because of a false accusation, although it is clear he was foolish to take Prünhilt's ring and girdle.

Turning to Norse sources, one of them is clear that Sigurd did have sexual relations with Brynhild, namely *Thidrek's Saga* 228–29. After Brynhild has refused Gunnar intercourse, Gunnar asks Sigurd to "take her virginity."[24] He can do this because of his strength and they agree on a pretence that Sigurd gets into bed with Brynhild while Gunnar leaves in Sigurd's clothes: "[Sigurd] went to Brynhild and quickly took her virginity." Further, "[i]n the morning he took from her hand a gold ring and put another in its place."[25] The key point is that the intercourse is done with Gunnar's approval and Brynhild is aware of the pretence.[26]

19. Av 7 (457; *NibE* 45).
20. Av 10 (678; *NibE* 65).
21. Av 10 (679–80; *NibE* 65).
22. Contrast Bjornsson, *Volsungs*, 245, who avers that no clear answer is given.
23. This scene was adapted in Wagner's *Lohengrin* Act II.
24. Haymes, *Thidrek*, 139.
25. Haymes, *Thidrek*, 140.
26. Björnsson, *Volsungs*, 246.

A second text, *Skaldskaparmal* 7 (*Prose Edda*), is more ambiguous. We read after Sigurd and Gunnar had changed shapes the following: "That evening [Sigurd] entered into marriage with Brynhild. But when they got into bed, he drew the sword Gram from its sheath and laid it between them." Although this suggests no intercourse took place, the continuation may suggest something different: "And in the morning when he got up and dressed, he gave Brynhild as morning gift the gold ring that Loki had taken from Andvari."[27] This "morning gift" or "linen fee" (línfe) "was a gift paid by the bridegroom to the bride on the morning after the marriage was consummated."[28] So there seems to be a certain ambiguity here.

There are Icelandic texts that seem clear that Sigurd did not have intimacy with Brynhild. We find this in the *Elder Edda*. See *Sigurdarkvida in skamma* 28 (the short lay of Sigurd) where, just before he dies, Sigurd says:[29]

> That girl [Brynhild] loves me above every man,
>
> but against Gunnar I did no harm;
>
> I spared our kinship, our sworn oaths,
>
> so I shouldn't be called his wife's lover.

See also *Helreid Brynhildar* 12 (*Brynhild's Hel ride*), where Brynhild, on her path to Hel, tells the ogress she meets:[30]

> We slept and were happy in but one bed,
>
> as if he'd been born my brother;
>
> not at all for the space of eight nights
>
> did we lay one arm over another.

Likewise, *Völsunga Saga* 29 suggests there was no intercourse. This text is remarkable because although the basic action is appropriated by Wagner at the end of Act I of *Götterdämmerung*, the atmosphere could not be more different. So Sigurd agrees to win Brynhild for Gunnar and to do this they "exchanged appearances" and Sigurd fights through the flames to find Brynhild.[31] The verbal exchange between Sigurd and Brynhild is civilized and polite and we read: "He stayed there for three nights and they shared the same bed. He took the sword Gram and laid it naked between them. She asked the reason. He said it was ordained that he should marry his wife in this way, or else die."[32]

Having considered these Germanic and Norse sources I turn to *Götterdämmerung*.

27. Faulkes, *Edda*, 102. Cf. Byock, *Prose Edda*, 99.
28. Byock, *Prose Edda*, 150 n. 4.
29. Orchard, *Elder Edda*, 187.
30. Orchard, *Elder Edda*, 195.
31. Finch, *Volsungs*, 48.
32. Finch, *Volsungs*, 50.

SIEGFRIED AND BRÜNNHILDE
The Drama of *Götterdämmerung*

The truly horrific scene at the end of *Götterdämmerung* Act I is made especially dark because of what Brünnhilde told Waltraute just moments earlier of the meaning of the ring from which Siegfried's love "shines blissfully forth from it":[33]

Mehr als Walhall's Wonne,	More than Valhalla's bliss,
mehr als der Ewigen Ruhm—	more than the glory of the immortals
ist mir der Ring:	the ring is to me:
ein Blick auf sein helles Gold,	one glance from its bright-shining gold,
ein Blitz aus dem hehren Glanz—	one flash of tis noble fire
gilt mir werther	is worth far more
als aller Götter	than all the gods'
ewig wärendes Glück!	eternal joy!
Denn selig aus ihm	For Siegfried's love
leuchtet mir Siegfried's Liebe.	shines blissfully forth from it.

After Waltraute's furious exit Brünnhilde thinks her lover is approaching, knowing nothing of Siegfried's being duped by the love potion.[34] Siegfried, wearing the magic tarnhelm to make him look like Gunther, fights through the flames that surround Brünnhilde's rock, and in the form of Gunther takes her as his bride.[35] But at the very end of Act I and in Act II Siegfried claims that he did not have intercourse with Brünnhilde. It is not immediately clear whether Siegfried did keep to this promise[36] and there is the possibility that Wagner wished to keep the question open; nevertheless, I think it is worth pursuing the question whether he does in fact rape her after the curtain falls at the end of Act I, since it may elucidate key moments in Acts II and III.

The music at the end of Act I is particularly menacing and whatever he says about his sword Nothung separating him from Brünnhilde, the music together with his words in this scene suggests he will overpower her sexually. Siegfried appears on Brünnhilde's rock in the form of Gunther, the tarnhelm covering his face, "leaving only his eyes free."[37] Brünnhilde asks who has forced his way onto her rock. Siegfried declares (and Brünnhilde's response alludes to Prometheus):[38]

33. *WagRS* 305.

34. The closest to this in the sources is *Völsunga Saga* 28, where it is neither Hogni nor Gudrun who administer the drink but Grimhild (Finch, *Volsung Saga*, 47; Björnsson, *Volsungs*, 231–32).

35. *WagRS* 306–8.

36. Hence, commentators such as Kitcher and Schacht, *Ending*, 173–74, leave the question open.

37. *WagRS* 306.

38. *WagRS* 307. In the dialogue with Brünnhilde he sings "with a disguised—rougher—voice" (*WagRS* 306). Note the allusion to Hermes' prophecy towards the end of Aeschylus, *Prometheus Bound*, 1021-25: "I tell you, the winged hound of Zeus, the bloodthirsty eagle, will greedily butcher your body into great ragged shreds, coming uninvited for a banquet that lasts all day, and will feast on your liver, which will turn black with gnawing" (Sommerstein, *Aeschylus I*, 556–57). Cf. Hesiod,

Siegfried:	Siegfried:
Ein Helde, der dich zähmt—	A hero who'll tame you,
bezwingt Gewalt dich nur.	if force alone can constrain you.
Brünnhilde:	Brünnhilde:
Ein Unhold schwang sich	A demon has leaped
auf jenen Stein;—	on to yonder stone;—
ein Aar kam geflogen	an eagle came flying
mich zu zerfleischen!—	to tear at my flesh!—

Then a little later we have language that suggests a sexual assault:[39]

Siegfried:	Siegfried:
Die Nacht bricht an:	Night draws on:
in deinem Gemach	within your chamber
mußt du dich mir vermählen.	you'll have to wed me.
Brünnhilde:	Brünnhilde:
Bleib' fern! Fürchte dieß Zeichen!	Keep away! Fear this token!
Zur Schande zwing'st du mich nicht,	You'll never force me into shame
so lang' der Ring mich beschützt.	as long as this ring protects me.
Siegfried:	Siegfried:
Mannesrecht gebe er Gunther:	Let it give Gunther a husband's rights:
durch den Ring sei ihm vermählt!	be wedded to him with the ring!
Brünnhilde:	Brünnhilde:
Zurück, du Räuber!	Away, you robber!
Frevelnder Dieb!	Impious thief!
Erfreche dich nicht mir zu nah'n!	Make not so bold as to near me!

There is then a shocking struggle at the end of which Siegfried tears the ring from her:[40]

Siegfried:	Siegfried:
Jetzt bist du mein!	Now you are mine!
Brünnhilde, Gunther's Braut—	Brünnhilde, Gunther's bride,
gönne mir nun dein Gemach!	allow me to enter your chamber!
Brünnhilde:	Brünnhilde:
Was könntest du wehren,	How could you stop him,
elendes Weib!	woman most wretched!

Theogony, 523–25 (Most, *Hesiod I*, 44–45).

39. *WagRS* 307–8.
40. *WagRS* 307.

Then after Brünnhilde has returned to the chamber, Siegfried "in his natural voice" calls on Nothung to be his witness:[41]

Nun, Nothung, zeuge du,	Now, Nothung, attest
daß ich in Züchten warb:	that I wooed her chastely:
die Treue wahrend dem Bruder,	keeping faith with my brother,
trenne mich von seiner Braut!	keep me apart from his bride!

In the letter of 25/26 January 1854 to his friend Röckel, Wagner writes of "[t]he terrible and daemonic nature of this whole scene":[42]

> everything collapses at Br.'s feet, everything is out of joint (Alles ist aus den Fugen); she is overpowered in a terrible struggle, she is "Godforsaken." And it is *Siegfried*, moreover, who in fact orders her to share his couch with him—*Siegfried* whom she (unconsciously—and therefore all the more bewilderingly) almost recognizes, by his gleaming eye, in spite of his disguise. (You feel that something "inexpressible" is happening here, and so it is very wrong of you to ask me to speak out on the subject!)[43]

From what we know of Siegfried so far in the *Ring*, he is morally far inferior to the hero of the *Nibelungenlied* or the Icelandic sources. We have yet to establish whether he raped Brünnhilde at the end of *Götterdämmerung* Act I, but even if he did not we are still left with a very unpleasant character. Perhaps one can excuse him in the later scenes in *Götterdämmerung* because he is drugged; but even before this he is belligerent as when he arrives at Gunther's court in *Götterdämmerung* Act I Scene 2: "nun ficht mit mir, / oder sei mein Freund!" ("now fight with me, / or be my friend").[44] At the same time, Brünnhilde is truly exalted in the *Ring*. This can be discerned in two ways. First, whereas in the Icelandic sources she is the daughter of Budli, i.e., she is simply a human being, in the *Ring* Wagner makes her the daughter of two gods, Wotan and Erda. As far as Prünhilt of the *Nibelungenlied* is concerned, although nothing is said of her ancestry, the assumption is that she is mortal despite her formidable strength. The second way Brünnhilde is exalted is that in *Walküre* we encounter her nobility and compassion. This contrasts starkly with the violent and aggressive Prünhilt of the *Nibelungenlied* and with the arrogant and quarrelsome Brynhild of the *Prose Edda* and *Völsunga Saga*.[45] However, Brünnhilde's character is somewhat tarnished as we shall see as we turn to *Götterdämmerung* Act II.

41. *WagRS* 307.
42. *SL* 310; *SB* 6:71. Cf Dawson-Bowling, *Experience*, 2:327.
43. *SL* 310; *SB* 6:71. "Alles ist aus den Fugen" is probably an allusion to *Hamlet* Act I Scene 5 in the translation of A. W. Schlegel (Shakespeare, *Werke*, 6:49: "Die Zeit is aus den Fugen").
44. *WagRS* 293; cf. Av 3 (106–110; *NibE* 14–15).
45. See Prose Edda, *Skaldskaparmal* 7, where Brynhild and Gudrun went down to the river to wash their hair. "When they got to the river, Brynhild waded out into the river away from the bank and

In Scene 2 of *Götterdämmerung* Act II Siegfried returns from Brünnhilde's rock having exchanged places back with Gunther. Siegfried, if not dishonest, either avoids answering questions or is somewhat misleading. So on his return Hagen asks Siegfried: "So you overpowered Brünnhild?" Siegfried avoids the question and asks "Is Gutrun' awake?"[46] He then explains what happened on the rock in what seems rather equivocal language. Answering Gutrune's question "So Brünnhilde's following my brother?" Siegfried answers: "The woman was easily wooed" ("Leicht ward die Frau ihm gefreit"). This is ambiguous in that the dative "ihm" could be taken to mean she was wooed "for him" (for Gunther by Siegfried) or "by him" (by Gunther).[47] Gutrune's reply suggests that she does not really understand what was going on since she assumes Gunther himself had gone through the fames: "Didn't the fire singe him?"[48] to which Siegfried does clarify that it was he who passed through the flames. Then the dialogue continues to be ambiguous:[49]

Gutrune:
So zwang'st du das kühne Weib?
Siegfried:
Sie wich—Gunther's Kraft.
Gutrune:
Und vermählte sie sich dir?
Siegfried:
Ihrem Mann gehorchte Brünnhild'
eine volle bräutliche Nacht.
Gutrune:
Als ihr Mann doch galtest du?
Siegfried:
Bei Gutrune weilte Siegfried.
Gutrune:
Doch zur Seite war ihm Brünnhild'?

Gutrune:
So you overcame the intrepid woman?
Siegfried:
She yielded to—Gunther's strength.
Gutrune:
And yet she was wed to you?
Siegfried:
Brünnhild' obeyed her husband
for the whole bridal night.
Gutrune:
But you yourself were deemed her husband?
Siegfried:
Siegfried stayed with Gutrun'.
Gutrune:
But Brünnhild was at his side?

---

said that she did not want to pour over her head the water that ran out of Gudrun's hair, since she had the more valiant husband" (Faulkes, *Edda*, 103). Gudrun then follows her out into the river and goes further upstream to wash her hair, claiming her husband is the more noble (i.e., Sigurd). A similar story is related in *Völsunga Saga* 30 (Finch, *Volsungs*, 50). Note also *Grípisspá* 27, which refers to Brynhild, daughter of Budli, but the "bold king" Heimir "is raising that harsh hearted girl" (Orchard, *Elder Edda*, 150). Note that although Siegmund accuses Brünnhilde of being "cold and hard" and an "unfeeling maid" (*WagRS* 163) in *Walküre* Act II this accusation proves to be unjustified.

46. *WagRS* 312.

47. *WagRS* 313.

48. *WagRS* 371 n. 161 suggests Gutrune seizes on the meaning "for him" for "ihm." But surely her reply assumes that Brünnhilde was wooed *by* Gunther.

49. *WagRS* 314; *SW* 13.II:48.

SIEGFRIED AND BRÜNNHILDE

Siegfried:
Zwischen Ost und West der Nord:
(*auf sein Schwert deutend*)
so nah'—war Brünnhild' ihm fern.

Siegfried:
Twixt east and west—the north:
(*pointing to sword*)
so close was the distance between them?

It may appear that Siegfried, by the "gesture" of pointing to the sword and by the use of musical motifs of "sword" and "spear"/"treaty," has allayed Gutrune's fears; but at the same time Hagen's motif, a falling diminished fifth, is heard also on the double basses and three bassoons (bar 326).[50] Siegfried then goes on to explain that he and Gunther only changed places back the next morning after Siegfried led her down from the fell into the valley to the shoreline of the Rhine.[51] So if Siegfried really did not have sexual relations with her she spent her wedding night "unconsummated." Provisionally I will take it that Gutrune is reassured that Siegfried did not have sexual relations with Brünnhilde and I will return to this.

We now move to a highly emotionally charged scene that I think shows Wagner as an outstanding dramatist. Gunther arrives at the Gibichung court with his bride Brünnhilde. He names the couples in this order: "Brünnhild'—and Gunther, / Gutrun'—and Siegfried!"[52] Porges, in his report of the 1876 rehearsals, overseen by Wagner himself, comments: "At the sound of Siegfried's name, Brünnhilde raises her eyes, horror-stricken, and Gunther involuntarily lets go of her hand."[53] So she sings "Siegfried . . . here! . . Gutrune . . . ?"[54] and then discovers the ring on his finger.[55] Brünnhilde: "Ha! . . . the ring . . . upon his hand! He . . . Siegfried?" She says it was taken from her by Gunther and asks how then did Siegfried get it? "I did not get / the ring from him" explains Siegfried. Gunther also says he gave it to no one.[56]

Brünnhilde then realizes that it was Siegfried who took the ring from her. Porges writes: "Siegfried, absorbed in thoughts of the past, answers this terrible indictment as if in a dream":[57] "It was not from a woman / the ring came to me, / nor was it a woman / from whom I took it: / I recognize clearly / the spoils from the fight / which I once won at Neidhöhl' / when slaying the mighty dragon."[58] This is half-true since although he took it from the dragon in the third opera of the cycle, he then gave it to Brünnhilde as a token of his love in the Prologue to *Götterdämmerung*, but then took it from her at the

50. Cf. Sabor, *Götterdämmerung*, 107.

51. *WagRS* 314.

52. *WagRS* 319.

53. Porges, *Rehearsing the Ring*, 131. The stage direction indicates: "Brünnhilde raises her eyes in alarm" (*WagRS* 319).

54. *WagRS* 319.

55. So for the exchange with Gunther to have worked he should have given the ring to Gunther as they exchanged places back.

56. *WagRS* 320.

57. Porges, *Rehearsing the Ring*, 132.

58. *WagRS* 321.

end of Act I. (Therefore, his amnesia extends from just after killing of Mime in *Siegfried* Act II, shortly after he killed the dragon, up until just after taking the potion in *Götterdämmerung* Act I).[59] But here he is being culpably dishonest for the sake of Gunther (i.e., he does not want to reveal to Brünnhilde that they exchanged shape).

Hagen intervenes to say that Siegfried must have obtained it by deceit (Trug) which Brünnhilde then takes up: "Deceit! Deceit!" ("Betrug! Betrug!").[60] We then see Brünnhilde again being "God-forsaken"[61] and she calls on the gods to teach her revenge. We again enter the realm of ambiguity. Brünnhilde claims that she is wed to Siegfried. But to what is she referring? Their former love (as seen in *Siegfried* Act III Scene 3 and *Götterdämmerung* Prologue), or the possible rape at the end of *Götterdämmerung* I? Her next words on the printed page may suggest the latter:[62]

Er zwang mir Lust	He forced delight
und Liebe ab.	from me, and love.

But the falling six note motif ("woman's worth") points us back to the scene where Siegfried discovers the sleeping Brünnhilde and opens up her breastplate. The notes are virtually the same, but the trill on the clarinets of a *major* third (based on c♭′ and e♭′) in *Siegfried* Act III Scene 3 ("sollt' ich auch sterbend vergehen"; see Example 10.1, bars 1043–44)[63] is placed later here in *Götterdämmerung* such that Brünnhilde's trill on the word "Liebe" ("love") is accompanied by violins playing a *minor* third trill (a♭′ and c♭′; see Example 10.2, bars 1037–38).

---

59. Note that in *Götterdämmerung* Act III Scene 2 he sings of killing Mime (*WagRS* 342). In the following discussion concerning whether it was Siegfried or Brünnhilde who was at fault, I am indebted to private communications with Lionel Friend.

60. *WagRS* 321.

61. *WagRS* 322; cf. *SL* 310; *SB* 6:71 ("von Gott verlassen"). I will discuss this further in the following chapter.

62. *WagRS* 322; Deathridge, *Ring*, 647 is similar: "He forced pleasure / and love from me." The translation of William Mann, *Götterdämmerung* 61, rather tones down, unjustifiably in my view, any sense of "assault": "He coaxed desire / and love from me."

63. Likewise there is a trill on the violas and cellos based on C♭ and E♭) in bar 1048.

SIEGFRIED AND BRÜNNHILDE

Example 10.1: *Siegfried* Act III bars 1040–50

Example 10.2: Götterdämmerung Act II bars 1034–40

Siegfried *then* has to admit he did have a part in wooing Brünnhilde for Gunther. He points to his sword Nothung, which "defended the oath of loyalty; / its sharp edge sundered me / from this unhappy woman."[64] Brünnhilde is then ambiguous, perhaps deliberately so.[65] She says that Siegfried is disingenuous in appealing to his sword: "Nothung, rested / serenely against the wall / while its master won him his sweetheart."[66] This must be referring to their happy days together and not the situation at the end of Act I of *Götterdämmerung*. Again the music suggests this and this interpretation is confirmed by Porges, who notes that the final words of the passage ("Wohl kenn' ich sein Schärfe [. . .] als die Traute sein Herr sich gewann"), "in which she voices her seething emotions in tones of biting irony fused with unutterable tenderness, should be veiled: she is referring to a secret known only to Siegfried and herself."[67] Further, her referring to Siegfried as the Nothung's lord ("sein Herr"), suggests she is speaking of their first meeting.

But the crowd, including the main protagonists (apart from Hagen), misunderstand this. They think that she is referring to the previous night when they think he tenderly loved her. The fact that Gutrune now accuses Siegfried of being "faithless" ("treulos") indicates that she had not taken Siegfried's private account to her earlier as an admission that he had made love to Brünnhilde the previous night. Siegfried cannot understand Brünnhilde's accusation because all he remembers was the meeting on the previous night. He then says he will swear an oath if anyone will offer a weapon (he cannot use Nothung now because people suspect he may have already falsely sworn on that in saying it separated him from Brünnhilde). Hagen menacingly offers his spear.

Siegfried's oath may sound convincing from words on the printed page but the music sounds rather hollow and Hagen's falling diminished fifth is heard again in the bass (see Example 10.3); Brünnhilde's counter oath on the other hand has a rich orchestration with a significant rhythmic variation (see Example 10.4).

---

64. *WagRS* 322–23.
65. Wapnewski, *Ring*, 278–79.
66. *WagRS* 323.
67. Porges, *Rehearing the Ring*, 133.

Example 10.3: Götterdämmerung Act II bars 1143–56

Example 10.4: Götterdämmerung Act II bars 1179–91

The hollowness of Siegfried's oath indicates that he has forgotten that crucial first encounter with Brünnhilde. Each tells the truth from what they know. The first six lines of each oath on Hagen's spear is identical (line 3 being "Hilf meinem ewigen Eide!" ("Assist my eternal oath!")). This is followed by six lines, Siegfried addressing the spear thus:[68]

Wo Scharfes mich schneide,	Where blade may bleed me,
scheide du mich;	be it you that bleeds me;
wo der Tod mich soll treffen	where death may strike,
treffe du mich:	be it you that strikes
klagte das Weib dort wahr,	if that woman's charge is true,
brach dich dem Bruder den Eid!	if I broke my vow to my brother!

Brünnhilde's counter charge after her introductory six lines is:[69]

Ich weihe deine Wucht,	I hallow your thrust
daß sie ihn werfe!	that it overthrow him!
Seine Schärfe segne ich,	I bless you blade
daß sie ihn schneide:	that it bleed him:
denn brach seine Eide er all',	for, just as he broke every oath he swore,
schwur Meineid jetzt dieser Mann!	this man has now forsworn himself!

Siegfried's words to Gunther in private afterwards simply say that the tarnhelm "must have only half concealed me."[70] This, he thinks, is the only reason Brünnhilde has decided falsely to accuse him. He tells the vassals to "cheer up" and calls on the women to help for the wedding preparation. The stage is then emptied apart from Brünnhilde, Gunther, and Hagen, who ruminate on what is to be done. Hagen says the only solution to this crisis is "Siegfried's death,"[71] hence the original title of the opera, and it is his death that these three plot. Neither Siegfried nor Brünnhilde come off particularly well in Act II.

However, towards the end of Act III both figures come to be exalted. In Scene 2 Hagen gives Siegfried "a sweet-tasting drink" to stir his memory afresh and Siegfried then narrates how he awoke the sleeping Brünnhilde; this then gives Hagen a pretext to bring Siegfried's life to an end by stabbing him in the back with his spear.[72] As he dies Siegfried is transfigured and we see the hero he could have been. In the first sketches for the *Ring* of 1848 he is made a sacrifice like Isaiah's Suffering Servant, not in that he takes on the sins of humankind but "[h]e has innocently taken on the

---

68. *WagRS* 324.
69. *WagRS* 324.
70. *WagRS* 325.
71. *WagRS* 328.
72. *WagRS* 342–43.

guilt of the gods" ("[e]r hat schuldlos die Schuld der Götter übernommen").[73] This is something entirely missing in the sources Wagner used and is one key to the theology of the *Ring*, which will be explored in the following chapter.

As we move through the "funeral march" and into the final scene we enter a new realm. There are signals of Siegfried's immortality[74] with the miraculous raising of his hand as Hagen attempts to take the ring,[75] which then appears to summon the transformed Brünnhilde.[76] Her transformed nature is highlighted by the fact that in her previous stage appearance at the end of Act II she calls upon Wotan, "avenging god," to hear her "oath of vengeance."[77] I would go to the point of saying that with her entrance she has recovered her lost divinity, and this has come about by her communion with the Rhinemaidens which has enabled her to come to understand everything. An aspect of Wagner's dramatic genius is that this key meeting is not portrayed on stage but is suggested in three ways. The first comes in *Götterdämmerung* III.1 when the Rhinemaidens tell Siegfried:[78]

Ein stolzes Weib	A proud-hearted woman
wird noch heut' dich Argen beerben:	will be your heir today, you wretch:
sie beut uns bess'res Gehör.	she'll give us a fairer hearing.
Zu ihr! Zu ihr! Zu ihr!	To her! To her! To her!

The second comes in a remarkable scene just after Siegfried's death and funeral march.[79] Gutrune, alone, is awaiting the return of Siegfried:[80]

Lachen Brünnhilde's	Brünnhilde's laughter
weckte mich auf.——	woke me up.——
Wer war das Weib,	Who was the woman
das ich zum Ufer schreiten sah?—	I saw going down to the shore?—
[. . .]	[. . .]
So war es sie [Brünnhilde],	So it was she [Brünnhilde]
die ich zum Rhein schreiten sah?—	whom I saw going down to the Rhine?—

Brünnhilde was presumably going down to the Rhine to commune with the Rhinemaidens.[81]

73. Haymes, *Ring*, 54–55.
74. Cf. Wintle, "Numinous," 215.
75. *WagRS* 347.
76. Cf. Abbate, *Unsung Voices*, 220.
77. *WagRS* 330.
78. *WagRS* 337.
79. On this scene see especially Wintle, "Numinous," 211–16, 223–34.
80. *WagRS* 344–45.
81. Wintle, "Numinous," 219, considers that through her "nocturnal communion" Brünnhilde

SIEGFRIED AND BRÜNNHILDE

The third hint of this meeting is in Brünnhilde's final words, where she thanks the Rhinemaidens for their "sound advice."[82] They have informed her of the reasons for Siegfried's apparent treachery and she comes to realize that Siegfried had been true to his oaths.[83] The issue is now finally settled for us that Siegfried did not in fact rape her at the end of *Götterdämmerung* Act I:[84]

Wie Sonne lauter	Purer than sunlight
strahlt mir sein Licht:	streams the light from his eyes:
der Reinste war er,	the purest of men it was
der mich verrieth!	who betrayed me!
Die Gattin trügend	False to his wife (i.e., Brünnhilde)
—treu dem Freunde—	—true to his friend—(i.e., Gunther)
von der eig'nen Trauten	from her who was faithful
—einzig ihm theuer—	—she alone who was loyal—
schied er sich durch sein Schwert.—	he sundered himself with his sword.
Ächter als er	Never were oaths
schwur keiner Eide;	more nobly sworn;
treuer als er	never were treaties
hielt keiner Verträge;	kept more truly;
laut'rer als er	never did any man
liebte kein and'rer:	love more loyally:
und doch alle Eide,	and yet every oath,
alle Verträge,	every treaty,
die treuste Liebe—	the truest love—
trog keiner wie er!—	no one betrayed as he did!
Wiss't ihr wie das ward?—	Do you know why that was so?—
(*Nach oben blickend*)	(*looking upward*)
O ihr, der Eide	Oh you, eternal
ewige Hüter!	guardians of oaths!
Lenkt eu'ren Blick	Direct your gaze
auf mein blühendes Leid:	on my burgeoning grief:
erschaut eu're ewige Schuld!	behold your eternal guilt!
Meine Klage hör',	Hear my lament,
du hehrster Gott!	most mighty of gods! [ie Wotan]

"has gained a hieratic authority aligning her with the eternally feminine forces of Erda, the Norns, and the Rhinemaidens."

82. *WagRS* 349.
83. *WagRS* 348.
84. *WagRS* 348–49 (modified); *SW* 13.III:236–47.

Durch seine tapferste That,	By the bravest of deeds,
dir so tauglich erwünscht,	which you dearly desired,
weihtest du den,	you doomed him
der sie gewirkt,	who wrought it to suffer
dem Fluche, dem du verfielest:—	the curse to which you in turn succumbed:—
mich—mußte	it was I whom the purest man
der Reinste verrathen,	had to betray,
daß wissend würde ein Weib!—	that a woman might grow wise.
Weiß ich nun was dir frommt?—	Do I know what you need?
Alles! Alles!	All things, all things,
Alles weiß ich:	all things I know,
alles ward mir nun frei!	I am free in respect to everything!

To atone for the gods' guilt Siegfried had to betray her "that a woman might grow wise."[85] This is extremely condensed and the idea seems to be that his death was necessary for he took on the curse that had fallen also on the gods and his death could only be brought about by Brünnhilde being betrayed. She understands all and now attains full freedom ("Alles ward mir nun frei!"; "all things became free to me"). Brünnhilde is free in that what she wants to do is exactly the right thing to do, i.e., sacrifice herself.[86] In *Götterdämmerung* Act II Scene 5 Hagen responds to Gunther's feeling of shame that Siegfried had sworn to him blood-brotherhood: "May blood now atone / for the broken bond!" ("Des Bundes Bruch / sühne nun Blut!").[87] Brünnhilde in this scene also uses language of sacrifice. She tells Gunther that Siegfried betrayed him but she too has been betrayed by all. Addressing Gunther and Hagen she declares": "If I had my due, / all the blood in the world / could never make good your guilt." She then adds these crucial lines:[88]

Doch des Einen Tod	But one man's death
taugt mir für alle:	will serve me for all:
Siegfried falle—	may Siegfried fall
zur Sühne für sich und euch!	to atone for himself and you!

The crucial twist in these words points to the deeper truth that Siegfried died not for any sin against Gunther or Brünnhilde. Rather he died for the world[89] and his *involuntary*

---

85. *WagRS* 349.
86. For the Hegelian background to this, see volume 1, chapter 6.
87. *WagRS* 328; cf. Haymes, *Ring*, 140–41.
88. *WagRS* 329; cf. Haymes, *Ring*, 140–41.
89. Here Brünnhilde is unconsciously speaking of the atoning work of Siegfried. Cf. Caiaphas who likewise unconsciously prophesies in the council of chief priests and pharisees of Jesus' atoning death: "'You do not understand that it is better for you to have one man die for he people than to have the whole nation destroyed,' He did not say this on his own, but being high priest that year he prophesied

sacrifice is completed by a more fundamental sacrifice: Brünnhilde's *voluntary* sacrifice, which leads to the redemption of the whole world.

The transformation of Brünnhilde at the end of *Götterdämmerung* is fundamental for understanding the Wagner's theological interests in the *Ring* and the way it points forward to his final stage work, *Parsifal*. As Apponyi writes: "In Brünnhilde's final song he shows he had already found the direction in which his mind was urging him. *Parsifal* is the goal he reaches. *Parsifal* completes the philosophy of the *Ring*, and solves the problems raised by it; it is the glorious close of a storm-tossed life, of a ceaseless search of a struggle to attain peace of soul. In *Parsifal* the solution of the problem is complete and final; it realises what Brünnhilde merely anticipated in her final song, namely, love."[90] He concludes: "The love of whose existence Brünnhilde is conscious and for which at the close of the *Ring* she longs, is the deeply felt, universal principle of self-sacrifice for others. This principle finds its most perfect and complete expression, freed from any other element, in the love of the Saviour—Jesus Christ. He is the real hero of the Parsifal saga. With this consummation the work of Richard Wagner was over."[91] The element of which this love is freed is the "repulsive modern exaggeration" of "one-sided emphasis on sex," which he relates to the "Freudian Doctrine" of which, he claims, there is no trace in Wagner.[92]

Theological Conclusions

The first theological conclusion to draw is that although the Siegfried of Wagner's *Ring* seems morally inferior to Sivrit of the Nibelungenlied or the Sigurd of the Norse sources (and, of course, if he were to have raped Brünnhilde this would bring him much further down the moral scale), he *is* transfigured just before his death. The question is why does Wagner want to present him so? One reason I think is that his death is seen as an atoning sacrifice, and this is stressed especially in the earlier sketches of the *Ring*.[93] But as Wagner developed the plot the focus moves from Siegfried's redemptive death to that of Brünnhilde. This may be because she is a much more sympathetic figure; but much more important is that as a suffering figure ("Godforsaken") she is also a divine figure.[94] She also can be understood to incorporate Siegfried into her being.[95] As I mentioned earlier she is the daughter of two gods. Wagner's portrayal of such a divine figure is possibly unique in religious

---

that Jesus was about to die for the nation" (John 11:50–51).

90. Apponyi, *Memoirs*, 104–5.

91. Apponyi, *Memoirs*, 105.

92. Apponyi, *Memoirs*, 105.

93. Haymes, *Ring*, 54–55.

94. Note, however, that her moments of greatest suffering (*Götterdämmerung* Acts I and II) are when she is emptied of her divinity.

95. See chapter 6 above.

tradition. At the end of *Walküre* she undergoes an incarnation in the sense that she becomes human *and* loses her divinity. This parallels a radical kenotic Christology whereby divinity is exchanged for humanity.[96] But in the final scene of *Götterdämmerung* she recovers her divinity. So when she dies she dies not only as a woman, and as a woman who has a human love for Siegfried, but also she dies as God. And as Martin Luther argued, it is only the death of God that can atone for sin.[97]

Although Brünnhilde is the key redeemer figure, Siegfried also has a key role. In the *Ring* of 1848 we saw that he was to take on the sin of the gods. Further, there has been a fairly consistent Siegfried-Christ relationship throughout the development of the *Ring*[98] and, as I will argue in chapter 12, Siegfried can sometimes be interpreted as an allegorical figure for Christ. It is also worth noting that Siegfried was born in a cave as in some traditions of Jesus' birth. We see this as early as the second century when Justin Martyr writes: "when the Child was born in Bethlehem, since Joseph could not find a lodging in that village, he took up his quarters in a certain cave near the village."[99] The same tradition is found in other early Christian and patristic writing,[100] e.g., in *Protoevangelium* 18.1: "And he [Joseph] found a cave there and brought her into it, and left her in the care of his sons and went out to seek for a Hebrew midwife in the region of Bethlehem."[101] I know of no instance where Wagner appealed to this tradition in his portrayal of Siegfried's birth and it would be fanciful to speculate that his placing Siegfried's birth in a cave was in any way influenced by this tradition. But the fact that both portrayals have Siegfried and Jesus born in primitive circumstances is worth reflecting upon and may strike those who know of both traditions. Note that the *Prose Edda* and *Elder Edda* give no details of Sigurd's birth;[102] the *Völsunga Saga* 12–13, tells that Hjördis gives birth to Sigurd in comfortable circumstance and is brought up in the court of King Hjalprek, whose son Alf she marries;[103] *Thidrek's Saga* narrates a traumatic birth in that two Counts, Artvin and Hermann, were engaged in combat since they could not agree what to do with the traitor Queen Sisibe; on giving birth to

---

96. The kenotic Christologies of the late nineteenth and early twentieth centuries did not generally go to such an extreme as in Wagner. So Thomasius distinguished between immanent attributes (truth, holiness, and love) and relative attributes (omnipotence, omniscience, omnipresence) of God. He argued that in the incarnation the relative attributes were surrendered but not the immanent attributes (Macquarrie, "Jesus Christus VI," 26–27).

97. See volume 1, chapter 6.

98. This has been clear in *Die Wibelungen*.

99. *Dialogue with Trypho* 78.5 (*ANF* 1:237). Justin earlier quotes Isa 33:16 (70.2): "he shall dwell in the lofty cave of the strong rock" (*Dialogue* 70, *ANF* 1:234), which has presumably influenced his telling of Jesus' birth in a cave. Goodspeed, *Apologeten*, 180, notes the link between Dan 2:34 ("a stone without hands was cut out of a great mountain"), quoted at the beginning of 70 (70.1), and Isa 33:16.

100. Origen, *Contra Celsum* 1.51; Jerome, *Letters* 58.3; 147.4.

101. Elliott, *Apocryphal New Testament*, 64.

102. *Skaldskaparmal* 7 (Faulkes, *Edda*, 101) and *Grípisspá* 3 (Orchard, *Elder Edda*, 147) simply tell us that his father was Sigmund and mother Hjördis.

103. Finch, *Volsung Saga*, 22.

Sigurd, she placed him in a glass casket, but when Artvin "struck his foot against the glass vessel so that it flew out into the river" she fainted and died.[104]

Another link between Siegfried and Christ can be perceived through the figure of Baldr in the Eddas.[105] Baldr's death parallels that of Christ and it may well be that the portrayal of his death has been influenced by Christian tradition. In *Völuspá* 31 we read of Baldr's "bloodstained sacrifice," which was ordained by his father Odin, and of the weeping mother (33). It may even be that "Loki is given an elaborate Judas-role to play"[106] since "[i]n achieving Baldr's death Loki is performing Óðinn's will"[107] and that Höðr, whose dart killed Baldr, is portrayed as blind since Longinus, whose spear pierced Christ's side, was blind according to tradition.[108] Now in the prose sketch for *Der junge Siegfried* (3–24 May 1851) the Wanderer actually speaks of "Balder": "Um der götter ende sorgen die götter, seit Balder sank der holdeste gott" ("Concerning the end of the gods, the gods fear, since Baldr, the fair god, has gone under").[109] This is drawing on the tradition of Ragnarök that Baldr's death will herald the end of the gods (*Völuspá* 31ff). But Baldr is here *not* identified with Siegfried since the Wanderer goes on to speak of the "hero" who does not know him and who will take away his guilt.[110] In the poem of 3–24 June 1851 Baldr is not explicitly mentioned, although he is referred to as "the gladdening one": "Um der seligen ende / sorgen die götter / seit der erfreuende sank / der im frieden siege schuf" ("Concerning the blessed end, / the gods fear / since the gladdening one has gone under / who made victory in peace").[111] These lines were not used in the final poem,[112] one possible reason being that he wished to simplify the plot and also to have Siegfried take on the role of Baldr.

---

104. *Thidrek's Saga*, 160 (Haymes, *Thidrek*, 104–5).

105. The story of Baldr in *Gylfaginning*, 49 (Faulkes, *Edda*, 48–51) is one of the finest of passages that are traditionally ascribed to Snorri (cf. Turville-Peter, *Myth*, 106).

106. Dronke, *Edda II*, 94.

107. Dronke, *Edda II*, 95.

108. Dronke, *Edda II*, 96–97, refers to the poems of Blathmac (c. 750–70) and an Irish Gospel book of c. 800.

109. Strobel, *Skizzen*, 88; TBRN1 229.

110. Strobel, *Skizzen*, 89: "Ein held entsproß, der nie mich gekannt, und doch tilgt er meine schuld." Cf. TBRN1 229.

111. Strobel, *Skizzen*, 172; TBRN1 308. Note the description of Baldr in *Gylfaginning* 22: "He is best, and all praise him. He is so fair in appearance and so bright that light shines from him. [. . .] He is the wisest of the Æsir and most beautifully spoken and most merciful" (Faulkes, *Edda*, 23). See also the versions used by Wagner: Rühs, *Edda*, 185; Simrock, *Edda*, 257.

112. WagRS 257.

Wagner as Siegfried

At the banquet following the first cycle of performances in 1876, Wagner's speech[113] was followed by that of the Reichstag deputy Max von Forckenbeck, which was described by Count Apponyi as "a string of rather bland eulogies, interspersed with critical allusions, but lacking all trace of warmth or enthusiasm."[114] The count then relates how two ladies "begged me to save the situation by making a speech."[115] Initially he resisted, but once an idea came to his mind he agreed. His own account corroborates that given by Cosima[116] and he recalls his speech thus:

> Him, the Master, and the growth and products of his genius, I compared to Siegfried, the youth who never learned the meaning of fear, who pressed forward undaunted by cliffs and abysses and raging fire to storm the heights wheron Brünnhilde slept her death-like sleep, and who wakened her to life again. Siegfried and Brünnhilde were Wagner and the Tragic Muse; and, in the name of all my fellow-guests, I offered to the Master Brünnhilde's rapturous greeting to Siegfried:—"Hail to thee, victorious light!"[117]

According to Kellermann, "Wagner was deeply moved and held him in a lengthy embrace."[118]

According to Apponyi this speech made not only a deep impression but also a lasting impression.[119] And Wagner was clearly delighted to be identified with Siegfried![120]

---

113. See volume 1, chapter 2.
114. Apponyi, *Memoirs*, 95.
115. Apponyi, *Memoirs*, 95.
116. *CD* 18 August 1876 (see volume 1, chapter 2).
117. Apponyi, *Memoirs*, 96.
118. Spencer, *Wagner Remembered*, 250.
119. Apponyi, *Memoirs*, 997–98, tells of how forty years later, in 1916, he met Prince Maximilian von Baden, the future chancellor, in neutral Stockholm. The Prince asked: "Are you Count Apponyi who made the famous speech at Bayreuth?"
120. Wagner also identified himself with the somewhat different figure of Hans Sachs.

— 11 —

Redemption

Wagner's Understanding of Redemption

In Wagner's thought redemption is multidimensional and often rather ambiguous and perhaps this is partly why the scholarly discussion can become somewhat nebulous. I hope some clarity can be gained by focusing first on the most probable fundamental source for his understanding of redemption: Martin Luther's German Bible. Here redemption ("Erlösung") in its basic sense means paying a price so as to free property or a person. Leviticus 25 explains that if someone falls into financial difficulty and has to sell their property, then their next of kin should then come and redeem what the relative has sold (v. 25): so a price is paid in order to free that property.[1] Of more interest for redemption in the *Ring* is the freeing of a prisoner, captive, or slave by paying a ransom. Again this is found in Lev 25:47–49, where an Israelite who has become a slave may be redeemed if "anyone of their family who is of their own flesh may redeem them" (Lev 25:49). Likewise, in the *Ring* cycle the goddess Freia is ransomed in Scene 4 of *Rheingold* by members of her wider family paying a price.[2] Addressing her fellow gods (especially Wotan) she asks:[3]

Dünkt euch Holda	Does Holda (ie Freia) really seem to you
wirklich der Lösung werth?	worthy of ransom?

She has been a prisoner of the giants, but when all the gold together with the tarnhelm and ring are given to them, Wotan exclaims to Freia "You are freed: / now it's bought back, / may our youth return!" ("Du bist befreit: / wieder gekauft / kehr' uns die Jugend zurück!").[4] Being "bought back" means she is redeemed, and one can compare Fricka's earlier words of Freia's "begging silently for redemption (Erlösung)."[5] The fact that Freia is redeemed with *gold* is striking when we come to look at Luther's view of redemption.

---

1. This corresponds to the English-language expression of "redeeming a mortgage."
2. Wotan, who pays the price, is her brother-in-law, Freia being Fricka's sister.
3. *WagRS* 113.
4. *WagRS* 113.
5. *WagRS* 109.

The view of redemption I now focus on is when the price paid is not gold but the price of a person's life. For Wagner the ultimate example of such a redemption is the sacrificial death of Christ and this can be found in the *Jesus of Nazareth* sketches: "Jesus announces his true mission, his quality as son of God, the redemption of all peoples of the earth through him" ("Jesus verkündigt seine wahre sendung—seine eigenschaft als gottes sohn, die erlösung aller völker der erde durch ihn") and he explicates this redemption in terms of "his sacrifice" ("sein opfer").[6] This idea of Jesus' redemptive death in the sense of "paying a price" is found in the Gospel tradition (Mark 10:45) and is expressed by St Paul, who tells the Corinthian Christians on two occasions: "you were bought with a price" (1 Cor 6:20; 7:23). The later Christian tradition sometimes added some theological confusion by asking *to whom* the price was paid. The church father Origen (c. 185–c. 254) argued that the price was paid to the devil[7] and others have argued the price was paid to God the father as a "satisfaction."[8] For the purposes of discussing the biblical background to Wager's understanding of redemption I assume that in Jesus' redemptive act a price *is* paid but that it stretches too far the metaphor within the myth to ask to whom the price was paid.[9]

The world of redemption in which Wagner was brought up was that of the Lutheran Church (into which he was baptized and confirmed)[10] and he was well acquainted with Luther's Bible, especially his translation of the New Testament.[11] Further, anyone being prepared for confirmation will have studied Luther's *Shorter Catechism*,[12] and Luther wished it to be learned by heart.[13] The *Shorter Catechism* contains three key texts of the Christian Faith, the Ten Commandments, the Apostles' Creed, and the Lord's Prayer, together with Luther's creative commentary on them in question and answer form. In the section on the creed, which he entitles "The Faith" ("Der Glaube"),[14] Luther goes through the three articles on Father, Son, and Holy Spirit. The

---

6. *PW* 8:291; *DTB* 244.

7. See Origen, *In Mattheum* 16.8, commenting on Matt 20:28 (Origenes, *Mattäus II* (ed. Vogt), 179; *MPG* 13:1397; cf. Aulén, *Christus Victor*, 49). Contrast Gregory of Nazianzus, who rejected the idea of a ransom, whether paid to God or the devil (Aulén, *Christus Victor*, 50).

8. See Anselm of Canterbury. Aulén, *Christus Victor*, 84–92. This view of satisfaction, whereby it is stressed what Jesus *as a human being* achieves, was then later adopted by Calvin and then by many evangelicals even to this day. Jeffrey, Ovey, Sach, *Pierced*, welcomed by many evangelicals and which puts forward a case for "penal substitution," is seriously deficient when it comes to key texts such as Rom 3:21–26. Such a theory of the atonement often forms the basis of many "evangelistic" sermons and is fundamental for Mel Gibson's film *Passion of the Christ*.

9. I will return to the question whether it is at all wise to speak of "theories of the atonement."

10. He was baptized on 16 August 1813 in the Thomaskirche Leipzig and confirmed on 4 April 1827 in the Kreuzkirche Dresden. In *My Life* 3; *Mein Leben* 1:9 he incorrectly claims he was christened two days after his birth.

11. See volume 1, chapter 7 and volume 2, chapter 2.

12. Although Wagner explains he did not particularly like his confirmation classes.

13. *BSELK* 503.

14. Schaff, *Creeds of Christendom*, 3:77.

heading for the second article on the Son is actually headed "Of Redemption" ("Von der Erlösung"), and included are these words: "I believe that Jesus Christ [. . .] has redeemed me, a lost and condemned human being, secured and delivered me [even] from all sins, from death, and from the power of the devil, not with gold or silver, but with the holy, precious blood, and with his innocent sufferings and death."[15] Whereas Freia is redeemed by gold, human beings, according to Luther and the biblical witnesses, are redeemed by Jesus offering his life (e.g., Rom 3:24–25).

According to this "second article," redemption is seen as release from three powers: sins, death, and the devil. Further, in this text redemption is just one stage in the salvation process (albeit a crucial one), and we find this view in other writings of Luther, such as the *Greater Catechism*.[16] But often he employs redemption for the whole process of salvation, found again in the *Greater Catechism,* which speaks of "a redeemer (ein Erlöser) who has taken us from the devil to God, from death to life and from sin to righteousness and thereby enlightens us."[17] In the *Ring* cycle redemption also can move between these two similar senses of redemption: a narrow sense, being redeemed from the curse of the ring, and a wider sense, which involves a renewal of the human person and of the created order.

In addition to the direct influence of Luther's Bible and Luther's theology there were other sources for Wagner's understanding of redemption that one could consider: Greek tragedy, Norse mythology, Goethe and Romantic writers, and minor strands in German idealism. In Wagner's mind all these sources were colored by Christian theology. Greek tragedy, although pre-Christian, had been "baptized" by Wagner;[18] Norse mythology, propagated by Christian writers, contained many Christian elements, and Wagner had further Christianized it as in his portrayal of Brünnhilde;[19] Romantic writers were all heavily influenced by Christian theology,[20] as were the German idealists.[21]

Of the great writers and dramatists, it was probably Goethe who influenced him most on the issue of redemption. The close of *Faust I* presents a Lutheran view of "justification of the ungodly" in the way the damning verdict of Mephistopheles

---

15. Schaff, *Creeds of Christendom*, 3:79; *BSELK* 511. This was quoted in full in chapter 2 above

16. Clemen, *Luthers Werke*, 4:82.3–4: "Selig werden aber /weis man wol das nichts anders heisset / denn von sunden / tod / Teuffell erlöset / ynn Christus reich komen / und mit yhm ewig leben."

17. Clemen, *Luthers Werke*, 4:55.10–12: "ein Erlöser / das ist / der vns vom Teuffel zu Gotte / vom tod zum leben / von sund zur gerechtikeit bracht hat und da bey erhelt." This all-encompassing sense of redemption and its centrality for Christ's "Amt und Werk" ("office and work") in many of Luther's writings was stressed by Hirsch, "Zu Luthers Theologie," 132, in his criticism of Seeberg's *Grundzüge der Theologie Luthers* of 1940.

18. See volume 1, chapter 4.

19. See volume 1, chapter 3 and volume 2, chapter 3.

20. See volume 1, chapter 5.

21. See volume 1, chapter 6.

is reversed.[22] One can also point to the final scene of *Faust II*, central for Wagner's thought, which presents a Christian (and Catholic!) view of redemption. However, Vaget argues that Wagner insists on "the human rather than a transcendental source of redemption"[23] and this "reflects Ludwig Feuerbach's influential critique of religion." Vaget argues that "by linking redemption so firmly to human sexuality Wagner betrays the often underestimated heritage in his thinking of *Das junge Deutschland* and of the Saint-Simonian philosophy."[24] Vaget further claims that the source of Wagner's Goethe criticism on this point comes from Vischer's essay (republished in *Kritische Gänge*, volume 2), where he argues that this scene of Faust's redemption was an incongruous borrowing from the Mount Olympus of the medieval world, Faust ending up a Catholic.[25] Vaget thinks Wagner read this essay since this same volume 2 of the *Kritische Gänge* contained Vischer's proposal for an opera based on the *Nibelungenlied*.[26] As pointed out in my first volume, it is unclear whether Wagner actually read Vischer's essay on the proposal for an opera and the same doubt surrounds the issue whether he read the Goethe essay. But even if he did I doubt very much whether Wagner would share Vischer's views on *Faust*. Having in mind *Faust II*, Wagner writes: "Before us Germans lies an equally uncomprehended artwork, a riddle still unsolved, in Goethe's *Faust*." Although he accepted that *Faust II* was idiosyncratic and "theatrically-speaking impracticable" he added that "when we possess a Theatre, a stage and actors who can set this Germanest of all dramas completely properly before us, will our æsthetic Criticism also be able to rightly judge this work: whereas to-day the coryphœi (Koryphäen) of that Criticism presume to crack bad jokes and parodies upon its second part."[27] The "Koryphäe" ("chorus leader") Wagner had in mind was Vischer himself who had produced a parody in 1862.[28]

As far as German idealism is concerned, redemption seemed to take a back seat.[29] The clearest sense of redemption is found in Schopenhauer,[30] and since Wagner knew something of him as he was completing the libretto there are cases where he could have affected Wagner's view of redemption, the clearest example being *Siegfried* Act

---

22. See volume 1, chapter 5.

23. Vaget, "Faust," 100. I assume he means "transcendent" rather than "transcendental."

24. Vaget, "Faust," 100.

25. Vischer, "Die Litteratur über Goethes Faust," 65, writes "und kommt die Rettung äußerlich nach, in Form eines Geschehens, die dem mittelalterlichen Olymp entlehnt ist, und der so ganz, so tief protestantische Faust, schließt katholisch."

26. Vaget, "Faust," 100. The Faust essay is pp. 49–215 and the proposal for an opera is pp. 397–436.

27. *PW* 5:212; *GSD* 9:214.

28. Vischer, *Faust: Der Tragödie dritter Theil*.

29. Hegel, for example, preferred the term "reconciliation" ("Versöhnung"); e.g., Miller, *Phenomenology*, 408 (§670); *HHW* 2:361.

30. Word occurrences do not tell the whole story but it is worth noting that there are just fourteen references to "Erlösung" ("redemption") in the index to the major works edited by von Löhneysen (*ASSW* 5:921).

III Scene 1.[31] Further, after the completion of the libretto at the end of 1852, he did later write an alternative Schopenhauer ending in 1856, but decided not to include this when he came to setting the words to music. Here Brünnhilde sings:[32]

nach dem wunsch- und wahnlos	to the holiest chosen land,
heiligstem Wahlland,	free from desire and delusion,
der Welt-Wanderung Ziel,	the goal of the world's migration,
von Wiedergeburt erlös't,	redeemed from reincarnation,
zieht nun die Wissende hin.	the enlightened woman now goes.

Having looked at how Wagner understood redemption and the various sources for his thought, I now turn to the questions of *what sort* of redemption Wagner envisaged in the *Ring* and immediately turn to ask *from what* is one supposed to be redeemed.

From What Is One Redeemed?

In the *Ring* cycle we see that the world is not as it should be. Nature has been desecrated, power is being abused, and we see the rise of the "unacceptable face of capitalism."[33] Many of the relationships are at breaking point: indeed there is theft, betrayal, and murder. As I argued in chapter 5 above, the world is "fallen."

The key thing of which one needs to be redeemed in the *Ring* is the curse of the ring. This is a demonic power. There are also demonic figures, the most threatening being Hagen, who meets his end at the very end of the drama. There are other demonic figures, but they are presented such that one can feel a certain sympathy for them, just as Wagner felt a certain sympathy for Alberich.[34] So Mime, despite his wish to kill Siegfried and his wish to gain the ring, has to be seen in the context that even if he had gained it, he would have little appetite for world rule and is essentially motivated by hate for and competition with his brother Alberich.[35] Even though Fafner may represent the power of the devil it is also possible to feel compassion for him. First, after Nothung has been lodged in his heart he accepts that Siegfried was goaded to do this and that it was not pre-meditated ("Your brain (Hirn) did not brood upon / what you have done").[36] Secondly, he at least acknowledges (if not confesses) killing Fasolt.[37] Thirdly, he warns the "bright-eyed boy" of the dangers awaiting him in that Mime

---

31. See volume 1, chapter 6 and chapter 12 below.
32. *WagRS* 363. See also volume 1, chapter 6.
33. This phrase was coined by Prime Minister Edward Heath in 1973 to describe the excesses of Lonrho, whose chief executive was "Tiny" Rowland.
34. See *CD* 2 March 1878 and chapter 6 above.
35. See chapter 5 above.
36. *WagRS* 241.
37. *WagRS* 242.

is plotting his death.[38] Wagner was clearly influenced here by *Fáfnir's lay* (*Fáfnismál*) stanzas 1–22 where the "Wurm"[39] seems somewhat more friendly than the "Satan" of Christian theology. Finally, Hunding is certainly a villain but he is only threatening in his role against Siegmund and Sieglinde and the only sense in which he could be a universal demonic menace is that he presents the idea of woman as "property." Hence, all these figures, apart from Alberich, are dealt with in that they do come to their end. In that "demonic" figures such as Hagen are destroyed, an adversary not only of Siegfried but of humanity generally, one can say that there is redemption in Luther's sense of being redeemed from the power of the "devil."[40]

I think a case can be made that the *Ring* is also concerned with redemption from "sins." The first sketch for the *Ring* speaks of the "guilt of the gods"[41] and throughout the development of the *Ring* the gods, especially Wotan, are portrayed as desperately in need of redemption. At least Wotan is aware of his "sin."[42] For others their "sin" is further exacerbated by the fact that there is simply no awareness of it. For example, Fricka is clearly unaware of her sin of self-righteousness[43] and although Fasolt in many ways is presented sympathetically, he is clearly oblivious of the fact that he is abusing Freia, and thinks solely of his own self-gratification and of fearing that he is to lose her.[44]

Finally, there is the question of redemption from death. The only figures for which death is an existential problem are the gods, as seen in Waltraute's narration where she tells of the "anxious gods" who fear death because Wotan refuses to touch Holda's apples;[45] Wotan is the only god who accepts death. Further, in the *Ring* it is assumed that death for human beings is a normal and natural process.

One can conclude so far that there is a need for redemption and a redeemer figure in respect to the curse of the ring, demonic figures, and "sin." But as Wagner worked on the libretto in the years 1848–52, his conception of this saviour and what this saviour figure was to achieve changed.

The Redeemer Figure

In the first sketches of the *Ring*, made in October 1848, this saviour figure was to be Siegfried. Wagner wrote "He has innocently taken on the guilt of the gods" ("Er hat

---

38. *WagRS* 242.
39. On the term "Wurm" and its Icelandic equivalent "ormr" see chapter 4 above.
40. On Luther and the "classic" idea of the atonement see Aulén, *Christus Victor*, 101–22.
41. Haymes, *Ring*, 54–55.
42. See especially his "confessions" to Brünnhilde in *Walküre* Act II Scene 2 (*WagRS* 149–54).
43. See her altercation with Wotan in *Walküre* Act II Scene 1 (*WagRS* 141–47).
44. See *Rheingold* Scenes 2 and 4 (*WagRS* 74, 110).
45. *WagRS* 303.

schuldlos die Schuld der Götter übernommen").[46] After Siegfried is killed by Hagen's spear, Brünnhilde explains "Hagen did not strike him down, no, he marked him for Wotan, to whom I shall now lead him."[47] Siegfried is to be the sole sacrifice. Addressing the "lordly gods" Brünnhilde declares "your injustice has been erased (euer Unrecht ist getilgt). Thank him, the hero, who took your guilt upon himself." This is reminiscent of the servant of Isaiah 53, applied to Jesus in 1 Pet 2:24: "He himself bore our sins in his body on the cross, so that, free for sins, we might live to righteousness; for by his wounds you have been healed." So in this early version, Siegfried's death was to redeem the gods and also to free the race of dwarves, the Nibelungs! In this earliest version of the *Ring* Brünnhilde's own death when she jumps into the fire does not seem to be sacrificial. Rather, the ring that bears Alberich's curse and that she has placed on her finger will be purified: "The fire that burns me will also purify the evil jewel."[48]

Essentially the same view is found in the libretto he wrote for *Siegfried's Tod* in 1848. But in a later addition Wagner made Siegfried's atoning death more explicit with these words of Brünnhilde:[49]

Selige Sühnung	Blessed atonement
ersah ich den hehren,	I saw for the holy,
heilig ewigen	sacredly ageless
einigen Göttern!	and only gods!
Freuet euch	Rejoice
des freiesten Helden!	in the freest of heroes!
Göttlichem Brudergruß	To the greeting of his brotherly gods
führt seine Braut ihn zu!	his bride is bringing him now!

This idea of Siegfried as redeemer recurs in the various drafts of the *Ring* right up until the verse draft for the third opera in the *Ring* cycle, *Siegfried* (this verse draft was completed 24 June 1851). So in the final section of Act III Scene 1 Wotan tells the earth goddess Erda that Siegfried "through a free deed / he takes away the guilt / which a god once created" ("durch freie that / tilgt er die schuld / die je ein gott einst schuf").[50] The verb "tilgen" ("to wipe out") is used in Luther's translation of the famous penitential psalm, Psalm 51. See Psalm 51:3b: "tilge meine Sünde / nach deiner grossen Barmherzigkeit" (51:1b: "blot out my sin according to your abundant mercy"); 51:11b: "Vud tilge alle meine Missethat" (51:9b: "and blot out all my iniquities"). Note also: Isa 43:25b: "Ich /Ich tilge deine Vbertrettung vmb Meinen Willen"[51]

46. Haymes, *Ring*, 54–55.
47. Haymes, *Ring*, 58–59.
48. Haymes, *Ring*, 58–59.
49. *SSD* 16:210 (*Götterdämmerung: Zu Brünnhilde's Schlußworten*).
50. Strobel, *Skizzen*, 173; *TBRN1* 309.
51. Isa 43:24b-25 is capitalised by Luther with comment in the margin: "Das ist alles so viel gesagt / Das vnser werck fur Gott nicht sunde tilgen / sondern allein seine Gnade" ("That all effectively says

("I, I blot out your transgression for my own sake").[52] Hence, Wagner has reversed this in that it is not God who takes away the sins of human beings but rather that the human being, Siegfried, takes away the guilt of the gods! It is he who achieves atonement or expiation (Sühnung/Sühne).

Although in the final version of the *Ring*, published in February 1853, Siegfried's death still has an atoning value,[53] the striking thing is that the key redeemer figure becomes Brünnhilde. We can discern this by the fact that as Wagner made final revisions to *Der junge Siegfried* at the end of 1852 the lines that Siegfried "through a free deed / he takes away the guilt / which a god once created" were removed and a highly significant new line was added. Wotan declares to Erda that their daughter Brünnhilde "will work the deed that redeems the world" ("erlösende Weltenthat").[54] Hence we have this comprehensive understanding of redemption, i.e., redemption of the world and not just redemption from the power of the cursed ring I mentioned earlier. And just to complicate matters further, the gods, rather than being redeemed and ruling, actually come to an end: *Götterdämmerung*. But even though they come to an end there is still the possibility that they are redeemed, but in a limited sense, a point to which I return.

We have then this fundamental shift in Wagner's development of his drama where the focus of the redemptive figure moves from Siegfried to Brünnhilde, and where Wagner introduces the idea of the end of the gods. And the way Brünnhilde emerges as this redeemer figure as the drama unfolds comes very much as a surprise in the second opera of the cycle. And it comes about because Wotan's plans to regain the ring go disastrously wrong.

Wotan's Failed Plans to Regain the Ring

Towards the end of *Rheingold*, as the gods are about to enter Valhalla, we hear a hint of Wotan's future plans:[55]

So—grüß' ich die Burg,	Thus I salute the stronghold,
sicher vor Bang und Grau'n.—	safe from dread and dismay.—

---

that our work for God does not wipe away sin but alone his grace").

52. Here I am translating Luther's version into English, not translating from the Hebrew or Greek. The verse numbers for Psalm 51 in English translations differ from those in Luther's translation (which follows the numbering in *Biblia Hebraica Stuttgartensia*).

53. Darcy, *Rheingold*, 30, avers that in the final version of *Siegfried's Tod/Götterdämmerung* that Siegfried's death has no atoning function whatsoever. To *some* extent he may be correct that "his actions may be understood as recreating all the mistakes Wotan made in *Das Rheingold*: embracing power, entangling himself in false treaties, and renouncing true love," but much more is at work in *Götterdämmerung*. I am also somewhat skeptical about the dramatic parallels Darcy discerns between *Rheingold* and *Götterdämmerung* (31–33).

54. *WagRS* 258.

55. *WagRS* 116.

The stage direction indicates he sings "very resolutely, as though seized by a grandiose idea" and the so-called sword musical motif[56] is introduced for the first time (here played by the second trumpet). The libretto says nothing of a sword[57] yet it seems highly significant that the sword motif is here played and for the first time in the *Ring* cycle. The reason Wagner uses this is to indicate, I think, that although Wotan is entering his stronghold Valhalla he still faces danger in that Alberich could recover the ring and wage war on Wotan and Valhalla. He explains to Brünnhilde in *Walküre* Act II: "Only were he / to win back the ring / would Valhalla then be lost: / he who laid a curse on love, / he alone / in his envy would use / the runes of the ring / to the noble gods' / unending shame; my heroes' hearts / he'd turn against me / forcing the brave / to battle with me / and, with their strength / wage war against me."[58] The sword motif points to the hero who, Wotan unconsciously hopes, will recover the ring. So we do not have the idea we find in the original sketch that Wotan plans a hero to redeem the gods and free the Nibelungs, but rather we have Wotan, a politician in the worst sense, who wants to recover the ring so as to rule the world. Wotan himself cannot recover the ring because he is constrained by his treaties, which are etched on his spear; so he needs a hero who can act independently of himself. As we have seen, Wotan's plan to recover the ring using Siegmund fails and Brünnhilde's act of disobedience proves her to be "das Andere"[59] who acts independently of Wotan, although whether she is independent or simply acting according to Wotan's deep wishes they debate in *Walküre* Act III. In opposing her father a series of events are set in place that lead to Wotan's downfall and the redemption of the whole world. And one of the key factors in this chain of events is Brünnhilde having to become fully human, fully "incarnate."

Brünnhilde's Divinity

It is not clear whether Brynhild is a Valkyrie in the *Elder Edda* but she does so appear in the *Prose Edda*, although not as a sympathetic character.[60] A Valkyrie literally means "chooser of the slain"[61] and some Icelandic sources suggest the Valkyries are rather

---

56. Wolzogen, *Leitfaden*, 32, terms it "divine sword" ("göttliche[s] Schwert").

57. The stage direction also says nothing about a sword. However, in rehearsals Porges (*Rehearsing the Ring*, 39) notes that Wagner wanted Wotan to take a sword and wield it: "As the new theme is sounded, signifying a new deed to be accomplished in the future [. . .,] Wotan, seized by a great thought, picks up the sword left by Fafner and, pointing to the castle, cries, 'So grüss ich die Burg, sicher vor Bang' und Grau'n!" This is a case where Wagner as director does not really shine! As Wintle, "Numinous," 206, points out, the sword motif "articulates a thought whose substance is concealed from the audience." Bailey, "Evolution," 55 n. 14, suggests the sword is a "visual symbol of the motive, rather than the motive as a musical tag for the sword."

58. *WagRS* 151.

59. See chapter 9 above.

60. Faulkes, *Edda*, 102–4.

61. Ellis Davidson, *Gods*, 61.

bloodthirsty women. So in *Njal's Saga* these "terrible female creatures" work out "the fate of warriors in battle" and bring down "blood and carnage upon men."[62] However, the Eddas present them as "more dignified and less blood-thirsty."[63] This may have happened because the poets who preserved these pagan myths and legends were themselves Christian. My contention is that Wagner has further Christianized the Valkyrie Brünnhilde. Her nobility and compassion in *Walküre* is striking. In his first sketch for the *Ring*, Wagner describes her as a "divine virgin,"[64] which could suggest either the Virgin Mary or even a female version of Christ himself.

This idea that she could be a female Christ may be underpinned by the significant changes Wager made to the Brynhild of his sources. In the *Poetic Edda* she is human, being the daughter of Budli (adopted by King Heimir).[65] But Wagner makes her fully divine, being the daughter of two gods, Wotan and Erda.[66] It may not be relevant but it is nevertheless interesting that in Doepler's costume design for the first *Ring* performance of 1876, Erda looks remarkably like the Virgin Mary.[67] There is the difference that her clothing is steel-blue[68] whereas Mary has a (deep) blue (ultra marine) because of her associations with nature, royalty, and peace. But the similarities are striking, especially considering that although she is supposed to be an *earth* goddess, Doepler has her coming out of the *clouds*, reminiscent of Mary as Queen of Heaven. Initially Cosima (and presumably her husband also) was pleased with the costumes[69] but later made very critical remarks, focussing on the *human* figures.[70]

Brünnhilde is therefore the daughter of the chief god Wotan and the goddess Erda who has some likeness to the Virgin Mary (the conception of Brünnhilde, however, was obviously not virginal). Further, we saw in chapter 8 that she is "immortal," referring to herself as Wotan's "eternal part" ("Dein ewig Theil").[71] Although the sug-

---

62. Ellis Davidson, *Gods*, 65. See Magnusson and Pálsson *Njal's Saga*, 349.

63. Ellis Davidson, *Gods*, 66.

64. Haymes, *Ring*, 48–49.

65. *Grípisspá* 27 (Orchard, *Elder Edda*, 150).

66. Note that the other Valkyries may not have this fully divine status since although Wotan was their father, their mother may not have been Erda but a mortal woman.

67. The photograph of Lousie Jaide as Erda from the 1876 performance though bears little resemblance to the Virgin Mary.

68. So described by Clara Steinitz. This is also the color of the cape of Wotan and Siegfried and the cloak of Wotan as Wanderer.

69. Cosima writes that "they are really lovely" but then adds: "I myself should have preferred a more mystical impression, everything too clearly defined visually is to my mind detrimental to the effect of the music and the tragic action" (*CD* 6 March 1876).

70. *CD* 28 July 1876: "The costumes are reminiscent throughout of Red Indians chiefs and still bear, along with their ethnographic absurdity, all the marks of provincial tastelessness." All we know of Wagner is that, according to Cosima, he agreed with her: "He agrees with me when I say that all the magic was lost through Doepler's *rags and patches*" (*CD* 23 February 1877).

71. *WagRS* 187.

gestion of Brünnhilde being a "super-woman" ("Über-Weib") is thought-provoking[72] I think it fails to do justice to Wagner's portrayal of this remarkable figure. She is divine even though one may consider in the normal ways of thinking of divinity that she is not. One may compare the way Paul speaks of Jesus Christ's divinity in terms of the "human being" (anthrōpos) in Rom 5:15–19; Brünnhilde, like Christ, makes us question our normal definition of "divinity."

Brünnhilde's Incarnation

It is not explicit in the libretto of *Walküre* that Brünnhilde is the redeemer figure, but it is clear in the next two operas, *Siegfried* and *Götterdämmerung*. But dramatically and musically there are indications already in *Walküre* that Brünnhilde will redeem the world. The final scene expresses the end of law and the beginning of love. The law is expressed by Wotan's spear on which his various treatises are etched. The form in which it appears at the end of *Walküre*, just before Wotan calls on Loge is shown in Example 11.1.

Example 11.1: *Walküre* III bars 1647–51

Wotan's spear is not *physically* broken until *Siegfried* Act III Scene 2, when he is confronted by Siegfried. But there is a musical indication in *Walküre* Act III, just after the exit of her eight Valkyrie sisters, that Wotan's spear is being broken. This is hinted by the bass clarinet in bars 984–86 (see Example 11.2) and again by the cor anglais and then oboe together with bass clarinet in bars 990–94, but then more clearly introduced by Brünnhilde's entry at bar 1004: "War es so schmählich . . . ." Then taking Brünnhilde's entry at bar 1020 ("War es so ehrlos was ich beging") this modified spear motif is seen in its definitive form. Wotan's descending spear motif (taken from late in Act III) is broken as she sings e´ d´ c´, then rather than singing the b below she jumps up to the octave above b´. Then she descends a´ g´ f#´ e´ and again rather than

---

72. Friedrich, "Philosophie," 56. He writes that Wagner does not have a philosophy of womanhood but a "Phantasmagorie des Weiblichen," an erotic or aesthetic ideal in which the human and the artistic are fused.

singing d´ jumps to the octave above d´´. Wotan's law (which can be almost equated with Wotan's power) is thus challenged by the Valkyrie, who has come to recognize that the key to the world is not love of power but rather the power of love.

This passage is also punctuated by three other motifs. First, the theme of Wotan's frustration appears right at the beginning of this passage and is woven into this transformation of the spear motif just discussed. Secondly we hear the so-called "fate" motif played twice, but this theme has a very specific identity in *Walküre* and *Siegfried*, namely "mutual recognition."[73] The use here is appropriate since Brünnhilde goes on to plead with her father "Look in my eyes" ("Sieh' mir in's Auge"). Thirdly, at the end of each of Brünnhilde's opening phrase we hear a motif that has the rhythm of the "mutual recognition" but the top line corresponds to the three final notes of the descending scale of "woman's worth" (included in example 11.4 below). Fourthly, the cellos in bars 1019–25 play the repeated motif of Siegmund's rebellion. This is first heard when Siegmund refuses the eternal bliss of Valhalla in Act II.[74] Its use here refers to the fact that Brünnhilde is defending her support for Siegmund in his rebellion.

---

73. Millington, "Musical Reforms," 16. E.g., in *Walküre* Act II it is heard in Brünnhilde's annunciation of death to her words "Siegmund!—Look on me!" (*WagRS* 159; bars 1490–92).

74. See chapter 8 above for further details.

REDEMPTION

Example 11.2: *Walküre* Act III bars 980–1036

257

Therefore, the end of *Walküre* presents us with a remarkable irony. Wotan, in punishing his daughter, *appears* to be the one in control and exercising power. He decides that she will no longer enjoy fellowship with him, will be banned from Valhalla, and put to sleep on the rock[75] where they find themselves. She loses her divine Valkyrie status and is to become fully human. Whoever awakens her will be her husband and she will have to submit to him. The only consolation is that the one who awakens her will be a fearless hero, since only such a person will be able to penetrate through the fire that will surround her rock. The key theological point is that Brünnhilde undergoes an incarnation as she loses her Valkyrie status. Wotan's final words to his beloved daughter are:[76]

---

75. On the links between Brünnhilde and Prometheus, see volume 1, chapter 4 and chapter 10 above.

76. *WagRS* 191.

REDEMPTION

Denn so—kehrt	And so—the god
der Gott sich dir ab:	turns away from you:
so küßt er die Gottheit von dir.	so he kisses your godhead away.

Again in this passage of Wotan kissing away her divinity Wagner makes his theological points. Just before Wotan's entry "And so turns the god now from you" (and overlapping it) we hear the first half of the renunciation motif (Example 11.4).[77] This motif first appears in *Rheingold* and is first sung by Woglinde (Example 11.3) to indicate the renouncing of love.[78] This renunciation motif[79] actually has two phrases, the second being a slight variant of the first:[80]

---

77. In a private communication (27 October 2016) Lionel Friend wrote that the "renunciation" motif "seems to be connected with the pains and agonies of those in love, the torment it brings, the confusions and contradictions." According to Ewans, *Aeschylus*, 92, "this motif is sounded when characters accept that they must pay the price of future torment for the gains they are making now."

78. Porges, *Rehearsing the Ring*, 10, notes that when Woglinde is delivering "the solemn passage, touched with tragedy [. . .] the individual feeling of the performer must be restrained" and when the woodwind declaim the melody at the end of the scene (bars 743–47) "[t]his mournful lament for the lost happiness of love accompanies the faint rustling of the water like a tragic epilogue."

79. See Wolzogen, *Leitfaden*, 15, who names the motiv "Entsagungsmotiv." Scruton, *Ring*, 160, 313, prefers the name "existential choice."

80. *WagRS* 68. Note that although both *GSD* 5:211 and *SW* 10.I:73 have "versagt," sometimes in performance "entsagt" is sung. The laconic first *Prosaskizze* has "Wer der liebe entsagt" (Strobel, *Skizzen*, 203; *TBRN1* 347). The *Prosaentwürf* expands this to "Die Mädchen:—nur durch einen Zauber könne der reif geschmiedet werden, und nur der gewänne den Zauber, der der liebe entsage." (Strobel, *Skizzen*, 215; *TBRN1* 351). As this was expanded again in the *Erschrift des Textbuches* one sees that "entsagt" is crossed out and replaced with "versagt" (*TBRN1* 374) hence rending the final form of the couplet "Nur wer die Minne / Macht versagt."

Example 11.3: *Rheingold* bars 617–28

REDEMPTION

Nur wer der Minne	Only the man who forswears
Macht versagt,	love's sway,
nur wer der Liebe	only he who disdains
Lust verjagt,	love's delights
nur der erzielt sich den Zauber	can master the magic spell
zum Reif zu zwingen das Gold.	that rounds a ring from the gold.

Note also that this is one of the few occasions in the *Ring* where Wagner uses end rhyme,[81] rather than his usual Stabreim, a form of alliterative verse. This renunciation motif has been used sparingly up until now. After its first occurrence in *Rheingold*, we have a second in *Walküre* Act I as Siegmund takes the sword Nothung out of the tree, and in the case considered here at the end of *Walküre* we have the third occurrence. In this instance Wagner's use of this motif points to two kinds of renunciation: Wotan's renunciation of his beloved daughter and also Brünnhilde's renunciation of her divinity. On a deeper level it may also point to the fact that after this Wotan is essentially a broken god, and in the next opera, *Siegfried*, he appears as a "Wanderer."

The first four notes of both halves of the renunciation motif is rather similar to the beginning of the Siegfried motif, and this I think is by no means coincidental, for Siegfried will be the hero who will rouse Brünnhilde from sleep and fall in love with her (see Figure 11.1).

Figure 11.1: Renunciation, Siegfried, and Woman's Worth

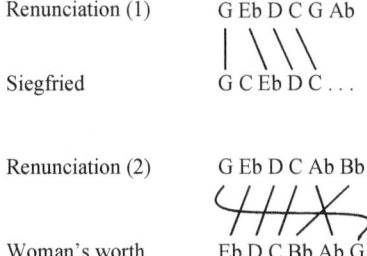

This renunciation motif (with a modified ending) also occurs towards the end of the confrontation between Brünnhilde and Waltraute in *Götterdämmerung* Act I Scene 3 with Brünnhilde's triumphant declaration "I shall never relinquish love, / they'll never take love from me" ("die Liebe ließe ich nie, / mir nähmen nie sie die Liebe").[82]

---

81. Also Westernhagen, *Forging*, 26, points out that quaver rests were inserted to emphasize "versagt" and "verjagt" (cf. the sketch, *Forging*, 25).

82. *WagRS* 305; *Götterdämmerung* I.1482–90.

THEOLOGY OF WAGNER'S *RING* CYCLE II

Example 11.4: *Rheingold* bars 1338–43; *Walküre* Act III bars 1608–29

Turning to Example 11.4 we see that after the first phrase of the renunciation motif is quoted, Wagner replaces the second part with a descending series of six notes. We hear this first in *Rheingold* Scene 2 when Loge speaks of "woman's delights and worth," sometimes just called the motif of "woman's worth" (bars 1338–40). This theme is actually formed by a permutation of the second phrase of the renunciation motif (see Figure 11.1).

Returning to Example 11.4, we then have a descending chromatic scale, the "sleep" motif. In the *Ring* Wotan's power is represented by a vigorous descending diatonic scale. Here we have this gentle descending chromatic scale that is then followed by the rocking lullaby of part of the "Walhalla" motif (the third segment of the motif). This same segment is used in *Götterdämmerung* when Brünnhilde tells Wotan to rest in peace, before the final conflagration that will spread to and engulf Valhalla. The irony is that a correlate of Brünnhilde's "incarnation" is that Wotan's power and his law begin to be diminished. Heinrich Porges, who made notes on Wagner's comments as he directed rehearsals for the first performance of the *Ring*, writes: "A remark of Wagner's that has an important bearing on the action must be cited: at the end, 'Denn so kehrt der Gott sich dir ab, so küsst er die Gottheit von dir' ['And so—the god / turns away from you: / so he kisses your godhead away'], one must for the first time see Wotan's spear slipping from his hand!"[83] After this Wotan is a broken god, and when he next appears on stage in *Siegfried* it is as the Wanderer who cannot act but only observe![84]

Although this final scene in *The Valkyrie* is heartbreaking it ends in a major key, that of E major. Using a major key and the whole atmosphere of the scene could indicate the future redemption. The prerequisite of this redemption is Brünnhilde's incarnation, for which she pays a high price. When Brünnhilde is awakened with the kiss of Siegfried in the next opera, although at first she expresses great joy, she also mourns the loss of her Valkyrie status. In *Siegfried* Act III Scene 3 there is a passage (bars 1279–1358)[85] with three exchanges, where Brünnhilde laments the loss of her Valkyrie status (beginning with "There I see Grane")[86] with the hero responding with successively increased passion; there is no communication, but rather they speak past each other. As Siegfried begins to express his desire for Brünnhilde, there is a possible allusion again to *Walküre* III (note the passionate music, bars 1294–1301): "My eyes now feast / on your lovely mouth: / yet with keen-edged thirst / my lips are burning, / longing to be regaled by this feast of my eyes!"[87] This contrasts starkly with Wotan's *non-sexual* reference to her lips: "when a kiss requited / your battle lust / and, childishly lilting, / the praise of heroes / flowed from your lovely kips."[88] It is also worth

83. Porges, *Rehearsing the Ring*, 76

84. *WagRS* 229.

85. See the musical analysis in McCreless, *Siegfried*, 216–17. Also Westernhagen, *Forging*, 174 (*Entstehung*, 207), notes that since Brünnhilde's awakening everything has been in triple time and the new theme, which in the sketch was also to be triple time (see Westernhagen, *Forging*, 161 Ex. 35; *Entstehung*, 193 Ex. 33), a sketch designed for "Act III or Tristan," is transformed into quadruple time which predominates for the rest of Act III.

86. *WagRS* 269.

87. *WagRS* 270.

88. *WagRS* 190–91.

stressing that Wotan kisses not her lips but her eyes![89] To Siegfried's sexual passion Brünnhilde responds by despondently looking on her shield and helmet, which no longer offer protection. Siegfried declares that she has pierced his heart and wounded his head, coming as he did with shield and helmet. She responds saying that she also lost her breastplate and is now "a weaponless, sorrowing woman."[90] Siegfried says he also was not protected and the fire about Brünnhilde's rock now burns in his breast: "O woman, quench the fire now! / Quell this chafing rage!"[91] This confrontation leads to Brünnhilde's fundamental declaration: "No god has ever dared draw near to me: / in awe the heroes bowed / before the virgin maid (Jungfrau)."[92]

But she has not only lost her protection against a lustful and passionate man; she has also lost her wisdom. She has passed this on to Siegfried (who does not seem to make great use of it!). She speaks of this loss in the Prologue to *Götterdämmerung*: "What gods have taught me / I gave to you: / a bountiful store / of hallowed runes; / but the maidenly source / of all my strength / was taken away by the hero / to whom I now bow my head. / Bereft of wisdom / but filled with desire; / rich in love / yet void of strength, / I beg you not to despise / the poor woman / who grudges you naught / but can give you no more!"[93]

The depths of Brünnhilde's vulnerability in her incarnation comes at the end of *Götterdämmerung* Act I and in Act II when she is betrayed by Siegfried and she, in Wagner's words, becomes "God-forsaken."[94] So in Act II she cries to the gods whom she feels are punishing her:[95]

Heil'ge Götter!	Hallowed gods!
Himmlische Lenker!	Heavenly rulers!
Rauntet ihr dieß	Was this what you whispered
in eurem Rath?	within your council?
Lehrt ihr mich Leiden	Would you teach me suffering
wie keiner sie litt?	as none yet suffered?

Wotan's final words to her suggest her incarnation involves *losing* her divinity: "So he kisses your Godhead away." Such loss entails losing fellowship with her father; another is losing her immortality; another is being vulnerable to the love of a man; and

89. A number of productions wish to make the father-daughter relationship here sexual, an unwise interpretation in my view.

90. *WagRS* 270.

91. *WagRS* 271.

92. *WagRS* 271.

93. *WagRS* 284–85.

94. Cf. *SL* 310; *SB* 6:71, where Wagner refers to the final scene of Act I. In placing "von Gott verlassen" in quotation marks he is probably alluding to Mark 15:34: "My God, my God, why have you forsaken me?" ("Mein Gott, mein Gott, warum hast du mich verlassen?")

95. *WagRS* 322.

another is, as we have just seen, being utterly "God-forsaken". But one aspect of her divinity remains: her love. One can compare the line in Charles Wesley's hymn "And can it be": Christ "emptied himself of all but love."[96]

It is not only that she "emptied herself of all but love" but love was also the very reason for her emptying. Brünnhilde becomes fully human because of her love for Siegmund and Sieglinde, which involved disobeying her father's command. As Wagner writes to Röckel: "Did you not feel that Brünnhilde has cut herself off from Wodan and all the other gods for the sake of—*love*, because—where Wodan clung to plans—she only—*loved*? Moreover, from the moment *Siegfr.* awakens her, she has no longer any other knowledge save that of love. [. . .] [S]he had renounced her divinity for the sake of love."[97]

Sacrifice of Siegfried and Brünnhilde

In the *Jesus of Nazareth* sketches Jesus' death occurs offstage but is indicated by events on stage ("Darkening of the heavens—thunder and lightning [. . .] Earthquake") and Peter presents his interpretation of Jesus' death.[98] This may be compared to Aeschylus, where, although Agamemnon's death occurs off-stage, one hears his cries and shortly afterwards Clytemnestra enters and explains what has occurred.[99] Siegfried's death is one of the key visual dramatic scenes in the *Ring* and for Brünnhilde, although the stage direction indicates that "[w]ith a single bound she urges the horse into the blazing pyre," we do not witness her actual death. The stage direction simply continues: "The flames immediately flare up so that the fire fills the entire space in front of the hall and appears to seize on the building itself."[100]

At the end of *Götterdämmerung* the world comes to be redeemed by her death and by that of Siegfried. Siegfried's death comes about through Hagen's devious plan. Brünnhilde though offers herself as a voluntary sacrifice. This is the deed that Wotan as Wanderer refers to in *Siegfried* Act III Scene 1, "the deed that redeems the world" ("erlösende Weltenthat").[101] But the redemption is actually achieved by the double sacrifice of Siegfried and Brünnhilde, and the necessity of this is partly related to Wagner's views on gender. As he wrote to Röckel: "Not even Siegfried alone (man alone (der Mann allein)) is the complete 'human being' ('Mensch'): he is merely the half,

---

96. See *Church Hymnal*, nr. 218 (416–17). The full second verse runs: "He left his Father's throne above — / so free, so infinite his grace — / emptied himself of all but love, / and bled for Adam's helpless race; / 'Tis mercy all, immense and free; / for, O my God, it found out me!"

97. *SL* 309; *SB* 6:70–71.

98. *PW* 8:297; *DTB* 246.

99. *Agamemnon*, ll. 1343, 1345; 1372–98 (Sommerstein, *Aeschylus II*, 164–71).

100. *WagRS* 351.

101. *WagRS* 258.

only with *Brünnhilde* does he become the redeemer."[102] Both in their different ways can be seen as Christ figures. In his writings Wagner often links Siegfried to Christ.[103] Many no doubt have difficulty with this idea since Siegfried is clearly an inspiration for Nietzsche's "Übermensch" (superman). But as Siegfried's death approaches, we may have an indication that Siegfried will die rather like Christ. Immediately after Siegfried explains to the hunting party that the Rhinemaidens *sang*[104] that he would be slain today the stage direction explains: "Siegfried settles down (lagert sich) between Hagen and Gunther."[105] Then after Hagen says it would be unfortunate for the hunter to be brought down by "a lurking head of game" Siegfried utters, rather out of the blue, "I thirst" ("Mich dürstet").[106] These happen to be exactly the words of the dying Christ in Luther's translation of John 19:28[107] and the rhythm and melodic shape Wagner employs corresponds to that used in Bach's *St John Passion*.[108]

---

102. *SL* 307; *SB* 6:68.

103. This has been discussed at various points in the two volumes. Note also that in *Jesus of Nazareth* Wagner has Jesus "sleeping under a tree" (*PW* 8:287; *DTB* 242). Cf. *WagRS* 237 "Siegfried stretches out comfortably under the lime tree" and 238 "He falls in to a silent reverie." Also after killing Mime Siegfried's "Gentle coolness / I choose beneath the lime!" is followed by the stage direction "He stretches out beneath the lime-tree" (*WagRS* 252).

104. *WagRS* 338: "I might have caught for you / three will waterbirds (Wasservögel), / who sang to me there on the Rhine / that I would be slain today." See the discussion of the woman as "music" in chapter 6 above and Brünnhilde, who is described by Siegfried as "singing" (*WagRS* 269, 271).

105. *SW* 13.III:108; *WagRS* 339. In the original *Siegfried's Tod* (Haymes, *Ring*, 160–61) and in *GSD* 6:241 this was placed *after* "Mich dürstet."

106. *WagRS* 339. See again *Siegfried's Tod* of 1848 (Haymes, *Ring*, 160–61).

107. Cf. Kitcher and Schacht, *Ending*, 188.

108. Whereas there is a fall of a perfect fifth on "dürstet" in Bach, Wagner has the fall of a diminished fifth on these two syllables, the interval associated with Hagen. The key signatures happen to be the same but the harmonies are quite different.

Example 11.5: Götterdämmerung Act III 579–85: "Mich dürstet"

Example 11.6: Bach *St John Passion:* "Mich dürstet"

It would be pressing the argument too far to say that Wagner was *influenced* here by Bach's *St John Passion*, especially since there is no extant reference to the work in Wagner's writings and it was not represented in either his Dresden or Wahnfried libraries;[109] further, Wagner's musical setting of "Mich dürstet" is quite natural. Nevertheless, an allusion to John 19:28 itself is not to be excluded for Siegfried will shortly face a violent death (and we know Wagner had a special interest in John's Gospel).[110] A further dramatic element to the scene for anyone familiar with the Gospel tradition is that just as Wagner places Siegfried between Gunther and Hagen, two figures who will also meet an unpleasant death, John 19:18 specifies that on Golgotha "[t]here they crucified [Jesus], and with him two others, one on either side, with Jesus between them."[111]

Whatever Siegfried's shortcomings as a hero, he does come into his own at his death, and, as I argued in chapter 10, we enter a numinous realm in the final scene. But the most striking Christ figure is Brünnhilde who, as I have argued, undergoes an incarnation, and voluntarily lays down her life. It is unclear whether *she* sees this as a fully redemptive death. She certainly knows that the ring she wears on her finger will be cleansed by the fire and her desire is certainly to follow Siegfried in his death. But whether she knows that her death will result in a new earth and a new heaven coming into being remains unclear. Wotan's prophecy that she would work the deed that redeems the world was made in private to Erda. But perhaps at that mysterious visit of Brünnhilde to the banks of the Rhine, of which there are only vague hints in *Götterdämmerung* Act

---

109. The *St John Passion* did not have the popularity of the *St Matthew Passion*. However, the vocal score was published together with the St Matthew passion in 1830 (a year after Mendelssohn's Berlin performance) and the first documented performance since Bach's death took place in 1833, conducted by Carl Friedrich Rungenhagen of the Berlin Singakademie, this leading to the publishing of the full score in 1834 (Leaver, "The Revival of the St. John Passion," 15). Schumann came to know the work in 1842 and in 1843 Eduard Krüger published in seven installments in *Neue Zeitschrift für Musik* (which Schumann then edited) an article that compared the two Bach passions ("Die beiden Bach'schen Passionen"). Before Schumann's performance of the majority of the work in Düsseldorf (13 April 1851) he used many of the choruses and chorales in performances. So the Dresden choral society that Schumann founded in 1848 performed individual movements accompanied by the piano only (Max, "Notes"). In a letter of 2 April 1849 (written from Dresden) he informs the composer and conductor Georg Dietrich Otten (of Hamburg) that "for about a year now I have been running a [. . .] concert society, which affords me the delight of hearing the works of Palestrina, Bach, and various other compositions. Do you know Bach's Passion-Music according to St. John, the so-called little one? [. . .] I wonder if you agree with me that it is much bolder, more powerful and poetical, than the St. Matthew version?" (Storck and Bryant, *Letters*, 260). An intriguing question is whether Wagner heard Schumann's performances of the St John Passion in Dresden.

110. See chapter 2 above and volume 1, chapter 7.

111. See also Mark 15:27; Matt 27:38, which specify that these were "bandits" who were crucified with him "one on his right and one on his left." Luke 23:32 says "[t]wo others also, who were criminals, were led away to be put to death with him" and adds a story unique to his gospel, one being unrepentant (23:39b) and one repentant (23:40–43). Again, anyone experiencing Wagner's scene in the light of the Gospel tradition may be tempted to identify the repentant with Gunther and the unrepentant with Hagen.

III, the Rhinemaidens disclosed that her death would indeed redeem the world. And Brünnhilde does say "All things, all things, / all things I know."[112]

A fair amount of Gospel criticism has also suggested that Jesus did not know that his death would be redemptive.[113] The Gospels however present a Jesus who did know that his death would have atoning value[114] and Wagner is faithful to this in his sketches *Jesus of Nazareth*.[115] But even if Brünnhilde were not aware that her death would be redemptive, this does not diminish the value of her laying down her life, just as the atoning value of Jesus' death would not be diminished had he not known of its significance.

In *Siegfried's Tod* of 1848 it is suggested that Brünnhilde offers her body to the gods:[116]

Sein Roß führet daher,	Lead his steed here.
daß mit mir dem Recken es folge:	So that it can accompany with me the warrior:
denn zu des Helden heiligster Ehre	For to the hero's highest honour
den Göttern erleg' ich den eig'nen Leib.	I offer to the gods my own body.
Vollbringet Brünnhild's letzte Bitte!	Carry out Brünnhilde's last wish!

There is however a significant change in *Siegfried's Tod* published in 1853. Lines 3–4 quoted above now become:[117]

denn des Helden heiligste	for my own body yearns
Ehre zu theilen	to share in the hero's
verlangt mein eigener Leib.	holiest honour.

Hence, in the final *Ring* neither the sacrifice of Brünnhilde nor of Siegfried are offered to a "god." Neither is their sacrifice seen as an expression of the love of a god, i.e., Wotan. What they offer are themselves and certainly for Brünnhilde it is an expression of her love not only for Siegfried but also for the world. This is because the whole train

---

112. *WagRS* 349. But as New Testament scholars realize "all" is not always what it is made out to be! See the discussion of texts such as Rom 11:32 (Bell, *Provoked to Jealousy*, 151–53)!

113. This was first put forward by Reimarus (see Talbert, *Reimarus Fragments*, 150).

114. See the debates on Mark 10:45 where Jesus says "For the Son of Man came not to be served but to serve, and to give his life a ransom for many"; note also the last supper narrative where, on taking the cup, he says "this is my blood of the covenant which is poured out for many" (Mark 14:24; cf. Matt 26:28; Luke 22:20; 1 Cor 11:25).

115. Cf *PW* 8:292 (*DTB* 244): Jesus speaks of "his sacrificial death (opfertod), after which the Holy Ghost shall be sent to them." Also *PW* 8:289 (*DTB* 243): "He foreshadows his redeeming death and second advent for the liberating of mankind"; *PW* 8:288 (*DTB* 242): "Jesus to his disciples, on his purpose and impending sacrificial death." *PW* 291(*DTB* 244): "Jesus announces his true mission, his quality as son of God, the redemption of all peoples of the earth through him, not of the Jews alone."

116. Haymes, *Ring*, 180–81 (modified).

117. Wagner, *Ring* (1853); *TBRN2* 480. Cf. *WagRS* 348.

of events leading to her death started with her intervening to try and save Siegmund. Therefore, no "theory of atonement" seems to be offered in the final *Ring* for the atoning deaths of Siegfried and Brünnhilde. This then poses a key question for Christian theology: should theologians be discussing Jesus' death in terms of a "theory of atonement" at all? It is the case, of course, that theologians discuss such theories at length, for example the nature of Christ's sacrifice and in what sense he stands in our place.[118] On rare occasions Wagner also discusses the nature of Christ's sacrifice[119] and it is difficult to avoid such discussions when employing words such as "redemption," which have a specific history of meanings. But perhaps the wisest way of interpreting the deaths of both Christ and Brünnhilde is simply to say that they were sacrificial deaths as expressions of their love for the world.

New Heaven and a New Earth

There can be no doubt that the world is redeemed at the end of this great art-work. But what about the redemption of the gods themselves? In the remarkable scene towards the end of Act I of *Götterdämmerung*, when the Valkyrie Waltraute comes to Brünnhilde on her rock and begs her to give the ring back to the Rhinemaidens, she quotes these words of Wotan:[120]

"des tiefen Rheines Töchtern	"If she gave back the ring
gäbe den Ring sie wieder zurück,	to the deep Rhine's daughters,
von des Fluches Last	from the weight of the curse
erlös't wär' Gott und Welt!"	both god and world would be freed!"

The first thing to notice is that reference is made to one god, i.e., Wotan ("Gott" in the singular). Further, the redemption of God and world is limited to redemption from the curse of the ring. For if the ring were simply returned to the Rhine there would be no sacrificial death of Siegfried and Brünnhilde and hence no renewal of the cosmos.[121]

---

118. Fischer, *Glaube*, 79–80, criticizes attempts to offer a theory of Christ's sacrifice in terms of both "exklusive Stellvertretung" ("exclusive place-taking") and "inklusive Stellvertretung" ("inclusive place-taking"). A key to understanding his approach is that one cannot speak objectively about God (see Bultmann, "Welchen Sinn hat es, von Gott zu reden?") and that there is no single reality but rather a multiplicity: "Die Wirklichkeit ist [. . .] kein einheitlicher Raum. Sie zerfällt vielmehr in eine unendliche Vielzahl von wirklichen und möglichen Räumen [. . .]" (Fischer, "Behaupten," 236).

119. In *Against Vivsection* Wagner makes the point that since Christ has been sacrificed any further sacrifices (he is thinking primarily of animal sacrifices) are simply not necessary: "The monstrous guilt of all this life a divine and sinless being (ein sündenloses göttliches Wesen) took upon himself, and expiated (sühnte) with his agony and death. Through this atonement (Sühnungstod) all that breathes and lives should know itself redeemed, so soon as it was grasped as pattern and example to be followed" (*PW* 6:203; *GSD* 10:202).

120. *WagRS* 304 (modified).

121. Compare the discussion of Jesus' atoning work, where New Testament scholars rightly

The situation would almost be equivalent in a theology where "keeping the law" would lead to an acquittal at the final judgement, but with no renewal of humanity or the cosmos, since there was no sacrifice of Christ. So if Brünnhilde gave back the ring any redemption would be of limited nature. Also, we know anyway that such a redemption is in principle impossible (just as keeping the law is in principle impossible) since for Brünnhilde the ring embodies Siegfried's love for her, a love she will never renounce: "I shall never relinquish love" ("die Liebe ließe ich nie").[122]

Going back to Waltraute's line "erlös't wär' Gott und Welt!" [123] we hear the third segment of the Valhalla motif, which is also used in Brünnhilde's "Schlussgesang" where she also could be pointing at least to Wotan's redemption.[124] "Rest now, rest now, you god" ("Ruhe, Ruhe du Gott").[125] Osthövener[126] thinks that this alludes to the promise of rest that God offers his people (Hebrews 4) and the famous line in Book I Chapter 1 of Augustine's *Confessions*: "for Thou hast formed us for Thyself, and our hearts are restless till they find rest in thee."[127] I am unsure whether Brünnhilde's words allude to these texts.[128] More likely is an allusion to Matt 11:28-29: "Come unto me all who are weary and heavy laden, and I will give you rest [. . .] and you will find rest for your souls" ("Kompt her zu mir / alle die jr mühselig und beladen seid / Jch wil euch erquicken, [. . .] So werdet jr Ruge finden fur ewre Seele"). Matthew 11:28-30 was marked in Wagner's New Testament and was quoted in the *Jesus of Nazareth* sketches,[129] so was significant for Wagner. Another possible allusion is to *requiescat in pace*,[130] a subjunctive to wish for someone to rest in peace. If this is the background then Brünnhilde here is neither *wishing* rest (a Catholic subjunctive

---

emphasize that it results in the renewal of creation. So the miracle of the "new creation" (2 Cor 5:17) is an integral part of the atonement. See Bell, *Evil*, 211, 223-24.

122. *WagRS* 305; note the use of the "Entsagung" motif at this point (*SW* 13.I:385, bars 1482-85).

123. *WagRS* 304.

124. Note also that the same segment is found after Brünnhilde is put to sleep in *Walküre* Act III (bars 1626-27). See Example 11.4 above.

125. *WagRS* 349.

126. Osthövener, "Konstellationen," 69.

127. *NPNF1* 1:45. *CCSL* 27:1: ". . . *inquietum est cor nostrum, donec requiescat in te.*"

128. Note that there are no markings for Hebrews 4 in Wagner's copy of Luther's New Testament (although other passages from the letter are marked). Note also that Wagner did not appear to show much interest in Augustine in the extant sources (Bell, *Parsifal*, 136 n. 3).

129. He marked Matt 11:28-30 in his NT with the Roman numeral II (suggesting it was relevant for his proposed Act II). It is quoted in the third section of the *Jesus of Nazareth* sketches (where texts for the respective Acts are quoted) but under Act I, not Act II (*PW* 8:323; *DTB* 260). The relevance for either Act is not clear; perhaps it is to do with Jesus' opposition to the Pharisees.

130. The closest biblical phrase is the Vulgate of Isa 57:2: "*veniat pax requiescat in cubili suo qui ambulavit in directione sua.*" But note also the reference to "sleep" for those who have died in Christ (1 Thess 4:13 etc.). *requiescat in pace* was used on gravestones and Wagner would obviously be aware of this usage. The other possible allusion of course is to the opening of the requiem *Requiem aeternam dona eis, Domine*.

requiescat in pace) or *stating* a rest (Protestant indicative, *requiescit in pace*) but giving a Wagnerian imperative (*requiesce in pace*; ruhe in Frieden).[131]

Overall the drama suggests that Wotan is put to rest before his destruction in the final conflagration; whether he has any future in the world to come is, I think, doubtful.[132] But there is a rebirth for the cosmos. This has been disputed by Darcy, who points to Wagner's writing that the *Ring* entails the world's "Untergang," which he translates as "destruction."[133] He refers to Wagner's letter to Liszt of 11 February 1853: "Mark well my new poem—it contains the world's beginning and its end (Untergang)!"[134] and to Cosima's comments: "R. says he must now compose his verses for the end of the world (Weltuntergangscouplet)."[135] There are around two hundred uses of "Untergang" in Wagner's extant works and the general sense is "going under," and this sense fits the above two texts. But in some key instances Wagner writes of "Untergang" in the context of redemption. A highly controversial one is at the end of *Judaism in Music*, where he writes of "the redemption of Ahasuerus—*Going under* (*Untergang*)."[136] However this may be interpreted,[137] Wagner nevertheless writes of a redemption; so the "going under" can be understood as one stage on the path to redemption. The same idea is present in *Communication to My Friends* where Wagner writes: "The Flying Dutchman, sure enough, had not as yet unveiled the newer world: his *Wife* could only redeem him by her and his going under (Untergang)."[138] It therefore seems reasonable to suggest that the use of "Untergang" for the ending of *Götterdämmerung* does not exclude a redemption and, as I have argued, there are so many pointers for such a redemption; and this is achieved by the dual sacrifice of Siegfried and Brünnhilde. Although it is often stressed in the secondary literature how many die at the end of the drama, it is worth bearing in mind that Wagner suggests that most do in fact survive,[139]

---

131. Note also the imperative in Feuerbach, *Thoughts*, 151: "Thought and conscious will / Now sleep there in eternal repose"; *LFW* 1:245: "Da schläft noch jetzt in ew'ger Stille / Gedanke und bewußter Wille."

132. The Icelandic "Ragnarök" is ambiguous since it could mean "doom of the powers" (from rök meaning doom) or "twilight of the powers" (from røkkr), which could imply a possible rebirth (I am grateful to Judith Jesch for these insights together with the philological study of Bernharðsson, "Ragnarök"). The German "Dämmerung" means "twilight" and hence "Götterdämmerung" as "twilight of the gods" could in theory allow for a rebirth of the gods; but it is unlikely Wagner understood a rebirth of the gods.

133. Darcy, "Pessimism," 27,

134. *SL* 281; *SB* 5:189.

135. *CD* 20 July 1872.

136. *PW* 3:100; *GSD* 5:85.

137. See Bell, *Parsifal*, 194–97.

138. *PW* 1:311 (modified); *GSD* 4:268.

139. I remain unconvinced by Darcy, "Pessimism," 43, who argues that Wagner engaged in a "daring experiment" in that those left on stage "no longer represent the Gibichung men and women" but are rather "*a projection of the audience*, which has been, so to speak, sucked into the vortex of the drama to preside over the concluding scene of cosmic destruction."

and more than survive, for they experience this new heaven and new earth.[140] Further, it may be significant that in Ettmüller's edition of the *Völuspá*, a work of which Wagner had clearly made much use, and which in many respects provides the framework for much of the *Ring*, the poem ends not on the grim note of the shadowy dragon carrying corpses away for consumption but rather the optimistic note of Hœnir prophesying that the sons of the two brothers Höd and Baldr will set up their home "in the wide wind realm."[141]

There is final pointer to the idea of redemption at the end of *Götterdämmerung*. The work ends on a plagal cadence: G♭ to D♭. Amongst the other stage works of Wagner which end with broadly similar cadential progressions are *Tristan* (E minor to B major) and *Parsifal* (D♭ to A♭).[142] Wagner, as we have seen, changed the ending of the *Siegfried's Tod/Götterdämmerung* poem several times and finally decided not to set to music either the Feuerbach or Schopenhauer endings, simply allowing the music to disclose in its own way what was going on. In the *Collected Writings* he included in a footnote both of these endings. For the Feuerbachian he writes that before the musical completion of the poem ("vor der musikalischen Ausführung des Gedichtes") these verses were inserted.[143] After quoting these lines he writes that he later composed verses that expressed the ending more suitably.[144] After quoting the Schopenhauer ending he then writes: "Finally it could not escape the composer that, since the meaning of these verses were already expressed with the greatest definition (mit höchster Bestimmtheit) in the tenor of the drama set to music (in der Wirkung des musikalisch ertönenden Drama's), their actual delivery had to be eliminated from the performance."[145] This could be taken to mean that the ending should be understood as a Schopenhauerian one.[146] Dahlhaus, however, writes that Wagner "seems to have been deceived as to the meaning of his own work. The really authentic ending is obviously the version of 1852, which was already prefigured in the first conception, the prose sketch of 1848."[147] I suggest that neither of these views are entirely satisfactory. I

---

140. In the final stage direction of the score (*SW* 13.III:295) we read that "[f]rom the ruins of the fallen hall, the men and women watch moved to the very depths of their being (in höchster Ergriffenheit)" but they nevertheless survive. Apart from earthly casualties (of which there are a fair few), the gods and the heroes perish in Walhalla (*WagRS* 351). Instead of "moved to the very depths of their being" ("in höchster Ergriffenheit") *GSD* 6:256 has "in speechless dismay" ("in sprachloser Erschütterung").

141. Dronke, *Edda II*, 24; Ettmüller, *Vaulu-spá*, 35. Dronke considers Hœnir to be the "priestly god of resurrection" (Dronke, *Edda II*, 60). Note also Ettmüller, *Vaulu-spá*, 35–36, includes as an appendix two verses that reflect the Christian vision of judgement in the sense of God settling "discord and strife" and the vision of virtuous people enjoying joy for ever.

142. I am grateful to Roger Allen for bringing this to my attention.

143. *GSD* 6:254.

144. *GSD* 6:255.

145. *GSD* 6:256; translation of Whittall in Dahlhaus, *Music Dramas*, 140 (modified).

146. Darcy, "Pessimism," 26.

147. Dahlhaus, *Music Dramas*, 140.

come back again to Wagner's view (see chapter 3 above) that the artist "stands before his own work of art—if it really *is* a work of art—as though before some puzzle, which is just as capable of misleading *him* as it can mislead another person."[148] He may consider the ending to be Schopenhauerian (although his interpretation of the Frankfurt sage was unusual) and it may be there are Schopenhauerian elements in it, but the ending is just as Feuerbachian and, as I have argued, Hegelian; and perhaps it could be the case that the "greatest definition" ("höchste Bestimmtheit") is offered by the final musical theme "glorification of Brünnhilde"[149] together with that plagal cadence.

The "Ending" of Götterdämmerung

Although the opening of the *Ring* is not clearly defined,[150] its ending, indeed the endings of every work in the cycle, proves to be well-defined. The cycle has a clear goal (telos), *Götterdämmerung* ending with that plagal cadence. But although the work is clearly *directional*, could it be said to represent a *linear* rather than a *cyclical* view of time?[151] One of the misleading contrasts in the discussion of religion is that between "Eastern" cyclical views of time (including ideas of reincarnation) and biblical "Western" linear views. This is so because Eastern views can have a linear aspect[152] and biblical views a circular one.[153] On the whole, one can say that biblical history is not simply "linear" or "cyclical" but is more like a spiral and is teleological.[154] The

---

148. *SL* 357 (translation modified); *SB* 8:152.

149. The theme is often wrongly termed the "redemption" or "redemption through love"; for the correct name see Cosima's letter to Eduard von Lippmann (given in Deathridge, "Reviews," 84).

150. See chapter 4 above.

151. On the question of whether the term "linear" is helpful see Begbie, *Time*, 58–61; Borthwick, Hart and Monti, "Eschatology." A work that could be said to be "linear" (although not one-dimensionally linear) is Beethoven's *Eroica symphony* (whose key the Prelude to *Rheingold* shares), opening with two forte E♭ chords and ending with a series of fortissimo E♭ chords.

152. Estes, *Mechanics*, 44, points out that what is called "cyclical time" in, say, Hinduism is a misnomer and should rather be categorized as "temporality as composed of cosmological cycles." Further, Hinduism can have "non-cyclical expanses of time" (46).

153. Augustine criticized circular views of time in *City of God* 12.13. He writes that some philosophers have introduced "cycles of time, in which there should be a constant renewal and repetition of the order of nature" (*NPNF1* 2:234). Augustine argues that such a view cannot be properly supported by Eccl 1:9–10. Such a text either speaks of "the succession of generations," etc., or the predestination of God whereby "all things have already existed, and that thus there is no new thing under the sun" (*NPNF1* 2:234). Against a cyclic view of time is the fact that "Christ died for our sins; and rising from the dead, He dieth no more" (*NPNF1* 2:234). Note also Augustine's psychological view of time in *Confessions* 11.20. He argues there are not three times of past, present, and future, but rather three presents, of past, present, and future that "somehow exist in the soul," and otherwise he "see[s] them not." Specifically they are "present of things past, memory; present of things present, sight; present of things future, expectation" (*NPNF1* 1:170). Again, see Estes, *Mechanics*, 44–46,

154. Estes, *Temporal Mechanics*, 46, finds that Christian time is "circular"; however, "it encompasses no true element of cyclicity or repetition" and "is more appropriately *teleological* rather than linear." He uses the ouroboros as his "conceptual symbol" and likens the Christian notion of time "to such

Bible concludes with a new heaven and a new earth in the book of Revelation and in a sense one returns to the paradise of Genesis 2. The *Ring* cycle likewise ends with a new creation and the cleansing of all that was wrong with the old order. Even more precisely, the cycle ends by returning to the Rhine and its Rhinemaidens. We have then a "cycle," a term Wagner himself used for his tetralogy, first in 1860,[155] but also a biblical view of history in that the drama is teleological, heading towards a definite goal (telos). Similarities are also to be found with Ragnarök of Norse mythology in that this represents "not the end," since "[e]arth will arise from the waves, fertile, green and fair as never before, cleansed of all its sufferings and evil."[156]

Hence the "ending" of *Götterdämmerung* also proves to be a new beginning and the sense of time is *both* directional *and* cyclical.

---

a closed circle." "The head and tail of the ouroboros is the Alpha and the Omega of the temporality of the Christian God in Christ" (Estes, *Temporal Mechanics*, 47, pointing to Rev 1:8, 11; 21:6; 22:13).

155. See *SB* 12:31 (7 January 1860); 13:249 (17 October 1861); *PW* 3:261; *GSD* 6:261 (*Epilogue to the "Nibelung's Ring"*).

156. Ellis Davidson, *Gods*, 38.

12

Aesthetics, Allegory, and Myth

Aesthetics

In this final chapter I ask in relation to questions of aesthetics, allegory, and myth, what may be at work in the process of the *Ring*'s composition and as it is experienced in the theatre. Elsewhere I have discussed issues of revealing the world and the "divine" in his final stage work, *Parsifal*, drawing on his later works on aesthetics, such as the *Beethoven* essay (1870) and employing a Kantian-Schopenhauerian framework.[1] I will return to some of these ideas at the end of the chapter but for now I employ a somewhat different approach, focusing on Wagner's earlier works on aesthetics.

Central for Wagner's process of composition and for the reception of his artworks was "the *emotionalising of the intellect*" ("die *Gefühlswerdung des Verstandes*").[2] One reason this was so essential was because Wagner saw the intellect as something that dissects, breaking down the "plastic" mythic "Gestalt" into its constituent parts.[3] In *Opera and Drama* Part II chapter 2, Wagner likened his work as artist to the Greek "Tragic-poet" before whom lay mapped out in the myth "[t]he unitarian Form of his artwork" ("[d]ie einheitvolle Form seines Kunstwerkes").[4] The mission of the artist was "to work up [the myth] into a living edifice, but in no wise to break in pieces and newly fit together in favour of an arbitrarily-conceived artistic building."[5] Hence, "[t]he Tragic-poet merely imparted the content and essence of the myth in the most conclusive and intelligible manner."[6] An element of this process is what I will later call the artist's "work *on* myth" ("Arbeit *am* Mythos").[7] However, in the "life-view

---

1. Bell, *Parsifal*, 273–312.
2. *PW* 2:208; *GSD* 4:78; *OD* 215.
3. Borchmeyer, *Theatre*, 140.
4. *PW* 2:156; *GSD* 4:34.
5. *PW* 2:156; *GSD* 4:34.
6. *PW* 2:156; *GSD* 4:34.
7. See the discussion below on "Myth and Mythic Allegories."

(Lebensanschauung) of the modern world" (which finds it artistic expression in the "Romance" ("Roman")) we see the breaking down of the whole:[8]

> So soon as the reflective Understanding (der reflektierende Verstand) looked aside from the image, to inquire into the actuality of the things summed-up in it, the first thing it saw was an ever waxing multitude of units, where the poetic view had seen a whole. Anatomical Science began her work, and followed a diametrically opposite path to that of the Folk's-poem. [. . .] The nature-view of the Folk has dissolved into physics and chemistry, its religion into theology and philosophy, its commonwealth into politics and diplomacy, its art into science and æsthetics,—and its Myth into the historic Chronicle.

Hence, as we saw in chapter 4 above, Wagner had a somewhat negative view of science[9] and this parallels what he here writes about the "historic Chronicle." Wagner's artistic project can to some extent be understood as reversing this "modern" trend: the move from "history" to myth is achieved precisely by "the emotionalising of the intellect."[10]

So how does Wagner go about reversing this "modern" trend? One way is through his music, through the "melodische Momente" (which I think is best translated "melodic impulses")[11] that are central to his "emotionalising of the intellect." Thorau writes: "What the composer had in mind for this layer was, precisely, an unconscious or at least pre-conceptual mode of perception. The musical motives are supposed to transfer the dramatic motives (or motifs) of the plot into the nonverbal artistic expression of the music."[12] So in *Opera and Drama* Wagner writes: "These Melodic Moments, in themselves adapted to maintain our Feeling at an even height, will be made by the orchestra into a kind of guides-to-feeling (Gefühlswegweisern) through the whole labyrinthine building of the drama."[13]

Wagner returns to the theme of "the emotionalising of the intellect" in *Communication to my Friends,* although he does not use exactly that phrase. He prefaces his discussion by comments on the organic nature of his drama and the point, which I think is entirely justified, that all unnecessary details are excluded:[14] "Just as the joinery of my

---

8. *PW* 2:157; *GSD* 4:34–35.

9. *PW* 2:158; *GSD* 4:36.

10. One can compare his comments from *Opera and Drama* Part II chapter 6: "Tone-speech is the beginning and end of Word-speech: as the *Feeling* is beginning and end of the Understanding, as *Mythos* is beginning and end of history, the *Lyric* beginning and end of Poetry" (*PW* 2:224); *GSD* 4:91: "Die *Tonsprache* ist Anfang und Ende der Wortsprache, wie das *Gefühl* Anfang und Ende des Verstandes, der *Mythos* Anfang und Ende der Geschichte, die *Lyrik* Anfang und Ende der Dichtkunst ist." Cf. volume 1, chapter 4.

11. Bell, "Death of God," 35 n. 27. See also volume 1, chapter 6.

12. Thorau, "Guides," 138.

13. *PW* 2:346; *GSD* 4:200.

14. Whatever one may feel about Wagner as a dramatist, surely one of his supreme gifts is to remove all unnecessary details. In volume 1, chapter 5 I gave the example of Puccini's *Tosca*, which

individual Scenes excluded every alien and unnecessary detail, and led all interest to the dominant Chief-mood (vorwaltende Hauptstimmung), so did the whole building of my drama join itself into one organic unity."[15] Then a few lines later he turns to questions of the development of the drama and the emotional understanding:

> Just as, in the progress of the drama, the intended climax of a decisory Chief-mood was only to be reached through a development, continuously present to the Feeling, of the individual moods already aroused: so must the musical expression, which directly influences the physical feeling (das sinnliche Gefühl), necessarily take a decisive share in this development to a climax; and this was brought about, quite of itself, in the shape of a characteristic tissue of principal themes, that spread itself not over *one* scene only (as heretofore in separate operatic "numbers"), but *over the whole drama*, and that in *intimate connection with the poetic aim (in innigster Beziehung zur dichterischen Absicht)*. The characteristic peculiarity of this thematic method, and its weighty consequences for the emotional understanding of the poetic aim (das Gefühlsverständniß der dichterischen Absicht), I have minutely described and vindicated, from the theoretic standpoint, in the third part of my book: *Opera and Drama*.[16]

Towards the end of the essay he writes that in composing *Siegfried's Tod* he feared that his "poetic purpose (dichterische Absicht) [. . .] could not be conveyed in all its bearings to the only organ at which I aimed, namely, the Feeling's-understanding (Gefühlsverständniß)."[17] His solution was to produce his myth "*in three complete dramas*, preceded by a lengthy *Prelude*" and hopes that in "a specially-appointed Festival [. . .] in the course of three days and a preliminary evening" that he, his artistic comrades, and performers shall succeed "in artistically conveying my purpose to the true Emotional (not the Critical) understanding of spectators who shall have gathered together expressly to learn it."[18] Hence, central to the emotionalising of the intellect is this gathering together at the "specially-appointed Festival," where he has in mind something analogous to the festival of Dionysus in ancient Athens.[19] In view of this analogy between Bayreuth and Athens, it is difficult to avoid the idea that such a gathering has a "religious" dimension.[20]

Another central means of achieving the emotionalising of the intellect is the music itself, as seen above in the discussion of the "melodic impulses" ("melodische Momente").

---

despite its gripping drama does not carry through the dramatic motif of Tosca's jealousy in Act I as well as it could.

15. *PW* 1:369; *GSD* 4:322–23.
16. *PW* 1:369; *GSD* 4:322–23.
17. *PW* 1:389–90; *GSD* 4:342.
18. *PW* 1:391; *GSD* 4:343.
19. See volume 1, chapter 4.
20. This is one essential reason why Nietzsche found Bayreuth so distasteful; see Nietzsche, *Anti-Christ*, 267 ("Wo ich Einwände mache," *FNKSA* 6:419), discussed in volume 1, chapter 6.

Such "impulses" are often first introduced by the orchestra and the complexity of the orchestra allows for a rich tapestry of motifs which can not only correspond to the "conscious" action on stage, rather like the Freudian "ego," but also point to the subconscious "id."[21] In other words, the orchestra is "omniscient."[22] Thereby it has the capacity to do the sort of thing a novel can do: illumine the drama from many perspectives. Borchmeyer draws a perceptive parallel between Wagner's vision of his "eschatological myth" and the triadic structure Schiller sets out in *Comments on Humboldt's Study of Antiquity*.[23] In the first period, the time of the Greeks, "the object stood immediately before us, but entangled and unclear (aber verworren und ineinanderfließend)." In the second, the modern (present) time, "we differentiate individual features and make distinctions." In the third period, which lies in the future, "the whole object (das Ganze) will once again stand before us, but now no longer entangled, but rather illumined from all sides."[24] Borchmeyer suggests that "[i]n much the same way, Wagner's eschatological myth is distinguished from primeval myth by the fact that it is 'lit from all sides.'"[25] Hence, "[j]ust as the chorus, together with the audience as represented by that chorus, could observe the stage characters from three sides, so, in the musical drama, myth was transformed by the orchestra into a 'phenomenon which is borne along on every side by the sound.'"[26] Borchmeyer here refers to Wagner's essay *Actors and Singers*, where he compares the Greek Chorus to the "merely audible Instrumental-orchestra." Wagner makes the remarkable assertion that this orchestra is "the only truly new creation entirely peculiar to our spirit, in all the realm of Art."[27] The fundamental role of the orchestra in the drama, and its relation to what happens on stage, is set out thus: "Here the infinitely potent orchestra" (adding in a footnote, that its "idealizing agency can only be ensured by making it invisible"), "there the dramatic mime; here the mother-womb of Ideal Drama, there its issue borne on every hand by sound (dort seine von jeder Seite her tönend getragene Erscheinung)."[28] Hence, it is the *orchestra* that is the "mother-womb" ("Mutterschooß") of the drama, and the *action on stage* is, as Ellis translates it, the "issue." And as this "mother-womb" the orchestra illumines the "dramatic mime" from all sides, hence facilitating for the "spectator" the holistic understanding that is requisite for the emotionalising of the intellect.

21. Cf. Magee, *Aspects*, 37.
22. Borchmeyer, *Theatre*, 141.
23. Borchmeyer, *Theatre*, 140, points out that this triadic structure underlines Schiller's *Über naïve und sentimentalische Dichtung* (1795), a work I noted in volume 1, chapter 5 that was important for Wagner. Wagner had access to this work in his 12 volume Schiller edition (*Sämtliche Werke*, 12:167–281).
24. *FSSW* 5:1042 (*Bemerkungen zu Wilhelm von Humboldt: Über das Studium des Altertums und des griechischen insbesondere*).
25. Borchmeyer, *Theatre*, 140.
26. Borchmeyer, *Theatre*, 140–41.
27. *PW* 5:198; *GSD* 9:199.
28. *PW* 5:198–99; *GSD* 9:199.

Identification and Representation

Although one can speak of the "spectator," as I have just done, the most profound experiences in the theatre can occur when one is drawn into the drama itself, having a sense that the protagonists represent us in some sense and even that one identifies with them. Not only do those experiencing the *Ring* have this sense of representation or identification but it seems that this is something Wagner would approve of. In volume 1, chapter 6 I noted Wotan's Schopenhauerian sentiment of "denial of the will" in *Siegfried* Act III Scene 1: "What I once resolved in despair, / in the searing smart of inner turmoil, / I now perform freely / in gladness and joy."[29] In a letter to Ludwig, Wagner not only explicates this Schopenhauerian understanding but writes that in some sense Wotan also represents us and is an example for us to follow:

> I too, like Wotan, must shut off the world of the will, firmly, unopenably (unentriegelbar) and with final resolution: this have I done! Nothing shall open it up again! In it and for it I suffered all I was capable of suffering: I have now acquired the right no longer to be a part of it!—You, my most gracious friend, will discover some day *what* I am telling you here and what I am hinting at!—And so I am now ready to cast myself into this final horror: for I can already hear the echo from the mountains resounding with the exultant clamour of redemption.[30]

The "echo from the mountain" must refer to the sleeping Brünnhilde, who will bring redemption.

Wotan is therefore an *example* for us of someone in need of redemption; but he could also be an allegorical figure, *pointing beyond himself*. In his letter to Röckel of 25/26 January 1854 Wagner contrasts Wotan and Siegfried. On Wotan as the Wanderer he writes: "observe him closely! he resembles *us* to a tee; he is the sum total of present-day intelligence, whereas Siegfried is the man of the future whom we desire and long for but who cannot be made by us, since he must create himself on the basis of *our own annihilation*."[31] This transition from Wotan (the sum total of present-day intelligence) to Siegfried (the man of the future) is portrayed in *Siegfried* Act III and there is a possible "symbolic intent" in the movement from G to C, "G as the key of Wotan's renunciation of power, and C as the key in which Siegfried assumes and transforms that power."[32] I suggest that both god and hero are not only *representative figures* but also *allegorical* figures. Wotan as Wanderer *represents* the human being in Adam and Siegfried *represents* the human being in Christ; further, the god and hero point beyond themselves as allegorical figures of Adam and Christ.

---

29. *WagRS* 257–8.

30. *SL* 740–41; *KB* 2:258. He derived "unentriegelbar" from "Riegel" meaning "bolt"; therefore, the sense is not just that you cannot "open it" but also that you cannot "unlock it" or "unbolt it."

31. *SL* 308; *SB* 6:69.

32. McCreless, *Siegfried*, 191.

That this interpretation is not so far from the truth may be suggested by Wagner's *Jesus of Nazareth*. Wagner raises the issue of the relationship between Adam and Christ in the second and third parts of the sketches (II.1, II.2). He explains that although Jesus was descended from David, ultimately he traced his lineage to Adam, "the immediate offspring of God, from whom spring all men."[33] Jesus came to understand the "universal" significance of this: "So Jesus brushed aside the House of David: through Adam had he sprung from God, and therefore all men were his brothers."[34] But there was a darker side to Adam. Although Adam (and Eve) were "innocent," in the process of gaining "knowledge" ("erkenntnis") they had to distinguish between the "helpful" and the "harmful." But "in the human heart the notion of the Harmful (der begriff des schädlichen) developed into that of the Wicked (bis zu dem von bösen)."[35] The dualism ("Zwiegespaltenheit") of the "Wicked" and "Good" "formed the basis of all Sin and Suffering of mankind."[36] One of the striking aspects of the *Ring* is that the fall is due not only to Alberich's theft of the Rheingold but also to Wotan's search for wisdom (missing in the 1848 *Mythus* and *Siegfried's Death* (1848)).[37] Wotan's "fall" opens up the possibility that he points beyond himself to the figure of Adam, who, like the god, fell in his search for knowledge.[38] In opposition to Adam is Christ. Although, as we have seen, Christ's lineage goes back to Adam in *Jesus of Nazareth*, his role is to undo the effects of Adam's fall and it is significant that the relevant New Testament text, Rom 5:18, was doubly marked in Wagner's copy of the New Testament and is quoted in *Jesus of Nazareth*: "Now, as through the sin of one the condemnation (verdamnis) came upon all, even so through the righteousness (gerechtigkeit) of one hath justification (rechtfertigung) of life come to all."[39]

Just as Wagner makes a Wotan/Adam link, so, as we have seen at many points in discussion, he makes a Siegfried/Christ link. In *Die Wibelungen*, composed at roughly the same time as he was working on his first sketch for the *Ring*, he likens the two figures ("in [that one native Stem-god, i.e., Siegfried] was found the striking likeness to Christ himself, the Son of God") and even identifies them: "In the German Folk survives the oldest lawful race of Kings in all the world: it issues from a son of God, called by his nearest kinsmen *Siegfried*, but *Christ* by the remaining nations of the earth; the welfare of his race, and the peoples of the earth derived therefrom, he wrought a deed most glorious, and for that deed's sake suffered death."[40] The

---

33. *PW* 8:297; *DTB* 248.

34. *PW* 8:298; *DTB* 248.

35. *PW* 8:310; *DTB* 254. Wagner returns to the theme of "innocence" and "Fall" later in his section on "woman" (*PW* 8:320; *DTB* 258).

36. *PW* 8:311; *DTB* 254.

37. See chapter 5 above.

38. As noted in chapter 5, this link between "error" and "knowledge" is central for the beginning of the *Artwork of the Future* (*PW* 1:69–70; *GSD* 42–43).

39. *PW* 8:338; *DTB* 266.

40. *PW* 7:287, 289; *GSD* 2:144, 146.

"race" ("Geschlecht") that issued from Siegfried/Christ should be understood in a "spiritual" sense since neither fathered any children.[41]

The *Ring* as Christian Allegory

At certain points in this book I have argued for a Christian allegorical interpretation of certain other scenes. First, the death of Siegmund as Wotan's only son who has to die because his father had issued various laws and he had to die because of Wotan's "love for the world."[42] Secondly, Brunnhilde's "incarnation" at the close of *Walküre* points to the second person of the Trinity becoming fully human and vulnerable to a world of suffering. This then leads to her becoming "God-forsaken" and eventually "working the deed that redeems the world."[43] A third type of allegory is again Siegfried as a Christ figure in overcoming Satan, in that he is the killer of the dragon, a point Wagner developed in *Die Wibelungen*, where he sets out a triangular relationship of Siegfried/Christ/Friedrich Barbarossa. We also saw in the previous chapter how Siegfried's sacrifice together with that of Brünnhilde achieves atonement.

It may be that we have no extant text where Wagner asserts his *Ring* is a Christian allegory, but I maintain it may nevertheless be seen as one. Further, even though Wagner may not have set out to write a Christian allegory, he may well have produced one. The power and mystery of Wagner's creation is such that even he himself felt he stood before his work "as though before some puzzle"[44] and the work he intended was not the work that transpired.[45] But if the work is to be understood as a Christian allegory there is this possible objection. How is it that we have *two* characters who are a "Christ figure," Siegmund and Brünnhilde? And how is it that Wotan is both a God the Father figure in *Walküre* II and III but then an Adam figure in *Siegfried* Act III? The answer to this is that like the best allegories, the *Ring* is not a consistent one; therefore it is not in the category of C. S. Lewis' *The Lion, the Witch and the Wardrobe*, which is written as a consistent allegory, with the lion Aslan as an allegorical figure for Christ. Realizing that the tetralogy is an inconsistent allegory George Bernard Shaw wrote: "an allegory is never quite consistent except when it is written by someone without dramatic faculty, in which case it is unreadable."[46] Such inconsistency is manifest in the way an allegorical figure such as Wotan can point to *different* entities beyond himself: in *Walküre* Acts II and III to "God the Father" and in *Siegfried* Act III Scene 1 to

---

41. Although Sigurd of *Saga of the Volsungs* fathers Aslaug through Brynhild (presumably in chapter 25) (cf. Faulkes, *Edda*, 105) Sivrit of the *Nibelungenlied* is childless; also no mention is made of Aslaug in the *Elder Edda*.
42. *WagRS* 186 (*Walküre* Act III Scene 3).
43. *WagRS* 258 (*Siegfried* Act III Scene 1).
44. *SL* 357; *SB* 8:152 (letter to August Röckel, 23 August 1856, discussed in chapter 3 above).
45. *SL* 357; *SB* 8:153.
46. Laurence, *Shaw's Music III*, 444.

Adam.⁴⁷ This observation confirms that Wotan cannot be understood simply in terms of "myth," a point to which I will later turn.

This now brings me to one of the fundamental characteristics of allegory: at its best it demonstrates a certain instability and it can spring surprises. Walter Benjamin speaks of allegory scattering and gathering. On the "confused court" he writes: "This court is subject to the law of 'dispersal' and 'collectedness.' Things are assembled according to their significance; indifference to their existence allowed them to be dispersed again."⁴⁸ Deathridge argues that the sources for the *Ring* "provided endless possibilities for allegory" and that "[i]n this labyrinth of images and ancient tales, its heroes, heroines, villains, and even stage props imbued with 'fate' such as the ring and the spear could be treated much as if they were disparate emblems gathering and dispersing around a figural center like Benjamin's 'confused court.'"⁴⁹ I suggest that Wagner's allegory "gathers" in the following way in *Walküre* Act II. Just as Wotan is fettered by his own treatises, so for Wagner God the Father is fettered by his laws and an important aspect of Christ's atoning work is to free God from these laws.⁵⁰ And so allegory "gathers" in that Wotan appears as "God the Father," who not only allows his Son to die but also plans it. Allegory "gathers" also at the end of *Walküre* Act III as Brünnhilde appears as a Christ figure through the act of "incarnation."⁵¹ But allegory not only "gathers"; it also "scatters." For Brünnhilde could appear as a Christ figure at the end of *Walküre* but then the allegory breaks down as she is awakened in *Siegfried* Act III and especially when we witness her behavior in *Götterdämmerung* Act II.

Myth and Mythic Allegories

Going back to *Siegfried* Act III Scenes 1–2, I therefore take Wotan and Siegfried as allegorical figures who *point beyond themselves*. But are they *solely* allegorical figures to whom we can choose to relate? Are they also not mythical figures? They certainly are, but it is important to ask what sort of myth we are dealing with. Schelling made a sharp distinction between allegory and mythology, claiming the latter was not "allegorical" but "tautegorical." Schelling argued that mythology is not something "artificial" ("kunstlich") but rather "natural" ("natürlich") and since myth comes into being by necessity, there is no distinction between form and content, stuff and dressing.⁵² I

---

47. Wagner even could conceive of Wotan as "a kind of Flying Dutchman" (*CD* 23 January 1879).

48. Benjamin, *Origin*, 188; *Ursprung*, 378: "'Zerstreuung' und 'Sammlung' heißt das Gesetz dieses Hofes. Die Dinge sind zusammengetragen nach ihrer Bedeutung; die Anteillosigkeit an ihrem Dasein zerstreute sie wieder."

49. Deathridge, *Beyond Good and Evil*, 94. On the confused court of Calderon, see below.

50. See Bell, *Parsifal*, 132–33.

51. Again Wotan appears as a "father God": "And so—the god turns away from you: / so he kisses away your godhead away" (*WagRS*, 191).

52. *SWMJ* 6:197 (*Einleitung in die Philosophie der Mythologie*): "Weil die Mythologie nicht ein künstlich, sondern ein natürlich, ja unter der gegebenen Voraussetzung mit Nothwendigkeit

think he is right in the sense that myth is not a freely produced work of art such as a novel but comes into being under key constraints. And so adopting a term from Coleridge, he argues that mythology is "tautegorical."[53] Therefore, the gods of myth are real existing beings and do not point beyond themselves.[54] This highlights the crucial point that whereas myth is inexchangeable, allegory (together with other tropes such as metaphor) is exchangeable. In C. S. Lewis' allegory *The Lion, the Witch and the Wardrobe* the lion Aslan is an allegorical figure for Christ. But the lion could be exchanged by another figure. Likewise if in metaphor (which is closely related to allegory) one says "Achilles is a lion," no one believes that Achilles really is a lion and so this metaphor can be replaced by another metaphor such as Achilles is an eagle (see Homer, *Iliad* 24.41; cf. 21.252). But in myth we are dealing with something that is inexchangeable (e.g., the sacrifice of Christ). In such myths one can work with Schelling's view that myth is tautegorical. But I suggest that in Wagner's *Ring* a different sort of myth is at work. Employing a distinction of Eberhard Jüngel, Wagner as an artist and allegoriser is concerned with "Arbeit *am* Mythos" (work *on* myth), which is a myth-critical reception as opposed to "Arbeit *des* Mythos" (work *of* myth), which is the reception of myth Schelling appears to have in mind.[55] Wagner certainly draws on myth but his myth, I suggest, seems to move over into allegory because of the composer's free artistic intent.[56] Even Coleridge can acknowledge in his lectures on Prometheus that in myths of "Jove's intrigues with Europa, Io, &c." that "symbol fades away into allegory," although symbol "never ceases wholly to be a symbol or tautegory."[57] The artist has a freedom that other myth-makers may not have and it is primarily the artist who has this freedom for the "invention of mythic allegories" ("Erfindung der mythischen Allegorien").[58] So going back to *Siegfried* Act III Scene

---

Entstandenes ist, lassen sich in ihr nicht *Inhalt* und *Form*, *Stoff* und *Einkleidung* unterscheiden."

53. *SWMJ* 6:197–98. Coleridge argued symbol was tautegorical (*Lay Sermons*, 30). Note, however, that although Schelling took this term from Coleridge he also influenced the poet in giving him a higher regard for Greek myth (see Halmi, "Coleridge," 354).

54. *SWMJ* 6:198: "Die Götter sind ihr wirklich existierende Wesen, die nicht etwas anderes *sind*, etwas anderes *bedeuten*, sondern *nur* das bedeuten, was sie sind."

55. Jüngel, "Wahrheit des Mythos," 43.

56. This freedom I believe is related to "conscious recollection" or "Besonnenheit" in E. T. A. Hoffmann. Wagner saw the need for an interaction of the "unconscious" and "conscious" for the creation of the artwork. See his letter to Hanslick (1 January 1847; *SL* 134; *SB* 2:538): "Do not underestimate the power of reflection; the unconsciously created work of art belongs to periods remote from our own: the work of art of the most advanced period of culture can be produced only by a process of conscious creation. [. . .] That the most fertile human nature [i.e., Goethe] can effect this wondrous combination between the power of the reflective intellect, on the one hand, & the fecundity of the more direct creative power on the other—that is what makes these highest manifestations of art such rare phenomena." Cf. Borchmeyer, *Theatre*, 35 n. 6.

57. Coleridge, *Shorter Works and Fragments*, 2:1280.

58. *PW* 6:213–14; *GSD* 10:212. Although in paragraph 2 of *Religion and Art* he writes of "the religious Founder" having this freedom, in paragraph 1 he writes that it is the artist who "freely and openly gives out his work as his own invention (Erfindung)" (*PW* 6:213; *GSD* 10:211). Note that he

1, it may be that myth takes on an allegorical dimension in that the figure of Wotan points beyond himself to Adam; and allegory takes on a mythic dimension in that we have the possibility of a mythological identification with the allegorical figure of the Wanderer and, later on, with Siegfried.

Therefore, although myth is often seen as fundamental for the *Ring*, allegory may well be equally central. Wagner rarely discusses allegory, but this may have something to do with the Romantic promotion of the symbol and the corresponding denigration of allegory as found in figures such as Goethe. He makes a clear contrast between symbol and allegory in his letter to Schelling (29 November 1803), where he asks him to explain to the painter Johann Martin Wagner the crucial distinction between the two: "Can you make clear to him the distinction between the allegorical and the symbolic; thus you will be his benefactor since so much revolves around this axis."[59] But in contrast, Schopenhauer makes no categorical distinction between allegory and symbol in plastic and pictorial art and indeed offers a positive evaluation of allegory in relation to poetry.[60]

I suggest that Wagner himself had a positive approach to allegory. Indeed, his leitmotifs[61] function rather like allegorical emblems. Returning to *Siegfried* Act III Scene 1, the nine musical motifs of the Prelude, skillfully woven together, in one way or another are related to the central figure of Wotan:[62] (1) the Valkyrie ride motif, here used for Wotan's riding, which forms the background texture for most of the Prelude; (2) the Erda motif; (3) the need of the gods;[63] (4) the spear or "treaty motif"; (5) twilight of the gods; (6) Wanderer; (7) power of the ring; (8) sleep motif; (9) "mutual recognition."[64] These motifs are, so to speak, "emblems" around the central figure of Wotan,[65] and roughly correspond to the "confused court" in Walter Benjamin's analy-

---

then goes on to speak of "a *sublime* distinction of the Christian religion" ("eine *erhabene* Eigenthümlichkeit der christlichen Religion"); my emphasis.

59. "Können Sie ihm den Unterschied zwischen allegorischer und symbolischer Behandlung begreiflich machen; so sind Sie sein Wohlthäther, weil sich um diese Axe so viel dreht" (Fuhrmans, *Schelling: Briefe und Dokumente III*, 32).

60. *WWR* 1:239, 240–42; *ASSW* 1:334. 335–36.

61. In his 1879 essay "On the Application of Music to the Drama" ("Über die Anwendung der Musik an das Drama,") Wagner refers to one of his "young friends" (i.e., Wolgozen) who writes of what he has called the "Leitmotive" ("der von ihm sogenannte 'Leitmotive'" (*GSD* 10:185; cf. PW 6:184). Wolzogen had not used this term in his *Leitfaden* of 1876 but had introduced it in writing in 1877 in an article in the *Musikalisches Wochenblatt* (Grey, "Origins," 191). The first to use it for Wagner's works was Ambos, "Streit," 142–43 (Grey, "Origins," 195) in 1860. Wagner's own terms are "melodic moments," "elements," "orchestral melody," "motifs" (Grey, "Leitmotif," 88).

62. Of these nine motifs, numbers eight and nine strictly belong to the beginning of Scene 1 into which the music of the Prelude seamlessly moves.

63. This first occurs in *Walküre* Act II Scene 2 (bars 815ff).

64. See the discussion in the previous chapter. The theme's use here, as Scene 1 begins (bars 64–71), presumably refers *ironically* to the mutual recognition between Wotan and Erda since only later in the scene does Erda realize that it is Wotan who stands before her.

65. Note that the motif often used for and associated with Wotan, the Valhalla motif, does not

sis of Barock dramas discussed above[66] whereby we find emblems placed around a central melancholic figure and illustrated so powerfully by Dürer's various depictions of *Melencolia*.[67] Wotan in this scene is not actually a figure of melancholy, although he certainly becomes one later as can be seen in Waltraute's description of him in *Götterdämmerung* Act I.[68] In fact, throughout the Prelude Wotan, far from being portrayed as melancholic, is full of "will," this being expressed through the "drive" of the music whose "elemental power" is driven "largely by the persistent ostinato-like repetition of the dotted figure associated [...] with the raw energy of the Valkyries"[69] but also by the five overlapping entries of the spear motif (bars 15–22). But all these allegorical emblems have a certain arbitrary nature. As allegorical emblems they are exchangeable; so although the stern downward minor scale is appropriate for Wotan's "spear"[70] one could conceive of Wagner composing a different motif. Further, Wagner's emblematic leitmotifs display a certain instability.[71]

Existential Displacement

There are times in the theatre when one is so overcome by Wagner's music and drama that one has a sense of "being taken out of oneself." Wagner may have been aware of the idea Luther puts forward of the "word of God" which addresses the human person who thereby undergoes an "existential displacement." It is perhaps less likely that he knew that Feuerbach shared Luther's view that language can effect a change in the world, thus anticipating "speech-act theory" or, as I prefer to understand it, "speech-event" ("Sprachereignis") theory,[72] something that figures such as Kant, Schleiermacher, and Hegel were unable to come to terms with.[73] A final matter to consider is

---

occur in the Prelude.

66. Benjamin, *Origin*, 188; "Ursprung," 364. Cf. Deathridge, *Good and Evil*, 83, 94.

67. Benjamin, *Origin*, 140; "Ursprung," 319.

68. Her description (*WagRS* 302–4) is then matched with that in the final stage direction of *Götterdämmerung* (*WagRS* 351). Deathridge, *Good and Evil*, 96–97, argues that this "image of the gods and their indecisive and resigned ruler" was probably introduced while Wagner was "recomposing the music of the ending of the *Ring* sometime between April and July 1872 (the period in which the full second draft of the music was finally completed)."

69. Allen, "Old order," 38.

70. See the musical example 11.1 in chapter 11. One way in which it is particularly appropriate is because it looks like a spear on the manuscript paper just as the "ring" motif provides a suitable acoustic picture. See Deathridge, "Leitmotifs in Wagner's Ring Cycle."

71. One example is the "Valhalla" motif, sometimes used for Valhalla itself, but sometimes for Wotan. Other such cases of "unstable" motifs have been discussed in secondary literature although often there is some dispute as to how "unstable" these motifs are in their reference. See, e.g., "love's denial" as used in *Rheingold* and *Walküre* (see the discussion in Cooke, *End*, 2–10). Further instability can be perceived as in the "fate" motif which in *Walküre* and *Siegfried* becomes a "mutual recognition motif" (see theme 9 in the Prelude to *Siegfried* Act III discussed above and chapter 11 above).

72. See volume 1, chapter 6.

73. Bayer, "Feuerbachs Lutherrezeption," 217–18.

whether Wagner's music addresses the hearers rather as the word of God addresses humankind, enabling an existential change.[74] Jüngel, who built upon the work of his teacher Ernst Fuchs, writes:

> In the language event, more is happening than merely communication from one consciousness to another. In the language event, the being of some content is expressed in language in such a way that it addresses the being of a person and summons that person out of himself through the word which addresses him, and in the word which addresses him that person is brought to himself or perhaps divorced from himself. In the language event what happens is that a person is drawn together into the word and there, "outside himself" (*extra se*), he comes to himself in the other word.[75]

Is this not also an apt analysis of those moments in the theatre that make life worth living?

---

74. See Bell, *Parsifal*, 290–91, 310.
75. Jüngel, *Mystery*, 12; *Geheimnis*, 13.

Bibliography

Orchestral Scores of the *Ring*

Voss, Egon, ed. *Das Rheingold*. 2 vols. SW 10.I–II. Mainz: Schott's Söhne, 1988–89.
Jost, Christa, ed. *Die Walküre* 3 vols. SW 11.I–III. Mainz: Schott Musik International, 2002–5.
Döge, Klaus, Egon Voss, and Annette Oppermann, ed. *Siegfried*. 3 vols. SW 12.I–III. Mainz: Schott Music, 2006–14.
Fladt, Hartmut, ed. *Götterdämmerung*. 3 vols. SW 13.I–III. Mainz: Schott's Söhne, 1981–82.

Vocal Scores

Johann Sebastian Bach. *Johannes-Passion/St John Passion. Klavierauszug/Vocal Score*. Edited by Walter Heinz Bernstein. English Translation by Henry S. Drinker. Kassel; Bärenreiter: Deutscher Verlag für Musik, 1981.
The Rhinegold. Complete Vocal Score by Otto Singer. English Translation by Ernest Newman. London: Breitkopf & Härtel, 1910.
Die Walküre. Vollständiger Klavierauszug von Karl Klindworth. English Translation by Frederick Jameson. Mainz: Schott, 1899.
Siegfried. Complete Vocal Score in a Facilitated Arrangement by Karl Klindworth. English Translation by Frederick Jameson. New York: Schirmer, 1904.
Götterdämmerung. Vollständiger Klavierauszug von Karl Klindworth. English Translation by Frederick Jameson. Mainz. Schott, 1899.

The Ring Poem

Wagner, Richard. *Der Ring des Nibelungen: Ein Bühnenfestspiel für drei Tage und einen Vorabend*. Privately published, 1853.
———. *Der Ring des Nibelungen: Ein Bühnenfestspiel für drei Tage und einen Vorabend*. 2nd ed. Leipzig: J. J. Weber, 1873 (1st ed. 1863).

Secondary literature

Abbate, Carolyn. "Analysis." *NGDO* 1:116-20.

———. *Unsung Voices: Opera and Musical Narrative in the Nineteenth Century*. Princeton Studies in Opera. Princeton, NJ: Princeton University Press, 1991.

Aichelle, Alexander. "Ending Individuality: The Mission of a Nation in Fichte's *Addresses to the German Nation*." In *The Cambridge Companion to Fichte*, edited by David James and Günter Zöller, 248–72. Cambridge: Cambridge University Press, 2016.

Allen, Roger. "'The old order changeth, yielding place to new': Siegfried Act III, Scene 1." *The Wagner Journal* 1.3 (2007) 35–48.

Ambos, A. W. "Der Streit um der sogenannte Zukunftsmusik." In *Cultur Bilder aus dem Musikleben der Gegenwart*. 2nd ed. Leipzig: Matthes, 1865 (1st ed. 1860).

Apponyi, Albert. *The Memoirs of Count Apponyi*. London: Heinemann, 1935.

Arnkiel, Trogillus. *Außführliche Eröffnung*. Hamburg: Thomas von Wierung, 1703 (in four parts, the first being *Cimbrische Heyden-Religion* 1702).

Auber, Daniel François. *La Muette de Portici: Libretto by Eugène Scribe und Germain Delavigne. Music by Daniel François Auber*. A facsimile edition of the printed orchestral score, with an introduction by Charles Rosen. 2 vols. New York: Garland, 1980.

Aulén, Gustaf. *Christus Victor: An Historical Study of the Three Main Types of the Idea of the Atonement*. Translated by A. G. Hebert. Foreword by Jaroslav Pelikan. London: SPCK, 1970.

Avemarie, Friedrich. *Tora und Leben: Untersuchungen zur Heilsbedeutung der Tora in der frühen rabbinischen Literatur*. TSAJ 55. Tübingen: J. C. B. Mohr (Paul Siebeck), 1996.

Bailey, Robert. "The Structure of the *Ring* and Its Evolution." *19th Century Music* 1 (1977–78) 48–61.

Baillie, J. B., ed. *G. W. F. Hegel: The Phenomenology of Mind*. 2nd ed. London: Allen & Unwin, 1949.

Barr, James. *The Garden of Eden and the Hope of Immortality*. London: SCM, 1992.

Barth, Herbert, Dietrich Mack, and Egon Voss, eds. *Wagner: A Documentary Study*. Translated by P. R. J. Ford and Mary Whittall. London: Thames and Hudson, 1975.

Bayer, Oswald. "Gegen Gott für die Menschen: Feuerbachs Lutherrezeption." In *Leibliches Wort: Reformation und Neuzeit im Konflikt*, 205–41. Tübingen: J. C. B. Mohr (Paul Siebeck), 1992.

Begbie, Jeremy S. *Theology, Music and Time*. Cambridge Studies in Christian Doctrine. Cambridge: Cambridge University Press, 2000.

Behler, Ernst. *Friedrich Schlegel in Selbstzeugnissen und Bilddokumenten*. Reinbek bei Hamburg: Rowohlt, 1966.

Beiser, Frederick C., ed. *The Early Political Writings of The German Romantics*. CTHPT. Cambridge: Cambridge University Press, 1996.

———. *Hegel*. London: Routledge, 2005.

Bell, Richard H. "Are Wagner's Views of 'Redemption' Relevant for the Twenty-first Century?" In *Das Kunstwerk der Zukunft: Perspektive der Wagnerrezeption im 21. Jahrhundert*, edited by Sven Friedrich, 71–86. Wagner in der Diskussion 11. Würzburg: Königshausen & Neumann, 2014.

———. *Deliver Us from Evil. Interpreting the Redemption from the Power of Satan in New Testament Theology*. WUNT 216. Tübingen: Mohr Siebeck, 2007.

———. *No one seeks for God: An Exegetical and Theological Study of Romans 1.18—3.20*. WUNT 106. Tübingen: Mohr Siebeck, 1998.

———. *Provoked to Jealousy: The Origin and Purpose of the Jealousy Motif in Romans 9–11*. WUNT 2.63. Tübingen: J. C. B. Mohr (Paul Siebeck), 1994.

———. "Richard Wagner's Prose Sketches for Jesus of Nazareth: Historical and Theological Reflections on an Uncompleted Opera." *Journal for the Study of the Historical Jesus* 15 (2017) 260–90.

———. "Sacrifice and Christology in Paul." *JTS* 53 (2002) 1–27.

———. "Teleology, Providence and the 'Death of God': A New Perspective on the *Ring* Cycle's Debt to G. W. F. Hegel." *The Wagner Journal* 11.1 (2017) 30–45.

———. *Wagner's Parsifal: An Appreciation in the Light of His Theological Journey.* Eugene, OR: Wipf & Stock, 2013.

———. "Wagner's Siegfried Act III Scene 1: A Study in 'Renunciation of the Will' and the 'Sublime.'" *The Wagner Journal* 10.2 (2016) 18–35.

Benjamin, Walter. *The Origin of German Tragic Drama.* Translated by John Osborne. London: NLB, 1977.

———. "Ursprung des deutschen Trauerspiels." *WBAW* 1:217–444.

Berger, Karol. *Beyond Reason: Wagner contra Nietzsche.* Oakland, CA: University of California Press, 2017.

Bermbach, Udo. *Der Wahn des Gesmtkunstwerkes: Richard Wagners politisch-ästhestische Utopie.* 2nd ed. Stuttgart: J. B. Metzler, 2004.

Bernharðsson, Haraldur. "Old Icelandic ragnarök and ragnarökkr." In *Verba Docenti: Studies in historical and Indo-European linguistics presented to Jay H. Jasanoff*, edited by Alan J. Nussbaum, 25–38. Ann Arbor, NY: Beech Stave, 2007.

Berry, Mark. *Treacherous Bonds and Laughing Fire: Politics and Religion in Wagner's Ring.* Aldershot: Ashgate, 2006.

Björnsson, Árni. *Wagner and the Volsungs: Icelandic Sources of Der Ring des Nibelungen.* University College London: Viking Society for Northern Research, 2003.

Borchmeyer, Dieter. *Drama and the World of Richard Wagner.* Translated by Daphne Ellis. Princeton, NJ: Princeton University Press, 2003.

———. *Richard Wagner: Ahasvers Wandlungen.* Frankfurt am Main: Insel, 2002.

———. *Richard Wagner: Theory and Theatre.* Translated by Stewart Spencer. Oxford: Clarendon, 2002.

———. "Wagners Mythos vom Anfang und Ende der Welt." In *Richard Wagner—"Der Ring des Nibelungen": Ansichten des Mythos*, edited by Udo Bermbach and Dieter Borchmeyer, 1–25. Stuttgart: J. B. Metzler, 1995.

Borthwick, Alastair, Trevor Hart and Anthony Monti. "Musical Time and Eschatology." In *Resonant Witness: Conversations between Music and Theology*, edited by Jeremy S. Begbie and Steven Guthrie, 271–94. Grand Rapids: Wm B. Eerdmans, 2011.

Böttger, Adolf, ed. *Byron's sämmtliche Werke.* 12 vols. Leipzig: Otto Wigand, 1841 (DB 13).

Boulez, Pierre. "A partir du présent, le passé." In *Histoire d'un "Ring"*, edited by Pierre Boulez, Patrice Chéreau, Richard Peduzzi, and Jacques Schmidt, 13–36. Paris: Laffont, 1980.

Brandon, S.G.F. *Jesus and the Zealots: a study of the political factor in primitive Christianity.* Manchester: Manchester University Press, 1967.

———. *The Trial of Jesus of Nazareth.* London: B. T. Batsford, 1968.

Brown, Andrew L. "Achilles." *OCD*³ 6–7.

Brown, Jane, K. "Faust." In *The Cambridge Companion to Goethe*, edited by Lesley Sharpe, 84–100. Cambridge: Cambridge University Press, 2002.

Brown, Raymond E. *The Gospel according to John.* 2 vols. London: Chapman, 1978.

Brueggemann, Walter. *Theology of the Old Testament: Testimony, Dispute, Advocacy.* Minneapolis: Fortress, 1997.

Bultmann, Rudolf. "New Testament and Mythology." In *Kerygma and Myth: A Theological Debate, Volume 1*, edited by Hans Werner Bartsch, 1–44. 2nd ed. Translated by Reginald H. Fuller. London: SPCK, 1964.

———. "Welchen Sinn hat es, von Gott zu reden?" In *Glauben und Verstehen: Gesammelte Aufsätze, Band I*, 26–37. 1933. 9th ed. Tübingen: J. C. B. Mohr (Paul Siebeck) 1993.

———. "What Does It Mean to Speak of God?" In *Faith and Understanding I*, edited with an introduction by Robert W. Fink, translated by Louise Pettibone Smith, 53–65. London: SCM, 1969.

Bury, R. G., ed. *Plato IX: Timaeus—Critias—Cleitophon—Menexenus Epistles*. LCL 234. 1929. Reprint. Cambridge: Harvard University Press, 1989.

Byock, Jesse, ed. *The Prose Edda*. London: Penguin, 2005.

———, ed. *The Saga of the Volsungs: The Norse Epic of Sigurd the Dragon Slayer*. London: Penguin, 1990.

Carlyle, Thomas. *Sartor Resartus and On Heroes, Hero-worship*. 1908. Reprint. Everyman's Library 278. London: Dent, 1948.

Carr, E. H. *Michael Bakunin*. 1937. Reprint. London: Macmillan, 1975.

Cassuto, U. *A Commentary on the Book of Genesis 1–11*. 2 vols. Translated by Israel Abrahams. Jerusalem: Magnes, 1961–64.

Catling, Richard W. V. "Delos." *OCD*[3] 442–44.

Chadwick, Mark B. "Wagner and Science: Twilight of the Gods Across the Multiverse." *The Wagner Journal* 9.1 (2013) 23–39.

Childress, James F. "Situation Ethics." In *A New Dictionary of Christian Ethics*, edited by John Macquarrie and James Childress, 586–88. London: SCM, 1987.

Church Hymnal: Full Music Edition. 5th ed. Oxford: OUP, 2000.

Cleasby, Richard, Gudbrand Vigfusson, and William A. Craigie. *An Icelandic-English Dictionary*. 2nd ed. 1957. Reprint. Oxford: Oxford University Press, 1969.

Clemen, Otto, ed. *Luthers Werke in Auswahl*. 4 vols. Bonn: Marcus und Weber, 1912–13.

Clement of Alexandria. "Exhortation to the Heathen." In *Ante-Nicene Christian Library Volume 4: Clement of Alexandria Volume 1*, edited by Alexander Roberts and James Donaldson, 17–110. Edinburgh: T. & T. Clark, 1867.

Coleridge, Samuel Taylor. *The Collected Works of Samuel Taylor Coleridge 6: Lay Sermons*. Edited by R. J. White. London: Routledge, 1972.

———. *The Collected Works of Samuel Taylor Coleridge, Vol. 11: Shorter Works and Fragments*. Edited by H. J. Jackson and J. R. de J. Jackson. 2 vols. London: Routledge & Kegan Paul, 1995.

Cooke, Deryck. *I Saw the World End: A Study of Wagner's Ring*. 1979. Reprint. Oxford: Clarendon, 1979.

———. "An Introduction to Wagner's *Der Ring des Nibelungen*." 2 CD set. 1958 (music); 1967 (speech).

———. "Wagner's Musical Language." In *The Wagner Companion*, edited by Peter Burbidge and Richard Sutton, 225–68. London: Faber and Faber, 1979.

Cormack, David. "Ellis, William Ashton." *CWE* 112–13.

———. "Faithful, All Too Faithful." *The Wagner Library* 4.9 (2002) 1–86.

Corse, Sandra. *Wagner and the New Consciousness: Language and Love in the Ring*. Rutherford: Associated University Press, 1990.

Crossley, James G. *The Date of Mark's Gospel: Insight from the Law in Earliest Christianity*. The Library of New Testament Studies. London: T. & T. Clark, 2004.

Dahlhaus, Carl. *Richard Wagner's Music Dramas*. Translated by Mary Whittall. Cambridge: Cambridge University Press, 1979.

Darcy, Warren. "Autograph Manuscripts." In *The Wagner Compendium: A Guide to Wagner's Life and Music*, edited by Millington, Barry, 217–21. London: Thames and Hudson, 1992.

———. "*Creatio ex nihilo*: The Genesis, Structure, and Meaning of the *Rheingold* Prelude." *19th Century Music* 13 (1989) 79–100.

———. "The Pessimism of the *Ring*." *The Opera Quarterly* 4.2 (1986) 24–48.

———. *Wagner's Das Rheingold*. 1993. Reprint. Studies in Musical Genesis and Structure. Oxford: Clarendon, 2002.

Darwin, Charles. *Evolutionary Writings*. Edited by James A. Secord. Oxford: Oxford University Press, 2008.

Dawson-Bowling, Paul. *The Wagner Experience and Its Meaning to Us*. 2 vols. Brecon, UK: Old Street, 2013.

Deathridge, John, ed. *Richard Wagner: The Ring of the Nibelung*. Translated and edited with an introduction by John Deathridge. London: Penguin, 2018.

———. "Cataloguing Wagner." In *The Richard Wagner Centenary in Australia*, edited by Peter Dennison, 185–99. Miscellanea musicologica 14. Adelaide: University of Adelaide Press, 1985.

———. "Reviews of A. D. Sessa, *Richard Wagner and the English*; J. L. DiGaetani (ed.), *Penetrating Wagner's Ring*; P. Burbidge and R. Sutton (ed.), *The Wagner Companion*; C. von Westernhagen, *Wagner: A Biography*." *19th Century Music* 5 (1981–82) 81–89.

———. *Wagner beyond Good and Evil*. Berkeley: University of California Press, 2008.

Defoe, Daniel. *Moll Flanders*. Edited with an introduction and notes by G. A. Starr. 1981. Reprint. Oxford World's Classics. Oxford: Oxford University Press, 1998.

Devrient, Eduard. *Aus seinen Tagebüchern, Berlin/Dresden/Karlsruhe*. Edited by Rolf Kabel. 2 vols. Weimar: Böhlhaus, 1964.

Dischner, Gisela, ed. *Friedrich Schlegels Lucinde und Materialien zu einer Theorie des Müßiggangs*. Hildesheim: Gerstenberg, 1980.

Doepler, Carl Emil. *Der Ring des Nibelungen: Figurinen*. Reprint. Mit Text von Clara Steinitz. Nachwort von Joachim Heinzle. Leipzig: Primus, 2012.

Donington, Robert. *Wagner's 'Ring' and Its Symbols*. 3rd ed. London: Faber and Faber, 1974.

Dreyfus, Laurence. *Wagner and the Erotic Impulse*. Cambridge: Harvard University Press, 2010.

Dronke, Ursula. *The Poetic Edda, Volume I: Heroic Poems*. Oxford: Clarendon, 1969.

———. *The Poetic Edda, Volume II: Mythological Poems*. Oxford: Clarendon, 1997.

———. *The Poetic Edda, Volume III: Mythological Poems II*. Oxford: Clarendon, 2011.

Dyson, Michael. "Sea, Mirror, Woman, Love: Some Recurrent Imagery in 'Opera and Drama.'" *Wagner Journal* 5.3 (2011) 16–33.

Ebeling, Gerhard. *Luther: An Introduction to his Thought*. Translated by R. A. Wilson. London: Collins, 1972.

———. "Luthers Wirklichkeitsverständnis." *ZThK* 90 (1993) 409–24.

Eberhardt, H. "Die Kyffhäuserburgen in Geschichte und Sage." *Blätter für deutsche Landesgeschichte* 96 (1960) 66–103.

Eichner, Hans. *Friedrich Schlegel*. New York: Twayne, 1970.

Eichrodt, Walther. *Theology of the Old Testament*. Translated by John Baker. 2 vols. London: SCM, 1961–67.

Elliott, J. K., ed. *The Apocryphal New Testament: A Collection of Apocryphal Christian Literature in an English Translation*. Oxford: Clarendon, 1993.

Ellis Davidson, H. R. *Gods and Myths of Northern Europe*. 1964. Reprint. Harmondsworth, UK: Penguin, 1976.

Engel, Erich W. *Richard Wagners Leben und Werke im Bilde*. 2 vols. Vienna/Leipzig: Emil M. Engel, 1913.

Engels, Frederick. *Ludwig Feuerbach and the Outcome of Classical German Philosophy*. Edited by C. P. Dutt. New York: International, 1970.

Estes, Douglas. *Temporal Mechanics of the Fourth Gospel: A Theory of Hermeneutical Relativity in the Gospel of John*. Biblical Interpretation Series 92. Leiden: E.J. Brill, 2008.

Ettmüller, Ludwig, ed. *Die Lieder der Edda von den Nibelungen: Stabreimende Verdeutschung*. Zurich: Drell, Füßli und Compagnie, 1837 (borrowed from Dresden Royal library).

———, ed. *Vaulu-spá: Das älteste Denkmal germanisch-nordischer Sprache, nebst einigen Gedanken über Nordens Wissen und Glauben und nordische Dichtkunst*. Leipzig: Weidmannsche Buchhandlung, 1830 (DB 149).

Eyth, Eduard, ed. *Hesiod's Werke*. 2nd ed. Stuttgart: Krais & Hoffmann, 1865.

Fairley, Barker, ed. *Goethe's Faust*. Toronto: University of Toronto Press, 1972.

Faulkes, Anthony. *Snorri Sturluson: Edda*. Everyman Library. London: J.M. Dent, 1987.

Feenberg, Andrew. *Lukács, Marx and the Sources of Critical Theory*. Totowa, NJ: Bowman and Littlefield, 1981.

Feuerbach, Ludwig. *The Essence of Christianity*. Translated by George Eliot. Introductory essay by Karl Barth. Foreword by H. Richard Niebuhr. New York: Harper & Brothers, 1957.

———. *Lectures on the Essence of Religion*. Translated by Ralph Manheim. New York: Harper & Row, 1967.

———. *Principles of the Philosophy of the Future*. Translated by Manfred H. Vogel. Indianapolis: Bobbs-Merrill, 1966.

———. *Thoughts on Death and Immortality*. Translated, with introduction and notes, by James A. Massey. Berkeley: University of California Press, 1980.

Fichte, Johann Gottlieb. *Addresses to the German Nation*. Edited by Gregory Moore. CTHPT. Cambridge: Cambridge University Press, 2008.

———. *Reden an die deutsche Nation*. Edited by Immanuel Hermann Fichte. Tübingen: Laupp, 1859 (Wahnfried).

———. *Science of Knowledge (Wissenschaftslehre) with the First and Second Introductions*. Edited and translated by Peter Heath and John Lachs. CPS. New York: Appleton-Century-Crofts, 1970.

Finch, R. G. *The Saga of the Volsungs*. Icelandic Texts. London: Thomas Nelson, 1965.

Finlay, Alison, and Anthony Faulkes, ed. *Snorri Sturluson, Heimskringla Volume I: The Beginnings to Óláfr Tryggvason*. University College London: Viking Society for Northern Research, 2011.

Fischer, Johannes. "Behaupten oder Bezeugen? Zum Modus des Wahrheitsanspruchs christlicher Reder von Gott." *ZThK* 87 (1990) 224–44.

———. *Glaube als Erkenntnis: Zum Wahrnehmungscharakter des christlichen Glaubens*. Munich: Christian Kaiser, 1989.

Fletcher, Joseph. "The New Look in Christian Ethics." *Harvard Divinity Bulletin* (1959) 7–18.

———. *Situation Ethics: The New Morality*. London: SCM, 1966.

Flew, Anthony, ed. *Body, Mind, and Death: From Hippocrates to Gilbert Ryle on the Question "What Is Consciousness?"* 1964. Reprint. London: Macmillan, 1974.

Foster, Daniel H. *Wagner's Ring Cycle and the Greeks.* Cambridge: Cambridge University Press, 2010.

Fouqué, Friedrich Baron de la Motte. *Sigurd der Schlangentödtner: ein Heldenspiel in sechs Abentheurer.* Berlin: Hitzig, 1808.

Fowler, Harold North, ed. *Plato I: Euthyphro—Apology—Crito—Phaedo—Phaedrus.* LCL 36. 1914 Reprint. Cambridge: Harvard University Press, 1995.

Frauer, Ludwig. *Die Walkyrien der skandinavisch-germanischen Götter- und Heldensage.* Weimar, 1846 (DB: Minna).

Frazer, James George, ed. *Apollodorus I.* LCL 121. 1921. Reprint. Cambridge: Harvard University Press, 1976.

Friedrich, Ernst F. *Das sogenannte hohe Lied Salomonis oder vielmehr das pathetische Dramation 'Sulamit', parallelistisch aus dem Hebräischen in's Dt. übers.v. Ernst F. Friedrich.* Königsberg: Schubert & Seidel, 1866.

Friedrich, Sven. "Gibt es eine 'Philosophie des Weiblichen' bei Wagner?" In *Das Weib der Zukunft: Frauengestalten und Frauenstimmen bei Richard Wagner,* edited by Susanne Vill, 44–56. Stuttgart: J. B. Metzler, 2000.

Fuchs, Hanns. *Richard Wagner und die Homosexualität: Unter besonderer Berücksichtigung der sexuellen Anomalien seiner Gestalten.* Berlin: Barsdorf, 1903.

Fuhrmans, Horst, ed. *F. W. J. Schelling: Briefe und Dokumente, Band III: 1803–1809 (Zusatzband).* Bonn: Bouvier, 1975.

Gerstenberger, Erhard S. *Theologies in the Old Testament.* Translated by John Bowden. London: T. & T. Clark, 2002.

Glasenapp, Carl Fr. *Das Leben Richard Wagners in sechs Büchern.* 1905–11. Reprint. Liechtenstein: Sändig, 1977.

Gobineau, Arthur. *Essai sur l'inégalité des races humaines.* 4 vols. Paris: Didot, 1853–55 (Wahnfried).

Goethe, Johann Wolfgang. *Goethe's sämmtliche Werke in vierzig Bänden.* Stuttgart: Cotta'scher, 1840 (DB 38).

———. *Goethe's sämmtliche Werke in dreißig Bänden.* Stuttgart: Cotta'scher, 1857–58 (Wahnfried).

Golther, Wolfgang. *Richard Wagner an Mathilde Wesendonk: Tagebuchblätter und Briefe 1853–1871.* Berlin: Duncker, 1908.

———. *Die sagengeschichtlichen Grundlagen der Ringdichtung Richard Wagners.* Berlin: Verlag der "Allgemeine Musik-Zeitung," 1902.

Goodspeed, Edgar J. *Die ältesten Apologeten: Texte mit kurzen Einleitungen.* Göttingen: Vandenhoeck & Ruprecht, 1914.

Göschel, Carl Friedrich. *Von den Beweisen für die Unsterblichkeit der menschlichen Seele.* Berlin: Duncker und Humblot, 1835.

———. *Die siebenfältige Osterfrage.* Berlin: Duncker und Humblot, 1836.

Gregor-Dellin, Martin. *Richard Wagner: His Life, His Work, His Century.* Translated by J. Maxwell Brownjohn. San Diego: Harcourt Brace Jovanovich, 1983.

———. *Richard Wagner: Sein Leben—Sein Werk—Sein Jahrhundert.* 1980. Reprint. Munich: Piper, 2005.

———. *Wagner-Chronik: Daten zu Leben und Werk.* 2nd ed. Kassel: Bärenreiter, 1983.

Grey, Thomas S. "Leitmotif, Temporality, and Musical Design in the Ring." In *The Cambridge Companion to Wagner*, edited by Thomas S. Grey, 87–97. Cambridge: Cambridge University Press, 2008.

———. *Wagner's Musical Prose: Texts and Contexts.* Cambridge: Cambridge University Press, 1995.

———. ". . . wie ein rother Faden: On the Origins of 'Leitmotif' as Critical Concept and Musical Practice." In *Music Theory in the Age of Romanticism*, edited by Ian Bent, 187–210. Cambridge: Cambridge University Press, 1996.

Grimm, Jacob. *Deutsche Mythologie.* 2 vols. 2nd ed. Göttingen: Dieterichsche Buchhandlung, 1844 (DB 44).

———. *Teutonic Mythology.* Translated from the fourth edition by James Steven Stallybrass, with notes and appendix. London: George Bell, 1882–88.

Grimm, Wilhelm, ed. *Die deutsche Heldensage.* Göttingen: Dieterichsche Buchhandlung, 1829 (DB 47).

Großmann-Vendrey, Susanna. *Bayreuth in der deutschen Presse. Dokumentendband 1: Die Grundsteinlegung und die ersten Festspiele (1872–76).* Regensburg: Bosse, 1977.

Hall, Jonathan M. *Ethnic Identity in Greek antiquity.* Cambridge: Cambridge University Press, 1997.

Halmi, Nicholas. "Coleridge on Allegory and Symbol." In *The Oxford Handbook of Samuel Taylor Coleridge*, edited by Frederick Burwick, 345–58. Oxford: Oxford University Press, 2009.

Harvey, Van A. *Feuerbach and the Interpretation of Religion.* Cambridge Studies in Religion and Critical Thought 1. Cambridge: Cambridge University Press, 1995.

Haymes, Edward R., ed. *The Saga of Thidrek of Bern.* Garland Library of Medieval Literature, Series B, 56. New York: Garland, 1988.

———. *Wagner's Ring in 1848: New Translations of the Nibelung Myth and Siegfried's Death.* Rochester, NY: Camden House, 2010.

Hébert, Marcel. *Le Sentiment Religieux dans l'Œuvre de Richard Wagner.* Paris: Librairie Fischbacher, 1895.

———. *Religious Experience in the Work of Richard Wagner.* Edited by C. J. T. Talar. Translated by C. J. T. Talar and Elizabeth Emery. Foreword by Stephen Schloesser. Washington, DC: The Catholic University of America Press, 2015.

Hegel, G. W. F. *Aesthetics: Lectures on Fine Art.* 2 vols. Translated by T. M. Knox. 1975. Reprint. Oxford: Clarendon, 2010.

———. *On Christianity: Early Theological Writings.* Translated by T. M. Knox. With an introduction, and fragments translated by Richard Kroner. Gloucester, MA: Smith, 1970.

———. *The Difference between Fichte's and Schelling's System of Philosophy.* Translated by H. S. Harris and Walter Cerf. Albany, NY: State University of New York Press, 1977.

———. *The Encyclopaedia Logic (with Zusätze): Part I of the Encyclopaedia of the Philosophical Sciences with the Zusätze.* A new translation with introduction and notes by T. F. Geraets, W. A. Suchting, and H. S. Harris. Indianapolis, IN: Hackett, 1991.

———. *Lectures on the Philosophy of World History. Introduction: Reason in History.* Translated by H. B. Nisbet. Introduction by D. Forbes. Cambridge Studies in the History and Theory of Politics. Cambridge: Cambridge University Press, 1975.

———. *Lectures on the Philosophy of Religion.* Edited by Peter C. Hodgson. 3 vols. 2007. Reprint. Oxford: Oxford University Press, 2011–12.

———. *Lectures on the Philosophy of History*. Preface by Charles Hegel. Translated by J. Sibree, 1861. Reprint. Meneola, NY: Dover 1956.

———. *Vorlesungen über die Philosophie der Geschichte*. Edited by Eduard Gans and Karl Hegel. Berlin: Duncker und Humblot, 1840 (DB 55).

———. *Vorlesungen über die Philosophie der Religion. Teil 1. Einleitung. Der Begriff der Religion*. Edited by Walter Jaeschke. Vorlesungen: Ausgewählte Nachschriften und Manuskripte 3. Hamburg: Meiner, 1983.

———. *Vorlesungen über die Philosophie der Religion. Teil 3. Die vollendete Religion*. Edited by Walter Jaeschke. Vorlesungen: Ausgewählte Nachschriften und Manuskripte 5. Hamburg: Meiner, 1984.

Heine, Heinrich. *Sämtlicher Werke, Band 9: Elementargeister. Die Göttin Diana. Der Doktor Faust. Die Götter im Exil*. Düsseldorfer Ausgabe. Hamburg: Hoffmann und Campe, 1987.

Helmholtz, Hermann. *Die Lehre von den Tonempfindungen, als physiologische Grundlage für die Theorie der Musik*. 4th ed. Braunschweig: Vieweg, 1877 (Wahnfried).

———. *On the Sensations of Tone as a Physiological Basis for the Theory of Music*. Adapted to the use of Music Students by Alexander J. Ellis. New introduction by Henry Margenau. New York: Dover, 1954.

Hengel, Martin. "Review of S. G. F. Brandon, *Jesus and the Zealots*." *JSS* 14 (1969) 231–40.

Herder, Johann Gottfried. "Essay on the Origin of Language." In *On the Origin of Language: Two Essays*, translated with afterwords by John H. Moran and Alexander Gode, 85–166. Chicago: University of Chicago Press, 1966.

Hirsch, Emmanuel. "Zu Luthers Theologie." *TLZ* 66.5/6 (May/June 1941) 129–34.

Hodgson, Peter C. *Shapes of Freedom: Hegel's Philosophy of World History in Theological Perspective*. 2005. Reprint. Oxford: Oxford University Press, 2012.

Hoffmeister, Johannes, ed. *Georg Wilhelm Friedrich Hegel: Phänomenologie des Geistes*. Der philosophische Bibliothek 114. 6th ed. Hamburg: Meiner, 1952.

Hofmann, Kurt. "Brahms and the Hamburg Musician 1833–1862." In *The Cambridge Companion to Brahms*, edited by Michael Musgrave, 3–30. Cambridge: Cambridge University Press, 1999.

Hooker, Brad, and Margaret Little, ed. *Moral Particularism*. Oxford: Clarendon, 2003.

Houlgate, Stephen. "Hegel's Theory of Tragedy." In *Hegel and the Arts*, edited by Stephen Houlgate, 146–78. Topics in Historical Philosophy. Evanston, IL: Northwestern University Press, 2007.

———. *Introduction to Hegel: Freedom, Truth and History*. 2nd ed. Oxford: Blackwell, 2005.

———. "G. W. F. Hegel: The Phenomenology of Spirit." In *The Blackwell Guide to Continental Philosophy*, edited by Robert C. Solomon and David Sherman, 8–29. Blackwell Philosophy Guides 12. Oxford: Blackwell, 2003.

———. *Hegel's Phenomenology of Spirit*. A Reader's Guide. London: Bloomsbury, 2013.

Huber, Herbert. *Der Ring des Nibelungen: Vollständiger Text mit Kommentar*. Weinheim: VCH, 1988.

Hübner, Kurt. "Wagners mythisches Christentum." In *Getauft auf Musik: Festschrift für Dieter Borchmeyer*, edited by Udo Bermbach and Hans Rudolf Vaget, with assistance from Yvonne Nilges, 275–90. Würzburg: Königshausen & Neumann, 2006.

———. *Die Wahrheit des Mythos*. Munich: C. H. Beck, 1985.

Hübscher, Arthur. *Arthur Schopenhauer: Gesammelte Briefe*. Bonn: Bouvier Verlag Herbert Grundmann, 1978.

Hutton, M., et al. *Tacitus I: Agricola, Germania, Dialogus*. LCL 35. 1914. Reprint. Cambridge: Harvard University Press, 1992.

Inwood, Michael J. *Hegel*. 1983. Reprint. London: Routledge, 1998.

———. *A Hegel Dictionary*. The Blackwell Philosopher Dictionaries. Oxford: Blackwell, 1992.

Iljin, Iwan. *Die Philosophie Hegels als kontemplative Gotteslehre*. Bern: Francke, 1946.

Jeans, James. *The Mysterious Universe*. Cambridge: Cambridge University Press, 1931.

Jeffrey, Steve, Mike Ovey, and Andrew Sach. *Pierced for Our Transgressions: Rediscovering the Glory of Penal Substitution*. Nottingham, UK: IVP, 2007.

Jüngel, Eberhard. *God as the Mystery of the World: On the Foundation of the Theology of the Crucified One in the Dispute between Theism and Atheism*. Translated by Darrell L. Guder. Edinburgh: T. & T. Clark, 1983.

———. *Gott als Geheimnis der Welt: Zur Begründung der Theologie des Gekreuzigten im Streit zwischen Theismus und Atheismus*. 5th ed. Tübingen: J. C. B. Mohr (Paul Siebeck), 1986.

———. *Paulus und Jesus: Eine Untersuchung zur Präzisierung der Frage nach dem Ursprung der Christologie*. HUzTh 2. 6th ed. Tübingen: J. C. B. Mohr (Paul Siebeck), 1986.

———. "Die Wahrheit des Mythos und die Notwendigkeit der Entmythologisierung." In *Indikative der Gnade—Imperative der Freiheit*, 40–57. Tübingen: Mohr Siebeck, 2000.

———. "'Die Weltgeschichte ist das Weltgericht' aus theologischer Perspektive." In *Die Weltgeschichte—das Weltgericht? Stuttgarter Hegel Kongreß 1999*, edited by Rüdiger Bubner and Walter Mesch, 14–33. Stuttgart: Klett-Cotta, 2001.

Kant, Immanuel. *Critique of the Power of Judgment*. Edited by Paul Guyer. Translated by Paul Guyer and Eric Matthews. CEWIK. Cambridge: Cambridge University Press, 2000.

———. *Natural Science*. Edited by Eric Watkins. Translated by Lewis White Beck, Jeffrey B. Edwards, Olaf Reinhardt, Martin Schönfeld, and Eric Watkins. CEWIK. Cambridge: Cambridge University Press, 2012.

———. *Religion within the Boundaries of Mere Reason and Other Writings*. Translated and edited by Allen Wood and George Di Giovanni. Introduction by Robert Merrihew Davies. CTHP. Cambridge: Cambridge University Press, 1998.

Käsemann, Ernst. *Jesus Means Freedom: A Polemical Survey of the New Testament*. Translated by Frank Clarke. London: SCM, 1969.

———. "The Problem of the Historical Jesus." In *Essays on New Testament Themes*, translated by W. J. Montague, 15–47. Studies in Biblical Theology 1.41. London: SCM, 1964.

Kaul, Camilla G. *Friedrich Barbarossa im Kyffhäuser: Bilder eines nationalen Mythos im 19. Jahrhundert*. Bonner Beiträge zur Kunstgeschichte 4. 2 vols. Cologne: Böhlau, 2007.

Kienzle, Ulrike. "*Parsifal* and Religion: A Christian Music Drama?" In *A Companion to Wagner's Parsifal*, edited by William Kinderman and Katherine R. Syer, 81–130. Rochester, UK: Camden House, 2005.

Kirchmeyer, Helmut. *Situationsgeschichte der Musikkritik und des musikalischen Pressewesens in Deutschland dargestellt vom Ausgange des 18. bis zum Beginn des 20. Jahrhunderts. IV. Teil. Das zeitgenössische Wagner-Bild*. Studien zur Musikgeschichte des 19. Jahrhunderts 7. 3 vols. Regensburg: Bosse, 1967–72.

Kirkpatrick, Robin, tr. and ed. *Dante Alighieri, The Divine Comedy I: Inferno*. London: Penguin, 2006.

Kitcher, Philip, and Richard Schacht. *Finding an Ending: Reflections on Wagner's Ring*. Oxford: Oxford University Press, 2004.

Knatz, Lothar. *Geschichte—Kunst—Mythos: Schellings Philosophie und die Perspektive einer philosophischen Mythostheorie*. Würzburg: Königshausen & Neumann, 1999.

Knox, T. M., ed. *G. W. F. Hegel: Outlines of the Philosophy of Right*. Revised, edited, and introduced by Stephen Houlgate. Oxford: Oxford University Press, 2008.

Koch, Michael. *Drachenkampf und Sonnenfrau: Zur Funktion des Mythischen in der Johannesapokalypse am Beispiel Apk 12*. WUNT 2.184. Tübingen: Mohr Siebeck, 2004.

Köhler, Joachim. *Richard Wagner: The Last of the Titans*. Translated by Stewart Spencer. New Haven: Yale University Press, 2004.

König, Eduard. *Die Genesis*. Gütersloh: Bertelsmann, 1919.

Kreckel, Manfred. *Richard Wagner und die französischen Frühsozialisten: Die Bedeutung der Kunst und des Künstlers für eine neue Gesellschaft*. EH 3.284. Frankfurt am Main: Lang, 1986.

Krömmelbein, Thomas. "Jacob Schimmelmann und der Beginn der Snorra Edda Rezeption in Deutschland." In *Snorri Sturluson: Beiträge zu Werk und Rezeption*, edited by Hans Fix, 109–30. Ergänzungsbände zum Reallexikon der Germanische Alterumskunde 18. Berlin: Walter de Gruyter, 1998.

Krüger, Eduard. "Die beiden Bach'schen Passionen." *Neue Zeitschrift für Musik* 18 (1843) 57–59, 61–62, 65–67, 69–71, 73–74, 77–79, 85–88.

Küng, Hans. *The Incarnation of God: An Introduction to Hegel's Theological Thought as Prolegomena to a Future Christology*. Translated by J. R. Stephenson. New York: Crossroad, 1987.

Kuzniar, Alice. *Outing Goethe and His Age*. Stanford, CA: Stanford University Press, 1996.

Lamb, W. R. M., ed. *Plato III: Lysis—Symposium—Gorgias*. LCL 166. 1925. Reprint. Cambridge: Harvard University Press, 1991.

Larrington, Carolyn, ed. *The Poetic Edda*. Oxford World's Classics. Rev. ed. Oxford: Oxford University Press, 2014.

———. *The Norse Myths: A Guide to the Gods and Heroes*. London: Thames & Hudson, 2017.

Lassen, Annette, ed. *Hrafnagaldur Óðins (Forspjallsljóð)*. University College London: Viking Society for Northern Research, 2011.

Laurence, Dan H., ed. *Shaw's Music: The Complete Musical Criticism of Bernard Shaw, Volume 3: 1893–1950*. London: The Bodley Head, 1989.

Leaver, Robin. "The Revival of the St. John Passion: History and Performance Practice." *American Choral Review* 1 (1989) 14–29.

Lehrs, Franz Siegfried (Levi, Samuel), ed. *Hesiodi carmina*. Paris, Didot, 1862.

Lohmeyer, Ernst. *Grundlagen paulinischer Theologie*. BzHTh 1. Tübingen: J. C. B. Mohr (Paul Siebeck) 1929.

Lorenz, Alfred. *Der musikalische Aufbau des Bühnenfestspieles* Der Ring des Nibelungen. 2nd ed. Tutzing: Schneider, 1966.

Luke, David, ed. *Goethe, Faust Part One*. Oxford World's Classics. 1987. Reprint. Oxford: Oxford University Press, 1998.

———, ed. *Goethe, Faust Part Two*. Oxford World's Classics. 1994. Reprint. Oxford: Oxford University Press, 1998.

———, ed. *Goethe: Selected Verse*. 1964. Reprint. London: Penguin, 1986.

Luther, Martin. *Die Gantze Heilige Schrift Deudsch 1545*. 3 vols. Edited by Heinz Blanke and Hans Volz. Munich: Rogner & Bernhard, 1972.

McClatchie, Stephen. *Analyzing Wagner's Operas: Alfred Lorenz and German Nationalist Ideology*. Rochester, NY. University of Rochester Press, 1998.

McCreless, Patrick. *Wagner's Siegfried: Its Drama, History, and Music.* Studies in Musicology 59. Ann Arbor, MI: UMI Research, 1982.

McManus, Laurie. "Feminist Revolutionary Music Criticism and Wagner Reception: The Case of Louise Otto." *19th Century Music* 37.3 (2014) 161–87.

McNaughton, David. "Intuitionism." In *The Blackwell Guide to Ethical Theory*, edited by Hugh LaFollette, 268–87. Blackwell Philosophy Guides. Oxford: Blackwell, 2000.

Macquarrie, John. "Jesus Christus VI." *TRE* 17:16–42.

Magee, Bryan. *Wagner and Philosophy.* London: Penguin, 2001.

———. *Aspects of Wagner.* 2nd ed. Oxford: Oxford University Press, 1988.

Magee, Elizabeth. *Richard Wagner and the Nibelungs.* Oxford: Clarendon, 1990.

Magnusson, Magnus, and Hermann Pálsson, ed. *Njal's Saga.* Harmondsworth, UK: Penguin, 1975.

Mann, Thomas. "Leiden und Größe Richard Wagners." In *Thomas Mann Essays, Band 4: Achtung, Europa! 1933–1938*, edited by Hermann Kurzke and Stephan Stachorski, 11–72. Frankfurt am Main: Fischer, 1995.

———. "Sorrows and Grandeur of Richard Wagner." In *Pro and Contra Wagner*, edited by Patrick Carnegy, 91–148. Translated by Allan Blunden. Introduction by Erich Heller. London: Faber and Faber, 1985.

Mann, William. *Siegfried: English Translation and Thematic Guide.* Royal Opera Texts. n.d.

———. *Götterdämmerung; English Translation and Thematic Guide.* Royal Opera Texts. n.d.

Marschner, Heinrich. *Hans Heiling: Romantischer Oper.* Libretto by Eduard Devrient. Piano reduction by Gustav F. Kogel. Leipzig: Friedrich Hofmeister, n.d.

Mason, Eudo C. *Goethe's Faust: Its Genesis and Purport.* Berkeley: University of California Press, 1967.

Matthews, Denis. *Beethoven.* Master Musicians. London: Dent, 1985.

Marx, Karl, and Friedrich Engels. *The Communist Manifesto.* With an introduction and notes by Gareth Stedman Jones. London: Penguin, 2002.

Max, Hermann. "Notes on the Performance of Bach's St. John Passion in the Version by Robert Schumann." CPO, 2006.

Melderis, H. *Raum—Zeit—Mythos: Richard Wagner und die modernen Naturwissenschaften.* Hamburg: Europäische Verlagsanstalt, 2001.

Miller, A. V., ed. *Hegel's Phenomenology of Spirit with an Analysis of the Text and Foreword by J. N. Findlay.* Oxford: Oxford University Press, 1977.

Millington, Barry, ed. *The Wagner Compendium: A Guide to Wagner's Life and Music.* London: Thames and Hudson, 1992.

———. "The Ring and Its Times: The Social and Political Background to the Tetralogy." In *Wagner's Ring and Its Icelandic Sources: A Symposium at the Reykjavík Arts Festival, 29 May 1994*, edited by Úlfar Bragason, 17–30. Reykjavík: Stofnun Sigurðar Nordals, 1995.

———. "Myths and Legends." In *The Wagner Compendium: A Guide to Wagner's Life and Music*, edited by Barry Millington, 132–38. London: Thames and Hudson, 1992.

———. "Wagner's Revolutionary Musical Reforms." *WagRS*, 14–16.

———. *Wagner.* MM. 1984. Reprint. Oxford: Oxford University Press, 2000.

Mohr, Wolfgang. "Mephistopheles und Loki." *Deutsche Vierteljahrsschrift für Literaturwissenschaft und Geistesgeschichte* 18 (1940) 173–200.

Most, Glenn W., ed. *Hesiod I: Theogony, Works and Days, Testimonia.* LCL 57. Cambridge: Harvard University Press, 2006.

Müller, Karl Otfried. *Geschichten hellenischer Stämme und Städte.* 3 vols. Breslau: Josef Max, 1844 (DB 96; Wahnfried).

Müller, Carl Otfried. *History and Antiquities of the Doric Race.* Translated by Henry Tufnell and George Cornewall Lewis. 1830. Reprint. 2 vols. Cambridge: Cambridge University Press, 2010.

Müller, Wilhelm. *Geschichte und System der altdeutschen Religion.* Göttingen: Vandenhoeck und Ruprecht, 1844.

Munz, Peter. *Frederick Barbarossa: A Study in Medieval Politics.* London: Eyre & Spottiswoode, 1969.

Murray, A. T., ed. *Homer: The Iliad.* 2 vols. 1924–25. Reprint. LCL 170–71. Cambridge: Harvard University Press, 1985.

Murray, A. T., ed. *Homer: The Odyssey.* 2 vols. LCL 104–5. Revised by George E. Dimock. Cambridge: Harvard University Press, 1995.

Nattiez, Jean-Jacques. *Wagner Androgyne: A Study in Interpretation.* Translated by Stewart Spencer. Princeton, NJ: Princeton University Press, 1993.

Nelis, Damien P. "Lyric Poetry." OCD^3 899–901.

Das Neue Testament, unseres Herrn und Heilandes Jesu Christi. Leipziger Jubelausgabe, nach der letzten Ausgabe Dr. Martin Luthers (vom Jahre 1545) revidiert von Hofrath Dr. (E. G.) Gersdorf und Dr. K. A. Espe. Leipzig: Möller, 1845.

Newman, Ernst. *The Life of Richard Wagner.* 4 vols. London: Cassell, 1933–47.

———. *A Study of Wagner.* 1899. Reprint. New York: Vienna House, 1974.

Nietzsche, Friedrich. *The Anti-Christ, Ecce Homo, Twilight of the Idols and Other Writings.* CTHP. Edited by Aaron Ridley and Judith Norman. 2005. Reprint. Cambridge: Cambridge University Press, 2012.

———. *Beyond Good and Evil.* CTHP. Edited by Rolf-Peter Horstmann and Judith Norman. 2002. Reprint. Cambridge: Cambridge University Press, 2018.

———. *Untimely Meditations.* Edited by Daniel Breazeale. Translated by R. J. Hollingdale. CTHP. 1997. Reprint. Cambridge: Cambridge University Press, 2001.

Nisbet, H. B. "Religion and Philosophy." In *The Cambridge Companion to Goethe*, edited by Lesley Sharpe, 219–31. Cambridge: Cambridge University Press, 2002.

Nolte, Erich. *Studien zu Richard Wagner's dramatischen Fragmenten im Zusammenhange seiner Entwicklung von 1841–56.* Berlin: Hermann Blanke, 1917.

Nordvig, Mathias. "Creation from Fire in Snorri's Edda: The Tenets of a Vernacular Theory of Geothermal Activity in Old Norse Myth." In *Old Norse Mythology—Comparative Perspectives*, edited by Pernille Hermann, Stephen A. Mitchell, and Jens Peter Schjødt, with Amber J. Rose, 269–88. Publications of the Milman Parry Collection of Oral Literature No. 3. Cambridge: Harvard University Press, 2017.

Nygren, Anders. *Commentary on Romans.* Philadelphia: Fortress, 1949.

Oberkogler, Friedrich. *Richard Wagner von Ring zum Gral: Wiedergewinnung seines Werkes aus Musik und Mythos.* Stuttgart: Freies Geistesleben, 1978.

Onnasch, Ernst-Otto. "Teleologie." In *Hegel-Lexikon*, edited by Paul Cobben, Paul Cruysberghs, Peter Jonkers, and Lu De Vos, 439–41. Darmstadt: Wissenschaftliche Buchgesellschaft, 2006.

Orchard, Andy, ed. *The Elder Edda.* London: Penguin, 2011.

Origenes. *Der Kommentar zum Evangelium nach Mattäus*, eingeleitet, übersetzt und mit Anmerkungen versehen von Hermann J. Vogt, Zweiter Teil. Bibliothek der griechischen Literatur 30. Stuttgart: Hiersemann, 1990.

Osthövener, Claus-Dieter. "Konstellationen des Erlösungsgedankens." In *Wagnerspectrum: Bayreuther Theologie*, 51–80. Würzburg: Königshausen & Neumann, 2009.

Peil, Peter. *Die Krise des neuzeitlichen Menschen im Werk Richard Wagners*. Cologne: Böhlau, 1990.

Perschmann, Wolfgang. *Die optimistische Tragödie: Sinndeutende Darsstellung*. Graz: Österreicher Richard-Wagner-Society, 1986.

Pfeiffer, Franz. "Volksbüchlein von Kaiser Friedrich." *Zeitschrift für deutsches Alterthum* 5 (1845) 250–67 (DB 168).

Porges, Heinrich. *Wagner Rehearsing the 'Ring': An Eye-Witness Account of the Stage Rehearsals of the First Bayreuth Festival*. Translated by Robert L. Jacobs. Cambridge: Cambridge University Press, 1983.

Praeger, Ferdinand. *Wagner, wie ich ihn kannte*. Leipzig: Breitkopf & Härtel, 1892.

Preuss, Horst Dietrich. *Old Testament Theology*. Translated by Leo G. Perdue. 2 vols. Edinburgh: T. & T. Clark, 1995–96.

Procksch, Otto. *Die Genesis*. KzAT 1. Leipzig: Deichertsche, 1924.

Proudhon, Pierre-Joseph. *Philosophie der Staatsökonomie oder Nothwendigkeit des Elends*. Translated by Karl Grün. 2 vols. Darmstadt: Carl Wilhelm Leske, 1847.

———. *Qu'est-ce que la propriété: ou Recherche sur le principe du droit et du gouvernement*. Paris: Libraire de Prévot, 1840.

Prutz, Hans. *Kaiser Friedrich I*. 3 vols. Danzig: A. W. Kasemann, 1871–74 (Wahnfried).

Rad, Gerhard von. *Old Testament Theology*. Translated by D. M. G. Stalker. 2 vols. London: SCM, 1975.

Ranke, Leopold. *Deutsche Geschichte im Zeitalter der Reformation*. 5 vols. Berlin: Dunker und Humblot, 1842–43 (1: 1842^2; 2: 1842^2; 3: 1843^2; 4: 1843; 5: 1843) (DB 111)

Rappl, Erich. "Aspekte einer musikalischen Weltschöpfung." In *Wagner 1976*, edited by Stewart Spencer, 8–29. London: The Wagner Society, 1976.

Rask, Rasmus. *Snorra-Edda*. Stockholm, 1818.

Raumer, Friedrich von. *Geschichte der Hohenstaufen und ihrer Zeit*. 2nd ed. 6 vols. Leipzig: F. A. Brockhaus, 1840–41. Wagner possessed vols 1 (1840); 2 (1841); 4 (1841) (DB 112).

Rawidowicz, S. *Ludwig Feuerbachs Philosophie: Ursprung und Schicksal*. 2nd ed. Berlin: Walter de Gruyter, 1964.

Resen, Peder (Resenius), Stephan Olafsen, and Gudmundur Andreae. *Edda Islandorum*. Copenhagen, 1665.

Ritter, Johann Wilhelm. *Fragmente aus dem Nachlasse eines jungen Physikers: Ein Tachenbuch für Freunde der Natur*. 2 vols. Heidelberg: Mohr und Zimmer, 1810.

Robertson, Ritchie. *Goethe: A Very Short Introduction*. Oxford; Oxford University Press, 2016.

Robinson, J. A. T. *Honest to God*. London: SCM, 1963.

Rousseau, Jean-Jacques. "Essay on the Origin of Languages, which Treats of Melody and Musical Imitation." In *On the Origin of Language: Two Essays*, translated with afterwords by John H. Moran and Alexander Gode, 1–74. Chicago: University of Chicago Press, 1966.

Rückert, Friedrich. *Gedichte von Friedrich Rückert*. Frankfurt am Main: Johann David Sauerländer, 1841.

Rückert, Heinrich, ed. *Friedrich Rückert's gesammelte poetische Werke in zwölf Bänden*. Neue Ausgabe. Frankfurt am Main: Johann David Sauerländer, 1882.

Ruffell, Ian A. *Aeschylus: Prometheus Bound*. Companions to Greek and Roman Tragedy. Bristol: Bristol Classical, 2012.

Rühs, Friedrich. *Die Edda nebst einer Einleitung über nordische Poesie und Mythologie und einem Anhang über die historische Literatur der Isländer*. Berlin: Realschulbuchhandlung, 1812 (DB 119).

Sabor, Rudolph. *Richard Wagner: Die Walküre*. London: Phaidon, 1997.

———. *Richard Wagner: Götterdämmerung* London: Phaidon, 1997.

Santaniello, Weaver. "A Post-Holocaust Re-examination of Nietzsche and the Jews." In *Nietzsche and Jewish Culture*, edited by Jacob Golomb, 21–54. London: Routledge, 1997.

Saxo Grammaticus. *Saxonis Grammatici Historia Danica. Recensuit et commentariis illustravit Petrus Erasmus Müller. Opus morte Mülleri interruptum absolvit Joannes Matthias Velschow*. 2 vols. Havniae [Copenhagen]: Gyldendal, 1839 (DB 125).

Schad, Martha, ed. *Cosima Wagner und Ludwig II. von Bayern—Briefe: Eine erstaunliche Korrespondenz*. Bergisch Gladbach: Gustav Lübbe, 1996.

Schaff, Philip, and David S. Schaff, ed. *The Creeds of Christendom. With a History and Critical Notes*. 3 vols. 1931. Reprint. Grand Rapids: Baker, 1983.

Schelling, Friedrich Wilhelm Joseph von. *Philosophical Investigations into the Essence of Human Freedom*. Translated and with an introduction by Jeff Love and Johannes Schmidt. SUNY Series in Contemporary Continental Philosophy. Albany, NY: State University of New York Press, 2006.

Schiller, Friedrich. *Sämtliche Werke*. 12 vols. Stuttgart: J. G. Cotta, 1838 (DB 126).

Schimmelmann, Jacob. *Die Isländische Edda*. Stettin: Stuck, 1777.

Schlegel, Friedrich. *Lucinde and the Fragments*. Translated with an introduction by Peter Firchow. Minneapolis: University of Minnesota Press, 1971.

———. "Über die Diotima." *KFSA* 1.1:70–115.

Schleiermacher, Friedrich Daniel Ernst. *Schriften aus der Berliner Zeit 1796–1799*, edited by Günter Meckenstock. Kritische Gesamtausgabe I.2. Berlin: Walter de Gruyter, 1984.

Schofield, Paul. The *Redeemer Reborn: Parsifal as the Fifth Opera of Wagner's Ring*. New York: Amadeus, 2007.

Schuler, John. *The Language of Richard Wagner's Ring des Nibelungen*. Lancaster, PA: Steinman & Foltz, 1909.

Schwally, Friedrich. "Die biblischen Schöpfungsberichte." *Archiv für Religionswissenschaft* 9 (1906) 159–84.

Scruton, Roger. *The Ring of Truth: The Wisdom of Wagner's Ring of the Nibelung*. Milton Keynes, UK: Allen Lane, 2016.

Seeberg, Erich. *Grundzüge der Theologie Luthers*. Stuttgart: W. Kohlhammer, 1940.

Seung, T. K. *Goethe, Nietzsche, and Wagner: Their Spinozan Epics of Love and Power*. Lanham, MD: Lexington, 2006.

Shakespeare, William. *Shakespeare's dramatische Werke nach der Uebersetzung von August Wilhelm Schlegel und Ludwig Tieck*. Revised by H. Ulrici. 12 vols. Berlin: Georg Reimer, 1867–71 (Wahnfried).

Simrock, Karl, ed. *Das Amelungenlied*. 3 vols. Das Heldenbuch, vols 4–6. Stuttgart: J. G. Cotta'scher, 1843–49 (DB 3).

———, ed. *Die Edda: die ältere und jüngere nebst den mythischen Erzählungen der Skalda*. Stuttgart: J. G. Cotta'scher, 1851.

Skelton, Geoffrey. "A Conflict of Power and Love." In *The Valkyrie/Die Walküre, Richard Wagner*, 7–13. Opera Guide 21. London: Calder, 1983.

Slotki, Judah J., ed. *Midrash Rabbah: Numbers*. 2 vols. London: Soncino, 1983.
Smith, Charles Forster, ed. *Thucydides I: History of the Peloponnesian War, Books I and II*. LCL 108. Cambridge: Harvard University Press, 2008.
Smith, Joseph P. *St. Irenaeus: Proof of the Apostolic Preaching*. Ancient Christian Writers. The Works of the Fathers in Translation 16. Westminster, MD: Longmans, Green and Co., 1952.
Smith, Margaret E. M. "Anaxagoras." *OCD*³ 85.
Sommerstein, Alan, ed. *Aeschylus*. 2 vols. LCL 145–46. Cambridge: Harvard University Press, 2008.
Spencer, Stewart. *Wagner Remembered*. London: Faber and Faber, 2000.
———. "The 'Romantic operas' and the turn to myth." In *The Cambridge Companion to Wagner*, edited by Thomas S. Grey, 67–73. Cambridge: Cambridge University Press, 2008.
Spencer, Stewart, and Barry Millington. *Wagner's Ring of the Nibelung: A Companion*. London: Thames & Hudson, 2010.
Stadtwald, Kurt. *Roman Popes and German Patriots: Antipapalism in the Politics of the German Humanist Movement from Gregor Heimbarg to Martin Luther*. Geneva: Libraire Droz, 1996.
Stein, Heinrich von. "Ueber Werke und Wirkungen Rousseau's." *Bayreuther Blätter* 4 (Dezember Zwölftes Stück 1881) 345–56.
Stewart, Jon. "Hegel's Philosophy of Religion of the Question of 'Right' and 'Left' Hegelianism." In *Politics, Religion, and Art: Hegelian Debates*, edited by Douglas Moggach, 66–95. Evanston, IL: Northwestern University Press, 2001.
Storck, Karl, ed. *Letters of Robert Schumann*. Translated by Hannah Bryant. London: John Murray, 1907.
Strobel, Otto. *Richard Wagner: Skizzen und Entwürfe zur Ring-Dichtung: Mit der Dichtung "Der junge Siegfried."* Munich: Bruckmann, 1930.
Stuhlmacher, Peter. *Biblische Theologie des Neuen Testaments. Band 1: Grundlegung: Von Jesus zu Paulus*. Göttingen: Vandenhoeck & Ruprecht, 1992.
Sturluson, Snorri. *Heimskringla: History of the Kings of Norway*. Translated with introduction and notes by Lee M. Hollander. 1964. Austin, TX: University of Texas Press, 1999.
Swanwick, Anna, ed. *Goethe's Faust*. Edited with an introduction by Karl Breul. London: Bell and Sons, 1928.
Talbert, Charles H, ed. *Reimarus Fragments*. Translated by Ralph S. Fraser. London: SCM, 1971.
Tappert, Theodore G. *The Book of Concord: The Confessions of the Evangelical Lutheran Church*. Philadelphia: Fortress, 1959.
Taylor, Charles. *Hegel*. Cambridge: Cambridge University Press, 1975.
Thorau, Christian. "Guides for Wagnerites: Leitmotifs and Wagnerian Listening." In *Richard Wagner and His World*, edited by Thomas S. Grey, 133–50. Princeton, NJ: Princeton University Press, 2009.
Thucydides, *History of the Peloponnesian War, Books I–II*. Translated by Charles Forster Smith. LCL 108. 1928. Reprint. Cambridge: Harvard University Press, 1991.
Trigg, Joseph Wilson. *Origen: The Bible and Philosophy in the Third-century Church*. London: SCM, 1985.
Turchin, Barbara. "The Nineteenth-century *Wanderlieder* Cycle." *The Journal of Musicology* 5 (1987) 498–525.

Turville-Petre, E. O. G. *Myth and Religion of the North: The Religion of Ancient Scandinavia*. London: Weidenfeld and Nicolson, 1964.

Uhland, Ludwig. *Gedichte*. Stuttgart: J. G. Cotta'scher, 1842 (DB 145).

Vaget, Han Rudolf. "Strategies for Redemption: *Der Ring des Nibelungen* and *Faust*." In *Wagner in Retrospect: A Centennial Reappraisal*, edited & with an introduction by Leroy R. Shaw, Nancy R. Cirillo, and Marion S. Miller, 91–104. Amsterdam: Rodopi, 1987.

Vazsonyi, Nicholas. *Richard Wagner: Self-Promotion and the Making of a Brand*. Cambridge: Cambridge University Press, 2010.

Villiers de l'Isle-Adam, Philippe-Auguste. "Souvenir." *Revue Wagnérienne* 3.5 (1897) 139–41.

Vischer, Friedrich. *Faust: Der Tragödie dritter Theil in drei Acten: Treu im Geiste des zweiten Theils des Goetheschen Faust gedichtet von Deutobold Symbolizetti Alegoriowitsch Mystifizinsky*. Tübingen: Laupp'schen, 1862.

———. "Die Litteratur über Goethes Faust." In *Kritische Gänge: Band 2*, 49–215. Tübingen: Ludwig Friedrich Fues, 1844.

———. "Vorschlag zu einer Oper." In *Kritische Gänge: Band 2*, 397–436. Tübingen: Ludwig Friedrich Fues, 1844.

Wagner, Nike. *The Wagners: The Dramas of a Musical Dynasty*. Translated by Ewald Osers and Michael Downes. London: Weidenfeld & Nicolson, 2000.

Walker, Alan. *Hans von Bülow: A Life and Times*. Oxford: Oxford University Press, 2010.

Wapnewski, Peter. *Weißt du wie das wird . . . ? Richard Wagner: Der Ring des Nibelungen*. Munich: Piper, 1996.

Warner, Emma. "The Artwork of the Future." *The Wagner Journal*, Special Issue (2013).

Warrack, John. "The Musical Background." In *The Wagner Companion*, edited by Peter Burbidge and Richard Sutton, 85–112. London: Faber and Faber, 1979.

Weder, Hans. "Der Mythos vom Logos (Johannes 1). Überlegungen zur Sachproblematik der Entmythologisierung." In *Mythos und Rationalität*, edited by Hans Heinrich Schmid, 44–75. Gütersloh: Gütersloher Verlagshaus Gerd Mohn, 1988.

Weinert, Friedel. *Copernicus, Darwin, & Freud: Revolutions in the History and Philosophy of Science*. Oxford: Wiley-Blackwell, 2009.

Weinhold, Karl. "Die Sagen von Loki." *Zeitschrift für deutsches Alterthum* 7 (1849) 1–94.

Weischedel, Wilhelm, ed. *Immanuel Kant. Werke in Zehn Bänden*. 1956-64. Reprint. Darmstadt: Wissenschaftliche Buchgesellschaft, 1983.

Weisse, Christian Hermann. *Grundzüge der Metaphysik*. Hamburg: Friedrich Perthes, 1835.

———. *Die philosophische Geheimlehre von der Unsterblichkeit des menschlichen Individuums*. Dresden: Ch. F. Grimmer, 1834.

Wellendorf, Jonas. "The Æsir and Their Idols." In *Old Norse Mythology—Comparative Perspectives*, edited by Pernille Hermann, Stephen A. Mitchell, and Jens Peter Schjødt, 89–110. Publications of the Milman Parry Collection of Oral Literature No. 3. Cambridge: Harvard University Press, 2017.

Wenham, Gordon. *Genesis 1–15*. Word Biblical Commentary. Waco, TX: Word, 1987.

Westermann, Claus. *Genesis 1–11: A Commentary*. Translated by John J. Scullion. London: SPCK, 1974.

Westernhagen, Curt von. *Die Entstehung des "Ring": Dargestellt an den Kompositionsskizzen Richard Wagners*. Zurich: Atlantis, 1973.

———. *The Forging of the "Ring": Richard Wagner's Composition Sketches for Der Ring des Nibelungen*. Translated by Arnold and Mary Whittall. Cambridge: Cambridge University Press, 1976.

———. *Richard Wagners Dresdener Bibliothek 1842 bis 1849*. Wiesbaden: F. A. Brockhaus, 1966.

———. *Richard Wagner: Sein Werk, sein Wesen, seine Welt*. Zurich: Atlantis, 1956.

———. *Wagner: A Biography*. Translated by Mary Whittall. 2 vols. Cambridge: Cambridge University Press, 1978.

Westernhagen, Dörte von. "Und was haben Sie vor 1945 gemacht? Der Wagner-Forscher Curt von Westernhagen." In *Wagnerspectrum: Wagner und Liszt*, 83–99. Würzburg: Königshausen & Neumann, 2011.

Whaley, Joachim. *Germany and the Holy Roman Empire, Volume 1: Maximilian I to the Peace of Westphalia, 1493-1648*. Oxford: Oxford University Press, 2012.

Whybray, R. N. *Isaiah 40–66*. New Century Bible Commentary. 1975. Reprint. Grand Rapids: Eerdmans, 1981.

Wille, Eliza. *Erinnerungen an Richard Wagner. Mit 15 Briefen Richard Wagners*. Zurich: Atlantis, 1982.

Williams, Simon. *Wagner and the Romantic Hero*. Cambridge: Cambridge University Press, 2004.

Windell, George G. "Hegel, Feuerbach, and Wagner's Ring." *Central European History* 9.1 (1976) 27–57.

Winterbourne, A. T. "Wagner's Ring and the Nature of Freedom; Some Kantian Speculations." *British Journal of Aesthetics* 28.4 (1988) 341–52.

Wintle, Christopher. "The Numinous in *Götterdämmerung*." In *Reading Opera*, edited by Arthur Groos and Roger Parker, 200–234. Princeton, NJ: Princeton University Press, 1988.

Wolzogen, Hans von. *Führer durch die Musik zu Richard Wagner's Festspiel Der Ring des Nibelungen: Ein thematischer Leitfaden*. Neue wohlfeile Ausgabe. Leipzig; Feodor Reinboth, n.d.

Wood, Allen W. "Fichte's Philosophy of Right and Ethics." In *The Cambridge Companion to Fichte*, edited by David James and Günter Zöller, 168–98. Cambridge: Cambridge University Press, 2016.

Young, Julian. *The Philosophies of Richard Wagner*. Lanham, MD. Lexington, 2014.

———. *Schopenhauer*. Routledge Philosophers. London: Routledge, 2005.

Zegowitz, Bernd. *Richard Wagners unvertonte Opern*. HBzdL 8. Frankfurt am Main: Lang, 2000.

Index of Authors

Abbate, Carolyn, 67, 238
Aichelle, Alexander, 104
Allen, Roger, 274, 287
Ambos, A.W., 286
Apel, Friedmar, xv
Apponyi, Albert, 241, 244
Aristotle, 76, 83
Arnkiel, Trogillus, 48
Auber, Daniel François, 116–17
Aulén, Gustaf, 246, 250
Avemarie, Friedrich, 15

Baader, Franz von, 159–60
Baeumlein, Wilhelm, 94
Bailey, Robert, 253
Baillie, J.B., 100
Barr, James, 91, 169
Barth, Herbert, xvii
Bauer, Hans-Joachim, xvi
Bayer, Oswald, 287
Begbie, Jeremy S., 275
Behler, Ernst, xv, 124
Beiser, Frederick C., 25, 76–77, 124, 161
Bell, Richard H., 3, 20, 31, 51, 72, 89, 93, 122, 138, 145, 162, 169, 183, 206–9, 215, 270, 272–73, 277–78, 284, 288
Benjamin, Walter, 284, 286–87
Berger, Karol, 103–4
Bergfeld, Joachim, xiii
Bermbach, Udo, 105
Bernharðsson, Haraldur, 273
Bernstein, Walter Heinz, 289
Berry, Mark, 41, 109, 115, 124, 197, 201–2
Björnsson, Árni, 20, 42, 61, 98, 223, 225
Borchmeyer, Dieter, xv–xvi, 55, 82, 96, 115, 126, 129, 145, 211, 277, 280, 285
Borthwick, Alastair, 275
Böttger, Adolf, 29
Boulez, Pierre, 116

Brandon, S.G.F., 11–12
Breig, Werner, xiv, xvii
Brown, Andrew L., 167
Brown, Jane K., 78
Brown, Raymond E., 19
Brueggemann, Walter, 33, 64
Bryant, Hannah, 269
Bultmann, Rudolf, 25, 113, 271
Burmeister, Klaus, xvi
Bury, R.G., 76
Byock, Jesse, 27, 162, 224
Byron (George Gordon), *see Index of Subjects and Names*

Carlyle, Thomas, 53–54, 105
Carr, E.H., 4
Cassuto, U., 160
Catling, Richard W.V., 36
Chadwick, Mark B., 53
Childress, James F., 186
Clement of Alexandria, 74
Cormack, David, 52–53
Cleasby, Richard, 88
Clemen, Otto, 247
Coleridge, Samuel Taylor, 285
Colli, Giorgio, xiv–xv
Cooke, Deryck, 47, 61, 69, 82, 97–98, 145, 173, 175, 178, 287
Corse, Sandra, 74, 99–100, 125, 128, 158, 196–97, 215
Crossley, James G., 184

Dahlhaus, Carl, 65, 274
Darcy, Warren, 61, 64, 66, 142, 252, 273–74
Darwin, Charles, 68, 72, 75
Dawson-Bowling, Paul, 61, 227
Deathridge, John, xvii, 4, 56–57, 66, 68, 141, 143, 147, 197, 230, 275, 284, 287
Defoe, Daniel, 140

307

INDEX OF AUTHORS

Descartes, René, 76, 83
Devrient, Eduard, 3–5, 83
Dimock, George E., 38
Dindorf, Wilhelm, 94
Dischner, Gisela, 124
Döge, Klaus, 289
Doepler, Carl Emil, 33, 254
Donington, Robert, 46, 153, 210
Dreyfus, Laurence, 117, 133–35, 164–68
Drinker, Henry S., 289
Dronke, Ursula, 22, 28–32, 34, 56, 88, 162, 180, 243, 274
Droysen, Johann Gustav, 105
Dürrer, Martin, xvi–xvii
Dyson, Michael, 74

Ebeling, Gerhard, 49–50
Eberhardt, H., 111
Edwards, Cyril, xvi
Eichner, Hans, 123
Eichrodt, Walther, 32
Elliott, J.K., 242
Ellis Davidson, H.R., 22, 202, 253–54, 276
Ellis, William Ashton, xiii, xvi, 6, 9, 52–53, 125, 128, 130, 133, 153, 155, 167, 183, 185, 215, 280
Engel, Erich, 3
Engels, Friedrich (Frederick), xv, 1, 103
Estes, Douglas, 275–76
Ettmüller, Ludwig, 28, 30–31, 56, 88, 274
Eyth, Eduard, 94

Fairley, Barker, 86
Faulkes, Anthony, 19, 27–28, 32, 42–43, 48–49, 60, 88, 145, 202, 224, 228, 242–43, 253, 283
Feenberg, Andrew, 125
Feuerbach, Ludwig, *see Index of Subjects and Names*
Fichte, Immanuel Hermann, xiv, 104
Fichte, Johann Gottlieb, *see Index of Subjects and Names*
Finch, R.G., 28, 145, 224–25, 228, 242
Finlay, Alison, 19, 145
Fischer, Johannes, 271
Fladt, Hartmut, xiv, 289
Fletcher, Joseph, 186, 188
Flew, Anthony, 206
Forner, Johannes, xvi
Foster, Daniel H., 35, 94, 104
Fouqué, Friedrich Baron de la Motte, 88, 220
Fowler, Harold North, 206
Frauer, Ludwig, 210–11
Frazer, James George, 39

Fricke, Gerhard, xiv
Friedrich, Ernst F., 123
Friedrich, Sven, xvi, 255
Friend, Lionel, 230, 259
Fuchs, Ernst, 288
Fuchs, Hanns, 162–63, 165, 167–69
Fuhrmans, Horst, 286

Gebhardt, Hans, xvi
Geck, Martin, xvii
Geraets, T.F., 216
Gerstenberger, Erhard S., 32
Glasenapp, Carl Fr., 8
Gobineau, Arthur, 221
Göpfert, Herbert G., xiv
Göschel, Carl Friedrich, 196
Goethe, Johann Wolfgang, *see Index of Subjects and Names*
Golther, Wolfgang, 20, 35, 171
Goodspeed, Edgar J., 242
Gray, Andrew, xv
Gregor-Dellin, Martin, xiii–xv, 6, 52, 95, 106, 116, 122, 126, 202–3
Grey, Thomas S., 71–72, 85, 119, 286
Grimm, Jacob, *see also Index of Subjects and Names*, 3, 22–23, 33–34, 42–44, 48, 50, 54, 56–57, 73, 82, 108–10
Grimm, Wilhelm, 54
Großmann-Vendrey, Susanna, 143

Hagen, Friedrich von der, 54
Hall, Jonathan M., 36
Halmi, Nicholas, 285
Harris, H.S., 216
Hart, Trevor, 275
Harvey, Van A., 121, 132
Haymes, Edward R., 10, 24, 27, 38, 41–42, 47, 88, 91–92, 95, 180, 184, 204–5, 220, 223, 238, 240–41, 243, 250–51, 254, 266, 270
Hébert, Marcel, 33
Hegel, G.W.F., *see Index of Subjects and Names*
Heine, Heinrich, 109
Helmholtz, Hermann, 52, 61, 69, 85
Hengel, Martin, 12
Herder, Johann Gottfried, 39, 72, 75, 103, 169
Hirsch, Emmanuel, 247
Hodgson, Peter C., 217
Hoffmann, Franz, xiv
Hofmann, Kurt, 143
Honderich, Ted, xvi
Hooker, Brad, 186
Hornblower, Simon, xvi
Hotho, Heinrich Gustav, 25

INDEX OF AUTHORS

Houlgate, Stephen, 16, 66, 75, 98–99, 122, 125–27, 138, 186, 196
Huber, Herbert, 86, 141, 195, 202
Hübner, Kurt, 25, 73, 110
Hübscher, Arthur, 68
Humberger, Julius, xiv
Hutton, M., 22

Inwood, Michael J., 75, 84, 182
Iljin, Iwan, 217

Jameson, Frederick, 289
Jeans, James, 53
Jeffrey, Steve, 246
Jesch, Judith, 273
Jestremski, Margret, xvi
Jost, Christa, 289
Jüngel, Eberhard, 15, 85, 217, 285, 288

Kalbeck, Max, 143
Kant, Immanuel, *see Index of Subjects and Names*
Käsemann, Ernst, 185, 188
Kaul, Camilla G., 106–8
Kienzle, Ulrike, 11
Kirchmeyer, Helmut, 203
Kirkpatrick, Robin, 56
Kitcher, Philip, 41, 142–44, 191, 225, 266
Kirschbaum, Engelbert, xv
Klindworth, Karl, 289
Knatz, Lothar, 84
Knaupp, Michael, xiv
Knox, T.M., 16, 125–26, 186
Koch, Michael, 51
Köhler, Joachim, 109
König, Eduard, 160
Kraft, Isabel, xvi
Kreckel, Manfred, 103
Krömmelbein, Thomas, 48, 50
Kropfinger, Klaus, xvi
Krüger, Eduard, 269
Küng, Hans, 216–17
Kuzniar, Alice, 168

Lamb, W.R.M., 161
Larrington, Carolyn, 27, 162
Lassen, Annette, 43
Laurence, Dan H., 95, 102, 178, 283
Leaver, Robin, 269
Lehmann, H.T., xv
Lehrs, Franz Siegfried (Levi, Samuel), 94, 115
Leibniz, Gottfried Wilhelm, 76, 85
Little, Margaret, 186
Lohmeyer, Ernst, 85
Löhneysen, Wolfgang Frhr. von, xiii

Lorenz, Alfred, 66–67
Luke, David, 26, 35, 37, 39–40, 44, 55, 57–60, 75, 78–79, 84–87, 163, 221
Luther, Martin, *see Index of Subjects and Names*

McClatchie, Stephen, 66
McCreless, Patrick, 263, 281
McManus, Laurie, 187
McNaughton, David, 186
Mack, Dietrich, xiii, xvii
Macquarrie, John, 242
Magee, Bryan, 91, 280
Magee, Elizabeth, 20, 28, 34, 42–44, 47, 82, 98, 101, 138, 219–20
Magnusson, Magnus, 46, 254
Mann, Thomas, 65, 158
Mann, William, 197, 230
Marschner, Heinrich, 203
Mason, Eudo C., 39
Matthews, Denis, 8, 95
Marx, Karl, xv, 1, 99, 103, 115, 218
Max, Hermann, 269
Medicus, Fritz, xv
Melderis, H., 53
Mielke, Andreas, xvi–xvii
Miller, A.V., 35, 98–100, 111, 168, 248
Millington, Barry, xvii, 11, 99, 103, 115–16, 197, 256
Mohr, Wolfgang, 44
Monti, Anthony, 275
Montinari, Mazzino, xiv–xv
Most, Glenn W., 95, 115, 226
Müller, Karl (Carl) Otfried, 35–37
Müller, Wilhelm, 98
Munz, Peter, 106, 108–11
Murray, A.T., 38, 94

Nattiez, Jean-Jacques, 71, 116, 130, 146–47, 151, 153, 156–61, 163, 196
Nelis, Damien P., 37
Newman, Ernst, 116, 141, 187, 203, 289
Nietzsche, Friedrich, *see Index of Subjects and Names*
Nisbet, H.B., 76, 216–18
Nolte, Erich, 6
Nordvig, Mathias, 55
Nygren, Anders, 9

Oberkogler, Friedrich, 174
Onnasch, Ernst-Otto, 84
Oppermann, Annette, 289
Orchard, Andy, 27–29, 31, 37, 43, 46, 48, 88, 144–45, 149, 173, 202, 204, 224, 228, 242, 254

INDEX OF AUTHORS

Osthövener, Claus-Dieter, 272
Ovey, Mike, 246

Pálsson, Hermann, 46, 254
Payne, E.F.J., xvi–xvii
Peil, Peter, 68
Pelikan, J., xv
Perschmann, Wolfgang, 61
Pfeiffer, Franz, 110–11
Porges, Heinrich, 68–69, 116–17, 229, 233, 253, 259, 263
Praeger, Ferdinand, 7
Preuss, Horst Dietrich, 32–33
Procksch, Otto, 160
Proudhon, Pierre-Joseph, 11–12, 102–3, 185
Prutz, Hans, 106

Rad, Gerhard von, 32
Raffel, Burton, xvi
Ranke, Leopold, 105–6
Rappl, Erich, 45
Rask, Rasmus, 48
Raumer, Friedrich von, 106
Rawidowicz, S., 50, 215
Resen, Peder (Resenius), 48
Richardson, Alan, xiv–xv
Ritter, Johann Wilhelm, 159
Robertson, Ritchie, 85–86, 163
Robinson, J.A.T., 188
Rousseau, Jean-Jacques, 71–72, 178
Rückert, Friedrich, 108
Ruffell, Ian A., 94
Rühs, Friedrich, 56, 243

Sabor, Rudolph, 173, 200, 203, 229
Sach, Andrew, 246
Sadie, Stanley, xv
Salaquada, Jörg, xvi
Salter, Lionel, xvii
Santaniello, Weaver, 8
Saxo Grammaticus, 173
Schacht, Richard, Philip, 41, 142–44, 191, 225, 266
Schad, Martha, 7
Schaff, David S., 17, 158, 246–47
Schaff, Philip, xvi, 17, 158, 246–47
Schelling, Friedrich Wilhelm Joseph von, *see Index of Subjects and Names*
Schiller, Johann Christoph Friedrich von, *see Index of Subjects and Names*
Schimmelmann, Jacob, 48, 50
Schlegel, A.W., *see Index of Subjects and Names*
Schlegel, Friedrich, *see Index of Subjects and Names*
Schleiermacher, Friedrich Daniel Ernst, *see Index of Subjects and Names*
Schofield, Paul, 97
Schopenhauer, Arthur, *see Index of Subjects and Names*
Schröter, Manfred, xvii
Schuler, John, 181
Schwally, Friedrich, 160
Scruton, Roger, 163, 259
Seeberg, Erich, 247
Seung, T.K., 39, 58, 78–79
Shakespeare, William, *see also Index of Subjects and Names*, 32, 227
Shaw, George Bernard, 95, 102, 178, 283
Sibree, J., 87, 123, 218
Simrock, Karl, *see Index of Subjects and Names*
Singer, Otto, 289
Skelton, Geoffrey, xiii, 115, 119, 172
Slotki, Judah J., 14
Smith, Charles Forster, 36
Smith, Joseph P., 74
Smith, Margaret, 79
Sommerstein, Alan, 225, 265
Spencer, Stewart, xiii, xvii, 110, 197, 244
Stadtwald, Kurt, 110
Stein, Heinrich von, 8
Steinsiek, Angela, xvi
Stewart, Jon, 196
Storck, Karl, 269
Strobel, Gertrud, xvi
Strobel, Otto, xv, 28, 34, 54, 61, 117–18, 133, 140, 150, 195, 200, 243, 251, 259
Stuhlmacher, Peter, 188
Sturluson, Snorri, 27, 243
Suchting, W.A., 216
Swanwick, Anna, 86

Tacitus, Cornelius, 22
Talbert, Charles H, 270
Tappert, T.G., 50
Taylor, Charles, 55
Thies, Erich, xv
Thorau, Christian, 278
Thucydides, 36
Trigg, Joseph Wilson, 206
Turchin, Barbara, 29
Turville-Petre, E.O.G., 30–31, 243

Uhland, Ludwig, 29

Vaget, Han Rudolf, 248
Vazsonyi, Nicholas, xiv, 65
Vetter, Isolde, xiv
Villiers de l'Isle-Adam, Philippe-Auguste, 20

INDEX OF AUTHORS

Vischer, Friedrich, 248
Vogt, Hermann J., 246
Voss, Egon, xiv, xvii, 289
Voss, Johann Heinrich, 94

Wagner, Nike, 100–101, 144
Wagner, Cosima, *see Index of Subjects and Names*
Wagner, Richard, *see Index of Wagner's Works; Index of Subjects and Names*
Walker, Alan, 143
Wapnewski, Peter, 233
Warner, Emma, 75, 84, 156, 166, 215–16
Warrack, John, 203
Weder, Hans, 25
Weinert, Friedel, 83
Weinhold, Karl, 43–44
Weischedel, Wilhelm, 83–84
Weisse, Christian Hermann, 84, 182, 196
Wellendorf, Jonas, 22

Wenham, Gordon, 86
Westermann, Claus, 64
Westernhagen, Curt von, 53–54, 94, 110, 211, 261, 263
Westernhagen, Dörte von, 53
Whaley, Joachim, 107
Whittall, Mary, xv, 274
Whybray, R.N., 64
Wille, Eliza, 54, 165
Williams, Simon, 28–29
Windell, George G., 113, 131–32
Winterbourne, A.T., 97, 113
Wintle, Christopher, 238, 253
Wolf, Werner, xvi
Wolzogen, Hans von, 67, 253, 259, 286
Wood, Allen W., 104
Young, Julian, 68, 129

Zegowitz, Bernd, 3, 12, 96, 106, 178–79, 183, 212

Index of Biblical Texts

I Old Testament

Genesis

1:1—2:25	73, 179, 185
1:1–19	97
1:2	64–65, 72
1:12	86
1:21	86
1:25	86
1:27	160
1:28	179
1:31	160
1:31a	93
2:2b—3:24	169, 215
2:4b–25	74, 276
2:9	73
2:11–12	73, 93
2:16–17	93
2:17	13
2:18	160
2:20	97
2:21–23	161
3:1–24	48, 74, 89, 91, 93
6:1–4	48
6:20	86
7:14	86
37:1—50:26	218

Exodus

3:2–3	211
3:5	211
20:2—31:17	50

Leviticus

11:14–29	86
25:47–49	245
25:49	245

Deuteronomy

21:23	30
24:1–4	185
32:1–43	33
32:8–9	49

1 Kings

17:1	22
18:41	22
18:45	22

Job

41:3	15

Psalms

42:1–2	7
51:1b	251
51:3b	251
51:9b	251
51:10 (12)	87
51:11b	251
82:6	14

INDEX OF BIBLICAL TEXTS

Isaiah

10:22	207
33:16	242
43:24b–25	251
43:25b	251
51:9	64
52:13—53:12	237, 251
57:2	272

Daniel

2:34	242

II New Testament

Matthew

5:17–48	188
5:17	188
5:21	188
5:27	188
5:31	188
5:33	188
5:38	188
5:43	188
11:18	17
11:28–30	272
11:28–29	188
12:28	272
19:3b–8	185
19:5–6	185
20:28	246
21:18–20	111
21:45–46	10
26:20	10
26:28	270
27:38	269

Mark

1:11	50
3:6	10
9:7	50
10:45	246, 270
11:12–14	111
11:20–21	111
12:29–34	15
14:24	270
15:27	269
15:34	30, 264

Luke

4:25	22
17:21	9
22:20	270
23:32	269
23:39b	269
23:40–43	269

John

1:1–18	25
1:1–4	76
1:4	76
1:18	19
3:16	51, 121
10:30	14
10:31–33	14
10:34–38	14
11:50–51	241
11:57	10
17:3	182
19:18	269
19:21	10
19:28	266, 269
19:34	30

Acts of the Apostles

5:30	30
10:39	30
13:29	30
17:23b–29	13
17:26–29	26
17:28	13, 26, 181

Romans

1:18	51
1:24–32	169
3:21–26	246
3:24–25	247
5:1—8:39	9
5:6–8	123
5:12–21	89
5:12	93
5:15–19	255
5:18	93, 282
7:6	13
7:6a	13
7:7	188
7:8	89
7:9–10	13

INDEX OF BIBLICAL TEXTS

7:12	208
8:2	188
8:3–4	13
8:32	19
9:1—11:36	207–8
9:17–29	207
9:18	207
9:19–21	207
9:27	207
10:3	15
11:25–27	207
11:28	207
11:32	270
13:8–10	188
13:8–9	188
13:10	188

1 Corinthians

6:20	246
7:23	246
11:25	270
13:9	216
14:11	166
15:24–26	18
15:31–32b	18
15:36	18
15:46	18
15:55–56	18

2 Corinthians

3:6	13
5:17	272

Galatians

3:13	30

Ephesians

5:25	144

1 Thessalonians

4:13	272

2 Thessalonians

2:8–12	198

1 Timothy

4:1	17
6:10	96

Hebrews

4:1–11	272
9:13–14	17

James

5:17	22

1 Peter

2:24	251

1 John

2:7	123
3:3–8	123
3:9	123
3:15–24	123
4:8	123
4:9–12	123
5:3–4	123

Revelation

1:8	50, 276
1:11	276
1:12–16	29
5:12	29
9:17–18	56
11:19—12:17	51
21:1	276
21:5–8	50
21:6	276
22:13	276

Index of Wagner's Works

I Der Ring des Nibelungen

Ring des Nibelungen, Der, see also Siegfried's Tod (1848); Rheingold; Walküre; Siegfried; Götterdämmerung
   Angelo Neumann's Berlin production of, 221
   first performance of, 61, 254, 263
Nibelungen-Mythus, Der
   "All-father" in, 27
   Brünnhilde as "divine virgin" in, 254
   children in, 24
   death of Brünnhilde in, 251
   death of Siegmund in, 38
   gods in, 24
   guilt of the gods in, 237–38, 250
   incest in, 184
   ring purified in, 251
   sacrifice of Siegfried in, 237–38, 250–51
   Urgesetz in, 180
Siegfried's Tod (1848)
   Brünnhilde enters Valhalla in, 204–5
   gods redeemed in, 251, 253
   Nibelungs liberated in, 251, 253
   Siegfried enters Valhalla in, 204–5
   sacrifice of Siegfried in, 251–52, 270
   Wotan as All-father in, 27, 204–5
   Wotan as ruling god in, 24, 205, 252
Rheingold, Das, see also Index of Subjects and Names (Alberich; Erda; Fafner; Freia; Fricka; Loge; Mime; Wotan)
   Alberich as "capitalist" in, 11, 89, 95–96, 102
   Alberich's sin in, 89, 91–93
   and "creator God", 65
   birth of consciousness in, 69–75
   creation in, 60–69, 84
   cursing of ring in, 44
   Erda's warning in, 40–41, 177, 189–91
   Fasolt in, 42, 44, 54, 61, 82, 94, 135, 139, 178, 249–50
   Fafner as *Wurm* in, 149
   Fafner in, 44, 54, 94, 178, 253
   father Rhine in, 65
   Flosshilde in, 65, 72, 74, 90, 93, 116
   Freia ransomed in, 245
   Loge on love in, 162–63
   lovelessness in, 89, 92
   Mime as "slave" in, 99
   music for Prelude of, 53, 65–68
   music for Scene 1 of, 71, 73
   Prosaskizza (prose sketches; November 1851) for, 54, 65, 113
   Prosaentwurf (prose draft; 23–31 March 1852) for, 65
   renouncing/cursing of love in, 69, 72, 89–92, 97, 127, 252, 259
   theft of Rhinegold in, 69, 113, 282
   Wellgunde in, 69, 72, 74, 90, 93
   Woglinde in, 61, 69, 71–74, 80, 90, 259
Walküre, Die, see also Index of Subjects and Names (Brünnhilde; Hunding; Sieglinde; Siegmund; Wotan)
   Brünnhilde as Wotan's will in, 150, 157, 210–11
   Brünnhilde's incarnation in, 20, 50, 197, 242, 253, 255–65, 269, 283–84
   Brünnhilde's loss of divinity in, 37, 121, 195, 242, 258
   Brünnhilde's freedom in, 211–13,
   death of Siegmund in, 19, 32, 38, 51, 200, 209, 283
   erotic love in, 135–40
   first (Munich) performances (1870) of, 203
   Fricka representing "law" in, 172, 187
   Fricka's self-righteousness in, 250
   Hunding in, 12, 79, 99, 101, 114–15, 137–40, 142, 145, 173–74, 184, 186, 197, 211, 250
   inspired by Mathilde Wesendonck, 133, 141, 171

Walküre, Die (continued)
   Prosaskizzen (prose sketches; November 1851) for, 133–34
   Prosaentwurf (prose draft; 17–26 May 1852) for, 140, 200
   Sieglinde "saves" Siegmund in, 164, 197
   Siegmund as "outsider" in, 128
   Siegmund's rejection of immortality in, 200, 203, 256
   Todesverkündigung in, 28, 119, 144, 198–200, 202–3, 256
   Wotan's loses power in, 263
   Wotan in Act I in, 140–41
   Wotan's Monologue (Act II) in, 91, 117–18, 120, 150, 179, 191–93, 253
Siegfried/Der junge Siegfried, see also Index of Subjects and Names (Brünnhilde; Erda; Fafner; Mime; Siegfried; Wanderer)
   androgyny in, 146, 153, 156–57, 162
   Brünnhilde as Siegfried's "mother" in, 149
   Brünnhilde as "singer" in, 150–51, 266
   Brünnhilde as *Wurm* in, 147–48, 151, 154–55
   Brünnhilde incorporates Siegfried in, 162, 164, 197
   Brünnhilde "saves" Siegfried in, 164, 197
   Erstschrift des Textbuches (verse draft; 3–24 June 1851) of, 27, 34, 118, 243
   Mime's desire for ring in, 96–97, 249
   music for Act III/3 of, 263
   Prelude to Act III of, 286–87
   Siegfried as Sun-god in, 146, 149, 157
   Prosaskizzen (prose sketches; c. 3–24 May 1851) for, 54, 243
   Prosaentwurf (prose draft; 24 May–1 June 1851) for, 117
   theme of "gratitude" in, 120
   Wanderer as powerless in, 212
   Wanderer's denial of will in, 281
   Woodbird in, 82, 87, 146, 151
   Wurm in, 34, 54, 86–87, 110, 120, 151, 249
Götterdämmerung/Siegfried's Tod, see also *Siegfried's Tod* (1848); Index of Subjects and Names (Brünnhilde; Gunther; Gutrune; Hagen; Siegfried; Wotan)
   betrayal of Brünnhilde in, 83, 240
   Brünnhilde as God-forsaken in, 227, 230, 241, 264–65, 283
   Brünnhilde as redeemer in, 51, 242, 252, 255, 265, 269, 281, 283
   Brünnhilde communes with Rhinemaidens in, 238–39, 269–70
   Brünnhilde incorporates Siegfried in, 156, 241
   Brünnhilde recovers divinity in, 156, 238, 242
   Brünnhilde's counter-oath in, 274
   Brünnhilde's freedom in, 216, 240
   ends on plagal cadence, 274
   Feuerbach ending of, 274–75
   "glorification of Brünnhilde" in, 275
   Hagen as demonic in, 249–50
   music for Act I/3 of, 225, 233
   sacrifice of Brünnhilde in, 19, 50, 127, 241, 265, 270–71, 273, 283
   sacrifice of Siegfried in, 83, 240, 251, 265, 270–71, 273, 283
   Schopenhauer ending of, 249, 274
   Siegfried as Christ in, 266, 269, 283
   Siegfried as "outsider" in, 128
   Siegfried as possible rapist in, 117, 222, 225, 227, 229–30, 239, 241
   Siegfried's death in, 37, 46, 237–38, 240–41, 252, 265–66, 269
   Siegfried's Funeral March in, 119, 238
   Siegfried's oath in, 233
   Siegfried on *Urgesetz* in, 180
   Siegfried's redemptive death in, 241–42, 251–52, 265–66
   Siegfried's transfiguration in, 221, 237, 241
   Wotan "put to rest" in, 32, 263, 272–73
Götterdämmerung: Zu Brünnhilde's Schlußworten, 251

II Other Musical and Stage works

Achilles, 6, 167, 202
Alexander, 6
Feen, Die, 142
Fliegende Holländer, Der, 129
   and Anton Mesmer, 159
   Dutchman as "outsider" in, 128
   love in, 131, 133
   redemption through love in, 122, 136
   Senta in, 136, 159
Friedrich I, 106–7, 110, 112
Jesus von Nazareth
   Adam (immediate offspring of God) in, 11, 282
   and *Lohengrin,* 5–6
   as tragedy, 4, 6, 16
   Bakunin on, 4
   Barabbas in, 9–10
   crucifixion in, 17
   death in, 183, 206
   death of Jesus in, 16, 265, 282
   Holy Spirit in, 198

House of David in, 11
Jesus as messiah in, 10, 198
Jesus as redeemer in, 16–17
Jesus' relation to Adam in, 11, 282
Jesus' relation to David in, 11, 282
Jesus' sacrifice in, 198
Judas in, 9–10
Liszt's support for, 6
Ludwig's enthusiasm for, 7
music for, 6, 8
music for "Christus im Schiffe", 5
on gratitude, 119–20
on love, 2, 9, 183–84, 212
on possession, 183
on property, 183
Peter in, 67, 265
Pharisees in, 10–11, 185, 187, 272
Pilate in, 10–11, 16
redemption through love in, 13
resurrection of Levi's daughter in, 198
second coming in, 109, 198
sin in, 12–14, 17, 183–84, 282
suffering of Jesus in, 212, 282
Liebesverbot, Das, 142
Lohengrin, 21, 129
and failed incarnation, 137
and failed redemption, 137
and *Jesus of Nazareth*, 5–6
Elsa in, 21, 129, 131, 134, 136–37
Lohengrin in, 21, 128–29, 131, 134, 136–37
love in, 134–37
Nibelungenlied in, 223
Ortrud in, 42, 203
passionate love in, 133
redemption through love in, 122, 136
Luthers Hochzeit, 108
Meistersinger von Nürnberg, Die
as comic opera, 6
cultural nationalism in, 103
"singing" in, 151
Walther as "outsider" in, 128
Parsifal
androgyny in, 162
as Christian work, 28
as goal of *Ring*, 241
Blick in, 138
"creation" of Parsifal in, 8
Parsifal as outsider in, 128
pessimistic anthropology in, 215
revelation in, 277
Schopenhauer modified in, 21
Rienzi, der Letzte der Tribunen, 142
Sarazenin, Die, 8, 106
Tannhäuser und der Sängerkrieg auf Wartburg

Elisabeth in, 136
love in, 133
Nietzsche on, 169
passionate love in, 133
"pornography" in 136
redemption through love in, 122, 136
sensuality in, 131
Venus in, 131, 136
Venusberg, 169
Tristan und Isolde, see also Index of Names and Subjects (Tristan; Isolde), 263
and androgyny, 158
and correction to Schopenhauer, 21, 171
and Ludwig II, 165
Blick in, 138
ends on plagal cadence, 274
Frau Minne in, 173
Liebestod in, 156
love in, 123
love and death in, 155–56
Tristan's wooing in, 181
union of lovers in, 158
Wieland der Schmied, 156

III Writings

Actors and Singers, 280
Against Vivisection (Open Letter to Ernst von Weber), 84
Annals, 3–4, 107, 202
Art and Revolution, 104
Apollo in, 36–37, 88, 181
dragon in, 37, 88
Jesus in, 37
on love, 13
on *Urgesetz*, 181
Artwork of the Future
and Ludwig II, 165
Feuerbach in, 215–16
Hegel in, 84, 216
on "amorphous" love, 133–34
on emergence of life, 75, 84, 215
on error, 75, 84, 93, 215, 282
on fall, 75, 215
on freedom, 215–16
on knowledge, 84, 93, 215, 282
on *Kunst*, 125
on masculine within femininity, 153, 156
on necessity, 215
on passionate love, 132
on property, 102–3
on same-sex love, 165–66
on the state, 104

INDEX OF WAGNER'S WORKS

Beethoven, see also Index of Subjects and Names, 277
Beethoven's Choral Symphony at Dresden, 1846, 4, 277–78
Brown Book, 3–4, 8, 107, 166, 202
Communication to my Friends, A
    on emotionalising of the intellect, 278
    on Flying Dutchman, 273
    on *Jesus of Nazareth*, 3, 8
    on *Liebesverlangen*, 133
    on love, 122, 134–35
    on music as love, 113
    on "purely human", 129
    on *Die Sarazenin*, 106
    on structuralist interpretation of myth, 21
Epilogue to the "Nibelung's Ring", 64, 181, 276
Happy Evening, A, 168
Herodom and Christianity, 220
Judaism in Music, 273
Music of the Future, 183
My Life, 3–4, 59, 102, 106–7, 158, 170, 186, 201, 219, 246
On German Opera, 116
Open Letter to Friedrich Nietzsche, 73
Open Letter to Herr Ernst von Weber, see *Against Vivisection*, 84
Opera and Drama
    handwriting for, 3
    on aesthetics, 277
    on annulling the state, 128–29
    on Antigone, 126–30, 212
    on fate, 213–14
    on *Gefühlsverständniß*, 279
    on incest, 144–46
    on Jocasta, 126, 129–30
    on *Liebesverlangen*, 133
    on love as cognitive, 125
    on melodic moments, 278
    on melody/harmony/poetry, 71
    on melody/speech, 71
    on music as woman, 74
    on Oedipus myth, 126–31
    on organicism, 77
    on poet (male)/music (female), 151–52, 164
    on poet (male)/musician (male), 164–65
    on purely human, 128–29
    on science and Christianity, 55
    on understanding (male)/feeling (female), 130–31
Pilgrimage to Beethoven, 63
    on creation, 63–64
    on nature, 64
Public and Popularity, 53
Reminiscences of Auber, 116
Religion and Art, 94, 207, 285
Toast on the Tercentenary of the Royal Kapelle at Dresden, 159
What is German, 166, 187
What Use Is This Knowledge? 26
Wibelungen, The
    Apollo in, 34–35, 110
    Christ in, 107, 110, 282–83
    dragon in, 34–35
    Friedrich Barbarossa in, 106–7, 109–12, 283
    hoard in, 15, 107, 109
    race in, 110, 282
    Siegfried in, 34–35, 107, 109–11, 282–83
    Wuotan in, 65

Index of Subjects and Names

absolute, the
    and *Lucinde*, 123
    Hegel on, 217
Achilles, 285
    love for Patroclus of, 167
    rejection of immortality of, 202–3
Adam
    and Christ, 11, 282
    and Odin, 50
    as androgynous, 160
    as "child of God", 74
    as Christ's ancestor, 11, 282
    as "offspring of God", 11, 282
    disobedience of, 93
    fall of, 13, 215, 282
    human being "in Adam", 281
    in *Jesus of Nazareth*, 11, 282
    in *Prose Edda*, 48
    naming animals, 97
    sin of, 93
    Wanderer as, 50, 281–84, 286
Aeschylus, 36
    Agamemnon, 265
    Eumenides, 39
    Prometheus Bound, 225
    on Patroclus, 167
Æsir, 22, 65–68, 86
aesthetics, 277–80
Ahasuerus
    Dutchman as, 21, 129
    "going under" (*Untergang*) of, 273
    redemption of, 273
Alberich (*Ring*), 43, 72, 86, 92, 115–16, 178, 191,
        193, 208, 212
    and Hagen, 89, 120
    and love, 90
    and power, 102
    as "capitalist", 11, 89, 95–96, 102
    as demonic figure, 93–94
    as "Jew", 10–11, 95–96
    as "Schwarz-Alberich", 97
    as survivor, 250
    desire for ring of, 103, 192, 253
    fall of, 89–94
    love-curse of, 127
    love for power of, 97, 102
    lust of, 74, 90, 113
    relationship to Mime of, 89, 94, 96, 99, 249
    renounces/curses love, 69, 89–91, 97, 127
    sin of, 89, 91–93
    steals Rhinegold, 69, 113, 282
    subjugates Grimhilde, 99, 118
    Wagner's sympathy for, 118, 249
Alexander the Great, 6
Alexander III, Pope, 110
Alhazen (Ibn al-Haytham), 33
allegory
    and Jesus' incarnation, 197
    and leitmotifs, 286
    and poetry, 286
    and symbol, 285–86
    W. Benjamin on, 284
    Christian, 50, 208, 242, 283–84
    Coleridge on, 285
    consistent, 283
    exchangeable nature of, 285
    Goethe on, 286
    inconsistent, 51, 283–84
    instability of, 19, 284
    in *Revelation*, 51
    mythic, 50, 277, 284–86
    Ring as, 19, 50, 208
    Schelling on, 284–86
    Schopenhauer on, 286
Amelungenlied, 55
Anaxagoras
    Goethe on, 59–60, 79, 218
    Hegel on, 217–18

INDEX OF SUBJECTS AND NAMES

androgyne
  immortality of, 159
androgyny
  and Siegfried, 156–57, 162
  and *Wieland*, 156
  Baader on, 159–60
  Gfrörer on, 162
  of Adam, 160, 162
  of Brünnhilde, 146, 153, 156–57, 162
  of Christ, 156, 159, 162
  Plato's *Symposium* on, 158–59
  J. W. Ritter on, 159
  F. Schlegel on, 161
  Schleiermacher on, 124, 161
  Wagner on, 164
Andvari, 224
Angrboda, 45
animals, *see also Fafner, as dragon; dragon; midgard serpent; ravens; Wolf (Fenrir)*
  Adam's naming of, 97
  desire for multiplication of, 160
  dragons, 48
  Hegel on, 87
  in J. Grimm's *Mythology*, 25
  in *Ring*, 86–88
  Old Testament sacrifice of, 17, 208, 271
  Siegfried and Brünnhilde acting like, 170
  Siegmund and Sieglinde acting like, 170
  Wagner's love of, 84, 87, 172
  Wotan and Erda acting like, 118, 170
  Wurm, 86–88
Anselm of Canterbury, 246
Antigone
  and music drama, 129–30
  annuls state, 127
  as patron saint of music drama, 129
  as virgin (*Jungfrau*), 212
  love of, 127, 129, 212
  love-curse of, 127
Apel, Theodor, 29
Apollo, 39, 79, 81, 147
  and Dorians, 36
  and Jesus, 37
  and Siegfried, 33, 36–37
  as sun-god, 33, 36–37, 149
  fights Python, 35–36, 88, 110
appearances (*Erscheinungen*), *see phenomenal world*
Aristotle, 76, 83
Arminius, 104
Arnkiel, Trogillus, 48
Arnold of Brescia, 107–8
art, *see also Index of Wagner's Works (Religion and Art)*
  and renewal/revolution, 1, 104–5, 128–29, 213–14
  cognitive nature of, 125
  commercialization of, 1
  for art's sake, 1
  origins of, 84
Artemis/Diana, 37, 79, 147
Aslaug (*Völsunga Saga*), 283
atonement
  and exclusive place-taking, 208, 271
  and inclusive place-taking, 208, 271
  and "new creation", 272
  and "satisfaction", 31, 246
  and Trinity, 31
  Anselm on, 246
  Calvin on, 246
  "classic" view of, 250
  in *Hávamál*, 30–31
  in *Ring*, 251–52, 271, 283
  Luther on, 250
  penal substitution, 208, 246
  "theories of", 271
  Wagner on, 17, 271
Auber, Daniel François Esprit, 116–17
Augustine of Hippo, 272
  Confessions, 272, 275
  on original sin, 21
  on predestination, 275
  on sexual sin, 169–70
  on time, 275
  pessimism of, 21, 93

Baader, Franz von, 159–60
Bach, Johann Sebastian,
  St Matthew Passion, 8, 269
  St John Passion, 6, 266, 268–69
Bakunin, Mikhail, 4, 102
Baldr, 115, 274
  death of, 37, 44, 46, 243
Baldrs draumar (Baldr's dreams/Vegtamskvida), 28, 43
Balzac, Honoré de, 95
baptism
  and Norse mythology, 30
  of Jesus, 11, 50
  of Wagner, 246
Bathilde (*Wieland der Schmied*), 156
Bayreuth Festival Theatre, *see Festspielhaus*
Beethoven, Ludwig van
  Christus am Ölberg, 8
  Symphony no. 3 (*Eroica*), 61, 275
  Symphony no. 7, 95
  Symphony no. 9, 4, 8, 57, 66, 78, 152
  Wagner's admiration for, 8, 104

INDEX OF SUBJECTS AND NAMES

Bendemann, E., 107
Berlioz, Hector (*Les Troyens*), 114
Bismarck, Otto von, 105
Blick (look)
    and erotic love, 138–39
    in *Parsifal*, 138
    in *Tristan*, 138
    of Brünnhilde, 154
    of Freia, 139
    of gods, 239
    of Sieglinde, 139
    of Siegmund, 210
    of Siegfried, 225
    of Wotan, 141
blood
    and Last Supper, 270
    and sexual arousal, 154–55
    as atonement, 240, 247, 270
    German, 22–23
    of animals, 17
    of Christ, 17, 247, 270
    of Fafner (*Wurm*), 151, 154–55
    of Python, 35
    of Volsungs, 138, 143
    of Ymir, 60
blood-brotherhood, 240
Bolin, Wilhelm, 50
Brahms, Johannes, 143
Brünnhilde (*Nibelungen-Mythus*)
    as divine virgin, 254
    death of, 251
    on *Urgesetz*, 180
    parentage of, 24
Brünnhilde (*Siegfried's Tod*, 1848)
    as child of Wotan, 24
    death of, 251
    enters Valhalla, 204–5
    immortality of, 204–5
    sacrificed *to gods*, 270
Brünnhilde (*Ring des Nibelungen*), see also marriage
    and Fricka, 38, 177
    and Wotan's "thought", 149
    as androgenous, 146, 153, 156–57, 162
    as "Christ", 19, 255, 269, 283–84
    as corporate personality, 162
    as divine, 9, 19, 26, 37–38, 253, 255
    as God-forsaken, 227, 230, 241, 264–65, 283
    as incorporating Siegfried, 156, 162, 164, 197, 241
    as "music", 151, 153
    as "the other", 212, 253
    as Prometheus, 225–26, 258
    as redeemer, 51, 242, 252, 255, 265, 269, 281, 283
    as Siegfried's "mother", 149
    as "singer", 150–51, 266
    as "slave", 99–101
    as *Über-Weib*, 25–55
    as virgin, 264
    as Wish-Maid (*Wunsch-Maid*), 27, 101
    as witness to love of Volsungs, 135, 143–44
    as "Woodbird", 151
    as Wotan's favorite daughter, 32, 51, 119, 172–73
    as Wotan's will, 150, 157, 210–211
    as *Wurm*, 147–48, 151, 154–55
    assaulted by Siegfried (Gunther), 225–26
    betrayal of, 83, 240
    character tarnished, 227, 233
    communes with Rhinemaidens, 238–39, 269–70
    compassion of, 227–28, 254
    death of, 50–51, 156, 251, 265, 269–71
    divinity of, 254
    embodies music, 151
    erlösende Weltenthat of, 51, 252, 265, 269, 283
    freedom of, 211–13, 215–16, 240
    "glorification of", 275
    "grows wise", 83, 240
    immortality of, 156, 194–95, 197, 199, 203, 254
    incarnation of, 20, 50, 197, 242, 253, 255–65, 269, 283–84
    incorporates Siegfried, 156, 162, 164, 197, 241
    in *Todesverkündigung*, 28, 119, 144, 198–200, 202–3, 256
    in "Wotan's monologue", 91, 117–18, 120, 150, 179, 191–93, 253
    laughter of, 238
    loss of divinity of, 37, 121, 195, 242, 258
    loss of immortality of, 197
    loss of Valkyrie status of, 258, 263–64
    love for the world of, 271
    love of, 51, 101, 120–21 149–50, 212, 271
    makes love like an "animal", 170
    nobility of, 227, 254
    oath (on Hagen's spear) of, 233, 235–37
    plots Siegfried's death, 237
    protected by Loge, 45
    puts Wotan to rest, 32, 263, 272–73
    recovers divinity, 156, 238, 242
    sacrifice of, 19, 50, 127, 241, 265, 270–71, 273, 283
    "saves" Siegfried, 164, 197

INDEX OF SUBJECTS AND NAMES

Brünnhilde (*Ring des Nibelungen*) (*continued*)
   self-consciousness of, 100, 125
   subjugated by Siegfried (Gunther), 99
   suffering of, 241, 264
   transfiguration of, 241
   transformation of, 113, 203,
Brynhild (Norse mythology), 37, 203–4, 222–24, 227–28, 253–54, 283
Budli, 227
Bülow, Cosima von, *see Wagner, Cosima*
Bülow, Daniela von, 54, 82
Bülow, Hans von, 143
Byron (George Gordon),
   Childe Harold, 29
   Manfred, 29

Caiaphas, 10, 240
Calderón de la Barca, Pedro, 184
   confused court of, 284, 286
Calvin, John, 246
capitalism, 2, 11, 88–89, 95–96, 102, 249
caprice (*Willkür*), 182, 212–16
Catholicism, 23, 104, 187, 248
cause (causation)
   efficient, 76
   final, 83–84
Chéreau, Patrice, 187
Christianity, *see Catholicism; Protestantism*
Church, Protestant, *see Protestantism*
Church, Roman Catholic, *see Catholicism*
civilization, 68, 145, 169
Clement of Alexandria, *Protrepticus*, 74
communism, 11, 103, 115
concept (*Begriff*), 20–21, 160, 82
consciousness, birth of, 69–75
cosmogony
   Ring as, 68
cosmology,
   Kant on, 83
   in *Ring*, 52, 68, 273
created order, *see also nature*
   goodness of, 51, 73, 89
   structuring of, 86
creation (act of)
   and Beethoven's *Ninth*, 63
   J. Grimm on, 56
   in 4004 BC, 5
   in *Book of Common Prayer*, 51
   in *Rheingold*, 60–61, 63–64, 66, 69, 84
   new (New Testament), 272
   new (*Ring*), 276
   of artwork, 65, 283, 285
   Wagner on, 5, 14

creation myth
   Norse, 60, 65–66, 75
   Old Testament, 64, 72–73, 93

"dance", 53, 55
Dante Alighieri, *see also Liszt, Dante Symphony*, 56
Darwin, Charles, 68, 72, 75
death
   acceptance of, 196–97, 250
   and birth, 206
   and immortality, ix, 2, 134, 189–206
   and kissing, 147–48, 156–57
   and law, 13
   and love, 123, 132, 147–48, 155–56
   and Pandora's box, 94
   and sexual union, 158
   and sin, 93
   as existential problem, 206, 250
   as natural, 250
   fear of, 99, 193, 250
   Feuerbach on, 206
   freedom from, 9
   Hegel on, 196–97, 218
   "laughing", 155, 157
   Liebestod, 123
   of Baldr, 37, 44, 46, 243
   of Brünnhilde, 50–51, 156, 251, 265, 269–71
   of Friedrich I, 110
   of God, 218, 242
   of gods, 47, 49
   of Jesus, 10, 12, 16–17, 30, 156, 184, 198, 212, 240, 243, 246–47, 265–66, 270–71, 275, 282
   of Odin, 32
   of Siegfried, 37, 46, 237–38, 240–41, 250–52, 265–66, 269, 282
   of Siegmund, 19, 32, 38, 51, 200, 209, 283
   of Sivrit, 223
   realm of, 35
   reconciliation with, 18
   redemption from, 9, 17–18, 247, 250
   Todesverkündigung, 28, 119, 144, 198–200, 202–3, 256
Delavigne, Germain, 116
Delphic oracle, 37, 181
Descartes, René, 76, 83
Deutschland, Das junge, 248
devil, *see also Satan*, 17, 25, 44, 50, 246–47, 249–50
Devrient, Eduard, 83
   Geschichte der deutschen Spielkunst, 3
   on *Jesus of Nazareth*, 4–5

INDEX OF SUBJECTS AND NAMES

Dionysus
    festival of, 279
divorce, 185, 188
Doepler, Carl Emil (costumes),
    for Erda, 254
    for Wotan/Wanderer, 33
    Cosima on, 254
dogma, religious, 128, 214
Donar (Norse mythology), 22
Donner (*Ring*), 19, 26, 42, 45, 47, 54, 77, 98, 162
Dorians, 36–37
dragon (*Art and Revolution*), 37, 88
dragon (*Die Wibelungen*), 34–36, 88
dragon (*Ring*), 33, 54, 102, 138, 151, 191, 229–30, 283
Dresden
    Dresden choral society, 269
    Kreuzkirche, 246
    library of Wagner in, 3, 12, 29, 43, 56, 76, 94, 106, 110, 112, 115, 158, 168, 185, 211, 269
    Royal library, 34
    uprising in, 11, 103
Dühring, Eugen, 8
Dürer, Albrecht (*Melencolia*), 287,
Dumas, Alexandre, 6
Dutchman (*Der fliegende Holländer*)
    as Odysseus, 21, 129
    as outsider, 128
    as wandering Jew, 21, 129
    love for Senta of, 136
    redemption of, 273
    Untergang of, 273
duty
    Fichte on, 124
    Hegel on, 16, 187
    Kant on, 124, 187
    Schleiermacher on, 124
    Wagner on, 120, 129

Ecken Ausfahrt (von der Hagen), 54
Edda, see Elder Edda, Prose Edda
egoism, 5, 18, 103, 131, 134, 152, 156, 158, 179, 182, 196
Elder Edda, see also *Völuspá*; *Hávamál*; *Vafthrúdnismál*; *Grímnismál*; *För Skírnis*; *Hymiskvida*; *Lokasenna*; *Thrymskvida*; *Grípisspá*; *Fáfnismál*; *Sigrdrífumál*; *Sigurdarkvida in skamma*; *Helreid Brynhildar*; *Baldrs draumar*, 27–28, 43, 56, 145, 222, 224, 242, 253, 283
elements of nature, four, 53, 55
    air, 57–59
    earth, 57–59
    Empedocles on, 33
    fire, 57–60
    gods related to, 54, 57
    Goethe, *Faust I* on, 57–58
    Goethe *Faust II* on, 58–59
    J. Grimm on, 25, 56–57, 73
    journeys through (in *Ring*), 56–57
    water, 57–60, 73
Elisabeth (*Tannhäuser*), 136
Ellis, William Ashton, xiii, xvi, 6, 9, 52–53, 125, 128, 130, 133, 153, 155, 167, 183, 185, 215, 280
Elsa (*Lohengrin*)
    as "redeemer", 137
    as Semele, 21, 129, 134
    love for Lohengrin of, 131, 136
emotionalising of the intellect (*Gefühlswerdung des Verstandes*), 149, 214, 278–80
Empedocles, 33
Engels, Friedrich, 1, 103
Erda, 24, 26–27, 39–41, 44, 47, 54, 57, 99, 115, 118, 153, 170, 177, 189–92, 194, 227, 239, 251–52, 254, 269
    as Virgin Mary, 254
"Erda" leitmotif, 86, 173, 286
erotic love, see also love; Wagner, on erotic love
    and knowledge, 125
    and shame, 169–70
    between men, 165–67
    in *Song of Songs*, 123
    in *Walküre*, 135–40
    redemption from, 21, 171
    redemption through, 21, 171
    renunciation of true, 91
eternal Jew, the (*ewige Jude, Der*), see Ahasuerus
eternal feminine/womanly, see also Goethe *Faust II*; Gretchen; love, 78, 157
ethics, see also intuitionism; particularism; situation ethics, 169
    love as criterion for, 186–88
    of duty, 124
    sexual, 38, 172–88
Euclid, 33
Euripides
    Iphigeneia at Aulis, 32
Eve/Eva (Genesis 1–3), 13
    and androgyny, 159–60
    as female Christ, 159
    as innocent, 282
    fall of, 215
    in *Jesus* sketches, 13
    in *Prose Edda*, 48

INDEX OF SUBJECTS AND NAMES

evolution, *see* Darwin, Charles; Lamarck, Jean-Baptiste
    Hegel on, 55, 68, 75
    Schopenhauer on, 53, 66, 68
existential displacement, 287–88
eye, *see also* Blick
    extramission theory, 33
    intramission theory, 33

Fafner (*Ring*)
    as "devil", 249
    as giant, 44, 54, 94, 178, 253
    as *Wurm*, 34, 54, 86–87, 110, 120, 151, 249
    representing papacy, 201, 221
Fáfnismál, 29, 37, 88, 250
faith, *see also* Jesus Christ, faith in; Index of Biblical Texts
    and God, 49–50
    and reason, 214
    Feuerbach on, 50
    Hegel on, 196
    Luther on, 49–50
    of Wagner, 185
fall
    Hegel on, 74, 87
    of Adam, 13, 215, 282
    of Alberich, 89–94
    of Eve, 215
    of Wotan, 82, 215, 282
    sexual element in, 91, 93
fate, 127, 129, 168, 173, 177, 182, 191, 213–14, 254, 284
"fate"/"mutual recognition" leitmotif, 203, 256, 286–87
Fasolt (*Rheingold*), 42, 44, 54, 61, 82, 94, 135, 139, 178, 249–50
Faust (Goethe)
    immortal part of, 168
feeling (*Gefühl*), *see also* emotionalising of the intellect; *Gefühlsverständiß*
    as beginning and end of understanding, 278
    as feminine, 129–31
    guides to, 278
    in composition, 128–31
    physical, 279
    "primitive", 63
Fenella (*La Muetta de Portici*), 117
Festspielhaus, 61, 279
Feuerbach, Ludwig
    Essence of Christianity, 19, 121, 140, 161, 182
    Essence of Religion, 170
    Principles of the Philosophy of the Future, 132
    Thoughts on Death and Immortality, 123, 132, 161, 201, 206, 274

    as Luther II, 50
    critique of religion, 248
    "Feuerbach ending", 274–75
    Marx on, 1
    on "amorphous" love, 133, 135
    on androgyny, 161
    on death, 206
    on egoism, 134, 157
    on faith, 50
    on God as love, 121–23
    on humanity of God, 19
    on immortality, 18, 200–202, 206, 273
    on love, 121–22, 140, 161, 201
    on sensuousness, 131–35, 138, 140, 213, 215–16
    on sex and sin, 169–70
    on species, 132, 140, 171
    on "speech-events", 287
    on Trinity, 161
    on *Urgesetz*, 182
Fichte, Johann Gottlieb, 125
    Orations to the German Nation, 104
    ethics of duty of, 124
    nationalism of, 103–4
    on *Entäusserung*, 130
    on *Urgesetz*, 182
    Schleiermacher's criticism of, 124
Flosshilde (*Rheingold*), *see also* Rhinemaidens (*Götterdämmerung*), 65, 72, 74, 90, 93, 116
Forckenbeck, Max von, 244
Formula of Concord, 19
För Skírnis/Skírnismál, 88
Förster-Nietzsche, Elizabeth, 162–63
Frankenhausen, battle of, 111
Frederick I (*Friedrich Barbarossa (Rotbart)*), 104–5
    as "Christ", 107, 110, 283
    as "Christian", 104
    as "Siegfried", 107, 110, 283
    as "Wotan", 107–9
    confrontation with papacy of, 106–8, 110
    death of, 110
    Hegel on, 112
    in Kyffhäuser legend, 88, 106–8, 111
    in *Volksbuch*, 108–11
    in *Die Wibelungen*, 106–7, 109–12
    Rückert's poem of, 108
    second coming of, 109
    sin of, 107
Frederick II (*Friedrich II*), 106, 108, 111
    in Kyffhäuser legend, 111
Frederick the Great (*Friedrich der Große*), 105

INDEX OF SUBJECTS AND NAMES

freedom
    and sin, 209
    from death, 9
    from law, 9, 11, 16, 188
    from sin, 9
    from wrath, 9
    Hegel on, 16, 186, 215–16
    Kant on, 214
    of Brünnhilde, 211–13, 215–16, 240
free will, 16, 186
Freia (*Grímnismál*), 173
Freia/Holda (*Ring*), 26, 96
    as abused, 92, 250
    as goddess of love, 41–42, 116, 135
    as sister of Fricka, 47, 245
    Blick of, 139
    golden apples of, 41–42, 45, 189
    redemption of, 44, 92, 245, 247
Freud, Sigmund
    ego, 280
    id, 280
    on sex, 241
Freyja (Norse mythology), 42, 47, 144
    identified as "Third", 48
Freyr, 47, 144
Fricka/Frikka (*Ring*), 26–28, 37–38, 47, 74, 86, 89, 91, 101, 114–15, 119, 135–36, 140, 142–43, 172–73, 175–77, 180, 192–93, 209–11, 245
    as goddess of marriage, 38, 41–42, 47, 115, 173–75, 178, 187
    as hypocrite, 175
    as "Pharisee", 187
    defenders of, 187
    law of, 177–78, 187
    represents "law", 172, 187
    self-righteousness of, 250
    sin of, 250
Frigg, 27, 32, 38, 47, 49, 115, 173
Froh (*Ring*), 26, 42, 45, 47, 127

Geirröd, 31
genetic sexual attraction, 140
Gibichungs, 24, 229, 273
Gibson, Mel (*Passion of the Christ*), 246
Gluck, Christoph Willibald, 116
Gobineau, Joseph-Arthur de, 221
God, *see also* absolute, the; Spirit
    and world, 14, 25–26, 68, 271
    as creator, 65
    as Father, 14, 17, 19–20, 31, 50–51, 76, 161, 246, 283–84
    as savior, 19
    as Son, 19, 76, 161
    constrained by own laws, 207
    death of, 196–97, 218, 242
    emotions of, 50–51
    Goethe on, 26
    humanity of, 9, 19, 51
    Jewish view of, 217
    kingdom of, 9, 17, 48, 188
    law of, 208, 284
    love of, 4, 51, 242
    promises of, 207
    suffering of, 13, 31, 51
    word of, 49, 287
gods
    anxiety of, 194, 250
    death of, 47, 49
    end of, 176–78, 190–94, 243, 252
    guilt of, 237–38, 250, 252
    ontological status of, 47, 49
    Siegfried and Brünnhilde acting like, 170
    Siegmund and Sieglinde acting like, 170
Goethe, Johann Wolfgang, *see also* Goethe Ur-Faust; Goethe, Faust I; Goethe Faust II
    Betrachtungen im Sinne der Wanderer, 85
    Briefe aus der Schweiz, 168
    Gott und Welt, 26
    Römische Elegien, 168
    Venetianische Epigramme, 168–69
    Weltseele, 76
    West-östlicher Divan, 168
    Wilhelm Meisters Lehrjahre
    Wilhelm Meisters Wanderjahre, 168
    Winckelmann und sein Jahrhundert, 168
    on allegory, 286
    on Christ, 26
    on compound nouns, 39
    on divinizing nature, 55
    on four elements, 57
    on God, 26
    on "justification of the ungodly", 247–48
    on organic worldview, 57, 75, 85
    on redemption, 247–48
    on same-sex love, 167–69
    on science, 55, 85
    on symbol, 286
    on *Theorie*, 85
    on *Urpflanze*, 192
    on *Urphänomen*, 86 182
Goethe, *Ur-Faust*, 85
Goethe, *Faust I*
    Prolog im Himmel, 35
    Nacht, 17, 78–79
    Studierzimmer I, 44, 57
    Wald und Höhle, 78
    Marthens Garten, 78

Goethe, *Faust I (continued)*
   Abend, 78
   Kerker, 247
   Earth spirit in, 39
Goethe, *Faust II*
   Klassische Walpurgisnacht, 58, 94
   Anaxagoras in, 59–60, 79, 218
   eternal feminine in, 78, 157
   Homunculus in, 59, 79
   Neptune/Vulcan opposition in, 59
   Thales in, 59–60
   water/fire opposition in, 59
Goldfriedrich, E.A., 107
Gospels, *see Index of Biblical Texts*
grace
   grace (*Gunst*) of gods, 209–10
   Luther on, 252
   C. Wesley on, 265
Greek history, *see Alexander the Great; Dorians; Herodotus; Thucydides*
Greek mythology, *see also Achilles; Apollo; Artemis; Dionysus; Hephaestus; Hera; Heracles; Hermes; Zeus*
   Coleridge on, 285
   divinizing of nature in, 55
Greek philosophy, *see Anaxagoras; Aristotle; Empedocles; Plato; Thales*
Greek tragedy, *see tragedy, Greek*
Gregory of Nazianzus, 246
Gregory of Tours, 112
Grenfell Tower, tragedy of, 46
Gretchen (*Faust*), 86–87, 221
   as eternal feminine, 78
   embodies nature, 78–79
   reconciliation with nature through, 80
Grimhilde (*Ring*), 99, 118
Grimhild (*Völsunga Saga*), 225
Grimm, Jacob, *see also Index of Authors*,
   on creation, 56
   on elements, 25, 56–57, 73
   on Loki/Logi, 43
   on paganism, 22–23
   on Protestantism, 23
   on Reformation, 22–23
   on revelation, 22
   on Siegfried, 109
Grimm, Wilhelm, *see Index of Authors*
Grímnismál, 27–29, 31, 48, 56, 60, 88, 173
Grípisspá, 228, 242, 254
Gudrun (Norse mythology), 222, 225, 227–28
Günther, Friedrich, 29
Gunnar (Norse mythology), 222–24

Gunther (*Götterdämmerung/Siegfried's Tod*), 99, 116, 222, 225–30, 233, 237, 239–40, 266, 269
Gunther (*Nibelungenlied*), 46, 222–23
Gutrune/Gudrune (*Götterdämmerung/Siegfried's Tod*), 41, 116–17, 222, 228–29, 233, 238
Gylfaginning, 19, 27–28, 39, 42, 47, 49, 88, 202, 243
   "High", 47
   "Just-as-High", 48
   "Third", 48
Gylfi, 47, 49

Hadrian IV, Pope, 108
Hagen (*Nibelungen-Mythus*), 251
Hagen (*Siegfried's Tod*, 1848), 24
Hagen (*Götterdämmerung*), 102, 117, 228, 230, 233, 240, 266, 269
   as demonic, 249–50
   as "Jewish", 10
   as son, 89, 120
   attempts to take ring, 238
   commands sacrifices, 42, 47
   drowning of, 60
   kills Siegfried, 237
Hagen (*Nibelungenlied*), 46, 223
Hagen, Friedrich von der, 54
Hans Sachs (*Meistersinger*)
   and cultural nationalism, 103
   Wagner identified with, 244
Hávamál, 31, 88
   crucifixion of Odin in, 29–31, 180
Haydn, Franz Joseph,
   The Creation, 61–64
Heath, Edward, 249
Hegel, Georg Wilhelm Friedrich, 13, 53
   Aesthetics, 16
   Encyclopedia I (Logic), 216
   Phenomenology of Spirit, 35, 98–100, 102, 124, 168, 248
   Philosophy of History, 87, 112, 123, 216–18
   Philosophy of Religion, 25, 122, 196
   Philosophy of Right, 16, 125–26, 186
   Positivity of the Christian Religion, 15
   Reason in History (Vernunft in der Geschichte), 216–18
   Spirit of Christianity, 16, 76, 186–87
   on the absolute, 217
   on Anaxagoras, 217–18
   on animals, 87
   on cunning of reason (*List der Vernunft*), 217
   on death, 196–97, 218
   on death of God, 196–97, 218
   on dialectic, 77

INDEX OF SUBJECTS AND NAMES

on diremtion (*Entzweiung*), 74–75, 90, 94–95, 178
on duty, 16, 187
on evolution, 55, 68, 75
on faith, 196
on fall, 74, 87
on finite, 25
on freedom, 16, 186, 215–16
on Friedrich Barbarossa, 112
on free will, 16, 186
on God and world, 25–26, 68
on history, 125, 216–18
on immortality, 196, 200
on incarnation, 217
on infinite, 25
on Islam, 217
on Judaism, 15, 217
on law/laws (moral), 16, 187
on love, 16, 113, 122–26, 134, 137–38, 187
on Luther, 123
on master/slave, 98–100, 210
on mutual recognition, 136, 197
on myth, 25
on natural religion, 35
on organic worldview 76
on pantheism, 25, 217,
on Plato, *Timaeus*, 76
on power, 97–98
on providence, 216, 218
on reason, 216, 218
on reconciliation, 218, 248
on society, 128
on spirit, 14, 84, 196, 216–18
on sublation (*Aufhebung*), 75, 196
on teleology, 84
on time and space, 66
on tragedy, 127
Hegelian Left, 141
Hegelian Right, 196
Heimskringla, 19, 98, 145
euhemerism of, 49
Heine, Ferdinand, 7
Heldenbuch, see Amelungenlied; Ecken Ausfahrt
Helreid Brynhildar, 224
Helmholtz, Hermann, 52, 61, 69
Wagner's poem for, 85
Hephaestus, 46, 115
Hera
as a mother, 115
as jealous wife, 37
marriage of, 144
persecutes Heracles, 220
Hercules, 36, 220
Herder, Johann Gottfried,
cultural nationalism of, 103
Nietzsche on, 169
on compound nouns, 39
on origin of language, 72
organic worldview of, 75
Hermes, *see also Mercury*, 46, 96, 225
Herwegh, Georg, 170
Hesiod
Theogony, 115, 225–26
Works and Days, 94–95
Wagner's editions of, 94, 115
heterosexuality, 163–64, 168
heterosexual love, 163–64
and homosexual love, 168
as selfish, 166
Hiller, Ferdinand, 111
Hinduism, 275
history
and "cunning of reason", 217
and myth, 278
as "slaughter bench", 217
biblical view of, 275–76
divinization of, 25
Hegel on, 125, 216–18
Marx on, 218
Wagner on, 278
Hitler, Adolf, 142
Hjördis, 242
hoard, 24, 35, 44, 65, 93, 96, 102, 107, 109
Höd, 46, 115, 274
Hogni (*Völsunga Saga*), 225
Hohenstaufens, 106–12
Holda, *see Freia*
Holy Roman Empire, 107, 111
Holy Spirit/Ghost,
in *Jesus of Nazareth*, 16, 198, 270
Luther on, 246
Homer
Iliad, 94, 115, 167, 285
Odyssey, 38, 115
Achilles in, 167, 285
as "indispensable", 94
Patroclus in, 167
Homeric Hymn to Apollo, 37
homosexuality, *see also same-sex love*
Goethe on, 167–69
of Loge, 163
of Mephistopheles, 163
of Winkelmann, 168
Schiller on, 167–68
Wagner on, 164–69
Hrafnagaldr Odhins (Odin's raven-magic), 43
human, purely (*rein menschlich*), 21, 104, 128–29, 131, 172, 214

329

INDEX OF SUBJECTS AND NAMES

Hunding (*Walküre*), see also marriage, 12, 79, 99, 101, 114–15, 137–40, 142, 145, 173–74, 184, 186, 197, 211, 250
Hunding (*Walküre* prose sketch 1852), 140
Hutton, James, 83
Hymiskvida, 29
Idunn, 42–43
immortality
    Achilles' rejection of, 167, 202–3
    and birth, 206
    and cognition, 196
    and death, ix, 2, 134, 189–206
    and Freia's apples, 189
    and love, 156
    as egotistic, 18
    Brünnhilde's loss of, 197, 264
    Feuerbach on, 134, 161, 200–201
    Göschel on, 196
    Hegel on, 196, 200
    in Valhalla, 202
    Kant on, 200, 206, 214
    lust for, 41
    of androgyne, 159
    of Brünnhilde, 156, 194–95, 197, 199, 203–5, 254
    of Faust, 163
    of Fricka, 193, 210
    of gods, 176, 189–94, 197, 225
    of Jesus, 197–98
    of Siegfried, 203–5, 238
    of soul, 198
    of spirit, 196
    of Wotan, 193
    Schopenhauer on, 206
    Siegmund's rejection of, 143, 200, 202–3
    Weisse on, 196
    Wotan gives up on, 194
    Wotan's loss of, 92
incarnation, ix, 24, 156
    Hegel on, 217
    of Brünnhilde, 20, 50, 197, 242, 253, 255–65, 269, 283–84
    of Christ, 197, 217, 242
incest, see also Oedipus
    in *Völsunga Saga*, 145
    of Odin and Earth, 27
    of Oedipus and Jocasta, 126, 129–30, 135, 143, 186
    of Siegmund and Sieglinde, 80, 142–45, 170, 172–75, 186
intuition (*Anschauung*), 20–21
intuitionism, 186

Irenaeus
    Proof of the Apostolic Preaching, 74
    on paradise, 74
Islam, 217
Israel, *see also* Jewish people; Index of Biblical Texts
    ancient, 32
    promises to, 207
    salvation of, 207
    Yahweh's love for, 209

Jaide, Louise, 254
Jerome, St (Hieronymus), 242
Jesuits, 187
Jesus Christ/Jesus of Nazareth
    and communication of attributes, 158
    as androgenous, 156, 159, 162
    as consciousness of love, 140
    as cursed, 31
    as friend of sinners, 10
    as "heir of David", 11
    as messiah, 10, 198
    as non-Jew, 11
    as redeemer, 16–17, 127, 246, 270
    as revolutionary, 11–12
    as savior, 107, 241
    as Son, 19, 76, 161
    birth of, 242
    blood of, 17, 247, 270
    crucifixion of, 4, 17, 30, 269
    death of, 10, 12, 16–17, 30, 156, 184, 198, 212, 240, 243, 246–47, 265–66, 270–71, 275, 282
    divinity of, 14, 158, 255, 271
    in *Die Wibelungen*, 107, 110, 282–83
    last supper of, 270
    love of, 13, 123, 144, 183–84, 186, 265
    resurrection of, 18, 198
    sacrifice of, 16–17, 127, 156, 198, 208–9, 246, 270–72, 285
    second coming of, 109, 198
    sinlessness of, 271
    suffering of, 9, 29, 212
    transfiguration of, 50
Jewish people
    "going under" (*Untergang*) of, 273
    laws of, 11–12, 15–16, 185, 187
    negative portrayal of, 10, 14–15, 187
    redemption of, 270, 273
    St Paul on, 15, 207
Jörd/Hlödyn, 39
Judaism, *see also* Index of Wagner's works (*Judaism in Music*)

INDEX OF SUBJECTS AND NAMES

Hegel on, 15, 217
Wagner on, 49
Judas Iscariot
    in *Jesus of Nazareth*, 9–10
    Loki as, 243
judgement of the world
    final, 272, 274
    reconciliation through, 217
Justin Martyr
    Dialogue with Trypho, 242
Kalbeck, Max, 143
Kant, Immanuel, *see also Index of Authors*
    Critique of the Power of Judgement, 83–84
    Natural Science, 83
    Theory of the Heavens, 83
    and Hegel, 125
    and practical reason, 16, 187, 200
    and revelation, 277
    categorial imperative of, 186
    on duty, 16, 124, 187
    on freedom, 214
    on God, 214
    on immortality, 200
    on radical evil, 96
    on teleology, 83–84
    reason/nature dualism of, 82
    Schleiermacher's criticism of, 124
Kellermann, Berthold, 244
kingdom of God, 9, 17, 48, 188
Kittl, Johann, 111
knowing
    through art, 125
    through "error" (*Irrthum*), 75, 84, 93, 215, 282
    through feeling, 214
    through love, 125
knowledge, *see also self-knowledge, wisdom*
    and desecration of nature, 92
    and fall, 13, 75, 82, 84, 93, 215, 282
    birth of, 75, 84
    of Adam and Eve, 13, 282
    of Brünnhilde, 83, 100, 151
    of Odin, 31, 180
    Wotan's search for, 8, 93, 118, 190–91
Kriemhilt (*Nibelungenlied*), 222–23
Kyffhäuser legend, 88, 106–8, 111

Lamarck, Jean-Baptiste, 55
Laussot, Jessie, 8
law/laws, moral
    and morality, 124, 186
    as lovelessness, 14
    Fichte on, 124
    freedom from, 9, 11, 16, 188

Hegel on, 16, 187
Kant on, 16, 124
of Fricka, 177–78, 187
of God, 208, 284
of Jewish people, 11–12, 15–16, 185, 187
of love, 5, 14, 183, 188
of Moses, 185, 188
of nature, 13
of Wotan, 89, 92, 176–78, 208, 283–84
opposed to love, 14, 16, 89, 183–84, 186–87, 255
primeval (*Urgesetz*), 179–83
Wagner on, 103
Lehrs, Franz Siegfried (Levi, Samuel), 94, 115
Leibniz, Gottfried Wilhelm, 76, 85
Leipzig
    Nikolaischule, 29
    Thomaskirche, 246
leitmotifs, *see also melodic moments/impulses*
    "Erda", 86, 173, 286
    "death", 203
    "glorification of Brünnhilde", 275
    "Hagen", 229, 235
    "love", 136
    "mutual recognition"/"fate", 203, 256, 286–87
    "nature (definitive)", 61, 67
    "need of the gods", 286
    "original nature", 61, 65
    "power of the ring", 286
    "rainbow bridge", 47
    "renunciation" (*Entsagung*), 97, 259, 261–63, 272, 287
    "ring", 287
    "Siegfried", 261
    "Sieglinde", 119
    "Siegmund's rebellion", 200, 256
    "sleep", 263, 286
    "spear"/"treaty", 68, 229, 255–56, 286–87
    "storm", 68
    "sword", 190, 253
    "twilight of the gods", 286
    "Valhalla", 263, 272, 287
    "Valkyrie ride", 286
    "Volsung", 203
    "Wanderer", 286
    "wave", 82
    "woman's worth", 230–32, 256–57, 261–62
    "Wotan's frustration", 119, 256–58
    "Wurm", 148–49, 154
    "Z", 175
    von Wolzogen on, 67, 253, 259
Leonardo da Vinci, 162
Lewis, C.S., 283, 285
Linnaeus, Carl, 85

INDEX OF SUBJECTS AND NAMES

Lippmann, Eduard von, 275
Liszt, Franz
   Dante Symphony, 65
   attends *Walküre* (1870), 203
   support for *Jesus of Nazareth*, 6
   Wagner's letters to, 4, 6–7, 52, 93–94, 113, 133–34, 151, 211, 273
Loge
   and Mephistopheles, 46, 179
   as "court jester", 43
   as Hephaestus, 46
   as Hermes, 46
   as tool of Wotan, 45–46, 255
   as "villain", 43
   on love, 162–63
   protects Brünnhilde, 45
   sexuality of, 162–63
Logi, 43
Lohengrin (*Lohengrin*)
   as outsider, 128
   as "redeemer", 137
   as Zeus, 21, 129, 134
   love for Elsa of, 131, 136
   needing redemption, 137
Lokasenna (*Oegisdrecka*), 39, 43, 144–45, 162
Loki, 43–46, 56, 145, 224
   and Baldr's death, 46, 243
   and *Ragnarök*, 45
   as Judas Iscariot, 243
   as Mephistopheles, 44
   as sin, 50
   begets Fenrir, 45
   begets Midgard Serpent, 45
   sexuality of, 162–63
look (of desire), *see Blick*
Lorenz, Alfred, 66–67
love, *see also erotic love; love for the world; same-sex love*, 113–71
   above religious belief, 203
   and cognition, 125
   and death, 123, 132, 147–48, 155–56
   and eternal feminine, 78
   and marriage, 12
   and power, ix, 89, 96
   and sensuousness, 131–33
   and *Urgesetz*, 181
   as "amorphous", 133, 135
   as criterion for ethics, 186–88
   as immanent attribute of God, 242
   as passionate, 132–33, 144
   between older and younger man, 164
   between parents and children, 118–19, 122
   chaste, 133
   confused with lechery, 113
   "conquers" God, 121
   curse of (subjective genitive), 127
   curse of (objective genitive), 90, 127, 192, 253
   eternal, 196
   Feuerbach on, 121–22, 140, 161, 201
   for God, 15
   for neighbor, 15, 120
   God as, 121–23
   greater than law, 12
   Hegel on, 16, 113, 122–26, 134, 137–38, 187
   heterosexual, 163–64, 166, 168
   homosexual, 164–69
   in *Artwork*, 133–34
   in *Communication*, 134–35
   in *Holländer*, 136
   in *Jesus of Nazareth*, 2, 9, 183–84
   in *Lohengrin*, 134–37
   in marriage, 12, 114, 117, 144
   in *Tannhäuser*, 122, 133, 136
   in Trinity, 161
   in *Tristan*, 123
   John's Gospel on, 121
   1 John on, 122
   kiss of, 148, 152
   law of, 5, 14, 188
   Loge on, 162–63
   Lucinde on, 123
   Männerliebe, 165–67
   "obviousness" of, 15
   of Antigone, 127, 129, 212
   of Brünnhilde, 51, 101, 120–21 149–50, 212, 242
   of Christ, 265
   of Fasolt, 135–36
   of Faust, 79
   of God, 4, 51, 242
   of Siegfried, 123, 221, 225, 239
   of Volsung twins, 80–82, 113–14, 124, 135–38, 141, 143, 164, 173, 180–81, 186, 197
   of Wotan, 118–19, 121, 208–9, 283
   opposed to law, 14, 16, 89, 183–84, 186–87, 255
   opposed to state, 126–29, 178
   Paul on, 51, 123, 188
   power of, 96, 113, 256
   reconciliation with nature through, 79
   redemption through, 13
   renunciation of, 9, 69, 72, 89–92, 97, 252, 259
   replaces Hegel's "spirit", 14, 196
   Schleiermacher on, 124
   sexual, 90, 114, 122, 160, 167–68, 179
   Sieglinde as, 142
   Song of Songs on, 123
   Spartan, 153

INDEX OF SUBJECTS AND NAMES

love for the world
    Brünnhilde's, 271
    Wotan's, 121, 209, 283
lovelessness
    fear of the end as source of, 41, 123
    gratitude as, 120
    in *Rheingold*, 89, 92
    in *Ring*, 120
    law as, 14
Ludwig II
    enthusiasm for *Jesus of Nazareth*, 7
    reads *Artwork*, 165
    "rescues" Wagner, 7, 105
    Ring dedicated to, 105
    Wagner's letters to, 164, 281
    Wagner's love for, 164–65
Luther, Martin
    Greater Catechism, 49, 96, 247
    Shorter Catechism, 17, 161, 246
    and existential displacement, 287
    and Feuerbach, 50
    bible translation of, 7, 9, 13, 17, 64, 87, 160, 166, 245–47, 251–52, 266, 272
    Hegel on, 123
    in Wartburg, 57
    on atonement, 250
    on death of God, 242
    on faith, 49–50
    on Friedrich I, 108
    on God's reality/faith, 49–50
    on grace, 252
    on redemption, 245, 247, 250
    on Word of God, 49, 287
    pessimism of, 21, 93, 170
    Wagner's admiration for, 93

Männerliebe (love between men), 165–67
Manfred (son of Friedrich II), 106
marriage, 142, 183, 185
    and love, 12
    and possession/property, 12, 114–15, 183–85, 250
    boredom within, 117
    love in, 12, 114, 117, 144
    loveless, 91–92, 114–15
    Marx on, 115
    of Gunnar and Brynhild, 224
    of Gunther and Brünnhilde, 116, 222, 225, 228–29, 233
    of Gunther and Prünhilt, 46, 222–23
    of Hunding and Sieglinde, 12, 114–15, 174–75, 186, 250
    of Oedipus and Jocasta, 130
    of poet and music, 152, 158
    of poetry and music, 71
    of Siegfried and Brünnhilde, 117, 222, 230
    of Siegfried and Gutrune, 116, 222, 228–29, 233
    of Siegmund and Sieglinde, 114
    of Sivrit and Kriemhilt, 222–23
    of Wotan and Fricka, 89, 91–92, 119, 136
    Röckel on, 185–86
Marschner, Heinrich (*Hans Heiling*), 203
Marx, Karl, 1
    on history, 218
    on marriage, 115
    on master/slave, 99
    on property, 103
melodic moments/impulses (*melodische Momente*), 278–79, 286
Melusina/e, 82
Mendelssohn, Felix Bartholdy
    and Bach's *St Matthew Passion*, 269
Mephistopheles/Mephisto, 58, 79
    and Loge, 44, 46, 179
    and Loki, 44
    as accuser, 247–48
    as "devil", 57
    attracted to boys, 163
    critic of medicine, 85
    critic of priests, 221
    critic of science, 55
    critic of theology, 85
    love of fire, 57
    on *Theorie*, 85
    on *Vernunft*, 84
Mercury, *see also Hermes*, 96
Mesmer, Anton, 159
metaphor
    and myth, 285
    depicting reality, 49
    exchangeable nature of, 285
    for Achilles, 285
    redemption as, 246
    sea of music, 130
Midgard serpent, 88
    as devil, 50
    begotten by Loki, 45
Mime (*Rheingold*; *Siegfried*), 33–34, 61, 86–87, 230, 266
    as "Jewish", 221
    as "slave", 99
    as smith, 220
    as step-father, 102, 119–20
    desire for ring, 96–97, 249
    on gratitude, 120
    on power, 96–97, 249
    on work, 96

INDEX OF SUBJECTS AND NAMES

Mime (*Rheingold; Siegfried*) (*continued*)
  on *Wurm*, 147
  plots Siegfried's death, 249
  relationship to Alberich, 89, 94, 96, 99, 249
miracle (*Wunder*), 214
  in *Jesus of Nazareth*, 198
  in poet's work, 214
  in religious dogma, 214
  of new creation, 272
Mommsen, Theodor, 52
Moses, 33, 211
  law of, 185, 188
Mozart, Wolfgang Amadeus,
  Don Giovanni, 65
  Zauberflöte, 65
music, *see also leitmotifs; melodic moments*
  and existential displacement, 287–88
  as *Abbild* of noumenon, 69
  as eternal feminine, 152
  as feminine, 74, 129, 131, 151–53, 158, 164, 266
  as love, 113
  belonging to language, 72
  Brünnhilde embodies, 151, 153
  erotic, 114, 133, 171
  linguistic nature of, 158
  music/poetry/dance, 53, 55
  praise of, 168
  Schopenhauer on, 68–69
  sexual union with poet of, 152, 158
  sexual union with poetry of, 129–30, 164
musician
  and poet, 152, 159, 164
  as male, 152, 159, 164
mutual recognition, 136, 197
"mutual recognition"/"fate" leitmotif, 203, 256, 286–87
myth, *see also creation myth; Greek mythology; Norse/Germanic mythology; paganism*
  and allegory, 2, 50, 277, 284–86
  and history, 278
  and metaphor, 285
  as inexchangeable, 285
  as tautegorical, 284–85
  Coleridge on, 285
  Hegel on, 25
  of Oedipus, 126–31
  ontology of, 285
  Schelling on, 284–85
  "work of" (*Arbeit des*), 285
  "work on" (*Arbeit am*), 277, 285
mythology, *see creation myth; Greek mythology; myth; Norse/Germanic mythology*

nationalism
  cultural, 103
  of Fichte, 103–4
  of Herder, 103
  of Wagner, 104
nature, *see also created order; elements of nature*
  desecration of, 1, 88–89, 92, 95
  divinizing of, 55
  goodness of, 51, 73, 89
  re-mystifying of, 53
necessity (*Nothwendigkeit*), ix, 2, 132
  freedom and, 207, 209, 215
  of free self-determination, 214
  of love, 135, 212
  of nature, 170, 213
  of self-annihilation, 212
  outer, 213
  spirit in itself as, 216
Neumann, Angelo (*Ring* production), 221
Nibelungs (*Siegfried's Tod*, 1848), 251, 253
Nibelungs (*Ring*), *see Alberich; Mime*
Nibelungenlied
  and German nationalism, 103
  Gunther in, 46, 222–23
  Kriemhilt in, 222–23
  Prünhilt in, 46, 222–23, 227
  Sivrit in, 46, 88, 222–23, 227, 241, 283
  Vischer's proposal for, 248
  Wagner's study of, 59
Nietzsche, Friedrich, 8, 52, 73
  Beyond Good and Evil, 183, 218
  The Case of Wagner, 169
  Ecce Homo, 8
  Homer and Hesiod, 94
  Nietzsche contra Wagner, 279
  Richard Wagner in Bayreuth, 77, 182
  Thus spake Zarathustra, 218
  on *Übermensch*, 102, 266
  on *Urgesetz*, 182–83
  on will to power, 218
Njal's Saga
  burning of Njal in, 46
  Valkyries in, 254
Njord, 47, 144
Norse/Germanic mythology, *see also Elder Edda; Heimskringla; Prose Edda; Thidrek's Saga; Völsunga Saga; Freyja; Freyr; Frigg; Odin; Thor; Brynhild; Gudrun; Gunnar; Sigurd*
  "baptized" by Wagner, 247
  divinizing nature in, 55
Nothung (sword)
  as witness, 225, 227, 233
  hews eternal rope, 180
  kills Fafner, 249
  removed from tree, 97, 261

INDEX OF SUBJECTS AND NAMES

Odin, 39, 43, 46
   and sacrifice of Baldr, 243
   as Adam, 50
   as All-father (*Alfödr*), 27
   as father of hosts (*Herfadir*), 100
   as father of the slain (*Valfadir*), 100
   as father of victory (*Sigfödr*), 100
   as husband of Frigg, 115, 173
   as law giver, 97–98
   as Oski, 27, 101, 141
   as storm god, 32–33
   as Wanderer, 28
   as war god, 32, 182
   as Ygg (dread), 29
   birth of, 49
   "crucifixion" of, 29–31, 180
   feasts of, 202
   Feuerbach on, 182
   has many sons, 19
   identified as "Just-as-High", 48
   in *Prose Edda* Prologue, 48–49
   likened to Zeus, 115
   lost eye of, 34
   names of, 27
   not creator god, 65
   sacrifice of, 31
   spear of (Gungnir), 98
   suffering of, 31
   swallowed by Fenrir, 32
   Valkyries as will of, 210–11
Odysseus
   Dutchman as, 21, 129
Oedipus (myth)
   and Jocasta, 126, 129–30, 135, 143, 186
   and Lauis, 126
   healthy children of, 186
   in *Opera and Drama*, 126–31
Old Testament/Hebrew Bible
   decalogue, 23
   sacrifices of, 17, 208, 271
   Völuspá as, 50
   Wagner's dislike of, 208
orchestra
   as "chorus", 280
   as "guides to feeling", 278
   as "id", 280
   as "mother-womb" of drama, 280
   as "omniscient", 280
   hidden, 61
   issuing from "womb of choir", 159
organic worldview
   of Goethe, 57, 75, 85
   of Hegel, 76
   of Herder, 75
   of Schelling, 75
Origen
   on birth of Jesus, 242
   on pre-existence of souls, 206
   on redemption, 246
original perfection, 5
original sin, 21, 87, 89, 93
Ortrud (*Lohengrin*), 42, 203
Otten, Georg Dietrich, 269

paganism, 20–23, 26, 30, 48, 54, 254
Palestrina, Giovanni Pierluigi da, 269
Pandora's box, 94
pantheism, 25, 217
Parsifal (Wagner's *Parsifal*), *see also* Index of
      Wagner's Works (*Parsifal*)
   as outsider, 128
   Wagner's "creation" of, 8
particularism, moral, 186
Patroclus, 167, 203
Paul of Tarsus/St Paul, *see also* Index of Biblical
      Texts,
   "abolishes" law, 13, 185
   Christology of, 255
   critique of Israel's religion of, 15
   on death of Christ, 30, 208–9, 246
   on election of Israel, 207
   on law of love, 188
   on law/spirit, 13
   on love, 51, 123
   on perseverance of the saints, 208
   on predestination, 51, 207
   on redemption, 30, 246
   on salvation of Israel, 207
   on sex and shame, 169
   on sin, 21, 93, 169–70
   on works of law, 15
   on wrath of God, 9, 51
   Wagner's admiration for, 93
Paulus Diaconus, 173
pederasty, 166
Pelasgians, 36
penal substitution, 208, 246
Pharisee/s
   Fricka as, 187
   in Gospels, 10–11, 185, 240–41, 272
   in *Jesus of Nazareth*, 10–11, 185, 187, 272
phenomenal world, *see also* world, of phenomena
   as embodied music, 69
   as embodied will, 69
Pilate, Pontius (*Jesus of Nazareth*), 10–11, 16
Pinder, Wilhelm, 231

Planer, Minna, *see Wagner, Minna*
Plato
   Critias, 76
   Laws, 76
   Phaedo, 206
   Symposium, 161, 158–59
   Timaeus, 76
   on pre-existence of souls, 206
   Schleiermacher's translation of, 158–59
Platonic Ideas, 76
poet
   and music, 152, 158
   and musician, 152, 159, 164
   as male, 158–59, 164
poetry
   and allegory, 286
   and music, 71, 129–31, 164
   poetry/music/dance, 53, 55
Porges, Heinrich, *see Index of Authors*
power, 97
   and love, ix, 89, 96
   as dominion, 184
   Hegel on, 97–100, 210
predestination
   Augustine on, 275
   Paul on, 51, 207
   Wagner on, 181
Prokofiev, Sergey Sergeyevich (*War and Peace*), 114
property, 9, 102, 183
   abolition of, 5, 103
   fair distribution of, 11, 103
   Marx/Engels on, 103
   protection of, 184
   Proudhon on, 103, 105
   "redemption of", 245
   woman as, 12, 114–15, 183–85, 250
Prose Edda, *see also Gylfaginning, Skaldskaparmal*, 145, 222, 242
   Brynhild in, 227, 253
   euhemerist view of gods, 47–48
   Loki and Logi in, 43
   Odin in, 27, 32
   Prologue of, 48–49
   Wagner's editions of, 49
Protestantism, *see also Formula of Concord; Luther; Reformation*
   Formula of Concord, 19
   Grimm on, 23
   Wagner on, 23, 104, 108
Proudhon, Pierre Joseph, 11–12, 102–3, 185
providence
   Hegel on, 216, 218
   in *Ring*, 207

   Wagner on, 216, 218
Prünhilt (*Nibelungenlied*), 46, 222–23, 227
psychoanalysis, *see also Freud, Sigmund*, 157
Puccini, Giacomo (*Tosca*), 114, 278–79
purely human (*rein menschlich*), 21, 104, 128–29, 131, 172, 214

Quantum Theory, 53

race
   Aryan, 220
   degeneration of, 185
   Germanic, 221
   Gobineau on, 221
   in *Die Wibelungen*, 110, 282
   of Hohenstaufens, 112
Radbod, Prince of Frisia, 203
Ragnarök, 32, 42, 45, 97, 119, 243, 273, 276
rainbow bridge, 35, 47
   leitmotif of, 47
ravens,
   and Kyffhäuser legend, 107–9
   of Wotan, 45, 107–9
reason (*Vernunft*)
   and faith, 214
   as freely self-determining thought, 216, 218
   coincides with desire, 216
   cunning of, 217
   Hegel on, 216, 218
   in history, 216–18
   in *Ring*, 218
   Kant on, 16, 82, 187, 200
   Mephistopheles on, 84
   Wagner on, 167
reconciliation
   Hegel on, 218, 248
   through judgement of world, 217
   with death, 18
   with nature, 79–80
Relativity
   general, 66
   special, 66
redemption
   and ransom, 245–46
   and sacrifice, 246
   catholic, 248
   from death, 9, 17–18, 247, 250
   from devil, 17, 247
   from erotic love, 21, 171
   from reincarnation, 249
   from sin, 17, 247
   Luther on, 245, 247, 250
   of Ahasuerus, 273
   of all people, 246, 270

INDEX OF SUBJECTS AND NAMES

of Dutchman, 273
of gods, 271
of Jewish people, 270, 273
of world, 113, 241, 252–53, 265
of Wotan, 271
Paul on, 30, 246
Schopenhauer on, 21, 171, 248
through Brünnhilde's death, 51, 242, 252, 255, 265, 269, 281, 283
through erotic love, 21, 171
through Jesus' death, 16–17, 246, 270
Reformation
   and German nationalism, 104
   J. Grimm on, 22–23
   Wagner on, 23, 110
Reformation Day, 110
Reiffrost, 54
reincarnation, 249, 275
Reimarus, Hermann Samuel, 270
renunciation
   of divinity, 121, 265
   of God, 121
   of love, 9, 69, 72, 89–92, 97, 127, 252, 259
"renunciation" ("*Entsagung*") leitmotif, 97, 259, 261–63, 272, 287
Rerir (*Völsunga Saga*), 145
resurrection
   general, 18
   in *Völuspá*, 274
   of Friedrich Barbarossa, 111
   of Jesus, 18, 198
   of Levi's daughter, 198
Rhinemaidens (*Götterdämmerung*), 238–39, 269–70, 180
ring
   Alberich's desire for, 103
   Alberich's plans to regain, 192, 253
   and wealth, 103
   as token of love, 229
   cursed, 44, 180, 251–52
   embodying love, 225, 272
   Froh on, 127
   Hagen attempts to take, 238
   Mime's desire for, 96–97, 249
   power of, 93, 252, 286
   purified by fire, 251, 269
   redemption from cursed, 252
   removed from Brünnhilde, 222, 226
   runes of, 180, 192, 253
   Siegmund to regain ring, 41, 97, 178, 191, 253
   Waltraute's plea concerning, 271–72
   Wotan's plans to regain, 252–53
Ritter, Johann Wilhelm, 159

Ritter, Karl, 134
Roberts, Richard, 97
Röckel, August, 4
Rousseau, Jean Jacques, 71–72, 178
Rückert, Friedrich, 108
Rüger, H.P., 15
Rungenhagen, Carl Friedrich, 269

sacrifice, *see also* atonement; Jesus Christ, sacrifice of; redemption
   as sin-offering, 208
   for sin, 19, 31, 240, 242
   in Old Testament, 17, 208, 271
   of Brünnhilde, 271. 19, 50, 127, 241, 265, 270–71, 273, 283
   of Jesus, 16–17, 127, 156, 198, 208–9, 246, 270–72, 285
   of Siegfried, 83, 240, 251, 265, 270–71, 273, 283
Sadducees, 11
Saga of Ynglings, 19
salvation, *see also* redemption
   of Jewish people, 207
   sexual union as, 164
same-sex love
   and heterosexual love, 168
   as eye-to-eye, 164–65
   as higher form of love, 166
   between older and younger man, 164
   Goethe on, 167–69
   in Sparta, 153
   of Ludwig and Wagner, 164–65
   of poet and musician, 164–65
   Schiller on, 167–68
Santayana, George, 206
Satan, *see also* devil, 17, 250, 283
savior, *see* Jesus Christ
Schelling, Friedrich Wilhelm Joseph von
   Ideas for a Philosophy of Nature, 75
   On the World Soul, 75
   and Plato, 76
   and J.W. Ritter, 159
   and J.M. Wagner, 286
   on allegory, 284–86
   on mythology, 284–86
   on nature, 53, 76
   on teleology, 84
   on *Urgesetz*, 182
   on will (*Wollen*), 84
   on world-soul, 26, 76
   organic worldview of, 75
Schiller, Johann Christoph Friedrich von, 69
   An die Freude (Ode to Joy),
   Die Freundschaft, 167–68

Schiller, Johann Christoph Friedrich von (*continued*)
   Die Götter Griechenlands, 55
   Über naïve und sentimentalische Dichtung, 280
   on nature, 55
   on same-sex love, 167–68
Schimmelmann, Jacob, 50
Schleiermacher, Friedrich Daniel Ernst, 287
   Athenæm Fragments, 161
   on androgyny, 161
   on love, 124
   translation of Plato, 76, 124, 158–59
Schlegel, A.W.
   Athenæm Fragments, 161
   on Hohenstaufens, 106
   on Shakespeare, 227
Schlegel, Friedrich, *see also Index of Authors*, 95, 124
   Athenæm Fragments, 161
   Lucinde, 123–24, 161
   On Diotima, 161
   on androgyny, 161
Schopenhauer, Arthur, *see also sufficient reason, principle of*
   and Darwin, 68
   and ending of *Ring*, 249, 274–75
   and *Liebestod*, 156
   and *Parsifal*, 277
   and revelation, 277
   on allegory, 286
   on denial of the will, 281
   on evolution of world-will, 53, 66, 68
   on immortality, 206
   on redemption, 21, 171, 248
   on sex/sin, 170–71
   on Wagner's *Ring*, 143
   on will, 84, 215, 218
   on will to life, 218
   pessimism of, 21, 93
   "Schopenhauer ending" of, 249, 274
   Wagner's knowledge of, 21, 41, 66, 170
Schumann, Robert, 269
Schwarz, Hanna, 187
science
   Goethe on, 55, 85
   Hegel on, 138
   mechanistic theories, 76
   Wagner on, 53, 55, 84–85, 159, 278
Scribe, Eugène, 6, 116
second coming
   of Friedrich Barbarossa, 109
   of Jesus, 109, 198
   of Siegfried, 109

self-consciousness
   Hegel on, 98, 126
   of Brünnhilde, 100, 125
   of Wotan, 125
self-knowledge
   God as, 14
Senta (*Der fliegende Holländer*)
   as redeemer, 273
   "going under" (*Untergang*) of, 273
   love for Dutchman of, 136
   "magnetic sleep of", 159
Sermon on the Mount, *see also Index of Biblical Texts*, 16, 187–88
sex, *see also sexual union etc*
   and shame, 169
   and sin, 169–71
   divorced from love, 91
sexual attraction, *see heterosexuality; homosexuality; sexual union*
   and Westermarck effect, 140
   genetic, 140
sexual desire, *see erotic love*
sexual ethics, *see also intuitionism; particularism; situation ethics*
   Fricka on, 38, 173–178
   in *Jesus of Nazareth*, 183–88
   law and, 172–88
   Wotan on, 173–78
sexual union, *see heterosexuality; homosexuality; sexual attraction*
   and acting like animals, 118, 169–70
   and acting like gods, 170
   and androgyny, 160
   and death, 158
   as salvation, 164
   in *Ring*, 157
   in *Tristan*, 158
   involving no sin, 170
   of music and poetry, 129–31
   of music and poet, 158, 164
sexuality, *see also heterosexuality; homosexuality*
Shaw, George Bernard, 95, 102, 178, 283
Shakespeare, William,
   Hamlet, 227
   King Lear, 32
   translation of A. W. Schlegel, 227
Siegfried (Grimm's *Mythologie*), 109
Siegfried (*Die Wibelungen*)
   as Apollo, 34–35, 110
   as Christ, 107, 110, 283
   as Friedrich I, 107, 110–11, 283
   as Sun-god, 34–35
   return of, 109

INDEX OF SUBJECTS AND NAMES

Siegfried (*Nibelungen-Mythus*)
    as redeemer, 250–51
    as sacrifice, 251
    as "suffering servant", 237–38
Siegfried (*Siegfried's Tod*, 1848)
    as sacrifice, 251–52, 270
    as Wotan's great-grandson, 24
    enters Valhalla, 204–5
Siegfried (*Ring*), *see also marriage*
    amnesia of, 156, 229–30, 233
    and androgyny, 156–58, 162
    and incest, 186
    and Woodbird, 82, 146, 151
    as allegorical figure, 284, 286
    as Apollo, 36–37, 149
    as Aryan, 220
    as Bakunin, 102
    as Baldr, 37, 243
    as Christ, 37, 156, 242–43, 266, 269, 282–83
    as "comic", 219
    as dishonest, 228–30
    as fearless, 123, 202, 244
    as Heracles, 36, 200
    as killer of Fafner, 249
    as mythical figure, 284
    as outsider, 128
    as possible rapist, 117, 222, 225, 227, 229–30, 239, 241
    as "singing", 151
    as "suffering servant", 252
    as sun-god, 34–36, 146, 149, 157
    as tragic hero, 219
    as wooer (Gunther), 181, 228, 233
    assaults Brünnhilde, 117, 225–26
    atoning death of, 240, 252
    betrays Brünnhilde, 230, 239–40, 264
    birth of, 120, 157, 242
    breaks Wotan's spear, 255
    Brünnhilde's love for, 195–96, 242
    calls on mother, 147
    consciousness of divine descent of, 220–21
    death of, 37, 46, 237–38, 240–41, 250–52, 265–66, 269, 282
    exercise of power of, 102
    faithful to Gunther, 230, 239
    immortality of, 203–5, 238
    learns fear, 100, 146–47, 154–55, 221–22
    love for Brünnhilde of, 221, 225, 239
    makes love like "animal", 170
    makes love like god, 170
    incorporated into Brünnhilde, 156, 162, 164, 197, 241
    oath on Hagen's spear of, 234, 237
    oath on Nothung of, 225, 227, 229, 233
    on animals/love, 87
    on death and fear, 194
    on "property", 102
    on *Urgesetz*, 180
    overcomes fear, 153
    redemptive death of, 241–42, 251–52, 265–66
    reflects on nature, 82
    reflects on parents, 118–19
    relationship to Brünnhilde, 117
    relationship to Mime, 119–20
    represents human being in Christ, 281
    sacrifice of, 83, 240, 251, 265, 270–71, 273, 283
    "saved" by Brünnhilde, 164, 197
    sexual passion of, 263–64
    subjugates (as Gunther) Brünnhilde, 225–26
    takes ring from Brünnhilde, 226
    transfiguration of, 237, 241, 221–22
    transformation of, 100, 221
    Wagner as, 244
Siegfried's Funeral March, 119, 238
"Siegfried" leitmotif, 261
Sieglinde (*Nibelungen-Mythus*), 184
Siegelind (*Siegfried's Tod*, 1848), 24
Sieglinde (*Ring*), *see also marriage*, 19, 24, 27, 36, 121, 176, 195, 202
    and mutual recognition, 136–38, 197
    as love, 142
    as property, 12, 114–15, 184, 250
    Blick of, 139
    death of, 120
    enters supernatural world, 199
    ethics of incest of, 173, 186
    in womb of mother, 138
    makes love like "animal", 170
    makes love like god, 170
    passionate love of, 79, 113–14, 124, 133, 135–36, 141, 143
    saved by Brünnhilde, 157
    "saves" Siegmund, 164, 197
    self-consciousness of, 125
    subjugated by Hunding, 99, 114
    takes initiative, 142
"Sieglinde" leitmotif, 119
Siegmund (*Nibelungen-Mythus*), 38, 184
Siegmund (*Siegfried's Tod*, 1848), 24
Siegmund (*Ring*), *see also marriage*, 36, 101, 145, 176
    abandoned by father, 211
    accuses Brünnhilde as cold and hard, 228
    adventures with Wolfe, 141
    agency of, 174, 177, 192–93, 210
    and mutual recognition, 136–38, 197
    as allegorical figure, 19, 50, 283

339

INDEX OF SUBJECTS AND NAMES

Siegmund (*Ring*) (*continued*)
   as only son of Wotan, 27–28
   as outsider, 128
   as "the other", 211–12
   as spring (*Lenz*), 142
   Brünnhilde tries to rescue, 271
   courage of, 202
   death of, 19, 32, 50, 209, 283
   ethics of incest of, 173, 186
   his love as witness, 143–44, 197
   in *Todesverkündigung*, 28, 119, 144, 198–99, 203, 256
   in womb of mother, 138
   loved by Brünnhilde, 120–21
   loved by father, 119
   makes love like "animal", 170
   makes love like god, 170
   meant to regain ring, 41, 97, 178, 191, 253
   passionate love of, 79, 113–14, 124, 133, 135–36, 141, 143
   pulls out Nothung from tree, 97, 140, 261
   puts Sieglinde before Valhalla, 200, 202–3
   rebellion of, 256
   rejects immortality, 200, 203, 256
   "saved" by Sieglinde, 164, 197
   self-consciousness of, 125
   "spring song" of, 80
   trusts father, 119
Siggeir (*Völsunga Saga*), 145
Sigi (*Völsunga Saga*), 145
Sigmund (*Grípisspá*), 242
Sigmund (*Skaldskaparmal*), 242
Sigmund (*Völsunga Saga*), 145
Signy (*Völsunga Saga*), 145
Sigrdrífa (Norse mythology), 37
Sigrdrífumál, 149
Sigurd (Norse mythology), 37, 204, 219–20, 222–24, 228, 241–43, 283
Sigurdarkvida in skamma, 224
Simrock, Karl
   Amelungenlied, 55, 220
   Edda, 28, 34, 43, 88, 243
   Nibelungenlied, xvi
sin, ix
   and freedom, 209
   and law, 208
   and sex, 169–71
   blotting out of, 251
   freedom from, 9
   in *Jesus of Nazareth*, 12–14, 17, 183–84, 282
   in marriage, 184
   Loki as, 50
   of Adam, 93
   of Alberich, 89, 91–93
   of Fricka, 250
   of Friedrich I, 107
   of self-righteousness, 250
   of the gods, 242
   of Wotan, 89, 92–93, 108, 250
   ontological view of, 169
   original, 21, 87, 89, 93
   origin of, 90
   redemption from, 17, 183, 247, 250
   sacrifice for, 19, 31, 240, 242
   wiping away of, 252
situation ethics, 186
Sivrit (*Nibelungenlied*), 46, 88, 222–23, 227, 241, 283
Skaldskaparmal, 42, 224, 227, 242
Skírnismál/För Skírnis, 88
Sleipnir, 162
society
   and law, 13, 177
   and love between men (*Männerliebe*), 167
   and Oedipus myth, 129, 145
   human misery in, 5, 95
   individual in, 125, 127–28, 213–14
   Marx on, 99
   potential for good, 178
   Rousseau on, 178
   sickness of, 1
   Wagner's hopes to transform, 1, 105
Sophocles
   Antigone, 122, 126–27
   Oedipus Tyrannus, 122
   Oedipus at Colonus, 122
soul, *see also* anthropology
   immortality of, 198
   of Jesus Christ, 198
   pre-existence of, 206
space and time, 66
spear (Hagen's), 233, 237, 251
spear (Longinus'), 243
spear (Wotan's), 28, 68
   and treaties, 253
   as "emblem", 284
   as expression of law, 255
   as weapon, 98
   broken, 255
   formed from Yggdrasil, 89, 92, 194, 215
   imposing order, 97–98
   slipping from Wotan's hand, 263
"spear"/"treaty" leitmotiv, 68, 229, 255–56, 286–87
Spinozism, 25
Spirit, *see also* Holy Spirit
   Hegel on, 14, 84, 196, 216–18

INDEX OF SUBJECTS AND NAMES

spring (*Lenz*)
    Siegmund as, 142
Stabreim, 137, 153, 155, 179, 187, 261
state
    and Creon, 126–27
    annulling of, 127–28, 214
    "going under" (*Untergang*) of, 129, 214
    opposed to love, 126–29, 178
Stein, Heinrich von, 8
Steinitz, Clara, 254
Sturluson, Snorri, 27, 243
subjectivity, 55
suffering
    of Brünnhilde, 241, 264
    of God, 13, 31, 51
    of humanity, 14, 201, 218, 282
    of Jesus, 9, 29, 212, 31, 283
    of Odin, 29, 31
    of Wotan, 9, 31, 51
symbol
    and allegory, 285–86
    Coleridge on, 285
    Goethe on, 286

Tacitus, Cornelius
    Germania, 22
Tannhäuser/Heinrich (*Tannhäuser*)
    as outsider, 128
    love for Elisabeth of, 136
tarnhelm, 225, 237, 245
teleology
    external, 84
    Hegel on, 84
    in biblical history, 275–76
    in *Ring*, 75, 77, 276
    internal, 84
    Kant on, 83–84
    Schelling on, 84
    Schopenhauer on, 68
Thales, 59–60
Thidrek's Saga, 219–20, 223, 242–43
thing-in-itself (Ding an sich) *see also* world, noumenal, 171, 206
Thor, 19, 22, 39, 47–48, 162
    identified as "High", 47–48
Thrymskvida, 39
Thucydides, 36
time and space, 66
Titian (*Assumpta*), 148
tragedy, Greek, *see also* Aeschylus; Antigone; Euripides; Oedipus; Sophocles, 104
    "baptized" by Wagner, 247
    chorus in, 280
    fate in, 213

    Hegel on, 127
    Jesus of Nazareth as, 4, 6, 16
transfiguration
    of Brünnhilde, 241
    of Jesus, 50
    of Siegfried, 221, 237, 241
Trinity
    and atonement, 31
    Feuerbach on, 161
    love in, 161
Tristan (*Tristan und Isolde*), 165, 181
Tübinger Stift, 76

Uhlig, Theodor
    Wagner's letters to, 4, 6, 113, 126, 133
understanding, *see also* emotionalising of the intellect, 128–30, 161, 278
understanding through feeling (*Gefühlsverständniß*), 214, 279
Untergang ("going under"),
    of Ahasuerus, 273
    of Dutchman, 273
    of Jewish people, 273
    of Senta, 273
    of world, 52, 273

Vafthrúdnismál, 28–29, 202
Valhalla
    Brünnhilde enters, 204–5
    Einherjar in, 202
    immortality in, 202
    Siegfried enters, 204–5
    Siegmund rejects, 200, 202–3
"Valhalla" motif, 263, 272, 287
Valkyries (Norse mythology)
    as blood-thirsty, 254
    as Odin's will, 210–11
Valkyries (*Ring*), *see* Brünnhilde; Waltraute
"Valkyrie ride" motif, 286
Vanir, *see also* Freyja, Freyr, 65, 86
Venus
    and "pornography", 136
    and sensuality, 131
Venusberg, 169
Vernunft, see reason
Verstand, see understanding; emotionalising of the intellect
Vidar, 115
Villiers de l'Isle-Adam, Philippe-Auguste, 20
virginal conception, 254
Virgin Mary
    and Antigone, 212
    Brünnhilde as, 254
    Erda as, 254

INDEX OF SUBJECTS AND NAMES

Virgin Mary *(continued)*
    Luther on, 17
vivisection, 84
Volksbuch (1519), 108–11
Volsung (*Siegfried's Tod*, 1848), 24
Volsung twins (*Nibelungen-Mythus*), 24, 184
Volsung twins (*Ring*), 80, 82, 117, 133, 135–44, 172, 176, 180, 186, 193, 211
Volsung (*Völsunga Saga*), 145
Völsunga Saga, 28, 145, 219, 222, 224–25, 227–28, 242
Völuspá, 28, 30–32, 34, 39, 45–46, 56, 59, 65, 88, 97, 274
    as "Old Testament", 50
    Christian theology in, 22, 243

Wagner, Adolf (uncle), 84
Wagner, Cosima, xiii–xiv, 7–8, 52, 54, 58, 73, 82, 104–5, 107–8, 111–12, 116, 118, 125, 147–48, 162, 169–70, 187, 203, 244, 254, 273, 275
Wagner, Johann Martin, 286
Wagner, Minna (née Planer), 4, 210
Wagner, Richard, *see also* Brünnhilde; Jesus Christ; Siegfried; Wotan; death; law; love; redemption; sacrifice
    admiration for Luther, 93
    admiration for Paul, 93
    anti-Judaism of, 49
    antisemitism of, 11, 49, 103
    as political revolutionary, 11
    as protestant, 23, 104, 108
    Dresden library of, 3, 12, 29, 43, 56, 76, 94, 106, 110, 112, 115, 158, 168, 185, 211, 269
    faith of, 185
    knowledge of Schopenhauer of, 21, 41, 66, 170
    love of animals of, 84, 87, 172
    nationalism of, 104
    on act of creation, 5, 14
    on androgyny, 164
    on atheism, 53
    on atonement, 17, 271
    on "dance", 53, 55
    on "denial of the will", 281
    on duty, 120, 129
    on erotic love, 21, 125, 135–40, 165–67, 171
    on Greek tragedy, 104, 247, 280
    on "historic Chronicle", 278
    on Judaism, 49
    on law of love, 5, 14, 183, 188
    on linguistic nature of music, 158
    on musicality of language, 158
    on the musician, 152, 159, 164–65
    on nature, 53, 55, 86, 89
    on orchestra, 159, 278, 280
    on pederasty, 166
    on predestination, 181
    on providence, 216, 218
    on race, 110, 220–21, 282
    on reason, 167
    on Reformation, 23, 110
    on salvation, 164
    on same-sex love, 164–69
    on science, 53, 55, 84–85, 159, 278
    on sublation (*Aufhebung*), 5, 14, 75, 196
    on the "saint", 221–22
    opposes legalism, 187
    study of New Testament of, 1, 3, 5, 12, 14, 17, 26, 93, 120, 122–23, 183, 186–87, 246, 272, 282
    Wahnfried library of, 12, 43, 54, 61, 94, 104, 106, 115, 123, 160, 221, 269
Wagner, Siegfried, 7–8, 52
Walther (*Meistersinger*), 128
Waltraute (*Götterdämmerung*), 28, 32, 107, 193–94, 225, 250, 261, 271–72, 287
Wanderer (*Siegfried*), *see also* Wotan
    as Adam, 50, 281–84, 286
    as broken god, 261, 263
    as Flying Dutchman, 28
    as romantic "Wanderer", 29
    in *Siegfried* Act II, 86
    in *Siegfried* Act III, 40, 118, 243, 265, 283–84, 286–87
    missing eye of, 34
Wandering Jew, *see* Ahasuerus
Warner, Keith, 20
Weisse, Christian Hermann
    on aesthetics, 196
    on Hegel, 84
    on immortality, 196
    on Schelling, 84
    on *Urgesetz*, 182
Welfs, 106–7
Wellgunde (*Rheingold*), *see also* Rhinemaidens (*Götterdämmerung*), 69, 72, 74, 90, 93
Wesendonck (Wesendonk), Mathilde
    Friedrich der Grosse, 105
    as inspiration for *Walküre*, 133, 141, 171
    Wagner's letters to, 92, 171
    Wagner's love for, 133, 141, 171
Wesley, Charles, 265
Westermarck, Edvard, 140
Wibelungs, 106–7
will (*Wille*)
    denial of, 281

INDEX OF SUBJECTS AND NAMES

divine, 214
Gattungs-Wille, 171
objectification of,
of Wotan, 211
pacification of, 171
Schelling on, 84
Schopenhauer on, 84, 218, 281
will to life, 202, 218
will to power, 218
Windfahrer, 54
wisdom, *see also knowledge*
of Brünnhilde, 100, 264
of primeval mothers, 40
well of, 115
Wotan's search for, 82, 92–93, 115, 215, 282
Wittgenstein, Carolyne von, 6–8
Woglinde (*Rheingold*), *see also* Rhinemaidens (*Götterdämmerung*), 61, 69, 71–74, 80, 90, 259
Wolf (Fenrir)
begotten by Loki, 45
swallows Odin, 32
Wolzogen, Hans von, *see also leitmotifs*, 67, 253, 259, 286
woman, *see also eternal feminine*
as property, 12, 114–15, 183–85, 250
as slave, 99
music as, 74, 129, 131, 151–53, 158, 164, 266
"woman's worth" leitmotif, 230–32, 256–57, 261–62
Woodbird (*Waldvogel*, *Siegfried*), 82, 87, 146, 151
world, *see also thing in itself; will*
"going under" (*Untergang*) of, 52, 273
of noumena, 171, 206
of phenomena, 69, 85, 206,
renewal of, 271
World Ash Tree, *see* Yggdrasil
world soul (*Weltseele*), 26, 76
Wuotan (*Die Wibelungen*), 65
Wotan (*Nibelungen-Mythus*)
as All-father (*Allvater*), 27
responsible for Siegfried's death, 251
Wotan (*Siegfried's Tod*, 1848)
as All-father (*Allvater*), 27, 204–5
as ruling god, 24, 205, 252
Wotan (Wodan; Wuotan), *see also gods; marriage; spear (Wotan's); Wanderer (Siegfried)*
accepts death, 250
and "will", 286–87
as "Adam", 50, 281–84, 286
as All-father (*Allvater*), 27
as avenging god, 238
as broken god, 261, 263

as father of battles (*Heervater*), 28, 32, 100, 177
as father of the slain (*Walvater*), 28, 100, 199–200
as father of victories (*Siegvater*), 28, 32, 100
as Flying Dutchman, 284, 286
as Friedrich I, 107–8
as god of Aryans, 170
as "God the father", 19–20, 50, 283–84
as "Licht-Alberich", 97
as mythical figure, 284
as Oski, 27, 101, 141
as politician, 253
as powerless, 212
as representing air, 57
as sky god, 33
as storm god, 33, 54
as sun-god, 34–35
as Wagner's mouthpiece, 141, 173, 186
as Wolfe, 141
as Yahweh, 32, 209
constrained by own laws, 177, 211
death of, 32
defies own laws, 176
denies will, 281
fall of, 82, 215, 282
in *Walküre* Act I, 140–41
law/s of, 89, 92, 176–78, 208, 283–84
loses power, 263
love for Brünnhilde of, 118–19
love for Siegmund of, 118–19, 208
love for the world of, 121, 209, 283
loved by Brünnhilde, 119
loved by Siegmund, 119
lust for power of, 96–97, 102–3
makes love like "animal", 118, 170
missing eye of, 33–35, 82, 140, 149
not creator god, 65
offered eye for Fricka, 115
ordering of world by, 11, 89, 97–98, 208
promises of, 208–9
prophecy of, 51, 121, 252, 265, 269
psychological complexity of, 9, 24, 31–32
put to rest, 32, 263, 272–73
redemption of, 271–72
rejects will to life, 202
renounces love, 92, 97, 252
searches for wisdom, 82–83, 93, 191, 282
shunning of ring by, 40–41, 189
sin of, 89, 92–93, 108, 250
subjugates/assaults Erda, 99, 117–18
suffering of, 9, 31, 51
trusted by Siegmund, 119
wrath of, 100

INDEX OF SUBJECTS AND NAMES

Wurm (Fafner), *see also Fafner*, 34, 54, 86–88, 109, 120, 151, 249
    as "devil", 249
    blood of, 151, 154–55
    Brünnhilde as, 147–48, 151, 154–55
"*Wurm*" leitmotif, 148–49, 154

Yahweh
    as storm god, 32
    as transcendent, 33
    as war god, 32
    distress of, 209
    represented by angel, 211
Yggdrasil, 23, 29, 73, 82, 88–89, 92, 194, 215
Ymir, 60

Zeus, 36–37, 79, 118, 144, 225
    likened to Lohengrin, 21, 129, 134–35
    likened to Odin, 115
    likened to Wuotan, 65

www.ingramcontent.com/pod-product-compliance
Lightning Source LLC
Chambersburg PA
CBHW060335010526
44117CB00017B/2832